THE BIBLICAL CANON LISTS FROM
EARLY CHRISTIANITY

The Biblical Canon Lists from Early Christianity

Texts and Analysis

EDMON L. GALLAGHER and JOHN D. MEADE

OXFORD
UNIVERSITY PRESS

OXFORD

UNIVERSITY PRESS

Great Clarendon Street, Oxford, OX2 6DP,
United Kingdom

Oxford University Press is a department of the University of Oxford.
It furthers the University's objective of excellence in research, scholarship,
and education by publishing worldwide. Oxford is a registered trade mark of
Oxford University Press in the UK and in certain other countries

First published 2017
First published in paperback 2019

Published in the United States of America by Oxford University Press
198 Madison Avenue, New York, NY 10016, United States of America

British Library Cataloguing in Publication Data
Data available

Library of Congress Cataloging in Publication Data
Data available

ISBN 978-0-19-879249-9 (Hbk.)
ISBN 978-0-19-883889-0 (Pbk.)

Printed and bound by CPI Group (UK) Ltd, Croydon, CR0 4YY

Ed dedicates this work to his cherished wife, Jodi

John dedicates this work to his children:
Charis, Magdalena, Emma June, and Peter
His joy and his delight

Preface

The contents of this book represent our primary objective: to seek understanding into the history of the Bible by returning to the ancient sources that comment on it. The ancient authors included in this work lived in a time of great tension, causing pressure from within and from without—the proto-orthodox faith (and its schisms) and the relationship of the church to the state not being least among them. These same authors also attested to the disputes about the contents of the canon of Scripture, but everywhere they affirmed that God had spoken and that these written, inspired records or Scriptures contained his revelation for the Church. The reader is invited to listen in on these early voices that contributed significantly to the conversation over and the question about the contents of the Bible—a conversation even by their time long underway. We hope our readers will benefit not only from our notes and analysis of the included texts, but also—and most importantly—from reading the texts themselves. Insight into these old questions comes primarily by returning to the sources. What the ancient authors in this volume show us is that many of our present questions regarding the canon of Scripture are not altogether new. They too wondered about which books had authority for church doctrine. They inquired about the role of scriptures that were ultimately not included in the canon of Scripture. So we invite readers to listen to the discussions over the canon at this early period with the hopes that they will gain greater clarity on how early Christians posed these questions and how they might provide the scaffolding for our own understanding of the history of the Bible.

Canon research requires great specialization. We would like to thank the following scholars for their insightful feedback and input on those parts of this work which intersect with their areas of expertise: John Barclay, David Brakke, Stephen Chapman, Stephen Dempster, Geoffrey Dunn, Michael Haykin, Ronald Heine, Charles Hill, Andrew Jacobs, Peter Martens, Lee Martin McDonald, Eva Mroczek, and Lucas Van Rompay. We are in their debt. We hope we have not overlooked anyone. Furthermore, we would like to thank Brian Arnold, John DelHousaye, and Michael Jackson for reading parts of the manuscript for clarity and for their encouragement during the writing of this book.

For ancient and modern works, we have generally tried to follow the abbreviations suggested in *The SBL Handbook of Style*, 2d edn (Atlanta, GA: SBL). Any deviations from what is found there should be self-explanatory.

We would like to thank our wives (Jodi and Annie) and children for their support during this project. We recognize the sacrifice on them that a project like this one becomes. We also thank the library staffs at Heritage Christian

University and Phoenix Seminary for their tireless service in tracking down the necessary sources in order for us to complete the work.

Edmon L. Gallagher
John D. Meade

Florence, Alabama and Phoenix, Arizona
September 2017

Contents

Introduction

The Bible took shape over the course of centuries, and still today Christian groups disagree over details of its contents. Christians in the Western world will most readily think of the differences between Roman Catholics and Protestants, the former having more books than the latter. Eastern Orthodox groups often have larger Bibles than Roman Catholics. The differences among these groups typically involve the Old Testament; for the most part, they accept the same twenty-seven-book New Testament. But some Christian groups have fewer or more NT books. All of these groups seem to agree that the practice of the early Church is, if not determinative, at least an important consideration in the task of delineating the Christian biblical canon. To contribute to such study, this book aims to present the evidence of the early Christian canon lists in an accessible form for the benefit of students and scholars.

DEFINITIONS

The study of the biblical canon has to do with identifying which books the Bible comprises. This simple description disguises the difficulties of arriving at a more precise definition. Because of our limited focus here on canon lists, we do not need to enter into the scholarly disagreements as to whether 'canon' should refer to the authority of a writing or to a list of scriptural books.[1] We will briefly survey the history of the term 'canon' and indicate how we define a canon list.

The use of the term 'canon' ($\kappa\alpha\nu\dot{\omega}\nu$) in reference to a collection of sacred Scripture dates to the fourth century.[2] The term had been used in a variety of ways in early Christianity, as in earlier Hellenistic Greek, generally indicating a 'standard' or a 'rule'. The apostle Paul used the word a few times in this way (2 Cor. 10:13–16; Gal. 6:16), and Irenaeus wrote about the 'canon' of faith

---

[1] Contrast the views of Chapman 2010 and Ulrich 2002, and see Spellman 2014: ch. 1.
[2] Metzger 1987: 289–93; Robbins 1993; Junod 2011; Markschies 2012: 11–17; 2015: 196–2012.

(*Haer.* 3.2.2). In the fourth century, Eusebius devised canon tables to aid comparison of parallel passages in the Gospels, and the decrees of ecclesiastical councils also received the label 'canons'. At nearly the same time, Athanasius described the Shepherd of Hermas as outside the canon (*Decrees of the Synod of Nicaea* 18), using here the word 'canon' for the first time (in our extant sources) in the sense of the canon of sacred Scripture. In his canon list (included in this volume), Athanasius labelled the authoritative books 'canonized' (*Ep. fest.* 39.16, 20, 21). The Synod of Laodicea likewise spoke of the canonical books (τὰ κανονικά) and the non-canonical books (τὰ ἀκανόνιστα). Latin adopted the Greek word, as did other languages, including English.

A canon list, then, should be a list of the books that an author or council considers to constitute the biblical canon.[3] This description fits most of the lists we have included in this volume. The lists by Athanasius, or Augustine, or Gregory of Nazianzus, or the list in the *Breviarium Hipponense* could hardly be described in any other way. We recognize that even these lists do not indicate that all Christians agreed completely on the contents of the biblical canon. The lists do not mean that the issue of the canon was settled for the entire church, just as today Christians have not achieved complete agreement in this area. But at the very least, these lists do indicate which books the individual Christian writer or the delegates of the Council accepted as canonical, and that in the fourth century especially the concern grew to restrict the books deemed authoritative for ecclesiastical doctrine. Close study of the lists also indicates a broad consensus on the majority of the books of the Bible, certainly by the mid-fourth century, though some doubt persisted regarding certain books (e.g., Esther, Revelation, the Shepherd of Hermas, the deuterocanonical literature).

Our description of a canon list as the list of books that an author or council considered canonical should be nuanced when considering certain lists. We have included a passage from Josephus often labelled the first Jewish canon list, but anyone reading the passage will be disappointed to find that Josephus fails to list the books, and his account—while it affords us a great deal of certainty on the majority of writings that made up his collection of twenty-two sacred books—is not so precise that we can have complete assurance that we know the contents of his canon. But we do know that Josephus had a canon, in the sense of a bounded collection of Scripture. Some authors included here do not allow such confidence. Our treatment of Origen in this volume includes one passage containing a list of Old Testament books and two passages containing lists of New Testament books. In none of these cases can we be sure that Origen is detailing the exclusive list of books that he accepted as canonical. Concerning the Old Testament list, Origen may be reporting the Jewish canon rather than his own; many scholars have read his introduction to the list in this way (even

---

[3] Some scholars might consider the term 'canon list' to involve a redundancy since they define 'canon' as a list; see Ulrich 2002: 32–3.

if Eusebius, who preserved the list, did not). As for the passages in Origen recording New Testament lists, one of them is overtly the product of Eusebius's editorial activity, compiling disparate passages from Origen's works that originally recorded merely the Gospels, on the one hand, or some apostolic letters, on the other. The other passage, from a homily on Joshua, does run through the majority of New Testament books, but Origen does not describe the passage as a canon list or anything similar, so it is not clear that he intended to list all of the books making up his New Testament canon (i.e., it might not be an exclusive list). In a similar manner, the Muratorian Fragment might not be an intentional canon list,[4] and the passage excerpted from Eusebius expresses doubts about some of the books he surveys (as do some other canon lists included here).

So the label 'canon list' is problematic for some of the passages compiled in this volume. Not all of them clearly list the bounded collection of Scripture as advocated by an author or council. Some of them, at least in their original context (e.g., the passages of Origen excerpted by Eusebius), intended to include only a portion of the Scriptures. One might then question why we have omitted other similar passages, such as Irenaeus's defence of four Gospels as alone authoritative (*Haer.* 3.11.8). We have aimed to include the passages generally considered canon lists in the history of interpretation, though we recognize the potential problems of such terminology.

IMPORTANCE OF THE CANON LISTS

The canon lists, in most cases, unambiguously report what the compilers of the lists considered to belong to the biblical canon (with the necessary caveats expressed in the previous section). For this reason, they bear an undeniable importance in the history of the canon. More than most other types of data, the lists directly inform us of the books considered canonical in early Christianity.

We are not claiming that the canon lists of the early centuries of the church tell the whole story of the biblical canon. A comprehensive study of the use of Scripture in the early church will give attention not just to the lists of books drawn up by early Christian writers but also to the citations of Scripture in their theological writings (commentaries, polemical works, doctrinal treatises, etc.), the contents of ancient manuscripts, the production and reception of translations of the Scriptures, comments about the reception of particular books, the liturgical use of various writings, and other elements of early Christian engagement with Scripture. Inasmuch as the church was influenced by Jewish opinion on the content of the Hebrew Bible, the same features on the Jewish side will also prove relevant for the history of the Christian Bible. This book focuses on

---

[4] See, e.g., Kaestli 1994: 615–17; Markschies 2015: 203, 205.

the canon lists, then, not because these lists merit exclusive attention, or even pride of place, in an account of the history of the canon, but rather for two other reasons, one practical and one theoretical. Presenting all of the evidence that should inform study of the development of the biblical canon would become a practical impossibility; we had to concentrate on a limited data set, and even in terms of which canon lists to present, we had to make choices. In regard to theory, early Christian writers used these lists to report their own biblical canon, which they also thought represented (or should represent) the canon of the church as a whole. While an account of the ancient biblical canon will need to consider evidence in addition to lists—and we have provided in our notes selective references to some of this other data—such an account would be completely inadequate if it did not present clearly and accurately the books Christians themselves listed as forming their canon.

Lists are not the only means by which early Christians expressed themselves on the subject of the biblical canon. Scattered comments on individual books or groups of books pepper patristic literature. We have not seen fit to collect all these comments. Some authors of fundamental importance—Irenaeus of Lyons, or Clement of Alexandria, or Tertullian, for example—left behind nothing that could be considered a canon list, though any canon history would have to give serious attention to their statements and practice. They do not receive extended treatment here because their works transmit no canon list, a decision which demonstrates that this book is not a full canon history but a tool for such research.

Canon histories often focus on other types of evidence besides lists, and sometimes this choice is appropriate. Study of authoritative Scripture at Qumran cannot rely on any list of authoritative books because the Dead Sea Scrolls did not preserve such a list. One must instead concentrate on the identity of the biblical scrolls that survived the centuries in the caves around Qumran, the way the non-biblical writings made use of the biblical works, and any comments in the scrolls—or contemporary Jewish literature more broadly—with bearing on the issue. All of these methods raise problems for the canon researcher: it is not clear that the presence of a manuscript at Qumran indicates canonicity, or scriptural or authoritative status, rather than simply popularity.[5] Citations often present similar difficulties of interpretation: does a citation of Esther, for example, indicate that the author of the quoting text considered Esther canonical, or merely useful, or authoritative in some way that would not entail scriptural status or canonicity? Manuscripts and citations provide valuable data but do not directly correspond to canonical categories.

Scholars have often used such data to construct pictures of the canon. For instance, Bart Ehrman wrote a well-respected article a few decades ago on 'The New Testament Canon of Didymus the Blind'.[6] Because Didymus, a

---

[5] See Lim 2013: 119–47.   [6] Ehrman 1983.

fourth-century Alexandrian theologian, did not produce a canon list, Ehrman had to determine the contents of his canon based on other criteria. He employed three: whether Didymus described a writing as divine; whether he used it in a 'canonical' way; and whether he cited it alongside another writing of incontestable canonical authority. This method led Ehrman to posit that Didymus's canon included many books in the modern New Testament, with the addition of the Shepherd of Hermas, the Epistle of Barnabas, the Didache, and perhaps 1 Clement and Ignatius's *Epistle to the Romans*. As already indicated, this method for determining canonicity in an ancient author encounters serious problems in the face of parallel evidence in the ancient world. Steve Mason, for instance, has argued in regard to Josephus that if we did not have his own canon list from *Against Apion*, his use of a wide variety of ancient Jewish writings especially in his *Jewish Antiquities*, which exhibits no difference whether the writing is now in the Hebrew Bible or not, would convince us that he had a very wide canon, perhaps no canon at all.[7] But instead, since Josephus does transmit a canon list, his writings caution us against assuming that using a writing, even using it as authoritative in some way, signals acceptance of that writing's canonical status. The same point can be made from many authors in this book, not least Athanasius, whose use of Sirach and Wisdom of Solomon 'as Scripture' does not mean that he includes them in his canon.[8] Citations prove to be a problematic criterion for determining which books someone would list as constituting the canon. Undoubtedly citations should receive intense scholarly study for the information they provide about early Christian use of a variety of writings and the value they placed on them, but the list of writings cited—even cited 'as Scripture'— does not always correspond to the list of canonical writings provided by individual authors.

Ancient manuscripts provide an important window into the early Christian encounter with Scripture, and scholars have often wanted to use their contents to determine the contemporary biblical canon, or at least the canon for the compiler of the manuscript. The fourth-century Greek manuscript Codex Sinaiticus contains at the end some writings that no major Christian group today considers canonical: the Shepherd of Hermas and the Epistle of Barnabas. A century later, Codex Alexandrinus included 1 Clement and 2 Clement. Does the inclusion of these writings in these biblical manuscripts indicate their canonicity? J.K. Elliott considers the answer fairly obvious: 'We must assume that the authorities behind Codex Sinaiticus and Codex Alexandrinus considered these works canonical and wished to promote them as such. Certainly the user of these codices would have accepted all the texts in their Bible codex as having equal status.'[9] Despite the confidence of this assertion, we rarely have solid information on what the users of manuscripts thought about the various compositions included in them. Again, the canon lists contemporary with these

---

[7] Mason 2002: 126–7.   [8] See Leemans 1997; 2003.   [9] Elliott 1996: 111.

codices render Elliott's assumption problematic. For instance, Athanasius promotes the reading (at least to catechumens) of writings that he does not include within the biblical canon. He explicitly says that these other writings do not have equal status with the canonical writings, but it is hard to argue that he would have objected to a biblical manuscript that included some of these non-canonical writings. And Athanasius is not the only early Christian to hold such views.[10] Like citations, manuscripts provide important data concerning the scriptural practices of early Christianity, but their contents are not equivalent to a canon list.

A chief importance of the canon lists resides, then, in their providing explicit statements on the canon. Additionally, some of the canon lists collected here hold fundamental importance for the development of the biblical canon. For the Old Testament, our earliest evidence for a clearly defined canon remains Josephus's statement about the scriptural books. The Talmudic list at Baba Bathra 14b provides the earliest clear attestation for the tripartite division of the Hebrew Bible, with the allocation (though not necessarily the sequence) of books among the three divisions still in use among Jews today. The Christian lists of Old Testament books also provide valuable evidence for alternative arrangements of the Jewish Bible.[11] Histories of the New Testament canon usually devote significant space to the Muratorian Fragment and the lists of Eusebius and Athanasius, all of which seem to provide glimpses of a solidifying canon. These early Christian lists not only offer the clearest expressions of the biblical canon, but some of them are prime evidence for the developing canon in early Judaism and early Christianity.[12]

Though the lists are of fundamental significance for study of the biblical canon, those approaching them should keep in mind some cautions. First, as we have already noted, these lists of canonical books do not bear a direct relation to the books used as religiously authoritative in early Christianity. If one were to make a list of books actually used by early Christians, it would likely feature either more or fewer books than those in the canon lists. For instance, though 2–3 John eventually secured their place in the biblical canon (for most Christian groups), they exerted relatively little impact on the surviving writings from the early church. The same could be said for some other books of both the Old and New Testaments (e.g., Chronicles, Ecclesiastes, James, 2 Peter). John Barton has explored the 'effective canon' of early Christianity, a term by which he means the books Christians commonly used.[13] But one might also look beyond the canon, to books like the Shepherd of Hermas and 1 Enoch, which,

---

[10] In the present volume, see the respective sections on Epiphanius, Rufinus, and Amphilochius in chs 3 and 4. See also Gallagher 2015b.

[11] See Dorival 2003.

[12] But on the limited role of lists in this regard, see Markschies 2015: 212.

[13] Barton 1997.

judging from citations of them and other data such as manuscript attestation, did find an esteemed place in early Christian thought. More obvious examples are the deuterocanonical books (Tobit, Judith, etc.), which eventually found their way into the canon lists. Those authors who did not include them in their canon lists often still cited them. A canon list was not a comprehensive list of valuable religious books.

A second caution is that lists often (not always) date to a time when the major formative stages of the biblical canon had already taken place. We usually see in the lists the results of a long process of development. All of the Old Testament lists collected here might fittingly receive such a description. By the time of our first canon lists (e.g., Josephus), there were still some open issues—the status of Esther, for instance, and Ecclesiastes, or, for Christians, whether a small selection of books (the deuterocanonicals) not included in the Jewish Bible should form a part of the Christian canon—but the process by which certain religious writings came to be distinguished from others began centuries before our first canon lists and had largely found resolution. The situation differs somewhat for the New Testament, since the Muratorian Fragment (regardless of the date) and the list of Eusebius, for instance, attest a developing process, but even by the late second century CE major features of the New Testament canon were already solidifying, at least for the group of Christians who came to call themselves catholic and orthodox. Especially the four Gospels and (most of) the letters of Paul, but also Acts and some of the Catholic Epistles and Revelation (for the most part), were generally received by the time our earliest lists catalogued these books. But other books also could claim widespread respect and significant authority—the Shepherd of Hermas, the Epistle of Barnabas, the Acts of Paul, etc.—and their status continued to meet with some uncertainty through the fourth century, an uncertainty that perhaps contributed towards the proliferation of lists at that time.

The canon lists do not answer all of our questions about which religious books early Christians considered important and worthy of reading, or how and why the biblical canon developed the way it did. But the lists are the best sources for telling us specifically which books early Christians considered canonical.

AIMS OF THIS BOOK

Despite the importance of these early lists of books, they have remained relatively inaccessible to most people interested in the subject, including most biblical scholars. Frequently, books on the biblical canon provide translated selections of the passages containing the lists, or they simply enumerate the books cited in the passages.[14] While these methods helpfully allow access to some of the important information contained in the early Christian writings, other information is obscured or omitted, so that the excerpt presents only a skewed version of the ancient source. In the nineteenth century, Theodor Zahn assembled many of the lists, presenting the original language and supplying them with extensive notes and discussion.[15] In more recent times, with the proliferation of good, modern editions of patristic works, one would need to collect dozens of volumes to find the best editions of each individual list. This book aims to obviate that need for students and most scholars.

In the lists that follow, we supply the most essential information to help readers understand the selected passages containing the lists of books. Most importantly, we have excerpted the relevant passages from the most authoritative modern editions. We provide the passage in the original language—usually Greek or Latin, occasionally Hebrew or Syriac—with a parallel English translation, sometimes our own, though often we have used previously published translations. Numerous footnotes accompany the translation, explaining the features of the passages, sometimes taking account of textual variants, frequently pointing readers to scholarly literature that provides further discussion. (Because we intend to benefit both scholar and student, we have not refrained from citing scholarly literature in languages other than English when we have determined that scholars would want to know about it.) Preceding the passage itself, some brief comments introduce the ancient author and work and offer a preview of the list of books. Each section within the chapters concludes with a summary of the canon list and additional comments on any matters that remain unclear.

We have tried to include every Christian canon list from the first four centuries, a terminus that corresponds generally to the period at which most scholars would say that the biblical canon had achieved a stable shape (or as close to it as it would achieve until the sixteenth century). The latest list included here— that of Pope Innocent I—dates to the first decade of the fifth century. Readers should not interpret our decision to omit lists following this point as an indication that medieval lists lack any interest; on the contrary, lists of canonical books up through the time of the Reformation continue to offer surprises and reward study. We hope that our presentation of the early Christian lists will offer a satisfactory gateway into this study. In a departure from our general principle of including early Christian lists, we have chosen to incorporate two Jewish lists, those of Josephus (which is technically not even a list) and the Babylonian Talmud. Those familiar with discussion on the formation of the Old Testament will immediately realize that these two lists—the only Jewish

---

[14] See Kaestli and Wermelinger 1984: 135–51, 197–210; Metzger 1987: 305–15. For the latter method, see McDonald and Sanders 2002: 585–97.

[15] Zahn 1888–92. More recently, Hennings (1994: 146–206) presents many of the Old Testament lists in the original language, but with very brief discussion. For the New Testament lists (without notes), see Grosheide 1948.

lists before the turn of the second millennium CE—often prove crucial in scholarly treatments of the Jewish or Christian canons, so that this book would seem incomplete without them.

Modern Canons

The following chart serves a dual purpose. First, it allows the reader easily to compare the biblical canons of four major religious traditions. It does not cover each religious tradition holding to a biblical canon, such as the Ethiopian Orthodox Church.[16] But the religious traditions represented here should enable the reader to see what is broadly shared and where the distinctions lie in terms of the biblical canon across a variety of traditions. Second, this chart attempts to present the biblical canons of these traditions in reliance on a significant Bible or canon list. The only tradition here that has offered an official list is that of the Roman Catholic Church, which listed the books of its Bible at the Council of Trent in 1546. As for Judaism, the Second Rabbinic Bible of 1524–5 proved highly influential, so it seemed appropriate to use its Table of Contents for the Jewish list, even though it was not especially innovative in regard to the elements represented here (the identity and arrangement of the books). Various Protestant groups have issued lists (such as the Belgic Confession of 1561 or the Westminster Confession of 1646). Because of its historical importance, we have chosen to use the Table of Contents from the first edition of Luther's complete Bible (1534), even though this Table of Contents might imply some dissatisfaction with certain books (e.g., Hebrews, James) that few Protestants today would share. In the absence of any official list representing all Orthodox churches,[17] we have chosen to use the Table of Contents of the Orthodox Study Bible as a good representative in English for those books commonly accepted as Scripture in Greek Orthodox congregations. Other Orthodox groups would dissent from certain elements in this list.[18]

Jewish canon	Protestant canon	Roman Catholic canon	Greek Orthodox canon
Second Rabbinic Bible, 1524–5[19]	Luther Bible, 1534[20]	Council of Trent, 1546[21]	Orthodox Study Bible, 2008
Torah Genesis	1. Genesis 2. Exodus	Five Books of Moses Genesis	Genesis Exodus

[16] On which see Bruk 2016: 202–2.   [17] See Lash 2007; Pentiuc 2014.
[18] E.g., the Russian Orthodox Church has tended to align its Old Testament canon with that of the Protestants more than with that of the Roman Catholics; see de Regt 2016.
[19] For a description, see Ginsburg 1897: 956–74.
[20] See the facsimile edited by Füssel 2002.   [21] Tanner 1990: 2.663–4.

Jewish canon	Protestant canon	Roman Catholic canon	Greek Orthodox canon
Exodus	3. Leviticus	Exodus	Leviticus
Leviticus	4. Numbers	Leviticus	Numbers
Numbers	5. Deuteronomy	Numbers	Deuteronomy
Deuteronomy	6. Joshua	Deuteronomy	Joshua
Nevi'im	7. Judges	Joshua	Judges
Joshua	8. Ruth	Judges	Ruth
Judges	9. Samuel	Ruth	1 Kingdoms
Samuel	10. Kings	1 Kings	2 Kingdoms
Kings	11. Chronicles	2 Kings	3 Kingdoms
Isaiah	12. Ezra	3 Kings	4 Kingdoms
Jeremiah	13. Nehemiah	4 Kings	1 Chronicles
Ezekiel	14. Esther	1 Paralipomenon	2 Chronicles
The Twelve	15. Job	2 Paralipomenon	1 Ezra
(Minor	16. Psalms	1 Esdras	2 Ezra
Prophets)	17. Proverbs of	2 Esdras (= Nehemiah)	Nehemiah
Ketuvim	Solomon	Tobit	Tobit
Psalms	18. Preacher of	Judith	Judith
Proverbs	Solomon	Esther	Esther
Job	(Ecclesiastes)	Job	1 Maccabees
Song of Songs	19. Song of Solomon	150 Psalms of David	2 Maccabees
Ruth	20. Isaiah	Proverbs	3 Maccabees
Lamentations	21. Jeremiah[22]	Ecclesiastes	Psalms
Qoheleth	22. Ezekiel	Song of Songs	Job
(Ecclesiastes)	23. Daniel	Wisdom	Proverbs of Solomon
Esther	24. Twelve Minor	Ecclesiasticus	Ecclesiastes
Daniel	Prophets	Isaiah	Song of Songs
Ezra-Nehemiah	Hosea	Jeremiah with Baruch	Wisdom of Solomon
Chronicles	Joel	Ezechiel	Wisdom of Sirach
	Amos	Daniel	Hosea
	Obadiah	The Twelve Minor	Amos
	Jonah	Prophets	Micah
	Micah	Hosea	Joel
	Nahum	Joel	Obadiah
	Habakkuk	Amos	Jonah
	Zephaniah	Obadiah	
	Haggai		
	Zechariah		
	Malachi		
	Apocrypha, that is,	Jonah	Nahum
	books not	Micah	Habakkuk
	considered equal to	Nahum	Zephaniah
	Holy Scripture, but	Habakkuk	Haggai
	which are still useful	Zephaniah	Zechariah
	and good to read.	Haggai	Malachi
	Judith	Zechariah	Isaiah

[22] Though Lamentations is not mentioned in the table of contents, it does follow Jeremiah in the text. Note that Luther arrives at the number twenty-four for the books of the Old Testament by counting Nehemiah separately from Ezra, whereas Jerome (see ch. 4) had counted Ezra and Nehemiah as one book but separated Lamentations from Jeremiah to reach the number twenty-four.

Jewish canon	Protestant canon	Roman Catholic canon	Greek Orthodox canon
	Wisdom	Malachi	Jeremiah
	Tobit	1 Maccabees	Baruch
	Sirach	2 Maccabees	Lamentations
	Baruch		Epistle of Jeremiah
	Maccabees		Ezekiel
	Parts of Esther		Daniel
	Parts of Daniel		
		The Four Gospels	
	1. Matthew	Matthew	Matthew
	2. Mark	Mark	Mark
	3. Luke	Luke	Luke
	4. John	John	John
	5. Acts	Acts of the Apostles	Acts
		Fourteen Letters of Paul the Apostle	
	6. Romans	Romans	Romans
	7. 1 Corinthians	1 Corinthians	1 Corinthians
	8. 2 Corinthians	2 Corinthians	2 Corinthians
	9. Galatians	Galatians	Galatians
	10. Ephesians	Ephesians	Ephesians
	11. Philippians	Philippians	Philippians
	12. Colossians	Colossians	Colossians
	13. 1 Thessalonians	1 Thessalonians	1 Thessalonians
	14. 2 Thessalonians	2 Thessalonians	2 Thessalonians
	15. 1 Timothy	1 Timothy	1 Timothy
	16. 2 Timothy	2 Timothy	2 Timothy
	17. Titus	Titus	Titus
	18. Philemon	Philemon	Philemon
	19. 1 Peter	Hebrews	Hebrews
	20. 2 Peter	1 Peter	James
	21. 1 John	2 Peter	1 Peter
	22. 2 John	1 John	2 Peter
	23. 3 John	2 John	1 John
		3 John	2 John
	Hebrews	James	3 John
	James	Jude	Jude
	Jude	Revelation	Revelation
	Revelation		

1

The Development of the Christian Biblical Canon

A Survey of the Early Period

On 8 April 1546 the Roman Catholic Council of Trent voted in favour of delineating the biblical canon, and they pronounced an anathema on anyone who did not accept it.[1] It was not the first time a council had voted on the biblical canon; earlier regional councils had considered the matter and issued (sometimes conflicting) canon lists—see the lists from the Synod of Laodicea (chapter 3) and the *Breviarium Hipponense* (chapter 4)—and the (Western) ecumenical Council of Florence a century before Trent had issued a biblical canon list (session 11, 4 February 1442).[2] But Trent was the first ecumenical council to pronounce an anathema on anyone who did not accept its ruling concerning the biblical canon,[3] and in this manner the council settled the matter for those it represented like no previous decision had. Yet, by the time Trent articulated the biblical canon, the Protestant Reformation was in its second generation and the churches of the East had for centuries refused to recognize the authority of Rome. Trent's decision on the biblical canon was binding for only a segment of the Christian world, and no previous council could claim to have settled the canon for all Christians because the ecumenical councils of the first millennium did not discuss the matter. The popular idea that a council of bishops, perhaps at Nicaea, restricted the holy books of the church in order to suppress dissident literature cannot find support in the evidence available to us. In the early period of the church's history, there was no official statement regarding the biblical canon, and the same is true for

---

[1] For Latin text and English translation, see Tanner 1990: 663–4. For an accessible introduction to Trent, see O'Malley 2013; on the biblical canon, see pp. 89–102.

[2] See the text and translation of this proclamation of the Council of Florence in Tanner 1990: 1.572.

[3] Florence, in connection with the biblical canon, anathematized groups who distinguished the God of the Old Testament from the God of the New Testament, naming the Manichees as one such group.

contemporary Judaism. The closest analogue to official statements, besides the regional councils,[4] comes only from individual bishops who at best enjoyed authority over a limited geographical area.[5] Up to the present day, there never has been a vote on the biblical canon which all Christians would feel bound to accept.

This situation has at least two important consequences for our study. First, given the lack of institutional control over this matter, we might be surprised by the basic unity of the two dozen early canon lists collected in this volume. There are differences among the lists, but a substantial core unites them all. Granted, these lists do all come from more or less orthodox writers whom we might expect to share much in common, and we know that other writers (e.g., Marcion) promoted a Bible that looked significantly different from the one evident in the lists. But many people commonly labelled heretics (e.g., Arius, Eunomius, even Priscillian) did not dispute which books should be considered binding but rather the interpretation of those books or the way to articulate the theological principles arising from them.[6] In short, there is a remarkable unity to the biblical canon even in the absence of a hierarchy able to impose that unity.[7]

The second consequence makes our task rather difficult. The lack of early official pronouncements on the canon means that the evidence for the development of the canon must be sought in disparate and contested locations, particularly the remains of manuscripts and scattered statements from various writers. The modern history of research into this question has demonstrated that such evidence will not drive all scholars, or even a majority of scholars, to a consensus position. Some scholars read the available evidence as pointing towards an early formation of the Bible: a basically stable Hebrew Bible in perhaps the second century BCE, and a basically stable New Testament in the late second century CE. The same evidence leads other scholars to insist that we should date the formation of the biblical canon centuries later, the Hebrew Bible in the second century CE or thereabouts, and the New Testament in the fourth century.

This chapter will not settle such disputes, nor will it even stake out a position among them. Instead, in keeping with the aims of this book, we intend to

---

[4] On the impact of these councils, see Verheyden 2013: 408: 'late and basically limited to technical matters and to confirming the consensus that had been growing'.

[5] On the role of bishops in the development of the biblical canon, see Markschies 2015: 202, 211.

[6] The same could be said for Gnostic groups and Montanists; see Gamble 2002: 292–3; Markschies 2015: 257 (on Gnostics specifically).

[7] Since this book focuses on those traditions that produced early lists—usually in Greek and Latin, but also Syriac—we pay less attention to other Christian traditions, such as the Ethiopian Orthodox Church, which has a Bible (not a canon in the narrow sense) that diverges in some significant ways from Western Bibles, even while the different traditions still share many things. See Bruk 2016.

survey—briefly—the evidence for canon formation and outline the major scholarly theories that seek to explain that data.[8] This overview of canon formation provides a context for the lists presented in the rest of the book. We start with the Old Testament, before turning to the New Testament.

THE HEBREW BIBLE/OLD TESTAMENT

The Hebrew Bible today consists of twenty-four books divided into three sections: the Torah (Law), Neviim (Prophets), and Ketuvim (Writings or Hagiographa), producing the acronym TaNaK, meaning the Jewish Bible.[9] This arrangement is attested by the Masoretic manuscripts from around the year 1000 CE, but we can trace the tripartite division and the number of books back much earlier than that. A passage of the Talmud lists the eight books of the Neviim and the eleven books of the Ketuvim, whereas it assumes everyone knows the five books of the Torah. This testimony, affirming the three divisions and the twenty-four books, dates no later than the redaction of the Talmud in the sixth century, and most scholars would date it well before then, perhaps as early as the second century.[10] Jerome, in the late fourth century, also testifies to the tripartite division of the Hebrew Bible, under the same three titles we know from Hebrew sources (or, rather, their Latin equivalents), and he divides the books among the three divisions similarly to the way the Hebrew sources do. But according to Jerome, only a minority, alternative Jewish opinion counts the books as twenty-four, with Ruth and Lamentations placed among the Ketuvim/ Writings. Jerome says that the dominant tradition among the Jews includes Ruth as a part of Judges and counts Lamentations as a part of Jeremiah—thus among the Prophets and not the Writings—and in this way the books number twenty-two.

We can thus confidently date to the fourth century or earlier (depending on the date of the Talmudic list) the Jewish enumeration of the Hebrew Bible as twenty-four books divided into three major sections. Our sources provide no consistent ordering of books within the third section (the Ketuvim/Writings), and there are some slight inconsistencies in the ordering of the second division (the Neviim/Prophets), but the Masoretic manuscripts, the Talmudic list, and Jerome's alternative ordering all situate the same books within the three divisions. But Jerome also tells us that the same books could be rearranged and

---

[8] For more comprehensive studies, see Beckwith 1985; Metzger 1987; McDonald and Sanders 2002; Lim 2013; Markschies 2015: 191–299; Mroczek 2016; McDonald 2017.

[9] On the term Tanak, see Ilan 2012.

[10] See ch. 2 on Baba Bathra. This list does not mention the total number of books, for which see b. Ta'an. 8a.

counted as twenty-two, while still maintaining the same divisions of Law, Prophets, and Writings (see chapter 4 on Jerome).

This alternative numbering of twenty-two is, in fact, the dominant tradition for counting the books of the Old Testament within the church. Origen is the earliest Christian author to mention this enumeration in a list still extant, and he relates the number twenty-two to the letters of the Hebrew alphabet: just as the Hebrews have twenty-two letters in their alphabet, so they have twenty-two books in their Bible. The books he lists more or less conform to the books Jerome lists, except in a few instances: (1) Origen's title Jeremiah includes the deutero-canonical Letter of Jeremiah (and probably Baruch); (2) his two books of Esdras probably refer to the canonical Ezra-Nehemiah (= Esdras B in the LXX tradition) along with 1 Esdras (= Esdras A in the LXX tradition), this latter book being canonical today only in the Eastern traditions; and finally (3) Origen does not mention the tripartite division of the Jewish Bible but rather arranges the canon in a very different manner.[11] Origen does say that he is transmitting the biblical canon of the 'Hebrews', so it may be that he is providing us with a Jewish arrangement for the canon that does not conform to the tripartite divisions of the Tanak.[12]

Other Christian sources also list the books as twenty-two, sometimes invoking the analogy with the Hebrew alphabet.[13] No Christian source (besides Jerome) in the first four centuries explicitly arranged the Old Testament in the three divisions of the Hebrew Bible;[14] patristic orders of the Old Testament vary widely, but always begin with the Pentateuch, usually followed by the books of history and prophetic literature, with the poetic books inserted here or there. The ordering of the books never achieved any sort of consistency, and sometimes different lists appear in the same author in different sequences.[15] In addition to the custom of counting the Old Testament as twenty-two books, some ecclesiastical writers did know about an alternative enumeration that reached to twenty-four books,[16] and some even mentioned another enumeration reaching to twenty-seven books, which, by a trick of counting, included the same contents as the lists numbering twenty-two.[17]

---

[11] Also, the Greek text transmitted in extant manuscripts of Eusebius—who preserves Origen's list for us—lacks the Twelve Minor Prophets, but that omission is clearly a mistake. See ch. 3 on Origen for more details.

[12] See Dorival 2003.

[13] The analogy with the Hebrew alphabet is mentioned by Origen, Athanasius, Epiphanius, Gregory of Nazianzus, Hilary of Poitiers, and Jerome. Cyril of Jerusalem and the disputed list of the Synod of Laodicea do not mention the alphabet but do mention the number twenty-two. See chs 3–4 below on these lists, and see the discussion of the number twenty-two in Gallagher 2012a: 85–92.

[14] Some Christian sources may have arranged the Old Testament into a tripartite structure different from the Tanak structure of the Rabbis. On Luke 24:44, see below. Ellis (1991: 11) sees a threefold structure in the canon list of Melito of Sardis.

[15] See the various OT lists in Epiphanius; also Jerome.

[16] See, e.g., the list by Hilary below.

[17] See the lists by Epiphanius and Jerome. Earlier than these lists, the Bryennios List implies the number twenty-seven.

But there are also Christian sources that include within the Old Testament some material not found in the rabbinic biblical canon, and this additional material is not limited to the expanded Jeremiah and the extra book of Esdras, as we have already seen in Origen. Augustine, for instance, includes within the Old Testament—not in any special category but intermixed with the other books—the works called Tobit, Judith, 1–2 Maccabees, Wisdom of Solomon, and Ecclesiasticus (= Sirach or Ben Sira). These are the writings that more than a thousand years later would receive the label 'deuterocanonical'.[18] Latin canon lists often include these books from the end of the fourth century.[19] There was some controversy about their inclusion, as Jerome says emphatically that they are not a part of the canon and that they are, instead, apocrypha.[20] Jerome knew that these books were not a part of the Jewish canon, so he thought Christians should not consider them canonical, either. Augustine also knew they were not in the Jewish canon, but he thought their usefulness for Christians granted them authority within the church.

Such information (and more) we obtain from the canon lists on which the current volume focuses. A great deal of scholarship on the canon concerns itself, however, with the developments prior to the lists, when the available evidence is much sparser and more difficult of interpretation. In the absence of lists in the earlier period, scholars often investigate how early they can trace certain elements of the later biblical canon, such as the enumeration as twenty-two or twenty-four, the tripartite division of the Hebrew Bible, or even simply the sanctity of the books. This backwards approach runs the real danger of anachronistically imposing on earlier sources the categories that may have been formulated only later.[21] Nevertheless, being awake to this danger will help us mitigate it. Moreover, these later categories have often given shape to the scholarly study of the earlier sources, and our concern here is with surveying not only the earlier sources but also scholarship on them. We will, therefore, take these issues one by one, followed by a look at the development of the Old Testament in Christian circles.

---

[18] The Roman Catholic deuterocanon also includes Baruch, but we have seen that in this early period this work was often considered a part of Jeremiah. In this way, it was also included by Augustine, but also by other Christians who did not include the other books of the deuterocanon (i.e., Tobit, Judith, etc.). The term 'deuterocanonical' was coined by Sixtus of Siena in his *Bibliotheca Sancta* (Venice, 1566), p. 10 (available on Google Books at <http://tinyurl.com/j8jj4rj>). The term refers to books that were not recognized as authoritative until a later time, and for Sixtus the deuterocanonical books include more books and sections of books than are commonly included under that label today.

[19] See the *Breviarium Hipponense*, Codex Claromontanus, the Mommsen Catalogue, and Innocent. Contrast Hilary, Jerome, and Rufinus.

[20] See in ch. 4 on Jerome's *Prologus Galeatus*.

[21] For a forceful argument against such a 'teleological' approach, see Mroczek 2016.

The Enumeration of the Old Testament Books

The earliest references we have to a specific number of books for the Jewish Bible come at the end of the first century CE and the beginning of the second century. Josephus tells his readers that whereas Greeks have innumerable contradictory books, Jews have only twenty-two containing the record of all time, from the creation of the world to the time of Artaxerxes, the Persian king in (what we now know as) the mid-fifth century BCE. Josephus does not mention that the significance of the number twenty-two relates to the Hebrew alphabet. He does not even tell us which books constitute these twenty-two: he merely says that five of them derive from Moses, thirteen derive from prophets who wrote the history of their times from Moses to Artaxerxes, and four of them contain hymns and precepts. It seems likely that Josephus has in mind the same books that later Christians would also number twenty-two, and thus essentially the same books that the Talmudic list would enumerate as twenty-four.[22]

Two other early sources mention this alternative reckoning of twenty-four books. The Christian Gospel of Thomas, probably dating to the second half of the second century, represents Jesus's disciples as saying to their master that 'twenty-four prophets have spoken in Israel, and they all spoke of you' (Gos. Thom. 52). There is no elaboration of this point, but it seems likely that the disciples are referring to the Jewish Scriptures and counting them as twenty-four books.[23]

From around the same time as Josephus, the Jewish work 4 Ezra provides the other reference to twenty-four books. The text purports to narrate events from the time of Ezra, but it was actually written by an anonymous author at the end of the first century CE. According to the narrative, the manuscripts of the Jewish Scriptures were destroyed along with the city of Jerusalem at the time of the Babylonian captivity. After the exile, Ezra and his five companions were charged by God to replace these Scriptures over a period of forty days.

> So during the forty days, ninety-four books were written. And when the forty days were ended, the Most High spoke to me, saying, 'Make public the twenty-four books that you wrote first, and let the worthy and the unworthy read them; but keep the seventy that were written last, in order to give them to the wise among your people. For in them is the spring of understanding, the fountain of wisdom, and the river of knowledge.' And I did so. (4 Ezra 14:44–8)

There are two sets of books mentioned in this passage, twenty-four public books and seventy books reserved for the wise. Both sets of books are inspired. Fourth Ezra thus seems to know a collection of sacred Scripture that includes twenty-four books, and it also knows of other books that are not in this collection but that are inspired. Most scholars have concluded that the author of 4 Ezra intended to legitimize pseudepigraphical books such as his own, and so he

---

[22] For more extensive discussion, see ch. 2 on Josephus.
[23] On this saying of Gos. Thom., see Gathercole 2014: 414–19.

mentioned the seventy inspired books that are reserved for the wise. But he also knew a public collection of twenty-four books that must have had relatively solid boundaries, since the seventy inspired books that he wanted to promote apparently could not form a part of the public collection.[24]

No earlier sources mention a particular number for the biblical books. The significance of an exact number is probably that the contents of the canon were determined, at least for the source that transmits the number. That is to say, a precise number of canonical books corresponds to a definite collection of canonical books, even if the number is symbolic and determines how the books are counted.[25] While 4 Ezra does not tell us which books constituted the twenty-four public books, the fact that it can enumerate them as twenty-four seems to indicate that their identity is certain; the canon is not open, but closed. The same is probably not true for the seventy books reserved for the wise. In that instance, the number seventy is probably purely symbolic, and it is very doubtful that the author of 4 Ezra could have actually named the seventy books, because there was no actual collection of seventy. If that is true for the number seventy, conceivably it could be true for the number twenty-four as well; perhaps it is also symbolic and it does not imply that there is an actual list of twenty-four books.[26] However, our earliest source that mentions a number—Josephus and the twenty-two books—obviously has in mind an actual list of books, since he divides those twenty-two books into different categories: five of Moses, thirteen of the prophets, and four of hymns and precepts. Probably both numbers (twenty-two and twenty-four) reflect an intentional enumeration aiming at the number of letters of the Hebrew and Greek alphabets, respectively, possibly under the influence of Alexandrian scholarship on Homer.[27] Most scholars argue that Josephus, 4 Ezra, and the Gospel of Thomas reflect a known biblical canon, even if not all Jews at the time would have accepted the same canon.[28]

The Divisions of the Old Testament

The tripartite structure of the Hebrew Bible—consisting of the five books of Torah, eight books of Neviim/Prophets, and eleven books of Ketuvim/Writings—certainly goes back to the fourth century CE, as confirmed by Jerome, and

[24] For discussion, see Lim 2013: 49–50; Steinberg and Stone 2015: 32–5. On the other hand, Dorival (2014: 29) proposes that 4 Ezra originally had groups of twenty-two and seventy-two books, which numbers fluctuated in the manuscript tradition. Epiphanius mentions two categories of books, one containing twenty-two books, the other seventy-two (see below, p. 165), which might be an echo or an adaptation of 4 Ezra.

[25] Darshan 2012. Note that the same is not true among Ethiopian Christians, for whom the symbolic number of eighty-one books in the Bible does not correspond to any definite collection, and Ethiopian theologians still disagree on how to make up the eighty-one books, or even the value of this enumeration. See Bruk 2016.

[26] See Mroczek 2016: 167–71.   [27] Darshan 2012.

[28] See, e.g., Barton (1986: 59), for whom Josephus is an anomaly.

perhaps earlier than that, depending on the date of the Talmudic list. The sources attesting the three divisions probably reflect a custom that had been known for some time, but scholars debate how early to date the tripartite arrangement. Earlier references to Scripture are bipartite more often than tripartite: they refer to 'the law and the prophets' or 'Moses and the prophets'.[29] Even early rabbinic (tannaitic) literature contains more bipartite references than tripartite ones.[30] While scholars of a previous generation typically understood such bipartite formulas as referring to the first two sections of the Tanak, before the formation of the Ketuvim, scholars often now are hesitant to assume that an earlier mention of 'prophets' must signify a canonical division (Neviim/Prophets) rather than non-Mosaic Scripture more generally.[31] Some pre-rabbinic statements, which we will survey in just a moment, might indicate that already in the second century BCE some Jews conceived of their Scriptures as inhabiting three divisions. Some scholars consider this discussion to have a bearing on the identity of books in the canon, since, they reason, if there are three sections of the Bible, the books occupying those divisions must also have been determined.

For most of the time period covered in this section, the concept of 'arrangement' of the Scriptures should probably be understood on a conceptual rather than physical level.[32] Since the codex did not become popular among Christians until the second century CE, and among other groups after that, we will mostly be concerned in this section with a period dominated by scrolls, which, for the most part, entailed individual biblical books written on individual scrolls.[33] The discussion of arrangement here then does not imply the arrangement of the biblical books in a codex. Possibly, the ancient indications of a canon structure point to some sort of arrangement of the scrolls in a library, but this

---

[29] Representative examples from Qumran and the New Testament: 1QS 1.2–3; Matt. 5:17. See further Barton 1986: 44–55.

[30] Leiman 1976: 58–9; Barton 1986: 52–4; Carr 1996: 57–8. The earliest rabbinic text that contains a tripartite formula is t. Roš. Haš. 2.12 (commenting on m. R.H. 4.6); for the text, see Leiman 1976: 63. However, Beckwith (1985: 166n6) believes the term '*Ketuvim*' in m. Yad. 3.5 refers to the third division of the Tanak and not to the 'Scriptures' more generally, as it is usually interpreted (also Danby 1933: 782n3). For Beckwith, then, there are two tannaitic references to the tripartite structure of the canon.

[31] See the discussion below. The view that 'prophets' refers to all non-Mosaic Scripture instead of the second division of the Tanak is most closely associated with John Barton (see esp. Barton 1986: 44–55). According to Steinberg and Stone (2015: 10), the NT phrase 'Moses and the Prophets' should be rendered 'Moses and the other inspired writers', thus not referring to the second division of the Tanak.

[32] For some reflections on conceptions of the Bible before the creation of full-Bible codices in the fourth century, see Kraft 2007: 10–18.

[33] There is some evidence among the Dead Sea Scrolls that multiple biblical books could appear on one scroll; see Tov 2004: 75. Most of the examples concern books of the Torah and the Minor Prophets. The only scroll that preserves the join between two books of the Torah is 4QpaleoGen-Exod¹ (first century BCE), in which the end of Genesis and the beginning of Exodus are in the same column, separated by three blank lines.

is only a guess.[34] Probably we have to do with a conceptual arrangement, the organization of the material in a person's head.

Six early statements have at least sometimes been interpreted as referring to the tripartite arrangement of the Hebrew Bible.

Prologue to Sirach 1–2; 8–10; 24–5

...the Law and the Prophets and the others that followed them...
...the Law and the Prophets and the other books of our ancestors...
...the Law itself, the Prophecies, and the rest of the books...

The book of Sirach, which became known in the Latin tradition as Ecclesiasticus, was written in Hebrew in the early second century BCE by a scribal teacher named Jesus Ben Sira.[35] Several decades later, the grandson of Ben Sira translated the book into Greek and added a prologue, from which the above statements are taken. Most scholars have regarded the prologue to Greek Sirach as good evidence for some sort of a tripartite canon, whether equivalent to the divisions of the later rabbinic Tanak or not.[36] This prologue is 'the most important witness for the formation of a tripartite canon' in the early period.[37] On this reading, the first two items mentioned in Sirach's prologue correspond to the first two divisions of the Tanak, while the third item—variously described as 'the others that followed them' or 'the other books of our ancestors' or 'the rest of the books'—corresponds to the Ketuvim, before any definite name for this third section had developed.[38] Some scholars question whether the third category mentioned by the grandson really describes the Ketuvim; perhaps the author simply refers to other Jewish literature besides the Law and the Prophets, which (as we have seen) was a common formula for describing Jewish Scripture at the time.[39] This revised view seems to have gained popularity over the past few decades, but many scholars still advocate the more traditional interpretation that the Sirach prologue attests to (perhaps an early form of) the tripartite canon. Steinberg and Stone's recent assessment helpfully provides the positive case for this view.

> Repeating the three-part formula three separate times in such a short passage suggests a common parlance, which gives the strong impression that the third group

---

[34] See Sarna 2000. For further bibliography, see Gallagher 2014c: 191n39.

[35] See Sir. 50:27 for the author's self-identification. Mroczek (2016: ch. 3) problematizes the authorship of Sirach.

[36] See Lange 2008: 55–6 with nn. 1–2.

[37] Steins 1995: 512. On the date and authenticity of the prologue, see Steinberg 2006: 158–9n183.

[38] See, e.g., Beckwith 1985: 112, 164.

[39] See Barton 1986: 47–8; Ulrich 2003a: 211–13; Carr 2011: 161–2; Lange 2008: 67–70 stresses that the threefold phrasing of the prologue refers to all of Jewish literature, and he thinks (pp. 70–2) that *Ep. Aristeas* cites the prologue to Sirach and confirms his interpretation.

regularly belongs with the other two. The use of the definite article in reference to all three sections indicates that each group is considered to be part of the same whole. The other books explicitly 'follow' the Law and the Prophets (v. 1); the word 'remaining' certainly does not refer to any remaining books that were known in the time of Ben Sira but, rather, to those that remain *of the sacred collection* in addition to the Law and the Prophets. All three collections are likewise accredited to the one authoritative tradition of the 'fathers' (v. 3). Therefore, we hold that the Ben Sira prologue witnesses to a three-part canon around 130 B.C.E.[40]

The issues continue to be debated. One of the points mentioned by Steinberg and Stone that continues to divide scholars is whether the presence of the definite article in relation to all the terms used in the prologue either signifies a definite collection of books[41] or, on the other hand, would be consistent with an open-ended and amorphous assortment of Jewish writings.[42] On the whole, probably most scholars still see in this prologue a reference to a third division of the canon, without necessarily thinking that the third division is closed and definite.[43]

4QMMT C 10–11

... we have [written] to you so that you may study (carefully) the book of Moses and the books of the Prophets and (the writings of) David [and the] [events of] ages past.[44]

This passage is found in the so-called Halakhic Letter from Qumran, one of the Dead Sea Scrolls. The writer of the letter encourages the readers to consider things written in some books, and the categories invoked have often been seen as reflecting the three divisions of the Hebrew Bible: the book of Moses (Torah), the books of the Prophets (Neviim), and David (Ketuvim). Such an interpretation assumes that the term 'David' refers to the book of Psalms,[45] which itself stands for the third section of the canon, the Ketuvim. If that were the case, then 'books of Moses', 'books of the prophets', and 'David' could essentially mean Torah, Neviim, Ketuvim.[46] But not everyone is convinced. When this Halakhic Letter was first fully published, the two editors responsible for it disagreed about the probability that 'David' referred not just to the Psalter

[40] Steinberg and Stone 2015: 12.
[41] Beckwith 1985: 166n2; van der Kooij 2003: 29; Steinberg and Stone 2015: 14.
[42] Trebolle Barrera 2002: 129; Lim 2013: 101.
[43] See, e.g., Dorival 2004: 98–9; Kaestli 2007: 108. Note also Sir. 38:34b–39:1, which describes the one devoted to the law, wisdom, and prophecies, a possible allusion to a tripartite conception of Scripture, though the passage goes on to mention also sayings and parables, and proverbs and parables (39:2–3).
[44] Translation from Qimron and Strugnell 1994: 59. The reconstructed Hebrew text is on the facing page.
[45] See the metrical list by Gregory of Nazianzus in ch. 3 for 'David' as the title of the Psalter, as well as the Syriac list from St Catherine's Monastery in ch. 5. Cf. also Heb. 4:7.
[46] Dempster 2008: 114–16.

but to the entire section of Ketuvim.[47] Others have pointed out that there are four—and not three—classifications of writings in the passage (Torah, Prophets, David, events of ages past), and Eugene Ulrich questioned the reconstruction of the Hebrew fragment, arguing that the reconstructed term 'David' might not have been in the scroll at all.[48] If 'David' is read in the scroll, one could also question whether the scroll intends to indicate the Psalter or some other composition.[49] Such arguments have weakened the weight of this testimony so that some recent advocates of an early tripartite Hebrew Bible do not invoke 4QMMT as positive evidence.[50]

2 Maccabees 2:13

> The same things are reported in the records and in the memoirs of Nehemiah, and also that he founded a library and collected the books about the kings and prophets, and the writings of David, and letters of kings about votive offerings.

In reporting about an action of collecting books by Judas Maccabeus in the second century BCE, this passage reflects back on a similar action earlier performed by Nehemiah. The categories of books mentioned here might correspond to the second and third divisions of the Tanak: books about the kings and prophets (i.e., Neviim), and the writings of David (i.e., Psalms, at the beginning of the Ketuvim) and letters of kings about votive offerings (cf. Ezra 6:3–12; 7:12–26, near the end of the Ketuvim). On this view, the first section, the Torah, is left unmentioned because it is self-evident.[51] Few scholars agree that this passage has reference to a tripartite canon.[52] Beckwith argues that the books in this library were non-Mosaic writings not limited to Scripture.[53]

Philo, On the Contemplative Life *25*

> In each house there is a consecrated room which is called a sanctuary or closet and closeted in this they are initiated into the mysteries of the sanctified life. They take nothing into it, either drink or food or any other of the things necessary for the needs of the body, but laws and oracles delivered

---

[47] See Qimron's interpretation at Qimron and Strugnell 1994: 59n10, and Strugnell's more cautious approach at ibid.: 112. (See also ibid.: ix for information about which editor was responsible for the different sections of the volume.)

[48] Ulrich 2003a; 2003b: 66–71; 2015: 300–2; Campbell 2000; Lim 2001. While the translation provided at Qimron and Strugnell 1994: 59 does not show the problem with the term 'David', the Hebrew text on p. 58 does show that the last two letters are uncertain.

[49] On texts associated in Antiquity with David, see Mroczek 2016: 78–83.

[50] See Steinberg and Stone 2015: 15n61.

[51] Dempster 2008: 116–17; cp. the omission of the Torah in Baba Bathra (ch. 2).

[52] Trebolle Barrera (2002: 130) suggests that the passage could be taken in such a way before arguing against it. For discussion of the passage, see Doran 2012: 59–60; Dorival 2014: 23.

[53] Beckwith 1985: 150–1.

through the mouths of prophets, and hymns and anything else which fosters and perfects knowledge and piety.[54]

This paragraph describes the habits of the desert-dwelling Jewish group that Philo calls the Therapeutae. He describes their literature as consisting of laws, prophetic oracles, and psalms (and anything else that promotes knowledge and piety). It does not take much imagination to see the first two categories as equivalent to the Torah and Neviim, while the hymns could refer to the Psalter, which in turn could stand for the entire Ketuvim.[55] Beckwith presented an extensive and complex argument that some ancient sources do refer to the third section of the canon by the title 'Psalms' or similar,[56] but his argument has persuaded few scholars.[57] If the Therapeutae's 'hymns' are biblical, it is difficult to see in them anything beyond the Psalter.[58]

Luke 24:44

Then he said to them, 'These are my words that I spoke to you while I was still with you—that everything written about me in the law of Moses, the prophets, and the psalms must be fulfilled.'

This paragraph describing a conversation between the resurrected Jesus and his disciples refers to Scripture as the law of Moses, the prophets, and the psalms. The argument for a reference to a tripartite canon here echoes the similar argument for the text from Philo noted above, so that here also some scholars see the reference to psalms as indicating the Hagiographa.[59] Many scholars doubt that the third element of Jesus's statement encompasses more than the Book of Psalms, though, even so, the threefold division of Scripture implied in this verse might suggest some sort of relationship (as a precursor?) to the Tanak structure familiar from rabbinic literature.[60]

Josephus, Against Apion *1.39–40*

Five of these are the books of Moses....From the death of Moses until Artaxerxes, king of the Persians after Xerxes, the prophets after Moses wrote the history of what took place in their own times in thirteen books; the remaining four books contain hymns to God and instructions for people on life.

While a much fuller discussion of this passage appears in chapter 2, here we should note that Josephus does divide his canon into three sections: books of Moses (five books), prophets after Moses (thirteen books), and hymns and

---

[54] Trans. Colson 1941: 127 (adapted).   [55] See Beckwith 1985: 117–18.
[56] Beckwith 1985: 112–15.   [57] See Steinberg and Stone 2015: 25.
[58] Barton 1986: 58.   [59] Beckwith 1985: 111–15; Dempster 2008: 120–1.
[60] Dorival 2014: 25–6; Steinberg and Stone 2015: 25.

instructions (four books). Such a structure does not precisely match the later Tanak divisions seen in Jerome and the Talmud. It may be that Josephus has adapted the Tanak categories in order to emphasize the historical nature of his sources.[61] Some scholars think that Josephus has divided these books according to genre without reference to any other canonical arrangement.[62]

Theories

Of these six proposed early references to a tripartite canon, only the Sirach prologue finds general acceptance as such a reference. Three passages mention in the third place the psalms or hymns (4QMMT [?]; Philo; Luke 24:44). Josephus's categories might in some way depend on the tripartite canon, but he also seems to have used genre as a structuring principle. So only one pre-rabbinic reference to the tripartite canon is relatively secure in the minds of a significant number of scholars.[63]

Various theories have sought to account for the development of the tripartite canon.[64] Ancient sources do not explicitly attribute the formation of the canon to any particular person, except perhaps for 4 Ezra, which narrates that Ezra and his companions wrote all twenty-four (or, rather, ninety-four) books after their destruction by the Babylonians. This general view—that Ezra assembled the Scriptures following the Babylonian exile—found wide acceptance in Christian sources in Antiquity and beyond.[65] Nearly five centuries ago, Elias Levita proposed a modified theory, that the men of the Great Synagogue in the early Second Temple Period fixed the three divisions of the Hebrew canon and its twenty-four books.[66] This theory was eventually displaced by what has been called the 'classic' or 'standard' theory of the canonization of the Hebrew Bible, which proposed that the canon developed in three stages corresponding to the three sections of the canon.[67] The Pentateuch was canonized first at the time of Ezra, before the Samaritans (who accept only the Pentateuch as Scripture) separated themselves from the Jews. The second section of the Tanak, the Neviim/Prophets, was canonized around 200 BCE, as indicated by Ben Sira's mention of the Twelve Prophets as a collection (49:10). This theory understands the law and the prophets in Sirach's prologue as the first two sections of the Tanak, while the prologue's reference to 'other books' implies that the Ketuvim were

---

[61] See Beckwith 1985: 118–27; Lim 2013: 49; Chapman 2016: 41.

[62] Mason 2002; Kaestli 2007: 109; Dorival 2014: 26; Steinberg and Stone 2015: 30–1.

[63] Dorival (2004: 96–9; 2014: 23–7) doubts that any of these passages indicates a tripartite canon, but rather argues that they display the inadequacy felt with the phrase 'law and prophets'.

[64] For a survey: Dorival 2004: 86–90; 2014: 14–18; for more detail, Chapman 2000: 3–70.

[65] Cf. Irenaeus, *Haer.* 3.21.2; Clement of Alexandria, *Strom.* 1.22; Tertullian, *Cult. fem.* 1.3; further references in Ryle 1892: 239–50; Fried 2014: 118–23.

[66] Ginsburg 1867: 120. On the reception of the idea, see Ryle 1892: 250–72.

[67] The classic articulation of the theory is Ryle 1892. On the background leading up to his formulation, see Chapman 2013.

still in the process of formation. This process would not achieve completion until the late first century CE, when the Rabbis finally settled the third section—and thus the canon as a whole—during a meeting at the Judean town of Yavneh (or Jamnia), a meeting often given the lofty title 'Council of Yavneh'.

This classic model of the Hebrew canon has been largely discarded over the last half-century. One of the first aspects of the theory to sustain heavy criticism was the final piece, the Council of Yavneh. In 1964, Jack P. Lewis pointed out that the rabbinic sources supposedly containing the records of such a council merely describe a discussion regarding whether two particular books (Qoheleth = Ecclesiastes, and Song of Songs) 'defile the hands' (m. Yad. 3.5), a phrase that rabbinic documents use to signify, paradoxically, the holiness of an object (m. Yad. 4.6).[68] Lewis argued that the ancient evidence does not support the idea of a council of Rabbis voting to close the Ketuvim or the biblical canon.[69]

Without this anchor, scholars are free to date the canonization of the Ketuvim earlier than the late first century, or later. Some have tried to locate the solidification of the tripartite Hebrew canon—more or less in its present form—within the second century BCE, in association with the Maccabean uprising.[70] This idea would explain the tripartite formula in Sirach's prologue and cohere with the high status enjoyed by the books of the Hebrew canon in the literature of Qumran, the Rabbis, Hellenistic Jewish authors Josephus and Philo, and the New Testament. But this view encounters problems: we have already seen that the Rabbis at Yavneh questioned the status of Qoheleth and Song of Songs, and they also discussed a few other books of the Hebrew Bible (e.g., Ezekiel, Esther, Proverbs).[71] Would they have been free to question these books had the canon been long settled? Moreover, some books not in the Jewish canon—as it would come to be defined—also had a very high status in Second Temple Judaism (e.g., Jubilees, Enochic writings, Tobit, Wisdom of Solomon, etc.), and Ben Sira was cited several times even in rabbinic literature.[72] Such evidence has led some scholars to consider the canon still open throughout the Second Temple Period, without achieving closure until perhaps the second or third century CE.[73] But an emphasis on the lateness of the canon fails to account for the high status that the books of the Jewish canon enjoyed at an earlier stage and their

[68] For a collection of rabbinic statements using the phrase 'defile the hands', see Leiman 1976: 102–20. For discussion, see Alexander 2007: 58–64; Lim 2010. Barton (1986: 68–72; 1997: 108–21; 2013: 160–1) pushes back against interpreting the phrase as referring to the canonicity or inspiration of a literary work.

[69] Lewis 1964; 2002. For the sources on Yavneh and further discussion, see Leiman 1976: 120–4.

[70] See Leiman 1976; Beckwith 1985; Dempster 2008.

[71] On the rabbinic sources, see Leiman 1976: 72–86; Beckwith 1985: 278–91.

[72] See, e.g., Sundberg 1964: 82, 103 ('a wide religious literature without definite bounds circulated throughout Judaism as holy scripture before Jamnia'); Charlesworth 2008. On Ben Sira, see Leiman 1976: 92–102; Labendz 2006; Ellis 2014.

[73] Mroczek 2016: 156–83; McDonald 2017: 1.415–18.

nearly exclusive use in Christian literature of the first two centuries. A number of scholars would combine both perspectives, arguing that the books of the Hebrew canon were basically settled at an early date, even if there continued to be some hesitation or uncertainty about certain books.[74] Sometimes Yavneh is still invoked as the place and time when the rabbinic canon achieved closure, though the idea of a council no longer plays a role in such proposals.[75]

A second major attack on the three-stage model of canon formation focused on the middle term, the Neviim/Prophets. In 1986, John Barton argued extensively that pre-rabbinic sources used the term 'prophets' in reference not merely to the eight books that would form the second section of the Tanak, but rather to all non-Torah Scripture.[76] This suggestion gains potency by observing the frequency of bipartite formulas in Second Temple Judaism ('law and prophets') and the instances in which the label 'prophet' is given to authors and books that the Rabbis would put in the Ketuvim. This latter point may be illustrated by references to Daniel (4Q174 1–3 II, 3–4; Matt. 24:15; etc.), David (11QPs^a XXVII.3–11; Acts 2:25–31), and Solomon (b. Sotah 48b) as prophets.[77] As for the first point, we noted earlier that the prevalence of the twofold formula 'law and prophets' extends across the Dead Sea Scrolls, the New Testament, and even early rabbinic literature. This evidence suggests that the Neviim, the second section of the Tanak, was not closed around 200 BCE, an idea for which there is little evidence. Instead, the phrase 'law and prophets' was a common way of referring to all Scripture, the Pentateuch and other Jewish Scripture, whether it eventually found a place in the Neviim or the Ketuvim (or, possibly, neither).[78] The phrase could be construed as 'the Torah and other inspired literature'.[79] This idea seems to have found general acceptance in recent scholarship, though—given the plethora of bipartite canonical references in Second Temple Judaism—scholars diverge regarding how they imagine the development of the tripartite canon. Barton himself, along with some others, believes that the Rabbis are responsible for dividing the older 'prophets' category into two sections, the Neviim and Ketuvim, and he proposed that they made this division for liturgical reasons.[80] Other scholars, emphasizing especially the

---

[74] Barton 2013: 158–61.

[75] Sundberg 1996: 100–3; Lim 2013.

[76] Barton 1986: 44–55; Barton had forerunners, as he himself acknowledges (p. 44), especially Barr 1983, on which influence see Chapman 2000: 56n23. Against Barton, see Beckwith 1985: 125–7; 1991.

[77] Further references and bibliography in Gallagher 2012a: 17.

[78] However, regarding this last possibility, Steinberg and Stone (2015: 24–5) point out that no Jewish sources use the phrase 'law and prophets' in reference to a book outside what would come to be defined as the Jewish Bible.

[79] See Steinberg and Stone 2015: 10.

[80] See Barton 1986: 75–82; Carr 2005: 265–6; 2011: 162n12. Portions of the Neviim are read during the Synagogue liturgy each week; see Fishbane 2002. On the possibility that the Ketuvim were once read in the liturgy, see Chapman 2016: 50–1n48. Ellis (1991: 45–6), Dorival (2003: 98–100; 2004: 93–5), and Kaestli (2007: 111) all suggest that the Rabbis transferred Daniel from the

prologue to Sirach, argue that the tripartite canon is early (second century BCE), but it coexisted alongside an alternative bipartite arrangement.[81]

The first section of the canon, the Torah, has also received its share of attention.[82] Most of this work is bound up with Pentateuchal criticism (a massive topic that should not divert us here), but we can note that there is currently no consensus on the time period at which the Pentateuch emerged, much less became canonical. Some scholars argue that those two concepts are inseparable for the Torah, that its emergence and its canonization are intertwined and simultaneous. Other scholars insist that even in the second and first centuries BCE, the authority apparently enjoyed by books like Jubilees and the Temple Scroll—books that could be viewed as rivals of the Pentateuch—indicates the contingent status of the Torah.[83] But Septuagint scholars still agree that the Pentateuch (basically as we have it) was translated into Greek in the third century BCE, which shows us that the Pentateuch existed at that time and that its status and/or authority seems to have exceeded what we might consider its literary competitors (at least in the minds of those involved in the translation project).[84] The Samaritans also consider (their own version of) the Torah to be Scripture, which again suggests the authority of the Torah before the final break between Jews and Samaritans, possibly as late as the end of the second century BCE.[85]

Besides the tripartite canon, ancient Jews may have conceptualized their Scriptures in other ways. We have already noted that, in light of the thesis of Barton that the term 'law and prophets' in the Second Temple Period denoted all of Scripture and not just the first two sections of the Tanak, most scholars are willing to imagine a bipartite arrangement in circulation at this time even if they also argue for the contemporary existence of a tripartite arrangement. Few Christian lists of Old Testament books, as the following chapters will show, conform to the tripartite arrangement, even if the author indicates his desire

---

Neviim to the more harmless Ketuvim specifically to diminish its apocalyptic influence on Jewish revolutionaries in the wake of the Jewish revolts (but see also Dorival 2014: 31–2). See also Sundberg 1964: 112–28 (on the anti-apocalypticism of the Yavnean Rabbis). But Leiman (1976: 59) points out that Daniel (along with David) is still considered a prophet in rabbinic literature. Also Dorival (2014: 28, 29) proposes that Ruth and Lamentations were transferred to the Ketuvim (on the authority of Jerome) due to liturgical reasons.

[81] Steinberg 2006: 167–72; Stone 2013: 50; Steins 1995: 510–12; Brandt 2001: 95–124.

[82] For a brief overview focused on canon, see Dorival 2014: 18–21.

[83] For scholarship on the development of the Pentateuch, see Moberly 2009: 430–2; or, for much more, Dozeman, Schmid, and Schwartz 2011. Among those scholars who maintain the authority of the Torah—and all Scripture—even during the process of its redaction, see Chapman 2000; 2016: 31–2; based on the earlier work of Childs 1979; cf. also Blenkinsopp 1977; Sanders 2005. On the contingent nature of the Torah's authority at Qumran and elsewhere, see Crawford 2008; Zahn 2011; Mroczek 2016: 114–55.

[84] On the Greek translation of the Torah, see Jobes and Silva 2015: 17–24; and the relevant articles in Aitken 2015a.

[85] See Knoppers 2013.

to transmit the canon as it existed among Jews (e.g., Origen; cf. Melito). Some scholars have argued that these Christian lists provide access to authentic Jewish lists of Scripture, so that some Jews may have continued to hold on to non-tripartite arrangements of their Scriptures even a few centuries into the common era.[86]

The evidence allows us fewer answers than we would like. The Tanak structure—Torah, Neviim, Ketuvim—for the Scriptures of at least some Jews certainly existed in Late Antiquity, even though the sequence of books within the Neviim and especially the Ketuvim was variable.[87] There may have existed at this time other Jewish arrangements reflected now in the Christian canon lists. Before the rabbinic period, the evidence becomes more meagre and permits little more than speculation. The prologue to Sirach convinces most scholars that some sort of tripartite arrangement dates to at least the second century BCE, perhaps alongside other arrangements. It is difficult to say more.

The Sanctity of Old Testament Books

At the end of the first century CE, Josephus offers the first explicit testimony that the sacred books received among the Jews had a fixed number and definite identity. While chapter 2 below will provide a fuller discussion of Josephus's list, here we should note that the Jewish historian asserts that all Jews have accepted this biblical canon for 'such a long time' (*C. Ap.* 1.42). Josephus does not name the twenty-two books, but scholars have usually assumed that he is speaking of more or less the same books the Rabbis include in their twenty-four-book canon. We have already seen that 4 Ezra 14, contemporary with Josephus, mentions twenty-four inspired books intended for the public. Evidence after the first century—see the lists in the following chapters—points to a settled Jewish canon (though certain Rabbis did raise questions about particular books; see below). But what about earlier? Josephus claims that all Jews had adhered to his twenty-two-book canon for a long time. Can we find evidence that would either substantiate or refute this claim?

Evidence before Josephus presents a problem: since Josephus gives us the first definite statement on the Jewish biblical canon, investigating the period before Josephus requires us to enter a realm without such clear statements. We must rely especially on manuscript discoveries (particularly the Dead Sea Scrolls) and comments on books or citations from them in other literature. Though the earliest comments and citations are found in the Hebrew Bible itself,[88] here we will consider only sources from the second century BCE onward.

---

[86] Katz 1956; Dorival 2003; Kaestli 2007: 113; see also Wolfenson 1924.
[87] On the sequence of books, see Gallagher 2014b; 2014c.
[88] See Chapman 2000; Talshir 2001; Carr 2011.

The issues driving this study concern the identity of the books Jews considered canonical and how early we can date such opinions. Given the difficulties with using the word 'canonical' in this context (discussed in the Introduction), we should perhaps replace this adjective with the description 'indisputably sacred and of inviolable authority'. Our sources once again will deny us definitive answers, but that does not mean they permit us no answers at all.

Part of the trouble is that we do not know what all Jews, or even all major Jewish groups, thought about Scripture in the Second Temple Period, and we have no guarantee that they all thought the same thing. Over the past several decades scholars have demonstrated the diversity within ancient Judaism, so much so that some scholars speak of Judaisms in the plural.[89] The varieties of Judaism in the period before the destruction of the temple in 70 CE coalesced into the relatively stable and harmonious rabbinic Judaism in the following centuries, starting in the wake of Jerusalem's destruction when a group of Jewish sages met at the Judean village of Yavneh.[90] But the pre-rabbinic diversity has significant implications for our investigation: evidence that a group of ancient Jews considered a certain book to be Scripture, or not to be Scripture, does not indicate that other Jewish groups shared the opinion. It is possible that different Jewish groups maintained different collections of Scripture.[91] It might be that Josephus was wrong, or, more likely, that he was exaggerating Jewish unity in a polemical context. A lack of unity on the biblical canon in ancient Judaism might have played an important role in the development of the Jewish canon. If divergent scriptural collections characterized the diversity of pre-rabbinic Judaism, then possibly the rabbinic biblical canon of twenty-four books represents the canon of the single Jewish group—usually identified as the Pharisees—that survived the destruction of 70 CE to take the leadership of rabbinic Judaism (Lim 2013). That is, on this view, the rabbinic biblical canon is merely the canon of the winners.

But we do not know that a diversity of scriptural collections characterized pre-rabbinic Judaism. That may or may not be the case. Philo wrote commentaries on the Pentateuch exclusively, and his citations from the Pentateuch far outnumber his citations from all other books combined. Such evidence has convinced some scholars that Philo's scriptural collection was limited to the Pentateuch.[92] Others have noted that while Philo cites other biblical books relatively infrequently, he does cite them and treat them as Scripture.[93] Further, Philo never mentions that his notion of Scripture extends no further than the

---

[89] For a critique of this terminology, see Schwartz 2011.

[90] This sentence greatly oversimplifies a complex historical development. For the thesis that Yavneh witnessed the demise of Jewish sectarianism, see Cohen 2010: 44–70, with the critique of Goodman 2009. For an account of the development of rabbinic Judaism, see Lapin 2012.

[91] A possible factor would be the availability of copies of texts. On the production and dissemination of texts in Antiquity, see Gamble 1995; Tov 2004; Goodblatt 2006: 28–48.

[92] Carr 1996: 35; Kamesar 2009: 72; Lim 2013: 91, 183.   [93] Chapman 2000: 271–3.

Pentateuch. In fact, we have no statements from this time period in which one Jewish group criticizes another group for their scriptural canon, and there is generally a large amount of coherence in the literature cited authoritatively among all Jewish groups, though groups do give prominence to some books more than others.[94] Our Introduction argued that judging an ancient author's canon from the citations found in his work is a precarious methodology, which is part of the reason the biblical canon lists presented later in this book serve such a valuable purpose. When investigating the period before the lists, we have no choice but to look at citations, but we should acknowledge their limited value in establishing the boundaries of an ancient scriptural collection. After all, apparently no Dead Sea Scroll cites the Book of Genesis.[95] All of this means that we should consider the possibility that the diversity within ancient Judaism entailed a diversity of scriptural collections, but we should also entertain the possibility that it did not.

At least two other ancient groups are also associated with a Torah-only canon: the Samaritans and the Sadducees. For these groups, unlike for Philo, we have ancient sources that make this claim. The Samaritans, of course, do not provide Jewish evidence, since they do not see themselves as a Jewish group, and Jews agree with them in that assessment, though both groups maintain that there is a close historical connection between them.[96] It is true that they have no Scripture except the Pentateuch, a circumstance that goes back at least to the time of Origen, our earliest source mentioning their limited canon.[97] About the Sadducees there is more reason for doubt. A number of church fathers claim that the Sadducees adhered to the Torah alone.[98] It is curious that no Jewish source, such as Josephus, mentions this distinction between Sadducees and other Jewish groups. Some scholars have thought that the church fathers simply confused the Sadducees with the Samaritans, and it is also possible that the fathers misinterpreted statements in Josephus (e.g., *Ant.* 13.297) such that the Sadducees accepted only the written Torah, not the oral Torah.[99] It is doubtful

---

[94] Lange 2004.   [95] See VanderKam 1998: 394; Ulrich 2015: 305.

[96] See Knoppers 2013; Pummer 2016: ch. 1. But see Carr (1996: 35), who argues that the Samaritan attitude towards Scripture should not be dismissed as non-Jewish because 'the Samaritan–Jewish split probably occurred fairly late in the Second Temple period'.

[97] See Origen, *Cels.* 1.49; and for an extensive collection and study of early Christian sources on Samaritans, see Pummer 2002; Lange 2004: 61n37. On the Samaritan canon, see also Zsengellér 1998. Ancient Jewish sources do not mention the Samaritan Torah-only canon. In the case of the Samaritans, the modern community's practice confirms the ancient Christian accounts limiting the group's Scripture to the Pentateuch (though the ancient sources do not permit us to know for certain what the Samaritan canon looked like before the third century CE; see Chapman 2016: 48n22.) As for the Sadducees, there is no such explicit evidence in addition to patristic testimony.

[98] For the sources, see Schürer 1973–87: 2.408n24. Some examples include Origen, *Cels.* 1.49; Jerome, *Comm. Matt.* 22:31–2.

[99] For these positions, see Schürer 1973–87: 2.408–9; Bruce 1988: 40–1. Some of the same arguments are found already in Eichhorn at the end of the eighteenth century; see Chapman 2013: 666. For the interpretation of the Josephan passage, see Mason 1991: 230–45. The argument of Satlow (2014: ch. 8) assumes that the Sadducees accept more Scripture than merely the Pentateuch.

that any of these Christians had first-hand knowledge of Sadducees.[100] So, it is plausible that patristic authors incorrectly reported on the Sadducean canon, though we have to reckon with the possibility that the Sadducees considered only the Torah to be Scripture and therefore provide evidence for Jewish diversity on the biblical canon.[101]

The majority of books in Josephus's canon were received as authoritative Scripture before the Jewish historian made his list.[102] The key indicators are the citations from these books in contemporary literature and the frequent appearance of scriptural shorthand expressions like 'the law and the prophets'—which seem to have in view, if not a fully determined content, then at least a generally acknowledged collection of literature. According to James VanderKam, such evidence 'does imply that [before 70 CE] there was a significant area of agreement among Jewish groups regarding which ancient writings were authoritative.'[103] Moreover, many Jews—all, according to Josephus—received these books as authoritative by the late first century, and it is unlikely that such reception constituted a radical change from the previous situation, especially in the absence of ancient statements disputing the status of these books. This negative argument carries a little more force than might at first appear. Some books were obviously important and authoritative early: the Torah, Psalms, and prophetic literature.[104] Other books did not attract much notice (Ruth, Chronicles, etc.), but they did feature later in the Jewish biblical canon, even though they remained relatively obscure. It seems likely that, for such books, the later reception continued a tradition rather than being an innovation, simply because we have little reason to suppose that at the end of the first century these books of little popularity enjoyed a sharp increase in their authority. In other words, why add them at that point? The major exception is the book of Esther: we do have ancient evidence that raises questions about this book, such as its absence at Qumran and from the canon lists of some early Christian writers.[105] A few other books were questioned by certain Rabbis, especially the three books of Solomon and Ezekiel. The nature of these rabbinic disputes has itself become a disputed question in scholarship, but it is unlikely that we should interpret these rabbinic discussions as indicating that the relevant books had not long

---

[100] However, for an argument that Sadducees possibly existed into the second or even third century—thus, against the common assumption of their dissolution around 70 CE—see Goodman 1994.

[101] Barthélemy 1984: 10–11; Carr 1996: 36–8; McDonald 2017: 1.251–8.

[102] Alexander 2007: 65; Barton 2013: 153, 161.   [103] VanderKam 2012: 60.

[104] Mroczek (2016: ch. 1) has problematized the idea of a Book of Psalms in Second Temple Judaism. Her intriguing analysis has not adequately addressed the evidence of the Septuagint, the evidence for which she diminishes by noting that our manuscripts of the Greek Psalter date long after the destruction of the temple (44–5).

[105] For the church fathers who omit Esther, see the lists in ch. 3 by Melito, Athanasius, Gregory of Nazianzus, and the more nuanced position of Amphilochius of Iconium. See also the Appendix for more details regarding the reception of Esther.

been considered sacred.[106] Probably almost all the books of the rabbinic Bible, or Josephus's Bible, were already considered authoritative long before, just as Josephus says.

The positive evidence for this view comes from citations and manuscripts. The New Testament, for instance, showcases the powerful influence and authority of a selection of Jewish documents that functioned as Scripture for these Jewish writers (as most, or all, New Testament authors were). The influence of Jewish Scripture in the New Testament is so pervasive and profound—and such a prominent topic in scholarship today—that we need hardly dwell on the point.[107] A few examples should suffice. Matthew 19 depicts a discussion between Jesus and the Pharisees on the topic of divorce. Both sides quote Scripture to demonstrate their positions. As James VanderKam writes, 'both the Pharisees and Jesus assume the question they are discussing is to be answered from the scriptures'.[108] In another passage, Jesus confounded the Pharisees with an unexpected interpretation of Psalm 110:1 (Matt. 22:41–6). Paul's major epistles (Romans, 1–2 Corinthians, Galatians) are brimming with biblical citations and allusions. Such citations in the New Testament establish the normative authority of especially the Torah, Isaiah, the Minor Prophets, and the Psalter, while other books appear relatively infrequently. And yet, even some of these rarely cited books clearly carried great authority, as evident from the use of Daniel in the Olivet Discourse (Matt. 24:15), or the reflections on Jeremiah's 'new covenant' passage in Hebrews 8.

The Dead Sea Scrolls present a similar, though opaque, picture. As John Collins aptly states, 'the Dead Sea Scrolls attest to a collection of authoritative scriptures that overlaps to a great degree with the later Bible of the rabbis'.[109] Unfortunately, the Qumran group did not leave behind a list of authoritative Scripture, so trying to decipher what they thought about certain books and which books might have comprised their scriptural collection becomes a difficult task. Scholars have formulated helpful criteria for determining whether the Qumran sectarians might have considered a book to be authoritative: whether the book exists in a significant number of manuscripts; whether the book was quoted in other literature; whether a commentary was written on the book.[110] None of these criteria alone suffices to establish a book's scriptural status, but cumulatively they can offer a strong impression that a book was received as authoritative, or, in other cases, a weak impression, or even no impression at all. As for the books later comprising the rabbinic canon, manuscripts of every book except Esther were recovered at Qumran, and some of these books existed in many manuscripts: most books of the Torah, Isaiah, and

---

[106] Leiman 1976: 72–86; Beckwith 1985: 297–323.   [107] See, e.g., Moyise 2015.
[108] VanderKam 2012: 54.   [109] Collins 2013: 202.
[110] See the varying criteria in Brooke 2007: 93–6; VanderKam 2012: 66; Barton 2013: 152–8; Ulrich 2015: 299–308.

the Psalter.[111] The number of manuscripts attested at Qumran for a book bears an uncertain relationship to sanctity,[112] but a high number of manuscripts apparently indicates at least the popularity of the book.[113] By that measure, the Book of Jubilees (fifteen scrolls), the Enochic literature (twelve scrolls), and the Community Rule (ten scrolls) were more popular compositions than some books that would comprise the Bible, such as the biblical historical books and wisdom literature. The Qumran group wrote commentaries on some prophetic works—Isaiah, some Minor Prophets, also Psalms—and there are citations from some biblical books.[114] The book of Jubilees was also cited at least once (CD 16:2–4; possibly 4Q228), and we have seen that the number of manuscripts of Jubilees at Qumran demonstrates its importance and popularity.[115]

It is difficult to know what the Qumran group considered Scripture, or rather what they did not consider Scripture, where they drew lines, since they must have excluded some books from being authoritative.[116] The evidence suggests that most books later comprising the rabbinic Bible were well-received at Qumran, and some clearly carried significant weight. Other books also were important to the group (especially Jubilees and the Enochic literature, but perhaps also Tobit, Ben Sira, the Temple Scroll, etc.) and also carried significant weight, as much as (or more than) some of the books in the Hebrew Bible, it would seem.[117] How the Qumran group parsed the authority of these books is hard—impossible—to determine, since they have not helped us by leaving behind much guidance.[118] If they considered Jubilees and 1 Enoch inspired, possibly they would have put these books in a separate category, along the lines of what we see in 4 Ezra 14, whose author knew that twenty-four books were accepted widely while another, larger group of books proved equally important for his constituency.[119] The Dead Sea Scrolls might serve as evidence for a wide collection of religious literature, encompassing most of the books now in the Hebrew Bible along with certain other works, as many scholars have determined,[120] but the nature of the evidence does not allow firm conclusions.

---

[111] For the numbers of manuscripts, see Tov 2010; Ulrich 2015: 320. Trebolle 2000 uses the manuscript evidence as one piece of his broader argument that there existed in Second Temple Judaism a 'canon within a canon' consisting of the Torah, Isaiah, the Minor Prophets, and Psalms. Note that Pajunen 2014 has demonstrated that the oft-repeated number of thirty-six Psalms scrolls from Qumran is fallacious; the number should be lower. See also Mroczek 2016: ch. 1.

[112] Lim 2013: 120.   [113] VanderKam 2012: 66; Ulrich 2015: 304.

[114] On the citations, see VanderKam 1998: 391–6; 2012: 67–70; on the commentaries, 2012: 36–8, 70–1.

[115] See VanderKam 1998: 399; García Martínez 2012: 537–9; Lim 2013: 131–5.

[116] VanderKam (2012: 51–2) gives the example of the Maccabean literature, which the Qumran group certainly did not consider authoritative.

[117] On 1 Enoch and Jubilees, see VanderKam 1998: 396–402. These two books also found a place within the Ethiopian Bible; see Baynes 2012.

[118] For a helpful discussion of different kinds of authority exerted by texts at Qumran, see Lim 2013: ch. 7.

[119] Brooke 2007: 87: 'every group held things in common with others as well as maintaining some compositions as authoritative for itself alone'.

[120] Sundberg 1964: 94–103; Carr 1996: 46–7; García Martínez 2012; cf. Ulrich 2015: 307–8.

Manuscript discoveries at Judean Desert sites other than Qumran suggest considerably more uniformity on the contents of Scripture. But in these cases, it is not so much the identity of the books discovered that carries the implications for the Jewish canon, but rather the textual form of those books. Qumran features books in a variety of textual forms—i.e., different editions of the same biblical book, such as a long and a short form of Jeremiah—only some of which (a significant percentage, to be sure, but not nearly all) correspond to the later rabbinic (Masoretic) text of the Bible. Qumran exhibits textual pluriformity, to use the wording of Eugene Ulrich.[121] On the other hand, Hebrew scrolls recovered from Wadi Murabba'at, Naḥal Ḥever, Masada, and other locations, which encompass a majority of the books in the rabbinic canon, all contain a conservative text corresponding closely to the Masoretic Text.[122] Emanuel Tov has argued that such conservatively copied scrolls owe their existence to a scribal headquarters responsible for the dissemination of the conservative text, and he connects this idea to the ancient testimony that the Jerusalem temple contained a storehouse of biblical scrolls.[123] Since the biblical books featuring this conservative text—both at Qumran and at the other sites—comprise nearly all of the books of the Hebrew Bible,[124] the Jerusalem temple library might provide a way for imagining the social location for an early scriptural collection. Furthermore, Greek manuscript discoveries indicate that at this same time period (around the turn of the era), the Greek text of several books underwent revision towards the conservatively copied Hebrew text within a literalizing translation tradition that probably also led to new Greek translations of some books of the Hebrew Bible (e.g., Song of Songs). Modern scholars have used the term '*kaige* tradition' to describe this literalizing translation tradition based on the conservatively copied Hebrew text.[125] Books known in the *kaige* tradition increase the total number of books that can be associated with the conservatively copied Hebrew text.[126] Many scholars associate the *kaige* tradition with Theodotion's

---

[121] Ulrich (2010: 155) finds this notion of pluriformity supported also by NT citations of the OT, the translations comprising the LXX, the Samaritan Pentateuch, and Josephus's use of the biblical text.

[122] The books represented include the Torah (each book), Joshua, Judges, Isaiah, Jeremiah, Ezekiel, the Twelve Minor Prophets, Psalms, Daniel, Ezra-Nehemiah. On the textual form, see Tov 2008: 171–88. The conservatively copied scrolls discovered at Qumran are generally recognized as not quite as close to the Masoretic Text as are the scrolls coming from other sites. Tov calls such Qumran scrolls 'second-circle' texts as opposed to the 'inner-circle' texts from other sites.

[123] See Tov 2008: 171–88; Lange 2009: 79; Carr 2011: 163. On the idea, see Gallagher 2015a.

[124] All the books except Chronicles and the Five Megillot (Ruth, Esther, Lamentations, Song of Songs, Ecclesiastes).

[125] The seminal study is Barthélemy 1963. For a more recent overview, see Jobes and Silva 2015: 28–9, 185–7, 320–3; Gentry 2016.

[126] Only Chronicles and Esther cannot be tied to the conservatively copied Hebrew text based on evidence derived from Qumran, other Judean Desert sites, and the *kaige* tradition of the Greek text. There are fragments, however, of Chronicles in the versions of Aquila and Symmachus, and a possible fragment of Theodotion's version. As for Esther, there is one possible fragment for Aquila's version (cf. Midrash Rabbah Esther 2.7).

Greek version,[127] traditionally dated to the late second century CE, though over the past few decades continued analysis of the translation technique of the Theodotion materials has led some scholars to reject this traditional date in favour of the mid-first century.[128] It is suggestive, therefore, that Theodotion's version, which is preserved for the most part only in patristic quotations, provides no evidence for any book outside the traditional Jewish Bible, although it did apparently include Baruch (as a part of Jeremiah?) and the Additions to Daniel.[129] While the Qumran group seems to have maintained a rather loose collection of authoritative literature, these other manuscript discoveries indicate that other groups, particularly those associated with the temple, may have held a view closer to that of Josephus.

Some Jewish sources indicate that the date at which a book was written might be determinative for its scriptural status. A passage in the Tosefta (a rabbinic document) says that 'the books of Ben Sira and all other books written from then on do not defile the hands' (t. Yad. 2.13). We have seen that Josephus mentioned a similar principle, limiting the divinely authoritative books to before the death of the Persian king Artaxerxes, because from that point Israel experienced 'the failure of the exact succession of the prophets' (C. Ap. 1.41). Josephus seems here to rely on an older tradition that prophecy had come to an end around the time of Ezra.[130] The opinion of Josephus himself is complicated by the fact that he does affirm the continuation of prophecy in some form,[131] and even in the passage quoted he does not rule out isolated instances of prophecy after Artaxerxes. But he does assert that something significant happened after the time of Artaxerxes, namely, that the line of succession of prophets stretching back to Moses came to an end. The tradition of the failure of prophecy is also known in rabbinic literature, where it is associated with the deaths of Haggai, Zechariah, and Malachi (t. Sotah 13.3), or the time of Alexander the Great (Seder 'Olam Rabba 30).[132] The story in 4 Ezra 14 about Ezra rewriting all the sacred books assumes that they had all been written by his time. Much earlier, 1 Maccabees mentioned three times (4:46; 9:27; 14:41) the absence of prophets during the Maccabean struggle. If we can associate this failure of prophecy with the cessation of the production of sacred and authoritative literature, as Josephus does, then we might imagine that other Jews besides Josephus also used the date of a work as a criterion for considering its scriptural status. Even if we cannot know when the ancients thought certain books

---

[127] Fernández Marcos 2000: ch. 9; Tov 2012: 142–3.

[128] Barthélemy 1963: 144–8; O'Connell 1972; Gentry 1995: 497–8; Gentry 2016: 225–7.

[129] There is even one testimony relating to a version of Baruch by Aquila. See the chart at Gentry 2016: 228–9.

[130] Alexander 2007: 69–71; Cook 2011; Gallagher 2012a: 14–17.

[131] Cf. B.J. 1.68; 3.399–408; 4.625.

[132] On the tradition regarding Haggai, Zechariah, and Malachi, cf. also b. Sanh. 11a; b. Yoma 9b; b. Sotah 48b. For the idea that the Second Temple lacked, among other things, the Holy Spirit, see b. Yoma 21b.

were written—would they have dated Jubilees to the second century BCE, like modern scholars, or to the Mosaic age, in accordance with the book's self-presentation?—the principle regarding a book's compositional date might still have served as a criterion of exclusion for some books.

It would appear that in the era before the canon lists, there was 'a limited set of books that was a functional collection of authoritative texts' on which all or most Jews could agree.[133] We cannot say for sure that Jews already received as Scripture every book of the rabbinic canon, though it is likely that at least some groups did. Esther experienced the most resistance, and the book does seem to have been excluded by the Qumran group,[134] but the celebration of Purim (a holiday based on events narrated in Esther) during the Second Temple Period probably entailed the authority of the book, and Josephus apparently included the book in his canon.[135] Neither can we say for sure that no other book was received as Scripture, though these other books would probably not have been embraced by everyone. That is to say, if the Qumran community accepted Jubilees as Scripture—possible, but not certain—probably they did not have many allies in this opinion. If we pursue this line of thought, we might say that Josephus was half-right, or even three-quarters: while every Jew (more or less) had for so long considered the twenty-two books to be divinely authoritative, some Jews may have attributed the same status to certain other books, as well. In the period before lists, we can still be confident about the reception of the core books—the Torah, the prophets, the Psalter—but the books at the fringe of the canon remain in uncertain territory.

The Old Testament in the Church

When the Council of Trent named the books of the canon, it included the books that would soon afterwards receive the label 'deuterocanonical': the books of Tobit, Judith, Wisdom of Solomon, Ecclesiasticus (Ben Sira), and 1–2 Maccabees.[136] About a decade earlier, Martin Luther published his complete German Bible (1534), which featured these same books not in the Old Testament proper but in a separate section which he labelled 'Apocrypha, which are books not considered of equal value to the Holy Scriptures, but are still useful and

---

[133] VanderKam 2012: 55; cf. Alexander 2007: 65: 'What the Rabbis were doing was defending a canon which they had received already more or less defined (save for a little fuzziness around the edges) from the pre-70 period.'

[134] Koller 2014: 129–35.

[135] ibid.: 156: 'Esther's inclusion in the canon should probably be explained as a result of the popularity of Purim and the fact that it is a wonderful story, to which many people were drawn.' On Josephus, see ibid.: 155n15.

[136] On the book of Baruch, see n. 18. In the early church, Baruch was often classified not as a separate work but as a part of Jeremiah.

good to read'.[137] The canon lists in the following chapters will show that both Luther and Trent can claim patristic precedent. These books were almost never included in the early Greek lists, and a few lists include a group of books that are non-canonical but useful to read, anticipating Luther's category.[138] Some fourth-century Latin lists did include these books within the canon, from which time they became a regular feature. Chapter 6 also shows that some of these books, along with some others not in the Jewish canon, appeared in some biblical codices from the fourth century and later. In this way, Trent's decision to include these books relied on earlier precedent, and the title 'deuterocanonical' hints at their 'secondary' reception: that is, the church did not reach agreement about them until after it had already acknowledged the canonicity of the other books, the books of the Jewish canon.

Scholars have long been curious about the role of these other books within early Christianity, and why the great biblical codices of the fourth and fifth centuries have more Old Testament books than appear in the Jewish Bible. One prominent explanation has been the Alexandrian canon hypothesis. First formulated near the beginning of the eighteenth century, the Alexandrian canon hypothesis proposes that the wider Old Testament canon of the Christian church corresponds to the biblical canon of Alexandrian Jews.[139] Whereas the Palestinian Jewish canon was the narrow canon attested by Josephus, the Jews of Alexandria accepted a wider assortment of religious literature, including most or all of the writings that had been translated from Hebrew to Greek, an activity usually associated with Alexandria. In 1964, Albert Sundberg argued strongly against the idea of an Alexandrian Jewish canon distinct from the Palestinian Jewish canon. He pointed out that even in Palestine there circulated a wide range of religious writings, as demonstrated by the Dead Sea Scrolls, and that citations of books in Alexandrian Jewish authors do not support the notion that they maintained a wider canon than their Palestinian counterparts. Sundberg accepted the then common notion that the tripartite canon developed in three stages, with a late-first-century Council of Yavneh closing the Ketuvim.[140] At the birth of Christianity, only the Torah and Neviim were closed, and the developing third section consisted of 'religious writings of undetermined proportions'.[141] The church, then, received from Jews two closed sections (Torah and Neviim) and an open third section with a great variety of literature. When the Jews closed their canon at Yavneh, the church was unaffected, as it had already split from

---

[137] See Fricke 1991. The Syriac canon list from the monastery of St Catherine may anticipate this move as it catalogues first the protocanonical books of the Old Testament and then the deuterocanonical books: that is, they are not mixed (cf. ch. 5, this volume).

[138] See especially the lists by Athanasius and Rufinus. On this non-canonical but useful category within the patristic period, see Gallagher 2015b.

[139] On the history of the idea, see Sundberg 1964: 7–40; Dorival 2014: 14–18. Chapman (2013: 685n118) points out that the Alexandrian Jewish canon hypothesis was not popular in the nineteenth century, which Sundberg (1964: 25–40) also recognized.

[140] Sundberg 1964: 81–2, 113–14, 127n71.   [141] ibid.: 82.

Judaism. Christians determined their own Old Testament without reliance on Jews, and the result was the wide canon, which found approval at Trent.[142]

Sundberg's monograph has had a profound impact on scholarship on the biblical canon, even on those scholars who still embrace the Alexandrian canon idea.[143] Some of the details of Sundberg's reconstruction must be modified in the light of developments in canon research that were occurring even while he was publishing his book, such as the demise of the Council of Yavneh idea and the three-stage theory of canon formation. Also, Sundberg considered the early statements about 'the law and the prophets' to refer to the first two sections of the Tanak, an interpretation generally now rejected in favour of the notion that 'prophets' in such a formulation refers to all non-Mosaic Scripture. Nevertheless, with such adaptations, many scholars have favoured Sundberg's basic thesis that the Jewish canon was not determined in the first century, so Christians did not inherit a canon but rather created one in subsequent centuries, a canon wider than the one the Jewish Rabbis defined.[144]

One difficulty with this interpretation of the Old Testament canon within the church is that the canon lists might be used to tell a different story. The Greek canon lists from the first four centuries attest a very stable collection that consistently mirrored the Jewish canon.[145] Of course, such a statement over-simplifies the reality, as chapter 3 shows. But chapter 3 will also show that the early Greek lists always have the same core books—constituting nearly the entire Jewish canon—with, perhaps, an additional book or two. For instance, the only book of the Jewish canon that is intentionally omitted from any of the lists is Esther, which is, nevertheless, usually included. It is possible that Melito of Sardis includes the Wisdom of Solomon, but his statement is open to varying interpretations, and neither the Wisdom of Solomon nor any of the other deuterocanonicals is included in any of the other early Greek lists, with one exception: the Apostolic Canons, composed perhaps in Antioch (Syria) in the late fourth century.[146] Some of the other lists do mention two books of Esdras, which would include the works known in the Septuagint as Esdras A and Esdras B. The book of Jeremiah would not only be the short Greek version of the book (as opposed to the longer Masoretic Text version) but would usu-ally include additional, brief compositions, such as Lamentations, Baruch, and the Epistle of Jeremiah. The books of Esther and Daniel would feature the expansions known in the Septuagint versions of these books. The different

---

[142] ibid.: 81–103.

[143] Joosten 2016; Guillaume 2004: 26–31; see also the literature cited by Lange 2014: 661–2.

[144] Barton 2013: 148–50; McDonald 2017: 1.227–9.

[145] For a possible exception, see the discussion in ch. 4 on the Latin list in the Codex Claromontanus, which scholars sometimes interpret as a translation from an early fourth-century Greek list.

[146] The textual history of the Apostolic Canons is complex, and some versions omit some or all of the deuterocanonical books. See ch. 3 for details.

versions of Esther and Daniel, and even the additional compositions included with Jeremiah and the alternative versions of the Ezra material,[147] were probably all considered to be issues of the textual form of these books, rather than matters of the canonicity of books. So, whereas we might say that such elements distinguish the Christian canon from the Jewish canon, probably most early Christians would not have thought about the matter in these terms, but rather would have seen the two canons as equivalent, though Christians and Jews use different versions of some of the books.

The early Latin canon lists present a somewhat different picture. Several fourth/fifth-century lists mirror the Greek lists by including only the books of the Jewish canon: Hilary, Rufinus, Jerome. Hilary does mention that some add Tobit and Judith. The deuterocanonical books appear in the lists by Augustine and Pope Innocent I, as well as in the Mommsen Catalogue and the *Breviarium Hipponense*, where they are not separated but intermixed with the books of the Jewish canon. Jerome and Rufinus both acknowledge the edifying nature of these extra books, explaining that they are not canonical, but useful.[148] Augustine, at least, recognizes that acceptance of the canonicity of books such as Sirach and Wisdom of Solomon was characteristic especially of the Western church (*City of God* 17.20).

One might interpret this evidence from the canon lists in different ways. Sundberg and those of a similar mindset acknowledge that some Christians began to limit their Old Testament to the books of the Jewish canon, but they believe this reflects a development in Christian thinking, that earlier Christians would have generally considered the deuterocanonical books as canonical. Sundberg thinks the fourth-century lists innovate in their advocacy of the Jewish canon for the church. 'The limitation of the Old Testament to the Hebrew canon in a Greek recension in the church in the East, however, does not have the credentials of long established practice. Rather, it shows signs of being recently accepted theory.'[149] Evidence for this interpretation could be found in the biblical manuscripts from the fourth and fifth centuries, and from contemporary scriptural citations, since manuscripts and citations include more books than those of the Jewish canon.

Other scholars believe that the lists accurately reflect the tradition of the church. There is no development in the canonical views reflected in the lists themselves, since the earliest lists we have, the Bryennios List and that of Melito of Sardis, already mirror the narrow Jewish canon.[150] Citations might

---

[147] Joosten (2016: 699) compares the LXX's Esdras A and Esdras B to the Old Greek and Theodotion versions of Daniel, i.e., different versions of the same book. On a similar opinion in Jerome, see Bogaert 2000: 16–17.

[148] For Jerome, see his *Preface to the Books of Solomon*; for Rufinus, see his canon list in ch. 4.

[149] Sundberg 1964: 146; see also Müller 2008; Law 2013: 87–9, 120–2.

[150] Law (2013: 123) minimizes the links between Melito's list and the Jewish canon before concluding that Melito still conforms to an early Christian pattern of 'aiming to mirror Jewish attitudes to the scriptural books'.

establish an early Christian acceptance of more books than in the Jewish canon, but about this point there is disagreement. Some scholars highlight the New Testament reliance on books outside the Hebrew Bible,[151] but others point out that the New Testament contains no formal citations of the deuterocanonical books and only one explicit citation of any apocryphal book, that of 1 Enoch 1:9 in Jude 14–15.[152] The lack of formal citation continues for the first couple of centuries of Christian history: according to Oskar Skarsaune, until Clement of Alexandria at the end of the second century, Greek Christian writers formally cite the deuterocanonical books only twice, both of which are quotations by Irenaeus of Baruch, which would have formed part of the book of Jeremiah at that time.[153] Such evidence suggests to some scholars that the Christian Old Testament canon began in conscious accord with the Jewish canon, and only later—especially in the Latin West—did the religious value and liturgical use of the deuterocanonical books secure them a place in canonical lists.[154]

The evidence demonstrates that the Jewish canon exercised a profound influence on the Christian pursuit for the correct Old Testament. While the lists indicate a widespread desire for the church to adopt the (LXX versions of the) books of the Jewish canon as its Old Testament, some Latin lists in the fourth century evince a desire to extend the canon beyond the bounds of the Hebrew Bible, and some comments from Christians even before the fourth century tend in the same direction. Tertullian, for example, used Jude's citation of 1 Enoch to argue for its scriptural status (*Cult. fem.* 1.3), and Origen's letter to Julius Africanus regarding the status of the story of Susannah—a deuterocanonical addition to Daniel—seemed to suggest not only that Christians should consider Susannah an authentic element of the text of Daniel, but also that the identity of scriptural books should be decided by the church and not by Jews.[155] The early Christian discussions of whether the Old Testament should correspond to the Jewish Bible or should encompass a wider variety of literature did not find resolution in Antiquity, but continued to reverberate throughout the Middle Ages and into the period of the Reformation, continuing even today, both in the West and the East.[156] The canon lists printed in this book provide a limited but important entry into this discussion.

---

[151] Sundberg 1964: 54–5; Law 2013: 87–9; McDonald 2017: 1.310–14 (see also McDonald 2007: 452–64).

[152] Skarsaune 1996: 445; Joosten 2016: 689. See also Lim 2013: 196, who minimizes the significance of Pauline parallels to apocryphal and pseudepigraphical texts. On Enoch, see VanderKam 1996; Hultin 2010.

[153] Skarsaune 1996: 444–6 (based on the data collected in *Biblia Patristica*). The two citations of Baruch in Irenaeus are found in *Epid.* 97 (Bar. 3:29–4:1) and *Haer.* 5.55.1 (Bar. 4:36–5:9). On Baruch as a part of Jeremiah, see Bogaert 2005: 288–92.

[154] See Ellis 1991: 6–36.   [155] See Gallagher 2012a: ch. 2.

[156] On the continuing disagreements over the Old Testament canon in the West, see Bogaert 2014; on the East, see Lash 2007.

THE NEW TESTAMENT

Just as he did every year, Bishop Athanasius of Alexandria dispatched a letter in 367 to the churches in his diocese, informing them of the date of that year's Easter celebration.[157] The annual Festal Letters that Alexandrian bishops wrote allowed them to comment on a variety of ecclesiastical matters, and the one Athanasius circulated in 367, the thirty-ninth Festal Letter he had written, contained an extended discussion of the biblical canon. This thirty-ninth Festal Letter of Athanasius has become famous in modern times because it contains the first listing of the twenty-seven-book New Testament that would become standard. It did not immediately have the effect of standardizing the New Testament, and in truth its influence in this regard is open to question: rather than signalling the end of a process of defining the New Testament canon, this letter seems to have merely marked a point along the way.[158] Subsequent canon lists did not always conform to Athanasius's New Testament: Greek canon lists sometimes omitted the Revelation of John;[159] the Syrian churches often expressed doubts regarding Revelation and some or all of the Catholic Epistles, and up until the fifth century Tatian's *Diatesseron* was more popular in Syrian churches than the four separated Gospels;[160] and other Eastern churches also had their own canonical peculiarities.[161] Latin lists correspond to Athanasius's canon more often, somewhat ironic since Athanasius's letter was not translated into Latin in Antiquity.[162]

The New Testament list of Athanasius represents a minor point—not a decisive event—in a long process, then, because his letter does not seem to have settled anything for the wider church. But, secondly, Athanasius's list carries less significance than modern students often attribute to it because the major developments in the history of the New Testament canon had occurred decades, even centuries, before Athanasius. We will see that before Athanasius was born, there were already established collections of the Fourfold Gospel, the

[157] According to von Lips (2004: 89), this Festal Letter tradition goes back to the middle of the third century or earlier.

[158] Brakke 1994: 418–19.

[159] See ch. 3 for the Apostolic Canons and the Synod of Laodicea. Gregory of Nazianzus fails to mention explicitly Revelation in his list, though he does seem to allude to it, accepting apostolic authorship. More than a decade before Athanasius, Cyril of Jerusalem had included twenty-six books, omitting only Revelation. Amphilochius of Iconium and Epiphanius of Salamis, subsequent to Athanasius, both include Revelation.

[160] See ch. 5 on the Syriac list from St Catherine's Monastery. On the *Diatessaron*, see below, and on its popularity, see Metzger 1987: 218.

[161] Metzger (1987: 223–8) briefly discusses the Armenian church, the Georgian church, the Coptic church, and the Ethiopian church.

[162] For Latin lists included in this volume that match Athanasius in the New Testament portion, see ch. 4 on Jerome, Rufinus of Aquileia, Augustine, the *Breviarium hipponense*, and Pope Innocent I. The two Latin lists included here that do not match Athanasius are the Mommsen Catalogue and the list found in Codex Claromontanus. Latin manuscripts often feature additional books such as *3 Corinthians* and the *Epistle to the Laodiceans* (Bogaert 2012: 90).

Pauline letters—with thirteen (in the West) or fourteen (in the East) letters, depending on the presence of Hebrews—and the seven Catholic Epistles, while Acts was also widely accepted, whereas Revelation, having previously enjoyed near universal reception, had now fallen into considerable doubt in some quarters.[163] The Alexandrian bishop merely had the privilege of writing down for the first time in a comprehensive and exclusive list the books that Christians had long considered Scripture.

Prior to Athanasius, only a handful of canon lists attempted anything like a comprehensive index of NT Scripture: those counting as such would include the lists of Cyril of Jerusalem and Eusebius of Caesarea, whereas the Muratorian Fragment, the list of the Synod of Laodicea, and Origen's NT list each encounters some problems. Briefly taking each of these lists in reverse chronological order,[164] we start with Cyril of Jerusalem, who in 350 listed the same books as did Athanasius, except that Cyril omitted Revelation. The same goes for the canon list associated with the Synod of Laodicea, though the dating of the Synod and the originality of its list are matters of dispute.[165] For Eusebius, in the first half of the fourth century, there are twenty-one books that are universally acknowledged (ὁμολογούμενα), or twenty-two if John's Revelation belongs here, whereas several further books are 'disputed' (ἀντιλεγόμενα): James, Jude, 2 Peter, 2–3 John, Acts of Paul, the Shepherd of Hermas, the Apocalypse of Peter, the Didache, the Revelation of John (again, if it belongs here), and the Gospel according to the Hebrews. These last six works are described not only as 'disputed' but also 'spurious' (νόθος), whereas this latter term is not used in reference to the first five, which might mean that the first five—all books that would later feature in Athanasius's canon—enjoyed already a higher status than the rest, either in the mind of Eusebius or in the wider church. In a homily on Joshua preserved only in Latin (*Hom. Jos.* 7.1), Origen once mentioned all of the authors of Athanasius's New Testament and even specified their works, resulting in a list closely approximating that of Athanasius already in the mid-third century. But Origen probably omitted Revelation and he failed to specify the number of Johannine letters. Finally, the contentious Muratorian Fragment—which may be the earliest list of all, possibly dating to the late second century, or may rather be contemporary with Athanasius—includes (implicitly) the Fourfold Gospel and thirteen Pauline letters (without Hebrews), along with Acts, some Catholic Epistles (1–2 John, 3 John [?], Jude), the Wisdom of Solomon (!), and the Revelations of John and of Peter, though with the admission that the latter Revelation encounters resistance from some as a liturgical document. The Fragment omits any reference to the letter to the Hebrews or

[163] On these 'mini-closures' of the canon, see Hahneman 1992: 175–7; Gamble 2002; Verheyden 2013; Bokedal 2014: 150–3.
[164] For more extensive discussion of each source, see chs 3–4.
[165] See ch. 3 on the Synod. It is not certain that even the Synod took place before Athanasius wrote his *Festal Letter* 39; see Markschies 2015: 196–7.

the letters of Peter and of James, and it includes a book (the Revelation of Peter) excluded by Athanasius (and considered 'spurious' by Eusebius) and another book (Wisdom of Solomon) included by Athanasius in the category of non-canonical books that are useful to read.

This review of the earliest New Testament lists shows that a great deal of the work was done before Athanasius. All of the lists include the four Gospels, Acts, and at least thirteen Pauline letters, along with some Catholic Epistles and other books. This survey also reveals which books were not definitely received: the Revelation of John, the Letter to the Hebrews, and several Catholic Epistles. The following pages explore the development of the sub-collections of the New Testament canon.[166] Athanasius secured his place in this history because he put all the pieces together in a list.

The Gospels

The Fourfold Gospel was widely—not universally—accepted from the end of the second century.[167] Irenaeus of Lyon in Gaul, about 180 CE, provides the pre-eminent testimony, to which we will give attention in a moment. Shortly after Irenaeus and on the other side of the Roman empire, Clement of Alexandria notes incidentally in a discussion of the *Gospel according to the Egyptians* that this latter work is not 'among the four Gospels passed down to us' (*Strom.* 3.13.93.1).[168] The Muratorian Fragment, which many scholars date to the end of the second century or beginning of the third, opens with a discussion of the four Gospels—unfortunately, only partially extant.[169] In the early third century, Tertullian chastises Marcion for relying solely on a mutilated copy of Luke when two apostles, Matthew and John, and two apostolic men, Mark and Luke, have written Gospels (*Marc.* 4.2).[170] Shortly thereafter, Origen, still in Alexandria, expresses the opinion that the four Gospels are like the elements of the faith of the church, naming specifically Matthew, Mark, Luke, and John (*Comm. John* 1.21–2), and later, after his move to Caesarea, he insists that while heretics have many Gospels, the church has only four (*Hom. Luc.* 1.2).[171]

But it is Irenaeus who provides the earliest explicit testimony to the four-fold Gospel.

---

[166] The same approach is followed in Gamble 2002; Verheyden 2013.

[167] See Schröter 2016: 24–8.

[168] On this passage, and Clement's use of a broad range of Gospels, see Hengel 2000: 15–19; Watson 2013: 418–36; Markschies 2015: 237–46.

[169] On the Muratorian Fragment, see ch. 4.

[170] On Tertullian, see, however, Hahneman 1992: 103–4.

[171] Watson (2013: 515) suggests that the charge of heresy derives from the translator Jerome rather than Origen's original Greek. On Origen's canon of the Gospels, see Heine 2010: 77–80.

Matthew, accordingly, produced a writing of the Gospel among the Hebrews in their own language, whereas Peter and Paul evangelized at Rome and founded the Church there. But after their departure, Mark, Peter's disciple and translator, handed down to us in writing what was preached by Peter. Luke too, Paul's follower, set down in a book the Gospel that was preached by Paul. Later, John likewise, the Lord's disciple who had also 'rested on His breast' [cf. John 13:23], issued the Gospel while living at Ephesus of Asia.[172]

Later, Irenaeus more explicitly insists that the authentic Gospels total precisely four.

It is not possible that there be more Gospels in number than these, or fewer. By way of illustration, since there are four zones in the world in which we live, and four cardinal winds, and since the Church is spread over the whole earth, and since 'the pillar and bulwark' [cf. 1 Tim. 3:15] of the Church is the Gospel and the Spirit of life, consequently she has four pillars, blowing imperishability from all sides and giving life to men.[173]

The rest of the paragraph expounds an analogy between the Gospels and the four living creatures of Revelation 4 and Ezekiel 1, such that John's Gospel corresponds to the lion, Luke's Gospel to the calf, Matthew's Gospel to the man, and Mark's Gospel to the eagle.[174]

While scholars agree that Irenaeus's explanations for the fourfold Gospel are unlikely to impress modern readers, they divide over how to interpret the background of his statements. Some scholars consider these statements by Irenaeus demonstrating the authority of the four Gospels to be a weak attempt to establish a new opinion,[175] while others, on the contrary, think his statements reveal an attempt to explain what Irenaeus had received as the church's traditional view.[176] In other words, some scholars think this passage from Irenaeus demonstrates the novelty of the idea of the fourfold Gospel, others think it demonstrates its antiquity. This debate is a symptom of the difficulty of interpreting the evidence earlier than Irenaeus.

This evidence for the reception of the Gospels before Irenaeus consists mostly of the ambiguous comments in writers such as Justin Martyr and Papias of Hieropolis, the harmonization of the Gospels by Tatian, and the use of the Gospels by groups that would become known as heretical, as well as the

---

[172] Irenaeus, *Haer.* 3.1.1; translation by Unger and Steenberg 2012: 30, slightly adapted. For commentary on this passage, see Unger and Steenberg 2012: 118–23nn4–7; Watson 2013: 454–72.

[173] Irenaeus, *Haer.* 3.11.8; translation by Unger and Steenberg 2012: 56, with commentary on pp. 148–50.

[174] On this analogy, see Watson 2016a: 44–6, and ch. 9. Jerome, *Comm. Matt.* praef. presents the more usual correspondences: Matthew = man; Mark = lion; Luke = calf; John = eagle.

[175] Hahneman 1992: 101–4; Gamble 2006: 206.

[176] Elliott 1996: 108; Stanton 2004: 67–8; Spellman 2014: 79; Schröter 2015: 170: 'Obviously, Irenaeus relies here on an older tradition about the four Gospels as a theological necessity for the church of God.'

tantalizing but disputed data provided by early Gospel codices. To take the last point first, our earliest certain four-Gospel codex is P[45], dating to the early third century, and thus after the time of Irenaeus.[177] The argument has been made, though, that two other extant codices, just as early or earlier than P[45], also originally featured all four Gospels: P[75] (early third century), which now contains only Luke and John; and a proposed combination of P[4] (fragments of Luke) with P[64] and P[67] (fragments of Matthew), dating perhaps to the late second century.[178] Since the resulting codex, if it did originally contain all four Gospels, would 'not look at all like an experiment by a scribe working out ways to include four gospels in one codex',[179] we could imagine predecessors, suggesting that the four-Gospel codex may originate in the mid-second century. However, not all scholars are convinced that P[64], P[67], and P[4] really do come from the same codex, and even if they do, whether that codex contained all four Gospels.[180]

As for early comments on the Gospels, we have very uncertain evidence in the collection of early Christian writings now known as the Apostolic Fathers, mostly from the late first or second century. These documents perhaps feature some interaction with written Gospels, but on this point scholars disagree.[181] For the most part, when these writings cite the words of Jesus, we cannot be sure whether they have access to one of our Gospels, to some other written source, or to oral tradition.[182] But some passages do seem to indicate that some of these early writings were familiar with, and highly valued, at least one of the Gospels now in the NT: 2 Clement 2:4 cites a statement found in Matt. 9:13 (//Mark 2:17) with the introduction 'another scripture says' ($\dot{\epsilon}\tau\dot{\epsilon}\rho\alpha$ $\delta\dot{\epsilon}$ $\gamma\rho\alpha\phi\dot{\eta}$ $\lambda\dot{\epsilon}\gamma\epsilon\iota$); and the Epistle of Barnabas 4:14 quotes the saying 'many are called but few are chosen' (cf. Matt. 22:14) with the introductory formula 'as it is written' ($\dot{\omega}s$ $\gamma\dot{\epsilon}\gamma\rho\alpha\pi\tau\alpha\iota$). In regard to the text from 2 Clement, Christopher Tuckett believes that '[i]t suggests that the NT gospel texts (or at least the Gospel of Matthew) were beginning to acquire the status of scripture alongside the books of the OT'.[183]

---

[177] For brief discussion, see Metzger and Ehrman 2005: 54; Spellman 2014: 71–4.

[178] See Epp 2002: 488; Stanton 2004: 71–5; Metzger and Ehrman 2005: 53; relying on Skeat 1997. Epp (2002: 488) and Stanton (2004: 73) consider the idea that the three fragments originally formed one codex to be secure. It has long been widely accepted that P[64] and P[67] originally formed one manuscript. On the date of the codex, see Stanton 2004: 73n37. But on the difficulties and vagaries of dating papyrus manuscripts, see Chapa 2016: 114–15.

[179] Stanton 2004: 74.

[180] For doubts raised about Skeat's argument, see Head 2005; S. Charlesworth 2007; Wasserman 2010. Hill 2011 defends the notion that the three fragments derive from a single codex, and he leaves open the possibility that it may have contained all four Gospels. For a summary of the debate, see Spellman 2014: 74–8.

[181] See the two volumes edited by Gregory and Tuckett 2005a; 2005c. See also the summary treatment by von Lips 2004: 33–40.

[182] See, e.g., the citation of Jesus' words in 1 Clem. 13:2; 46:7–8, neither of which matches precisely any text in one of the four Gospels; and see the discussion of Gregory 2005.

[183] Tuckett 2012: 145. See also Gregory and Tuckett 2005b: 254–5; and, on Barn. 4:14, Carleton Paget 2005: 232–3.

Papias of Hierapolis (early second century) was somewhat more explicit, but his testimony presents numerous difficulties, not least of which is that his works are preserved only fragmentarily in later writers, such as Irenaeus (*Haer.* 5.33.4) and Eusebius (*Hist. eccl.* 3.39).[184] He wrote five books on the *Interpretation of the Oracles of the Lord*, which were still available to Eusebius, and in which he reports that Mark wrote down the words of Peter and 'Matthew collected the oracles in the Hebrew language' (Eusebius, *Hist. eccl.* 3.39.15–16).[185] At the same time, Papias himself prefers 'the living and abiding voice' (3.39.4).[186] Some scholars have argued for a knowledge of the Gospel of John on the part of Papias, but the point continues to be debated.[187]

The comments of Justin Martyr in the mid-second century are again too ambiguous to occasion agreement among scholars.[188] He does not even mention any authors associated with Gospels. He does use the term 'Gospel' for a written document, and he apparently knows multiple Gospels (εὐαγγέλια; *1 Apol.* 66.3).[189] But more often Justin uses the phrase 'the memoirs of the apostles' (τὰ ἀπομνημονεύματα τῶν ἀποστόλων) or a close variation.[190] Once he explains that these memoirs are read in the public assembly (67.3). His citations reveal that he knew both Matthew and Luke, and he cites once a passage known from Mark (3:16–17) as coming from the memoirs of Peter (*Dial.* 106.3), which, in accordance with other early Christian tradition, probably refers to the Gospel of Mark.[191] At *Dialogue* 103.8, he mentions that these memoirs were composed by the apostles and those who followed them, a comment that, if pressed, could indicate that Justin was familiar with at least two Gospels by apostles and at least two Gospels by those who followed the apostles, and possibly then he has in mind the same four Gospels that Irenaeus would later extol.[192] This interpretation may be an overreach.[193] In any case, according to

---

[184] For a collection of fragments of Papias, see Holmes 2007: 722–67.

[185] For an interpretation, see Hengel 2000: 65–73. On Mark's connection to Peter, see Bond 2015.

[186] See Markschies 2015: 221.

[187] Favouring knowledge of John's Gospel are Hill 1998 (with a response by Manor 2013); Bauckham 2017: ch. 16. Watson (2013: 463) is doubtful.

[188] On Justin's evidence, see Metzger 1987: 143–8; Stanton 2003; Watson 2013: 473–7; Markschies 2015: 232–4.

[189] Trypho also seems to know εὐαγγέλιον as the title of a written work (*Dial.* 10.2), and Justin uses the title at *Dial.* 100.1; cf. Didache 8.2; 15.4. On the development of the term, see Koester 1990: 1–48; Stanton 2004: 52–9. Origen reflects on the significance of the title 'Gospel' at *Comm. John* 1.27.

[190] *1 Apology* 66.3; 67.3–4; and thirteen times in his *Dialogue with Trypho*: 100.4; 101.3; 102.5; 103.6, 8; 104.1; 105.1, 5, 6; 106.1, 3, 4; 107.1.

[191] On this last point, see above on Papias, and Bauckham 2017: 212–13. On Justin's knowledge of Mark, see Koester 1990: 40; and on his use of Matthew and Luke, ibid.: 360–402. On the phrasing at *Dial.* 106.3—'his memoirs' as a reference to Peter's memoirs rather than Christ's—see Stanton 2003: 362.

[192] Hengel 2000: 20; Stanton 2003: 362; 2004: 76.

[193] Watson 2013: 476n106: '[t]here is no suggestion of a fourfold gospel here'.

Schröter, it is 'rather improbable that Justin knew of any other gospel' besides those that would soon become canonical.[194] Still, scholars debate whether Justin knew John's Gospel,[195] and he evinces no desire to fix the number of Gospels.[196] Moreover, many of his citations do not match precisely anything in our written Gospels, and scholars often attribute to him either some sort of harmonizing activity or, perhaps, use of a prior harmony.[197]

As it happens, Justin's student Tatian (ca. 170) becomes 'our first incontest-able witness to the common availability and use of four gospels'.[198] Tatian com-posed his own new Gospel using as his sources the four Gospels that would enter the NT.[199] This new Gospel is now called the *Diatessaron*, a name first attested in Eusebius (τὸ διὰ τεσσάρων [εὐαγγέλιον], 'the Gospel through the four'; *Hist. eccl.* 4.29.6),[200] but it seems that this name does not descend from Tatian himself, who simply called his creation the Gospel and did not sign his own name to it.[201] We cannot say that Tatian regarded his sources as canonical; rather, he seems to have viewed them as problematic in some way, perhaps because of their differences or a perceived lack of order, problems that could best be solved, he thought, through a harmonized Gospel.[202] His Gospel enjoyed wide circulation and esteem in Syrian churches, so much so that we have 'good reason to believe that this work served as the standard gospel text for many Syriac-speaking churches until at least the mid-fifth century....'[203] Tatian thus presents a paradoxical picture of the reception of the Gospels: on the one hand, he apparently considered their narratives about Jesus to be the most authori-tative available;[204] on the other hand, he apparently did not regard them as sacrosanct, and he intended to replace them with his new composition.[205]

Tatian's work thus serves as an example of the different approaches Christians took in the second century (and beyond) to the narratives of Jesus's life. Not everyone latched onto the four Gospels; in fact, immediately prior to his strange

---

[194] Schröter 2016: 25; Stanton 2004: 76; for bibliography on this question, see Cirafesi and Fewster 2016: 187n3.

[195] Hengel (1989: 12–14) argues for dependence on John's Gospel for the formation of Justin's Logos Christology (see also Hill 2004: 316–42, esp. 316–25), a point accepted by Markschies 2015: 234n206, and conceded as possible by Watson 2013: 477, who also wants to point out that Justin never cites John's Gospel. Stanton (2003: 363–4) would prefer to say that he cites the Fourth Gospel only once, at *1 Apol.* 61.4–5, but he acknowledges that it is a 'free rendering' of John 3:4–5.

[196] Norelli 2010: 182.

[197] Koester 1990: 365–75; Hengel 2000: 20; Stanton 2003: 364–5; Watson 2013: 474–5; Markschies 2015: 232.

[198] Gamble 2002: 280.

[199] Tatian possibly used other sources as well, an idea hard to demonstrate; see Petersen 1994: 27–9; N. Perrin 2003: 604; Baarda 2012: 338n14; Schmid 2013: 115n4. For a survey of scholarship since the mid-1990s, see Schmid 2013, who describes the period as one characterized by a 'new perspective' on the *Diatessaron*.

[200] For this reading, see M. Crawford 2013: 363 with n. 2.

[201] See M. Crawford 2013; Watson 2016b: 96–7.   [202] Norelli 2010: 183; M. Crawford 2015.

[203] M. Crawford 2013: 364; see also Norelli 2010: 183.   [204] N. Perrin 2003.

[205] Norelli 2010: 183; M. Crawford 2016.

defence of the fourfold Gospel, Irenaeus reported that some groups chose to use only one Gospel (*Haer.* 3.11.7): the Ebionites used Matthew; Marcion's followers used their teacher's version of Luke; Mark was chosen by those 'who separate Jesus from Christ, alleging that Christ remained impassible, but that it was Jesus who suffered'; and the Valentinians used John. The most important of these 'heretics', at least in terms of scholarly discussion of the New Testament canon, has been Marcion, who arrived in Rome from his native Pontus around the year 140. Unfortunately, none of Marcion's works survive, compelling us to access remnants of them in the quotations made by his opponents. These opponents reported that a Gospel was associated with Marcion, and they identified this text with the Gospel of Luke, in an altered (corrupted) form edited by Marcion himself.[206] Whether this means that Marcion intentionally rejected the other Gospels, or that he simply was familiar with only one Gospel, we cannot finally know.[207] Perhaps all these groups chose a single Gospel as a way of answering the difficulty Tatian tried to solve in his own way, the difficulty posed by different accounts of the life of Jesus.

But other Gospels also proliferated, beyond those that have so far occupied our attention. After complaining that some groups accept only one Gospel, Irenaeus accuses the Valentinians of accepting more Gospels than there really are (*Haer.* 3.11.9). We have noticed Origen's comment from his first homily on Luke that 'heretics have many' Gospels; he names the Gospel according to the Egyptians, the Gospel according to the Twelve Apostles, the Gospel according to Thomas, the Gospel according to Matthias, and the Gospel according to Basilides (*Hom. Luc.* 1.2). Most of these Gospels we know only by name, but many other Gospels have been preserved in one form or other, often only fragmentarily.[208]

These Gospels outside the fourfold Gospel circulated more widely than the statements by Irenaeus and Origen indicate. Eusebius (*Hist. eccl.* 6.12) tells the story of a late-second-century bishop, Serapion of Antioch, who permitted the church at Rhossus to read the Gospel of Peter, before reversing his decision when he perceived that some people in that community inclined towards heresy; nevertheless, he acknowledged the orthodoxy of most of the content of the Gospel of Peter. This account 'shows that in the second century a bishop could regard it as generally possible that a Christian community might use a gospel that does not belong to the accepted four Gospels'.[209] Moreover, both Origen

---

[206] See Irenaeus, *Haer.* 1.27.2; 3.12.12; Tertullian, *Marc.* 4.6.2; Epiphanius, *Pan.* 42.9.1; 42.11.3–6. For a reconstruction of Marcion's Gospel, see Roth 2015. For an English translation of a different reconstruction, see BeDuhn 2013: 99–127. Scholars debate whether Luke actually did form the basis for Marcion's Gospel; see the history of research in Roth 2015: 7–45.

[207] See the discussion in Gamble 2006: 205–8.

[208] For basic information on several of the 'apocryphal Gospels', see the appendix to this volume. For a survey of these documents, see Frey 2015; and for a collection of texts, see Ehrman and Pleše 2011.

[209] Schröter 2015: 173. On Clement, see Metzger 1987: 130–5; Hahneman 1992: 105–6. On Origen's use of Gos. Thom., see Carlson 2014.

and his Alexandrian predecessor Clement refused to allow their acceptance of the fourfold Gospel to prevent them from making positive use of other Gospels.[210] In fact, in the very passage in which Clement acknowledged that the Gospel according to the Egyptians is not one of the four received Gospels, he offered an allegorical interpretation of its contents (*Strom.* 3.13.93).[211] In his discussion of the New Testament canon, Eusebius noted that some include the Gospel according to the Hebrews among the disputed writings (*antilegomena*); Eusebius apparently did not consider it heretical (*Hist. eccl.* 3.25.5).[212] While some Gospels—such as the Gospel of Thomas and the Gospel of Judas—were more closely associated with groups that someone like Irenaeus would label heretical,[213] writers outside of these groups could still use positively such Gospels. Origen, for example, found in the Gospel of Thomas at least one saying of Jesus that he regarded as authentic.[214]

These other Gospels, which apparently began to appear in the latter half of the second century,[215] were popular for a long time among a variety of Christian groups.[216] A survey of second- and third-century Christian manuscripts suggests that 'owners of gospel texts were as likely to possess a noncanonical gospel as a copy of Luke or Mark'.[217] But the manuscripts might also indicate that their early users (or the scribes producing them) often recognized a distinction between those documents that would become canonical and those that would not. For example, writings that would become canonical almost always appear in codex format, while other writings could as likely inhabit scrolls; additionally, there seems to be more textual variation in the case of the writings that would not become canonical, perhaps indicating less careful transmission.[218] No manuscript attests the presence of an apocryphal Gospel bound with a Gospel eventually considered canonical,[219] even though multiple canonical Gospels sometimes occupied the same manuscript, at least from the late second or early third century, as we have seen. Such evidence, along with the other data we have already examined, supports Schröter's evaluation that early Christians

---

[210] Schröter 2015: 170.

[211] On this Gospel, for which Clement is essentially our only source, see Frey 2015: 25–6.

[212] On this Gospel, see ibid.: 23.   [213] Schröter 2015: 172–5.

[214] Origen (*Hom. Jer.* 27.3.7; cf. *Hom. Jos.* 4.3) seems to regard Gos. Thom. 82 as authentic, though he does not name the Gospel (Carlson 2014: 142–4). At *Cels.* 8.15–16, Origen rejects the authenticity of Gos. Thom. 74, again, without naming the text (ibid.: 145–6). See also Carlson's (2014: 146–50) discussion of Origen's *De pascha*, which uses Gos. Thom. 23, and the prologue of a catena fragment on John 20:25.

[215] Schröter 2015: 171; see generally Frey 2015.

[216] Reed 2015. For a popularizing account of the widespread and long-lasting influence of these Gospels, see Jenkins 2015.

[217] Watson 2016a: 4; similarly Chapa 2016: 117. For a brief account of this manuscript evidence, see Watson 2016a: 2–4; for more detail, see Chapa 2016. Chapa 2016 (117–18) questions whether the preserved manuscripts (often from the Oxyrhynchus garbage dump) can be considered representative of books valued at the time.

[218] See Chapa 2016: 119–29.

[219] Elliott 1996: 110 (see also 107); Hill 2013a: 322–3; Chapa 2016: 122.

often 'did not think these gospels had the same status as the four Gospels, but they did not entirely reject all of these other gospels.'[220]

Our survey has shown that the second century was the decisive time for the formation of the fourfold Gospel that Athanasius would promote in his thirty-ninth *Festal Letter*.[221] The limited evidence from that fateful century will continue to be parsed and debated by scholars. The end of the century witnessed the solidification of the fourfold Gospel in the writings of Irenaeus, followed not long after by less enthusiastic but no less definitive testimony from Clement of Alexandria, Tertullian, and Origen. Not every question is settled with Irenaeus, as some Christian leaders a few decades later would express reservations regarding the Gospel of John,[222] and of course Syrian Christians replaced their Gospel harmonized by Tatian (the so-called *Diatessaron*) with the fourfold Gospel only in the fifth century. But the major developmental period for the formation of the four-Gospel canon is to be sought in the second century.

The Pauline Letter Collection

Athanasius included in his canon list 'fourteen letters by the apostle Paul', and he names the addressees of the letters, in the traditional order, except that Hebrews precedes the Pastoral Epistles, a sequence common at the time.[223] Of course, most modern scholars are convinced that Paul did not compose Hebrews, and a number of ancient authors harboured similar doubts about the letter, which sometimes resulted in its exclusion from the canon, a situation characteristic especially of the West. Of the lists collected in this book, all of them include the fourteen epistles of Paul, except for the Muratorian Fragment, which omits Hebrews and also surprisingly omits the letters of Peter and James;[224] the Mommsen Catalogue, which mentions thirteen letters of Paul (thus excluding Hebrews); and the list in the Codex Claromontanus, which actually includes only ten letters (not Hebrews, Philippians, or 1–2 Thessalonians), the probable result of scribal error.[225] The inclusion of a collection of Pauline letters within the canon seems to have been a foregone conclusion prior to the

---

[220] Schröter 2015: 170–1.

[221] This is not a surprising insight; see, e.g., Norelli 2010, or almost any survey of the NT canon.

[222] Contrast Watson 2013: 477–93 with Hill 2004: ch. 4.

[223] This order is found in all three of the great whole-Bible codices from the fourth and fifth centuries: Vaticanus, Sinaiticus, and Alexandrinus (see ch. 6). See also the canon list of the Synod of Laodicea.

[224] In fact, these omissions are so surprising that some scholars propose they result from scribal error. See the discussion of the Fragment in ch. 4.

[225] See the discussion of the Codex Claromontanus list in ch. 4. Some of the other lists do present some difficulties in relation to Paul's letters. The Syriac list from St Catherine's monastery (ch. 5) has two letters to the Philippians and no reference to 1 Timothy, though it does mention 2 Timothy; such deviations from the usual list of Pauline letters likely result from scribal corruption.

time of our earliest lists;[226] the question involved which letters to include, and even this question concentrated—by the time of our canon lists—on a single letter, that to the Hebrews. Our discussion will give attention to this issue, but first we will explore the evidence available for the development of the Pauline letter collection.

The earliest phase of the collection remains veiled to us, subject to little more than conjectures, which have abounded. Usually these theories have posited someone near the end of the first century travelling among the churches receiving Paul's letters on a quest to collect and edit them.[227] Some scholars are also willing to entertain the notion that Paul himself, or a close associate, may have possessed authors' copies of some letters, which served as (at least) the kernel for the collection.[228] As Gamble remarks, 'It seems unlikely that Paul would have written the kinds of letters he wrote without retaining copies.'[229] The limited evidence available to us includes the following points: the Acts of the Apostles occupies a great deal of its narrative with Paul's travels without ever mentioning his letters; 2 Peter 3:15–16 observes that Paul's letters can cause problems for interpreters; apparently we do not have all of Paul's letters, since the apostle seems to reference such letters not in our possession (e.g., 1 Cor. 5:9); Col. 4:16 refers to the exchange of Pauline letters between churches; most scholars maintain that some of the letters in the collection were not actually written by Paul (e.g., Ephesians, the Pastorals); and possibly some of his letters have been preserved fragmentarily, as imagined by some scholars to be the case for several letters now constituting our 2 Corinthians. Such data and hypotheses, restricted as they are, need to be addressed by theories of the early formation of the Pauline letter collection. We can content ourselves here by noting our lack of knowledge and move on in search of more explicit information.

Like the fourfold Gospel, but somewhat less definitely, the Pauline letter collection seems to have coalesced by the end of the second century. This view does not depend on a late-second-century date for the Muratorian Fragment, though it would receive additional support from such a dating, since the Fragment mentions all thirteen letters (not Hebrews).[230] Origen apparently accepted the entire fourteen-letter Pauline corpus, though only in a passage preserved in Latin (*Hom. Jos.* 7.1) does he actually mention the number fourteen.[231] The fifth

---

[226] Lindemann 2003: 321.

[227] For a survey of theories, see Gamble 1985: 36–41; Porter 2004; 2008; 2011.

[228] Gamble 1995: 100; Porter 2008. Gamble earlier (1985: 36–41) did not consider the possibility of Pauline involvement in the collection, but more recently (2002: 286) he considered something like this scenario worthy of 'more attention.'

[229] Gamble 1995: 101.

[230] See the section on the Muratorian Fragment in ch. 4. The discussion of Paul's letters occupies lines 39–65.

[231] For this passage, see the section on Origen in ch. 3. On Origen's citations of Paul, see the brief remarks of Metzger (1987: 137–8).

book of Tertullian's *Against Marcion* is entirely taken up with a detailed critique of Marcion's collection of Pauline letters (the *Apostolikon*, on which, see below), during the course of which Tertullian defends what he considers the correct text of each of the thirteen letters (without Hebrews).[232] Clement of Alexandria does not say how many letters Paul wrote; he quotes, and attributes to Paul, every document in the fourteen-letter collection with the exception of Philemon, perhaps due to its brevity.[233] Likewise, Irenaeus quotes or alludes to all of the Pauline letters, excepting only Philemon.[234] Such evidence establishes the availability and acceptance of the entire collection (with or without Hebrews) by the end of the second century, though we do not have such a firm statement on the unalterable state of the collection as Irenaeus provides for the Gospels.

The same time period saw the production of our earliest and most extensive papyrus codex of Paul's letters, P[46].[235] This manuscript preserves nine letters in the following sequence: Romans, Hebrews, 1–2 Corinthians, Ephesians, Galatians, Philippians, Colossians, 1 Thessalonians. The manuscript cuts off near the end of 1 Thessalonians, and it is missing its last fourteen pages, so we cannot be sure of the complete contents of the original manuscript. Scholars have generally assumed that 2 Thessalonians would have appeared, and possibly Philemon, but there would not have been enough room to include the Pastoral Epistles.[236] Nevertheless, 'it can be cogently argued that the Pastorals did have a place in' this manuscript.[237] Possibly, therefore, P[46] attests a Pauline letter collection without the Pastorals, but the current evidence does not allow certainty in the matter.

It is more certain that Marcion omitted the Pastorals, since Tertullian tells us as much and criticizes Marcion for it (*Marc.* 5.21). Marcion regarded Paul as the truest and greatest apostle, so that beside his Gospel—a redacted form of Luke—he was willing to place only Pauline compositions. Marcion's *Apostolikon*, his edition of apostolic letters, encompassed ten letters of Paul, in the following order: Galatians, 1–2 Corinthians, Romans, 1–2 Thessalonians, Ephesians,[238]

---

[232] Tertullian ascribes Hebrews to Barnabas (*De pudic.* 10; 20), as noted also below.

[233] Brooks 1992: 42–3. He does not name 1–2 Thessalonians, but he does quote them as Pauline. Every other epistle he quotes by name.

[234] Blackwell 2011. On his treatment of Hebrews, which he does not explicitly attribute to Paul, see below.

[235] The website for the Virtual Manuscript Room (<http://ntvmr.uni-muenster.de/liste>) offers the date 200–225.

[236] Hahneman 1992: 115–16.

[237] Gamble 2002: 285, citing Trobisch 1989: 27–38; Duff 1998. For a critique of Duff, see Epp 2002: 498–502; Parker 2008: 253–4. Trobisch (1994: 16), Duff (1998: 589), Epp (2002: 502), and Parker (2008: 254) all ultimately conclude that we simply do not know which books the scribe included after 1 (or 2) Thess., but scholars can imagine various possibilities.

[238] According to Tertullian, *Marc.* 5.17, Marcion referred to Ephesians as the Epistle to the Laodiceans. Epiphanius, *Pan.* 42.12.3, does not report this information.

Colossians, Philippians, Philemon.[239] Marcion thus provides our earliest hard evidence of a collection of Pauline letters, omitting the Pastorals and Hebrews. Some scholars have argued that this collection of ten letters existed before Marcion, deriving evidence for this idea in part from the so-called Marcionite Prologues.[240] These prologues appear first in the Latin *Codex Fuldensis* (sixth century) and then commonly in Latin manuscripts, but already in the fourth century Marius Victorinus appears to have drawn on them for the prologues to his Latin commentary on some of Paul's letters.[241] For most of the twentieth century, scholars believed that these prologues had originated in Marcionite circles, but Nils Dahl argued forcefully that the prologues are not Marcionite but 'catholic', and thereby provide evidence for a catholic edition of Paul's letters similar in shape to the one Marcion would later promote, i.e., totalling ten letters, without Hebrews or the Pastorals, and arranged according to the seven-churches model.[242] While Dahl's theory has won adherents,[243] other scholars continue to advocate the view that Marcionite circles produced these prologues.[244] The position one takes on this matter will have consequences for how readily one envisions a ten-letter Pauline collection preceding Marcion.

In the period before Irenaeus, aside from Marcion, our evidence remains rather slim for a Pauline collection, or sometimes even for usage of individual Pauline letters. In Justin Martyr there is a 'strange, almost deathly, silence' in regard to Paul generally,[245] whereas gnostic groups did tend to value Paul.[246] Within the Apostolic Fathers, only a few writings exhibit awareness of Paul or his letters.[247] Ignatius (*Eph.* 12.2; *Rom.* 4.3), Polycarp (*Phil.* 3.2; 9.1; 11.2, 3), and Clement of Rome (1 Clem. 5.5; 47.5) mention Paul by name. Ignatius is aware of several Pauline letters (cf. *Eph.* 12.2), most probably including at least 1 Cor., Eph., 1 Tim., and 2 Tim.[248] Polycarp mentions 'letters' that Paul wrote (*Phil.* 3.2), and he most likely also knew 1 Cor., Gal., Eph., 1 Tim., and perhaps 2 Tim.[249] Clement certainly knew Paul's letter to the Romans (e.g., 1 Clem. 35:5–6; cf. Rom. 1:29–32) and his first letter to the Corinthians (1 Clem. 47:1–4), whereas evidence for his knowledge of other Pauline Epistles is ambiguous.[250] Clement's exhortation at 1 Clem. 47 that the Corinthians should take up the letter Paul

[239] Tertullian, *Marc.* 5.2–21; for a modern reconstruction, see Schmid 1995; for a study of Marcion's editorial principles in relation to the Pauline letters, see Scherbenske 2013. On the somewhat conflicting testimony found in Epiphanius, *Pan.* 42.12.3, see the brief remarks of Verheyden 2003: 522n170. Gamble (2006: 208–9) favours Epiphanius's testimony.

[240] So Schmid 1995: 284–308; Gamble 2002: 283–4; 2006: 208–10; Verheyden 2013: 395.

[241] For a brief introduction, see Houghton 2016: 198; or, for more, Scherbenske 2013: 85–93. Scherbenske includes an English translation (87–8) and the Latin text (282–3n79) of each prologue. On the use made of the prologues by Marius Victorinus, see Cooper 2005: 92–3.

[242] See Dahl 1978.   [243] Hahneman 1992: 111–15; Schmid 1995.

[244] Scherbenske 2013: 91–2, 237–42; Jongkind 2015.   [245] Foster 2011: 123.

[246] N. Perrin 2011.   [247] See Lindemann 1990.   [248] Foster 2005: 164–72.

[249] Holmes 2005: 201–18. On the plural 'letters' at Polycarp's *Phil.* 3.2, see ibid.: 201–2n55; Spellman 2014: 83.

[250] Gregory 2005: 142–53.

sent to them 'shows that Clement considered it to be self-evident that he should make use of Paul's letter in support of his own argument; that he assumed that the letter of Paul sent some forty years before is still available in the Corinthian church; and that he saw no reason to comment on the fact that a copy of the letter already existed in Rome'.[251] Finally, the *Epistle to Diognetus* attributes to 'the apostle' the saying that 'knowledge puffs up, but love builds up' (12.5; cf. 1 Cor. 8:1).[252] In this early period, we know that some authors were familiar with multiple Pauline letters—Clement, Ignatius, Polycarp, the author of 2 Peter (3:16)—but we have little information about the shape of the collection.

The status of the Pastorals and Hebrews in this era is especially hard to pin down. While these books were traditionally transmitted as Pauline letters, as we have seen, modern scholars are nearly unanimous in rejecting Pauline authorship for the anonymous Hebrews and, with slightly less unanimity, for the Pastorals, which do claim Pauline authorship. Marcion included none of these books in his canon, while P[46] contains Hebrews but not the Pastorals, at least not in the manuscript as it now survives. Certainly, Irenaeus knew the Pastorals as Pauline compositions,[253] as does the Muratorian Fragment. Before Irenaeus, they are harder to track, as are all the Pauline letters, but the difficulty for the Pastorals is increased somewhat by their absence from Marcion's canon and P[46]. It is probable that Polycarp knew 1–2 Timothy.[254] Theophilus of Antioch, the late-second-century apologist, from around the time of Irenaeus, quotes portions of 1 Tim. 2:2 and Tit. 3:1 as 'the divine word' (ὁ θεῖος λόγος).[255] According to Jerome (*Comm. Tit.* praef.), Tatian rejected 1 Timothy but accepted Titus. It is hard to say, then, at what date the Pastorals began to circulate as part of the Pauline letter collection, though this seems to have taken place by the time of Irenaeus, and thereafter their position seems secure.

The matter stands differently with regard to Hebrews, which features no internal claim of Pauline authorship.[256] It appears in P[46], obviously as a Pauline letter, but the Muratorian Fragment never mentions it. Irenaeus cites it, but not as from Paul,[257] and Tertullian (*De pudic.* 10; 20) ascribes it to Barnabas, Paul's travelling companion from Acts.[258] Apparently, already Clement of Rome makes use of Hebrews (1 Clem. 36), but he neither mentions an author, nor

---

[251] ibid.: 144–5.

[252] See Bird 2011: 74–5, and see Bird's entire discussion, leading him to conclude, 'The *Epistle to Diognetus* is undoubtedly a document with strong Pauline influences (esp. from Romans, Titus, and 1 Corinthians)' (87).

[253] Cf. *Haer.* 1, praef., where 1 Tim. 1:4 is cited as from 'the apostle'; *Haer.* 1.16.3, where Tit. 3:10 is cited as from Paul; *Haer.* 3.14.1, where 2 Tim. 4:10–11 is cited as from Paul.

[254] Cf. Polycarp, *Phil.* 4.1 (1 Tim 6:7, 10); *Phil.* 9.2 (2 Tim. 4:10); see Holmes 2005: 215–18.

[255] *Apol. Ad Autolycum* 3.14.

[256] On the reception of Hebrews in early Christianity, see Hahneman 1992: 119–25; Armstrong 2006: 122–9.

[257] Cf. *Haer.* 2.30.9; 3.6.5; 5.32.2. See also Eusebius, *Hist. eccl.* 5.26.

[258] See de Boer 2014.

even acknowledges that he is interacting with a text.[259] According to Eusebius, both Clement of Alexandria (see *Hist. eccl.* 6.14.2–3) and his predecessor Pantaenus (i.e., 'the blessed presbyter', *Hist. eccl.* 6.14.4) regarded Hebrews to be Pauline. Origen affirmed its Pauline authorship many times, once even saying that he intended to write a defence of the epistle as Paul's (*Ep. Afr.* 14), though in his *Homilies on Hebrews* (preserved by Eusebius, *Hist. eccl.* 6.25.13–14) he admits that only God knows the author's identity.[260] As for the manuscript evidence, 'it seems as if there are no Greek manuscripts of the Pauline corpus extant that excluded Hebrews'.[261] In the West, there continued to be doubts about its authorship, as Eusebius acknowledged (*Hist. eccl.* 3.3.5; 6.20.3), and as we have already seen in Tertullian and the Muratorian Fragment (if the latter is indeed a product of the West). But we previously noticed that the Western canon lists from the fourth century onwards typically mention the fourteen epistles of Paul. Whereas Jerome admits the doubts held by his countrymen about the letter (e.g., *Vir. ill.* 5), he also says that the acceptance of the epistle does not depend on its authorship (*Epist.* 129.3),[262] an opinion similar to that expressed by Origen in his *Homilies on Hebrews*.

During the first half of the second century, then, we have good evidence for the circulation of some of Paul's letters, as writers start to cite them as authoritative statements of the Christian faith. Around mid-century, Marcion promoted a ten-letter collection, which he may not have invented. The end of the century attests the collection in more or less the form that became traditional, with thirteen or, usually, fourteen letters.

Catholic Epistles

Immediately after his treatment of the Gospels, Athanasius mentions Acts and the Catholic Epistles, specifying that these latter number seven and attributing one to James, two to Peter, three to John, and one to Jude. We will wait until the next section to discuss the reception of Acts, but here we should note that by grouping Acts with the Catholic Epistles, this list of Athanasius conforms to the practice of the Greek manuscript tradition. Just as it was common for codices of the Gospels and codices of the Pauline Epistles to circulate independently, so also the Catholic Epistles and Acts formed a unit, though the earliest such example, P[74], comes from the seventh century.[263] But contemporary with Athanasius (or close to it), the three great biblical codices feature the grouping Acts–James–Peter–John–Jude, whether after the Pauline Epistles and before Revelation (Sinaiticus), or after the Gospels and before Paul (Vaticanus and

---

[259] Cf. Eusebius, *Hist. eccl.* 3.38.1; see Gregory 2005: 152–3.
[260] Armstrong 2006: 127n85.   [261] Elliott 1996: 109.
[262] For this passage, see the section on Jerome in ch. 4.   [263] Parker 2008: 283.

Alexandrinus).[264] Though there is variation in the grouping before the seventh century, 'the order of the seven Catholic letters is very uniform, especially among Greek manuscripts'.[265]

We do see some variation in the canon lists. While several of the lists in this book group Acts with the Catholic Epistles in different arrangements,[266] several other lists separate Acts from the Catholic Epistles by inserting between them the Pauline letters.[267] Moreover, the lists do not always present the Catholic Epistles in the same internal sequence: while the single most common sequence is James–Peter–John–Jude (especially in Greek sources),[268] the lists (especially Latin ones) attest several alternate sequences:

John–Peter–Jude–James: Innocent
Peter–John–Jude–James: *Breviarium Hipponense*, Augustine
Peter–James–Jude–John: Rufinus, Origen (*Hom. Jos.* 7.1)
James–John–Jude–Peter: Apostolic Canons

Of course, there are occasions when not all seven letters appear in the list. The Syriac list from St Catherine's Monastery omits reference to any of these letters, reflecting the Syrian church's widespread doubt about these letters, where perhaps none of these letters were accepted until the fifth century.[269] The Mommsen Catalogue omits James and Jude, apparently reflecting hesitations about these books in the West in the mid-fourth century. Such doubts were explicitly noted in the East a couple decades later, when Amphilochius of Iconium reported that some accept three (James, 1 Peter, 1 John) and others seven Catholic Epistles. At the beginning of the fourth century, Eusebius had placed only two of these epistles (1 Peter and 1 John) in the category of 'universally received writings' (ὁμολογούμενα), while the other five were 'disputed' (ἀντιλεγόμενα). Eusebius also preserves a fragment from the fifth book of Origen's *Commentary on John*, in which the Alexandrian mentions 'one acknowledged epistle' (μία ἐπιστολὴ ὁμολογουμένη) of Peter and another that is doubted (ἀμφιβάλλεται), and three epistles of John, but some doubt the authenticity of two of them.[270] Finally, the Muratorian Fragment comments only on Jude and two epistles of John; the absence of other Catholic Epistles perhaps results from scribal error.[271]

---

[264] See ch. 6.   [265] Parker 2008: 283–6, quotation from 285–6.
[266] Acts-Catholic Epistles, after Paul: Jerome. Catholic Epistles-Acts, after Paul: Epiphanius, Augustine, Innocent. Acts-Catholic Epistles, before Paul: Cyril of Jerusalem, Laodicea. Catholic Epistles-Acts, before Paul: Origen (*Hom. Jos.* 7.1).
[267] Eusebius, Muratorian Fragment, Rufinus, *Breviarium Hipponense*, Gregory of Nazianzus, Amphilochius of Iconium. The Mommsen Catalogue has Revelation between Acts and the Catholic Epistles.
[268] Cyril of Jerusalem; Gregory of Nazianzus; Amphilochius of Iconium; Epiphanius; canon list of the Synod of Laodicea; Jerome, *Epist.* 53.9.5. On the variety of orders, see Elliott 1996: 109.
[269] Hahneman 1992: 126; Nienhuis and Wall 2013: 31.
[270] See the section on Origen in ch. 3.
[271] See the section on the Muratorian Fragment in ch. 4.

By the end of the fourth century, Greek and Latin canon lists routinely included seven Catholic Epistles without any hesitation: Gregory of Nazianzus, Epiphanius, the Apostolic Canons (with some additional writings), the list of the Synod of Laodicea, Jerome,[272] Augustine, the *Breviarium Hipponense*, Rufinus, Innocent. The earliest source to include all seven letters without wavering is Cyril of Jerusalem, who mentions the 'seven Catholic Epistles'. Other Greek sources also call these letters 'catholic',[273] but Latin sources from our period tend not to see these letters as a distinct canonical collection—and do not label them 'catholic'—but rather group them with Paul as apostolic letters.[274] The idea of seven Catholic Epistles is found already in Eusebius (*Hist. eccl.* 2.23.25), though he himself lists some of these as doubted, as we have seen.[275] The earliest attestation for the term 'catholic' is in Origen, who labelled individual letters, and not a collection of letters, as catholic.[276] He frequently describes 1 John as a catholic letter (e.g., *Comm. John* 1.138; 2.149),[277] and sometimes uses the word in reference to 1 Peter (*Sel. in Psa.* 3.6; *Comm. John* 6.175.9),[278] and once in reference to the Epistle of Barnabas (*Cels.* 1.63.9). The word apparently signifies for Origen the general nature of the addressees of these letters; the epistles are not addressed to specific individuals or churches but to the church catholic.[279]

Origen is also the first author to attest clear knowledge of all seven Catholic Epistles, as he is the first writer on record to mention James, 2 Peter, and 2–3 John. He makes extensive use of James,[280] though he knows that not everyone accepts the letter (*Comm. John* 20.10.66), just as Eusebius will later report that 'not many of the ancients' make use of James (*Hist. eccl.* 2.23.25).[281] It is not clear what Origen thought about the shorter Petrine and Johannine letters. We have already seen that in the fifth book of his *Commentary on John*, he acknowledges contemporary doubts about 2 Peter and 2–3 John, and the only

---

[272] See his *Epist.* 53.9.5, below in ch. 4. Jerome does elsewhere admit to doubts about some Catholic Epistles: 2 Peter (*Vir. ill.* 1.3), but he also suggests that both Petrine epistles are authentic and their stylistic differences result from different amanuenses (*Epist.* 120.11.5); 2–3 John (*Vir. ill.* 9; 18), but he also quotes 2–3 John as apostolic (*Comm. Tit.* 1.8–9; *Epist.* 123.11; 146.1).

[273] Gregory of Nazianzus, Epiphanius, Amphilochius of Iconium, the list of the Synod of Laodicea.

[274] See the sections on Rufinus, the *Breviarium Hipponense*, Augustine, and Innocent in ch. 4. Jerome, on the other hand, considers the Catholic Letters a collection in so far as he numbers them as seven (*Epist.* 53.9.5). Here he does not use the label 'catholic', but he does at *Vir. ill.* 1.3; 2.2; 4.1–2. See Nienhuis and Wall 2013: 33.

[275] See the section on Eusebius in ch. 3, where *Hist. eccl.* 2.23.25 is quoted.

[276] However, a Latin translation (produced under the direction of Cassiodorus) of portions of the *Hypotyposes* of Clement of Alexandria refers to Jude as a catholic epistle; see Nienhuis and Wall 2013: 223. Moreover, Clement (*Strom.* 4.15) described the apostolic letter found in Acts 15:23–9 as a catholic epistle; see Armstrong 2006: 114, and on the reception of the terminology, see 114–15.

[277] See also fragments preserved in Eusebius, *Hist. eccl.* 5.18.5; 7.25.7–10.

[278] See also the fragment preserved by Eusebius, *Hist. eccl.* 6.25.5.

[279] Nienhuis and Wall 2013: 27.   [280] ibid.: 25–7.   [281] See ibid.: 77–9.

quotations of these three letters in Origen's œuvre are some quotations of 2 Peter in works preserved only in Latin.[282] No earlier writer mentions these letters,[283] though (at least content from) 2 John was used from the late second century (Irenaeus).[284] 'That 1 John should have been mentioned and used before there is any reference to a second or third Epistle is hardly surprising for it is longer and has much more theological content. Whether this may on occasion mean that 2 and 3 John were either not known or not accorded authority is difficult to determine.'[285] As Lieu further points out, even when these letters were included in fourth-century canon lists, they continued to be seldom used.[286]

The other three Catholic Epistles were certainly known and valued from the second century onwards, though Jude's status was more uncertain than that of the other two. According to Eusebius (*Hist. eccl.* 3.39.17), Papias made use of 1 Peter and 1 John, and these two letters were typically accorded a high position. Attestation for them includes Polycarp, Irenaeus, Clement, Tertullian, and Origen.[287] The strongest testimony in support of Jude is surely Tertullian's defence of the inspiration of 1 Enoch based on Jude's use of it (v. 14),[288] but other witnesses include Clement, the Muratorian Fragment (68), and Origen.[289] But Origen does acknowledge that others may hesitate to accept the letter (*Comm. Matt.* 17.30.9–10), as does Eusebius (*Hist. eccl.* 2.23.25).[290]

---

[282] *Princ.* 2.5.3; *Hom. Lev.* 4.4; *Hom. Num.* 13.8.1; *Comm. Rom.* 8.7.7. Kruger (2015: 107n43) cites also *Princ.* 4.1.31. At *Comm. John* 1.26 (preserved in Greek), Origen mentions the 'writings of Peter'. On the absence of 2–3 John from Origen's works, see Lieu 1986: 10–11.

[283] Gamble 2002: 287. On the reception of 2 Peter, see Nienhuis and Wall 2013: 112–14; on the reception of 2–3 John, see Lieu 1986: 5–36.

[284] Cf. Irenaeus, *Haer.* 3.16.5, 8, but Irenaeus represents the material from 2 John as coming from the same letter as the material from 1 John. Earlier, Polycarp (*Phil.* 7.1) mentions the antichrist in language that recalls 1 John 4:2 and 2 John 7. Also, Clement (*Strom.* 2.15.66) calls 1 John 'the larger epistle', implying at least two Johannine letters, but Tertullian mentions only 'the letter' of John (*De pud.* 19.10; *Scorp.* 12.4; *Idol.* 2.3). Lieu (1986: 8–9) shows that while Cyprian did not use 2–3 John, a council held at Carthage under Cyprian in 256 included a quotation of 2 John 10–11 from one of the delegates. Dionysius of Alexandria seems to accept 2–3 John (Eusebius, *Hist. eccl.* 7.25.11). Didymus the Blind never cited 2–3 John, though he did accept 2 Peter (Ehrman 1983: 6–11).

[285] Lieu 1986: 6.   [286] ibid.: 15.

[287] Polycarp: *Phil.* 1, 8; cf. Eusebius, *Hist. eccl.* 4.14.9 (1 Peter); *Phil.* 7 (1 John); Irenaeus: *Haer.* 4.9.2 (1 Peter); *Haer.* 3.16.5, 8 (1 John); Clement: *Strom.* 3.18.10; 4.20.129 (1 Peter); *Strom.* 2.15.66 (1 John); Tertullian: *Scorp.* 12 (1 Peter); *De pud.* 19.10; *Scorp.* 12.4; *Idol.* 2.3 (1 John); Origen: *apud* Eusebius, *Hist. eccl.* 6.25.8, 10. For 1 Peter, there is also the evidence of 2 Peter, which labels itself a 'second letter' (2 Pet 3:1). See Nienhuis and Wall 2013: 108–12 (1 Peter), 171–4 (Johannine letters). Justin also possibly shows familiarity with 1 John at *1Apol.* 32.7–8 (cf. 1 John 3:9); see ibid.: 19n7, who cite also *Dial.* 123.9.

[288] Cf. Tertullian *Cult. fem.* 1.3. On the other hand, Jerome says that Jude's citation of 1 Enoch caused people to doubt the authority of Jude (*Vir. ill.* 4).

[289] Clement, *Paed.* 3.8.44; cf. Eusebius, *Hist. eccl.* 6.14.1; Origen, *Comm. Matt.* 10.17. On Origen's use of Jude, see Nienhuis 2007: 54. Moreover, 2 Peter apparently makes extensive use of Jude.

[290] On Jude's reception, see Moore 2013: 510–15; Nienhuis and Wall 2013: 223–5.

Our brief survey has found that Eusebius was largely correct in his evaluation of the reception of these letters: while 1 Peter and 1 John enjoyed early and widespread acceptance as authoritative statements from apostles, the other five letters encountered various levels of resistance. They apparently circulated in different combinations in Antiquity; our earliest text of the epistles of Peter and Jude (P^{72}) is found in a codex that contains these three letters with other writings, none of which entered the canon.[291] There may have been a Johannine collection, as well.[292] For the Gospels and the Pauline letters, we saw that the second century was the key period for the formation of the collection. Our evidence suggests that the formation of the Catholic Epistle collection occurred about a century later. By the end of the second century, we have clear references to 1 Peter, 1–2 John, and Jude, without any suggestion that these letters form a collection. By the end of the third century, all seven letters are known and, according to Eusebius (*Hist. eccl.* 2.23.25), form a collection called the Catholic Epistles, though some of them still faced uncertainty.[293] This uncertainty especially found expression in Syrian churches, where even today most of these letters are usually excluded from Syrian Bibles.[294] But Greek and Latin sources from the mid-fourth century generally accept all seven Catholic Epistles, Cyril of Jerusalem providing the first extant list to do so.

Acts

We mentioned earlier that Athanasius places Acts and the Catholic Epistles immediately after the fourfold Gospel, and we have seen that this arrangement stands in harmony with some other canon lists and some manuscripts. All of the canon lists collected in this volume that contain a list of New Testament books include the Acts of the Apostles, but in various positions: usually in its familiar position immediately after the Gospels,[295] but not always.[296] By the time Christians produced lists of authoritative books, there was no question that Acts belonged somewhere on the list.

---

[291] On this codex, see Wasserman 2006: 30–50.

[292] See Hill 2004. Parker (2008: 283–5) guesses that Bezae (GA 05) might have contained the Johannine writings together.

[293] Hahneman 1992: 125; Gamble 2002: 288. On recent attempts to evaluate the Catholic Epistles as a collection, see Lockett 2015.

[294] Metzger 1987: 220.

[295] Muratorian Fragment (34), Eusebius, Cyril of Jerusalem, Gregory of Nazianzus, Amphilochius, the list from the Synod of Laodicea, the *Breviarium Hipponense*, Rufinus, and the Syriac list from St Catherine's Monastery.

[296] Sometimes it is immediately before Revelation: Mommsen Catalogue, Augustine, Innocent, Epiphanius (maybe: his Greek syntax makes the exact placement—whether before or after the Catholic Epistles—difficult to determine). Codex Claromontanus puts it after Revelation but before the Shepherd of Hermas. Jerome (*Epist.* 53.9.4) puts it after Paul and before the Catholic Epistles; possibly this is what Epiphanius also intends. Origen (*Hom. Jos.* 7.1) puts it before Paul and after the Catholic Epistles. Acts is the final work mentioned in the list in the Apostolic Canons, after several writings not found in the canon of Athanasius.

The earlier reception of Acts is somewhat less clear. Irenaeus unquestionably knew Acts, citing it by name (*Haer.* 3.13.3) and using it extensively in *Haer.* 3.13–15.[297] Clement of Alexandria and Tertullian also provide testimony to Acts.[298] Evidence prior to Irenaeus is controverted. Some scholars believe Justin's reference to Jesus's post-resurrection teaching, his ascension, and the apostle's reception of power (*1Apol.* 50.12) relies on Acts, but others disagree.[299] The *Epistula Apostolorum* may make use of Acts, but not everyone finds this evidence convincing.[300] The *Epistle of Lyons and Vienne* (177 CE, *apud* Eusebius, *Hist. Eccl.* 5.1–2), slightly earlier than Irenaeus, seems to rely on Acts, especially in its citation of Stephen's dying prayer (Acts 7:60; *Hist. eccl.* 5.2.5), but, again, other explanations are possible.[301] What we can say with certainty is that Christians from the late second century generally regarded Acts as authoritative and received it as part of their Scriptures.

Revelation

The conclusion to Athanasius's NT canon list says simply, 'And again, the Revelation of John', a brief note that reveals none of the doubts about this final book that continued to plague its reception in the East for many centuries. John's Apocalypse experienced a curious reception history, widely received, considered apostolic and inspired, until the mid-third century, when the tide began to turn against the book, from which point doubts about its authorship and its suitability as Christian Scripture prevented Christian leaders, especially in the East, from attributing to it full canonical authority. This uncertainty is reflected in the canon lists collected in this book; most of the lists, like that of Athanasius, include Revelation without any hint of doubt,[302] some note the doubts about the book,[303] and some fail to mention the book at all.[304] While all of the Western lists include Revelation, the hesitations in the East reverberated

---

[297] On Irenaeus' use of Acts, see Mount 2002: 12–29.

[298] Clement, *Strom.* 5.12.82; see Brooks 1992: 42. Tertullian, *Marc.* 5.1–4; *Praescr.* 22; see Metzger 1987: 159.

[299] Rowe 2010: 74–5, favouring dependence on Acts; on the other hand, see Gregory 2003: 317–21; 2010: 82–3.

[300] Schröter (2013: 278) thinks it is certain, Gregory (2003: 306) regards it as tenuous; see his further discussion at pp. 322–6.

[301] Gregory 2003: 326–8.

[302] Muratorian Fragment, Origen (*apud* Eusebius, *Hist. eccl.* 6.25.9, although Revelation goes unmentioned in *Hom. Jos.* 7.1), Epiphanius, Mommsen Catalogue, Jerome (*Epist.* 53.9.6), Augustine, *Breviarium Hipponense*, Rufinus, Innocent, Codex Claromontanus.

[303] Eusebius says that it is either accepted or spurious; Amphilochius says that the majority regard it as spurious.

[304] Cyril of Jerusalem, the list of the Synod of Laodicea, Gregory of Nazianzus (who does, however, regard the book as genuinely apostolic; see the discussion of his list in ch. 3), the Apostolic Canons, and the Syriac list from St Catherine's Monastery.

throughout the centuries, so that the Greek Orthodox biblical canon did not definitely admit Revelation until the seventeenth century, and it has never formed a part of the Orthodox liturgy.

But from the beginning it was not so, according to the evidence available to us. Early on, both the Eastern and Western Christians accepted the book.[305] Important second- and third-century writers claimed for the book apostolic authorship and, thus, inspiration, including Justin Martyr, Irenaeus, Tertullian, and Origen.[306] Papias affirmed the trustworthiness of the book, and the second-century *Epistle of Lyons and Vienne* introduce a quotation of Rev. 22:11 with the phrase, 'that the scripture might be fulfilled'.[307] Irenaeus (*Haer.* 3.11.8) defended the four Gospels by drawing on the image of the four living creatures in Rev. 4, as if the authority of Revelation were more widely acknowledged than that of the fourfold Gospel.[308] The Muratorian Canon argues for the Pauline Epistles on the basis of Revelation: Paul wrote to seven churches just as John did (cf. Rev. 2–3). And when the Muratorian Canon says that 'some' do not accept the Apocalypse of Peter, it implies that the same is not true for the Apocalypse of John.

In the second century, the belief developed that Christ would return to earth to reign for a thousand years, a belief that coheres with Rev. 20. This literalistic view of the millennium found support already in Papias,[309] Justin Martyr (*Dial.* 80–1), and others.[310] Soon millenarianism generated such controversy that some of its opponents sought to discredit the Johannine writings upon which the doctrine was based. The third-century presbyter Gaius disputed the authorship of Revelation, attributing it instead to the heretic Cerinthus.[311] Other opponents of millenarianism would accept Revelation's authority but offer a spiritual rather than literal interpretation, such as Origen and Methodius of Olympus.[312] 'Origen reproached [the millenarians] for abandoning all intellectual effort, and for sticking solely to the literal sense of Scripture. He himself

---

[305] Hahneman 1992: 23–5; McGinn 2009; Constantinou 2013: 1–46; Kruger 2016; cf. Bokedal 2014: 152.

[306] Justin Martyr, *Dial.* 81; Irenaeus, *Haer.* 5.26.1; 35.2; Tertullian, *Marc.* 4.5; Origen, *Comm. John* 5 (*apud* Eusebius, *Hist. eccl.* 6.25.9). But Pagels (2012: 112) argues that the identification of John of Patmos with the apostle was a response to the rejection of Revelation.

[307] *Apud* Eusebius, *Hist. eccl.* 5.1.58. The use of Revelation by Papias is attested by Andrew of Caesarea, *Comm. Apoc.* prol. (available in the translation by Constantinou 2011: 53–4); see also Hill 2004: 111, 394–5.

[308] Irenaeus apparently relied on an earlier source; see Skeat 1992.

[309] See Eusebius, *Hist. eccl.* 3.39.12–13. Eusebius explains this belief on the part of Papias as due to his stupidity.

[310] For the entire discussion, see Hill 2001; McGinn 2009.

[311] This is the usual interpretation of Eusebius, *Hist. eccl.* 3.28.1–6; 7.25.2; see Pagels 2012: 103–6. Scholars often connect Gaius to a group called the *Alogoi* by Epiphanius, *Pan.* 51 (Grant 1993: 96–8). For sceptical investigations into the foundations of this scholarly reconstruction of ancient opposition to the Johannine writings, see Hill 2004: 174–204; Manor 2016.

[312] Cf. Origen, *Princ.* 2.11.2; cf. Hill 2001: 176–89. On Methodius, see ibid.: 39–41. On the emergence of the spiritual reading, see McGinn 2009: 89–105.

interprets all these passages spiritually, i.e. allegorically: e.g. the precious stones of the New Jerusalem are the saints, and so on (*De Princ.* II 11:2–3). Thus he deprives the millenarians of the scriptural basis of their teaching.'[313]

However, Dionysius of Alexandria, a student of Origen who became bishop of Alexandria in 248, suggested that John's Apocalypse was written by a different John from the apostle. He sought to demonstrate this position through literary analysis, intending to show that the same author could not have written the Gospel and Revelation.[314] Dionysius's opinion became influential when Eusebius of Caesarea featured it prominently in his *Ecclesiastical History* (7.25) and gave favour to the view. Eusebius explained in his own review of the biblical canon that Revelation was either universally accepted or spurious.[315] We have seen that canon lists in the East wavered on its status. No Greek commentary on Revelation would appear until the late sixth century,[316] and its position in the East continued to be uncertain until early modern times.

In the West, the spiritual interpretation dominated, and there did not exist the same anxiety with millenarianism, so there was not as much opposition to the book. The first Latin commentary on Revelation was produced by Victorinus (d. 304), bishop of Pettau (modern Ptuj in Slovenia), who did advocate a literal millennial reign of Christ, but his commentary was reworked by Jerome, who removed the millenarian elements and made other changes.[317] It was this adjusted commentary by Victorinus-Jerome, along with another commentary by the fourth-century Donatist writer Tyconius, that exerted a strong influence on later Latin authors and established the spiritual interpretation of Revelation in the West.[318] As we saw earlier, no early Western canon list omits Revelation.[319]

The hesitations regarding Revelation in the East had a strong impact on the transmission of the book. According to a recent survey,[320] there are only 307 Greek manuscripts containing John's Apocalypse.[321] The oldest fragment is P[98] (second century), the oldest complete text is in Codex Sinaiticus. (Vaticanus suffers a lacuna at the end of the New Testament, so that we cannot be sure whether it originally included Revelation.)[322] There are seven papyri (each

---

[313] Simonetti 1994: 45; see also Dorival 2013: 614, citing *Princ.* 1.2.10; 4.2.3.

[314] Grant 1993: 104–6.

[315] *Hist. eccl.* 3.25; see ch. 3 on Eusebius; and see Hill 2004: 461–3.

[316] Constantinou 2013: 7–9.

[317] For Victorinus' commentary, see Dulaey 1997; for a brief description, see McGinn 2009: 101–4.

[318] Constantinou (2013: 2–6) briefly describes the Latin commentary tradition. For more extensive treatment, see Gryson 1997.

[319] Much later, in the sixteenth century, doubts about Revelation would arise in the West; see Backus 2000: ch. 1.

[320] Elliott 2015; see also Epp 2002: 503, 505.

[321] For basic information about most of these manuscripts, see Aune 1997: cxxxiv–clx. See also Schmid 2015.

[322] Parker (2008: 72) suggests we discontinue referring to Vaticanus as a full-Bible codex because of our uncertainty as to whether it originally contained Revelation.

containing only the Apocalypse),[323] twelve majuscules,[324] and 289 minuscules, of which 138 contain only the Apocalypse (usually with a commentary), while the rest include also other portions of the New Testament. Some manuscripts include Revelation alongside patristic literature.[325] There are 150 Greek manuscripts that contain the entire New Testament except for Revelation.[326]

The strange reception history of Revelation is perhaps the best illustration of the fraught and contentious nature of canon history. Whereas Western churches have consistently accepted Revelation as apostolic and authoritative from earliest times, Eastern churches have consistently entertained doubts about the book. It attained a secure position in the Greek church only in relatively recent times, and it has also held a dubious position within the Syrian churches.[327] These later hesitations stand in contrast to the widespread authority enjoyed by the book in the second and third centuries. Perhaps it is fitting that this strange and difficult book should experience such a strange and difficult reception.

Closing the NT Canon

Athanasius's list was an attempt not only to include all of the writings he considered inspired and authoritative, but also to exclude other writings that he judged without value, or even dangerous. Aside from these two extremes, Athanasius also omitted from his NT canon some writings that he considered valuable expressions of the Christian life and edifying for believers, especially neophytes. The value of these writings ensured them a respected place in Christian literature, so that Athanasius did not want to class them among the rejected works but among those that, while not canonical, should be read by the faithful. These in-between books—not canonical but not rejected—include most of the deuterocanonical books of the Old Testament and, in terms of the New Testament, the Shepherd of Hermas and the Didache. Long before Athanasius, these two writings, along with several others that would not feature within the twenty-seven-book New Testament, enjoyed a high status among Christians, a status seemingly equal to that accorded to some books that Athanasius did deem canonical.

Beside the core writings of the Gospels and major Pauline Epistles, which were used very often, even more often than the Old Testament,[328] Christians

---

[323] P18, P24, P43, P47, P85, P98, P115.

[324] 01, 02, 04, 025, 046, 051, 052, 0163, 0169, 0207, 0229, 0308, the last eight containing only the Apocalypse.

[325] Metzger 2003: 205–6.   [326] Elliott 1996: 110.

[327] On the position of Revelation within the Syrian churches, see Metzger 1987: 218–22. The book was not translated into Syriac until the sixth century; see Brock 2006: 36. The Peshitta does not contain it, though the Harklean does.

[328] For the concept of 'core' writings, see Barton 1997: 19; Spellman 2014: 42–3.

used (less often) other writings, some later classified as canonical and some not.[329] The high status of some of the useful non-canonical books is also evident by their appearance in manuscripts of the Bible, such as Sinaiticus (which ends with the Epistle of Barnabas and a substantial portion of the Shepherd of Hermas) and Alexandrinus (which ends with 1–2 Clement).[330] It is not clear that this manuscript evidence indicates the canonicity of these books for the creators or users of these manuscripts (on this issue, see the Introduction), but the inclusion of these additional books at the end of the New Testament does clearly establish the value these books held for Christian readers in the fourth century.

The Appendix contains basic information regarding the majority of these writings that might at times have been considered Scripture but did not find a place in Athanasius's canon. In terms of these extra-canonical books, the lists included in this book mention the following early Christian writings in a positive way, whether that means inclusion in the biblical canon or merely counting them as useful but without canonical authority.

Apocalypse of Peter	The Muratorian Fragment includes the Apocalypse of Peter within its survey of Christian Scripture, but the Fragment also says that some exclude this Apocalypse from public reading. Eusebius (*Hist. eccl.* 3.25.4) lists the Apocalypse of Peter as among the *antilegomena* ('disputed') and *notha* ('spurious'). The list in Codex Claromontanus includes the Apocalypse of Peter under obelus.
Shepherd of Hermas	The Muratorian Fragment says that the Shepherd should not be read publicly but should be read privately. Eusebius (*Hist. eccl.* 3.25.4) considers the Shepherd to be *antilegomena* and *notha*, though he elsewhere acknowledges significant early Christian use of this work (3.3.6; 5.8.7). Athanasius includes the Shepherd among those non-canonical books that should be read. Jerome lists the Shepherd as non-canonical (*Prol. Gal.*). Rufinus includes it among the 'ecclesiastical' books that are useful but cannot establish doctrine. The list in Codex Claromontanus includes the Shepherd under obelus. Codex Sinaiticus includes the Shepherd after the Epistle of Barnabas.
Epistle of Barnabas	Eusebius (*Hist. eccl.* 3.25.4) lists Barnabas as *antilegomena* and *notha*. The list in Codex Claromontanus includes Barnabas under obelus. Codex Sinaiticus includes Barnabas after Revelation.
Acts of Paul	Eusebius (*Hist. eccl.* 3.25.4) classifies the Acts of Paul as *antilegomena* and *notha*. The list in Codex Claromontanus includes Acts of Paul under obelus.

[329] Stuhlhofer 1988, summarized and developed by Barton 1997: ch. 1.
[330] See ch. 6. In its table of contents, Alexandrinus lists Psalms of Solomon after 2 Clement, but 2 Clement is the final writing in the manuscript today. Codex Vaticanus contains no Christian writings considered non-canonical by Athanasius, but the manuscript is not complete at the end, breaking off at Heb. 9:14.

Didache	Eusebius (*Hist. eccl.* 3.25.4) considers the Didache to be *antilegomena* and *notha*. Athanasius includes the Didache among those non-canonical books that should be read. The work (mentioned below) called the Two Ways by Rufinus no doubt has a close relationship with the Didache.
Gospel according to the Hebrews	Eusebius (*Hist. eccl.* 3.25.5) lists this Gospel as *antilegomena*.
1 Clement	Eusebius does not mention Clement at all in his major discussion of the NT canon at *Hist. eccl.* 3.25, even though he elsewhere describes 1 Clement as a 'recognized [ὁμολογουμένη] epistle of Clement, long and wonderful [μεγάλη τε καὶ θαυμασία]', and he says that it 'was publically read in the common assembly in many churches both in the days of old and in our own time' (3.16; cf. 4.23.11). He later (3.38.1) says that 1 Clement is 'recognized by all' (ἀνωμολογημένη παρα πᾶσιν). The Apostolic Canons include 1 Clement within the biblical canon, and we have seen that Codex Alexandrinus puts 1 Clement after Revelation.
2 Clement	Eusebius is not convinced that ancient writers knew 2 Clement (3.38.4). The Apostolic Canons include 2 Clement within the biblical canon, and Codex Alexandrinus joins 2 Clement to 1 Clement at the conclusion of the NT, following Revelation.
Two Ways	Rufinus names the Two Ways as an 'ecclesiastical' work that is useful but cannot establish doctrine. This work surely shares a great deal with the Didache, and perhaps they are identical. Moreover, the following work, the Judgement of Peter, possibly also serves as another name for this work.
Judgement of Peter	Rufinus mentions the Judgement of Peter immediately following his reference to the Two Ways in such a way that has left scholars in some doubt as to whether Rufinus intends by these two titles to refer to two different works or only one.

Aside from the information available in lists and the major biblical codices, one should also consider the use made of these books in early Christian literature (quotations and allusions), as well as the manuscript attestation for each book, including ancient translations, which can indicate something of the popularity of the literary work.[331] Especially in the case of the Shepherd of Hermas, the number of early manuscripts transmitting this work suggests its high status, perhaps on—or surpassing—the level of several books now in the NT. Origen, for one, considered the Shepherd 'divinely inspired' (*Comm. Rom.* 10.31), though he acknowledged that not everyone shared his view (e.g. *Comm. Matt.* 14.21).[332] Gamble emphasizes that 'in respect of many of these documents, especially 1 Clement, Barnabas, the Shepherd and the Didache,... the esteem and use attaching to them was appreciably earlier, more continuous,

---

[331] The Appendix briefly surveys such information for many of these books.
[332] This comment survives only in Rufinus's translation. The Latin is *divinitus inspirata*.

and more widespread than to many of the writings that were finally accepted in the canon, including Hebrews, 2 Peter, James, and 2 and 3 John.[333] Early on, it is difficult to tell a difference between the reception of these diverse books, except in so far as some were associated with apostles while others were not. It is also difficult to determine the historical causes that led to the non-canonicity of some writings and the acceptance of others; scholars discuss various factors, not only apostolicity, catholicity, and orthodoxy, but also more institutional factors, and the role of heretics, especially Marcion, in prodding the church towards a canon.[334] Given the importance of the sub-collections of the NT, as we have seen throughout this survey, it is probably significant that the Shepherd and Barnabas, for instance, never secured a position within one of these sub-collections.[335]

There were other works often classified now—as in Antiquity—as New Testament Apocrypha, including apocryphal Gospels, apocryphal Acts, apocryphal epistles, and apocryphal Apocalypses.[336] Sometimes these works were associated with heretics, but in other cases they were composed and embraced in orthodox circles, becoming in their own way 'useful for the soul'.[337] The Acts of Thomas may serve as an example, since it seems to have been considered Scripture in some circles, serving as the basis for some sermons by Jacob of Serugh.[338] Only a few of these apocrypha were used on a wide enough basis to merit a comment from Eusebius in his classification of this literature (*Hist. eccl.* 3.25), and at best Eusebius called them *antilegomena* ('disputed') and *notha* ('spurious').[339] Other writings are the 'forgeries of heretics' (αἱρετικῶν ἀνδρῶν ἀναπλάσματα), 'altogether wicked and impious' (ἄτοπα πάντῃ καὶ δυσσεβῆ), to which no orthodox writer has ever referred (3.25.6–7). These writings include various apocryphal Gospels and Acts.[340]

The canon lists brought clarity to these issues for their authors and the communities they represented. Athanasius surely did not have to tell anyone that

[333] Gamble 2002: 290.
[334] See Metzger 1987; Markschies 2015; for a brief statement, Gamble 2002: 294. Some scholars consider Marcion to have played a crucial role: Campenhausen 1972: 148; BeDuhn 2013: 4. Others think he played a negligible role: Barton 1997; Gamble 2006. On this discussion, see Markschies 2015: 217–18. According to Gamble (2002: 292), 'It is quite uncertain, for example, that Marcion considered his canon to be closed and exclusive; his followers, in any case, apparently did not' (citing Hahneman 1992: 90–3).
[335] Noted by Bokedal 2014: 152.
[336] For a collection, see Elliott 1993, or the more recent German edition that has started to appear; for the first volume, see Markschies and Schröter 2012.
[337] For this terminology, see Bovon 2012. On the orthodox use of apocrypha, see also Jenkins 2015; Nicklas 2016.
[338] On the Acts of Thomas as Scripture, see Henry 2014; on Jacob of Serugh, see ibid.: 169.
[339] He so treats the Acts of Paul, the Apocalypse of Peter, and the Gospel according to the Hebrews.
[340] For the full list of apocryphal writings condemned by Eusebius, see the section on Eusebius in ch. 3.

the fourfold Gospel or the letters of Paul were authoritative, but he did feel it necessary to compose a precise list of canonical books so that his readers could know which writings were not authoritative Scripture. According to Athanasius, the canon was closed: 'let no one add or subtract anything from them' (*Ep. fest.* 39.19). These books are the 'springs of salvation', and in them alone 'the teaching of piety is proclaimed'. Likewise, Gregory of Nazianzus considered his list to include all of the authoritative Scriptures, so that any others are not genuine. The Synod of Laodicea prohibited the reading of non-canonical books in church. Cyril of Jerusalem recommended to catechumens to read privately only what the church reads publicly, and he put all writings not on his list in a secondary rank. The Councils of Carthage and Hippo (represented by the *Breviarium Hipponense*) allowed only the divine Scriptures on their canon lists to be read in worship. Despite these attempts to settle the discussion, we saw at the beginning of this section on the New Testament that some books continued to waver in and out of the canon for many centuries (e.g., Revelation in the East, *Laodiceans* in the West), up to the time of the Reformation and even beyond, while biblical canons in other parts of the Christian world (e.g., the Syrian church, the Ethiopian church) continued to reflect their own traditions, sharing many things in common with the Greek and Latin lists, but not every-thing. The lists collected in this book show both the unity and the diversity of the NT canon in Antiquity.

*   *   *

While this survey of the early history of the biblical canon has not attempted to resolve the many problems faced by such study, we hope that it has provided readers with guidance to the data at our disposal and the major scholarly inter-pretations of that data. And we hope that it has provided not only a context for the biblical canon lists that follow, but also encouragement to the reader to dive in to these ancient sources for the insights they yield about how ancient Christians understood and classified these writings containing, in many cases, what they took to be divine revelation. Study of these lists illuminates a crucial aspect of the development of the Bible, showing us how early Christians clari-fied distinctions that sometimes had long been vague, with the intention of helping the church grow in the knowledge of the word of God.

2

Jewish Lists

INTRODUCTION

The lists in this chapter may seem strange for the presently entitled book, but we include them because it would be even stranger for a book on canon lists to omit a discussion of them.

Josephus's list is the earliest in this book, even though we cannot properly describe it as a 'list'. He does not provide us with a specific catalogue of books, but he does provide us with an exclusive number of books ('twenty-two') and a further categorization of five books of the lawgiver (i.e. Moses), thirteen books of the prophets, and four remaining books. Josephus mentions twenty-two books and he may be the influence on many of the church fathers in this volume, who also record the number of books for the Old Testament as twenty-two. Josephus, of course, records this 'list' in Greek.

The second list in this chapter is written in Hebrew from around 200 CE. The list of books in Baba Bathra, if one assumes the five books of the Torah, number twenty-four, which is another ancient way of reckoning the books (cf. the discussion of the number of OT books on pp. 6–7).

In this chapter, we observe the earliest Jewish attestation to fixed lists of sacred books. It is a curiosity that there are only two Jewish lists before the late medieval period, while early Christians proliferated canon lists of Scripture in the earlier period. The comparisons and contrasts between these lists and the rest of the lists in chapters 3–5 illuminate the relationship between Jewish and Christian views of the contents and orders of the Hebrew Bible and the Christian Old Testament.

TITUS FLAVIUS JOSEPHUS

Josephus (37–ca. 100), named at birth Yoseph bar Mattityahu, was born to an aristocratic family. This status explains his Greek education and his high-level friendships in the city, among other aspects of his life.[1] In 67 CE, the Roman army of 60,000 drove his Galilean forces back to the fortified hill at Jotapata, where he surrendered to General Vespasian and his son Titus. For the rest of the war he remained a captive, aiding the Romans with translation, interrogation, and negotiation until the siege of Jerusalem in 70 CE. After Jerusalem fell, Josephus accompanied the general and his son back to Rome, where he lived the rest of his life. In Rome, he received his new name, Titus Flavius Josephus, although he only used the name Josephus in his own writings.

In Rome (71 CE) he began a writing career that produced four works: *Jewish War* in seven volumes (mostly written by 79 CE, completed by 81), explaining the causes of the Judean rebellion against Rome and narrating the history of the war that led to the destruction of Jerusalem in 70 CE; *Jewish Antiquities* in twenty volumes (completed in 93/94 CE), narrating Jewish history from the biblical account of creation up to the point where his *Jewish War* had begun; the autobiographical *Life* of Josephus (appendix to the *Antiquities*; uncertain date of composition); and *Against Apion*, a two-volume apologetic sequel to the *Antiquities* in which Josephus responded to the criticisms of the Jewish nation propagated by, among others, a certain Egyptian named Apion who had died about fifty years before Josephus answered him. In this last work, Josephus endeavours to show that, despite Apion's assertions, Judean history actually predates Greek history, and Judean historiography rests on a surer foundation than that of the Greeks. As part of this argument, he contrasts the Jewish twenty-two trusted books with the thousands of Greek books which contradict one another.

Jewish canon: Josephus did not list the exact contents of the canon. He does, however, say that, in contrast to the Greeks, the Jews have 'only twenty-two books', and he divides these books into three categories: five books of Moses, thirteen prophetic books, and four books of hymns and divine precepts. While this description is sufficient to identify the majority of books in Josephus's canon, scholars debate whether Josephus included certain books such as Ecclesiastes or Song of Songs, and in which category (the second or third) he would have placed which books.

Studies: Höffken 2001: 159–77; Mason 2002: 110–27; Barclay 2007: 28–32; Lim 2013: 43–9; Steinberg and Stone 2015: 26–31; Dempster 2016: 321–61 (esp. pp. 326–41).

Against Apion 1.37–42

Date: post 94[2]

Introduction: Although the work is entitled *Against Apion*, Apion is not mentioned until *C. Ap.* 2.2. Apion was a well-known scholar in Greek language

---

[1] For biography and bibliography related to Josephus, cf. Mason 2010: 828–32.

[2] Dates of 96 (the death of Domitian), 98 (brief reign of Nerva), or any time within the reign of Trajan (98–117) have been suggested as possible dates of *Against Apion*. Josephus wrote *Apion*

and literature in Alexandria in the first century CE.[3] Based on the argument of Book 1, in Book 2 Josephus ventures a counter-statement against him and other detractors (*C. Ap.* 2.2), and Josephus reserved the most space for Apion (*C. Ap.* 2.8–144). Josephus dedicated this work as well as his earlier works to an Epaphroditus, whom we cannot identify with certainty.[4]

Modern scholars classify *Apion* under the genre of 'apology' or defence literature. This work is filled with a defence of Judaism against specific accusations from 'outsiders' (1.3; 2.296), even if it contains elements of polemics and encomium (i.e., propaganda; 2.145–286).[5] Though the work is directed at outsiders, it may have been composed to encourage and strengthen the convictions of those inside the Jewish community.[6]

The outline of Book 1 is as follows:[7]

1.1–5:	Introduction
1.6–218:	Part One: The Antiquity of the Judeans
1.6–56:	Prolegomenon: Comparative Historiography
	1.6–27: The inadequacies of Greek historiography
	1.28–56: The superiority of non-Greek/Judean historiography
1.57–59:	Preliminary Conclusion and Announcement of Agenda
1.60–68:	Reasons for Greek Ignorance of Judeans
1.69–218:	Evidence for Judean Antiquity
	1.69–72: Introduction
	1.73–105: Egyptian evidence
	1.106–27: Phoenician evidence
	1.128–60: Chaldean evidence
	1.161–214: Greek evidence
	1.215–18: Conclusions

The relevant paragraph on the Jewish canon supports Josephus's argument that Jewish historiography is superior to non-Jewish historiography. The significant claims in this paragraph are that: (1) only prophets who learned by the inspiration of God wrote the history of the events of the remote past and of events close to them (1.37); (2) only twenty-two books contain the entire record of all time and are rightly trusted (1.38–40); (3) the later record is not deemed worthy of the same trustworthiness as the former (1.41); and (4) in the next paragraph, Josephus will also claim that although this record in twenty-two books is ancient, no one has ever dared to add, to take away, or to alter anything (1.42).

---

after the *Jewish Antiquities* (cf. *C. Ap.* 1.1; 2.287), the conclusion of which is dated to 94 CE, the thirteenth year of the reign of Domitian and the fifty-sixth year of Josephus' life (*Ant.* 20.267). Only this sure criterion aids the dating of *Apion*. Josephus wrote *Apion* between this date and his death, a date which cannot be established with precision. For the challenge of dating *Apion*, cf. Barclay 2007: XXVI–XXVIII.

[3] ibid.: 170–1n7.   [4] ibid.: 3–4n3.   [5] ibid.: XXXV.   [6] ibid.: LI.
[7] ibid.: XXI.

Text[8]	Translation[9]
(37) Εἰκότως οὖν, μᾶλλον δὲ ἀναγκαίως, ἅτε μήτε τὸ ὑπογράφειν αὐτεξουσίου πᾶσιν ὄντος μήτε τινὸς ἐν τοῖς γραφομένοις ἐνούσης διαφωνίας, ἀλλὰ μόνον τῶν προφητῶν τὰ μὲν ἀνωτάτω καὶ παλαιότατα κατὰ τὴν ἐπίπνοιαν τὴν ἀπὸ τοῦ θεοῦ μαθόντων, τὰ δὲ καθ᾽ αὑτοὺς ὡς ἐγένετο σαφῶς συγγραφόντων,	(37) Naturally, then, or rather necessarily— seeing that it is not open to anyone to write of their own accord, nor is there any disagreement present in what is written, but the prophets alone[10] learned, by inspiration from God, what had happened in the distant and most ancient past and recorded plainly events in their own time just as they occurred—
(38) οὐ μυριάδες βιβλίων εἰσὶ παρ᾽ ἡμῖν ἀσυμφώνων καὶ μαχομένων, δύο δὲ μόνα πρὸς τοῖς εἴκοσι βιβλία τοῦ παντὸς ἔχοντα χρόνου τὴν ἀναγραφήν, τὰ δικαίως πεπιστευμένα.	(38) among us there are not thousands of books in disagreement and conflict with each other, but only[11] twenty-two books,[12] containing the record[13] for all time, which are rightly trusted.

---

[8] Niese: 1889 (repr. 1955): 8–9.   [9] Barclay 2007: 28–32.

[10] The prophets in this section are Moses and the prophets after him (cf. Deut. 34:10–12; cp. Deut. 18:15–22) who wrote the history in thirteen books.

[11] Josephus claims that there are only twenty-two books among the Jews that contain the record for all time and that are rightly trusted. 'Only' twenty-two books echoes his earlier point that the prophets 'alone' learned by the inspiration of God (1.37). Josephus does not use the word 'canon', but his use of the word 'only' indicates an exclusive and closed list of books. Josephus used many works outside of these books in his *Antiquities*, which might have suggested that he had an open canon, but this statement in *Apion* shows that he considered the canon closed a long time ago (cf. Mason 2002: 126). Furthermore, Josephus claims to present the viewpoint of Jews for many of whom it is innate to regard these books as decrees of God (cf. *C. Ap.* 1.42).

[12] Josephus does not connect the number twenty-two with the alphabet of the Hebrews as many later Christians would do (cf., e.g., ch. 3 on Origen and Epiphanius; for an extended discussion of the meaning of the symbolism of the twenty-two books in Origen and other early fathers, cf. Gallagher 2012a: 86–92). Jub. 2.23 (second-century BCE) established the significance of the 'twenty-two chief men from Adam to Jacob' and the 'twenty-two kinds of works made before the seventh day', showing this number to be foundational to creation and the history of Israel. (For a full development of the numerical symbolism of the number twenty-two, cf. ch. 3 on Epiphanius for discussion of Epiphanius's canon list in *Mens.* 22–3.) If the number twenty-two had this or any symbolic value to Josephus, he does not explain it. However, his listing and numbering of the books probably assumes the presence of double books—two books reckoned as one book (e.g. Ruth and Judges are probably reckoned as one book). Perhaps, therefore, the symbolic value of the number twenty-two determined Josephus's numbering of the books, even though without the double books the number would be closer to twenty-seven (cf. the lists of Epiphanius in ch. 3). Alternatively, Hengel 2002 suggests that Josephus's twenty-two books did not combine Ruth with Judges nor Lamentations with Jeremiah, but rather his canon excluded the Song of Songs and Ecclesiastes, both of which were still controversial among the rabbis in the second century (p. 101). Around the same time, 4 Ezra 14:45–6 notes the publishing of the *twenty-four* books for all, worthy and unworthy, to read. The Babylonian Talmud also implies a numbering of twenty-four books (cf. below). Jerome explains that the Jews had an alternative way of numbering the books, since they sometimes counted combined books as two (e.g. Judges–Ruth was sometimes reckoned as two separate books: Judges and Ruth; cf. ch. 4 on Jerome).

[13] Josephus uses ἀναγραφή 'record' forty-two times, twenty-four times in the plural and eighteen times in the singular. Here he uses the term to denote the whole of history. In *Ant.* 1.12, he tells how King Ptolemy II failed to obtain 'the whole record' (πᾶσαν τὴν ἀναγραφήν), but only the portion containing the Law. At the end of the *Antiquities*, he says he 'attempted to preserve *the record* of the high priests throughout the period of two-thousand years … as the sacred books contain *the record* concerning everything' (*Ant.* 22.261).

Text	Translation
(39) καὶ τούτων πέντε μέν ἐστι Μωυσέως, ἃ τούς τε νόμους περιέχει καὶ τὴν ἀπ' ἀνθρωπογονίας παράδοσιν μέχρι τῆς αὐτοῦ τελευτῆς· οὗτος ὁ χρόνος ἀπολείπει τρισχιλίων ὀλίγῳ ἐτῶν.	(39) Five[14] of these are the books of Moses, which contain both the laws and the tradition from the birth of humanity up to his death;[15] this is a period of a little less than 3,000 years.[16]
(40) ἀπὸ δὲ τῆς Μωυσέως τελευτῆς μέχρι τῆς Ἀρταξέρξου τοῦ μετὰ Ξέρξην Περσῶν βασιλέως οἱ μετὰ Μωυσῆν προφῆται τὰ κατ' αὐτοὺς πραχθέντα συνέγραψαν ἐν τρισὶ καὶ δέκα βιβλίοις· αἱ δὲ λοιπαὶ τέσσαρες ὕμνους εἰς τὸν θεὸν καὶ τοῖς	(40) From the death of Moses[17] until Artaxerxes,[18] king of the Persians after Xerxes,[19] the prophets[20] after Moses wrote the history of what took place in their own times in thirteen books;[21] the remaining four books[22] contain

---

[14] Philo (d. ca. 50 CE) has the earliest reference to the five books of Moses (*Eternity* 19). Philo calls these books 'Holy Books' and he claims that Moses, the lawgiver of the Jews, named the first one Genesis. These books were probably ordered as follows: Genesis–Exodus–Leviticus–Numbers–Deuteronomy. Later church fathers, such as Melito, had a different order: Genesis–Exodus–Numbers–Leviticus–Deuteronomy, but this order is not widely attested in the sources.

[15] The first book is Genesis, and Deut. 34:1–8 records the death of Moses.

[16] In a context of historiography and the antiquity of the Jewish people, Josephus emphasizes the historical nature of the five books of Moses, though noting the presence of laws in these books as well.

[17] According to Deut. 34:9ff, Joshua would be Moses's successor. However, Epiphanius's canon list in *Mens.* 4 has Job directly after the books of Moses, and it is also possible to construe Josephus's thirteen books in this way.

[18] Josephus, with the Old Greek version of Esther, understood king Ahasuerus (cf. Esth. 1:1) as Artaxerxes, the fifth king of Persia (reigned 465–424 BCE; cf. *Ant.* 11.184ff). He, therefore, would be the last king mentioned in the prophetic record of the thirteen books, and therefore, Esther was probably the final book of this section.

[19] Elsewhere, Josephus locates Xerxes, the fourth king of Persia (reigned 486–465 BCE), as the king who ruled during the time of Ezra-Nehemiah (cf. *Ant.* 11.120ff). Though Josephus claims this chronology, Ezra 7:1 (cp. also Esdras A 8:1) shows that Artaxerxes was king during the time of Ezra. Xerxes is the king who invaded Greece, the war about which Herodotus wrote his *Histories*. Given that Herodotus was already acclaimed the 'father of history' by Cicero (*De legibus* 1.5), Josephus shows that at about the time the biblical record is finishing, the Greek records are commencing (cf. Barclay 2007: 30n164).

[20] The so-called latter prophets (e.g. Isaiah) are easily identified among these 'prophets'. Josephus also follows the tradition established by Chronicles (cf., e.g., 1 Chr. 29:29; 2 Chr. 9:29, 12:15, 20:34, 32:32), which assigns the authorship of the history books of Samuel–Kings to prophets. Chronicles mentions prophets and seers near the time period of each of the kings of Israel and Judah as the ones who wrote down the accounts of each king. In 2 Chr. 32:32, the Chronicler notes that the acts of Hezekiah are written down in the vision of Isaiah the prophet in the book of the Kings of Israel and of Judah. Here, the Chronicler does not refer to independent prophetic sources, only those sources which are recorded in the historical books. Cf. Talshir 2001: 386–403, esp. 391–2.

[21] Even though researchers do not agree on the order of these books (see the various listings below), they do mostly agree on the contents of these thirteen books: Job, Joshua, Judges–Ruth, Samuel, Kings, Chronicles, Jeremiah–Lamentations, Isaiah, Ezekiel, the Twelve Prophets, Daniel, Ezra–Nehemiah, and Esther. For the suggestion that Josephus could have prefixed Ruth to Psalms, see Beckwith 1985: 80. For a notable exception, see Zevit (1998:140n20), who believes Josephus, due to his sole interest in the historical books, omitted Isaiah, Jeremiah, Ezekiel, the Twelve, the Song of Songs, and Lamentations, since he would not have regarded these books as useful for his purpose. Instead, according to Zevit, Josephus reckons twenty-two books by counting 1 and 2 Samuel and 1 and 2 Kings and 1 and 2 Chronicles as two books each and Ezra and Nehemiah as two books. For a recent response and rejection of this view, see Steinberg and Stone 2015: 29–30.

[22] Josephus's point here is that the Judeans have fewer books that contain the record of history than do the Greeks. These remaining four books do not contribute to Judean historiography or the inspired

Text	Translation
ἀνθρώποις ὑποθήκας τοῦ βίου περιέχουσιν.	hymns to God[23] and instructions[24] for people on life.
(41) ἀπὸ δὲ Ἀρταξέρξου μέχρι τοῦ καθ᾽ ἡμᾶς χρόνου γέγραπται μὲν ἕκαστα, πίστεως δ᾽ οὐχ ὁμοίας ἠξίωται τοῖς πρὸ αὐτῶν διὰ τὸ μὴ γενέσθαι τὴν τῶν προφητῶν ἀκριβῆ διαδοχήν. (42) δῆλον δ᾽ ἐστὶν ἔργῳ, πῶς ἡμεῖς πρόσιμεν τοῖς ἰδίοις γράμμασι· τοσοῦτο γὰρ αἰῶνος ἤδη παρῳχηκότος οὔτε προσθεῖναί τις οὐδὲν οὔτε ἀφελεῖν αὐτῶν οὔτε μεταθεῖναι τετόλμηκεν, πᾶσι δὲ σύμφυτόν ἐστιν εὐθὺς ἐκ πρώτης γενέσεως Ἰουδαίοις τὸ νομίζειν αὐτὰ θεοῦ δόγματα καὶ τούτοις ἐμμένειν καὶ ὑπὲρ αὐτῶν, εἰ δέοι, θνήσκειν ἡδέως.	(41) From Artaxerxes to our own time every event has been recorded,[25] but this is not judged worthy of the same trust,[26] since the exact line of succession of the prophets did not continue.[27] (42) It is clear in practice how we approach our own writings. Although such a long time has now passed, no one has dared to add, to take away, or to alter anything;[28] and it is innate in every Judean, right from birth, to regard them as decrees of God, to remain faithful to them and, if necessary, gladly to die on their behalf.

prophetic record, and therefore, it would have been advantageous for Josephus to have omitted them from his list all together. However, once he mentioned the previous eighteen books of Moses and the tradition written by prophets, he included the four remaining books as a matter of course because they were integral to the Jewish canon (cf. Höffken 2001: 162–4 (esp. 162n9); Barclay 2007: 30n166).

[23] The 'hymns to God' refer to the Psalms. Prior to Josephus, Philo used 'hymns' (ὕμνοι) as a title for the Psalms regularly (cf., e.g., *Plant.* 29.4; *Conf.* 39.5; *Migr.* 157.5). Elsewhere, Josephus refers to the Levites singing 'hymns to God . . . as they had been instructed by David' (*Ant.* 9.269). Though we do have evidence for alternative collections of Psalms in Hebrew among the Dead Sea Scrolls (cf. Mroczek 2015), the Greek Psalter evidences a relatively stable transmission history.

[24] The last three books probably refer to the three Solomonic wisdom books, which appear nearly ubiquitously (cf. the discussion on the order of these three books in ch. 3 on Gregory of Nazianzus) in the following order: Proverbs–Ecclesiastes–Song of Songs. See Beckwith (1985: 80), for the remote possibility that Lamentations, if separated from Jeremiah, would appear among these three books, and either Ecclesiastes or Song of Songs, disputed among the Pharisees, would be omitted from Josephus's canon.

[25] Significantly, Josephus notes that from Artaxerxes to the current time there are Judean records—thus no gaps. He even includes his own record of the War (*C. Ap.* 1.47). See Barclay 2007, who indicates a gap of about a hundred years between *Ant.* 11.296 (the death of Artaxerxes in 424 BCE) and *Ant.* 11.304 (the death of Philip of Macedon in 336 BCE) (p. 30n167). Josephus does not cite his sources, but presumably they include the record of the succession of priests down to the present day (*C. Ap.* 1.36). His inattentiveness to these records after the death of Artaxerxes shows that his foundation for the history of Antiquity is the twenty-two-book canon.

[26] Although each event was written down after the death of Artaxerxes, these records are not worthy of the same trust as the previous ones. In *C. Ap.* 1.38, he already stated that only the twenty-two books are rightly trusted. Therefore, the record after Artaxerxes is not as trustworthy as the record before him in the canonical books.

[27] More literally, because there was no exact succession of the prophets. The failure of the line of prophets to write history *and the events of their own day as they occurred* (*C. Ap.* 1.37; cp. 1.40) led to the unreliability of the later record. According to Barclay 2007, Josephus crafts a 'motif that looks like an artificial creation to emphasize, by comparison, the unimpeachable authority of the 22 books' (pp. 30–1n169). However, if Josephus has in mind that each generation needed contemporary prophets to relate its history (as Barclay suggests earlier, and a plain reading of the books of Chronicles indicates [cf. n. 20 above]), then the broken succession would lead to less trustworthy accounts than the previous record, at least according to Josephus's own logic. Nevertheless, Josephus does trust these later histories enough to base upon some of them (e.g., the Maccabean literature) his own narration of Second Temple Jewish history. His *Antiquities* contain no reference to the other deuterocanonical literature (Tobit, Judith, Sirach, Wisdom of Solomon).

[28] For an exhaustive study of the phrase, 'neither to add nor to take away', cf. van Unnik 1949: 18. In ancient literature, the phrase denotes a faithful adherence to a text or tradition that

The Canon List of Josephus

Since Josephus does not list the exact contents of the books in his canon list, we only list his headings and brief descriptions of the types of works within the twenty-two books. Scholars have attempted to reconstruct Josephus's list, and these conjectures are presented below, illustrating that most scholars agree on the identification of Josephus's books but hold slightly different opinions over how he ordered them.

Five Books of Moses

    Laws

    Tradition

Thirteen Books of the Prophets

    History from the Death of Moses to Artaxerxes

Four Remaining Books

    Hymns to God

    Instructions for People on Life

Barclay[29]	Beckwith[30]	Leiman[31]	Thackeray[32]
The Law	The Law	The Law	The Law
Joshua	Job	Joshua	Joshua
Judges + Ruth	Joshua	Judges + Ruth	Judges + Ruth
Samuel	Judges + Ruth	Samuel	Samuel
Kings	Samuel	Kings	Kings
Isaiah	Kings	Isaiah	Chronicles
Jeremiah +	Isaiah	Jeremiah +	Ezra–Nehemiah
Lamentations	Jeremiah +	Lamentations	Esther
Ezekiel	Lamentations	Ezekiel	Job
The Twelve	Ezekiel	The Twelve	Isaiah
Chronicles	The Twelve	Job	Jeremiah +
Ezra–Nehemiah	Daniel	Daniel	Lamentations
(= Esdras)	Chronicles	Ezra-Nehemiah	Ezekiel
Daniel	Ezra-Nehemiah	Chronicles	The Twelve
Job			

one would not dare change, as Josephus describes the Scriptures here. Furthermore, Inowlocki 2005 shows that Josephus used the expression within its Greco-Roman context to signal that he was being both faithful to the original content and adapting the *lexis* according to the context of reception (p. 64). He probably depends on Deut. 4:2, 13:1; and *Aristeas* 311 for this phrase. The expression is found, though with a slight change in wording, in Athanasius *Ep. fest.* 39.19. Some modern scholars (e.g., Lange 2007) are suspicious of Josephus on this point given the textual pluriformity discovered at Qumran. Others have understood Josephus's statement not against the background of the Qumran community but against the text stored in the Temple guarded by the chief-priests (cf. *C. Ap.* 1.29); see van der Kooij 2012: 29–40 (esp. pp. 35–6).

[29] Barclay 2007: 30n165–6.   [30] Beckwith 1985: 206–7.
[31] Leiman 1991: 32–3.   [32] Josephus, *C. Ap.* 1.40nb–c (Thackeray, LCL).

Barclay	Beckwith	Leiman	Thackeray
Esther	Esther	Esther	Daniel
Psalms	Psalms	Psalms	Psalms
Proverbs	Proverbs	Proverbs	Song of Songs
Song of Songs	Ecclesiastes	Ecclesiastes	Proverbs
Qoheleth[33]	Song of Songs	Song of Songs	Ecclesiastes

Sections within Josephus's canon list: Scholars dispute whether Josephus's canon list can be construed according to sections or divisions. Some scholars have discerned a tripartite structure from this account, while others have interpreted it as containing no divisions. Steve Mason argued that Josephus does not confirm or deny the presence of a tripartite structure of the Jewish canon. Rather, Josephus's 'generic' classification of the books is according to genre (laws, tradition, hymns, and advice), and these genres do not correlate to divisions within the Jewish scriptures.[34] Mason further suggested that if Josephus were dividing the canon into sections, he would be advocating for a five-part canon: Mosaic laws, Mosaic tradition, later history, hymns, and practical advice.

Julius Steinberg and Timothy Stone argue that Josephus does not present the canon according to structural divisions or genre distinctions. Rather, given Josephus's historiographical purpose in the context, they suggest that he is only concerned to reckon the books in terms of historical or non-historical.[35]

Timothy Lim, along with most others,[36] argues that although Josephus may have classified the Judean records according to genre, he also grouped the various genres into sections, marked off by the number of books in each: 'the books of Moses', 'the Prophets', and 'the remaining four books'.[37]

Josephus's use of numbers to create three sections of books does suggest that he (and probably his source as well) divided the canon along these lines. However, his tripartite structure of the canon is nowhere replicated exactly in either later Jewish or Christian lists—neither in the section headings themselves nor in the exact contents of each section (cf. the other lists in this volume).

---

[33] Aquila, the Jewish reviser who flourished around 130 CE, probably would have referred to this book as κωλέθ (*koleth*), a Greek transliteration for Hebrew *qoheleth* due to his rendering of the Hebrew at Eccl. 1:1 (cf. Field 1875: 2.380). Josephus could have entitled the work *koleth*, or Ecclesiastes as it is known traditionally.

[34] Mason 2002: 113–15. Barclay (2007: 30n166) acceded with Mason's conclusion on this point.

[35] Steinberg and Stone 2015: 31. They conclude that 'Josephus does not provide evidence for the structure of the Jewish canon, and consequently he should not be used as a witness against its possible tripartite structure' (p. 31).

[36] See the literature in Mason 2002: 114n12. Höffken (2001: 162) also dissents from Mason's opinion that Josephus's list is generic and ordered according to literary genres. Rather, he interprets everything here as 'tradition' (παράδοσις).

[37] Lim 2013: 46.

The Babylonian Talmud has an implied tripartite structure (the Torah is not listed explicitly) and contains different books than Josephus probably had in each of the last two sections (e.g. Daniel is probably among the Prophets in Josephus but certainly among the Writings in the Talmud). For example, Cyril of Jerusalem, among other fathers, maintained the twenty-two books of the Old Testament, but he divided them according to four sections: (1) five books of Moses; (2) history books; (3) five books in verse; and (4) five prophetic books.

Josephus, therefore, attests the boundaries of the canon (i.e. 'only twenty-two books'), and many fathers, especially in the East, followed his lead in their enumeration and boundaries of the books of the Old Testament.[38] The headings and contents of each section appear to be fluid in the first century CE. They contrast with the New Testament's earlier sections of 'Law and Prophets' (e.g. Matt. 5:17) or 'Law, Prophets, and Psalms' (Luke 24:44; cp. the Prologue to Sirach 1–2; 8–10; 24–5).[39] Later Christian fathers adopt almost the exact same contents but do not reflect a tripartite structure for the Old Testament.

THE BABYLONIAN TALMUD

The Babylonian Talmud is a massive medieval Jewish compilation of rabbinic law and legend, completed around the sixth century.[40] It is organized as a commentary on the Mishnah, itself a compilation of Jewish law from around 200 CE. The Mishnah is written in Hebrew, while the commentary on the Mishnah in the Talmud is usually in Aramaic. Two different rabbinic communities, one in Palestine and one in Babylonia, prepared commentary on the Mishnah, and each produced a Talmud, the Palestinian Talmud (Talmud Yerushalmi) and the Babylonian Talmud (Talmud Bavli). The latter has enjoyed much more authority to the present day and has informed traditional Jewish life more than any other literary work besides the Bible. When one speaks of the 'Talmud' without further qualification, the reference is to the Babylonian Talmud.

The Mishnah contains six major sections or 'orders' (Hebrew: *seder*, pl.: *sedarim*), with each order comprising a number of tractates.[41] These tractates

---

[38] Cf. Gallagher 2012a: 27.

[39] Cf. ch. 1 for a survey of these texts and the meanings of these terms.

[40] This is the traditional date. For an introduction to rabbinic literature, see Strack and Stemberger 1996. See also the relevant articles in Katz 2006. On the traditional date, see Strack and Stemberger 1996: 193–4. According to Ben-Eliyahu, Cohn, and Millar (2012: 34), 'it is now generally accepted that the *Bavli* was not considered to be a closed work until the sixth to seventh centuries, or perhaps early in the eighth'.

[41] Two widely available English translations of the Mishnah are Danby 1933 and Neusner 1988.

constitute the major organizing feature for the Talmud, and in editions and translations of the Talmud, often each tractate will occupy its own volume. One of these Talmudic tractates, Baba Bathra, contains the earliest list of books we have in a Hebrew source. The date of this list is somewhat uncertain. Since the Talmud collects many earlier traditions, one cannot necessarily use the date of the final compilation of the Talmud to date any given tradition contained in it. Moreover, the list as presented in the Talmud is a *baraita* (Aramaic for 'outside'), a particular type of tradition bearing this name because of its omission from the Mishnah, despite its being early rabbinic (Tannaitic) tradition.[42] *Baraitot* are preserved in Hebrew and introduced with particular formulas (such as 'Our Rabbis taught', as below in our *baraita*) identifying them as Tannaitic traditions. Consequently, all *baraitot* are traditionally dated to about the year 200, the time of the redaction of the Mishnah. Of course, a Tannaitic tradition may reflect still earlier tradition, and Beckwith, for one, has associated our *baraita* containing the list of books with a much earlier period, the gathering of books by Judah the Maccabee in the second century BCE (2 Macc. 2:14).[43] Few scholars have been persuaded by Beckwith's argumentation in this instance.[44] Other scholars would push the date of the *baraita* somewhat later than the time of the Mishnah.[45] Since all such datings essentially rely on educated speculation, it seems safest at this time to maintain the traditional date of about 200 CE.[46]

Jewish canon: The list in Baba Bathra is organized according to the divisions of the traditional Jewish canon, the TaNaK (Torah/Law, Neviim/Prophets, Ketuvim/Writings).[47] The passage is framed in terms of a discussion of the order of books within the Neviim and Ketuvim, apparently intending to establish a definitive sequence for these sections. There is no mention of the Torah because there could be no doubt at this time in regard to the Torah,[48] whereas doubt persisted, it seems, about the sequence of books in the Neviim and Ketuvim. The contents of the list correspond precisely to the contents of the traditional Jewish biblical canon, except for the absence of the Torah here. The sequence of books in this list, however, has not become traditional.

Studies: Leiman 1976: 51–3; Beckwith 1985: ch. 4; Jacobs 1991: 31–41; Brandt 2001: 63–6; Wyrick 2004: 21–79; Alexander 2007.

---

[42] Strack and Stemberger 1996: 177–8, 198–9.
[43] Beckwith 1985: 122–7, 152–3.   [44] See, e.g., Ellis 1991: 44n140.
[45] See the survey of dates at Brandt 2001: 64n211.
[46] Jacobs 1991: 32; Alexander 2007: 77.
[47] On the Tanak structure, see ch. 1, 'The Hebrew Bible/Old Testament'.
[48] Leiman 1976: 53; Brandt 2001: 64. There are a few unexpected arrangements of the Pentateuch in the canon lists; see the sections on the Bryennios List and the list of Melito of Sardis in ch. 3 and the Mommsen Catalogue in ch. 4.

Baba Bathra 14b

Date: ca. 200 CE[49]

Introduction: This passage cites a *baraita* concerning the order of the Neviim (Prophets) and Ketuvim (Writings) and then discusses the reasons behind the order. Louis Jacobs explains why this passage appears where it does in Baba Bathra:

> Tractate *Bava Bathra* deals with jurisprudential topics—conveyancing, inheritance, and the like—and seems, at first glance, to be the last place in which to expect a discussion on the Biblical books. The reason why the passage appears where it does is, following the usual pattern of Talmudic material, by association. The preceding section of the tractate considers the case of joint-owners of an article who wish to divide it—a typical '*Bava Bathra*' theme. How is the division to be effected, and what if only one of the joint-owners wishes to divide or give the other the option of buying him out? In this context it is ruled that if two have joint-ownership of a book of the Bible it must not be divided, i.e. cut in two, even if both agree to the division, since the sanctity of a Biblical book requires that it be left intact. This leads, purely by association, to the discussion on the order and authorship of the Biblical books.[50]

After the discussion of the order of the books, the passage continues with a lengthy discussion of the authorship—or, perhaps better, editing[51]—of the books.[52]

Text[53]	Translation[54]
ת״ר סדרן של נביאים יהושע ושופטים שמואל ומלכים ירמיה ויחזקאל ישעיה ושנים עשר	Our Rabbis taught: the order[55] of the Neviim is, Joshua, Judges, Samuel, Kings, Jeremiah, Ezekiel, Isaiah, and the Twelve.[56]

[49] The Vilna (= Vilnius, capital of Lithuania) edition of the Talmud—the standard edition for more than a century—assigned each folio page a number, and each side of the page is called the a-side or b-side of that page (relying on conventions established earlier; see Heller 1995: 40–51). The canon list appears on the b-side of p. 14. The date is traditional; see earlier discussion.

[50] L. Jacobs 1991: 31–2.   [51] Leiman 1976: 163n259.

[52] For a discussion of this material on authorship/editing, see Wyrick 2004: 21–79.

[53] Epstein and Simon 1960: 18.14b. The Hebrew/Aramaic text is a reprint of the standard Vilna edition first published by the Romm publishing house in 1880–1886.

[54] ibid.: slightly adapted. This translation was first published (without the Hebrew/Aramaic text) by the Soncino Press in 1935–1952.

[55] The emphasis on order here demands explanation. Order for what purpose? The rabbinic commentary on this *baraita*, contained in the subsequent passage, understands it in terms of chronological order (see also L. Jacobs 1991: 33–4). It should not refer to order of copying the books in a codex, since rabbinic biblical codices did not appear for several more centuries (Alexander 2007: 76). Perhaps it refers to the order of copying the books in scrolls, in those cases when a single scroll featured more than one book (see ibid.: 76n41; Leiman 1976: 202n644).

[56] This sequence for the prophetic books is often reproduced in manuscripts (see Beckwith 1985: 450), but there are also several other orders—again, Beckwith (1985: 208) mentions nine orders for the Prophets. See also Brandt 2001: 142–8. The major codices from the tenth and eleventh centuries—the Aleppo Codex and the Leningrad Codex—have the order Isaiah–Jeremiah–Ezekiel–Twelve.

Text	Translation
מכדי הושע קדים דכתיב תחלת דבר ה' בהושע וכי עם הושע דבר תחלה והלא ממשה ועד הושע כמה נביאים היו וא"ר יוחנן שהיה תחלה לארבעה נביאים שנתנבאו באותו הפרק ואלו הן הושע וישעיה עמום ומיכה	Let us examine this. Hosea came first, as it is written, *God spoke first to Hosea* [Hos. 1:2].[57] But did God speak first to Hosea? Were there not many prophets between Moses and Hosea? R. Joḥanan, however, has explained that [what it means is that] he was the first of the four prophets who prophesied at that period, namely, Hosea, Isaiah, Amos, and Micah.[58]
וליקדמיה להושע ברישא כיון דכתיב נבואתיה גבי חגי זכריה ומלאכי וחגי זכריה ומלאכי סוף נביאים הוו חשיב ליה בידייהו וליכתביה לחודיה וליקדמיה איידי דזוטר מירכס	Should not then Hosea come first?—Since his prophecy is written along with those of Haggai, Zechariah, and Malachi,[59] and Haggai, Zechariah, and Malachi came at the end of the prophets,[60] he is reckoned with them.[61] But why should he not be written separately and placed first?—Since his book is so small, it might be lost [if copied separately].[62]
מכדי ישעיה קדים מירמיה ויחזקאל ליקדמיה לישעיה ברישא כיון דמלכים סופיה חורבנא וירמיה כוליה חורבנא ויחזקאל רישיה חורבנא וסיפיה נחמתא וישעיה כוליה נחמתא סמכינן חורבנא לחורבנא ונחמתא לנחמתא:	Let us see again. Isaiah was prior to Jeremiah and Ezekiel. Then why should not Isaiah be placed first?—Because the Book of Kings ends with a record of destruction and Jeremiah speaks throughout of destruction and Ezekiel commences with destruction and ends with consolation and Isaiah is full of consolation; therefore we put destruction next to destruction and consolation next to consolation.[63]
סידרן של כתובים רות וספר תהלים ואיוב ומשלי קהלת שיר השירים וקינות דניאל ומגילת אסתר עזרא דברי הימים	The order of the Ketuvim is Ruth, the Book of Psalms, Job, Proverbs, Ecclesiastes, Song of Songs, Lamentations, Daniel and the Scroll of Esther, Ezra and Chronicles.[64]

[57] For an introduction to rabbinic interpretation of Scripture, see Elman 2004.

[58] These eighth-century prophets were all roughly contemporaneous, according to the first verse of their respective books.

[59] Hosea appears on the same scroll as Haggai, Zechariah, and Malachi—and, of course, eight other prophets, thus forming the Book of the Twelve Prophets.

[60] These three prophets were post-exilic prophets, as the content of their books makes clear.

[61] The Rabbis explain that since Hosea appears on a scroll with other prophets who came much later than Isaiah, Amos, and Micah, the writing associated with Hosea stands not at the head of the prophetic collection but at its end, even though Hosea prophesied first (according to the interpretation of Hos. 1:2 here).

[62] This passage explains the formation of the Book of the Twelve, due to the brevity of their writings and the fear that individual scrolls of each book could easily be misplaced. For more recent scholarly approaches to the formation of the Book of the Twelve, see Ben Zvi and Nogalski 2009. An example of an early scroll of the Book of the Twelve is MurXII (Murabbaʿat 88; ca. 100 CE), though the preserved portion now contains only fragments of Joel, Amos, Obadiah, Jonah, Micah, Nahum, Habakkuk, Zephaniah, Haggai, and Zechariah.

[63] The Rabbis here reveal that the concern with ordering the writings is not limited to chronology but also involves thematic connections between books.

[64] This sequence for the Ketuvim is unusual, but there seems to be no usual order for the Ketuvim. Beckwith (1985: 208–11) talks about seventy-nine different orders (see ibid.: 452–64). See also Brandt 2001: 148–64. One striking feature of this list is that the Megillot (Ruth, Song of Songs, Ecclesiastes, Lamentations, Esther) are not grouped together, as they are in most Masoretic manuscripts. For an argument for the priority of the order in the Masoretic manuscripts, thus against the usual scholarly assumption, see Stone 2013. Chronicles rarely appears last among the OT books in patristic lists, but see Innocent's list for one such example.

Text	Translation
ולמ״ד איוב בימי משה היה ליקדמיה לאיוב ברישא אתחולי בפורענותא לא מתחלינן רות נמי פורענות היא פורענות דאית ליה אחרית דאמר רבי יוחנן למה נקרא שמה רות שיצא ממנה דוד שריוהו להקב״ה בשירות ותושבחות	Now on the view that Job lived in the days of Moses,[65] should not the book of Job come first?—We do not begin with a record of suffering. But Ruth also is a record of suffering?—It is a suffering with a sequel [of happiness], as R. Joḥanan said: Why was her name called Ruth?—Because there issued from her David who replenished[66] the Holy One, blessed be He, with hymns and praises.

The Canon List of the Babylonian Talmud

[Torah—assumed]
Neviim (Prophets)
    Joshua
    Judges
    Samuel
    Kings
    Jeremiah
    Ezekiel
    Isaiah
    The Twelve (Minor Prophets)
Ketuvim (Writings)
    Ruth
    Book of Psalms
    Job
    Proverbs
    Ecclesiastes
    Song of Songs
    Lamentations
    Daniel
    The Scroll of Esther
    Ezra
    Chronicles

[65] This tradition is perhaps reflected in the Job manuscripts at Qumran that were written in paleo-Hebrew script, as were some Torah scrolls; see Tov 2004: 246–7.

[66] The note in the Epstein–Simon edition explains that the passage connects Ruth's name with this word, 'replenish' (Hebrew רוה), which bears some resemblance to Ruth in Hebrew.

3

Greek Christian Lists

INTRODUCTION

Eastern Christians from around 150 CE to 400 CE composed many Greek lists of scriptural books. In some cases, we cannot discern the author of the list (cf. the Synod of Laodicea, Apostolic Canons) or even where and exactly when it was composed (cf. the Bryennios List), but in many cases we know the author of the list, the place where he composed it, when he composed it, and even some of the circumstances in which he crafted it. Mainly, Christian bishops from Egypt, Cyprus, Asia Minor (modern-day Turkey), and Palestine took responsibility to draft these lists.

Some of these lists were composed as poems for didactic purposes (Gregory of Nazianzus, Amphilochius of Iconium), while others were clearly intended to instruct new converts (catechesis) and churches generally on the contents of Scripture (Cyril of Jerusalem, Athanasius of Alexandria). Other authors used lists of scriptural books in creative ways in their writings and sermons (Origen of Alexandria, Epiphanius of Salamis), while others merely wanted to investigate which books were disputed and which were not (Eusebius of Caesarea, perhaps Melito of Sardis).

For each list below we have provided introductions to the list and the author of the list when known, summaries of the information pertaining to the canon, the text, and translation (in synoptic columns) of the work in which the list is located, analysis and commentary on the lists themselves, a summary list of books, and, if relevant, any concluding comments on the canon list.

THE BRYENNIOS LIST

In 1873, Philotheos Bryennios was working in the library of the Jerusalem Monastery of the Most Holy Sepulchre in the city of Constantinople when he discovered a manuscript (copied in 1056) containing the previously lost Didache, the two epistles of Clement, and several other compositions. Among these other compositions was a list of the OT books that has become known as the Bryennios List (BL).[1] The list of biblical books filled about twelve lines in the manuscript on fol. 76a, appearing between 2 Clement and the Didache itself. Bryennios published the contents of the manuscript in 1883, simply transcribing the list of biblical books. The surprising rediscovery of the Didache overshadowed the other works in the manuscript, so that it was not until 1950 that a full-scale analysis of this list was published. Jean-Paul Audet's seminal study brought the list to the attention of scholars and spawned further analysis. Various issues are disputed, including the list's language, provenance, date, and significance for the history of the canon of the Old Testament.

BL contains a list of 'the names of the books among the Hebrews'. Its twenty-seven book titles appear first in a Semitic form (in Greek transliteration) and then in the usual Greek form. The Semitic names for the books relate clearly to the titles in Epiphanius's list in *Mens.* 23, though the two lists also have differences, to be discussed below.[2]

Old Testament canon: This canon list contains a similar catalogue of books to the Jewish and Protestant canons in twenty-seven books. The identification of Esdras A and Esdras B is an open question, as well as whether Lamentations, Baruch, and the Epistle or a combination of these works are subsumed under the title of 'Jeremiah'. This list does not contain any of the deuterocanonical books.

Studies: Bryennios 1883: ρμζ'–ρμη'; Katz 1956, 1974; Jepsen 1959; Audet 1950, 1974; Goodblatt 1982; Cross 1998: 221–2; Brandt 2001: 78–80; Lim 2013: 41–3.

The Text of the Bryennios List

Date: 100–150 CE

Text[3]	Translation
ὀνόματα τῶν βιβλίων παρ' ἑβραίοις	Names of the books among the Hebrews
βρισίθ · γένεσις · ἐλσιμόθ · ἔξοδος · ὁδοικρά · λευϊτικόν · διησοῦ · ἰησοῦ υἱοῦ ναυή · ἐλεδεββαρί · δευτερονόμιον · οὐιδαβίρ · ἀριθμοί · δαρούθ · τῆς ῥούθ · διὼβ · τοῦ ἰώβ · δάσοφτιμ(ν)[4] · τῶν κριτῶν · σφερτελίμ ·	Brisith: Genesis. Elsimoth: Exodus. Odoikra: Leviticus. Diiēsou: Joshua son of Nauē. Eledebbari: Deuteronomy. Ouidabir: Numbers. Darouth: Of Ruth. Diōb: of Job. Dasophtim(n): Of the Judges. Sphertelim:[5] Psalter. Diemmouēl:

[1] Cf. Audet 1974: 52, for the details. We cite the reprint page numbers of this article throughout. For the initial publication of the list, see Bryennios 1883: ρμζ'–ρμη'.
[2] See the section on Epiphanius below for details.
[3] MS *Hierosolymitanus* 54. For the photograph of the MS, see Harris 1885. Cf. Audet 1974 for transcription.
[4] The *nu* is raised over the *mu* in the MS.
[5] For a study of this title in the Second Temple Period, cf. Mroczek 2015: 13–17. She did not note the evidence of BL in her article, but if BL's usual date is maintained, then this list would contain the earliest evidence for the Greek transliteration of ספר תהלים *sepher tehelim* or Book of Psalms.

Text	Translation
ψαλτήριον · διεμμουήλ · βασιλειῶν α´ · διαδδουδεμουήλ · βασιλειῶν β´ · δαμαλαχήμ · βασιλειῶν γ´ · ἀμαλαχήμ · βασιλειῶν δ´ · δεβριιαμίν · παραλειπομένων α´ · δεριιαμίν · παραλειπομένων β´ · δαμαλεώθ · παροιμιῶν · δακοέλεθ · ἐκκλησιαστής · σιρὰ σιρίμ · ἆσμα ἀσμάτων · διερέμ · ἱερεμίας · δααθαρσιαρ · δωδεκαπρόφητον · δησαΐου · ἠσαΐου · διεεζεκιήλ · ἰεζεκιήλ · δαδανιήλ · δανιήλ · δέσδρα · ἔσδρα α´ · δαδέσδρα · ἔσδρα β´ · δεσθής · ἐσθήρ	Of Kingdoms First. *Diaddoudemouēl*: Of Kingdoms Second. *Damalachēm*: Of Kingdoms Third. *Amalachēm*: Of Kingdoms Fourth. *Debriiamin*: Of Paralipomena First. *Deriiamin*: Of Paralipomena Second. *Damaleōth*: Of Proverbs. *Dakoeleth*: Ecclesiastes. *Sira Sirim*: Song of Songs. *Dierem*: Jeremiah.[6] *Daatharsiar*: Twelve Prophets. *Dēsaiou*: Of Isaiah. *Dieezekiēl*: Of Ezekiel. *Dadaniēl*: Of Daniel. *Desdra*: Esdras A. *Dadesdra*: Esdras B.[7] *Desthēs*: Esther.

The Canon List of the Bryennios List

Bryennios		Epiphanius, *Mens.* 23	
Semitic	Received Greek	Semitic	Received Greek
1 βρισίθ	γένεσις	1 Βιρσήθ	ἣ καλεῖται Γένεσις κόσμου
2 ἐλσιμόθ	ἔξοδος	2 Ἐλησιμώθ	ἡ Ἔξοδος τῶν υἱῶν Ἰσραὴλ ἐξ Αἰγύπτου
3 ὀδοικρά	λευϊτικόν	3 Οὐαϊεκρά	ἣ ἑρμηνεύεται Λευιτικόν
4 διησοῦ	ἰησοῦ υἱοῦ ναυή	6 Οὐαϊδαβήρ	ἥ ἐστιν Ἀριθμῶν
5 ἐλεδεββαρί	δευτερονόμιον	5 Ἐλλεδεβαρείμ	τὸ Δευτερονόμιον

---

[6] Διερεμίου in *Mens.* 23, which corresponds closely to the name of Jeremiah in MT: יִרְמְיָהוּ *Yirmᵉyahu* and exactly to the spelling which Origen conveys for the Hebrew and the Three: λόγοι Ἱερεμίου υἱοῦ Χελχίου 'the words of Jeremiou son of Chelchiou' (*Hom. Jer.* 20.5). The spelling could reflect the simple genitive form of the name, but it is interesting that this list does not use the Hebrew form of the name as found in Origen's list (Ἱερεμια; cp. δησαΐου BL with Ιεσσια 'Isaiah' in Origen). Audet supposed that the spelling in BL and *Mens.* 23 is older and indicative that -ιου was an indeclinable form similar to the slightly later -ιαου of Aquila (cf. 2 Kings 23:24 Ελκιαου as nominative for חִלְקִיָּהוּ; Audet 1974: 63–4). This list gives no details on the exact contents of Jeremiah, whether Lamentations, Baruch, and the Epistle are included under its title or not. The modern Jewish Bible includes Lamentations, but not the other two. Because of this list's early date (as presumed by most scholars; see below), the later LXX codices do not necessarily provide insight into the nature of the title 'Of Jeremiah'. Melito only listed 'Of Jeremiah', while Origen included Lamentations and the Epistle of Jeremiah. We have no evidence that Jews ever doubted the sanctity of Lamentations, and the fact that Origen only mentioned Jeremiah with Lamentations and the Epistle 'in one' under the Greek title but not the Hebrew title may indicate that his Jewish informant counted Lamentations as a part of the book bearing the Hebrew title, *Jeremia*. When Epiphanius comments on a list similar to BL in *Mens.* 23 he says, 'And there is another small book, which is called *Kinōth*, which is translated Lamentations of Jeremiah. This one is joined to Jeremiah....' Since Epiphanius transmits a list similar to BL, one may speculate whether he also transmitted a traditional interpretation of it. This third list from Epiphanius does not mention Baruch or the Epistle, but only Lamentations.

[7] The identity of these books has long been disputed, given the presumed antiquity of this list. Audet (1974: 69) suggested that Esdras A relates to a Targum of the Masoretic Esdras B (Ezra–Nehemiah). Katz (1974: 85) expressed doubts about this assumption.

Bryennios		Epiphanius, *Mens.* 23	
Semitic	Received Greek	Semitic	Received Greek
6 οὐιδαβίρ	ἀριθμοί	4 Διησοῦ	ἡ τοῦ Ἰησοῦ τοῦ Ναυῆ
7 δαρούθ	τῆς ῥούθ	8 Διώβ	ἡ τοῦ Ἰώβ
8 διώβ	τοῦ ἰώβ	9 Δεσωφτείμ	ἡ τῶν Κριτῶν
9 δάσοφτιμ(ν)	τῶν κριτῶν	7 Δερούθ	ἡ τῆς Ῥούθ
10 σφερτελίμ	ψαλτήριον	10 Σφερτελείμ	τὸ Ψαλτήριον
11 διεμμουήλ	βασιλειῶν α΄	15 Δεβριαμείν	ἡ πρώτη τῶν
			Παραλειπομένων
12 διαδδουδεμουήλ	βασιλειῶν β΄	16 Δεβριαμείν	Παραλειπομένων δευτέρα
13 δαμαλαχήμ	βασιλειῶν γ΄	11 Δεσαμουήλ	Βασιλειῶν πρώτη
14 ἀμαλαχήμ	βασιλειῶν δ΄	12 Δαδουδεσαμουήλ	Βασιλειῶν δευτέρα
15 δεβριὰμίν	παραλειπομένων α΄	13 Δμαλαχείμ	Βασιλειῶν τρίτη
16 δεριαμίν	παραλειπομένων β΄	14 Δμαλαχείμ	Βασιλειῶν τετάρτη
17 δαμαλεώθ	παροιμιῶν	17 Δμεθαλώθ	ἡ Παροιμιῶν
18 δακοέλεθ	ἐκκλησιαστής	18 Δεκωέλεθ	ὁ Ἐκκλησιαστής
19 σιρὰ σιρίμ	ᾆσμα ἀσμάτων	19 Σιραθσιρείν	τὸ Ἆσμα τῶν Ἀσμάτων
20 διερέμ	ἱερεμίας	21 Δαθαριασαρά	τὸ Δωδεκαπρόφητον
21 δααθαρσιαρ	δωδεκαπρόφητον	22 Δησαίου	τοῦ προφήτου Ἡσαίου
22 δησαίου	ἡσαίου	20 Διερεμίου	ἡ τοῦ Ἱερεμίου
23 διεεζεκιήλ	ἱεζεκιήλ	23 Διεζεκιήλ	ἡ τοῦ Ἱεζεκιήλ
24 δαδανιήλ	δανιήλ	24 Δεδανιήλ	ἡ τοῦ Δανιήλ
25 δέσδρα	ἔσδρα α΄	25 Δέσδρα	ἡ τοῦ Ἔσδρα πρώτη
26 δαδέσδρα	ἔσδρα β΄	26 Δέσδρα	ἡ τοῦ Ἔσδρα δευτέρα
27 δεσθής	ἐσθήρ	27 Δεσθήρ	ἡ τῆς Ἐσθήρ

This table places the books of BL and *Mens.* 23 in their respective orders. All researchers agree that these two lists are related due to their unique preservation of the spellings of the Semitic titles, particularly their use of the *d/dy* ('of') particle appearing before the majority of the titles. One can see that not all Semitic spellings of the books agree. The different orthographies resulted from the long textual transmission of the list, in all probability. Also, Epiphanius's list has much fuller Greek titles than BL. The agreements and differences probably demonstrate that these lists descend from a common source and that Epiphanius's list has undergone more revision or correction than BL. This contrast may be observed in the different ordering of the books as well.

The identity of the language of the Semitic titles has provoked much debate. Audet originally assessed the titles in the list as 'Hebrew-Aramaic' (see the title of his article). Specifically, he noted that books 1, 2, 3, 6, 5, 10, 19, 16 are transliterated directly from Hebrew.[8] So far all sides agree. The debate is over the nature of the spellings of the rest of the books: are these Hebrew or Aramaic spellings or some combination of the two? Audet held that the majority of these titles were Aramaic, with at least one mixed form (δαμαλεώθ, 'of Proverbs' from

---

[8] Audet 1974: 56. The numbers correspond to the numbers next to BL in the table above.

Aramaic *math°lā'* with the Hebrew plural ending *-ōth*).[9] The strongest evidence of Aramaic, according to Audet, was the use of the *d/dy* ('of') particle (transcribed as δ/δι/δα before eighteen of the twenty-seven titles).[10] These strands of evidence led Audet to conclude that BL has elements of both Aramaic and Hebrew. The language of the list and its unusual order of the books suggested to Audet an early second century date (ca. 100–50).

Not all subsequent research agreed with Audet's conclusions regarding the language of the titles. Most notably, David Goodblatt, following Jepsen, challenged the idea that any of the titles are Aramaic. First, the ending -ιν (*-in*) is not exclusively Aramaic, since Mishnaic/Middle Hebrew (ca. 400 BCE–400 CE) used this ending for the masculine plural absolute forms just as often as *–im*, the form in Standard Biblical Hebrew. Secondly, the Aramaic *d/dy* ('of') particle is used in Hebrew titles of books. The Aramaic *sypr' d*, 'book of', is found in combination with Hebrew titles such as *spr' d'ywb* 'the book of Job'.[11] Therefore the combination of Aramaic prefixes on Hebrew titles is attested among Jews in the early centuries of the Christian era. Thirdly, the one truly Aramaic title, δααθαρσιαρ (*tĕrê 'asar*; 'of the Twelve') had already become a loanword and appears in Hebrew contexts in rabbinic literature. Thus it is the exception that proves the rule according to Goodblatt.[12]

The identification of the list's source language has had a considerable influence on whether the list is interpreted as Jewish or Jewish-Christian. BL uses only the Greek alphabet and therefore was of primary use in a Greek-speaking community. As for the Semitic source of the Greek list, Audet considered either a Jewish or Jewish-Christian community as the ultimate origin of the list.[13] Audet believed that the Aramaic titles pointed to Aramaic Targums corresponding to each of the books of the Old Testament, which could only be read by Jews or Jewish Christians. On Audet's view, the putative Aramaic titles of the books could indicate an Aramaic-speaking Christian milieu.[14] Goodblatt, on the other hand, concluded that nothing in the titles (including the Aramaic prefixes) prevents attributing those titles to a strict Jewish milieu.[15] If the Semitic titles are not Aramaic but Hebrew, as Goodblatt argued, then Audet's proposal that the list arose among Armaic-speaking Christians loses credibility and the evidence shifts in favour of a Jewish provenance. Assuming the Jewish origin of the list based on its original language, the questions still to be answered are: (1) when did Christians receive it; and (2) how did they adapt it? We will see later that Melito's list provides a plausible context for BL and might show that it was received by Christians before the end of the second century. As for Christian adaptations of BL, the prime candidate is the order of books, which does not resemble any known Jewish list (cf. discussion below). If the list comprises primarily Hebrew titles in Middle/Mishnaic Hebrew, the evidence of the list's

---

    [9] ibid.: 57.   [10] ibid.: 57.   [11] Goodblatt 1982: 83.   [12] ibid.: 81–2.
    [13] Audet 1974: 61–3.   [14] ibid.: 62.   [15] Goodblatt 1982: 84.

language dates it before the fifth century. Other considerations such as the ordering of the books, its relation to other lists, and the reception history of individual books, provide a more precise basis for dating the list.

Most scholars have dated this list to some time during the first or second centuries. All scholars agree that Epiphanius's list in *Mens.* 23 and BL share a common source.[16] Therefore 392 is the *terminus ad quem* for the source of BL.

The ordering of the books in BL provides more evidence for its date. The order is unique among the lists:

Genesis
Exodus
Leviticus
Joshua
Deuteronomy
Numbers
Ruth
Job
Judges
Psalter
1 Kingdoms   (= 1 Samuel)
2 Kingdoms   (= 2 Samuel)
3 Kingdoms   (= 1 Kings)
4 Kingdoms   (= 2 Kings)
1 Paralipomena   (= 1 Chronicles)
2 Paralipomena   (= 2 Chronicles)
Proverbs
Ecclesiastes   (= Qoheleth)
Song of Songs
Jeremiah   (+ Lamentations? + Baruch? + Epistle?)
The Twelve Prophets
Isaiah
Ezekiel
Daniel
Esdras A
Esdras B
Esther

---

[16] On this reconstruction, Epiphanius's version of the list is usually viewed as a later revision of the common source from which *Mens.* 23 and BL descended (cf. the section on Epiphanius later in this chapter). BL was probably a more faithful copy of the source than *Mens.* 23, since the latter shows a greater conformity to the other lists of the fourth century. Cf. Audet 1974: 59. Audet was open on the question of whether Epiphanius was the reviser or whether he received an already revised list. Furthermore, the Greek names in *Mens.* 23 also show an updated and fuller form with the addition of the definite article ἡ, 'the', which probably stands for ἡ βίβλος, 'the book'. It is still far from clear who revised this catalogue of books.

By far its most interesting feature is the order of the first six books: Genesis–Exodus–Leviticus–Joshua–Deuteronomy–Numbers. The first three books are in their usual sequence, while the final three are in the exact opposite sequence found in other lists. This ordering still leaves Deuteronomy as the fifth book.[17] Scholars explain this odd sequence as either a copying error of some kind, or perhaps dependent on the view that Joshua belongs with the Pentateuch.[18]

Other features of the sequence are also peculiar. The grouping Ruth–Job–Judges attests a connection between Job and Judges also known elsewhere,[19] but Ruth's position before Job rather than after Judges is unusual. Also, the placement of the Psalter after Judges and before the history books of Samuel–Kings–Chronicles is unique. Brandt suggested that maybe there was a tendency to introduce important figures before the historical accounts of those figures, but he immediately discounts this possibility since Proverbs–Qoheleth–Song of Songs, the Solomonic books, come after Samuel–Kings–Chronicles, rather than before.[20]

Despite some of these idiosyncrasies, there are clear agreements between this list and others: Samuel–Kings–Chronicles (= Melito, Origen; ≠ Babylonian Talmud) and the Solomonic sequence of Proverbs–Qoheleth–Song of Songs (= Melito, Origen, Babylonian Talmud). The conclusion of the list with Esdras A–Esdras B–Esther (= Jerome *Prologus Galeatus*) is the earliest attestation of this order.[21] Origen's list ends with Esther, while Melito's list ends with the books of Esdras and omits Esther.

The sequence of the prophets in BL is both contrastive and comparative with known traditions: Jeremiah–The Twelve Prophets–Isaiah–Ezekiel–Daniel. On the one hand, Daniel appears among the prophets in this list, while

---

[17] The list of Melito has a slight variation in the first six books: Genesis–Exodus–Numbers–Leviticus–Deuteronomy–Joshua. And it is interesting that Amphilochius in the second half of the fourth century must add, 'and Leviticus, the middle book', which reveals perhaps that there was still some uncertainty about the order of the first five books. Cf. the respective lists of Melito and Amphilochius later in this chapter.

[18] Brandt (2001: 80) points to b. Ned. 22b: 'Had Israel not sinned, only the Pentateuch and the book of Joshua would have been given to them, [the latter] because it records the apportionment of Palestine [among the tribes]'; cf. Leiman 1991: 67. This statement attests the relationship between Joshua and the Pentateuch, but it does not necessarily confirm the order of the books in BL. Audet (1974: 67) had considered BL's unusual sequence to be due to haphazard copying. Katz (1974: 87) more specifically proposed the idea of a mistaken *boustrophedon* reading, such that a scribe read the first line left-to-right (as normal) but mistakenly read the second line right-to-left. Lim (2013: 42) seems to accept Katz's explanation.

[19] Cf. Epiphanius's list from *Mens.* 23 later in this chapter; cf. B. Bat. 15b, where Rabbi Eliezer suggests that Job lived during the period of the Judges; see Beckwith 1985: 190.

[20] Brandt 2001: 79–80.

[21] Esdras A and Esdras B refer to Ezra-Nehemiah or Esdras 1 and Esdras 2. The list's early date could support both possibilities. Most later Christian lists refer to the books in the Greek tradition known as Esdras A and Esdras B, but some question over the identity of Esdras in Melito's list persists (cf. p. 81 n. 43 below). Cf. the Appendix in this volume for a discussion of the books of Esdras.

the Babylonian Talmud and Jerome's *Prol. Gal.* place it in the Writings.[22] Grouping Daniel with the prophets agrees with the earliest lists of Melito and Origen. On the other hand, this exact sequence of books is not known from other lists. The only other list to place Jeremiah at the head of the prophets is the Babylonian Talmud. Most lists have The Twelve or Isaiah at the head of these books.[23]

The idiosyncrasies of the order of the books in BL led Audet and subsequent scholars to conclude that this list antedates the other lists.[24] Audet suggested that the letter written by Melito of Sardis to his 'brother' Onesimus (preserved by Eusebius, *Hist. eccl.* 4.26.12–14) provides a plausible context for BL. In Melito's letter to Onesimus, the former is replying to an inquiry of the latter concerning both the exact number (ἀριθμόν) and the exact order (τάξιν) of the ancient books. Audet drew the correct inference that Onesimus and Melito were not satisfied with the state of information they had on this question. A list such as BL may have been in circulation in the mid-second century and contributed to the confusion that Melito and Onesimus sought to redress.

Thus there are contrasting features within BL. The title of the list, 'Names of the books among the Hebrews', and the Hebrew titles of the books indicate a Jewish milieu, while the order of the books, although sharing limited overlap with Jewish lists, points mainly in the direction of a Christian provenance.[25] Goodblatt posited that the list originated in a Jewish milieu but that a Gentile Christian was responsible for the order of the books.[26] It is the sequence of books that indicates to most scholars that BL dates early (second century or earlier), under the assumption that the earlier confusion on this matter gave way to more strict and standardized lists.[27] It is difficult to imagine a third- or fourth-century Christian or Jew providing such a list of books in the order found in BL. Epiphanius's list in *Mens.* 23 shows that in the late fourth century the Hebrew titles were still transmitted, but the book order had been corrected. It is possible that the unusual order in BL could result at a later time, but most researchers have considered it more probable that the list reflects a time of greater instability. The second century attests both very few canonical lists

---

[22] Cf. Matt. 24:15 for an early designation of 'Daniel the Prophet'. For other citations, see Gallagher 2012a: 17n14.

[23] The Twelve at the head: Origen *apud* Rufinus (i.e., Rufinus's Latin translation of Eusebius, *Hist. eccl.* 6.25.2); Jerome, *Epist.* 53. Isaiah at the head: Melito; Jerome, *Prol. Gal.*

[24] Audet 1974: 60–1.   [25] Brandt 2001: 80.   [26] Goodblatt 1982: 84.

[27] Audet 1974 suggested a date in the first half of the second century; see also Katz 1974: 85–9; Lim 2013: 41–3, esp. 43. Cross 1998: 222n8 would date it even earlier. Jepsen 1959 appears to date it considerably later on the basis of the analogous lists of Origen and Jerome, who, like BL, also included Semitic names for the books (pp. 131–2). McDonald's earlier view (2007: 203–4), dating the list to the fourth century based on its similarities to Epiphanius, *Mens.* 23, is now updated in McDonald (2017: 1.358–60), where he appears more favourable towards a second century dating. But the order of the books in BL does not closely align with any of these third- and fourth-century lists (Origen, Jerome, Epiphanius), and both Origen and Jerome enumerate the books as twenty-two, unlike BL.

and documented confusion on the number and order of the biblical books (cf. Melito, discussed above and also the section on Melito below), so it seems to provide a more likely context for BL than the fourth century, when canonical lists become much more numerous, reflecting more awareness of the issues and more stability.

If the usual dating of BL can be accepted, then we have an early-second-century Jewish list of books received among Christians, comprising the twenty-seven books of the Old Testament. The contents of the list cohere closely with the other canonical lists preserved from the patristic era, though the order of books diverges significantly from other known examples, perhaps indicating continuing uncertainty on that matter.

MELITO OF SARDIS

According to Eusebius (*Hist. eccl.* 4.26.1), Melito served as bishop of Sardis in western Asia Minor in the late second century.[28] In a letter written by the Ephesian bishop Polycrates to Victor of Rome (*apud* Eusebius, *Hist. eccl.* 5.24), Melito appears as an especially pious eunuch who was a quartodeciman, celebrating Easter in conjunction with the Jewish Passover, beginning on the fourteenth day of the Jewish month Nisan (usually in March–April of our calendar). According to Eusebius (*Hist. eccl.* 4.26.2), Melito wrote a number of works, of which only fragments survive, except for his *On Passover* (*Peri Pascha*), rediscovered in the first half of the twentieth century in a complete copy.[29] One of his lost works comprised six books of *Extracts*, a collection of passages from the Old Testament that had bearing on the Christ and the Christian faith. Eusebius preserves the preface to this work, containing a list of OT books.

Old Testament canon: Melito's list contains all the books of the Jewish canon except for Esther. He includes a single book of Esdras, unlike several canon lists in this volume, which contain two books of Esdras. This title could refer to 1 Esdras or to Ezra–Nehemiah (known in Greek manuscripts as Esdras B). After Proverbs, Melito mentions a book of Wisdom, which possibly indicates the deuterocanonical Wisdom of Solomon, or could be another name for Proverbs. Melito does not elaborate on what may have been included within the title 'Jeremiah'.

Studies: Sundberg 1964: 133–4; Ellis 1991: 10–12; Hennings 1994: 152–4; Gallagher 2012a: 21–4.

---

[28] Hall (1979: xii) casts doubt on whether Melito was actually a bishop.
[29] For the *Peri Pascha*, see Hall 1979. On Melito's other works, see ibid.: xiii–xvii.

Extracts *Preface*

Date: 170 CE

Introduction: Melito's *Extracts* apparently contained a collection of what he considered to be messianic prophecies in the Old Testament—the Law and the Prophets, as he calls it—along with other verses thought to be especially related to the church. A preliminary issue concerns which books one might expect to provide messianic prophecies; that is, which books belonged to the Law and the Prophets. He begins this work by narrating his journey to the East (Palestine, 'where these things were proclaimed and accomplished'), where he inquired about the books of the Old Testament, and he immediately records the answer he received. The work is unfortunately lost, but Eusebius preserves the portion of the preface containing the list of books (*Hist. eccl.* 4.26.12–14). Melito does not inform us of the source of his canon, whether Jews or Christians. Some scholars have pointed out that had Melito wanted to ask Jews about their canon, he could have done so in his native Sardis, where a large Jewish community flourished. Moreover, it seems likely that Melito would have sought out a Christian source to inform him of the books of the Old Testament, rather than a Jewish source.[30] Kaestli asserts that the list does not necessarily represent Melito's own OT canon, but rather he intends simply to list the books of the Jewish canon that could provide messianic testimonies useful in debates with Jews.[31] Eusebius clearly does not share this interpretation of Melito's intentions, since he introduces Melito's preface by stating that it contains a list of the recognized books of the Old Testament.

Text[32]	Translation
(12) ἀλλὰ ταῦτα μὲν ἐν τῷ δηλωθέντι τέθειται λόγῳ· ἐν δὲ ταῖς γραφείσαις αὐτῷ Ἐκλογαῖς ὁ αὐτὸς κατὰ τὸ προοίμιον ἀρχόμενος τῶν ὁμολογουμένων τῆς παλαιᾶς διαθήκης γραφῶν ποιεῖται κατάλογον· ὃν καὶ ἀναγκαῖον ἐνταῦθα καταλέξαι, γράφει δὲ οὕτως.	(12) Now these were set down in the work indicated; but in the *Extracts* written by him, the same author, beginning in the preface, makes a catalogue of the recognized writings of the Old Testament.[33] It is necessary to provide this catalogue here, and he writes thus:
(13) «Μελίτων Ὀνησίμῳ τῷ ἀδελφῷ χαίρειν. ἐπειδὴ πολλάκις ἠξίωσας, σπουδῇ τῇ πρὸς τὸν λόγον χρώμενος, γενέσθαι σοι ἐκλογὰς ἔκ τε τοῦ νόμου καὶ τῶν προφητῶν περὶ τοῦ σωτῆρος καὶ πάσης τῆς πίστεως ἡμῶν,	(13) 'Melito to Onesimus his brother,[34] greetings. Since you have often asked, employing urgency in the request, that there be extracts for you from the law and the prophets concerning the Saviour and our entire faith, and moreover you desired to learn the facts of the old books, in regard to their

---

[30] See Beckwith 1985: 184–5; Hahneman 1992: 77; Gallagher 2012a: 24; against Buhl 1892: 20; Ryle 1892: 215; Katz 1956: 196n11.

[31] Kaestli 2007: 112.   [32] Schwartz 1903: 386–8.

[33] For the significance in Eusebius of the term 'recognized books' (ὁμολογούμεναι γραφαί), see discussion of Eusebius's list later in this chapter.

[34] 'Brother' perhaps means in this context 'fellow bishop'; cf. Audet 1950: 143.

Text	Translation
ἔτι δὲ καὶ μαθεῖν τὴν τῶν παλαιῶν βιβλίων ἐβουλήθης ἀκρίβειαν πόσα τὸν ἀριθμὸν καὶ ὁποῖα τὴν τάξιν εἶεν, ἐσπούδασα τὸ τοιοῦτο πρᾶξαι, ἐπιστάμενός σου τὸ σπουδαῖον περὶ τὴν πίστιν καὶ φιλομαθὲς περὶ τὸν λόγον ὅτι τε μάλιστα πάντων πόθῳ τῷ πρὸς τὸν θεὸν ταῦτα προκρίνεις, περὶ τῆς αἰωνίου σωτηρίας ἀγωνιζόμενος.	number and their order, I have diligently accomplished this, knowing your diligence in regard to the faith and love of learning in regard to the word, and that more than all things you prefer these because of your love for God, as you struggle concerning eternal salvation.
(14) ἀνελθὼν οὖν εἰς τὴν ἀνατολὴν καὶ ἕως τοῦ τόπου γενόμενος ἔνθα ἐκηρύχθη καὶ ἐπράχθη, καὶ ἀκριβῶς μαθὼν τὰ τῆς παλαιᾶς διαθήκης βιβλία, ὑποτάξας ἔπεμψά σοι· ὧν ἐστι τὰ ὀνόματα· Μωυσέως πέντε, Γένεσις Ἔξοδος Ἀριθμοὶ Λευιτικὸν Δευτερονόμιον, Ἰησοῦς Ναυῆ, Κριταί, Ῥούθ, Βασιλειῶν τέσσαρα, Παραλειπομένων δύο, Ψαλμῶν Δαυίδ, Σολομῶνος Παροιμίαι ἡ καὶ Σοφία,	(14) Having gone, then, to the east and having gotten to the place where these things were proclaimed and accomplished,[35] and having learned accurately the books of the Old Testament,[36] I have arranged them and sent them to you, of which the names are: of Moses—five, Genesis, Exodus, Numbers, Leviticus,[37] Deuteronomy, Joshua [the son] of Nun, Judges, Ruth, of Kingdoms—four,[38] of Paralipomena—two,[39] of the Psalms of David, of Solomon—Proverbs which is also Wisdom,[40] Ecclesiastes, Song of Songs, Job,

[35] Palestine. Hall (1979: 66–7n10) notes that Melito here becomes the first recorded Christian pilgrim to the Holy Land, and Hall defends the veracity of Melito's statement to have travelled to Palestine against others who see here a 'literary figment'.

[36] It might seem odd that a Christian bishop would need to learn the books of the Old Testament. This statement might indicate some confusion in Asia Minor regarding the precise contents of the Old Testament (McDonald 2017: 1.317), perhaps due to the circulation of pseudepigrapha, or the continuing questions raised by Jews or disagreements among Christians. Or Melito might here be referring specifically to the issues he has already broached—namely, the number and order of the OT books, and not necessarily their identity. Given the apparent circulation in some Christian sources of a list such as the Bryennios List (see the previous section in this chapter), we might well imagine some confusion regarding the sequence and enumeration of books. At any rate, Melito apparently thinks that there does exist a definite collection of 'Law and Prophets', and he can discover the precise contents—including their number and order—in the East.

[37] The sequence Numbers–Leviticus is striking, especially in light of Melito's earlier stress on the precise order of books. This transposition of Leviticus and Numbers is attested in some other sources as well (cf. the Mommsen Catalogue; *De Sectis*, formerly attributed to Leontius of Byzantium, PG 86/1.1200d–1201a). It could conceivably be intentional; see Leiman 1976: 165n264; Kaestli 2007: 112n35. See also 4QReworked Pentateuch[b] (4Q364; DJD 13), which contains nothing from Leviticus in its preserved fragments (though perhaps originally it did; Crawford 2008: 40), while it preserves extensive sections of the other four books of the Pentateuch. But if Melito's order actually reflects an alternative sequence for the Pentateuch, it cannot have been very widespread, both because of the paucity of attestation and because Leviticus takes place at Sinai (7:38; 25:1; 26:46; 27:34) and thus between Exodus (in which Israel arrives at Sinai, ch. 19) and Numbers (in which Israel leaves Sinai, 10:10).

[38] The four books of Kingdoms correspond to the books known in English as 1–2 Samuel and 1–2 Kings.

[39] 'Paralipomena' is the Greek title for Chronicles.

[40] This phrase has occasioned some disagreements. Either Melito means that 'Wisdom' is an alternative title for the book of Proverbs (cf. Stuart 1845: 259; Perler 1966: 225: 'Proverbes ou Sagesse de Salomon'; Hall 1979: 67n15), or he means that both the Proverbs of Solomon and the Wisdom of

Text	Translation
Ἐκκλησιαστής, Ἆισμα Ἀισμάτων, Ἰώβ, Προφητῶν Ἡσαΐου Ἱερεμίου τῶν δώδεκα ἐν μονοβίβλῳ Δανιὴλ Ἰεζεκιήλ, Ἔσδρας· ἐξ ὧν καὶ τὰς ἐκλογὰς ἐποιησάμην, εἰς ἓξ βιβλία διελών». καὶ τὰ μὲν τοῦ Μελίτωνος τοσαῦτα.	of prophets—of Isaiah, of Jeremiah,[41] of the Twelve in one book,[42] of Daniel, of Ezekiel, of Esdras;[43] from which also I have made extracts, dividing into six books.' And such are the things of Melito.

The Canon List of Melito

Of Moses, five:
Genesis
Exodus
Numbers
Leviticus
Deuteronomy
Joshua
Judges
Ruth
1–4 Kingdoms   (= 1–2 Samuel and 1–2 Kings)
1–2 Paralipomena (= 1–2 Chronicles)
Psalms
Proverbs (or Wisdom?)
(Wisdom?)

Solomon—two separate books—are included in the list. The Wisdom of Solomon is a deutero-canonical book, not a part of the modern Jewish canon or of the Protestant canon, but it was certainly an important book in early Christianity; see Larcher 1969; Horbury 1995; Stuhlhofer 1988: 147. Evidence for the use of the title 'Wisdom' as an alternative title for Proverbs, comes from Eusebius: 'And not only he [= Hegesippus] but also Irenaeus and the whole company of the ancients (ὁ πᾶς τῶν ἀρχαίων χορός) called the Proverbs the All-virtuous Wisdom (πανάρετος Σοφία)' (*Hist. eccl.* 4.22.9). At the turn of the fifth century, Rufinus of Aquileia translated Euebius's *Hist. eccl.* into Latin, and for the phrase under dispute Rufinus offered *Salomonis Proverbia quae et Sapientia* ('Proverbs of Solomon, which is also his Wisdom'), indicating that he understood the two titles to refer to the same book. Possibly, the Greek grammar points in the same direction (we owe this insight to personal communication with Adam McCollum): the titles in Melito's list are all anarthrous, suggesting that the Greek *eta* in the phrase ἡ καὶ Σοφία (as printed by Schwartz) might not be an article but could be either a relative pronoun (ᾗ; as in Rufinus's translation, and attested in some Greek manuscripts, according to Schwartz's apparatus) or a conjunction (ἤ; 'or'). The Muratorian Fragment contains a reference to the Wisdom of Solomon, and the book is also found along with the other deuterocanonical books in the Mommsen Catalogue, Augustine's canon list, and the canon list contained in the *Breviarium Hipponense*, all from the later fourth century (see ch. 4 for these lists). Hengel (2002: 120) is doubtful that Melito relies on Wisdom within his *Peri Pascha*.

[41] There is no indication here whether other books were included under this title, such as Lamentations, Baruch, or the Epistle of Jeremiah, all of which are sometimes in patristic lists mentioned as a part of the book of Jeremiah, but none of which receives any mention from Melito.

[42] The Twelve Minor Prophets often counted as a single book in patristic lists, as also in Jewish reckoning.

[43] It is not clear whether Melito has in mind the book we know as 1 Esdras or Ezra–Nehemiah. Sundberg (1964: 133) and Hall (1979: 67n16) assume the latter. For other Old Testament lists that end with the books of Esdras and Esther, see the Bryennios List and Epiphanius, *Mens.* 22–3; cf. Kaestli 2007: 113. The Leningrad Codex of the Hebrew Bible ends with Ezra(–Nehemiah).

Ecclesiastes
Song of Songs
Job
of Prophets:
Isaiah
Jeremiah
The Twelve
Daniel
Ezekiel
Esdras

Two issues merit brief comment.

Esther: Melito does not mention Esther. It is possible that the omission was an accident,[44] committed either by Melito or Eusebius (who preserves the list), or an early scribe of Eusebius's *Ecclesiastical History*. Some scholars believe that the list requires Esther in order to make up the number of books at which Melito was aiming, but we cannot be certain what number this may have been (see below). Many scholars regard the omission of Esther as intentional on the part of Melito's source. As the Appendix to this volume shows, some Jewish sources evince uncertainty about the book,[45] and some other patristic canon lists also omit the book: Gregory of Nazianzus, Amphilochius of Iconium (noting also its acceptance by some Christians), and Athanasius, who included Esther among the non-canonical books that should be read by catechumens.[46]

Number of books: Melito does not specify the number of books constituting the Old Testament, and his list has led to divergent enumerations among scholars. He names twenty-one separate book titles (not counting Wisdom as a separate book; see n. 40 above), but he asserts that some of these titles apply to multiple books (the four books of Kingdoms and two books of Paralipomena). If we count those separate books individually, we would arrive at twenty-five books. But it would become customary in Christian lists to count the four books of Kingdoms only twice, and the two books of Paralipomena only once, on analogy with the Jewish enumeration.

Origen, Athanasius, and others, assert that the Old Testament totals twenty-two books, and they connect this number with the Hebrew alphabet, which has twenty-two letters. Some scholars believe that Melito also intended a twenty-two-book canon.[47] Melito's twenty-one separate titles could easily be adapted to this numbering scheme either by (1) considering Wisdom to be a separate book from Proverbs; (2) assuming that Esther, accidentally omitted, makes up the difference; or (3) counting the four books of Kingdoms twice, as customary

---

[44] Stuart 1845: 227; Ryle 1892: 215; Ellis 1991: 11; Cavalier 2012: 117.

[45] Note, e.g., its absence from the Dead Sea Scrolls and the questions raised in rabbinic literature (b. Meg. 7a, etc.).

[46] Each of these lists appears later in this chapter. For further discussion, see Leiman 1976: 160n239; Hennings 1994: 151n85.

[47] Buhl 1892: 20; Kaestli 2007: 112.

in canon lists.[48] If Melito aimed for a total of twenty-two books, this last sugges-tion seems the most probable, since no other source counts the four books of Kingdoms as a single book.[49] According to Katz, Melito's statement that the Twelve Minor Prophets count as one book indicates his concern to arrive at a total of twenty-two books.[50]

However, Melito did not mention the total number of books, so we cannot be certain that he had ever heard of a twenty-two-book canon, much less that he aimed for one here. Possibly he did not aim for any particular symbolic number, though he does say that he wanted the number to be accurate.[51]

ORIGEN OF ALEXANDRIA

Origen (ca. 185–254) was a seminal figure in early Christianity for his ground-breaking work in theology, biblical interpretation, and textual scholarship.[52] He earned his nickname *Adamantios* ('man of steel'; Eusebius, *Hist. eccl.* 6.14) from his prodigious literary output, which prompted Jerome to exclaim 'Who could ever read as much as he has written!' (*Epist.* 33.5). Origen began his car-eer in Alexandria as a teacher of Greek grammar and literature, which contrib-uted to his expertise in Greek philosophy and textual scholarship, skills he would put to good use. Soon he became the director of a catechetical school in Alexandria. His move to Caesarea in about 230 coincided with his ordination and, hence, his preaching. He suffered during the persecutions under the emperor Decius (249–50), and died a few years later. He wrote many commen-taries, composed many sermons, published the great apologetic work *Against Celsus*, and compiled the enormous *Hexapla*, an edition of the Old Testament featuring the Hebrew text in two columns (in Hebrew letters and Greek trans-literation) and four different Greek translations.

Old Testament canon: In a comment on Psalm 1, Origen finds occasion to list the twenty-two books of the Old Testament 'as the Hebrews transmit them'. His list corresponds to the Protestant Old Testament, except for the presence of the Epistle of Jeremiah (as part of the book of Jeremiah), the possible inclusion of 1 Esdras alongside Ezra–Nehemiah, and the absence—clearly unintentional—of the Minor Prophets. What is not clear is whether Origen is advocating this canon 'according to the Hebrews' as also the church's Old Testament, or whether he is merely report-ing the contents of the Jewish Bible. Origen cited a variety of Jewish literature not found in the Jewish Bible. The *Commentary on the Psalter* in which the list appeared has perished, but Eusebius (*Hist. eccl.* 6.25.1–2) preserved the list itself.

---

[48] For another view, with regard to Lamentations, see Sundberg (1964: 133–4), but he later realizes the improbability of his view (p. 146).

[49] Katz 1956: 196. [50] ibid. [51] See Beckwith 1985: 184–5.

[52] For an introduction, see Heine 2010. On his biblical scholarship, see Martens 2012. See also McGuckin 2004.

New Testament canon: Our extant texts preserve two passages sometimes identified as NT canon lists from Origen, though scholars have also questioned the suitability of such a label. Eusebius (*Hist. eccl.* 6.25.3–14) extracts a few passages from different works by Origen to attempt a reconstruction of the NT canon according to Origen: the result is the fourfold Gospel (based on a passage in Origen's *Commentary on Matthew*), a collection of letters from Paul, Peter, and John, and John's Apocalypse (based on a passage in Origen's *Commentary on John*). Eusebius did not preserve here any comment on James or Jude—though we otherwise know that Origen valued each of these writings— and the only comment on the Acts of the Apostles in Eusebius's materials from Origen here comes in an offhand way in a third extract (from Origen's *Homilies on Hebrews*) dealing with the authorship of Hebrews, which Origen accepts as authoritative, whether or not Paul wrote it. In the earlier extract from the *Commentary on John*, Origen reported contemporary doubts about the authenticity of 2 Peter and 2–3 John. As Eusebius presents Origen's opinion in this series of extracts, one would conclude that Origen's NT canon approximated the modern twenty-seven-book canon with the possible exceptions of 2 Peter, 2–3 John, James, and Jude, five books corresponding precisely to the earlier *antilegomena* ('disputed') category in Eusebius's own NT canon list.

The second list from Origen appears in his *Homilies on Joshua*, where the entire twenty-seven-book New Testament is listed, with the possible omission of John's Apocalypse and 3 John. Unfortunately, the original Greek of the *Homilies* no longer survives, so that we depend on Rufinus's Latin translation. Some scholars suspect Rufinus of tampering with the translation, reducing its value as a witness to Origen. Whether or not these lists provide secure attestation of Origen's NT canon, Origen remains important to the history of the canon in many ways, not least in his being 'the first ancient churchman to have offered some comment on all twenty-seven writings that are now part of the NT canon.'[53]

Studies: Ruwet 1943; 1944; Hanson 1954: 127–56; Sundberg 1964; de Lange 1976: 49–61; Junod 1984; Metzger 1987: 135–41; Kalin 1990: 274–82; Hennings 1994: 154–61; Nienhuis 2007: 52–63; Heine 2010: 65–82; 2011; Gallagher 2012a: 30–49, 69–85; Kruger 2015; Gallagher 2016b.

Selecta in Psalmos 1

Date: 220s[54]

Introduction: Origen's first *Commentary on the Psalter*—now preserved only in excerpts from other authors—covered Psalms 1–25. While commenting on

---

[53] Nienhuis 2007: 53.
[54] See the chart at Nautin 1977: 410. Nautin examines the extant remains of Origen's Alexandrian *Commentary on Psalms 1–25* at pp. 262–75. See also Heine 2010: 115–22.

the first psalm, he expounds on the significance of the number twenty-two, perhaps owing to his knowledge of a rabbinic tradition that the first word of the Psalter (*ashrei*, 'blessed') appears twenty-two times in the book.[55] The twenty-two letters of the Hebrew alphabet serve as an introduction to wisdom, just as the twenty-two books of the Jewish Bible introduce readers to spiritual knowledge. He lists the twenty-two encovenanted books 'as the Hebrews transmit them'. With the loss of Origen's commentary, we rely on Eusebius's citation of the list at *Hist. eccl.* 6.25, where the great historian attempted to compile Origen's scattered comments on the biblical canon (both testaments). Whether or not Origen intended this list to guide the church's reception of Jewish Scripture, there is little doubt that Eusebius understood the list in this way.[56]

Origen's list provides the Greek name for each biblical book, and then the Hebrew name in Greek transliteration, followed sometimes by a translation of the Hebrew name. He says that he is reporting the Jewish canon. It seems likely that he received from the Jews a list of Hebrew names for the biblical books, which he has correlated with the Greek Bible by lining up the names; that is, probably the Hebrew names are Jewish tradition but the rest of this list is the work of Origen.[57]

Text[58]	Translation[59]
(1) τὸν μέν γε πρῶτον ἐξηγούμενος Ψαλμόν, ἔκθεσιν πεποίηται τοῦ τῶν ἱερῶν γραφῶν τῆς παλαιᾶς διαθήκης καταλόγου, ὧδέ πως γράφων κατὰ λέξιν· "οὐκ ἀγνοητέον δ' εἶναι τὰς ἐνδιαθήκους βίβλους, ὡς Ἑβραῖοι	(1) Now while expounding the first Psalm he set forth the catalogue of the sacred Scriptures of the Old Testament, writing somewhat as follows in these words: 'But it should be known that there are twenty-two encovenanted books,

---

[55] See the additional material preserved from Origen's *Selecta in Psalms* 1 in the *Philocalia* 3, in the edition of Harl 1983: 260–8. Harl (262–3) explains about the rabbinic tradition, for which see *Midrash Tehillim* 1.8 in the translation of Braude 1959: 1.12. Braude (399n33) points out that '[t]he word *Blessed* actually occurs twenty-five times in the Psalter. Perhaps Rabbi disregards the three linked with malediction, which occur in Psalm 127 and in Psalm 137.'

[56] On this issue, see the discussion, with bibliography, in Gallagher 2012a: 37–8.

[57] See Sundberg 1964: 134–8.

[58] Schwartz 1908: 572–6. This edition also prints Rufinus's Latin translation (ed. Theodor Mommsen) of Eusebius's *History* on pages facing the Greek. For this passage, Rufinus's translation runs:

(1) Exponens sane primum psalmum designat etiam ipse, qui sit canon veteris testamenti, hoc modo scribens: 'Non est ignorandum,' inquit, 'viginti et duo esse libros in canone veteris testamenti, sicut Hebraei tradunt, secundum numerum scilicet elementorum, quae apud ipsos habentur.' (2) Et paulo post addit haec: 'Sunt autem viginti et duo libri: Genesis, Exodus, Leviticus, Numeri, Deuteronomium, Iesus Nave, Iudicum, Regnorum primus et secundus unus liber est apud illos, quem nominant Samuhel. item tertius et quartus unus est apud ipsos, quem appellant Regnum David, et Paralipomeni primus et secundus in uno habentur, quem dicunt Sermones dierum. Esdras primus et secundus in uno est. item liber Psalmorum, Salomonis Proverbia, et alius Ecclesiastes, et tertius eiusdem, Cantica canticorum. sed et duodecim prophetarum liber unus est et Esaias propheta, Hieremias, Ezechiel, Danihel, Iob et Hester. in his concludunt voluminum divinorum. Machabaeorum vero libros extrinsecus habent.'

[59] Loeb (Oulton).

Text	Translation
παραδιδόασιν, δύο καὶ εἴκοσι, ὅσος ἀριθμὸς τῶν παρ' αὐτοῖς στοιχείων ἐστίν." (2) εἶτα μετά τινα ἐπιφέρει λέγων· "εἰσὶν δὲ αἱ εἴκοσι δύο βίβλοι καθ' Ἑβραίους αἴδε· ἡ παρ' ἡμῖν Γένεσις ἐπιγεγραμμένη, παρὰ δ' Ἑβραίοις ἀπὸ τῆς ἀρχῆς τῆς βίβλου Βρησιθ, ὅπερ ἐστὶν 'ἐν ἀρχῇ'· Ἔξοδος, Ουελλεσμωθ, ὅπερ ἐστὶν 'ταῦτα τὰ ὀνόματα'· Λευιτικόν, Ουϊκρα, 'καὶ ἐκάλεσεν'· Ἀριθμοί, Αμμεσφεκωδειμ· Δευτερονόμιον, Ελλεαδδεβαρειμ, 'οὗτοι οἱ λόγοι'· Ἰησοῦς υἱὸς Ναυῆ, Ιωσουεβεννουν· Κριταί, 'Ρούθ, παρ' αὐτοῖς ἐν ἑνί, Σωφτειμ· Βασιλειῶν α' β', παρ' αὐτοῖς ἕν, Σαμουηλ, 'ὁ θεόκλητος'· Βασιλειῶν γ' δ' ἐν ἑνί, Ουαμμελχδαυιδ, ὅπερ ἐστὶν 'βασιλεία Δαυΐδ'· Παραλειπομένων α' β' ἐν ἑνί, Δαβρηϊαμειμ, ὅπερ ἐστὶν 'λόγοι ἡμερῶν'· Ἔζρας α' β' ἐν ἑνί, Εζρα, ὅ ἐστιν 'βοηθός'· βίβλος Ψαλμῶν, Σφαρθελλειμ· Σολομῶνος	according to the Hebrew tradition; the same as the number of the letters of their alphabet.[60] (2) Then further on he adds as follows: 'These are the twenty-two books according to the Hebrews: that which is entitled with us Genesis, but with the Hebrews, from the beginning of the book,[61] *Brēsith*, that is "In the beginning". Exodus, *Ouelle smōth*, that is, "These are the names". Leviticus, *Ouïkra*, "And he called". Numbers, *Ammes phekōdeim*.[62] Deuteronomy, *Elle addebareim*, "These are the words". Jesus the son of Nave, *Iōsoue ben noun*. Judges, Ruth, with them in one book, *Sōphteim*.[63] Of Kingdoms i, ii, with them one, *Samuel*,[64] "The called of God". Of Kingdoms iii, iv, in one, *Ouammelch david*, that is, "The kingdom of David".[65] Paralipomenon i, ii, in one, *Dabrē iamein*, that is, "Words of days".[66] Esdras i, ii, in one, *Ezra*, that is, "Helper".[67] Book of Psalms,

[60] Origen used 'encovenanted' on one other occasion to indicate that the Jews contest the Book of Tobit as not encovenanted (ἐνδιαθήκῳ) (*De oratione* 14.4). Jews today count the number of their books as twenty-four, a number assumed already by the Talmud (B. Bat. 14b, on which see ch. 2), 4 Ezra 14:45, and the Gospel of Thomas 52. Josephus reported that the Jews had twenty-two books (see the section on Josephus in ch. 2), though he is the only Jewish source for this enumeration. Josephus neither listed all of his twenty-two books, nor did he explicitly relate the number of books to the Hebrew alphabet. The number twenty-two became a common way of counting the Old Testament books among early Christians; see Gallagher 2012a: 85–92.

[61] Jewish titles for the biblical books often (though not always) derive from the first few words of the book.

[62] Origen does not provide a translation of the Hebrew name for Numbers. Oulton in a note, suggests 'fifth (book) of the precepts' or 'of the mustered men'. The customary Hebrew name for Numbers is *Bᵉmidbar*, 'in the wilderness'.

[63] This is the Hebrew name for the book of Judges. Origen includes Ruth with Judges under this title. We have no evidence that Jews ever counted Ruth as a part of the book of Judges, though Josephus may have done such. This reckoning—Ruth and Judges together as one book—became common in Christianity.

[64] The books of Samuel count as one in the Hebrew Bible. In Greek tradition these books, along with 1–2 Kings, went under the title 'Kingdoms', of which there were four books.

[65] The customary Hebrew title for Kings is *Mᵉlachim*, 'kings'.

[66] The Greek title for Chronicles is Paralipomenon, 'things omitted'. See Knoppers and Harvey 2002.

[67] The books Origen has in mind under the titles Esdras A and Esdras B are perhaps the books known by those names in the LXX tradition (such as in Codex Vaticanus), which English-speaking scholars customarily call 1 Esdras (= Esdras A) and Ezra–Nehemiah (= Esdras B); see Janz 2010: 36–7. The other possibility is that Esdras A refers to Ezra and Esdras B refers to Nehemiah, in which case Origen's comment that the Hebrews reckon both books together would be more accurate. Ezra and Nehemiah do count as one book in the Jewish Bible, but 1 Esdras is not a part of the Jewish Bible, a fact that Origen presumably would have known from his *Hexapla*. See below on this issue, pp. 94–5. First Esdras, contains material covering most of the book of Ezra, along with the last two chapters of 2 Chronicles, a brief passage from Nehemiah (7:73–8:13a), and an

Text	Translation
παροιμίαι, Μελωθ· Ἐκκλησιαστής, Κωελθ· Ἆισμα ᾀσμάτων (οὐ γάρ, ὡς ὑπολαμβάνουσίν τινες, Ἄισματα ᾀσμάτων), Σιρασσιρειμ· Ἡσαΐας, Ιεσσια· Ἰερεμίας σὺν Θρήνοις καὶ τῇ Ἐπιστολῇ ἐν ἑνί, Ιερεμια· Δανιήλ, Δανιηλ· Ἰεζεκιήλ, Ιεζεκιηλ· Ἰώβ, Ιωβ· Ἐσθήρ, Εσθηρ. ἔξω δὲ τούτων ἐστὶ τὰ Μακκαβαϊκά, ἅπερ ἐπιγέγραπται Σαρβηθσαβαναιελ."	*Sphar thelleim*. Proverbs of Solomon, *Melōth*. Ecclesiastes, *Kōelth*. Song of Songs (not, as some suppose, Songs of Songs), *Sir assireim*. Esaias, *Iessia*. Jeremiah with Lamentations and the Letter,[68] in one, *Jeremia*. Daniel, *Daniēl*. Ezekiel, *Ezekiēl*. Job, *Jōb*. Esther, *Esthēr*. And outside these[69] are the Maccabees, which are entitled *Sar bēth sabanai el*.[70]

Commentary on Matthew 1

Date: 248/9

Introduction: Origen wrote twenty-five volumes on Matthew, of which books 10–17 survive in Greek (covering Matt. 13:36–22:33), while an extant ancient Latin translation, traditionally called *Commentariorum series*, starts at book 12.9 (covering Matt. 16:13–27:63). The rest survives only in scattered fragments, of which our passage below is one example. In book one, Origen made a comment on the fourfold Gospel, which Eusebius then quoted to demonstrate Origen's opinion on which Gospels should be received. Origen mentions only the traditional four Gospels. The passage is preserved in *Hist. eccl.* 6.25.3–6.

additional story near the beginning known as the Story of the Three Pages. The dating of the composition of this work depends on its relationship to Ezra–Nehemiah, an issue of intense debate; for a summary, see Patmore 2015. The Greek translation probably dates to the second century BCE; ibid.: 183–4. Esdras B is a literal Greek translation of the Hebrew/Aramaic Ezra–Nehemiah, produced perhaps in the first century BCE (Janz 2010: 163, 150–1) or even as late as the second century CE (Wooden 2015: 196–7).

[68] The Letter of Jeremiah is reckoned in Roman Catholic Bibles as the sixth chapter of the book of Baruch. It became common among Christians to consider the Lamentations to be a part of Jeremiah, as also Baruch and the Letter of Jeremiah, the last two items being absent from the Jewish Bible. This is Origen's only reference to the Letter of Jeremiah in his extant corpus. None of his sixteen citations of Baruch give it the label 'Scripture', but he does use the formula 'it is written' once in reference to it (*Fr. Jer.* 56); see Heine 2011: 394. According to Bogaert (2005: 291), Origen may have been the one who discovered that Baruch was not a part of the Hebrew book of Jeremiah and thus separated it from Jeremiah and gave it its own name, Baruch. Bogaert (ibid.: 298) also thinks it very likely that the presence of the 'Letter' here implies the presence of Baruch as well, even though Origen does not mention it.

[69] With this comment, Origen acknowledges that the books of the Maccabees do not belong to the encovenanted books of the Hebrews. His comment also seems to imply that Jews continue to use 1 Maccabees, which is also suggested by Jerome's comment in his *Prologus Galeatus* that he had seen a Hebrew copy of this book (if that is what Jerome means). On Origen's own use of the books of Maccabees, see Heine 2011: 395.

[70] This Semitic name for 1 Maccabees provides some evidence that the original language of the book was not Greek, and that a Semitic text survived into Origen's day. Jerome (*Prologus Galeatus*) also says that the book existed in Hebrew, and he apparently claims to have seen a copy. The meaning of this Semitic name reported by Origen is difficult to determine; we are dealing with a Greek transliteration of perhaps an Aramaic translation of a Hebrew title. For suggestions, see Williams 2015: 266.

Text[71]	Translation[72]
(3) ταῦτα μὲν οὖν ἐν τῷ προειρημένῳ τίθησι συγγράμματι· ἐν δὲ τῷ πρώτῳ τῶν εἰς τὸ κατὰ Ματθαῖον, τὸν ἐκκλησιαστικὸν φυλάττων κανόνα, μόνα τέσσαρα εἰδέναι εὐαγγέλια μαρτύρεται, ὧδέ πως γράφων·	(3) These things he inserts in the above-mentioned treatise.[73] But in the first of his [*Commentaries*] *on the Gospel according to Matthew*, defending the canon of the Church, he gives his testimony that he knows only four Gospels, writing somewhat as follows:
(4) "ὡς ἐν παραδόσει μαθὼν περὶ τῶν τεσσάρων εὐαγγελίων, ἃ καὶ μόνα ἀναντίρρητά ἐστιν ἐν τῇ ὑπὸ τὸν οὐρανὸν ἐκκλησίᾳ τοῦ θεοῦ, ὅτι πρῶτον μὲν γέγραπται τὸ κατὰ τόν ποτε τελώνην, ὕστερον δὲ ἀπόστολον Ἰησοῦ Χριστοῦ Ματθαῖον, ἐκδεδωκότα αὐτὸ τοῖς ἀπὸ Ἰουδαϊσμοῦ πιστεύσασιν, γράμμασιν Ἑβραϊκοῖς συντεταγμένον·	(4) '... as having learnt by tradition concerning the four Gospels, which alone are unquestionable in the Church of God under heaven, that first was written that according to Matthew,[74] who was once a tax-collector but afterwards an apostle of Jesus Christ,[75] who published it for those who from Judaism came to believe, composed as it was in the Hebrew language.[76]
(5) δεύτερον δὲ τὸ κατὰ Μάρκον, ὡς Πέτρος ὑφηγήσατο αὐτῷ, ποιήσαντα, ὃν καὶ υἱὸν ἐν τῇ καθολικῇ ἐπιστολῇ διὰ τούτων ὡμολόγησεν φάσκων· ἀσπάζεται ὑμᾶς ἡ ἐν Βαβυλῶνι συνεκλεκτὴ καὶ Μάρκος ὁ υἱός μου.	(5) Secondly, that according to Mark, who wrote it in accordance with Peter's instructions,[77] whom also Peter acknowledged as his son in the catholic epistle, speaking in these terms: "She that is in Babylon, elect together with you, salutes you; and so doth Mark my son" [1 Peter 5:13].

---

[71] Schwartz 1908: 576. Rufinus's translation:

(3) De novi autem testamenti canone in primo libro commentariorum euangelii secundum Matthaeum hoc modo scribit: (4) 'Ex traditione', inquit, 'didici de quattuor euangeliis, quia haec sola absque ulla contradictione suscipi debent in omnibus quae sub caelo sunt ecclesiis dei. ita etenim tradiderunt patres, quia primo omnium scriptum sit euangelium a Matthaeo, qui aliquando fuerat publicanus, Hebraeicis litteris et traditum his, qui ex circumcisione crediderant, (5) secundum vero scriptum esse a Marco iuxta ea, quae sibi tradiderat Petrus, de quo et in epistula sua commemorat, dicens: "salutat vos filius meus Marcus". (6) tertium esse secundum Lucam, quod Paulus apostolus conlaudat tamquam his, qui ex gentibus crediderant, scriptum. super omnia vero euangelium esse Iohannis.'

[72] Loeb (Oulton).

[73] The statement refers to the passage quoted previously in this section from Origen's *Selectae in Psalmos* on the Jewish canon.

[74] The order of the Gospels reported by Origen here corresponds to the so-called Eastern order, and Origen here also attests what would become a common idea (but already in Irenaeus, *Haer.* 3.1.1), that the canonical order of the Gospels corresponds to the chronology of their composition. Clement of Alexandria had assumed a different chronology of composition (cf. Eusebius, *Hist. eccl.* 6.14.6–7). Irenaeus attests several sequences, including the order Matthew, Luke, Mark, John (*Haer.* 3.9.1–11.6; 3.11.7; 4.6.1; cf. 3.11.8: John, Luke, Matthew, Mark), probably identical to Clement's order. The so-called Western order placed the two apostles first, usually in the order Matthew, John, Luke, Mark. See Hahneman 1992: 183–7. On the origin of the Gospel titles, see the evidence collected in Hengel 2007.

[75] Cf. Matt. 9:9; 10:3.

[76] On the tradition of Matthew's original composition in Hebrew, widely attested in patristic literature (already by Papias; Eusebius, *Hist. eccl.* 3.39.16), see Evans 2007; Edwards 2009: 1–96.

[77] The tradition that Mark records Peter's reminiscences goes back to Papias; see Eusebius, *Hist. eccl.* 3.39.14–15. For a recent defence and interpretation of such a view, see Bauckham 2017: 155–82, 202–39.

Text	Translation
(6) καὶ τρίτον τὸ κατὰ Λουκᾶν, τὸ ὑπὸ Παύλου ἐπαινούμενον εὐαγγέλιον τοῖς ἀπὸ τῶν ἐθνῶν πεποιηκότα· ἐπὶ πᾶσιν τὸ κατὰ Ἰωάννην."	(6) And thirdly, that according to Luke, who wrote, for those who from the Gentiles [came to believe], the Gospel that was praised by Paul. After them all, that according to John.'

Commentary on John 5

Date: ca. 230

Introduction: Origen wrote thirty-two books on John, ending at John 13:33. Partial or complete texts survive for books 1, 2, 6, 10, 13, 19, 20, 28, and 32. The present passage from book 5 is preserved in Eusebius, *Hist. eccl.* 6.25.7–10, where the church historian had cited it as a demonstration of what Origen had to say on the epistles he accepted. Origen mentions the letters of Paul, two letters of Peter (of which one is doubted), three letters of John (of which two are doubted), and John's Apocalypse. Nevertheless, the passage does not serve Eusebius's purpose well, as it does not specify the number of Pauline letters, and has nothing to say about James or Jude, both of which Origen elsewhere treated positively. Kalin is certainly correct that 'Origen is by no means giving in this paragraph quoted from *Commentary on John* 5 a list of the writings in the apostle (i.e. non-gospel) section of a New Testament canon list.'[78] Presumably, though, Eusebius considered this passage the most convenient and complete presentation of Origen's views on the subject, and favoured quoting this single passage instead of assembling several scattered quotations on the various epistles.

Instead of providing a list of canonical books, Origen in our passage intended to show that the apostles wrote but a few books.[79] This intention becomes clear not only from a reading of the passage, but also from an examination of its context, which is preserved in *Philocalia* 5. We find there that at the beginning of *Comm. Joh.* 5 Origen is trying to justify his verbosity in light of the scriptural warning against making many books (Eccl. 12:12). He solves this problem by suggesting that all of Scripture is in fact one book, and anyone who writes truth in accordance with Scripture does not come under the censure of Ecclesiastes. Before arriving at this conclusion he highlights the problem—the seeming unseemliness of composing many books—by admitting that the individual inspired writers did not multiply books. For instance, Moses only wrote five books. Here, the Philocalists interrupt their quotation of Origen and insert the comment: 'Then, after enumerating prophets and apostles, and showing how each of them wrote but a little, or not even that, he continues...' (*Philoc.* 5.2). It is a portion of this section, omitted in the *Philocalia*, that Eusebius has excerpted as evidence of Origen's views on the authorship and reception of the apostolic letters.

---

[78] Kalin 1990: 279.   [79] See Ruwet 1942: 20.

Text[80]	Translation[81]
(7) καὶ ἐν τῷ πέμπτῳ δὲ τῶν εἰς τὸ κατὰ Ἰωάννην Ἐξηγητικῶν ὁ αὐτὸς ταῦτα περὶ τῶν ἐπιστολῶν τῶν ἀποστόλων φησίν· "ὁ δὲ ἱκανωθεὶς διάκονος γενέσθαι τῆς καινῆς διαθήκης, οὐ γράμματος, ἀλλὰ πνεύματος, Παῦλος, ὁ πεπληρωκὼς τὸ εὐαγγέλιον ἀπὸ Ἱερουσαλὴμ καὶ κύκλῳ μέχρι τοῦ Ἰλλυρικοῦ, οὐδὲ πάσαις ἔγραψεν αἷς ἐδίδαξεν ἐκκλησίαις, ἀλλὰ καὶ αἷς ἔγραψεν, ὀλίγους στίχους ἐπέστειλεν.	(7) And in the fifth of his *Expositions on the Gospel according to John* the same person says this with reference to the epistles of the apostles: 'But he who was made sufficient to become a minister of the new covenant, not of the letter but of the spirit [cf. 2 Cor. 3:6], even Paul, who fully preached the Gospel from Jerusalem and round about even unto Illyricum [cf. Rom. 15:19], did not so much as write to all the churches that he taught; and even to those to which he wrote he sent but a few lines.[82]
(8) Πέτρος δέ, ἐφ᾽ ᾧ οἰκοδομεῖται ἡ Χριστοῦ ἐκκλησία, ἧς πύλαι Ἅιδου οὐ κατισχύσουσιν, μίαν ἐπιστολὴν ὁμολογουμένην καταλέλοιπεν, ἔστω δὲ καὶ δευτέραν· ἀμφιβάλλεται γάρ.	(8) And Peter, on whom the Church of Christ is built, against which the gates of Hades shall not prevail [cf. Matt. 16:18], has left one acknowledged epistle, and, it may be, a second also; for it is doubted.[83]
(9) τί δεῖ περὶ τοῦ ἀναπεσόντος ἐπὶ τὸ στῆθος λέγειν τοῦ Ἰησοῦ, Ἰωάννου, ὃς εὐαγγέλιον ἓν καταλέλοιπεν, ὁμολογῶν δύνασθαι τοσαῦτα ποιήσειν ἃ οὐδ᾽ ὁ κόσμος χωρῆσαι ἐδύνατο, ἔγραψεν δὲ καὶ τὴν Ἀποκάλυψιν, κελευσθεὶς σιωπῆσαι καὶ μὴ γράψαι τὰς τῶν ἑπτὰ βροντῶν φωνάς;	(9) Why need I speak of him who leaned back on Jesus' breast [cf. John 13:23], John, who has left behind one Gospel, confessing that he could write so many that even the world itself could not contain them [John 21:25]; and he wrote also the Apocalypse, being ordered to keep silence and not to write the voices of seven thunders [Rev. 10:4]?
(10) καταλέλοιπεν καὶ ἐπιστολὴν πάνυ ὀλίγων στίχων, ἔστω δὲ καὶ δευτέραν καὶ τρίτην· ἐπεὶ οὐ πάντες φασὶν γνησίους εἶναι ταύτας· πλὴν οὔκ εἰσιν στίχων ἀμφότεραι ἑκατόν."	(10) He has left also an epistle of a very few lines, and, it may be, a second and a third; for not all say that these are genuine.[84] Only, the two of them together are not a hundred lines long.'

[80] Schwartz 1908: 576–8. Rufinus's translation:

(7) De apostolicis quoque litteris ita dicit: 'Is vero, qui idoneus factus est minister novi testamenti, non litterae, sed spiritus, Paulum dico, qui replevit euangelium ab Hierusalem in circuitu usque ad Illyricum, nec ad omnes ecclesias, quas docuerat, scripsit, sed quattuordecim solas epistolas et in ipsis plures brevissimas scribit.

In an effort to make the discussion tidier, Rufinus here inserts Origen's comments about the authorship of Hebrews, which Eusebius presents in the next extract (6.25.11–14). Rufinus's translation does not, then, follow the exact order of Eusebius. After the comments on Hebrews, Rufinus comes back to the present extract:

(8) Petrus vero, super quem Christi fundatur ecclesia, duas tantummodo epistulas scribit, e quibus a nonnullis et de secunda dubitatur. (9) Iohannes quoque, qui supra pectus domini recubuit, post euangelium scribit et Apocalypsin, in qua tamen reticere iussus est, quid septem tonitruorum locutae sunt voces. (10) scripsit autem et tres epistulas, in quibus duae perbreves, de quibus et apud quosdam dubia sententiae est.

[81] Loeb (Oulton).
[82] Origen does not state here how many Pauline letters he accepts. He seems to have accepted thirteen or fourteen letters of Paul, depending on the status of Hebrews; see Metzger 1987: 137–8.
[83] For Origen's statements on Peter's epistles, see below on the *Homilies on Joshua*.
[84] For Origen's statements on John's epistles, see below on the *Homilies on Joshua*.

Homilies on Joshua 7.1

Date: ca. 250 for the lost Greek original, ca. 400 for the extant Latin translation (Rufinus)

Introduction: While preaching about the fall of Jericho (Josh. 6), Origen compares the trumpets that brought down Jericho's walls to the books of Christian Scripture, which trumpet forth the gospel and demolish the walls of unbelief. If this text authentically derives from Origen, it could represent our earliest testimony to the twenty-seven-book New Testament, depending on the textually problematic mention of Revelation and the number of Johannine epistles included. Unfortunately, the passage is available only in the Latin translation made by Rufinus, whose notoriously loose translation technique was criticized in Antiquity as in the Modern Period.[85] Some scholars have doubted that the passage derives from Origen, attributing its creation instead to the translator.[86] Other scholars consider such a position to be exaggerating the liberties taken by Rufinus.[87] These scholars argue that even if Rufinus made changes in certain details, the passage as a whole accurately reflects the Greek *Vorlage*. If the passage does originate with Origen, possible modifications made by Rufinus will be indicated in the notes.

Text[88]	Translation[89]
Sacerdotali tuba primus in Evangelio suo Matthaeus increpuit; Marcus quoque, Lucas et Iohannes suis singuli tubis sacerdotalibus cecinerunt; Petrus etiam duabus epistolarum	Matthew first sounded the priestly trumpet in his Gospel; Mark also; Luke and John each played their own priestly trumpets. Even Peter cries out with trumpets in two of his

[85] For a summary of this issue, see Bruce 2002: 13–17. Rufinus himself claims that he translated the Joshua homilies 'literally and without great effort'—that is, without the effort of filling in gaps he perceived in Origen's text or polishing the rough style; cf. Rufinus's translation of Origen, *Comm. Rom.* epilogue, in the translation of Scheck 2002: 311.

[86] Robbins 1986: 89–97; Kalin 1990: 279–81.

[87] Metzger 1987: 139–40; Ferguson 2002: 50; Kruger 2015; Gallagher 2016b. McDonald (2017: 2.82–83) modifies the opinion he had expressed earlier (2007: 305–8).

[88] Baehrens 1921: 327–8.   [89] Bruce 2002: 74–5.

Text	Translation
suarum personat tubis; Iacobus quoque et Iudas. Addit nihilominus adhuc et Iohannes tuba canere per epistolas suas[90] et Lucas Apostolorum gesta describens. Novissimus autem ille veniens, qui dixit: 'Puto autem, nos Deus apostolos novissimos ostendit' et in quatuordecim epistolarum suarum fulminans tubis muros Hiericho et omnes idolatriae machinas et philosphorum dogmata usque ad fundamenta deiecit.	epistles;[91] also James and Jude.[92] In addition, John also sounds the trumpet through his epistles,[93] and Luke, as he describes the Acts of the Apostles. And now that last one comes, the one who said, 'I think God displays us apostles last' [1 Cor. 4:9], and in fourteen of his epistles,[94] thundering with trumpets, he casts down the walls of Jericho and all the devices of idolatry and dogmas of philosophers, all the way to the foundations.[95]

[90] Baehrens notes that textual witnesses, *Cg*, *Del*, have 'et apocalypsin' (and the Apocalypse). Metzger (1987: 139n51) agrees with Baehrens that it is 'probably a scribal expansion of the text'; see also Stenzel 1942: 53; Armstrong 2006: 113–14n49. Other scholars assume that Revelation is original: Robbins 1986: 89–97; Kalin 1990: 280; Kruger 2015: 108n47. The translator Rufinus certainly accepts Revelation as canonical; he includes it in his canon list at *Comm. Symb.* 35 (see on Rufinus in ch. 4). As for Origen, he gives no indication of harbouring doubt over its authorship, asserting it to be by John the apostle (Eusebius, *Hist. eccl.* 6.25.9, quoted above). On the reception of Revelation in early Christianity, including its 'frequent' citations by Origen, see Hahneman 1992: 23–5; also Constantinou 2012; 2013: chs 2–3.

[91] Armstrong (2006: 116–17) points out that if we can attribute the reference to 2 Peter here to Origen rather than Rufinus (see the introduction to this passage on the issue of Rufinus's translation technique), this passage would represent the first Christian testimony favouring the authority of 2 Peter. He continues: 'On three occasions Origen speaks of 1 Peter simply as "the Catholic Epistle," thus tacitly affirming the singularity of Peter's received epistolary corpus [cf. *Comm. in Joh.* 6.175; *Sel. in Psa.* 3.6; Eus. *Hist. eccl.* 6.25.5]. Nevertheless, Origen also twice refers to 1 Peter as the apostle's "first epistle" and he once even quotes 2 Pet 1:4 and specifically references Peter as his source [cf. *Princ.* 2.5.3; *Comm. Matt.* 15.27; *Hom. Lev.* 4.4].' Kruger (2015: 107n43) adds these instances of Origen's citing 2 Peter approvingly: *Hom. Num.* 13.8.1; *Comm. Rom.* 8.7; *Princ.* 4.1.31; *Comm. in Joh.* 1.26. Eusebius (*Hist. eccl.* 6.25.8, quoted earlier) has preserved Origen's statement that 2 Peter 'is disputed' (ἀμφιβάλλεται).

[92] James and Jude are not included in the catalogue of books attested by Origen as compiled by Eusebius, *Hist. eccl.* 6.25.

[93] Only rarely does 2 John appear without 3 John, so the plural 'epistles' here—whether it belongs to Origen or Rufinus—likely would include not only two letters (1 John and 2 John) but all three Johannine letters; see Hahneman 1992: 14–16. Metzger (1987: 139n52) suggests that a variant 'three' in connection with the letters of Peter may originally have been associated with the letters of John. Eusebius (*Hist. eccl.* 6.25.10, quoted above) has preserved Origen's statement about the second and third letters of John that 'not all say these are genuine'. There are no citations of 2–3 John in Origen's extant works. But see Heine 2010: 82.

[94] The catalogue of Origen compiled by Eusebius (*Hist. eccl.* 6.25) mentions the epistles of Paul but omits a number, while the translation by Rufinus of the same text inserts the number 'fourteen'. Since the present text is available only in Rufinus's translation, we cannot know whether the Greek original included the number 'fourteen' or not, but possibly the translator inserted this detail. In any case, it does appear from Origen's comments elsewhere that he accepted thirteen or fourteen letters of Paul, depending on the status of Hebrews; see Metzger 1987: 137–8. The number 'fourteen' here assumes that Hebrews counts as a Pauline epistle, an issue on which Origen gave divergent answers. Origen attributes Hebrews to Paul at *Princ.* 4.1.13 (and elsewhere in *Princ.*, though in passages preserved only in Rufinus's translation: preface; 1.5.1; 2.6.7; 3.1.10; 3.2.4; 4.1.24); *Cels.* 3.52; 7.29; *Ep. Afr.* 9. For Origen's doubts, see Eusebius, *Hist. eccl.* 6.25.11–14. On the wider reception of Hebrews in the early church, see Hahneman 1992: 119–25.

[95] This list—if it derives from Origen—has surprised some scholars because of its omission of the Shepherd of Hermas and the Epistle of Barnabas; see Kalin 1990: 281. See also Heine 2010:

The Canon Lists of Origen

Selectae in Psalmos 1

The following chart displays Origen's OT canon list.[96]

Greek recension in Christian use	Hebrew canon	Meaning of Hebrew	Rufinus[97]
ἡ παρ' ἡμῖν Γένεσις ἐπιγεγραμμένη, παρὰ δ' Ἑβραίοις ἀπὸ τῆς ἀρχῆς τῆς βίβλου	Βρησιθ	ὅπερ ἐστὶν 'ἐν ἀρχῇ'	Genesis
Ἔξοδος	Ουελλεσμωθ	ὅπερ ἐστὶν 'ταῦτα τὰ ὀνόματα'	Exodus
Λευιτικόν	Ουϊκρα	'καὶ ἐκάλεσεν'	Leviticus
Ἀριθμοί	Αμμεσφεκωδειμ		Numeri
Δευτερονόμιον	Ελλεαδδεβαρειμ	'οὗτοι οἱ λόγοι'	Deuteronomium
Ἰησοῦς υἱὸς Ναυῆ	Ιωσουεβεννουν		Iesus Nave
Κριταί, Ῥούθ, παρ' αὐτοῖς ἐν ἑνί	Σωφτειμ		Iudicum
Βασιλειῶν α' β', παρ' αὐτοῖς ἕν	Σαμουηλ	'ὁ θεόκλητος'·	Regnorum primus et secundus unus liber est apud illos, quem nominant Samuhel
Βασιλειῶν γ' δ' ἐν ἑνί	Ουαμμελχδαυιδ	ὅπερ ἐστὶν 'βασιλεία Δαυίδ'	item tertius et quartus unus est apud ipsos, quem appellant Regnum David
Παραλειπομένων α' β' ἐν ἑνί	Δαβρηϊαμειν	ὅπερ ἐστὶν 'λόγοι ἡμερῶν'	et Paralipomeni primus et secundus in uno habentur, quem dicunt Sermones dierum
Ἔζρας α' β' ἐν ἑνί	Εζρα	ὅ ἐστιν 'βοηθός'	Esdras primus et secundus in uno est
βίβλος Ψαλμῶν	Σφαρθελλειμ		item liber Psalmorum
Σολομῶνος παροιμίαι	Μελωθ		Salomonis Proverbia
Ἐκκλησιαστής	Κωελθ		et alius Ecclesiastes
Ἆισμα ᾀσμάτων (οὐ γάρ, ὡς ὑπολαμβάνουσίν τινες, Ἄισματα ᾀσμάτων)	Σιρασσιρειμ		et tertius eiusdem, Cantica canticorum
			sed et duodecim prophetarum liber unus est
Ἡσαΐας	Ιεσσια		et Esaias propheta
Ἰερεμίας σὺν Θρήνοις καὶ τῇ Ἐπιστολῇ ἐν ἑνί	Ιερεμια		Hieremias
Δανιήλ	Δανιηλ		Ezechiel

81–2; Kruger 2015: 109–11. If Rufinus did omit a reference to the Shepherd here, it is strange that he did not also alter Origen's comment at *Comm. Rom.* 10.31 (available only in Rufinus's translation) such that the Shepherd is 'divinely inspired'.

[96] Chart adapted from Sundberg 1964: 136.

[97] Rufinus of Aquileia translated Eusebius's *Ecclesiastical History* into Latin around the year 400. His complete translation of Origen's Old Testament canon is given above in n. 58.

Greek recension in Christian use	Hebrew canon	Meaning of Hebrew	Rufinus
Ἰεζεκιήλ	Ιεζεκιηλ		*Danihel*
Ἰώβ	Ιωβ		*Iob*
Ἐσθήρ	Εσθηρ		*et Hester*
ἔξω δὲ τούτων ἐστὶ τὰ Μακκαβαϊκά, ἅπερ ἐπιγέγραπται	Σαρβηθσαβαναιελ		*in his concludunt voluminum divinorum. Machabaeorum vero libros extrinsecus habent.*

As mentioned earlier, it seems likely that Origen received only the Hebrew names from his Jewish source. He then correlated this list to his Christian Bible as best he could. It is therefore difficult to know whether Origen's Jewish informant would have considered both Judges and Ruth to be implied by the title Σωφτειμ (Judges), as Origen says, though other Christian authors (such as Jerome, *Prologus Galeatus*) also claim that Jews reckon these books together, and some scholars assume that Josephus counted the books in this way. The same doubt applies to the books included with Jeremiah. On the other hand, we have Jewish evidence for 1–2 Samuel, 1–2 Kings, 1–2 Chronicles (Paralipomenon) each counting as one book.

Jews also count Ezra and Nehemiah as one book, but it is uncertain whether Origen has made the correct correlation to his Greek Bible. His Jewish informant probably simply said that the Hebrews possess a book called Ezra, which is really two books in one.[98] Origen's Greek Christian titles Esdras A and Esdras B may refer either to the Greek translations known today as 1 Esdras and Ezra–Nehemiah, or to Ezra (Esdras A) and Nehemiah (Esdras B). The former possibility receives support from the fourth-century codices (e.g., Codex Vaticanus, Codex Sinaiticus), but the titles of the books of Esdras in Greek and Latin are notoriously variable and we cannot be certain what titles would have been familiar to Origen. There is no certain evidence how the various books of Esdras were distinguished before the fourth-century codices. The Lucianic Greek manuscripts reverse the titles, calling our Ezra–Nehemiah 1 Esdras.[99] Nevertheless, it is most likely that Origen intends to include both Esdras A (i.e., 1 Esdras) and Esdras B (i.e., Ezra-Nehemiah) together as one book, despite the fact that this correlation does not accurately reflect contemporary Jewish practice. Jerome makes the same implication in his comment on Ezra in his Prologus Galeatus.

Origen's usage elsewhere does not help us identify the books he has in mind here. He twice refers to material in Nehemiah as 'in the second book of Ezra'

[98] Cf. b. B. Bat. 14b (see ch. 2), where the list includes a reference to 'Ezra' without any mention of Nehemiah, which must be assumed as a part of Ezra. The Masoretic notes also assume these two books are one. It is not certain how early this Jewish practice is; cf. VanderKam 2000: 60–80.

[99] See Janz 2010: 33. Janz also points out that Melito of Sardis is the first author to use Esdras as the title of a book (p. 35), and that no Greek author ever used Nehemiah as the title of a book (p. 36). See the Appendix on Esdras, p. 269.

(both times at *Comm. Matt.* 15.5), but this designation does not clarify whether for him Esdras A would correspond to Ezra or to 1 Esdras. Early Christian authors often speak of 'Esdras' without clearly identifying which book they have in mind.[100] Origen cited 1 Esdras three times.[101] At least twice he quotes the literal Greek translation of Ezra–Nehemiah.[102]

The twelve Minor Prophets also count as a single book in Jewish tradition, but Origen's list (as we have it) fails to include the Minor Prophets. This omission is clearly a mistake, as the listed books total only twenty-one, and Origen has said that the list should equal twenty-two. Whether the accidental omission is due to Origen or Eusebius (or some scribe), we cannot tell. Rufinus has supplied the missing notation (was it present in his copy of Eusebius? Or perhaps he checked Origen's original text?) at the customary spot for the Minor Prophets at this time, at the head of the prophetic corpus.[103]

One book for which Origen knew that his own text diverged from the Jewish text was that of Daniel. Origen's *Epistle to Africanus* argues against the idea that Christians ought to adopt the Jewish form of the biblical text as opposed to the traditional Christian form of the LXX, which sometimes diverged widely from the Jewish text. The main point of contention in that epistle is the LXX additions to Daniel, especially Susannah. Though Origen knows that the Jews do not accept this story as an authentic part of Daniel, he insists that Christians ought to continue to receive the story as Scripture.

Origen says that a book of Maccabees stands 'outside of these', i.e., it is not received among the Hebrews as an encovenanted book. Origen surely has in mind the book we know as 1 Maccabees, since it is the only book of the Maccabees (there are four total) that probably originated in Hebrew.

Origen's list includes the following books:

Old Testament
  Genesis
  Exodus
  Leviticus

---

[100] See Janz 2010: 35–6.

[101] *Hom. Ezech.* 9.2.5 (1 Esd. 1:19, but cf. 2 Chron. 35:18); *Comm. Ioh.* 6.1(5) (1 Esd. 4:37–47); *Hom. Jos.* 9.10 (1 Esd. 4:40; cf. 4:59–60); see Canessa 1997: 2.357–9. Canessa lists fifty citations of 1 Esdras for the first four or five centuries of the church (ibid.; see also 1.17–26; and Myers 1974: 17–18).

[102] *Comm. Matt.* 15.5; *Ep. Afr.* 19, both referring to Neh. 1:11. On the reception of this translation of Ezra–Nehemiah, see Janz 2010: 164–77. No Jewish author clearly knows this translation; Josephus relies on a source more similar to 1 Esdras for the material on the return from exile, and his material on Nehemiah—not contained in 1 Esdras—diverges widely from the translation called in Vaticanus Esdras B, suggesting the possibility of a separate source. But Janz (2010: 166) also points out that the Jewish revisions (*kaige*, Aquila) demonstrate some Jewish interest in this translation. On the reception of the Ezra materials generally, see Denter 1962.

[103] Hilary of Poitiers, who follows Origen closely, lists the Twelve Minor Prophets in the same location as Rufinus (see on Hilary in ch. 4). However, Rufinus's own canon list (see ch. 4) places the Twelve Minor Prophets at the close of the prophetic corpus, as is common today.

Numbers
Deuteronomy
Joshua
Judges-Ruth
1–2 Kingdoms   (= 1–2 Samuel)
3–4 Kingdoms   (= 1–2 Kings)
1–2 Paralipomena   (= Chronicles)
1–2 Esdras   (= ? see comments above)
Psalms
Proverbs
Ecclesiastes
Song of Songs
[Twelve Minor Prophets, missing from the list in Eusebius, supplied by Rufinus]
Isaiah
Jeremiah–Lamentations–Epistle of Jeremiah[104]
Daniel
Ezekiel
Job
Esther
Outside of these:
Maccabees

Commentary on Matthew 1

Gospels
  Matthew
  Mark
  Luke
  John

In other passages, Origen also indicates that he—and the church—accepts only four Gospels.[105] He does mention other Gospels on occasion. He acknowledges that he has read numerous non-canonical Gospels, naming explicitly the Gospel according to the Egyptians, the Gospel according to the Twelve Apostles, a Gospel written by Basilides, the Gospel of Thomas, the Gospel of Matthias (*Hom. Luc.* 1.2). He cites the Gospel of the Hebrews three times, introducing each quotation with the qualification, 'if one accepts'.[106] He also knows the

---

[104] For an argument that the reference to the 'Letter' of Jeremiah is a scribal gloss, see Ellis 1991: 14–15.

[105] Cf. *Comm. Joh.* 1.21–2; *Hom. Luc.* 1.2 ('the Church has four Gospels, but heresy has many'). See Heine 2010: 77–80.

[106] *Comm. Joh.* 2.87; *Hom. Jer.* 15.4; *Comm Matt.* 15.14.

Gospel of Peter, and cites approvingly a tradition derived from it regarding Mary's perpetual virginity (*Comm. Matt.* 10.17).

Commentary on John 5

> Epistles and Apocalypse
> Paul
> Peter: one epistle and maybe another
> John: Gospel, Apocalypse, one epistle and maybe two more

This passage does not offer much. Its only use is in specifying Origen's opinion regarding the Petrine and Johannine letters. He reports that the church has doubts about the authenticity of 2 Peter and 2–3 John. Origen himself never quotes 2–3 John, but he does cite 2 Peter a few times.[107]

In this excerpt by Eusebius, no reference is made to James or Jude. About the latter, 'Origen demonstrates nothing but approval.'[108] Origen's treatment of James is more complicated but also generally positive.[109]

As for Paul, Origen apparently accepted a fourteen-letter collection. While he never says so outright (unless the Latin translation of the *Homilies on Joshua* 7.1 can be trusted), he does make 'frequent citations from the Pauline Epistles, including even the brief letter to Philemon'.[110] In the case of 2 Timothy, he admits that 'some have dared to reject this Epistle, but they were not able'.[111] Origen also frequently cites Hebrews as a Pauline letter,[112] even promising in one passage that he would write a defence of the Pauline authorship of Hebrews (*Ep. Afr.* 14).[113] In the chapter in which Eusebius cites Origen's opinions on the scriptural books, he concludes with a lengthy quotation from Origen's *Homilies on Hebrews*, where Origen admits the difficulty of the authorship issue and confesses that only God knows the true author of Hebrews (*Hist. eccl.* 6.25.11–14). He never doubts the authority of the epistle, no matter the author.

Homiliae in Josuam 7.1

> New Testament
> Matthew
> Mark

---

[107] Cf. *Princ.* 2.5.3 (Latin); *Hom. Lev.* 4.4 (Latin). See nn. 91 and 93 above.

[108] Nienhuis 2007: 54, citing *Comm. Matt.* 10.17.40ff., and other passages. According to Nienhuis, Origen only once revealed that anyone harboured any concerns about Jude (*Comm. Matt.* 17.30.9–10).

[109] ibid.: 55–60. [110] Metzger 1987: 137–8.

[111] *Comm. ser. Matt.* 117; quoted in Metzger 1987: 138.

[112] Cf. *Comm. Joh.* 1.141; 2.72; 2.82; 10.84; *Or.* 27.5, 13, 15; *Princ.* praef.

[113] For a list of passages where Origen affirms the Pauline authorship of Hebrews, see Armstrong 2006: 127n85. See also n. 94 above.

Luke
John
Peter (two)
James
Jude
John (plural)
Acts
Paul (fourteen)
(Revelation)

Revelation is not included in the text as printed by Baehrens, but his apparatus records its appearance in some witnesses. Origen indicates his acceptance of Revelation in other passages, where he cites it as an authentic work of the apostle John. If Revelation is included, this list would correspond to the modern twenty-seven-book New Testament, depending on how many letters of John are included in the plural 'epistles' of John. The fourteen letters of Paul would encompass Hebrews.

Some scholars have doubted the authenticity of this passage, attributing it to Rufinus (the translator), rather than to Origen. But there is no doubt that the main contours of this list match what Origen did consider authoritative Scripture. The only real room for doubt is whether he accepted two epistles of Peter and three epistles of John. He mentions these three letters as doubted in his *Commentary on John* 5; the only quotations of them appearing in Origen's preserved works amount to a few quotations of 2 Peter preserved in Latin. If the passage essentially derives from Origen, possibly Rufinus inserted the number 'two' for Peter's letters and 'fourteen' for Paul's, but assuming such a scenario, it is curious that he did not do the same for John's letters.

One final comment: Origen did not restrict his reading or quotations to books he considered canonical or scriptural. He considered some books that he called *apocrypha* to be authentic testimonies from biblical times, sometimes preserving historical material or sometimes offering edification. For example, despite his acknowledgment of the fourfold Gospel accepted in the church, he did make use of the Gospel of Thomas and considered some of its content to reflect accurately sayings of Jesus.[114] As for OT apocrypha (or pseudepigrapha), occasionally he cites the books of Enoch (e.g., *Princ.* 4.4.8), though he also criticizes Celsus for his ignorance that the writings of Enoch are not received by Christians (*Cels.* 5.54).[115] Origen is also suspicious that some OT apocrypha may have been tampered with by Jewish leaders

---

[114] See Carlson 2014: 137–51. On the status of the Epistle of Barnabas, 1 Clement, and the Shepherd of Hermas in Origen, see Heine 2010: 82.
[115] See Gallagher 2012a: 46–9.

(*Ep. Afr.* 13–15). These examples, which could be multiplied, show Origen finding value in a variety of religious texts, not merely those generally received by Christians.[116]

EUSEBIUS OF CAESAREA

Eusebius (ca. 260–339), the father of Church History, became bishop of Caesarea in 313.[117] His many important literary works—especially his *Preparation for the Gospel*, *Demonstration of the Gospel*, and *Ecclesiastical History*—preserve a great deal of early Christian material that would otherwise be lost. One of his objectives in writing the *Ecclesiastical History* was to collect statements regarding which books particular early Christian authors received as Scripture. 'As the narrative proceeds I will take pains to indicate successively which of the orthodox writers in each period used any of the doubtful books (τῶν ἀντιλεγομένων), and what they said about the encovenanted (ἐνδιαθήκων) and accepted (ὁμολογουμένων) Scriptures and what about those which are not such' (*Hist. eccl.* 3.3.3; cf. 5.8.1).[118]

Old Testament canon: In his *Ecclesiastical History*, Eusebius recorded three lists of OT books, those of Josephus (3.10.1–5), Melito of Sardis (4.26.12–14), and Origen (6.25.1–2), all more or less agreeing in content.[119] He apparently intended readers to understand that these lists, despite their minor disagreements, represented the OT canon of the church. He introduced Josephus's list with this comment: 'In the first of these [aforementioned] books [= *Against Apion*] he gives the number of the encovenanted scriptures (τῶν ἐνδιαθήκων γραφῶν) of the so-called Old Testament, and showed as follows which are undisputed (ἀναντίρρητα) among the Hebrews as belonging to ancient tradition' (3.9.5). Similarly, his introduction to Melito's list describes it as 'a list of the recognized (ὁμολογουμένων) scriptures of the Old Testament' (4.26.12), and before quoting Origen's list he says that it is 'the catalogue of the sacred Scriptures of the Old Testament' (6.25.1). Eusebius seems to have thought that the OT canon was settled.

---

[116] For more on Origen's use of apocrypha, see Ruwet 1944; Hanson 1954: ch. 8.

[117] For an introduction to his life and works, see Johnson 2014.

[118] For a helpful presentation of references to such comments in Eusebius, *Hist. eccl.*, see Dungan 2007: 141–7 (Appendix 1).

[119] Josephus numbered the books as twenty-two, but he did not provide a list of those books. Origen (or Eusebius) accidentally omitted the Twelve Minor Prophets. Melito omitted Esther, probably not by accident, and he mentioned a book called 'Wisdom', which may either be the deuterocanonical Wisdom of Solomon or an alternative name for the book of Proverbs. See the discussion of Josephus in ch. 2, and the discussions of Melito and Origen earlier in this chapter.

New Testament canon: Matters stood differently in regard to the NT canon. Eusebius knew that, despite widespread agreement on some books—especially the Gospels and the Pauline Epistles—the churches did not completely agree on every book to be received as Scripture. Disagreement persisted regarding the Catholic Epistles and the Apocalypse (the Book of Revelation). While the Apocalypse had enjoyed widespread support in the second and third centuries, Eusebius records some later doubts about the authenticity and authority of the book, and he himself is not sure what to do with it. As for the Catholic Epistles, the first epistles of Peter and John are the only ones that Eusebius knows to have achieved unanimous support. On the other hand, James, Jude, 2 Peter, 2 John, and 3 John may be useful, but are not accepted everywhere. There is also some doubt about Hebrews, but Eusebius feels comfortable ascribing it to Paul and granting it authority. Other books not now included in the New Testament, such as the Shepherd of Hermas and the Epistle of Barnabas, also receive attention in the *Ecclesiastical History*. While Eusebius discusses the acceptance or canonicity of certain Christian literature throughout the *History*, he tries to offer a coherent discussion of the entire NT canon at *Hist. eccl.* 3.25.1–7, where he categorizes the books according to their level of acceptance.

Studies: Grant 1980: 126–41; Robbins 1986; Hahneman 1992: 133–40; Baum 1997; Kalin 2002; Armstrong 2006; Junod 2011.

Ecclesiastical History 3.25

Date: ca. 325[120]

Introduction: Eusebius here classifies Christian Scripture according to three basic categories: writings accepted universally by orthodox Christians (*homologoumena*), writings disputed by Christians (*antilegomena*), and heretical writings. Within his discussion of the *antilegomena*, he labels certain writings spurious (*notha*), though scholars disagree as to whether Eusebius intends this term to apply to all of the *antilegomena* or only those explicitly so named.

---

[120] The date of the *Ecclesiastical History* has elicited numerous theories of multiple editions of the work; for a brief survey, see Young with Teal 2010: 3–4. The final edition of the *History* followed the Council of Nicaea, which garners a discussion in book 10.

Text[121]	Translation[122]
(1) Εὔλογον δ᾽ ἐνταῦθα γενομένους ἀνακεφαλαιώσασθαι τὰς δηλωθείσας τῆς καινῆς διαθήκης γραφάς. καὶ δὴ τακτέον ἐν πρώτοις τὴν ἁγίαν τῶν εὐαγγελίων τετρακτύν, οἷς ἕπεται ἡ τῶν Πράξεων τῶν ἀποστόλων γραφή·	(1) At this point it seems reasonable to summarize the writings of the New Testament which have been quoted. In the first place should be put the holy tetrad of the Gospels.[123] To them follows the writing of the Acts of the Apostles.
(2) μετὰ δὲ ταύτην τὰς Παύλου καταλεκτέον ἐπιστολάς, αἷς ἑξῆς τὴν φερομένην Ἰωάννου προτέραν καὶ ὁμοίως τὴν Πέτρου κυρωτέον ἐπιστολήν· ἐπὶ τούτοις τακτέον, εἴ γε φανείη, τὴν Ἀποκάλυψιν Ἰωάννου, περὶ ἧς τὰ δόξαντα κατὰ καιρὸν ἐκθησόμεθα. καὶ ταῦτα μὲν ἐν ὁμολογουμένοις·	(2) After this should be reckoned the Epistles of Paul.[124] Following them the Epistle of John called the first, and in the same way should be recognized the Epistle of Peter.[125] In addition to these should be put, if it seem desirable, the Revelation of John, the arguments concerning which we will expound at the proper time.[126] These belong to the Recognized Books.

[121] Schwartz 1908: 250-2. This edition also prints Rufinus's Latin translation (ed. Theodor Mommsen) of Eusebius's *History* on pages facing the Greek. For this passage, Rufinus's translation runs:

(1) Ut ergo, quando quidem in hos devenimus locos, omnem novi testamenti canonem designemus, primo nobis omnium euangeliorum caelestis quadriga iungatur, his Actus apostolorum copulentur. (2) post hos Pauli epistulae socientur, consequantur vero has prima Iohannis epistula, similiter et Petri prima. haec sunt, de quibus nulla umquam prorsus extitit dubitatio. (3) sequenti loco iam sunt illa, de quibus a nonnullis dubitatum est: Revelatio Iohannis, de qua quid singuli veterum senserint, suis in locis ostendemus, et epistula Iacobi, sed et Iudae, Petri quoque secunda et item Iohannis secunda et tertia, sive hae ipsius euangelistae sive etiam alterius eius cognominis ostendentur. (4) post haec iam scriptura est, quae dicitur Actus Pauli, sed et libellus qui appellatur Pastoris, et Revelatio Petri, de quibus quam maxime dubitatur. fertur etiam Barnabae epistula et Doctrina quae dicitur apostolorum. (5) quidam autem his sociant etiam euangelium quod dicitur secundum Hebraeos, quo praecipue utuntur illi Hebraei qui Christum suscipere videntur, sed in ecclesia ei contradicitur. (6) quae omnia tamen a nobis necessario enumerata sunt, ut absque ulla ambiguitate claresceret, quae sint in veteri auctoritate et quae sint, in quibus vel contradictio aliqua vel etiam cunctatio, cum tamen a quam plurimis ecclesiis recipiantur, soleat admitti. sed et de illis sciendum est, quae sub nomine apostolorum ab haereticis proferuntur, velut Petri et Thomae et Matthiae et ceterorum similiter apostolorum quae appellant euangelia, sed et Andreae et Iohannis atque aliorum apostolorum Actus, quod nusquam prorsus in scriptis veterum, eorum dumtaxat, qui apostolis successerunt, aliqua mentio eorum aut commemoratio habetur. (7) in quibus et ipse stilus multum ab ecclesiastica consuetudine deprehenditur esse diversus. sensus quoque ipse et omnia, quae in his inferuntur, longe ab apostolica dissonant fide, ex quo figmenta esse pravitatis haereticae conprobantur. unde ne inter illa quidem, de quibus dubitari diximus, conlocanda sunt, sed ut aliena penitus et a pietatis regula discrepantia propellenda.

[122] Lake 1926: 257-9 (adapted).

[123] Eusebius does not find it necessary to name individually Matthew, Mark, Luke, and John because they are so well known. On the early reception of the Fourfold Gospel, see ch. 1, pp. 32-9. On Eusebius specifically, see Watson 2013: 436-52.

[124] Eusebius does not specify here which letters of Paul he accepts, but earlier (3.3.5) he had given the number as fourteen, which includes Hebrews.

[125] Eusebius elsewhere makes clear that of the Catholic Epistles only 1 Peter and 1 John were universally accepted.

[126] Eusebius's confusing opinion on the Apocalypse apparently went through some development during the course of his life, and perhaps during the course of his work on his *History*. For a reconstruction of this development, see Grant 1980: 126-7, 130-6. The Apocalypse appears in this list both in the undisputed category and in the spurious category.

Text	Translation
(3) τῶν δ᾽ ἀντιλεγομένων, γνωρίμων δ᾽ οὖν ὅμως τοῖς πολλοῖς, ἡ λεγομένη Ἰακώβου φέρεται καὶ ἡ Ἰούδα ἥ τε Πέτρου δευτέρα ἐπιστολὴ καὶ ἡ ὀνομαζομένη δευτέρα καὶ τρίτη Ἰωάννου, εἴτε τοῦ εὐαγγελιστοῦ τυγχάνουσαι εἴτε καὶ ἑτέρου ὁμωνύμου ἐκείνῳ.	(3) Of the Disputed Books which are nevertheless known to most are the Epistle called of James, that of Jude, the second Epistle of Peter, and the so-called second and third Epistles of John, which may be the work of the evangelist or of some other with the same name.[127]
(4) ἐν τοῖς νόθοις κατατετάχθω καὶ τῶν Παύλου Πράξεων ἡ γραφὴ ὅ τε λεγόμενος Ποιμὴν καὶ ἡ Ἀποκάλυψις Πέτρου καὶ πρὸς τούτοις ἡ φερομένη Βαρναβᾶ ἐπιστολὴ καὶ τῶν ἀποστόλων αἱ λεγόμεναι Διδαχαὶ ἔτι τε, ὡς ἔφην, ἡ Ἰωάννου Ἀποκάλυψις, εἰ φανείη· ἥν τινες, ὡς ἔφην, ἀθετοῦσιν, ἕτεροι δὲ ἐγκρίνουσιν τοῖς ὁμολογουμένοις.	(4) Among the books which are not genuine must be reckoned the Acts of Paul, the work entitled the Shepherd, the Apocalypse of Peter, and in addition to them the letter called of Barnabas and the so-called Teachings of the Apostles.[128] And in addition, as I said, the Revelation of John, if this view prevail.[129] For, as I said, some reject it, but others count it among the Recognized Books.
(5) ἤδη δ᾽ ἐν τούτοις τινὲς καὶ τὸ καθ᾽ Ἑβραίους εὐαγγέλιον κατέλεξαν, ᾧ μάλιστα Ἑβραίων οἱ τὸν Χριστὸν παραδεξάμενοι χαίρουσιν.	(5) Some have also counted the Gospel according to the Hebrews in which those of the Hebrews who have accepted Christ take a special pleasure.[130]
(6) ταῦτα δὲ πάντα τῶν ἀντιλεγομένων ἂν εἴη, ἀναγκαίως δὲ καὶ τούτων ὅμως τὸν κατάλογον πεποιήμεθα, διακρίνοντες τάς τε κατὰ τὴν ἐκκλησιαστικὴν παράδοσιν ἀληθεῖς καὶ ἀπλάστους καὶ ἀνωμολογημένας γραφὰς καὶ τὰς ἄλλως παρὰ ταύτας, οὐκ ἐνδιαθήκους μὲν ἀλλὰ καὶ ἀντιλεγομένας, ὅμως δὲ παρὰ πλείστοις τῶν ἐκκλησιαστικῶν γινωσκομένας, ἵν᾽ εἰδέναι ἔχοιμεν αὐτάς τε ταύτας καὶ τὰς ὀνόματι τῶν ἀποστόλων πρὸς τῶν αἱρετικῶν προφερομένας ἤτοι ὡς Πέτρου καὶ Θωμᾶ καὶ Ματθία ἢ καί τινων παρὰ τούτους ἄλλων εὐαγγέλια περιεχούσας ἢ ὡς Ἀνδρέου καὶ	(6) These would all belong to the Disputed Books, but we have nevertheless been obliged to make a list of them, distinguishing between those writings which, according to the tradition of the Church, are true, genuine, and recognized, and those which differ from them in that they are not encovenanted but disputed, yet nevertheless are known to most of the writers of the church, in order that we might know them and the writings which are put forward by heretics under the name of the apostles containing Gospels such as those of Peter, and Thomas, and Matthias, and some others besides,[131]

[127] The second and third letters of John do not bear his name but instead are written in the name of 'the elder', traditionally identified as John the apostle (or 'the evangelist', since to him is ascribed the authorship of the Fourth Gospel). Eusebius expresses doubt about whether to identify the author of these two small letters with John the Apostle or someone else.

[128] Commonly known now as the Didache (Greek for 'teaching'). On all of these spurious books, see the Appendix.

[129] See above for Eusebius's placing of the Apocalypse among the 'recognized' group, 'if it seem desirable' (3.25.2).

[130] Eusebius mentions this Gospel at 3.27.4; 3.39.17; 4.22.8. For other ancient Christian references to this Gospel according to the Hebrews, see Edwards 2009: 1–96; see also Evans 2007.

[131] See Ehrman and Pleše 2011. Ehrman and Pleše do not include the Gospel of Matthias, which was mentioned by Clement of Alexandria, *Strom.* 3.4; Jerome, *Comm. Matt.* preface. With regard to Peter, Eusebius elsewhere says: 'On the other hand, of the Acts bearing his name, and the Gospel named according to him and Preaching called his and the so-called Revelation, we have no knowledge at all in Catholic tradition, for no orthodox (ἐκκλησιαστικός) writer of the ancient time or of our own has used their testimonies' (3.3.2). Somewhat of an exaggeration: according to Eusebius, Serapion had written against the Gospel of Peter (6.12), but Clement of Alexandria had commented on the Apocalypse of Peter (6.14.1).

Text	Translation
Ἰωάννου καὶ τῶν ἄλλων ἀποστόλων πράξεις· ὧν οὐδὲν οὐδαμῶς ἐν συγγράμματι τῶν κατὰ τὰς διαδοχὰς ἐκκλησιαστικῶν τις ἀνὴρ εἰς μνήμην ἀγαγεῖν ἠξίωσεν, (7) πόρρω δέ που καὶ ὁ τῆς φράσεως παρὰ τὸ ἦθος τὸ ἀποστολικὸν ἐναλλάττει χαρακτήρ, ἥ τε γνώμη καὶ ἡ τῶν ἐν αὐτοῖς φερομένων προαίρεσις πλεῖστον ὅσον τῆς ἀληθοῦς ὀρθοδοξίας ἀπᾴδουσα, ὅτι δὴ αἱρετικῶν ἀνδρῶν ἀναπλάσματα τυγχάνει, σαφῶς παρίστησιν· ὅθεν οὐδ' ἐν νόθοις αὐτὰ κατατακτέον, ἀλλ' ὡς ἄτοπα πάντῃ καὶ δυσσεβῆ παραιτητέον.	or Acts such as those of Andrew, and John, and the other apostles.[132] To none of these has any who belonged to the succession of the orthodox ever thought it right to refer in his writings. (7) Moreover, the type of phraseology differs from apostolic style, and the opinion and tendency of their contents is widely dissonant from true orthodoxy and clearly shows that they are forgeries of heretics. They ought, therefore, to be reckoned not even among spurious books but shunned as altogether wicked and impious.

The Canon List of Eusebius

Recognized, Encovenanted Books:
    Four Gospels
    Acts of the Apostles
    Epistles of Paul
    1 John
    1 Peter
    (?) Revelation of John (?)
Disputed Books:
    James
    Jude
    2 Peter
    2 John
    3 John
    Spurious Books:
        Acts of Paul
        Shepherd (of Hermas)
        Apocalypse of Peter
        Epistle of Barnabas
        Teachings of the Apostles (Didache)
        (?) Revelation of John (?)
        (?) Gospel according to the Hebrews (?)
Heretical Books:
    Gospel of Peter
    Gospel of Thomas
    Gospel of Matthias
    other Gospels
    Acts of Andrew

[132] For translations of these apocryphal Acts, see Elliott 1993: 229–535. For discussion, see Klauck 2008.

Acts of John
other Acts

Several issues require elaboration.

Paul's letters: Eusebius had specified the number of Paul's letters earlier in the same book. The only one that merited further discussion was Hebrews, whose authenticity had been questioned.

> And the fourteen letters of Paul are obvious (πρόδηλοι) and plain (σαφεῖς), yet it is not right to ignore that some dispute (ἠθετήκασι) the Epistle to the Hebrews, saying that it was rejected (ἀντιλέγεσθαι) by the church of Rome as not being by Paul, and I will expound at the proper time what was said about it by our predecessors. Nor have I received his so-called Acts among undisputed (ἐν ἀναμφιλέκτοις) books. (3.3.5)[133]

At 3.38, Eusebius suggests that either Luke or Clement translated into Greek the Epistle to the Hebrews, which had been written by Paul in Hebrew.[134]

The Apocalypse of John: Eusebius is inconsistent in his treatment of John's Apocalypse. His initial positive opinion—in line with the majority of Christian writers who preceded him—seems to have yielded to concerns over how millenarians were using the book to support their views. His opinion seems to have reversed again when he understood the argument of Dionysius of Alexandria that the Apocalypse was authentically composed by a person named John, but not the apostle.[135] Immediately before the canon list, Eusebius had said:

> Of the writings of John in addition to the gospel the first of the epistles has been accepted (ὡμολόγηται) without controversy (ἀναμφίλεκτος) by ancients and moderns alike but the other two are disputed (ἀντιλέγονται), and as to the Apocalypse there have been many advocates of either opinion up to the present. (3.24.17–18)

In fact, Eusebius has not cited any opinions against John's Apocalypse, only opinions in its favour.[136] He will later discuss the views of Dionysius of Alexandria (7.25), who also seemed generally positive toward the book, though denying its apostolic authorship because of various stylistic peculiarities. Some scholars think that Eusebius tried to redeem the status of the Apocalypse against critics who considered it forged in the name of the apostle John.[137]

---

[133] Hebrews is an *antilegomenon* in terms of its Pauline authorship but not in terms of its origins within the apostolic timeframe (cf. 6.13.6); see Robbins 1986: 118–20; Baum 1997: 345.

[134] He cites a similar opinion in the name of Clement of Alexandria at 6.14.2–4, and he cites Origen's opinion at 6.25.11–14. For more on Eusebius on Hebrews, see Grant 1980: 136–7; Baum 1997: 327–8.

[135] See Gustafsson 1961: 439–41; Grant 1980: 126–41; Mazzucco 1982.

[136] See the testimonies collected by Eusebius from Justin (4.18.8), Theophilus (4.24), Melito (4.26.2), Irenaeus (3.18.1–3; 5.8.5–6), Apollonius (5.18.4), Clement of Alexandria (3.23.6), and Origen (6.25.9–10), and see Hahneman 1992: 23.

[137] See, e.g., Robbins 1986: 117.

Others take the exact opposite view, that Eusebius overturned the unanimous Christian approval for the Apocalypse because he wanted to exclude it from the canon.[138]

The Catholic Epistles: Eusebius is the first witness to a seven-letter collection called the Catholic Epistles (2.23.25, quoted below).[139] Nevertheless, he admits that only two of the seven enjoy universal reception in the church: 1 Peter and 1 John. The other Catholic Epistles constitute the entirety of the *antilegomena*, the disputed writings, except for the documents that Eusebius specifically says are spurious (the Acts of Paul, etc.). The passage from 3.24.18 on the writings of John was quoted just above, where again he classifies 2–3 John as *antilegomena*. Regarding James and Jude, Eusebius earlier had said:

> Such is the story of James, whose is said to be the first of the Epistles called Catholic. It is to be observed that its authenticity is denied (ἰστέον δὲ ὡς νοθεύεται μέν), since few of the ancients quote it, as is also the case with the Epistle called Jude's, which is itself one of the seven called Catholic; nevertheless we know that these letters have been used publicly with the rest in most churches. (2.23.24–5)

And with regard to Peter's writings:

> Of Peter, one epistle, that which is called his first, is admitted (ἀνωμολόγηται), and the ancient presbyters used this in their own writings as unquestioned (ὡς ἀναμφιλέκτω), but the so-called second Epistle we have not received as encovenanted (οὐκ ἐνδιάθηκον μὲν εἶναι παρειλήφαμεν), but nevertheless it has appeared useful (χρήσιμος) to many, and has been studied with other Scriptures. (3.3.1)

> Now the above are the books bearing the name of Peter, of which I recognize only one as genuine (γνησίαν) and admitted (ὁμολογουμένην) by the presbyters of old. (3.3.4).

Eusebius is correct that earlier Christian writers interact with these five Catholic Epistles rather sparingly. Origen is the first to mention explicitly a second epistle of Peter, and while 2 John (and maybe even 3 John) had been used and cited even in the second century, Origen notes contemporary doubts about all three of these letters and does not quote them in his works extant in Greek.[140] Origen makes extensive use of James and approves also of Jude.[141] Clement of Alexandria quotes Jude a few times,[142] and Tertullian so assumes the unimpeachable

---

[138] See Constantinou 2012.   [139] Nienhuis 2007: 66–7; see pp. 41–8 above.

[140] There are a few citations of 2 Peter in Origen's works preserved in Latin. See the discussion of Origen earlier in this chapter. On the use of 2–3 John in the second century, see the chart at Hill 2004: 450. Irenaeus, for example, quotes 2 John as a letter from the Lord's disciple John (*Haer.* 3.16.8; cf. 3.16.5). The Muratorian Fragment (possibly second century) is aware of multiple letters of John (possibly the canonical three; see ibid., 136).

[141] See Nienhuis 2007: 54 (on Jude) and 55–60 (on James).

[142] Clement of Alexandria, *Paed.* 3.8.44.3–45.1; *Strom.* 3.2.11.2. Eusebius reports that Clement commented on Jude (*Hist. eccl.* 6.14.1). There is no certain evidence for Irenaeus's use of Jude; Nienhuis 2007: 35.

authority of Jude that he uses its citation of 1 Enoch 1:9 (Jude 14) as a proof for the inspiration of this latter text (*Cult. fem.* 1.3), though Jerome reports that Jude's use of Enoch had led to doubts about Jude (*Vir. ill.* 4). Pre-Origenic use of James is more difficult to uncover, despite Eusebius's statement that Clement of Alexandria commented on the Catholic Epistles (*Hist. eccl.* 6.14.1).[143] The relative brevity of each of these letters may have played a role in their poor attestation in pre-fourth-century sources.

The spurious writings: Eusebius names as spurious five writings, and suggests that two others—the Apocalypse of John and the Gospel according to the Hebrews—might be added to the category. These spurious writings are distinguished from the heretical writings—which Eusebius later calls 'completely spurious' (παντελῶς νόθα; 3.31.6)—apparently because he considered them orthodox. They do not, however, count as genuinely apostolic, despite their positive value. Three of these spurious writings feature in the modern collection of early Christian works known as the Apostolic Fathers:[144] the Shepherd of Hermas, the Epistle of Barnabas, and the Didache (the Teachings of the Apostles). Each of these works enjoyed respect in early Christian circles, and at least the Shepherd and the Didache found an occasional place in ecclesiastical liturgy.[145] On the Shepherd, Eusebius had reported:

> But since the same Apostle [= Paul] in the salutations at the end of Romans has mentioned among others Hermas [Rom. 16:14], whose, they say, is the Book of the Shepherd,[146] it should be known that this also is rejected (ἀντιλέλεκται) by some, and for their sake should not be placed among accepted books (ἐν ὁμολογουμένοις), but by others it has been judged most valuable (ἀναγκαιότατον), especially to those who need elementary instruction. For this reason we know that it has been used in public in churches, and I have found it quoted by some of the most ancient writers. (3.3.6)[147]

---

[143] It is difficult to know how firm such evidence is for Clement's knowledge of James; see Nienhuis 2007: 48–50. On whether Irenaeus used James, see ibid., p. 36. Eusebius himself uses James more than Jude; see Westcott 1889: 424n2; Robbins 1986: 124–5.

[144] On the origin of the term, see Lincicum 2015.

[145] Eusebius testifies to the practice of reading the Shepherd in church (3.3.6). Rufinus acknowledges that the Shepherd and the Didache (if that is what Rufinus means by his title 'The Two Ways') were read in church (*Comm. Symb.* 36). Athanasius appointed these same two writings for catechetical instruction (*Ep. fest.* 39). Tertullian, on the other hand, in his Montanist phase rejected the Shepherd as dangerous (*Pud.* 10, 20). We are not aware of testimony regarding the liturgical use of the Epistle of Barnabas.

[146] Origen (*Comm. Rom.* 10.31) is the first writer to associate the Hermas of the Shepherd with the Hermas mentioned by Paul in Rom. 16:14; cf. Jerome, *Vir. ill.* 10.

[147] Besides this reference, Eusebius mentions the Shepherd only twice more in his *History*, once where he calls it spurious (3.25.4), and once where he says that Irenaeus's description of the Shepherd as 'Scripture' (γραφή; *Haer.* 4.20.2) indicates his 'reception' of the document (5.8.7), presumably as inspired Scripture. The earliest writers to mention the Shepherd were Irenaeus and Clement of Alexandria, on whom see Batovici 2013; Hill 2013b. On the reception of the Shepherd more generally, see Osiek 1999: 4–7.

The Shepherd is also preserved in a great many manuscripts: eighteen Greek papyri from the first four centuries, along with an appearance of a significant portion of the text in the Codex Sinaiticus.[148] Eusebius has little to say about the Epistle of Barnabas, but it was an important document for Clement of Alexandria (as Eusebius recognized; 6.14.1) and Origen, and it appears between Revelation and the Shepherd of Hermas in Codex Sinaiticus.[149] The Didache held a prominent position in early Christianity, though our available evidence suggests that Christians preferred to praise it for its usefulness rather than actually use it.[150] It left little trace among Greek manuscripts, and it was eventually incorporated within the fourth-century Apostolic Constitutions.[151]

The other two spurious writings, the Acts of Paul and the Apocalypse of Peter, also achieved varying levels of acceptance in Christian communities and came to exert tremendous influence. Eusebius knew that Clement of Alexandria had made use of the Apocalypse of Peter (*Hist. eccl.* 6.14.1), though he had earlier said that this Apocalypse, along with other Petrine apocrypha, went unmentioned by all ecclesiastical authors (3.3.2). According to the author of the Muratorian Fragment, 'we receive' (*recipimus*) the Apocalypses of John and Peter, though some objected to the liturgical use of the Apocalypse of Peter (lines 70–1). Sozomen reports that in fifth-century Palestine the Apocalypse of Peter was still read on Good Friday (*Hist. eccl.* 7.19). Elliott collects seven patristic citations of this Apocalypse.[152] The text is preserved complete only in Ethiopic.

---

[148] For the papyri, all fragmentary, see Wayment 2013: 81–169. On the Shepherd in Sinaiticus, see Batovici 2014. There were also translations into Latin, Coptic, and various languages, which must sometimes serve to fill in the lacunose Greek text. Jerome says, however, that few Latins are aware of the Shepherd (*Vir. ill.* 10).

[149] Cf. Clement of Alexandria, *Strom.* 2.6.31; 2.7.35; 2.15.67; 2.18.84; 2.20.116; 5.8.51–2; 5.10.63; Origen, *Princ.* 3.2.4; *Cels.* 1.63 (where he refers to it as a 'catholic epistle'); see also Didymus the Blind, *Comm. Zach.* 259.21–4; *Comm. Ps.* 300.12–13. For the use by Clement and Origen, see Metzger 1987: 134 (with note 43), 140. Jerome considers Barnabas an authentic letter from the companion of Paul, regards it as useful, but also calls it apocryphal (*Vir. ill.* 6); see Metzger 1987: 236. Only one Greek papyrus fragment of the text from the first four centuries has survived, for which see Wayment 2013: 37–9.

[150] On the reception of the Didache, study of which is complicated by the various forms of the text circulating in antiquity, see Niederwimmer 1998: 4–18. It is mentioned as a useful work by Athanasius (*Ep. fest.* 39) and possibly by Rufinus (*Comm. Symb.* 36), and, of course, Eusebius includes it in our passage as a spurious—but not heretical—document. The few extant early quotations might include Clement of Alexandria, *Strom.* 1.20, 100.4; Ps-Cyprian, *De aleat.* 4, and a few other more questionable cases.

[151] See Niederwimmer 1998: 17, 28–9. The Greek manuscripts attesting the work are limited to the Bryennios Manuscript from the eleventh century (discovered in 1873) and a couple of leaves from a fourth- or fifth-century papyrus codex, on which see Wayment 2013: 41–2. On the several ancient translations (Coptic, Ethiopic, Georgian), see Niederwimmer 1998: 24–27.

[152] Elliott 1993: 598–600. The citations are from Clement of Alexandria (*Ecl.* 41.1–2; 48.1); Methodius of Olympus (*Symposium* 2.6); Macarius Magnes (*Apocritica* 4.6.7, *bis*); and Theophilus of Antioch (*Ad Autolycum* 2.19, *bis*). On the reception of the Apocalypse of Peter, see Jakab 2003. See also Lapham 2003: 193–216.

Even though only about two-thirds of the Acts of Paul now survives, many extant manuscripts attest portions of this work, including eleven papyri in Greek and Coptic, and over forty Greek manuscripts of the Acts of Paul and Thecla alone (= Acts of Paul chs 3–4).[153] Several early Christians cite the text, and they especially appreciated the character of Thecla and the story of Paul's baptizing a lion (ch. 9).[154] On the other hand, Eusebius recognizes that the work is not undisputed (*Hist. eccl.* 3.3.5); Tertullian (*Bapt.* 17.5) did not appreciate the work, and Jerome (*Vir. ill.* 7) classifies it as apocrypha. But 3 Corinthians, which sometimes formed a section of the Acts of Paul and also circulated independently, appears in several manuscripts and editions of the Bible in Latin, Syriac, and Armenian.[155]

Eusebius's categories: The nature of the categories into which Eusebius divides the NT writings in our passage has been the subject of intense scrutiny, partly because Eusebius fails to clarify the precise relationship between the first set of *antilegomena* (disputed writings) and the second set, which he labels 'spurious' (*notha*). The other two categories—the *homologoumena* (accepted) and the heretical writings—are clear, with the exception of Eusebius's peculiar treatment of the Apocalypse of John. The *homologoumena*, as writings accepted by the church universal, constitute the encovenanted writings (ἐνδιάθηκοι).[156] None of the *antilegomena* can boast such widespread recognition, and therefore they cannot be considered encovenanted (3.25.6).

But is there a distinction between the two sets of *antilegomena*? Parallel statements in Eusebius might indicate a negative answer. At 3.31.6, Eusebius mentions three groups: holy writings (= *homologoumena*), *antilegomena*, and writings that are 'completely spurious' (= heretical writings). Some scholars point to such statements, along with other features of Eusebius's discussion, as indicating that the terms *antilegomena* and spurious (*notha*) are for Eusebius essentially two different ways of saying the same thing, so that in his mind there is little difference between the reception accorded, for instance, 2 Peter and that accorded the Acts of Paul. In favour of this view is the summary statement Eusebius makes at 3.25.6, after describing the spurious books: 'these all belong to the *antilegomena*'.[157]

On the other hand, such statements from Eusebius ensure only that he considered the term *antilegomena* applicable to each of these writings, not

---

[153] On the manuscript evidence, see Pervo 2013: 59–60.

[154] Cf. Hippolytus, *Comm. Dan.* 29.3; Origen, *Princ.* 1.2.3; *Comm. Joh.* 20.12. On the reception of the Acts of Paul, see Pervo 2013: 42–59.

[155] On the Latin manuscripts, see Bogaert 2012: 90. On the Syriac and Armenian evidence, see Metzger 1987: 219, 223. Bodmer Papyrus X also preseves 3 Corinthians in Greek.

[156] On the other hand, 1 Clement—not mentioned here—is 'recognized' (*homologoumenos*) in terms of its Clementine authorship but is not encovenanted (3.16; 3.38), and it is an *antilegomenon* (6.13.6). It was read in some churches (3.16; 4.23.11).

[157] See Robbins 1986: 137–41; Kalin 2002: 394–7.

necessarily the term spurious. Consequently, some scholars believe that the spurious writings constitute a subcategory of *antilegomena*, to be distinguished from other *antilegomena* which could not be described as spurious (e.g., James, 2 Peter, etc.).[158] Even so, clearly Eusebius did not emphasize any such division. Part of the reason Eusebius may not have cared to stress a distinction between the two sets of *antilegomena* is that this distinction held less significance for him than the distinction between the orthodox books (including the *homologoumena* and all of the *antilegomena*) and the heretical books.[159] Perhaps in Eusebius's mind the disputed Catholic Epistles were less disputed (or ought to be less disputed; see below) than those books he explicitly labels 'spurious', but since all of these books contained orthodox content and none could be considered *homologoumena* and therefore 'encovenanted', any distinction between them carried less weight than the distinction between all of these books and the heretical books that went unmentioned by orthodox writers.

Eusebius's canon: Eusebius did not use the word 'canon' (κανών) to designate a collection of scriptural books.[160] Instead, he used *endiathēkos* (ἐνδιάθηκος), translated above as 'encovenanted', to designate those books belonging to New Covenant Scripture. Scholars like to debate how closely *endiathēkos* overlaps with the way later authors would use the term *canōn*, but most agree that *endiathēkos* is essentially Eusebius's way of saying 'canonical' in the sense of 'bearing unassailable authority'.[161] The books described as *endiathēkoi* would then constitute what would pass as the canonical books in Eusebius's day, and these are the *homologoumena*, the books in the first category, encompassing twenty-one or twenty-two writings, depending on the status of John's Apocalypse.[162] Some scholars have thought that Eusebius also included within the canon the first set of *antilegomena*, but such an interpretation relies on concepts foreign to this passage.[163] It may be that Eusebius harboured a personal opinion distinct from what he could verify as the general practice of the church, and the use of the term 'spurious' in reference to the second set of *antilegomena* and not the first set might bolster such an interpretation. Baum suggests that though the first set of *antilegomena* were disputed within the church, and so could not be considered *homologoumena* or *endiathēkoi*, Eusebius himself

---

[158] See Baum (1997: 338) and Junod (2011: 345), who argue that Eusebius regards the first set of *antilegomena* to be genuine (i.e., authentic works by the authors to whom they are ascribed) and so necessarily not spurious.

[159] Baum 1997: 335.

[160] Robbins 1993. There is, however, some disagreement over the meaning of κανών at *Hist. eccl.* 6.25.3. Contrast the opinions of Grant 1980: 141n28 and Hahneman 2002: 406.

[161] Metzger 1987: 292; Baum 1997: 334 (cf. 345); Bokedal 2014: 66, 75–6. Junod 2011: 351, however, believes the term *kanōn* implies a fixity not connoted by *endiathēkos*.

[162] See Kalin 2002: 397–403, who points out that at 3.3.3 Eusebius equates the *homologoumena* with the *endiathēkoi*, he distinguishes the *endiathēkoi* from the *antilegomena* at 3.25.6, and at 3.3.1 he says that 'we have not received' 2 Peter as *endiathēkos*. See also Baum 1997: 334.

[163] See Metzger 1987: 201–7.

considered these writings authentic and genuine, and thought they should be treated as *endiathēkoi*.[164]

CYRIL OF JERUSALEM

Cyril (ca. 315–ca. 387) was born in Jerusalem where he first served as a priest.[165] When his bishop, Maximus, died in 348, Acacius of Caesarea and Patrophilus of Scythopolis ensured that Cyril replaced him. However, the fourth-century Christological controversies combined with the changing emperors created problems for Cyril's continuous leadership over the church in Jerusalem, but scholars remain uncertain about the details.[166] In 357, he was deposed at a local synod, a decision which he had reviewed by the synod of Seleucia in 359. Probably, at this time the Homoiousians or Homoians, those who believed the Son was of 'similar substance' as the Father, reinstalled him in the see of Jerusalem.[167] In 360, the synod of Constantinople upheld the prior decision to depose Cyril. Although he was deposed as bishop over the recognized church of the empire, he was not formally exiled by the emperor according to the evidence. From 360 to 379, the church of Jerusalem was split into two factions, the Homoians and the Homoeans—those who believed the Son was of the 'same substance' as the Father. Although Cyril was deposed, he was still acting as bishop over the Homoian group in Jerusalem until 367, when he joined the Homoeans. At this time, many of the churches of the city were probably under his oversight. Under the orthodox Emperor Theodosius I (379), Cyril had an uninterrupted episcopacy for eight years until his death in 387.

Cyril's corpus contains twenty-four catecheses, or instructions; a homily on John 5:5; and a letter to Emperor Constantius. He gave the catecheses while he was still a priest, or shortly after he became bishop (ca. 350). The first catechesis is introductory; the next eighteen (2–19) address 'those being enlightened'; that is, those who await baptism at Easter. Catecheses 20–4, called *Mystagogical Catecheses*, address the newly baptized and explain the meaning of the sacraments and the liturgy. This series of catecheses provides ample information on the catechumenate and liturgy in use in Jerusalem at this time. *Catechesis* 4 contains Cyril's canon list.

---

[164] Baum 1997: 341–2. According to Baum, Eusebius thought some disputed works were authentic, and one universally received work (John's Apocalypse) was inauthentic (p. 346), so that his own personal list of *endiathēkoi* Scripture would include twenty-six books.

[165] For biography and bibliography on Cyril, cf. Simonetti 2014: 654–5.

[166] For a detailed and plausible reconstruction of the events of Cyril's career, see van Nuffelen 2007: 142–3.

[167] On the modern confusion over Cyril's Christology, see Simonetti 2014: 654. In sum, Cyril does not use the Nicene term *homoousios* (that is, the Son is of the 'same substance' as the Father), which means he did not align with the pro-Nicene camp. However, he did not align with the pro-Arian camp either, since he claimed that the Son is coeternal with the Father and the Son was the Son by nature—not adoption.

Old Testament canon: Cyril's OT canon list agrees mainly with the twenty-two-book Jewish canon, except he includes Baruch and the Epistle of Jeremiah as part of the book of Jeremiah.

New Testament canon: Cyril's NT canon list follows the Eastern order, placing the Catholic Epistles before the Pauline Epistles. Furthermore, it omits the Book of Revelation.

Studies: Mullen 1997; Junod 2005: 180–3.

Catechesis 4.33–6

Date: ca. 350

Introduction: In *Catechesis* 4, 'Of the Ten Points of Doctrine', Cyril introduces catechumens to the following fundamentals of the Christian faith:

1–3:	Introduction: Virtue and Piety
4–6:	Of God
7–9:	Of Christ and his Birth of a Virgin
10–15:	Of Christ's Cross, Burial, Resurrection, Ascension, and Future Judgment
16–17:	Of the Holy Spirit
18–21:	Of the Soul
22–6:	Of the Body
27–9:	Of Meats and Clothing
30–1:	Of the Resurrection of Believers
32:	Of the Laver
33–6:	Of the Divine Scriptures
37:	Final Exhortation

The final doctrine mentioned and described in this lecture is 'Of the Divine Scriptures', and here Cyril introduces the scriptures of the Old and New Testaments (33); tells the story of how the Seventy-two Interpreters rendered the Hebrew Scriptures into Greek (34); lists by name the books of the Old Testament (35); and lists the major sections of the New Testament and concludes the matter (36).

Text[168]	Translation[169]
ΠΕΡΙ ΤΩΝ ΘΕΙΩΝ ΓΡΑΦΩΝ.	Of the Divine Scriptures.
(ΛΓ') Ταῦτα δὲ διδάσκουσιν ἡμᾶς οἱ θεόπνευστοι γραφαὶ τῆς παλαιᾶς τε καὶ καινῆς διαθήκης. Εἷς γάρ ἐστιν ὁ τῶν δύο διαθηκῶν Θεὸς,	(33) Now the divinely inspired Scriptures of both the Old and the New Testament teach us these things. For the God of the two Testaments is One,

---

[168] Reischl and Rupp 1967a: 124–30.
[169] Adpated and slightly revised from *NPNF*².

Text	Translation
ὁ τὸν ἐν τῇ καινῇ φανέντα Χριστὸν ἐν τῇ παλαιᾷ προκαταγγείλας· ὁ διὰ νόμου καὶ προφητῶν εἰς Χριστὸν παιδαγωγήσας. Πρὸ γὰρ τοῦ ἐλθεῖν τὴν πίστιν, ὑπὸ νόμον ἐφρουρούμεθα· καὶ ὁ νόμος παιδαγωγὸς ἡμῶν γέγονεν εἰς Χριστόν. Κἄν ποτε τῶν αἱρετικῶν ἀκούσῃς τινὸς βλασφημοῦντος νόμον ἢ προφήτας, ἀντίφθεγξαι τὴν σωτήριον φωνὴν, λέγων· Οὐκ ἦλθεν Ἰησοῦς καταλῦσαι τὸν νόμον, ἀλλὰ πληρῶσαι. Καὶ φιλομαθῶς ἐπίγνωθι, καὶ παρὰ τῆς Ἐκκλησίας, ποῖαι μέν εἰσιν αἱ τῆς παλαιᾶς διαθήκης βίβλοι, ποῖαι δὲ τῆς καινῆς. Καί μοι μηδὲν τῶν ἀποκρύφων ἀναγίνωσκε. Ὁ γὰρ τὰ παρὰ πᾶσιν ὁμολογούμενα μὴ εἰδὼς, τί περὶ τὰ ἀμφιβαλλόμενα ταλαιπωρεῖς μάτην; Ἀναγίνωσκε τὰς θείας γραφὰς, τὰς εἴκοσι δύο βίβλους τῆς παλαιᾶς διαθήκης ταύτας, τὰς ὑπὸ τῶν ἑβδομήκοντα δύο Ἑρμηνευτῶν ἑρμηνευθείσας.	Who in the Old Testament foretold the Christ Who appeared in the New; Who by the Law and the Prophets led us to Christ's school. *For before faith came, we were shut up under the law* (Gal. 3:23), and *the law has become our tutor to bring us to Christ* (Gal. 3:24). And if ever you hear any of the heretics[170] speaking evil[171] of the Law or the Prophets, answer in the sound of the Saviour's voice, saying, *Jesus came not to destroy the Law, but to fulfil it* (Matt. 5:17). Learn also diligently, and from the church, what are the books of the Old Testament, and what those of the New. And, pray, read none of the apocryphal writings:[172] for why do you, who does not know those which are accepted[173] among all, trouble yourself in vain about those which are doubtful?[174] Read the Divine Scriptures, the twenty-two books of the Old Testament, these that have been translated by the Seventy-two Interpreters.[175]

[170] Perhaps the Marcionites are in view.   [171] Lit. 'blaspheming'.

[172] Cyril uses ἀπόκρυφα on four occasions (*Cat.* 4.22, 33, 35; 15.16). In *Cat.* 4.22, he describes the human body, including the 'hidden' lungs which breathe the air continuously. The other three uses refer to the 'apocryphal writings'. In *Cat.* 4.35, he instructs the catechumens to read the twenty-two books of the Old Testament, which are read openly in the church, but to stay away from the apocryphal writings. Cyril reminds the catechumens that the far wiser and more pious apostles and subsequent leaders of the church have handed down these twenty-two books, and that they, as children of the church, should not infringe upon its statutes (cf. below for Athanasius's *Ep. fest.* 39.16 for a similar explanation). Thus, Cyril appears to define 'the apocryphal writings' as the books not read openly in the church. The books read openly are the books in his canon list. For the usage of the term in *Cat.* 15.16, see n. 203.

[173] ὁμολογούμενα; NPNF²: acknowledged. Origen used the same term in his *Commentary on John* 5 (*apud* Eusebius) in order to describe the authenticity of 1 Peter (cf. Origen above for details). Eusebius also uses this term to describe the accepted and *encovenanted* books; that is, undisputed books (cf. Eusebius above for details). By ca. 350, this term appears as a technical term to describe the authentic and canonical books of the Old and New Testaments.

[174] ἀμφιβαλλόμενα; NPNF²: disputed. In the same section of his *Commentary on John* 5, Origen used this term to describe 2 Peter. However, Origen probably used the term to indicate that the book was truly disputed among the churches. Cyril used the conjunction γάρ ('for') to explain what he meant by 'apocryphal writings'. Thus he probably intends to use the term 'doubtful' synonymously for 'apocryphal writings' (cf. Junod 2005: 181).

[175] Epiphanius also recounted the story of the Seventy-two translators in his discussion of the OT canon in *Mens.* 3.76–95; 5.143–8. In *Mens.* 5, he says that the Seventy-two translated the twenty-two books and seventy-two apocryphal books (cf. Epiphanius below for details). For the earliest account of the Seventy-two, which reports that they translated only the Law or the five books of Moses, see the *Letter of Aristeas* (ca. 100 BCE). Cyril accedes with other early Christian fathers that the Seventy(-two) translated the whole Old Testament (cf., e.g., Justin Martyr, *Dial.* 78; Irenaeus, *Haer.* 3.21.2). Jerome, however, did recognize that the original Greek translation involved only the Pentateuch (cf. *Comm. Ezech.* 5:12).

Text	Translation
(ΛΔ´) Ἀλεξάνδρου γὰρ τοῦ Μακεδόνων βασιλέως τελευτήσαντος καὶ τῆς βασιλείας εἰς τέσσαρας διαιρεθείσης ἀρχὰς, εἴς τε τὴν Βαβυλωνίαν καὶ τὴν Μακεδονίαν, Ἀσίαν τε καὶ τὴν Αἴγυπτον· εἷς τῶν τῆς Αἰγύπτου βασιλευόντων, Πτολεμαῖος ὁ Φιλάδελφος, φιλολογώτατος γενόμενος βασιλεὺς καὶ τὰς κατὰ πανταχοῦ βίβλους συναθροίζων, παρὰ Δημητρίου τοῦ Φαληρέως, τοῦ τῆς βιβλιοθήκης προνοητοῦ, περὶ τῶν νομικῶν καὶ προφητικῶν θείων γραφῶν ἐπακούσας· καὶ πολὺ κάλλιον κρίνας, οὐ παρὰ ἀκόντων ἀναγκαστῶς τὰ βιβλία κτήσασθαι, ἀλλ᾽ ἐξιλεώσασθαι δώροις μᾶλλον καὶ φιλίᾳ τοὺς ἔχοντας· καὶ γινώσκων, ὅτι τὸ μὲν ἀναγκαστὸν δολοῦται πολλάκις, ἀπροαιρέτως διδόμενον· τὸ δὲ ἐκ προαιρέσεως παρεχόμενον σὺν ἀληθείᾳ τῇ πάσῃ δωρεῖται· Ἐλεαζάρῳ τῷ τότε ἀρχιερεῖ πλεῖστα δῶρα πέμψας εἰς τὸν ἐνταῦθα τῶν Ἱεροσολύμων ναόν, ἐξ κατὰ φυλὴν τῶν δώδεκα τοῦ Ἰσραὴλ φυλῶν, πρὸς ἑαυτὸν εἰς ἑρμηνείαν ἐποίησεν ἀποστεῖλαι. Εἶτα καὶ τοῦ, θείας ἢ μὴ τὰς βίβλους εἶναι λαμβάνων ἀπόπειραν, καὶ πρὸς τὸ μὴ συνδυάσαι πρὸς ἀλλήλους τοὺς ἀποσταλέντας ὑποπτεύσας· ἐν τῇ λεγομένῃ Φάρῳ, τῇ πρὸς Ἀλεξάνδρειαν κειμένῃ, τῶν παραγενομένων ἑρμηνευτῶν ἑκάστῳ ἴδιον οἶκον ἀπονείμας, ἑκάστῳ πάσας τὰς γραφὰς ἐπέτρεψεν ἑρμηνεῦσαι. Τούτων δὲ ἐν ἑβδομήκοντα [καὶ] δύο ἡμέραις τὸ πρᾶγμα πληρωσάντων, τὰς ὁμοῦ πάντων ἑρμηνείας, ἃς κατὰ διαφόρους οἴκους ἀλλήλοις μὴ προσιέντες ἐποιήσαντο, συναγαγὼν ἐπὶ τὸ αὐτό, οὐ μόνον ἐν νοήμασιν, ἀλλὰ καὶ ἐν λέξεσιν εὗρεν συμφώνους. Οὐ γὰρ εὑρεσιλογία καὶ κατασκευὴ σοφισμάτων ἀνθρωπίνων ἦν τὸ γινόμενον· ἀλλ᾽ ἐκ Πνεύματος ἁγίου ἡ τῶν ἁγίῳ Πνεύματι λαληθεισῶν θείων γραφῶν ἑρμηνεία συνετελεῖτο.	(34)[176] For after the death of Alexander, the king of the Macedonians, and the division of his kingdom into four principalities, into Babylonia, and Macedonia, and Asia, and Egypt, one of those who reigned over Egypt, Ptolemy Philadelphus, being a king very fond of learning, while collecting the books that were in every place, heard from Demetrius Phalereus, the curator of his library, of the Divine Scriptures of the Law[177] and the Prophets, and judged it much nobler, not to get the books from the possessors by force against their will, but rather to propitiate them by gifts and friendship; and knowing that what is extorted is often adulterated, being given unwillingly, while that which is willingly supplied is freely given with all sincerity, he sent to Eleazar, who was then High Priest, a great many gifts for the Temple here at Jerusalem, and caused him to send him six interpreters from each of the twelve tribes of Israel for the translation. Then, further, to make experiment whether the books were Divine or not, he took precaution that those who had been sent should not combine among themselves, by assigning to each of the interpreters who had come his separate chamber in the island called Pharos, which lies over against Alexandria, and committed to each the whole Scriptures to translate.[178] And when they had fulfilled the task in seventy-two days, he brought together all their translations, which they had made in different chambers, without sending them one to another, and found that they agreed not only in the sense but even in words.[179] For the process was no word-craft, nor contrivance of human devices: but the translation of the Divine Scriptures, spoken by the Holy Spirit, was of the Holy Spirit accomplished.

[176] For a discussion of the ancient sources related to the origins of the Septuagint, see Fernández Marcos 2000: 35–51. Much of Cyril's account of the translation corresponds to the *Letter of Aristeas*, but he includes also some later embellishments.

[177] Lit. 'laws'.

[178] The idea that Ptolemy separated the translators is first clearly articulated by Irenaeus (*Haer.* 3.21.1–3), though Philo may hint at it (*Mos.* 2.37). The story is also found in rabbinic literature (cf. b. Meg. 9a–b).

[179] οὐ μόνον ἐν νοήμασιν, ἀλλὰ καὶ ἐν λέξεσιν. For a similar idea, see Philo, *Mos.* 2.37–40, on the interpretation of which see Kamesar 2009: 65–72.

Text	Translation
(ΛΕ΄) Τούτων τὰς εἴκοσι δύο βίβλους ἀναγίνωσκε· πρὸς δὲ τὰ ἀπόκρυφα μηδὲν ἔχε κοινόν. Ταύτας μόνας μελέτα σπουδαίως, ἃς καὶ ἐν Ἐκκλησίᾳ μετὰ παρρησίας ἀναγινώσκομεν. Πολύ σου φρονιμώτεροι καὶ εὐλαβέστεροι ἦσαν οἱ ἀπόστολοι καὶ οἱ ἀρχαῖοι ἐπίσκοποι, οἱ τῆς Ἐκκλησίας προστάται, οἱ ταύτας παραδόντες. Σὺ οὖν, τέκνον τῆς Ἐκκλησίας ὢν, μὴ παραχάραττε τοὺς θεσμούς. Καὶ τῆς μὲν παλαιᾶς διαθήκης, καθὼς εἴρηται, τὰς εἴκοσι δύο μελέτα βίβλους· ἃς, εἰ φιλομαθὴς τυγχάνεις, ἐμοῦ λέγοντος, ὀνομαστὶ μεμνῆσθαι σπούδασον. Τοῦ νόμου μὲν γάρ εἰσιν αἱ Μωσέως πρῶται πέντε βίβλοι, Γένεσις, Ἔξοδος, Λευιτικόν, Ἀριθμοί, Δευτερονόμιον· ἑξῆς δὲ, ἡ Ἰησοῦ υἱοῦ Ναυῆ· καὶ τὸ τῶν Κριτῶν βιβλίον μετὰ τῆς Ῥούθ, ἕβδομον ἀριθμούμενον. Τῶν δὲ λοιπῶν ἱστορικῶν βιβλίων, ἡ πρώτη καὶ ἡ δευτέρα τῶν Βασιλειῶν μία παρ᾽ Ἑβραίοις ἐστὶ βίβλος· μία δὲ καὶ ἡ τρίτη καὶ ἡ τετάρτη. Ὁμοίως δὲ παρ᾽ αὐτοῖς καὶ τῶν Παραλειπομένων ἡ πρώτη καὶ ἡ δευτέρα μία τυγχάνει βίβλος· καὶ τοῦ Ἔσδρα ἡ πρώτη καὶ ἡ δευτέρα μία λελόγισται· δωδεκάτη δὲ βίβλος ἡ Ἐσθήρ. Καὶ τὰ μὲν ἱστορικὰ ταῦτα. Τὰ δὲ στιχηρὰ τυγχάνει πέντε· Ἰώβ, καὶ βίβλος Ψαλμῶν, καὶ Παροιμίαι, καὶ Ἐκκλησιαστὴς, καὶ Ἄισμα ᾀσμάτων ἑπτακαιδέκατον βιβλίον. Ἐπὶ δὲ τούτοις τὰ προφητικὰ πέντε· τῶν δώδεκα προφητῶν μία βίβλος, καὶ Ἡσαΐου μία,	(35) Of these read the twenty-two books, but have nothing to do with the apocryphal writings.[180] Study earnestly these only which we read openly in the church. Far wiser and more pious than you were the Apostles, and the bishops of old time, the rulers[181] of the church who handed down[182] these books.[183] Being therefore a child of the church, do not infringe[184] upon its statutes. And of the Old Testament, as we have said, study the twenty-two books, which, if you are desirous of learning, strive to remember by name, as I recite them. For of the Law, the books of Moses, are the first five, Genesis, Exodus, Leviticus, Numbers, Deuteronomy. And next, Joshua the son of Nave, and the book of Judges, including Ruth,[185] counted as seventh. And of the other historical books, the first and second books of the Kingdoms[186] are among the Hebrews one book; also the third and fourth one book.[187] And in like manner, the first and second of Paralipomenon[188] are with them one book; and the first and second of Esdras[189] are counted one. Esther[190] is the twelfth book; and these are the Historical writings. But those which are written in verses are five, Job, and the book of Psalms, and Proverbs, and Ecclesiastes, and the Song of Songs, which is the seventeenth book. And after these come the five Prophetic books: of the Twelve Prophets one book, of Isaiah one, of Jeremiah one, including Baruch,[191] and

[180] Lit. 'but have nothing in common with the apocrypha'.　　　[181] *NPNF²*: presidents.

[182] παραδίδωμι. Cf. Athanasius's similar use of this term in *Ep. fest.* 39.16 later in this chapter.

[183] Not only does Cyril think that the biblical canon is closed, but he also implies that it has been closed since the days of the apostles.

[184] *NPNF²*: trench.

[185] Lit. 'with Ruth'. Origen is the first to attest 'Judges with Ruth' as one book. There is no evidence that Jews coupled Ruth with Judges, although Josephus's twenty-two books probably depends in part on numbering Ruth with Judges.

[186] *NPNF²*: Kings. In the Jewish and English Bible traditions these are the books of 1–2 Samuel.

[187] In the Jewish and English Bible traditions these are the books of 1–2 Kings.

[188] *NPNF²*: Chronicles. Paralipomenon ('The Things Omitted') is the title of these books in Greek. In the Jewish and English Bible traditions these are the books of 1–2 Chronicles.

[189] In *Cat.* 16.28, Cyril introduces a short citation from Esdras B 19:20 (cf. Neh. 9:20) with ὁ Ἔσδρας φησίν 'Ezra says'. There is no parallel text to this one in Esdras A. Certainty in this matter is precluded, though Cyril probably intended the two works known in the Greek tradition as Esdras A and Esdras B with the use of these titles, not Ezra and Nehemiah.

[190] Cyril does not use Esther according to *Biblia Patristica*.

[191] Lit. 'with Baruch, and Lamentions, and the Epistle'. Cyril cites Baruch 3:36–8 introducing it with 'Hear the prophet saying…' (Ἄκουε τοῦ προφήτου λέγοντος) (*Cat.* 11.15), probably indicating the prophet Jeremiah. In a spurious work attributed to Cyril, the author cites Baruch 3:38 with

Text	Translation
καὶ Ἱερεμίου μετὰ Βαροὺχ, καὶ Θρήνων, καὶ Ἐπιστολῆς· εἶτα Ἰεζεκιὴλ, καὶ ἡ τοῦ Δανιὴλ, εἰκοστηδευτέρα βίβλος τῆς παλαιᾶς διαθήκης. (ΛϚ′) Τῆς δὲ καινῆς διαθήκης, τὰ τέσσαρα μόνα εὐαγγελία· τὰ δὲ λοιπὰ ψευδεπίγραφα καὶ βλαβερὰ τυγχάνει. Ἔγραψαν καὶ Μανιχαῖοι κατὰ Θωμᾶν εὐαγγέλιον, ὅπερ εὐωδίᾳ τῆς εὐαγγελικῆς ἐπωνυμίας ἐπικεχρωσμένον, διαφθείρει τὰς ψυχὰς τῶν ἁπλουστέρων. Δέχου δὲ καὶ τὰς Πράξεις τῶν δώδεκα ἀποστόλων. Πρὸς τούτοις δὲ καὶ τὰς ἑπτὰ, Ἰακώβου, καὶ Πέτρου, καὶ Ἰωάννου, καὶ Ἰούδα καθολικὰς ἐπιστολάς· ἐπισφράγισμα δὲ τῶν πάντων, καὶ μαθητῶν τὸ τελευταῖον,	Lamentations,[192] and the Epistle;[193] then Ezekiel, and the Book of Daniel,[194] the twenty-second book of the Old Testament. (36) Then of the New Testament there are the four Gospels[195] only, for the rest have false titles[196] and are mischievous. The Manichæans also wrote a Gospel according to Thomas,[197] which being infused[198] with the fragrance of the evangelic title corrupts the souls of the simple sort. Receive also the Acts of the Twelve Apostles; and in addition to these the seven Catholic Letters of James, Peter,[199] John,[200] and Jude;[201] and as a seal upon them all, and the last work of the disciples, the fourteen Letters of

the introduction 'Jeremiah cries' (Ἱερεμίας βοᾷ) (*Homilia in occursum domini* 11; Reischl and Rupp 1967b: 452). Many fourth-century Greek and Latin fathers appealed to these verses as a prophecy of the incarnation of the Son of God (cf., e.g., the sections on Amphilochius of Iconium and Gregory of Nazianzus below).

[192] Cyril believed that Jeremiah the prophet wrote the work entitled 'the Lamentations'. In *Cat.* 13, he exposits the words of the creed concerning Christ's 'being crucified and buried'. When Cyril cites Lam 4:20, he introduces the book by noting that Jeremiah wrote things worthy of lamentations in 'the Lamentations' (*Cat.* 13.7). Cyril cites Lam. 4:20 a second time, introducing it with ὥς φησιν Ἱερεμίας ὁ προφήτης 'as Jeremiah the prophet says' (*Cat.* 17.34). He also cites Lam. 3:53, introducing it with πάλιν προφήτης ἄλλος λέγει 'Again another prophet says…' (*Cat.* 13.35). The words 'in a pit' or 'in a well' from this verse allude to Jeremiah going to the 'cistern house' or the 'house of the well' in Jer. 37:16 (LXX 44:16).

[193] Cyril does not use the Epistle of Jeremiah according to *Biblia Patristica*.

[194] Cyril probably conceived the title 'Daniel' as including Susanna and Bel and the Dragon, and, therefore, he probably thought this longer version of the book was canonical. In a treatment of OT witness to the Holy Spirit, Cyril introduces a quotation of Theodotion Daniel 13:45 ('God raised up the Holy Spirit upon a young lad') with the words 'for it has been written' (γέγραπται γάρ) (*Cat.* 16.31). In the next and concluding section of the same catechesis (16.32), Cyril says, 'And it was truly possible to select numerous texts from the Old Testament and to discourse more widely concerning the Holy Spirit.' Cyril, therefore, includes Susanna (i.e. Daniel 13) as part of the book of Daniel and therefore as part of the canon of the Old Testament. Cyril alludes to Bel and the Dragon (Dan. 14:36) in *Cat.* 14.25. He recounts the story of an angel transporting Habakkuk from Judea to Babylon as support for the teaching of Christ's ascension into heaven.

[195] The four Gospels are not even named, for they are well known by this time. Athanasius puts the four Gospels in the following order: Matthew, Mark, Luke, and John; cf. the section on Athanasius below.

[196] Lit. 'pseudepigrapha'.

[197] In *Cat.* 6.30–5, Cyril describes Manes and the Manichæans. In 6.31, he says, 'Let none read the Gospel according to Thomas: for it is the work not of one of the twelve Apostles, but of one of the three wicked disciples of Manes.' An apocryphal Gospel of Thomas is known to Hippolytus (*Haer.* 5.2) and Origen (*Hom. Luc.* 1; PG 13: 1801), but Cyril is the first to link its authorship to the Manichæans. See Gathercole 2012: 58.

[198] *NPNF²*: tinctured.

[199] In *Cat.* 10.15, Cyril may allude to 2 Peter 1:19. In *Cat.* 15.22, he may allude to 'righteous Lot' in 2 Peter 2:7. He does not cite this book directly.

[200] Cyril does not use 2–3 John according to *Biblia Patristica*.

[201] Cyril does not use Jude according to *Biblia Patristica*.

Text	Translation
τὰς Παύλου δεκατέσσαρας ἐπιστολάς. Τὰ δὲ λοιπὰ πάντα, ἐν δευτέρῳ κείσθω. Καὶ ὅσα [μὲν] ἐν ἐκκλησίαις μὴ ἀναγινώσκεται, ταῦτα μηδὲ κατὰ σαυτὸν ἀναγίνωσκε, καθὼς ἤκουσας. Καὶ τὰ μὲν περὶ τούτων, ταῦτα.	Paul.[202] But let all the rest[203] be put aside in a secondary rank.[204] And whatever books are not read in churches, these read not even by yourself, as you have heard me say. Thus much of these subjects.

The Canon List of Cyril

The Twenty-Two Books of the Old Testament
    Five Books of Moses
        Genesis
        Exodus
        Leviticus
        Numbers
        Deuteronomy
    The History Books
        Joshua
        Judges + Ruth
        1–2 Kingdoms   (= 1–2 Samuels)
        3–4 Kingdoms   (= 1–2 Kings)
        1–2 Paralipomenon   (= 1–2 Chronicles)
        1–2 Esdras   (= ?Esdras A and Esdras B or Ezra–Nehemiah?)
        Esther
    Five Books in Verse
        Job
        Book of Psalms
        Proverbs

[202] Cyril includes Hebrews within the fourteen letters of Paul as is standard among the fourth-century Eastern fathers (cf., e.g., Athanasius below).

[203] Cyril omits the book of Revelation from his list, which in a community in Palestine is not surprising (Junod 2005: 182). Further evidence that he probably considered the book outside of the canon comes from *Cat.* 15.16, where Cyril explains the great tribulation and the Antichrist who shall reign for three-and-a-half years. He says, 'We do not speak from *apocryphal writings* but from Daniel', and he goes on to cite Theodotion Daniel 7:25 and other passages from Daniel. In contrast, when Irenaeus teaches the same doctrine, he cites texts from Daniel (*Haer.* 5.25.3–4), and then in the next chapter says, 'In a still clearer light has John, in the Apocalypse, indicated to the Lord's disciples what shall happen in the last times…' (*Haer.* 5.26.1; cp. Hippolytus, *Antichr.* 31, 36, et al.; cf. *NPNF*², 109n4). However, in *Cat.* 1.4 Cyril does allude to the 'paradise' in Rev. 2:7. Furthermore, in *Cat.* 10.3 Cyril perhaps alludes to Rev. 5:5 when he says that the Christ is also called a Lion.

[204] Of the deuterocanonical books, Cyril uses sparingly Wisdom and Sirach. In *Cat.* 9.2, 16, Cyril cites Wis. 13:5 and attributes it to Solomon 'according to Solomon who says' (κατὰ τὸν Σολομῶντα τὸν λέγοντα). In *Cat.* 11.19, Cyril cites Sir. 1:30a and 3:22a without attribution or introductory formula. In *Cat.* 6.4, he cites Sir. 3:21–2a without attribution or introductory formula. He may allude to these works a few more times according to *Biblia Patristica*, but he only cites them in these places.

> Ecclesiastes
> Song of Songs
The Five Prophetic Books
> > The Book of the Twelve
> > Isaiah
> > Jeremiah + Baruch + Lamentations + the Letter
> > · Ezekiel
> > Daniel   (+ Susanna + Bel and Dragon)
The New Testament
> The Four Gospels
> The Acts of the Twelve Apostles
> The Seven Catholic Letters
> > James
> > Peter   (= 1–2 Peter)
> > John   (= 1–3 John)
> > Jude
> The Fourteen Letters of Paul

Cyril's canonical books: Cyril does not use the word 'canon' to describe the books in his list. Rather, he prefers to use the term 'acknowledged' or 'accepted' books (*homologoumena*), a term which Origen and Eusebius had used to designate the undisputed books among the churches. Cyril's list of NT books vis-à-vis Eusebius's list of books admits of no disputes. Eusebius's disputed Catholic Letters (James, 2 Peter, 2–3 John, Jude) are included in Cyril's canon list without question.

Cyril's second-tier books: Modern scholars dispute the interpretation of the phrase 'but let all the rest be put aside in a secondary rank' (*Cat.* 4.36). Some hold that Cyril maintains a trifold schema of religious writings: the canonical books, the books of 'second rank' (which may also be read or cited in churches), and the heretical apocryphal books.[205] Others think that Cyril holds only to a bifold schema of religious literature: the canonical books and the apocryphal books. He uses three terms to describe the second category: apocryphal writings (*Cat.* 4.33), doubtful writings (*Cat.* 4.33), and the phrase 'in second rank' with its instruction not to read in private anything that is not read publicly in the church (*Cat.* 4.36). The books read publicly in the church were already defined according to his canon list.[206]

The first option accedes with the trifold schema of religious literature observed in Athanasius and Rufinus. On the second option Cyril does something novel. Whereas Athanasius used the intermediate books for the instruction of catechumens, Cyril instructs them to stay away from all books not read in the church. Cyril's own use of the Wisdom of Solomon and Sirach present

---

[205] Ellis 1991: 19–21 (esp. 20–1).   [206] Junod 2005: 182–3.

a bit of inconsistency to his theory, but perhaps Cyril intended the prohibition for the catechumens alone.[207]

ATHANASIUS OF ALEXANDRIA

Athanasius (295/300–373) succeeded Alexander as bishop of Alexandria in 329 while still probably younger than thirty years of age.[208] His staunch and unwavering support for Nicene Christology brought him into repeated conflict with powerful churchmen, including Eusebius of Nicomedia, resulting in five separate periods of exile from his episcopal see: (1) 335–7 at Trier in Gaul; (2) 339–46 in Rome; (3) 356–62 in Egypt; (4) 362–3 in Egypt; and (5) 365–6 in the Alexandrian suburbs. Throughout his time in and out of Alexandria, Athanasius produced an extensive corpus of ecclesial and theological works. He may have written his *Contra gentes–De incarnatione Verbi* sometime between the Council of Nicaea (325) and his first exile at Trier. After his return from Trier, he wrote most of his anti-Arian works such as his *Discourses Against the Arians* I–II (ca. 340–1). Probably subsequent to his second exile he composed his *Discourse Against the Arians* III. More treatises followed: *The Synods* (ca. 359–62), *The Decrees of the Council of Nicaea* (ca. 350–6), *Life of Anthony* (ca. 356–62), *Defense of His Flight* (ca. 357–8), *History of the Arians* (ca. 357–8), and numerous letters throughout. His annual *Festal Letters* (329–73) announced the coming of Easter and discussed a variety of issues he felt compelled to address: the lifestyles of Christian communities, the cult of the martyrs, the sins of ordinary believers, the value of human sexuality, irregular ordinations, the proper celebration of Easter, the meaning of fasting, and the promise of eternal life. In *Ep. fest.* 39 (367), Athanasius wrote to the churches of Alexandria concerning the canon of Scripture.

Old Testament canon: Athanasius's OT canon list agrees mainly with the modern Jewish canon. However, he does not list Esther and he explicitly lists Baruch and the Letter of Jeremiah as part of the book of Jeremiah. Furthermore, there is some question about what he meant by 1 and 2 Esdras (reckoned as one book), but he probably intended the books in the Greek Old Testament with those names (Esdras A and Esdras B)—not Ezra and Nehemiah, respectively.

New Testament canon: Athanasius's NT canon list contains the twenty-seven books contained in today's New Testament. His list transposes the Catholic Epistles and the Pauline Epistles and includes the Revelation of John without acknowledgment of the disputes encompassing this book.

Studies: Ruwet 1952; Brakke 1994; Camplani 2003: 498–518; Junod 2003; Ernest 2004: 336–52; Aragione 2005; Brakke 2010.

---

[207] Gallagher 2012a: 29n62.
[208] For biography and bibliography on Athanasius, cf. Camplani 2014: 274–84.

Epistula festalis 39.15–21

Date: 367

Introduction: The text presented here constitutes the entire portion of this letter preserved in Greek (paragraphs 15–21). This text was not transmitted with the rest of the writings of Athanasius. Rather, because of its focus on the canon of Scripture, it was included and preserved with collections of canon law of Greek fathers from the fifth century.[209] The Council of Trullo (691) names Athanasius among other fathers who were the sources of its canonical collections. The fact that these patristic letters were included in these canonical collections 'conferred on them an authority to all without distinction, certainly not equal to that of the canons of synods and even less to that of councils, but all the same higher than that of a simple case law, as they all represent tradition, adorned by such great names'.[210] The Greek manuscript tradition (tenth–thirteenth centuries) names three of Athanasius's letters which were included in these canonical collections: the letter to the monk Ammoun, our excerpt from *Ep. fest.* 39, and the letter to Rufinien.[211]

Before the twentieth century all that was known of *Ep. fest.* 39 came from this Greek excerpt (it was also known from other versions such as Syriac). In the mid-fourth century Theodore of Tabennese (ca. 314–68) had a letter of Athanasius translated and transcribed into Egyptian (Coptic), since he thought that this letter had defined 'the sources of living water' (i.e., the canonical Scriptures in *Ep. fest.* 39.19).[212] Researchers have now published translations of the Coptic version, which present text for paragraphs 6–34. Scholars refer to 'fragments' of *Ep. fest.* 39 and the *Festal Letters* in general. 'Fragments' refer to excerpts from a festal letter, but one should not imagine, for example, a fragment of a Dead Sea Scroll. Rather, in some cases, these fragments are whole folios in manuscripts. Camplani has critically reconstructed the text of the letter on the basis of all of the available evidence, especially the Greek excerpt and the Coptic fragments or excerpts from seven different Coptic manuscripts, which modern scholars have grouped into two codices.[213] These fragments provide the essential context for understanding the canon list. Camplani helpfully summarizes the structure of the letter as follows:[214]

> 6–12: After a small lacuna, we read an elaborate discourse on Christ as the teacher. Athanasius declares that Christ is the only true teacher, the teacher by nature, while men are only such by teaching that comes from him.

---

[209] Ernest 2004: 336–7; Aragione 2005: 216–17.   [210] Joannou 1962: XIII–XIV.

[211] Aragione 2005: 217. For the texts of these three letters, cf. Joannou 1963: 2.71–6.

[212] Aragione 2005: 198; Lefort 1953: 178. For the French translation, see Lefort 1943: 206–7.

[213] A codex in this discussion is the modern scholar's construct. Three manuscripts constitute one codex, MONB.AS, while four other manuscripts constitute another codex, MONB.AT. Cf. Camplani 2003: 503; Aragione 2005: 202.

[214] Camplani 2003: 503–4; cf. Junod 2003: 199–200 for a similar analysis of Athanasius's flow of thought in this letter.

13–14: This characteristic of the Lord is, however, rejected by the Jews, and after them by the Arians, in turn followed by the Melitians.

15–16: Instead Christians celebrate Easter according to the traditions of the masters and fathers and the scriptures designed to educate fully. Athanasius fears that heretics may mislead the simple with the apocryphal books, and therefore feels the duty to proclaim the canon, even if the faithful know it.

17–20: Athanasius proposes the canon of the OT, the canon of the NT, and the list of books 'not canonized, but prescribed by the fathers to be read to those who have recently joined'.

21–3: Athanasius finds that in none of these categories of inspired books is there mention of apocryphal books. He starts at this point a long polemical attack against these books. Although he does not name them as Apocalypse of Elijah and the Ascension of Isaiah, he makes allusion to works named after these figures. These books contain useful lessons, but also ungodly things.

24–5: Instead the Scriptures are sufficient for the faith: they speak of the Father, Son, and Holy Spirit. They talk about the divinity and humanity of the Savior. They contain the doctrine of the resurrection and the final judgment. They, themselves, are able to refute heresies: the Manicheans, the Marcionites, the Montanists, Arians, and their parasites, the Melitians.

26–32: Against those who cite 1 Cor. 2:9 as evidence that the apostle Paul used and cited apocryphal literature, Athanasius argues at length that Paul was quoting the canonical Old Testament, though in a way that accorded more with the meaning than with the actual words.

33: Proclamation of the dates of the Easter season.

34: Episcopal List (incomplete?).

Athanasius, therefore, drafted this canon list (paras 15–21) to promote a unified piety around Jesus, the only true Teacher (paras 6–14), and to protect the church against heresy (paras 21–32).

Text[215]	Translation[216]
Περὶ τῶν θείων γραφῶν.	Concerning the Divine Scriptures
(15) Ἀλλ᾽ ἐπειδὴ περὶ μὲν τῶν αἱρετικῶν ἐμνήσθημεν ὡς νεκρῶν, περὶ δὲ ἡμῶν ὡς ἐχόντων πρὸς σωτηρίαν τὰς θείας γραφάς, καὶ φοβοῦμαι μήπως, ὡς ἔγραψε Κορινθίοις	(15) [...] But inasmuch as we have mentioned that the heretics[217] are dead but we have the Divine Scriptures for salvation, and I am afraid that, as Paul wrote to the Corinthians,[218] a few

[215] Joannou 1963: 2.71–6. For a presentation of the Coptic evidence and a translation of the Coptic version of *Ep. fest.* 39, cf. Aragione 2005: 201–16. The paragraph numbers are not from Joannou, but are taken from Camplani's translation, followed also by Brakke 2010.

[216] Brakke 2010: 60–1. We have slightly revised his translation and noted the instances throughout.

[217] In para. 25 of this letter, Athanasius names the Manichaeans, Marcion, the Montanists (= 'the people in Phrygia'), the Arians, and the Melitians as these heretics.

[218] Cf. 2 Cor. 11:1, 3, 4 et al. Researchers have noted how Athanasius speaks in the first person in this letter and how he establishes 'high protections' by imitating Paul in 2 Cor. 11:3 (para. 15) and Luke in Luke 1:1–4 (para. 16) as a rhetorical device (Junod 2003: 202–3; cf. Ernest 2004: 339).

Text	Translation
Παῦλος, ὀλίγοι τῶν ἀκεραίων ἀπὸ τῆς ἁπλότητος καὶ τῆς ἁγνότητος πλανηθῶσιν ἀπὸ τῆς πανουργίας τῶν ἀνθρώπων, καὶ λοιπὸν ἐντυγχάνειν ἑτέροις ἄρξονται τοῖς λεγομένοις ἀποκρύφοις, ἀπατώμενοι τῇ ὁμωνυμίᾳ τῶν ἀληθῶν βιβλίων, παρακαλῶ, ἀνέχεσθε, εἰ περὶ ὧν ἐπίστασθε, περὶ τούτων κἀγὼ μνημονεύων γράφω διά τε τὴν ἀνάγκην καὶ τὸ χρήσιμον τῆς ἐκκλησίας. (16) Μέλλων δὲ τούτων μνημονεύειν, χρήσομαι πρὸς σύστασιν τῆς ἐμαυτοῦ τόλμης τῷ τύπῳ τοῦ εὐαγγελιστοῦ Λουκᾶ, λέγων καὶ αὐτός· Ἐπειδή πέρ τινες ἐπεχείρησαν ἀνατάξασθαι ἑαυτοῖς τὰ λεγόμενα ἀπόκρυφα καὶ μῖξαι ταῦτα τῇ θεοπνεύστῳ γραφῇ, περὶ ἧς ἐπληροφορήθημεν, καθὼς παρέδοσαν τοῖς πατράσιν οἱ ἀπ᾽ ἀρχῆς αὐτόπται καὶ ὑπηρέται γενόμενοι τοῦ λόγου, ἔδοξε κἀμοί, προτραπέντι παρὰ γνησίων ἀδελφῶν καὶ μαθόντι ἄνωθεν ἑξῆς ἐκθέσθαι τὰ κανονιζόμενα καὶ παραδοθέντα, πιστευθέντα τε θεῖα εἶναι βιβλία, ἵνα ἕκαστος, εἰ μὲν ἠπατήθη, καταγνῷ τῶν πλανησάντων,	of the simple folk might be led astray from sincerity and purity through human deceit and might then begin to read other books, the so-called apocrypha,[219] deceived by their having the same names as the genuine[220] books, I exhort you to bear with me if, to remind you, I write about things that you already know, on account of the church's need and advantage. (16) As I begin to mention these things, in order to commend my audacity,[221] I will employ the example of Luke the evangelist[222] and say myself: Inasmuch as certain people have attempted to set in order for themselves the so-called apocryphal books[223] and to mix these with the divinely inspired Scripture,[224] about which we are convinced it is just as those who were eyewitnesses from the beginning and assistants of the Word handed down to our ancestors,[225] it seemed good to me, because I have been urged by genuine brothers and sisters and instructed from the beginning, to set forth[226] in order the books that are

[219] Athanasius will later be somewhat more explicit regarding the apocrypha that should be avoided. In para. 21, Athanasius probably alludes to two apocryphal works—the Book of Enoch and the Ascension of Isaiah—as examples of these kinds of works (cf. Camplani 2003: 512n22 and n23; cf. Junod 2003: 201). He also mentions an apocryphal work attributed to Moses (Testament of Moses?) in the same paragraph. In para. 26, Athanasius mentions an individual ('he' in Brakke 2010: 64, p. 50; a 'generic heretic' according to Camplani 2003: 515n34) who evidently believed that in 1 Cor. 2:9 Paul cites as Scripture ('as it is written') material from an apocryphal book. Early Christians proposed different solutions to this problem. Origen refers to the Secreti Eliae Prophetae, 'Apocrypha of the Prophet Elijah,' as the source for Paul's citation in 1 Cor. 2:9 in *Comm. Matt.* 23.37 (GCS 38, 250). The Apocalypse of Elijah does not contain the phrase in question, but there were probably a number of works attributed to Elijah from this period (Charlesworth 1983: 728). Jerome thought that the base of the citation in 1 Cor. 2:9 was from Isa 64:4 in *Comm. Isa.* 17 on Isa 64:4 (CCL 73A, 735). Athanasius rejects the heretic's position by claiming that Paul gathered the meaning of these words from the Prophet Isaiah in 29:18–19. The origin of Paul's citation remains unknown. Cf. Norelli (1995: 590–2), for adept commentary on this problem.

[220] Brakke 2010 uses 'genuine' for both ἀληθής (as here) and γνήσιος.

[221] Ernest observes that Athanasius presents his canon list to the churches with no argument, no conciliar pronouncement, and no authority of any kind. Rather he uses imitation of the apostles as a protection (σύστασις) of his boldness (τόλμη) (Ernest 2004: 339). Cf. Junod 2003: 203.

[222] Cf. Luke 1:1–4. For detailed analysis of the linguistic parallels between Luke 1:1–4 and this section of the letter, cf. Junod 2003: 204–5 and Ernest 2004: 339–40.

[223] Cf. n. 219 above.   [224] Cf. 2 Tim. 3:16.

[225] Or 'fathers'. Junod 2003 notes that mention of the 'fathers' is important since they constitute the link in the tradition between 'the witnesses from the beginning' and the church of Athanasius's day (p. 204).

[226] Ernest 2004 notes that where Luke (1:3) simply 'writes' (γράψαι), Athanasius sets forth 'a manifesto or statement of faith' (p. 339).

Text	Translation
ὁ δὲ καθαρὸς διαμείνας χαίρῃ πάλιν ὑπομιμνησκόμενος.	canonized,[227] transmitted,[228] and believed to be divine, so that those who have been deceived might condemn the persons who led them astray,[229] and those who have remained pure might rejoice to be reminded (of these things).[230]
(17) Ἔστι τοίνυν τῆς μὲν παλαιᾶς διαθήκης βιβλία τῷ ἀριθμῷ τὰ πάντα εἰκοσιδύο, τοσαῦτα γάρ, ὡς ἤκουσα, καὶ τὰ στοιχεῖα τὰ παρ᾽ Ἑβραίοις εἶναι παραδέδοται, τῇ δὲ τάξει καὶ τῷ ὀνόματι ἔστιν ἕκαστον οὕτως· πρῶτον Γένεσις· εἶτα Ἔξοδος· εἶτα Λευιτικόν· καὶ μετὰ τοῦτο Ἀριθμοί· καὶ λοιπόν, τὸ Δευτερονόμιον· ἑξῆς δὲ τούτοις ἐστὶν Ἰησοῦς ὁ τοῦ Ναυῆ· καὶ Κριταί· καὶ μετὰ τοῦτο ἡ Ῥούθ· καὶ πάλιν ἑξῆς, Βασιλειῶν βιβλία τέσσαρα· καὶ τούτων τὸ μὲν πρῶτον καὶ δεύτερον εἰς ἓν βιβλίον ἀριθμεῖται, τὸ δὲ τρίτον καὶ τέταρτον ὁμοίως εἰς ἕν· μετὰ δὲ ταῦτα, Παραλειπομένων πρῶτον καὶ δεύτερον,	(17) There are, then, belonging to the Old Testament in number a total of twenty-two, for, as I have heard, it has been handed down[231] that this is the number of the letters in the Hebrew alphabet.[232] In order[233] and by name they are as follows: first, Genesis; then, Exodus; then, Leviticus; and after this,[234] Numbers; and finally Deuteronomy. After these is Joshua, the son of Nun; and Judges; and after this, Ruth;[235] and again, next four books of Kingdoms,[236] the first and second of these being reckoned as one book,[237] and the third and fourth likewise being one.[238] After these are First and Second Paraleipomenon,[239] likewise reckoned as one

[227] For a discussion of this term in Athanasius, cf. the summary of Athanasius's canon below.

[228] In addition to describing these books as 'canonized', Athanasius describes them as 'transmitted'. The Greek word has the meaning 'transmit or hand down as a tradition' (cf. Lampe 1961: s.v. παραδίδωμι). Earlier in this paragraph, he referred to the eyewitnesses and servants of the Word as transmitting to 'the ancestors' the tradition from the beginning. In para. 20, Athanasius refers to the books to be read as 'prescribed by the ancestors'. These intermediate figures come after the apostles and before Athanasius and are significant to the transmission of the tradition related to the canonized books.

[229] Cf. n. 217 above.

[230] Luke aims to inform his already catechized readers, while Athanasius writes so that those who have been misled might condemn those who led them astray and those who were not misled might rejoice at the reminder (Ernest 2004: 339–40).

[231] Cf. n. 228 above for the meaning of παραδίδωμι. Athanasius claims that the twenty-two books corresponding to the letters in the Hebrew alphabet is a tradition he has heard. Given his use of the word παραδίδωμι, he means that the ancestors or fathers passed this tradition down to him.

[232] For the tradition of twenty-two books corresponding to twenty-two letters in the Hebrew alphabet, see, e.g., Origen above for details.

[233] Melito also claimed to provide the 'order' of the Old Testament books. Cf. above for his list and discussion.

[234] Perhaps 'after this [i.e. Leviticus]' stresses that Numbers comes after Leviticus since there are other known lists where Leviticus follows Numbers. Cf. the list of Melito above and ch. 4 for the Mommsen Catalogue.

[235] Athanasius reckons Ruth as a separate book from Judges, thus preserving the number of books as twenty-two, since he will later omit Esther. For details of an example of Ruth included with Judges, cf. the section on Origen above.

[236] Brakke 2010: Kings.

[237] In the Jewish and English Bible traditions these are the books of 1–2 Samuel.

[238] In the Jewish and English Bible traditions these are the books of 1–2 Kings.

[239] Brakke 2010: Chronicles. Paralipomenon ('The Things Omitted') is the title of these books in Greek. In the Jewish and English Bible traditions these are the books of 1–2 Chronicles.

Text	Translation
ὁμοίως εἰς ἓν βιβλίον πάλιν ἀριθμούμενα· εἶτα Ἔσδρα πρῶτον καὶ δεύτερον ὁμοίως εἰς ἕν· μετὰ δὲ ταῦτα, βίβλος Ψαλμῶν· καὶ ἑξῆς Παροιμίαι· εἶτα Ἐκκλησιαστής· καὶ Ἄσμα ᾀσμάτων· πρὸς τούτοις ἔστι καὶ Ἰώβ· καὶ λοιπόν, Προφῆται, οἱ μὲν δώδεκα εἰς ἓν βιβλίον ἀριθμούμενοι, εἶτα Ἡσαΐας, Ἰερεμίας, καὶ σὺν αὐτῷ Βαρούχ, Θρῆνοι καὶ ἐπιστολή, καὶ μετ᾽ αὐτὸν Ἰεζεκιὴλ καὶ Δανιήλ. Ἄχρι τούτων τὰ τῆς παλαιᾶς διαθήκης ἵσταται. (18) Τὰ δὲ τῆς καινῆς πάλιν οὐκ ὀκνητέον εἰπεῖν. Ἔστι γὰρ ταῦτα· Εὐαγγέλια τέσσαρα, κατὰ Ματθαῖον, κατὰ Μάρκον, κατὰ Λουκᾶν καὶ κατὰ Ἰωάννην· εἶτα μετὰ ταῦτα Πράξεις ἀποστόλων, καὶ ἐπιστολαὶ καθολικαὶ καλούμεναι τῶν ἀποστόλων ἑπτά, οὕτως· Ἰακώβου μὲν μία, Πέτρου δὲ δύο, εἶτα Ἰωάννου	book; then First and Second Esdras, likewise as one.[240] After these is the book of Psalms; and then Proverbs; then Ecclesiastes and the Song of Songs. After these is Job;[241] and finally the Prophets, the Twelve being reckoned as one book; then Isaiah; Jeremiah, and with it, Baruch, Lamentations, and the Letter;[242] and after it, Ezekiel and Daniel.[243] To this point are the books of the Old Testament.[244] (18) Again, one should not hesitate to name the books of the New Testament. For these are the four Gospels, Matthew, Mark, Luke, and John; then after these, Acts of the Apostles and seven letters,[245] called catholic, by the apostles, namely: one by James; two by Peter; then three by John; and after these, one by Jude. After

[240] Athanasius introduces 2 Esdras (Neh.) 18:10 in para. 33 of this festal letter with 'the word of Esdras' (Brakke 2010: 66). In *Apol. Const.* 18, Athanasius depends on the wording of 1 Esdr. 5, not 2 Esdr. 3. Ernest notes that 'the two books of Esdras do not correspond to Ezra and Nehemiah; rather 2 Esdras translates Ezra–Nehemiah, while 1 Esdras is a Greek work covering some of the same ground; but Athanasius, who prefers 1 Esdras, probably did not know that' (Ernest 2004: 342n110 and pp. 239–40).

[241] In Melito's list and the list of the Synod of Laodicea, Job follows Song of Songs and appears before the prophetic books.

[242] Athanasius includes explicitly Baruch, Lamentations, and the Epistle of Jeremiah with the book of Jeremiah. His list resembles that of the Synod of Laodicea and to a lesser degree the first two lists of Epiphanius, which include Baruch, Lamentations, and the Epistle of Jeremiah with Jeremiah. Origen had earlier included Lamentations and the Epistle of Jeremiah but not Baruch unless the latter was part of the work entitled 'the Epistle'. Cf. Origen above for details. Athanasius makes one reminiscence to Lamentations 3:27 (*Ep. Amun.* 68). Athanasius cites Baruch five times, and in each case he attributes the work to Baruch or the book bearing his name—not Jeremiah. He cites Baruch 3:12 twice (*C. Ar.* 1.19; 2.42; in each case, Athanasius attributes 'Fountain of wisdom' to the book of Baruch [ἐν δὲ τῷ Βαροὺχ γέγραπται] and Baruch, respectively), Baruch 3:36 (*C. Ar.* 2.49; according to Athanasius, Baruch 3:36, as part of the Scriptures, teaches that the Son is not ranked among creatures), Baruch 4:20 (*C. Ar.* 1.12; Athanasius introduces Baruch 4:20 and 4:22 with 'And Baruch was writing' [ὁ δὲ Βαροὺχ ἔγραφε]), and Baruch 4:22 (*C. Ar.* 1.12). He never uses the Letter of Jeremiah (Ernest 2004: 346–7).

[243] Athanasius cites Theodotion's version of Susannah 1:42 with the formula ἐν δὲ τῷ Δανιήλ, 'in Daniel' (*C. Ar.* 1.13). He introduces a citation of Theodotion's Bel 1:5 with the phrase ὡς Δανιὴλ εἴρηκε τῷ Ἀστυάγῃ, 'as Daniel spoke to Astyages' (*C. Ar.* 3.30), but such wording does not necessarily imply that Athanasius considered Bel to be a part of the book of Daniel (cf. Ernest 2004: 347n130).

[244] The book of Esther has been omitted from this list of canonical books but will be included in the 'to be read' category in para. 20 below. On the omission of Esther, Athanasius agrees with the earlier list of Melito and the later list of Gregory of Nazianzus (cf. these lists in the present chapter for details); cf. also the list of Amphilochius of Iconium below; he lists Esther with an acknowledgement of the issue.

[245] Athanasius includes all seven catholic letters in his list without dispute (cp. Cyril of Jerusalem's list above). Cf. the section on Eusebius above for a record of the disputes over James, Jude, 2 Peter, and 2–3 John. Cf. below for Amphilochius's record of the dispute over Jude, 2 Peter, and 2–3 John, while he regarded James as undisputed.

Text	Translation
τρεῖς, καὶ μετὰ ταύτας Ἰούδα μία· πρὸς τούτοις Παύλου ἀποστόλου εἰσὶν ἐπιστολαὶ δεκατέσσαρες, τῇ τάξει γραφόμεναι οὕτως· πρώτη, πρὸς Ῥωμαίους, εἶτα πρὸς Κορινθίους δύο, καὶ μετὰ ταῦτα πρὸς Γαλάτας, καὶ ἑξῆς πρὸς Ἐφεσίους, εἶτα πρὸς Φιλιππησίους, καὶ πρὸς Κολοσσαεῖς, καὶ μετὰ ταῦτα πρὸς Θεσσαλονικεῖς δύο, καὶ ἡ πρὸς Ἑβραίους, καὶ εὐθὺς πρὸς μὲν Τιμόθεον δύο, πρὸς δὲ Τίτον μία, καὶ τελευταία ἡ πρὸς Φιλήμονα μία· καὶ πάλιν Ἰωάννου Ἀποκάλυψις.	these there are fourteen letters by the apostle[246] Paul, written in this order: first to the Romans; then two to the Corinthians; and after these, to the Galatians; and next to the Ephesians; then to the Philippians and to the Colossians; and after these, two to the Thessalonians; and that to the Hebrews;[247] and additionally, two to Timothy, one to Titus, and finally that to Philemon, one. And again,[248] the Revelation of John.[249]
(19) Ταῦτα πηγαὶ τοῦ σωτηρίου, ὥστε τὸν διψῶντα ἐμφορεῖσθαι τῶν ἐν τούτοις λογίων· ἐν τούτοις μόνοις τὸ τῆς εὐσεβείας διδασκαλεῖον εὐαγγελίζεται· μηδεὶς τούτοις ἐπιβαλλέτω, μηδὲ τούτων ἀφαιρείσθω τι. Περὶ δὲ τούτων ὁ κύριος Σαδδουκαίους μὲν ἐδυσώπει, λέγων· ʻΠλανᾶσθε μὴ εἰδότες τὰς γραφὰς μηδὲ τὴν δύναμιν αὐτῶν᾽, τοῖς δὲ Ἰουδαίοις παρήνει· ʻἘρευνᾶτε τὰς γραφάς, ὅτι αὐταί εἰσιν αἱ μαρτυροῦσαι περὶ ἐμοῦ᾽.	(19) These are the springs of salvation, so that someone who thirsts may be satisfied by the words they contain. In these books alone[250] the teaching of piety is proclaimed. Let no one add or subtract anything from them.[251] Concerning them the Lord put the Sadducees to shame when he said, ʻYou err because you do not know the Scriptures or their meaning᾽ (Matt 22:29//Mark 12:24), and he reproved the Jews, ʻSearch the Scriptures, for it is they that testify to me᾽ (John 5:39).
(20) Ἀλλ᾽ ἕνεκά γε πλείονος ἀκριβείας προστίθημι καὶ τοῦτο γράφων ἀναγκαίως, ὡς ὅτι ἔστι καὶ ἕτερα βιβλία τούτων ἔξωθεν, οὐ κανονιζόμενα μέν, τετυπωμένα δὲ παρὰ τῶν πατέρων ἀναγινώσκεσθαι τοῖς ἄρτι	(20) But for the sake of greater accuracy, I add this, writing from necessity. There are other books, outside of[252] the preceding, which have not been canonized,[253] but have been prescribed[254] by the ancestors[255] to be read to

[246] Brakke 2010 omitted ʻapostle᾽ from his translation.

[247] Aragione 2005: 210 notes that in the Coptic tradition Hebrews comes after the two letters to the Corinthians. Athanasius does not mention the dispute over Hebrews as Eusebius did (cf. section on Eusebius above.). Later (ca. 380), Amphilochius would mention the dispute over Hebrews, even though he would accept it without reservation (cf. section on Amphilochius below for details).

[248] Brakke 2010: ʻbesides᾽. Athanasius uses πάλιν ʻagain᾽ purposefully, since he probably refers to the same John here that also wrote the Gospel and the three letters mentioned earlier in the list.

[249] Athanasius lists John's Apocalypse without any notice of dispute, though other authors spanning the fourth century acknowledged such disputes, on which cf. the sections in this chapter on Eusebius and on Amphilochius for details.

[250] The bishop believes his list of canonical books to be an exclusive list of books which preach the instruction of piety.

[251] Cf. Deut 4:2, 13:1 (12:32 EV); Rev 22:18–19. In the context of his canon list of twenty-two books, Josephus (*C. Ap.* 42) likewise makes allusion to Deut 4:2 (cf. ch. 2 on Josephus), as does the Letter of Aristeas 311 with regard to the fidelity to the wording of the Greek translation of the Law.

[252] Brakke 2010: ʻin addition to᾽. Athanasius's expression resembles Origen's ἔξω τούτων ʻoutside of these᾽, which he applied to the book of Maccabees in his canon list (cf. section on Origen above for details).

[253] Cf. the summary of meaning of this term in Athanasius below.

[254] Brakke 2010: ʻappointed᾽. The books in this paragraph are not ʻcanonical᾽ or ʻapocryphal᾽ but ʻprescribed to be read to catechumens᾽. For a discussion of this term in Athanasius, cf. the summary of Athanasius's books to be read below.

[255] Or ʻfathers᾽. Cf. nn. 225, 228, and 231 above for explanation of this term and the function of these ʻfathers᾽ in the argument of Athanasius.

Text	Translation
προσερχομένοις καὶ βουλομένοις κατηχεῖσθαι τὸν τῆς εὐσεβείας λόγον· Σοφία Σολομῶντος καὶ Σοφία Σιρὰχ καὶ Ἐσθὴρ καὶ Ἰουδὶθ καὶ Τωβίας καὶ Διδαχὴ καλουμένη τῶν ἀποστόλων καὶ ὁ Ποιμήν.	those who newly join[256] us and want to be instructed in the word of piety: the Wisdom of Solomon,[257] the Wisdom of Sirach,[258] Esther,[259] Judith,[260] Tobit,[261] the book called Teaching of the Apostles,[262] and the Shepherd.[263]

[256] Athanasius refers to new converts, those willing to be catechized or instructed with regard to the word of piety. Ernest notes that Athanasius assigned these 'other books' to be read to the new converts who need simple instruction in morality and monotheism (Ernest 2004: 343–4). In para. 28 of the letter, Athanasius says, '...but instead to place before them the teaching they [i.e. catechumens] need: what will teach them how to hate sin and to abandon idolatry as an abomination...' (trans. Brakke 2010).

[257] Ernest notes that Athanasius does not differentiate with citation formulas the books categorized as canonical and the books prescribed to be read to catechumens (Ernest 2004: 80; 359n139). In *Apol. sec.* 3.4 Athanasius introduces two citations—Prov. 19:5 and Wis. 1:11, respectively—with one formula (τὸ ἐν ταῖς ἁγίαις γραφαῖς γεγραμμένον, 'what is written in the Holy Scriptures'). Although the apology is from 357, the encyclical letter containing these citations is from 339. Leemans (1997) concluded that Athanasius did not use Wisdom differently than the other canonical books but 'valued the writings of both categories on an equal level' (p. 368).

[258] In *C. Ar.* 2.79, Athanasius introduces a long citation from Sir. 1:9–10 with ὥσπερ οὖν καὶ ὁ τοῦ Σιράχ φησιν, 'therefore just as also the Son of Sirach says'. In this context, Athanasius alludes to Wis. 6:24 and Prov. 14:16. He cites Eccl. 8:1 and 'the apostle' Paul at 1 Cor. 1:21. From this instance and others like it, Ernest concludes that Athanasius cites Sir. 1:9–10 in the same way as canonical Scripture (Ernest 2004: 351n139). Leemans 2003 concluded that Athanasius's 'theoretical position' on the canon differed from his 'practical use' of books (pp. 276–7). Leemans attributes this situation not to inconclusiveness or incoherence on the part of Athanasius, but to the process of canonization as full of uncertainties and far from closed in the second half of the fourth century.

[259] In *Ep. fest.* 4.2, Athanasius alludes to Esth. 4:16 and establishes Esther as an example of one who saved her people through fasting and prayer to God (PG 26: 1377; text preserved in Syriac, translated into Latin in PG; Eng. trans. *NPNF*² 4:516). Cf. *Ep. fest.* 10.11 for an allusion to Esth. 3:10–11 and 9:20–1. Cf. Lorenz 1986: 62 ln. 1 in Syriac; Engl. trans. *NPNF*² 4:531–2. Other than these references, Athanasius does not use Esther.

[260] In the works of Athanasius studied by Ernest 2004, the bishop quotes five words of Jdt 8:16 (οὐκ ἔστιν ὡς ἄνθρωπος ὁ θεός 'God is not as a human') on five occasions (*C. Ar.* 1.21, 27, 28 (2x) 2.35). Athanasius also alludes to Jdt 9:1 and 13:7–8 in *Ep. fest.* 4.2 and presents Judith as an example of one who overcame enemies through fasting and prayers (PG 26: 1377; text preserved in Syriac, translated into Latin in PG; Eng. trans. *NPNF*² 4:516). Other than these references, Athanasius does not use Judith.

[261] In *Apol. sec.* 11.2, Athanasius cites four words from Tobit 12:7 introducing it as Scripture (ὡς γέγραπται, 'as it is written'). Cf. Opitz 1938: 96 ln. 9. Ernest 2004 provides a few more references from Tobit (3:3 [*Ep. Ors.* 1], 4:14 [*Vit. Ant.* 3.1], and 4:18 [*Apol. Const.* 17]) in Athanasius's writings. Otherwise, Athanasius does not use Tobit in his writings.

[262] Ernest is not aware of any use of the Didache in the writings of Athanasius (Ernest 2004: 350–1).

[263] Athanasius's position on the Shepherd has been a matter of dispute. Both here and in *Decr.* 18.3.2 (ca. 350) he excludes the Shepherd from the canon. In *Inc.* 3.1 (ca. 326–8), Athanasius calls the Shepherd 'most useful' (ὠφελιμωτάτη) and cites 26:1 in parallel with Gen. 1:1 to show that God is the creator of all things. Some scholars have considered this latter passage evidence that Athanasius maintained a wider canon (at least at one point in his life) than our festal letter would indicate; cf. Ehrman 1983: 18–19. Ernest argues from *Inc.* 3.1 that Athanasius does not use citation formulas to differentiate between the canonical books and the books to be read (Ernest 2004: 80–81n51). For the adjective 'useful' (ὠφέλιμος) in a description of non-canonical religious literature, see the section on Epiphanius below.

Text	Translation
(21) Καὶ ὅμως, ἀγαπητοί, κἀκείνων κανονιζομένων, καὶ τούτων ἀναγινωσκομένων, οὐδαμοῦ τῶν ἀποκρύφων μνήμη, ἀλλὰ αἱρετικῶν ἐστιν ἐπίνοια, γραφόντων μὲν ὅτε θέλουσιν αὐτά, χαριζομένων δὲ καὶ προστιθέντων αὐτοῖς χρόνους, ἵνα ὡς παλαιὰ προφέροντες, πρόφασιν ἔχωσιν ἀπατᾶν ἐκ τούτου τοὺς ἀκεραίους.	(21) Nevertheless, beloved the former books are canonized; the latter are (only) read; and there is no mention of the apocryphal books.[264] Rather, (the category of apocrypha) is an invention of heretics, who write these books whenever they want and then generously add time to them, so that, by publishing them as if they were ancient, they might have a pretext for deceiving the simple folk [...].

The Canon List of Athanasius

The Twenty-Two Books of the Old Testament
 Genesis
 Exodus
 Leviticus
 Numbers
 Deuteronomy
 Joshua
 Judges
 Ruth
 1–2 Kingdoms   (= 1–2 Samuels)
 3–4 Kingdoms   (= 1–2 Kings)
 1–2 Paralipomenon   (= 1–2 Chronicles)
 1–2 Esdras
 Book of Psalms
 Proverbs
 Ecclesiastes
 Song of Songs
 Job
 The Prophets
  The Twelve
  Isaiah
  Jeremiah + Baruch + Lamentations + the Letter
  Ezekiel
  Daniel   (+ Susanna + ?Bel and Dragon?)
The New Testament
 The Four Gospels
  Matthew
  Mark
  Luke
  John

---

[264] Athanasius probably intends that the ancestors or fathers did not mention the apocryphal books, as he has claimed they mentioned the canonical books and the books to be read.

Acts of the Apostles
Seven Catholic Letters
    James
    1–2 Peter
    1–3 John
    Jude
Fourteen Letters of Paul
    Romans
    1–2 Corinthians
    Galatians
    Ephesians
    Philippians
    Colossians
    1–2 Thessalonians
    Hebrews
    1–2 Timothy
    Titus
    Philemon
Revelation of John
The Books to be Read
    Wisdom of Solomon
    Wisdom of Sirach
    Esther
    Judith
    Tobit
    Didache
    Shepherd
Apocryphal Books
    Book of Enoch (?)
    Ascension of Isaiah (?)
    Testament of Moses (?)
    Apocalypse of Elijah (?)

Athanasius's canon: Athanasius had a fixed canon as shown from *Ep. fest.* 39 (367) and perhaps as early as *Decr.* 18.3.2 (ca. 350). However, he continued to cite religious literature not found in his canon list in similar ways to how he cited canonical literature.[265] Éric Junod comments that Athanasius uses the word 'canonized' as a received technical term, which requires no definition, though this letter contains the first attested use of κανονίζειν ('to include in the canon') in reference to the books of Scripture. But Athanasius's failure to cite any documentation suggests that he was not basing himself on a catalogue previously set down in writing.[266] In *Decr.* 18.3.2, Athanasius used the noun κανών

---

[265] See Ehrman 1983: 18–19 and Leemans 2003: 276–7. Cf. the Introduction for a brief discussion of this issue.
[266] Junod 2003: 205 with n25.

'canon' to indicate that the Shepherd of Hermas is not in the canon (μὴ ὂν ἐκ τοῦ κανόνος). Interestingly, in the same passage Athanasius introduces a citation of the Shepherd with γέγραπται ('it has been written').[267]

Questions remain regarding (1) Athanasius's motivation to promulgate this list; (2) his detractors; (3) his sources for this list; and (4) the effect of this list on other books used by the Alexandrian church. Recent researchers have noted that Athanasius's list is 'apodictic' and 'prescriptive' rather than descriptive of 'alternative understandings or variegated historical actualities', as Eusebius's earlier list had been.[268] David Brakke views Athanasius's 'bounded and unchangeable "episcopal canon"' as replacing 'the flexible and indeterminate "academic canon"' of Christian teachers like Origen or Eusebius.[269] However, Ernest accedes with Westcott's conclusion that Athanasius's list reflects his understanding of the canon that he had inherited from his Christian Alexandrian predecessors rather than a revision of Eusebius's list.[270] Athanasius drafted the canon list to promote a unified instruction of piety around Jesus and to protect the church against heresy. He claims to be transmitting what was handed down by the ancestors of the Alexandrian church. The inevitable consequences of this action were that Eusebius's NT list would be revised and the competing lists of heretics in Alexandria would be stamped out. Books such as Enoch and the Testament of Moses would be relegated to apocryphal status and would not be considered canonical within wider Eastern Orthodoxy.[271] The effect on the deuterocanonical books is less clear and is addressed in the next paragraph.

Athanasius's books to be read: Athanasius appears to be the first to develop an explicit schema for a threefold categorization of religious literature. However, he was not alone in categorizing some religious books as neither canonical nor apocryphal but useful and worthy of study.[272] Later patristic authors such as Epiphanius, Rufinus, Amphilochius, and Jerome had similar categories.[273] In *Ep. fest.* 39.20, Athanasius claims that the middle category, 'the books to be read to catechumens', was prescribed by the fathers of the church in Alexandria. The churches were to use these books to instruct or catechize the new converts in the word of piety. In para. 19, only the canonical books proclaim 'the teaching of piety' (τὸ τῆς εὐσεβείας διδασκαλεῖον). The bishop, therefore, envisions the middle category of books not proclaiming the teaching of piety but being

---

[267] Cf. Metzger 1987: 289–93, for an overview of the history of the term κανών 'canon'.

[268] Cf. Ernest 2004: 342–3, esp. n111 and n112. Cf. above for the list of Eusebius.

[269] Cf. Brakke 2010: 55.

[270] Cf. Ernest 2004: 342–3n111. For the opinion of Westcott, cf. Westcott 1896: 456n3.

[271] The *de facto* canonicity of today's Ethiopian Orthodoxy includes Enoch within the canon.

[272] Ellis 1991 sees the distinction between useful and canonical Scripture in Origen (who implicitly ascribed it to Jews) and Josephus, and with less probability, in the Prologue to Ben Sira (pp. 17–18).

[273] Cf. the respective sections in this chapter and in ch. 4. Cf. Gallagher 2012a: 27–9 and the literature noted there for a discussion of the history of this threefold categorization of religious literature (i.e. canonical, ecclesiastical, and apocryphal).

useful in the instruction of new converts in the word of piety. Although Athanasius described these books positively, he used them comparatively fewer times than the books he designated canonical.[274]

Athanasius's apocryphal books: For Athanasius the first two categories of books are related to the instruction and word of piety. The apocryphal books are not. The church has traditionally not used them; on the contrary, they are the inventions of heretics, who 'added time' to these books to give them the appearance of antiquity (para. 21). The bishop appears to have made no use of the books he named apocryphal, nor did he think the apostles had done so.[275]

SYNOD OF LAODICEA

The Synod of Laodicea (SoL) probably occurred sometime between 342 and 381. All of the Greek and Latin canonical collections of this synod have as part of their title 'the canons of the Synod in Laodicea of Phrygia'.[276] Theodoret of Cyrrhus (ca. 430) mentions the synod gathered in Laodicea of Phrygia (i.e. north central Asia Minor).[277] Thus 430 is the *terminus ante quem* for the synod.[278] The number of bishops who attended is not clear. Joannou notes the

[274] Cf. Ernest's Appendix B, 380–418, in which all of the deuterocanonical and noncanonical references are listed on one page, while the references to the canonical books comprise thirty-seven pages. Ernest 2004 considers Athanasius's use of the books from the middle category as 'a harbinger of the instability of his halfway category: these books were destined either to be accepted as canonical or not to be read as Scripture at all.... The distinctions that scholars have noted between Scripture and canon, and between different senses of canon, were eroding' (p. 351n141). The following centuries confirm Ernest's conclusion regarding the destiny of these books. However, the threefold categorization of books appears to have strongest support in the fourth century and does not appear to be eroding at this time.

[275] Cf. n. 219 above. Ernest (2004) holds that if Athanasius had paid much attention to Jude 14–15, he would not have been able to argue against the books of Enoch in the way he did (p. 347n131). However, while recognizing this distinct possibility, Athanasius may have been concerned only where the apostles used γέγραπται, 'it is written', as Paul did in 1 Cor. 2:9.

[276] Cp. also the west Syrian *Synodicon* in Vööbus 1975: 115. Wagschal (2015) notes that the west Syrian tradition adopted the Antiochian corpus (though he prefers to call it the 'Nicene corpus' on pp. 33–4) ca. 500 (p. 35).

[277] PG 82: 613. In his commentary on Colossians 2:18, Theodoret mentioned the Synod in Laodicea of Phrygia to show that some in the churches were worshipping angels. Furthermore, he reported its decision to prohibit the praying to angels. Canon 35 of SoL clearly prohibits the worship of angels.

[278] We cannot date the synod precisely. Wagschal (2015) notes the uncertain date of the synod but dates it before 380 (p. 33). Joannou 1962: 128 believes that the internal contents of the canons (e.g. the liturgical prescriptions of canons 14–23 and 25–30) situate the synod towards the end of the second half of the fourth century. For the date ca. 363, probably because the Photinians, a heretical group, are mentioned in canon 7, see Metzger 1987: 210. Photinus of Sirmium was condemned as an Arian by the Synod of Antioch (344 CE) and he died in exile in 366; cf. Joannou 1962: 127n5. Perhaps the Synod gathered right before he died to rule on this heresy among other matters. For the view that considers the mention of the Photinians in canon 7 suspect and opts for a later date within the fourth century, see Joannou 1962: 127.

Decretum Gratiani (ca. 1200), which says the synod consisted of twenty-two bishops.[279]

The individual, original conciliar collection is not preserved.[280] The oldest collection of conciliar decrees, called the *Corpus canonum Oriente* (*Syntagma Antiochenae* or *Syntagma canonum*) was probably compiled in Antioch ca. 342–81. As a chronological collection, it included the canons of the synods of Ancyra (ca. 314), Neocaesarea (314/25), Gangra, Antioch, and Laodicea (343–80). Eventually, the canons of the general Councils of Nicaea (325), Constantinople (381), and Chalcedon (451) were included in it. The *Corpus canonum* furnished the foundation of all later Byzantine canonical collections.[281] It is known chiefly through the later compilations of Dionysius Exiguus (ca. 500, or as late as 523) and John Scholasticus (ca. 550; patriarch of Constantinople 565–77).

In Rome, Dionysius used the *Corpus canonum* for his base to which he added later canons from the Council of Carthage. He also compiled many papal decrees. Later he combined the canons of the councils and the papal decrees into one work, which modern scholars refer to as the *Collectio Dionysiana*. Together, the canons of the fourth-century Eastern Greek councils and the papal decretals form the foundation of Western Latin canon law.[282]

John Scholasticus, a priest from Antioch, compiled his *Synagoge of 50 titles* (*Collectio L titulorum* or simply *Coll50*) ca. 550. John based his collection on a previous but now lost collection known as *Collectio LX titulorum*, the basis of which was the Greek conciliar canons from the previous councils. This part of the collection was very similar to Dionysius's collection. If Dionysius's innovation was to add papal decrees to church law, John's was to include important patristic letters such as the so-called 'canonical letters' of Basil (*Letters* 199 and 217). John's collection was the oldest and most important collection of canon law in the East and it occupies as significant a place as Dionysius's collection in the West.[283]

Both collections of SoL contain fifty-nine canons.[284] Joannou noted that Dionysius's canon four is the fifth of John Scholasticus's collection and John's fifth is the fourth in Dionysius's collection.[285] The only major difference

---

[279] Joannou 1962: 127n2. Metzger (1987) notes that one account says there were thirty-two members in attendance, while another account had only twenty-four, but he did not cite his sources (p. 210).

[280] Pennington 2007: 393. For the most recent, accessible history of Byzantine canon law, see Wagschall 2015: 32–50.

[281] Pennington 2007: 393.   [282] ibid.: 396–7.   [283] ibid.: 399.

[284] Some scholars divide the original canon 59 into canon 59 and canon 60 (e.g. Zahn 1888–92: 2.197ff; Markschies 2012: 127; see discussion below). On this scheme, canon 60 is the actual list of books of the Old and New Testaments, while canon 59 contains only the prefatory material.

[285] Joannou 1962: 128n9.

between these collections pertains to canon 59, the list of the canonical books (see discussion below).

Old Testament canon: The canon list of SoL agrees with the twenty-two books of the Jewish canon except that it includes Baruch and the Epistle of Jeremiah together with Jeremiah as the twentieth book. SoL included Esther, and it excluded the deuterocanonical books.

New Testament canon: SoL's list of NT books contains twenty-six of the twenty-seven books of the traditional New Testament. It omits the Revelation of John, characteristic of Eastern lists from the middle of the fourth century (cf., e.g., the section on Cyril of Jerusalem above). It includes all of the Catholic Letters in their Eastern order after Acts. It, therefore, agrees with many of the Eastern lists from the second half of the fourth century.

Studies: Zahn 1888–92: II,1.195–202; Jonkers 1954: 86–96; Joannou 1962: I,2.127–9; Markschies 2012: 126–8; Wagschal 2015.

Synod of Laodicea Canon 59

Date: before 380

Introduction: Although the *Corpus canonum* is no longer extant, the collections of Dionysius and John Scholasticus preserve canon 59, which contains a ruling on the canon of Scripture. The original form of canon 59 is a matter of dispute, since only the Greek collection contains the list of books, while the Latin and Syriac collections omit it. Some scholars argue that the actual list of books was added to the Greek collection by a later scribe after the synod but before Chalcedon (451), and therefore the Latin collection represents the more original form of canon 59.[286] However, the canon list could be authentic to the actual proceedings of the synod since (1) it agrees with many of the Eastern lists from the fourth century;[287] and (2) Dionysius was probably motivated to omit the Eastern list of books because he had already included the papal letter of Innocent I in his collection of western canon law, which included the wider biblical canon for the church of Rome.[288]

---

[286] Markschies (2012), following Zahn (1888–92: 2.197ff) and Metzger (1987: 210), says, 'However, this list represents, from what we know, a later addition to the Canons of the synod. It has, however, been included in the pre-Chalcedonian *Corpus Canonum* of the Byzantine Church' (p. 127).

[287] The Old Testament section does not include the deuterocanonical books. Furthermore, the New Testament section omits the book of Revelation, which was common in the fourth-century lists from the East.

[288] Joannou 1962: 129n11. For the canon list of Innocent I, see ch. 4 , pp. 231–5.

Text[289]	Translation
ΝΘ *Περὶ τῶν ὀφειλόντων ἐν τῇ ἐκκλησίᾳ* *ψάλλεσθαι καὶ ἀναγινώσκεσθαι.*	59 Concerning the books which ought to be sung[290] and read[291] in the church.
Ὅτι οὐ δεῖ ἰδιωτικοὺς ψαλμοὺς λέγεσθαι ἐν τῇ *ἐκκλησίᾳ, οὐδὲ ἀκανόνιστα βιβλία* *ἀναγινώσκεσθαι, ἀλλὰ μόνα τὰ κανονικὰ τῆς* *καινῆς καὶ παλαιᾶς διαθήκης.*	For it is not fitting to speak secular[292] psalms in the church nor to read non-canonical[293] books, but only the canonical[294] books of the New and Old Covenant.[295]
Ὅσα δεῖ βιβλία ἀναγινώσκεσθαι καὶ *αὐθεντεῖν. (Τὰ) τῆς παλαιᾶς διαθήκης· α´* *Γένεσις κόσμου· β´ Ἔξοδος ἐξ Αἰγύπτου· γ´* *Λευιτικόν· δ´ Ἀριθμοί· ε´ Δευτερονόμιον· στ´* *Ἰησοῦς τοῦ Ναυῆ· ζ´ Κριταί, Ῥούθ· η´ Ἐσθήρ·* *θ´ βασιλειῶν α´ β´· ι´ Βασιλειῶν γ´ δ´· ια´* *Παραλειπομένων α´ β´· ιβ´ Ἔσδρας α´ β´· ιγ´* *βίβλος ψαλμῶν ρν´· ιδ´ Παροιμίαι* *Σολομῶντος· ιε´ Ἐκκλησιαστής· ις´ Ἄσμα* *ἀσμάτων· ιζ´ Ἰώβ· ιη´ οἱ δώδεκα Προφῆται·* *ιθ´ Ἡσαΐας· κ´ Ἰερεμίας, Βαρούχ, Θρῆνοι καὶ* *ἐπιστολή· κα´ Ἰεζεκιήλ· κβ´ Δανιήλ.*	All of these books are fitting to read and to have authority.[296] (The books) of the Old Covenant: one, Genesis of the world; two, Exodus out of Egypt; three, Leviticus; four, Numbers; five, Deuteronomy; six, Joshua of Naue; seven, Judges, Ruth; eight, Esther; nine, first and second of Kingdoms;[297] ten, third and fourth of Kingdoms;[298] eleven, first and second of Paralipomenon; twelve, first and second of Esdras;[299] thirteen, Book of One-Hundred-and- Fifty Psalms;[300] fourteen, Proverbs of Solomon; fifteen, Ecclesiastes; sixteen, Song of Songs;

[289] ibid.: I,2.154–5.

[290] *ψάλλεσθαι.* 'To be sung' is used only here in the canon lists and refers to the Psalms that ought to be sung in the liturgy of the church. This point is elaborated in the next line.

[291] *ἀναγινώσκεσθαι.* 'To be read' is used in two different ways in the canon lists. (1) The books to be read in church refers to the canonical books just as Cyril of Jerusalem used the expression to indicate his list of canonical books (*Cat.* 4.33, 36). SoL clearly uses the term in this way in the next line. (2) The books to be read indicates useful books, which were not canonical. Athanasius refers to the books to be read to the catechumens, which suggests that these books are not to be read in the broader assembly (*Ep. fest.* 39.20), and Rufinus refers to a list of similar books that are to be read in the churches but are not to support points of doctrine (*Symb.* 36).

[292] The meaning could also be 'private psalms' (Lampe 1961: 668).

[293] *ἀκανόνιστα.* 'Noncanonical'. The books not found in the following list are considered outside of the canon. Books outside of the canon should not be read in church. SoL does not treat the matter of private reading. Cyril prohibited the catechumens from reading any book that was not read in the church (*Cat.* 4.36).

[294] *τὰ κανονικά.* Only 'the canonical' books of the Old and New Testaments about to be listed are to be read in the church.

[295] Both the Greek and Latin collections agree to this point. The Latin version ends here. Likewise the Syriac version of SoL's canon 59 ends at this point (cf. Vööbus 1975: 124–5). Only the Greek version presents the list of books. Some scholars refer to the list of books as canon 60, but all of the sources have canon 59.

[296] Although many canon lists imply the notion of authoritative books, SoL makes explicit that these books have authority. The scope of the authority of these books is not detailed. Perhaps this expression refers to the function of the canonical books, as Jerome says, 'for the authoritative confirmation of ecclesiastical doctrines' (*Preface to the Books of Solomon*; cp. ch. 4 on Rufinus, *Symb.* 36).

[297] 1–2 Samuel in the Jewish and Protestant traditions.

[298] 1–2 Kings in the Jewish and Protestant traditions.

[299] Probably a reference to Esdras A and Esdras B.

[300] The title of the work specifically excludes the reading and authority of a version of the Psalter containing Psalm 151. Contrast this title with some of the manuscripts of the Apostolic Canons below that list the Book of One-Hundred-and-Fifty-One Psalms.

Text	Translation
	seventeen, Job; eighteen, The Twelve Prophets; nineteen, Isaiah; twenty, Jeremiah, Baruch, Lamentations, and Epistle; twenty-one, Ezekiel; twenty-two, Daniel.
Τὰ τῆς καινῆς διαθήκης· Εὐαγγέλια τέσσαρα Ματθαίου Μάρκου Λουκᾶ Ἰωάννου· Πράξεις καθολικαὶ τῶν ἀποστόλων καὶ ἐπιστολαὶ καθολικαὶ ἑπτὰ οὕτως· Ἰακώβου αʹ, Πέτρου αʹ βʹ, Ἰωάννου αʹ βʹ γʹ, Ἰούδα μία· ἐπιστολαὶ Παύλου δεκατέσσαρες οὕτως· πρὸς Ῥωμαίους μία, πρὸς Κορινθίους αʹ βʹ, πρὸς Γαλάτας αʹ, πρὸς Ἐφεσίους μία, πρὸς Φιλιππησίους αʹ, πρὸς Κολασσαεῖς αʹ, πρὸς Θεσσαλονικεῖς αʹ βʹ, πρὸς Ἑβραίους αʹ. πρὸς Τιμόθεον αʹ βʹ, πρὸς Τίτον αʹ, πρὸς Φιλήμονα αʹ.	The (books) of the new covenant: four Gospels of Matthew, of Mark, of Luke, of John; General Acts of the Apostles and the seven general epistles are thus: one of James, first and second of Peter, first, second, and third of John, one of Jude; the fourteen epistles of Paul are thus: one to the Romans, first and second to the Corinthians, one to the Galatians, one to the Ephesians, one to the Philippians, one to the Colossians, first and second to the Thessalonians, one to the Hebrews,[301] first and second to Timothy, one to Titus, one to Philemon.[302]

The Canon List of the Synod of Laodicea

Of the Old Covenant
1. Genesis of the world
2. Exodus out of Egypt
3. Leviticus
4. Numbers
5. Deuteronomy
6. Joshua of Naue
7. Judges-Ruth
8. Esther
9. 1–2 Kingdoms
10. 3–4 Kingdoms
11. 1–2 Paralipomenon
12. 1–2 Esdras
13. Book of One-Hundred-and-Fifty Psalms
14. Proverbs of Solomon
15. Ecclesiastes
16. Song of Songs
17. Job
18. The Twelve Prophets

---

[301] The order of Thessalonians-Hebrews is known from the fourth- and fifth-century magisterial codices and the canon list of Athanasius.

[302] The Book of Revelation is omitted from the canon list. Although Athanasius included Revelation without dispute in 367, Amphilochius (ca. 380) still reported that the majority say the Revelation of John was spurious. Around 350, Cyril of Jerusalem also omitted the book of Revelation from his list. Thus SoL's list fits the general pattern of the Eastern lists in the middle-to-late fourth century.

19. Isaiah
20. Jeremiah, Baruch, Lamentations, and Epistle
21. Ezekiel
22. Daniel

Of the New Covenant
   Four Gospels
      Matthew
      Mark
      Luke
      John
   General Acts of the Apostles
   Seven General Epistles
      James
      1–2 Peter
      1–3 John
      Jude
   Fourteen Epistles of Paul
      Romans
      1–2 Corinthians
      Galatians
      Ephesians
      Philippians
      Colossians
      1–2 Thessalonians
      Hebrews
      1–2 Timothy
      Titus
      Philemon

APOSTOLIC CANONS

The Apostolic Canons is a series of eighty-four or eighty-five canons (Syriac versions have as few as eighty and eighty-one canons) occurring in book 8, chapter 47 of the Apostolic Constitutions. Generally, this collection is considered to be the literary output of the compiler(s) or editor(s) responsible for the Apostolic Constitutions itself.[303] The Apostolic Constitutions is a composite work, comprising the Didascalia (Books 1–6), the Didache (Book 7), and the Apostolic Tradition, together with some other material (Book 8).[304]

---

[303] Hess 2002: 49. Apos. Con. VIII.47.85 names a Clement, probably meant to be Clement of Rome, as the compiler/author of the eight books of the Constitutions.
[304] Bradshaw 2002: 84.

Researchers generally agree that the Apostolic Constitutions was written in Syria, probably in Antioch, sometime between 375 and 380. Due to its reference to the feast of Christmas (Apos. Con. V.13.1), which was only beginning to surface in Eastern churches around this time, an earlier date than 375 is not probable. Furthermore, a later date than 380 is not likely, since its doctrine of the Holy Spirit is contrary to the definition of the Council of Constantinople (381).[305] By the synod of Trullo (692), the orthodoxy of the work was called into question and the synod concluded that heretics must have corrupted the work of the apostles. Before 891, Photius criticized the work for its Arianism.

Modern researchers present the following options for the authorship of the work:[306] (1) F.X. Funk advocated for the orthodoxy of the work by choosing orthodox textual variants and claimed that any heterodox elements were from the compiler's source and thus pre-dated the Arian controversy. (2) C.H. Turner argued strongly for an Arian compiler.[307] (3) Georg Wagner attempted to establish a connection to Eunomius through verbal parallels (d. 393; one of the leaders of the extreme Arians). (4) Dieter Hagedorn attributed authorship to an obscure bishop named Julian. (5) Marcel Metzger, who built upon Hagedorn's suggestion, concluded that, although Julian's Arianism was more explicit than the more moderate subordinationism of the Apostolic Constitutions, this inconsistency could be attributed to the difference between a commentary and a liturgical work that drew upon traditional material. However, Metzger did not think that the compiler could be considered a strict Arian.

The manuscript tradition of the Apostolic Canons is complex.[308] In Greek it was transmitted through collections of canon law (the oldest MSS of which date to ca. 800) and manuscripts of the Apostolic Constitutions. For his edition, Marcel Metzger has added Greek MSS to the previous editions of Funk and Lagarde, making his edition the standard work for the Apostolic Constitutions.[309] His manuscript stemma demonstrates the relationship between the Greek and Latin MSS.[310] In Latin, Dionysius Exiguus only transmitted the first fifty canons of the Apostolic Canons. The Latin Verona fragment (fifth/sixth centuries; siglum FV in Metzger's edition) contains the complete number of the Apostolic Canons. In Syriac, there are three copies of the Apostolic Canons from the British Museum: Add. 12,155 fol. 203b (eighth century), Add. 14,526 fol. 4b (seventh century, 641), and fol. 44b (eighth century).[311] To these we add

---

[305] Metzger 1985: 55–60; Bradshaw 2002: 84–5.
[306] For details and bibliography on the authorship question, see Bradshaw 2002: 85–6.
[307] Turner 1913; 1914; 1920.
[308] Turner 1915 summarizes Greek, Latin, Syriac, Coptic, and Ethiopic evidence. More Greek and Syriac evidence has come to light since 1915.
[309] See Metzger 1985 for the most up-to-date list of Greek and Latin MSS (pp. 65–6).
[310] Metzger 1985: 78.
[311] For more information on these MSS, see Wright 1871: 921, 949; p. 1033; and p. 1036 respectively. We were not able to access these MSS, and therefore, they are merely listed.

MS. DS 31 (seventh/eighth centuries), which contains the Apostolic Canons in eighty canons.[312] The Apostolic Canons are also found in Syriac as part of the Apostolic Constitutions.[313] Finally, there are versions of the Apostolic Canons in Coptic and Ethiopic.[314]

Old Testament canon: The OT canon list incorporates many books that were not finally included in the Jewish and Protestant Bibles, including Judith, Tobit (in Syriac and Ethiopic traditions), the three or four Books of Maccabees, Psalm 151 (in the Latin and one Greek manuscript), Wisdom of Solomon, and perhaps Wisdom of Sirach. The prophets are numbered as sixteen, with Jeremiah perhaps including Lamentations, Baruch, and the Epistle of Jeremiah according to tradition.

New Testament canon: The NT canon list contains the four Gospels, the fourteen letters of Paul, the seven Catholic Epistles, and Acts. It also contains the two letters of Clement. Furthermore, the Ethiopic tradition includes the Apocalypse of John.

Studies: Schodde 1885; Turner 1912a, 1912b, 1912c, 1913, 1914, 1915, 1920, 1930; Metzger 1985; 1986; 1987; Bradshaw 2002: 73–97, esp. 80–6; Haelewyck 2008: 152–3.

Apostolic Canons 85

Date: ca. 375–80

Introduction: The biblical canon list is the content of the last canon of the Apostolic Canons (canon 85 in the Greek tradition which is Apos. Con. VIII.47.85). However, earlier in the Apostolic Constitutions, instruction was provided regarding which books were to be read and in what order:

> (5) Let the reader, standing in the middle on a certain high place, read the books of Moses and Joshua of Naue, the books of Judges and Kingdoms, the books of Paralipomenon and the books of the Return [i.e. Esdras], in addition to these the books of Job and the books of Solomon and the Sixteen Prophets. (6) Now after the readings have occurred two by two, let a different person sing the hymns of David, and let the people sing the refrains in response. (7) After this let our Acts be read and the Epistles of Paul our fellow worker, which he sent to the churches according to the guidance of the Holy Spirit. And after these let an elder or deacon

---

[312] See Brock and Van Rompay 2014: 235–7. Although we were not able to check this manuscript, the catalogue contains an English translation of the listing of the canonical books from the final canon, which we include below.

[313] The editions by Lagarde 1856 and Vööbus 1975 are presented below. Haelewyck 2008 also includes the Eastern Syriac Nomocanon of ʻAbdishoʻ de Nisibe which contains a similar, though later, list of books to the MSS of Lagarde and Vööbus (p. 152).

[314] Turner 1915: 529–30. For the Ethiopic in English translation, cf. Schodde 1885. We were not able to verify Schodde's translation, but we included the significant differences in the notes below.

read the Gospels, which we, Matthew and John, handed down to you, and the fellow workers associated with Paul, Luke and Mark, left behind for you (Apos. Con. II.57.5–7).[315]

The canon list, therefore, has a liturgical function, regulating what should be read in the assembly.

Text[316]	Translation
πε´.[317] Ἔστω δὲ ὑμῖν πᾶσι κληρικοῖς καὶ λαϊκοῖς βιβλία σεβάσμια καὶ ἅγια τῆς μὲν παλαιᾶς διαθήκης Μωσέως πέντε·[318] Ἰησοῦ δὲ τοῦ Ναυῆ ἕν, τῶν Κριτῶν ἕν, τῆς Ῥοὺθ ἕν,[319] τῶν Βασιλειῶν τέσσαρα, Παραλειπομένων τῆς βίβλου τῶν ἡμερῶν δύο, Ἔσδρα δύο,[320] Ἐσθὴρ ἕν, Ἰουδὶθ ἕν,[321] Μακκαβαίων τέσσαρα,[322] Ἰὼβ ἕν, βίβλος Ψαλμῶν ἑκατὸν πεντήκοντα καὶ ἑνός,[323] Σολομῶντος βιβλία πέντε· [324] Προφῆται δέκα ἕξ.[325] Ἔξωθεν ὑμῖν προσιστορείσθω μανθάνειν ὑμῶν τοὺς νέους τὰς Σοφίας τοῦ πολυμαθοῦς Σιράχ. Ἡμέτερα δέ, τοῦτ᾿ ἔστι τῆς καινῆς διαθήκης, Εὐαγγέλια μὲν τέσσαρα, ὡς καὶ ἐν τοῖς προλαβοῦσιν εἴπομεν, Ματθαίου, Μάρκου, Λουκᾶ, Ἰωάννου·[326] Παύλου ἐπιστολαὶ δεκατέσσαρες,[327] Ἰακώβου μία, Ἰωάννου τρεῖς, Ἰούδα μία, Πέτρου δύο,[328] Κλήμεντος δύο, καὶ αἱ Διαταγαὶ ὑμῖν τοῖς ἐπισκόποις δι᾿ ἐμοῦ Κλήμεντος ἐν ὀκτὼ βιβλίοις προσπεφωνημέναι, ἃς οὐ χρή δημοσιεύειν ἐπὶ πάντων διὰ τὰ ἐν αὐταῖς μυστικά· καὶ αἱ Πράξεις ἡμῶν τῶν ἀποστόλων.	85. Now let the venerated and holy books be for all of you, clerics and laypeople.[329] Of the Old Covenant: Five of Moses; now one of Joshua of Naue, one of the Judges, one of Ruth,[330] four of the Kingdoms, two of Paralipomenon of the book of days,[331] two of Esdras, one of Esther,[332] one of Judith,[333] four of Maccabees,[334] one of Job, Book of One-Hundred-and-Fifty-One Psalms;[335] five books of Solomon;[336] sixteen Prophets;[337] outside of these, let it be added to you as further instruction that your youth learn the Wisdom of Sirach, the polymath.[338] Now our (books), that is, of the New Covenant: four Gospels, as also we spoke in the preceding, of Matthew, of Mark, of Luke, of John; fourteen epistles of Paul,[339] one of James, three of John, one of Jude, two of Peter,[340] two of Clement,[341] and the Constitutions are for you, the bishops, invoked by me, Clement,[342] in eight books, which are not fitting to display for all because of the mysteries in them; and the Acts of our Apostles.[343]

[315] (5) Μέσος δὲ ὁ ἀναγνώστης ἐφ᾿ ὑψηλοῦ τινος ἑστὼς ἀναγινωσκέτω τὰ Μωϋσέως καὶ Ἰησοῦ τοῦ Ναυῆ, τὰ τῶν Κριτῶν καὶ τῶν Βασιλειῶν, τὰ τῶν Παραλειπομένων καὶ τὰ τῆς Ἐπανόδου, πρὸς τούτοις τὰ τοῦ Ἰὼβ καὶ τὰ Σολομῶντος καὶ τὰ τῶν Ἑκκαίδεκα προφητῶν. (6) Ἀνὰ δύο δὲ γενομένων ἀναγνωσμάτων, ἕτερός τις τοῦ Δαυὶδ ψαλλέτω τοὺς ὕμνους, καὶ ὁ λαὸς τὰ ἀκροστίχια ὑποψαλλέτω. (7) Μετὰ τοῦτο αἱ Πράξεις αἱ ἡμέτεραι ἀναγινωσκέσθωσαν καὶ αἱ ἐπιστολαὶ Παύλου τοῦ συνεργοῦ ἡμῶν, ἃς ἀπέστειλε ταῖς Ἐκκλησίαις καθ᾿ ὑφήγησιν τοῦ ἁγίου Πνεύματος· καὶ μετὰ ταῦτα πρεσβύτερος ἢ διάκονος ἀναγινωσκέτω τὰ Εὐαγγέλια, ἃ ἐγὼ Ματθαῖος καὶ Ἰωάννης παρεδώκαμεν ὑμῖν καὶ οἱ συνεργοὶ Παύλου παρειληφότες κατέλειψαν ὑμῖν Λουκᾶς καὶ Μάρκος.

[316] M. Metzger 1987: 306–8.

[317] Canon 82 in Lagarde's MS and canon 81 in Vööbus's MS.

[318] Greek MS a (Metzger's siglum; tenth century) lists them as follows: γένεσις, ἔξοδος, λευϊτικόν, ἀριθμοὶ καὶ δευτερονόμιον (Genesis, Exodus, Leviticus, Numbers, and Deuteronomy). The Syriac MSS also do not list the five books of Moses individually (see below).

[319] Vööbus's MS places 'one of Judith' after Ruth.

[320] The Ethiopic has 'one book of Job' after the books of Ezra and before Esther.

[321] The Ethiopic does not include Judith among the canonical books but among the writings to teach children. Rather, the book of Tobit appears after Esther in the Ethiopic.

[322] Latin MS FV reads *tria* 'three'. The Syriac tradition agrees with the Latin's 'Three of Maccabees'. The Syriac tradition has 'one of Tobit' before the books of Maccabees. The Ethiopic tradition omits the books of Maccabees.

[323] Greek MS a reads: $\Psi \alpha \lambda \mu o i \ \dot{\epsilon} \kappa \alpha \tau \dot{o} \nu \ \pi \epsilon \nu \tau \dot{\eta} \kappa o \nu \tau \alpha$, 'One-Hundred and Fifty Psalms'. The Syriac MSS also affirm only One-Hundred and Fifty Psalms (see below). The Ethiopic has 'One-Hundred and Fifty Psalms of David'.

[324] Greek MS a reads: $\tau \rho i \alpha, \ \pi \alpha \rho o \iota \mu i \alpha \iota, \ \dot{\epsilon} \kappa \kappa \lambda \eta \sigma \iota \alpha \sigma \tau \dot{\eta} \varsigma, \ \ddot{\alpha} \sigma \mu \alpha \ \dot{\alpha} \sigma \mu \dot{\alpha} \tau \omega \nu$, 'Three, Proverbs, Ecclesiastes, Song of Songs'. The Syriac MSS contain the tradition of five books of Solomon without listing them. The Ethiopic lists Ecclesiastes earlier in the catalogue after Tobit. After Psalms, the Ethiopic has 'the proverbs of Solomon, Ecclesiasticus, and Song of Songs'.

[325] Lagarde's MS has 'Of the Prophets: Twelve one, of Isaiah one, of Jeremiah one, of Ezekiel one, of Daniel one' (see below). Similarly, the Ethiopic lists the Twelve Prophets, Isaiah, Jeremiah, Daniel, Ezekiel.

[326] After the Gospels, the Ethiopic has: Acts of the Apostles, two letters of Peter, three letters of John, one letter of James, and one letter of Jude.

[327] After the letters of Paul and before the letters of Clement, the Ethiopic has the Apocalypse of John.

[328] Lagarde's MS (BL Add. 14,526) has: one letter of James, two of Peter, three of John, one of Jude. Vööbus's MS has: two letters of Peter, three letters of John, one letter of James, one letter of Jude.

[329] The canonical books are for all, while Sirach is for the youth and the eight books of Clement mentioned below are only for the bishops.

[330] Ruth and Judges are separate works.

[331] Vööbus's MS 'The Book of the Words of the Days' has a title close to the Greek 'The Book of Days'. Lagarde's MS has 'Of Necessities'.

[332] Esther is disputed in the fourth century, but included in this catalogue.

[333] Judith is not listed in the other fourth-century Eastern catalogues.

[334] The three or four books of Maccabees are not listed among the other fourth-century Eastern catalogues.

[335] The Book of One-Hundred-and-Fifty-One Psalms is rare among the lists; see also the Mommsen Catalogue, and cp. Synod of Laodicea's Book of One-Hundred-and-Fifty Psalms.

[336] The first four books are probably Proverbs, Ecclesiastes, Song of Songs, and Wisdom of Solomon. The identity of the fifth book is not clear, since Sirach is explicitly named and said to be 'outside' later in the list. The Wisdom of Solomon is not catalogued in any of the other Eastern lists. Turner 1912c notes that the Latin MS should probably be followed, except probably for the reference to the five books of Solomon, since later the Wisdom of Sirach is said to be outside of the canonical books. However, he does allow for an 'unintelligent combination' of Athanasius's list with a tradition of five canonical books of Solomon (p. 512).

[337] Among the early lists, only Innocent I counts the prophets as sixteen Prophets.

[338] The useful, non-canonical status of Sirach is well attested in the fourth century (cf., e.g., the respective sections in this chapter on Epiphanius and Athanasius for details). The Ethiopic version contains the following books to be taught to children: the Wisdom of Solomon, Judith, three books of Kufâlê [Book of Jubilees], and Jesus the son of Sirach.

[339] Hebrews is included among the fourteen letters of Paul.

[340] The seven Catholic Epistles are included in the catalogue without any dispute.

[341] Probably, these are the two letters of Clement of Rome which form part of the corpus known as the Apostolic Fathers. Cf. Metzger 1987: 216, 225; Holmes 2007: 38. These Epistles are also included at the end of Codex Alexandrinus (cf. ch. 6 for the contents of this codex).

[342] The compiler of the Apostolic Constitutions probably used the pseudonym Clement of Rome, since he was considered the 'secretary' of the Apostolic College, and St Peter in particular (cf. Metzger 1985: 36).

[343] The Book of Revelation is omitted from the catalogue in accord with the majority of Eastern lists from the fourth century.

The Canon List of the Apostolic Canons

Old Testament
    Five of Moses
    Joshua of Naue
    Judges
    Ruth
    1–4 Kingdoms   (= 1–2 Samuel + 1–2 Kings)
    1–2 Paralipomenon (= 1–2 Chronicles)
    1–2 Esdras
    Esther
    Judith
    1–4 Maccabees
    Job
    Book of 151 Psalms
    Five Books of Solomon
    Sixteen Prophets
    Outside of these:
        Sirach
        (Ethiopic: the Wisdom of Solomon, Judith, three books of Kufâlê
        [Book of Jubilees], and Jesus the son of Sirach)
New Testament
    Four Gospels
        Matthew
        Mark
        Luke
        John
    Fourteen Epistles of Paul
    One of James
    Three of John
    One of Jude
    Two of Peter
    (Ethiopic: The Apocalypse of John)
    Two of Clement
    For the bishops:
        Eight books of the Constitutions
    Acts of the Apostles

Appendix: Syriac Version

Lagarde MS

Date of MS: eighth/ninth century

Text[344]	Translation
(Syriac text)	82. Now let these venerated and holy books be for them, clerics and laity. Of the Covenant from old thus: Of Moses five books. Of Joshua son of Nun one. Of Judges one. Of Ruth one. Of Kingdoms four. Of Things Omitted two.[345] Of Ezra two. Of Esther one. Of Judith one. Of Tobit one. Of Maccabees three. Of Job one. The accepted book of Psalms one. Of Solomon five books. Of the Twelve Prophets one. Of Isaiah one. Of Jeremiah one. Of Ezekiel one. Of Daniel one. Outside let the Wisdom of that great of learning, Sirach, be for you all as instruction of the young.
(Syriac text)	Now our own [sacred books], that is, of the New Covenant: The Gospels, indeed four, as we spoke of these previously: of Matthew, of Mark, of Luke, of John. Of Paul fourteen letters. Of Jacob one letter. Of Peter two. Of John three. Of Judah one. Of Clemis two letters. And these [Apostolic Constitutions], which are entrusted to you, O bishops, by my own hands, Clemis and they were invoked in eight books. Therefore these, which are not fit to show before anyone, [are for you, bishops] because of the mystic content in them. Further also the Acts or Actions of us, of the Apostles.

Vööbus MS

Date of MS: 1204 according to colophon[346]

Text[347]	Translation
(Syriac text)	81. Now let these be the venerated and holy books for you all, clerics and laity.

---

[344] Codex Sangermanensis (MS Syr. 62 Bibliothèque Nationale, Paris). Cf. Lagarde 1856: ‏ܣܒ-ܣܡ‎ (esp. ‏ܣܡ-ܠܕ‎ ln. 19–23; ln. 1–14).

[345] Title for Chronicles. Marginal gloss in the ms: ‏ܡܝܡܝܐ‎ cf. the title for Chronicles above.

[346] Vööbus 1975: X–XII.   [347] ibid.: 58–72, esp. 71, ln. 8–26.

Text	Translation
(Syriac)	Of the Old Covenant: Of Moses five. Of Joshua son of Nun one. And of Judges one. Of Ruth one. Judith one. Of Kingdoms four. Of the book of Chronicles[348] two. Of Ezra two. Esther one. Tobias one. Maccabees three. Job one. Book of One-Hundred-and-Fifty Psalms one. Of Solomon five books. Sixteen Prophets. Now from outside let the wisdom of that one great of learning, Bar Sira, one, be listed by you for instruction of the young.
(Syriac)	Now our own [sacred books], that is, of the New Covenant: indeed, there are four Gospels just as we spoke of these previously: of Matthew, of Mark, of Luke, of John. Of Paul fourteen letters. Of Peter two letters. Of John three letters. Of Jacob one letter. Of Judah one letter. Of Clemis two letters. And these [Apostolic Constitutions] which are entrusted to you, bishops, by my own hands, Clemis, which were ordered in eight books, these which are not permissible that they be shown before anyone because of the mystical content in them. And the Acts of us, of the Apostles.

MS. DS 31

Date of MS: seventh–eighth centuries[349]

Old Testament: Moses: five; Joshua son of Nun; Judges: Ruth; Kingdoms: four; Chronicles: two; Ezra: two; Esther; Judith; Tobith; Maccabees: three; Job; 150 Psalms; Solomon: five books; Prophets: sixteen; in addition, for the instruction of young people: Wisdom of Bar Sira.

New Testament: Gospels: four; Paul's Epistles: fourteen; Peter's Epistles: two; John's Epistles: three; James' Epistle; Jude's Epistle; Clement's Epistles: two (and assigned to bishops: Clement, which consists in eight books, not to be shown in front of everyone due to their secret content); Acts of the Apostles.

GREGORY OF NAZIANZUS

Gregory of Nazianzus (329/30–390/1), known as 'the Theologian', was bishop of Sasima in Cappadocia Secunda (modern southeast Turkey) for a brief stint

---

[348] Payne Smith (1879a: 814) suggests the Syriac is a corruption from the Hebrew title דברי הימים 'the words of the days'.

[349] List from the catalogue by Brock and Van Rompay 2014: 237.

in 372. He became bishop of Constantinople in 380, but he was pressured to resign from this post in 381. At different points in his ministry he served at an administrative level in his father's church in Nazianzus.[350]

After leaving Constantinople Gregory retired to a secluded life in Nazianzus and Cappadocia, where he probably wrote all of the poetry (about 19,000 lines) that we possess today in the last nine years of his life.[351] In addition to his poetry, forty-five Orations and some two-hundred-and-fifty letters of his body of work remain. According to Gilbert, Gregory's poetry may be broadly classified in four groups: (1) the *Poemata Arcana* (overview of Christian doctrine in verse); (2) poems relating to ethics; (3) autobiographical poems; and (4) poetry pertaining to literary criticism.[352] The Theologian's work contributed greatly to the church's doctrinal formulations of the Trinity and the person of Christ, to name only a couple of examples. From his works it is evident that he roamed the Scriptures, citing and alluding to them ubiquitously within his speeches and letters. Finally, he also composed several specific poems on Scripture.[353]

Old Testament canon: Gregory's canon of the Old Testament agrees mainly with the contents of the twenty-two books of the Jewish canon except that he omitted Esther and presumably included Lamentations, Baruch, and the Epistle of Jeremiah under the title of Jeremiah. He does not include any of the deuterocanonical books.[354]

New Testament canon: Gregory's canon of the New Testament contains twenty-six or twenty-seven books. It possibly contains an allusion to the book

---

[350] Cf. McGuckin (2001) for a substantive account of Gregory's life.
[351] Gilbert 2001: 1. Jerome recorded that Gregory composed some 30,000 lines (*Vir. ill.*, 117).
[352] ibid.: 6–13.   [353] Cf. Dunkle 2009.
[354] Although Gregory does not list the deuterocanonical books, he does use these books throughout his writings. According to *Biblia Patristica*, Gregory uses some fifty references from Wisdom of Solomon in his works (cf., e.g., 7:26 [*Orat*. 29.17 (PG 36:96 C,13)]. His writings contain twenty-five references to Sirach or Ecclesiasticus (cf., e.g., 38:16 [*Orat*. 7.1 (PG 35: 757 A,3)]). He alludes to Judith 10:3 once in *Epistle* 44.4 (GCS 53, 40 ln. 15–16). He alludes to Tobit 5:18 and 10:4 four times, respectively (the examples listed in *Biblia Patristica* from PG 36: 541, 604, PG 38: 63, and SC 270, 130 ln. 28 were not clear allusions to Tobit 5:18 or 10:4). He alludes to 1 Macc, 3:45 and 4:60 in *Orat*. 22.2 (SC 270, 220 ln. 2–3). He uses seventeen references in 2 Macc. (cf., e.g., 6:18 (PG 35: 913 C,1). Surprisingly, Gregory only uses γέγραπται, 'it has been written', on two occasions to introduce Scripture, once to introduce 1 Cor. 14:21 (*Orat*. 41.15; PG 36: 449), and once to introduce John 17:12 in *Significatio in Ezechielem* (PG 36: 668). He does use ἡ (θεία) γραφή φησιν(ν), 'The (divine) Scripture says', on nine occasions. Seven times this introductory formula precedes books in Gregory's canon list (Isa. 42:14; Job 3:9; Jer. 5:7, 9:21, 10:19, 15:18; Hos. 8:11; Ps 117:12). The other two instances appear to refer to Scripture generally. In addition to these instances, *TLG* yielded some 105 occurrences of γραφή and its derivatives in Gregory and none of these introduced a deuterocanonical book. However, forms of the noun 'Scripture' introduced readings from the following books: 1 Sam. 16:7; Job 5:26, 12:22; Prov. 31:3, 10; Amos 5:8; Hag. 2:6/ Heb. 12:26–7; Jer. 4:31, 5:7. 28:34; Isa. 62:1; Ps. 93 (94):17, 143(144):12; Matt. 7:14. Other uses of the word were less clear as to what Gregory might be referring to. Since Gregory cites and alludes to many books without introducing them as Scripture—those in his canon list and those outside of it—the list becomes the key to discerning his canon. Therefore, one cannot conclude, as Norris (1997) does, that Gregory read the canon of the Septuagint 'for he quotes as Scripture passages from Tobit, Judith, 1 & 2 Maccabees, Wisdom of Solomon, Ben Sirach and Baruch' (pp. 151–2).

of Revelation after the Gospel of John and therefore Gregory's order would agree with other known eastern orders of the New Testament books.

Studies: Westcott 1896; Norris 1997; Thielman 1998; Gilbert 2001: 1–26, 85–6; McGuckin 2001; Dunkle 2009.

Carmina Theologica, Book I, Section I, Carmen XII

Date: 381–90

Introduction: The first seven lines of this poem provide a two-fold rationale for the list. First, according to Gregory, the Scriptures in this list are a place for one to roam in tongue and mind. They are given (1) to illumine hidden things; (2) to be nudged by the commands of God; and (3) to lead one away from earthly things. Thus this list of Scriptures was intended to promote piety. Secondly, given the Arian, Neo-Arian, Pneumatomachian, and Apollinarian controversies in Cappadocia, the Theologian was conscientious to record a list of the genuine books of divinely inspired Scripture to keep one from deception due to the many strange books and interpolated evils that have come into being. Therefore, Gregory's list intended both to promote piety on the one hand and to protect from heterodoxy on the other.

Text[355]	Translation
IB΄. Περὶ τῶν γνησίων βιβλίων τῆς θεοπνεύστου Γραφῆς.	Twelfth. Concerning the genuine books of the divinely inspired[356] Scripture.
Θείοις ἐν λογίοισιν ἀεὶ γλώσσῃ τε νόῳ τε	Among divine oracles in tongue and mind always
Στρωφᾶσθ'· ἢ γὰρ ἔδωκε Θεὸς καμάτων τόδ' ἄεθλον,	Roam;[357] for either God bestowed this prize due to troubles,
Καί τι κρυπτὸν ἰδεῖν ὀλίγον φάος, ἢ τόδ' ἄριστον,	A small light even to see some hidden thing, or this is best,
Νύττεσθαι καθαροῖο Θεοῦ μεγάλῃσιν ἐφετμαῖς·	To be nudged by the great commands of the pure God;
5 *Ἢ τρίτατον, χθονίων ἀπάγειν φρένα ταῖσδε μερίμναις.*	Or third, to lead away the heart from earthly things by these thoughts.
Ὄφρα δὲ μὴ ξείνῃσι νόον κλέπτοιο βίβλοισι	Now lest you be deceived in your own mind by strange books
(Πολλαὶ γὰρ τελέθουσι παρέγγραπτοι κακότητες),	(For many interpolated[358] evils have come into being)

---

[355] PG 37: 472–4.　　[356] Cf. 2 Tim. 3:16.

[357] *LSJ* does not list a metaphorical meaning 'to ruminate on,' and Dunkle (2009) notes that this meaning is 'unusual' but provides no instances of the word with that meaning (p. 66). We have preferred to maintain the meaning of 'roam' or 'wander' in the translation because of these factors.

[358] Lampe (1961) also lists 'spurious' as a meaning for παρέγγραπτος (p. 1029). Gregory envisions foreign or strange books as these interpolated or imported evils that have come into being.

Text	Translation
Δέχνυσο τοῦτον ἐμεῖο τὸν ἔγκριτον, ὦ φίλ᾽, ἀριθμόν.	Receive, O friend, this approved[359] number[360] of mine.
Ἱστορικαὶ μὲν ἔασι βίβλοι δυοκαίδεκα πᾶσαι	These are all twelve historical books
10　Τῆς ἀρχαιοτέρης Ἑβραϊκῆς σοφίης.	Of the rather ancient Hebrew wisdom.[361]
Πρωτίστη, Γένεσις, εἶτ᾽ Ἔξοδος, Λευιτικόν τε.	The very first, Genesis, then Exodus, and Leviticus.
Ἔπειτ᾽ Ἀριθμοί. Εἶτα Δεύτερος Νόμος.	Then Numbers. Then Deuteronomy.[362]
Ἔπειτ᾽ Ἰησοῦς, καὶ Κριταί. Ῥοὺθ ὀγδόη.	Then Joshua, and Judges. Ruth eighth.[363]
Ἡ δ᾽ ἐνάτη δεκάτη τε βίβλοι, Πράξεις βασιλήων,	Now the ninth and tenth books, Acts of the Kingdoms,[364]
15　Καὶ Παραλειπόμεναι. Ἔσχατον Ἔσδραν ἔχεις.	And Paralipomena. Last you have Esdras.[365]
Αἱ δὲ στιχηραὶ πέντε, ὧν πρῶτός γ᾽ Ἰώβ·	Now the five in verse, of which, first is indeed Job;
Ἔπειτα Δαυΐδ· εἶτα τρεῖς Σολομωντίαι·	Then David;[366] then three pertaining to Solomon:
Ἐκκλησιαστής, Ἄσμα καὶ Παροιμίαι.	Ecclesiastes, Song, and Proverbs.[367]
Καὶ πένθ᾽ ὁμοίως Πνεύματος προφητικοῦ.	And likewise five of the prophetic Spirit.

[359] ἔγκριτον ('approved'). Under the verb, ἐγκρίνω, Lampe (1961) lists 'scripture as canonical' as a gloss (p. 404). In the context of a list of the genuine books, Gregory appears to use the phrase 'approved number' as a way to refer to the canonical books.

[360] Gilbert (2001) renders the Greek as 'list', but since the 'number' of the books is a common theme throughout the canon lists of this period, it is best to retain it here as well (p. 85).

[361] 'Hebrew wisdom' refers generally to the teachings of the Old Testament and it also indicates that Gregory thinks his canon list of the OT books comes from the Jews and corresponds to their ancient twenty-two books, which corresponds to the letters of their alphabet (see below).

[362] Gregory has Δεύτερος Νόμος, lit. 'Second Law', while the standard title for the book is Δευτερονόμιον (cf., e.g., Amphilochius below).

[363] Ruth is reckoned as its own book apart from Judges, even though the more standard reckoning was to include Ruth with Judges as one book.

[364] The ninth book must be 1–2 Kingdoms (= 1–2 Samuels) and the tenth book must be 3–4 Kingdoms (= 1–2 Kings).

[365] Gregory counts Esdras as one book. By listing one book, Esdras, Gregory probably relies on the tradition of counting Esdras A and Esdras B as one book. Origen combined these two books into one work, Ezra (cf. Origen above, p. 86n67). Gregory omits Esther, but, since he counted Ruth as its own book, he preserved twelve history books (cf. McDonald 2007: 203). He does allude to the book of Esther six times in his work *Carmen moralium* 29 (*Adversus mulieres se nimis ornantes*). See Knecht (1972: 34) at ln. 291, where 'Esther' is mentioned by name (= Esther 2:15, 17), ln. 292 (= Esther 8:3, 11), and ln. 295 (= Esther 3:11, 13).

[366] Gregory's title 'David' for the Psalter is unique among the Greek lists. It is, however, the title of the Psalter in the Syriac canon list from St Catharine's monastery (cf. ch. 5 on this list). Traditionally, David is the chief author of the psalms of the Psalter. Around 100 BCE, a Dead Sea Scroll, 11Q13 col. II at ln. 10, contains a reference to the 'Songs of David'. Furthermore, the New Testament contains a number of examples of David speaking in the Psalter (cf., e.g., Acts 2:25). For a recent treatment of David's relationship to the Psalms in the Second Temple Period, cf. Mroczek 2016: 51–85.

[367] Ecclesiastes–Song–Proverbs is a strange order for the Solomonic books. The poem's metre (iambic trimetre) probably determined this unusual sequence. In all of the other Jewish and Christian lists, as well as the codices of Vaticanus, Sinaiticus, and Alexandrinus, the order is Proverbs–Ecclesiastes–Song.

Text	Translation
20 Μίαν μέν εἰσιν ἐς γραφὴν οἱ δώδεκα·	In one writing are the Twelve:[368]
Ὡσηὲ κ᾿ Ἀμὼς, καὶ Μιχαίας ὁ τρίτος·	Hosea, and Amos, and Micah third;
Ἔπειτ᾿ Ἰωὴλ, εἶτ᾿ Ἰωνᾶς, Ἀβδίας,	Then Joel, then Jonah, Obadiah,
Ναούμ τε, Ἀββακούμ τε, καὶ Σοφονίας,	And Nahum, and Habakkuk, and Zephaniah,
Ἀγγαῖος, εἶτα Ζαχαρίας, Μαλαχίας.	Haggai, then Zechariah, Malachi.
25 Μία μὲν οἴδε. Δευτέρα δ᾿ Ἡσαΐας.	These are one. Now second is Isaiah.
Ἔπειθ᾿ ὁ κληθεὶς Ἱερεμίας ἐκ βρέφους.	Then Jeremiah,[369] the one called from infancy.[370]
Εἶτ᾿ Ἰεζεκιὴλ, καὶ Δανιήλου χάρις.	Then Ezekiel, and the favour of Daniel.
Ἀρχαίας μὲν ἔθηκα δύω καὶ εἴκοσι βίβλους,	I have set down the ancient two and twenty books,
Τοῖς τῶν Ἑβραίων γράμμασιν ἀντιθέτους.	Corresponding to the letters of the Hebrews.[371]
30 Ἤδη δ᾿ ἀρίθμει καὶ νέου μυστηρίου.	Now immediately count those of the new mystery.[372]
Ματθαῖος μὲν ἔγραψεν Ἑβραίοις θαύματα Χριστοῦ·	Matthew wrote to the Hebrews[373] the wonders of Christ;[374]

[368] Gregory makes explicit that the Twelve Prophets are in one book (cp. ln. 25). The order of the Twelve Prophets here conforms to the sequence known in LXX manuscripts rather than the Hebrew sequence popularized in the West by Jerome's translation. The difference is limited to the first six books, which in the Hebrew sequence runs Hosea, Joel, Amos, Obadiah, Jonah, Micah. Furthermore, Gregory's list differs slightly from Amphilochius's, which has Joel–Obadiah–Jonah.

[369] Gregory uses fifteen references to the book of Lamentations in his writings. He mentions specifically the 'Lamentations of Jeremiah' (τῶν Ἱερεμίου Θρήνων) in a context in which he alludes to various parts of the book in *Orat*. 6.18 (PG 35: 745 A,7). He uses five references to the book of Baruch in his writings. Most of these instances allude to 3:36–8, which was used to support the doctrine of the incarnation of the Son of God, for it predicts a time when God will not only *appear* to humanity but also *dwell* with them (e.g. *Orat*. 19.13 [PG 35: 1057 D,2]; cp. section on Amphilochius, below, for the use of this same passage). Gregory cites Baruch 3:36, 38 in *Orat*. 30.13, and interestingly he does not introduce the citation as Scripture or as from Jeremiah or Baruch (cf. Gallay 1978: 254, at ln. 32–4). According to *Biblia Patristica*, he does not use the Epistle of Jeremiah, but some fathers included it in their canon lists, probably because they considered it to belong to the works of the prophet (cf. above on Origen, p. 87n68, and Athanasius, p. 123n242). Epiphanius makes clear that the Jews accepted Lamentations but rejected Baruch and the Epistle (cf. below, p. 165, along with p. 161n431).

[370] Cf. the allusion to Jer. 1:5.

[371] By equating the books of the Old Testament with the twenty-two letters of the Hebrew alphabet, Gregory has patterned his list after many of the early patristic lists, and the Hebrew canon has influenced his own canon theory. For more references to the twenty-two books as patterned after the Hebrew alphabet, cf. Gallagher 2012a: 85–92.

[372] Gregory uses the expression 'new mystery' in one other place to describe 'the august and new mystery of Christ' (Χριστοῦ τὸ σεπτὸν καὶ νέον μυστήριον) (*Carmina moralia* PG 37: 730). The books of the new mystery relate to the revelation of Christ. Gregory's expression is an adaptation of one in Eusebius where he refers to 'the mystery of the new covenant' (τῆς καινῆς διαθήκης μυστηρίου; *Dem. Ev.* 7.1.152).

[373] Perhaps Gregory alludes to the tradition that Matthew's gospel was written in Hebrew. Cf. Gallagher 2012a: 127n78 for patristic references to this tradition. Dunkle (2009) notes that Gregory's other Scripture poems also comment on the intended audiences of each gospel (p. 69). See below. In addition, Dunkle (2009) also suggests that these three languages—Hebrew, Greek, and Latin—represent the main languages of the early church, and furthermore, each of these languages was inscribed above the cross (p. 69).

[374] Cf. Matt. 21:15 for a reference to the 'wonders' Christ performed in the presence of the Jewish leaders. Furthermore, Gregory composed a special poem, 'The Wonders of Christ

Text	Translation
Μάρκος δ' Ἰταλίη, Λουκᾶς Ἀχαϊάδι·	And Mark to Italy,[375] Luke to Greece;[376]
Πᾶσι δ' Ἰωάννης, κῆρυξ μέγας,	And John to all, a great preacher, one who
οὐρανοφοίτης.	entered heaven.[377]
Ἔπειτα Πράξεις τῶν σοφῶν ἀποστόλων.	Then Acts of the wise apostles.
35 Δέκα δὲ Παύλου τέσσαρές τ' ἐπιστολαί.	Now the ten and four epistles of Paul.[378]
Ἑπτὰ δὲ καθολικαί, ὧν, Ἰακώβου μία,	And the seven general ones, of which, one of James,
Δύω δὲ Πέτρου, τρεῖς δ' Ἰωάννου πάλιν·	and two of Peter, and three of John again;[379]
Ἰούδα δ' ἐστὶν ἑβδόμη. Πάσας ἔχεις.	And Jude is seventh.[380] You have all.
Εἴ τι δὲ τούτων ἐκτὸς, οὐκ ἐν γνησίαις.	If there is any outside of these, they are not among the genuine.[381]

according to Matthew', in which he enumerates some twenty wonders of Christ in that Gospel (PG 37: 488–91).

[375] In the poem, 'The Wonders of Christ according to Mark', Gregory introduces Mark as one who wrote to the Ausonians (Αὐσονίοισι; classical Greek designation for the Romans/Italians) (PG 37: 491).

[376] In the poem, 'The Wonders according to Luke', Gregory introduces Luke as the one who wrote of august miracles to Greece (PG 37: 492–4).

[377] Gregory does not mention the Book of Revelation by name. Most scholars reasonably interpret this omission as indicating that Gregory did not consider Revelation to be canonical, a not uncommon view in the fourth-century Eastern church (cf. above, pp. 104–5, on Eusebius, and below, p. 154, on Amphilochius, both of whom comment on this uncertainty). See Westcott 1896: 453; Metzger 1987: 212. However, the description of John as 'one who entered heaven' may make reference to Revelation (cf. 4:1–2), implying that Gregory accepted the genuine apostolic authorship of the book. Gregory does cite Revelation on several occasions, holding it and its author in high esteem; cf., e.g., *Orat.* 42.9 (PG 36: 469 A,10); *Orat.* 29.17 (PG 36: 96 D,3); *Orat.* 40.45 (PG 36: 424 C,4), and see Thielman, 1998: 157. As Thielman suggests, these considerations should caution one from concluding that Gregory definitely excluded John's Apocalypse from his canon. Possibly he intends this reference to John as one who entered heaven—an allusion to Revelation— to include the book within his list, though he expresses himself allusively in this poem. If so, the placement of Revelation immediately after the Gospels would conform to a known ancient sequence of the books (cf. Thielman 1998: 156). We are, however, unable to make any confident assertions either way.

[378] *Pace* Gilbert (2001) who translates 'ten' epistles of Paul (p. 86), apparently a typographical error. Gregory includes Hebrews in the fourteen epistles of Paul.

[379] 'Again' perhaps indicates that Gregory thought the John of the three letters was the same as the John of the Fourth Gospel mentioned earlier.

[380] *Pace* Gilbert (2001), who translates Jude as 'eighth' (p. 86), apparently a typographical error. Gregory considers all seven of the Catholic Epistles to be genuine.

[381] Gregory says the reader has all of the books, and if there are any outside of these, they are not among the genuine. The title of the poem designates these books as the genuine books of the divinely inspired Scriptures. 'Genuine' appears to mean 'canonical' in this context and therefore this list represents Gregory's canon of Scripture. Given Gregory's use of the deuterocanonical books, it would be premature to conclude that he had a simple 'genuine' versus 'spurious' division of books. Rather, 'outside of these genuine books' probably means non-canonical writings. Gregory may still have an intermediate category of books between 'canonical' and 'spurious', in which he would place Esther and the deuterocanonical books.

The Canon List of Gregory of Nazianzus

Twenty-Two Books of the Ancient Hebrew Wisdom
    Twelve Historical Books
        Genesis
        Exodus
        Leviticus
        Numbers
        Deuteronomy
        Joshua
        Judges
        Ruth
        Acts of the Kingdoms   (= 1–2 Samuels + 1–2 Kings)
        Paralipomena   (= 1–2 Chronicles)
        Esdras   (= 1–2 Esdras)
    Five books in Verse
        Job
        David   (= Book of Psalms)
        Ecclesiastes
        Song
        Proverbs
    Five of the Prophetic Spirit
        Twelve Prophets
            Hosea
            Amos
            Micah
            Joel
            Jonah
            Obadiah
            Nahum
            Habakkuk
            Zephaniah
            Haggai
            Zechariah
            Malachi
        Isaiah
        Jeremiah   (+ Lamentations + Baruch + ? Epistle of Jeremiah?)
        Ezekiel
        Daniel
Books of the New Mystery
    Matthew
    Mark
    Luke
    John
    ?Revelation?   (= if 'one who entered heaven' alludes to it)
    Acts of the Apostles
    Fourteen Epistles of Paul

Seven General Epistles
James
1–2 Peter
1–3 John
Jude

AMPHILOCHIUS OF ICONIUM

Amphilochius (ca. 340/5–398/404) became bishop of Iconium in 373 after Basil of Caesarea invited him to the post. Before assuming this position, he held two posts that we know about: (1) he was a rhetorician in Constantinople; and then (2) he resided in the desert as an ascetic. He was first cousin to the famous Cappadocian father Gregory of Nazianzus.[382] Not many of his writings come down to the present time. There remains a treatise, *Contra haereticos*, an *Epistola synodalis*, and a limited number of homilies. In addition to these works, a well-composed didactic poem, *Iambi ad Seleucum*, survives. It is this composition which contains the canon (κανών) list of Amphilochius (ln. 251–319).

The *Iambi ad Seleucum* was preserved among the works of Gregory of Nazianzus, but with an attribution to Amphilochius. Nevertheless, some sixteenth-century editors argued for Gregory's authorship of the poem, an idea reflected in J.-P. Migne's printing the poem as a work of Gregory.[383] More recent editors have followed the manuscripts in attributing the work instead to Amphilochius.[384]

Amphilochius probably wrote this poem for his young nephew, Seleucus. It displays the rhetoric which characterized all of his works.[385] Its 340 poetic lines address several topics, including characteristics of the godly life (ln. 8–180) and the study of the sacred books and the devotion to the rule of faith (ln. 181–319). In the second section, Amphilochius reviews the books of Scripture and doctrines such as the Trinity.[386] Like that of Gregory of Nazianzus, the canon list in verse is presumably crafted to facilitate its memorization. These two lists are unique among the corpus of the canon lists in this respect and they are monuments to the great learning of the Cappadocian theologians.

Old Testament canon: The first part of the list treats the books of the Old Covenant. Amphilochius does not claim to be imparting the twenty-two books of the Hebrews, nor does he mention the twenty-seven books of the Old Testament,

---

[382] Cf. Bonis 1959 for more details on the life of Amphilochius.

[383] PG 37: 1577–1600. Cf. Joannou (1963: 232) and the discussion of this history in Oberg (1969: 1–2) and also his list of *testimonia*, which attribute the work to Amphilochius, beginning with Severus of Antioch and Cosmas Indicopleustes in the sixth century (pp. 90–3).

[384] Joannou 1963: 232; Oberg 1969: 1–2.   [385] Joannou 1963: 232.

[386] For a full listing of the topics in *Iambi*, cf. Oberg 1969: 4.

as many of the lists from the third and fourth centuries do. His list includes thirty-eight books, if the double books (e.g. 1–2 Kingdoms) are not reckoned as one book and the Twelve Prophets are reckoned as individual books. The contents of his Old Testament correspond closely to the Jewish canon, except that there is some doubt about the position of Esther in the list (ln. 288). He does not mention any book outside the Jewish canon.

New Testament canon: The second part of the list records the books of the New Covenant. Amphilochius's list corresponds to the twenty-seven-book canon of Athanasius, but Amphilochius does note the disputed books of Hebrews, the Catholic Epistles (2 Peter, 2–3 John, and Jude), and the Apocalypse of John. He does not mention other books such as the Shepherd of Hermas or the Epistle of Barnabas.

Studies: Holl 1904; Moss 1930; Bonis 1959; Joannou 1963: 232–7; Oberg 1969; Datema 1978; Bruce 1988: 81, 212–13; Barkhuizen 2001.

Iambi ad Seleucum 251–320

Date: ca. 380

Introduction: In lines 181–320, Amphilochius presents Seleucus with 'the study of the sacred books and the order of the rule of faith'.[387] The canon list of the books of the Old and New Testaments concludes this long section. In lines 183–192, Amphilochius exhorts Seleucus as follows:[388]

Now since you should train (προγυμνάσῃς) your mind moderately beforehand
As in school (παλαίστρᾳ) with various treatises,
Contend (ἐνάθλει) with the divinely inspired Scriptures themselves
Collecting the great wealth of the two covenants,
On the one hand, the Old, but, on the other hand, always the New.
For the New has been written second
And after it there will be no third.
Allot (νέμε) all diligence to these (i.e. the two covenants),
From which you should learn to practise the useful way (χρηστὸν τρόπον)
And to worship (σέβειν) the true and only God.

---

[387] Oberg 1969: 4.

[388] ἐπὰν δὲ τὸν νοῦν μετρίως προγυμνάσῃς
ὡς ἐν παλαίστρᾳ ποικίλοις συγγράμμασιν,
αὐταῖς ἐνάθλει ταῖς θεοπνεύστοις γραφαῖς
διττῶν διαθηκῶν συλλέγων πλοῦτον μέγαν,
τῆς μὲν παλαιᾶς, τῆς δέ γε καινῆς ἀεί.
καινὴ γάρ ἐστι δευτέρα γεγραμμένη
καὶ μεθ’ ἑαυτὴν μηκέθ’ ἕξουσα τρίτην.
ταύταις ἅπασαν ἀσμένως σπουδὴν νέμε,
παρ’ ὧν μαθήσῃ χρηστὸν ἐξασκεῖν τρόπον
καὶ τὸν ἀληθῆ καὶ μόνον θεὸν σέβειν.

The two covenants are great wealth. Seleucus is to contend with or engage in them. From these two covenants, Seleucus is to learn how to practise the useful or worthy way of life and how to worship God. This introduction shows the purpose of the canon list to appear several lines later. Primarily, Amphilochius devised his canon list to promote the divinely inspired books which taught one how to live usefully and how to be pious towards God. The actual preface to his canon list in lines 251–60 presents a more negative purpose: the list should protect Seleucus from the fraudulent and unsafe 'scriptures' in circulation. Amphilochius, therefore, drafted his canon list to promote piety on the one hand and to protect one from dangerous forgeries of the canonical books on the other.

Text[389]	Translation
251 Πλὴν ἀλλ' ἐκεῖνο προμαθεῖν μάλιστά σοι προσῆκον· οὐχ ἅπασα βίβλος ἀσφαλὴς ἡ σεμνὸν ὄνομα τῆς γραφῆς κεκτημένη.	But this especially for you to learn Is fitting: not every book is safe, Which has acquired the venerable name of Scripture.[390]
εἰσὶν γάρ, εἰσὶν ἔσθ' ὅτε ψευδώνυμοι	For there are times when there are pseudonymous[391]

---

[389] Oberg 1969: 36–9.

[390] 'Scripture' is considered to be a 'venerable name' for the books in the list, but, as Amphilochius notes, it has been applied to pseudonymous books as well. He, therefore, appears to reserve this name, Scripture, for the books in this list. In ln. 319, he refers to the list as the canon of the 'divinely inspired scriptures'.

[391] Amphilochius does use the term 'pseudonymous' to indicate non-canonical works, but this term does not immediately make any book 'spurious'. Rather, under the label 'pseudonymous' Amphilochius includes books 'intermediate' and 'neighbors... to the words of truth' and also the 'spurious' and 'utterly unsafe' books. He does not provide any examples of books from the intermediate category in this list, but elsewhere he does allude to other works which he did not include in the list. In his work, *Contra Haereticos* 24.934–7, he alludes to Sirach 21:2: 'φύγε ἀπὸ γυναικὸς ὡς ἀπὸ προσώπου ὄφεως' ('Flee from a woman as from the face of a serpent'), but immediately following this, he cites Proverbs 6:27–8 as Scripture: 'ὥς φησιν ἡ γραφή· 'καὶ Τίς ἀποδήσει πῦρ ἐν τῷ κόλπῳ αὐτ<ο>ῦ καὶ τὰ ἱμάτια οὐ κατακαύσει; ἢ τίς περιπατήσει ἐπ' ἀνθράκων, τοὺς δὲ πόδας οὐ κατακαύσει' ('As the Scripture says, "and who will give fire in his bosom and it will not burn his garments? Or who will walk upon coals, and will not burn his feet?"') (*Contra Haereticos* 24.934–7; CCG 3, 210). By alluding to the book of Ecclesiasticus positively but not calling it Scripture and excluding the work from his canon list, Amphilochius would probably call the work 'intermediate'; that is, books which are not canonical Scripture but are useful Scripture or books that neighbour the words of truth. In the same work, Amphilochius may allude to Tobit 1:6: 'ἐκ<ε>εῖ τὰς ἀπαρχὰς καὶ τὰς δεκάτας καὶ πάσας τὰς εὐχὰς ἀνέφερες' ('there you were bringing first fruits and tithes and all vows'), but the evidence for this allusion is weaker than for Ecclesiasticus (*Contra Haereticos* 16.589–590; CCG 3, 200). In another sermon, extant mainly in Syriac along with a few Greek and Latin fragments, Amphilochius uses Wisdom of Solomon 1:7 in defence of the full divinity of the Holy Spirit. For the Syriac text, cf. Moss 1930: 337, ln. 13–14; for the English translation see ibid.: 351–2. Amphilochius does not cite the work as Scripture but only alludes to it. Unfortunately, we do not possess the Greek form of the text and the form, as it comes to us, deviates from the extant Syriac Peshitta version. Regarding the differences between these text forms, Moss queries, 'Is it possible that he [the Syriac translator of the sermon] was not well acquainted with the text of those books not in the Jewish canon? Is it possible that these books were not regarded as authoritative by the school to which he belonged?' (ibid.: 328). These questions

Text	Translation
255 βίβλοι· τινὲς μὲν ἔμμεσοι καὶ γείτονες,	Books, some are intermediate and neighbours,
ὡς ἄν τις εἴποι, τῶν ἀληθείας λόγων.	As one might say, to the words of truth.
αἱ δ' αὖ νόθοι τε καὶ λίαν ἐπισφαλεῖς	But others are spurious[392] and surely unsafe,
ὥσπερ παράσημα καὶ νόθα νομίσματα,	Like counterfeit and spurious coins,
ἃ βασιλέως μὲν τὴν ἐπιγραφὴν ἔχει,	Which have the king's inscription,
260 κίβδηλα δ' ἐστί, ταῖς ὕλαις δολούμενα.	But they are fraudulent, being disguised with respect to their material.
Τούτων χάριν σοι τῶν θεοπνεύστων ἐρῶ	For these reasons I will say to you
βίβλων ἑκάστην· ὡς δ' ἂν εὐκρινῶς μάθῃς,	Each of the divinely inspired books,[393] in order that you might learn them clearly,
τὰς τῆς παλαιᾶς πρῶτα διαθήκης ἐρῶ.	Those of the Old Covenant I will say first.
ἡ πεντάτευχος τὴν κτίσιν, εἶτ' ἔξοδον,	The Pentateuch has The Creation,[394] then Exodus,
265 λευιτικὸν δὲ τὴν μέσην βίβλον ἔχει,	And Leviticus, the middle book,[395]
μεθ' ἣν ἀριθμούς, εἶτα δευτερονόμιον.	After which is Numbers, then Deuteronomy.
τούτοις Ἰησοῦν προστίθει καὶ τοὺς κριτάς,	To these add Joshua, and the Judges,
ἔπειτα τὴν Ῥοὺθ βασιλειῶν τε τέσσαρας	Then Ruth[396] and of Kingdoms four
βίβλους, παραλειπομένων δέ γε ξυνωρίδα.	Books, and of Paralipomena indeed a pair of books.

pertain only to the reception of the text of Wisdom within the Syriac community, which is an interesting question in its own right. However, Amphilochius probably cited the received Greek version of Wisdom 1:7 and he considered it at the least to illustrate the divinity of the Holy Spirit, and at the most to establish the doctrine itself. Since Amphilochius does not include the book of Wisdom in his canon list and he does not refer to it as Scripture here, he probably only alludes to it in order to illustrate the filling power of the Spirit of the Lord. The doctrine of the divinity of the Spirit is established properly from the Gospel of John according to Amphilochius.

[392] He provides the reader with two instances of this word (νόθος) applied to two books in the list itself. He notes that some consider Hebrews to be spurious, but he does not consider it to be so. Also, the majority consider the Apocalypse of John to be spurious. Thus some do not reckon these two books to be in the canon, and these same groups must therefore reckon them to be unsafe as well. It is unclear as to whether Amphilochius would consider the Apocalypse of John to be unsafe. Since he includes it among what might also be described as disputed books, perhaps he would consider it to be in the intermediate category. Earlier in the fourth century, Eusebius listed examples of spurious works: 'Among the books which are not genuine (νόθοι) must be reckoned the Acts of Paul, the work entitled the Shepherd, the Apocalypse of Peter, and in addition to them the letter called of Barnabas and the so-called Teachings of the Apostles. And in addition, as I said, the Revelation of John, if this view prevail. For, as I said, some reject it, but others count it among the Recognized Books' (*Hist. eccl.*" 3.25.4; quoted above, p. 102). For a discussion of the relationship between spurious works and disputed works in Eusebius, see pp. 106–9.

[393] 2 Tim 3:16 probably refers to the Scriptures of the Old Testament as 'divinely inspired', and Amphilochius expands this sense to include the books of the Old and New Covenants.

[394] Κτίσις 'creation' instead of γένεσις 'genesis' is unique among the Greek and Latin lists (cf. ch. 5, on Syriac MS 10 from St Catherine's Monastery, which has 'Creation' as a title for Genesis). Perhaps the two-syllable word was more desirable for the poetic line than the three-syllable word. In any case, this title for Genesis indicates that Amphilochius considered the book to emphasize the Creation.

[395] Given the lists in Melito (170 CE; see above, p. 80n37) and the Mommsen Catalogue (before 365 CE; see below, p. 190), which transpose Leviticus and Numbers, Amphilochius may be making a strong point to keep Leviticus as the middle book of the Pentateuch.

[396] Ruth is placed directly after Judges, but it is counted as a separate book rather than as 'with Judges', as is found in many of the lists.

Text	Translation
270 Ἔσδρας ἐπ᾽ αὐταῖς πρῶτος, εἶθ᾽ ὁ δεύτερος.	Upon them first Esdras, then the second.[397]
ἑξῆς στιχηρὰς πέντε σοι βίβλους ἐρῶ·	Next I will say to you the five books in verse:
στεφθέντος ἄθλοις ποικίλων παθῶν Ἰὼβ	Job, having been crowned with the contests of manifold sufferings,
ψαλμῶν τε βίβλον, ἐμμελὲς ψυχῶν ἄκος,	And the book of Psalms, a soothing remedy for souls,
τρεῖς δ᾽ αὖ Σολομῶντος τοῦ σοφοῦ, παροιμίας,	Moreover three books of Solomon the Wise: Proverbs,
275 ἐκκλησιαστὴν ᾆσμά τε τῶν ᾀσμάτων.	Ecclesiastes and Song of Songs.
ταύταις προφήτας προστίθει τοὺς δώδεκα,	To these add the Twelve Prophets:[398]
Ὡσηὲ πρῶτον, εἶτ᾽ Ἀμὼς τὸν δεύτερον,	Hosea first, then Amos second,
Μιχαίαν, Ἰωήλ, Ἀβδίαν καὶ τὸν τύπον	Micah, Joel, Obadiah, and the type
Ἰωνᾶν αὐτοῦ τοῦ τριημέρου πάθους,	Of him who suffered three days, Jonah,[399]
280 Ναοὺμ μετ᾽ αὐτούς, Ἀββακούμ, εἶτ᾽ εἴνατον	Nahum after them, Habakkuk; then ninth
Σοφονίαν, Ἀγγαῖόν τε καὶ Ζαχαρίαν	Zephaniah, and Haggai, and Zechariah
διώνυμόν τε ἄγγελον Μαλαχίαν.	And the angel with two names, Malachi.[400]
μεθ᾽ οὓς προφήτας μάνθανε τοὺς τέσσαρας,	After these, learn the four prophets:
παρρησιαστὴν τὸν μέγαν Ἠσαίαν	The great and courageous Isaiah,
285 Ἰερεμίαν τε συμπαθῆ, καὶ μυστικὸν	And the sympathetic Jeremiah,[401] and mysterious
Ἰεζεκιήλ, ἔσχατον δὲ Δανιήλ,	Ezekiel, and last Daniel,

[397] First and Second Esdras are counted as two distinct books. See the Appendix, p. 269.

[398] The 'Twelve Prophets' (οἱ προφῆται) is in the plural not the neuter singular (τὸ δωδεκαπρόφητον) as in, e.g., Epiphanius. Not many early canon lists include a complete catalogue of the Twelve Prophets. Cf. the previous section on Gregory of Nazianzus for a similar list. The order of the Twelve Prophets here conforms to the sequence known in LXX manuscripts rather than the Hebrew sequence popularized in the West by Jerome's translation. The difference is limited to the first six books, which in the Hebrew sequence runs: Hosea, Joel, Amos, Obadiah, Jonah, Micah.

[399] Perhaps, Amphilochius's exegesis of Jonah as the τύπος 'type' of the one who suffered three days provided some rationale for why it is in the canon (Matt. 16:4 has the word 'sign' (σημεῖον), as does Luke 11:29–30).

[400] The comment 'two-named angel/messenger' is not clear. The Jewish revisions of Aquila, Symmachus, and Theodotion have Μαλαχίου as a proper name (Field 1875b: 2.1031). Jerome discusses Malachi's name in the prologue to his *Commentary on Malach*, where he confirms that 'the other interpreters translated the name *Malachi* as it is read in the Hebrew'. However, LXX–Malachi has rendered the Hebrew as ἀγγέλου αὐτοῦ 'of his angel/messenger'. Furthermore, Targum Jonathan has 'by the hand of my messenger whose name is called Ezra the scribe'. Jerome rejects the opinion of some (Origenists?) who think the phrase refers to 'an angel (*angelum*) come from heaven and assumes a human body'. For his part, Jerome understood the name to mean 'my messenger (*nuntius*)'. Thus Amphilochius's short comment on the book of Malachi may refer to the debate over whether Malachi was a heavenly angel or a human messenger. In the case of the latter, that messenger was Ezra, which was the tradition of the Jews according to the Targum and Jerome's own report in the prologue to his commentary on the book.

[401] Amphilochius does not list the books of Lamentations, Baruch, or the Epistle of Jeremiah. We have no extant citations of Lamentations or the Epistle of Jeremiah. Since Lamentations was included in the early Jewish and Christian lists, it is probably included under the title of Jeremiah. The same may be the case for the Epistle (cf., e.g., p. 87 on Origen and p. 123 on Athanasius for details). In *Oratio* or Homily 1, entitled 'On the Nativity', 1.2.50–52", Amphilochius cites Baruch 3:38 as 'from the other saying of the prophet that says' (ἐκ τῆς ἑτέρας τοῦ προφήτου φωνῆς λεγούσης). Cf. the English translation in Barkhuizen 2001: 4. For the critical edition, cf. CCG 3, p. 6, ln. 50–2. Amphilochius's wording indicates that he thought Baruch was a part of the

Text	Translation
τὸν αὐτὸν ἔργοις καὶ λόγοις σοφώτατον.	The rather wise one in deeds and words.[402]
τούτοις προσεγκρίνουσι τὴν Ἐσθήρ τινες.	Some include Esther in addition to these.[403]
Καινῆς διαθήκης ὥρα μοι βίβλους λέγειν.	It is time for me to say the books of the New Covenant.
290 εὐαγγελιστὰς τέσσαρας δέχου μόνους·	Accept only the four Evangelists:
Ματθαῖον, εἶτα Μάρκον, ᾧ Λουκᾶν τρίτον	Matthew, then Mark, to whom adding Luke as third
προσθεὶς ἀρίθμει τὸν Ἰωάννην χρόνῳ	Number John as fourth in time,[404]
τέταρτον, ἀλλὰ πρῶτον ὕψει δογμάτων.	But first in sublimity of doctrine.
βροντῆς γὰρ υἱὸν τοῦτον εἰκότως καλῶ	For I fairly call the son of thunder
295 μέγιστον ἠχήσαντα τῷ θεοῦ λόγῳ.	Him who proclaimed most loudly the Word of God.
δέχου δὲ βίβλον Λουκᾶ καὶ τὴν δευτέραν	Now receive the book of Luke, even the second
τὴν τῶν καθολικῶν πράξεων ἀποστόλων.	One of the general Acts of the Apostles.
τὸ σκεῦος ἑξῆς προστίθει τῆς ἐκλογῆς,	Next add the Elect Vessel,[405]
τὸν τῶν ἐθνῶν κήρυκα, τὸν ἀπόστολον	The Preacher of the Gentiles, the Apostle
300 Παῦλον σοφῶς γράψαντα ταῖς ἐκκλησίαις	Paul who wisely wrote to the churches
ἐπιστολὰς δὶς ἑπτά· Ῥωμαίοις μίαν,	Twice seven epistles:[406] one to the Romans,
ᾗ χρὴ συνάπτειν πρὸς Κορινθίους δύο,	To which it is necessary to join two to the Corinthians,

book of the prophet Jeremiah. Baruch was Jeremiah's scribe (cf. Jer. 36:4), and therefore, he may have thought that the book of Baruch was from Jeremiah the prophet, as well. This introduction to Baruch differs from the way he introduces Isa 9:5 a few lines later: 'Or have you not heard what has been written' (ἢ οὐκ ἀκηκόατε τὸ γεγραμμένον), which clearly indicates the scriptural status of this book. Cf. the English translation in Barkhuizen 2001: p. 4. For the critical edition, cf. CCG 3, p. 6, ln. 62–3. Even though the introductions to the citations of Baruch and Isaiah differ, Amphilochius does appear to cite Baruch as Scripture and he cites it in order to show that the Old Testament does not simply teach about the appearances of God, but also about his *dwelling* among mankind. Cf. Barkhuizen (2001: 13–14) for this interpretation. Amphilochius cites the book of Baruch to make a theological point because he was probably convinced that the book belonged to the corpus of Jeremiah the prophet, a common view among Christians at this time. See the Appendix, pp. 262–3.

[402] Amphilochius combines two traditional understandings of Daniel: (1) he is grouped among the prophets; and (2) he was rather wise in deeds and words. Perhaps the second comment about him does recognize that his book was sometimes considered to be among the Writings, which included the works of wisdom, not the prophets (cf. ch. 2, pp. 67–9, on the Babylonian Talmud for details).

[403] There is no evidence of Amphilochius's use of Esther in his extant works. Although Amphilochius does not clearly add Esther to the canon, many earlier than him and during his time did (cf. the Bryennios List, p. 72; Origen, p. 87; Epiphanius pp. 161, 164, 167; and in ch. 4, Jerome, pp. 201, 208, 211). If he is excluding Esther from the canon, he would agree with the lists of Melito (see p. 82), Athanasius (p. 125), and Gregory of Nazianzus (pp. 143–6), which do not include the book either. Amphilochius does not describe the book as spurious (νόθος), as he does with the Apocalypse of John and Hebrews. It would therefore fit into either his canonical books or his intermediate books. If he considered Esther as intermediate, he would then agree with Athanasius's judgement that Esther be placed among the books to be read to the catechumens.

[404] The comment, 'fourth in time', probably indicates that this ordering of the four Gospels was done according to chronological principles.

[405] Cf. Acts 9:15.   [406] Paul's fourteen epistles include the book of Hebrews.

Text	Translation
τὴν πρὸς Γαλάτας τε καὶ πρὸς Ἐφεσίους, μεθ᾽ ἣν	The one both to the Galatians and to the Ephesians, after which
τὴν ἐν Φιλίπποις, εἶτα τὴν γεγραμμένην	The one to the Philippians, then the one written
305 Κολασσαεῦσι, Θεσσαλονικεῦσιν δύο,	To the Colossians, two to the Thessalonians,
δύο Τιμοθέῳ, Τίτῳ καὶ Φιλήμονι	Two to Timothy, to Titus, and to Philemon
μίαν ἑκατέρῳ καὶ πρὸς Ἑβραίους μίαν.	One to each of them and one to the Hebrews.[407]
τινὲς δέ φασι τὴν πρὸς Ἑβραίους νόθον	Now some say the one to the Hebrews is spurious
οὐκ εὖ λέγοντες· γνησία γὰρ ἡ χάρις.	They do not speak well; for the grace is genuine.
310 εἶεν, τί λοιπόν; καθολικῶν ἐπιστολῶν	So far so good, what is the rest? Of the catholic epistles
τινὲς μὲν ἑπτά φασιν, οἱ δὲ τρεῖς μόνας	Some say seven; others only three
χρῆναι δέχεσθαι· τὴν Ἰακώβου μίαν,	Is it necessary to accept: the one of James,
μίαν δὲ Πέτρου τῶν τ᾽ Ἰωάννου μίαν.	And one of Peter, and of those of John, one,
τινὲς δὲ τὰς τρεῖς καὶ πρὸς αὐταῖς τὰς δύο	But some receive three, and in addition to them the two
315 Πέτρου δέχονται, τὴν Ἰούδα δ᾽ ἑβδόμην.	Of Peter, and that of Jude, the seventh.[408]
τὴν δ᾽ ἀποκάλυψιν τὴν Ἰωάννου πάλιν	And the Apocalypse of John[409] again
τινὲς μὲν ἐγκρίνουσιν, οἱ πλείους δέ γε	Some accept, but the majority indeed
νόθον λέγουσιν. οὗτος ἀψευδέστατος	Say it is spurious.[410] This could be the most truthful
κανὼν ἂν εἴη τῶν θεοπνεύστων γραφῶν.	Canon[411] of the divinely inspired scriptures.
320 Αἷς εἰ σὺ πεισθῇς, ἐκφύγοις κόσμου πάγας.	If you are persuaded by these, you may escape the snares of the world.

[407] Amphilochius cites and alludes to Hebrews on many occasions. A good example of an allusion to Hebrews 3:1 is in *Oratio* or Homily 1.5.130: διό, ἀδελφοὶ μακαρίας κλήσεως ἐπουρανίου μέτοχοι (CCG 3, 8, ln. 130). See the English translation in Barkhuizen 2001: 7.

[408] The Catholic Epistles are treated similarly to Esther earlier in the list. Amphilochius reports on the debate over the exact number of them: some say three must be received (= James, 1 Peter, and 1 John), while others say seven (= James, 1–2 Peter, 1–3 John, and Jude). It is interesting that Amphilochius does not apply the term spurious (νόθος) to the latter four epistles, which may show that these are at least intermediate and neighbours to the words of truth in his mind. In the few works of Amphilochius that come down to the present time, there is no record of his use of 2 Peter, 2–3 John, or Jude. Gregory of Nazianzus accepted all seven of the Catholic Epistles as canonical, perhaps indicating that his first cousin, Amphilochius, would do the same, but this must remain only a probability.

[409] There is no evidence of Amphilochius's use of the book of Revelation in the paucity of his extant works.

[410] Amphilochius comments that some accept the Apocalypse of John, but the majority say it is spurious (νόθος). This view also seems to be the position Gregory of Nazianzus, who did not include the Apocalypse explicitly in his list, though he cites it and alludes to it on at least a couple of occasions. For details, see above, p. 146n377.

[411] The word κανών is used to denote an exclusive list of divinely inspired scriptures. The use of the superlative 'most unerring' or 'most truthful' (ἀψευδέστατος) to describe 'canon' is interesting. He does not include any of the deuterocanonical books in this list. Amphilochius holds a few books in dispute, but these books are held to be in the canon by many others.

The Canon List of Amphilochius

Books of the Old Covenant
    The Pentateuch
        The Creation   (= Genesis)
        Exodus
        Leviticus
        Numbers
        Deuteronomy
    Joshua
    Judges
    Ruth
    1–4 Kingdoms   (= 1–2 Samuels + 1–2 Kings)
    1–2 Paralipomena   (= 1–2 Chronicles)
    1–2 Esdras
    Five Books in Verse
        Job
        Book of Psalms
        Proverbs
        Ecclesiastes
        Song of Songs
    The Twelve Prophets
        Hosea
        Amos
        Micah
        Joel
        Obadiah
        Jonah
        Nahum
        Habakkuk
        Zephaniah
        Haggai
        Zechariah
        Malachi
    The Four Prophets
        Isaiah
        Jeremiah   (+ Lamentations + Baruch + ?Epistle of Jeremiah?)
        Ezekiel
        Daniel
    ? Esther ?   (= disputed book)
Books of the New Covenant
    The Four Gospels
        Matthew
        Mark
        Luke
        John

Acts of the Apostles
Fourteen Epistles of Paul
    Romans
    1–2 Corinthians
    Galatians
    Ephesians
    Philippians
    Colossians
    1–2 Thessalonians
    1–2 Timothy
    Titus
    Philemon
    Hebrews
Seven Catholic Epistles
    James
    ?1–2 Peter?   (= 2 Peter is disputed)
    ?1–3 John?   (= 2–3 John are disputed)
    ?Jude?   (= disputed)
?Revelation?   (= disputed)

Amphilochius's intermediate books: In the introduction to the list, Amphilochius says that 'not every book which has received the venerable name of Scripture is safe. For there are extant pseudonymous books, some of which are intermediate and neighbors . . . to the words of truth (ἔμμεσοι καὶ γείτονες . . . τῶν ἀληθείας λόγων) but others are spurious and surely unsafe (αἱ δ' αὖ νόθοι τε καὶ λίαν ἐπισφαλεῖς).' He classifies both kinds of books as pseudonymous. Unfortunately, he does not provide any examples of books from this category. We note that he alluded to Tobit, Sirach/Ecclesiasticus, and the Wisdom of Solomon in his extant writings (see above, n. 391). He found the teachings in these books useful for exhorting the church, but he did not refer to them as Scripture and he did not include them in his canon list. Thus he used the deuterocanonical books without attributing canonical status to them. These books were intermediate or neighbours to the words of truth. Therefore, Amphilochius's intermediate category aligns with the view of other fourth-century fathers that these books were useful and to be read.[412] In the final analysis, one cannot be certain about all of the books that would be in Amphilochius's intermediate category, but he certainly had such a category and the evidence suggests that he abided by his categories in practice.

    Amphilochius's spurious books: In the introduction to his list, Amphilochius also mentioned a second type of pseudonymous work, the spurious and surely unsafe books. He then draws the following comparison, 'Like counterfeit and spurious coins, which have the king's inscription, but they are fraudulent, being disguised with respect to their material' (ln. 258–60). Unfortunately, again there

---

[412] For details, see pp. 124–5, 128–9 on Athanasius, and p. 173 on Epiphanius.

is not much evidence for what Amphilochius considered to be a spurious book. From the list itself some were claiming that Hebrews and Revelation were spurious. Amphilochius clearly contradicts that position regarding Hebrews, for he says about the book that its grace is genuine or authentic (γνησία). For the Revelation of John he mentions that the majority consider that book to be spurious, but it is unclear what Amphilochius would say about the book, since he inserts it into his list.[413] We have no evidence of his use of the book of Revelation. Since his list instructs Seleucus to accept only the four evangelists of Matthew, Mark, Luke, and John, we can suggest that he would classify other gospels (e.g. Gospel of Thomas) as spurious.

Amphilochius's canon: Amphilochius's canon list of the books of the Old and New Covenants essentially reflects the contemporary Protestant Bible except for the probable inclusion of Baruch and the Epistle of Jeremiah, since these works were considered to be from the prophet himself. He did not include any of the deuterocanonical books in his list. Amphilochius drafted his canon list for two purposes: (1) to teach one the useful way of life and how to worship God, and the converse, how to escape from the traps of the world; and (2) to teach which books only appear to bear the king's inscription but actually are forgeries and very unsafe. Amphilochius believed that this exclusive list of books was vital to promoting piety and protecting the church from heresy and therefore he called it 'the most truthful canon of the divinely inspired Scriptures'.

EPIPHANIUS OF SALAMIS

Epiphanius (ca. 315–402/3) was born in Besanduc near Eleutheropolis in Palestine, southwest of Jerusalem. While living in Egypt during his teenage years he probably received monastic training and education.[414] He returned to Palestine in ca. 335 and established a monastery near the place of his birth. In 366/7, he became bishop of Salamis[415] (in Cyprus), a position he maintained until his death 402/3.[416] His residency in Palestine and Egypt placed him in an ideal context to learn the history of the scriptures. He embodied the antiquarian spirit, and his knowledge of ancient languages combined with his impulse

---

[413] For other fourth-century descriptions of forgeries of the canonical books, cf. the respective sections on Athanasius and Cyril of Jerusalem in this chapter.

[414] For more on Epiphanius's relation to Egyptian monasticism, see Kim 2015: 17–28.

[415] In the 360s, the city was technically called Constantia, refounded by Constantius II. The older city was destroyed in an earthquake, but people in the fourth century still called it Salamis. See ibid.: 152.

[416] For an account of Epiphanius's life and ministry see ibid. He lays out a probable account of Epiphanius's final days, in which he dies in 403. Therefore the beginning of his episcopate would be 367 (ibid.: 225–36). For an older account see Dechow 1988.

to refer to ancient sources flowed into his biblical scholarship.[417] Jerome celebrated him as a *pentaglōssos*, a five-tongued man.[418] From the *Hexapla* or the
hexaplaric recension he was able to cite the Hebrew in Greek transliteration
and multiple Greek versions in order to buttress an argument about a particular meaning of the words of Scripture.[419] His *Panarion* or 'chest of remedies
for those bitten by beasts' was written as a polemic against various heretical
sects. He compared their deeds to 'poisons and toxic substances' and his own
writing to 'the antidotes'.[420] His *De mensuris et ponderibus* or 'Concerning
Weights and Measures' is a true antiquarian work.[421] In addition to these two
works, he composed *De XII Gemmis* or 'Concerning the Twelve Stones',
which is a commentary on Aaron's breastplate (cf. Exod. 28).

Old Testament canon: Epiphanius included three OT canon lists in his writings (*Pan.* 8.6.1–10; *Mens.* 4–5; *Mens.* 22–3). Each time he reckons the books
as twenty-seven, but says that the Hebrews reckon them as twenty-two. Both
numbers correspond to the Hebrew alphabet, which has twenty-two letters, five
of which have two forms (a medial and a final form), these letters corresponding to five doubled books (1–2 Kingdoms, 3–4 Kingdoms, 1–2 Paralipomenon,
1–2 Esdras, Judges-Ruth).[422] He does not use the term 'canon' ($\kappa\alpha\nu\dot\omega\nu$)[423] to refer

---

[417] Jacobs 2013.

[418] *Ruf.* 3.6. In 2.22 of the same work, Jerome credits Epiphanius with knowing Greek, Syriac,
Hebrew, Egyptian (Coptic?), and in part also, Latin. Although see the discussion in ibid.: 449n66,
as to whether Jerome was sincere in this context, or simply trying to score points against Rufinus
during the Origenist controversy. See also Dummer 1968.

[419] *Pan.* 65.4.4–6 contains a good example. In order, he cites the respective versions of the
Seventy, Aquila, Symmachus, Theodotion, *Quinta, Sexta*, and the Hebrew in Greek transliteration
of Psalm 109:3 (EV 110:3) and then relates each word of the Hebrew to its respective equivalent in
the Seventy. In addition, he describes Origen's *Hexapla* in some detail in *Pan.* 64.3.5–7 and *Mens.*
7, 18–19 and the use of the aristarchian signs in the early sections of *Mens.*

[420] *Pan.* Prooemium I 1.1.2.

[421] The Greek version of *Mens.* trails off at the end, but the Syriac version, whose MSS are
earlier and more extensive than the Greek, appears to be complete. For the Syriac version and
English translation, see Dean 1935.

[422] The LXX books 1–4 Kingdoms usually have in English the titles 1–2 Samuel and 1–2 Kings.
Jerome (see p. 199) also reported this tradition of counting the OT books as either twenty-two or
twenty-seven and explained the difference as related to the five doubled Hebrew letters, but in his
telling the five doubled books included Jeremiah–Lamentations rather than Judges–Ruth.

[423] Epiphanius does use the word 'canon' and derivatives some twenty-five times in his writings. The word refers to the 'rule of faith and hope…founded…in those not denying the resurrection…' (*Ancoratus* 89.4). He also uses the phrase 'ecclesiastical rule' to refer to the teachings
constituted ($\delta\iota\alpha\tau\acute\alpha\sigma\sigma\omega$) by the apostles (*Pan.* 48.9.5). He then uses this phrase to contrast the
teachings and instructions of the church with the teachings of various sects. In *Pan.* 60.1.5, he
compares and contrasts the Apostolikoi (or Apotaktikoi) with another heretical group known as
the Katharoi: 'the Katharoi use only the specified scriptures ($\tau\alpha\hat\iota\varsigma$ $\dot\rho\eta\tau\alpha\hat\iota\varsigma$ $\gamma\rho\alpha\phi\alpha\hat\iota\varsigma$), but these (i.e.
the Apostolikoi) depend mostly ($\tau\dot o$ $\pi\lambda\epsilon\hat\iota\sigma\tau o\nu$) on the works called The Acts of Andrew and of
Thomas, since these (Apostolikoi) are completely foreign to the ecclesiastical rule' ($\pi\alpha\nu\tau\acute\alpha\pi\alpha\sigma\iota\nu$
$\dot\alpha\lambda\lambda\acute o\tau\rho\iota o\iota$ $\tau o\hat v$ $\kappa\alpha\nu\acute o\nu o\varsigma$ $\tau o\hat v$ $\dot\epsilon\kappa\kappa\lambda\eta\sigma\iota\alpha\sigma\tau\iota\kappa o\hat v$ $\dot\upsilon\pi\acute\alpha\rho\chi o\nu\tau\epsilon\varsigma$). Given Epiphanius's use of the word $\kappa\alpha\nu\dot\omega\nu$
elsewhere, he is likely saying here that the Apostolikoi are too dependent on literary works which
are foreign to the ecclesiastical rule. These teachings would probably include the list of specified
books that Epiphanius provides in his writings, but they would not be limited to those lists.

to these twenty-seven(two) books. Rather, in the course of describing how the Seventy-two Translators worked he concluded, 'And so the twenty-seven specified[424] (ῥηταί) and established[425] (ἐνδιάθετοι) books were translated, being numbered as twenty-two according to the letters of the alphabet of the Hebrews' (*Mens.* 3, ln. 92–5). He also made distinctions between these books and others. In his discussion of the translation method of the Seventy-two Translators, he notes that they produced both the twenty-two books *and* the seventy-two apocrypha (ἑβδομήκοντα δύο τῶν ἀποκρύφων; *Mens.* 5, ln. 147–8).[426] He also mentioned that the Jews have certain books in dispute (ἐν ἀμφιλέκτῳ), 'separate from some other apocryphal books' (χωρὶς ἄλλων τινῶν βιβλίων ἐναποκρύφων; *Pan.* 8.6.4). He did not mention the names of the books in the apocryphal category, but in the disputed category he placed the books of Sirach and Wisdom. In another place he says Sirach and Wisdom are 'useful' (χρήσιμοι) and 'beneficial' (ὠφέλιμοι) but they are not offered up to the number of the specified books (τῶν ῥητῶν; *Mens.* 4, ln. 122–3).

New Testament canon: Epiphanius lists the books of the New Testament while offering a summary of all of the Divine Scriptures (*Pan.* 76.22.5). The list is abbreviated but does contain four Gospels, fourteen Epistles of Paul, the Acts of the Apostles, the Catholic Epistles of James, Peter, John, and Jude, and

---

[424] ῥητός is difficult to translate in these contexts. Lampe's lexicon supplies 'canonical' when the word describes writings. However, in light of more recent scholarly discussion it seems best that we reserve the translation 'canon' for the actual Greek term κανών (and derivatives), and even then only in specific circumstances; see Metzger 1987: 289–93. Even so, Epiphanius appears to use the word ῥητός as equivalent to our 'canonical', just as Origen and Eusebius used the word ἐνδιάθηκος; see the section on Eusebius above, pp. 109–10. Since Epiphanius in *Mens.* uses ῥητός to describe the *specified number* of books of the Old Testament, we have used 'specified' as its equivalent. Cp. *Mens.* 22, ln. 676.

[425] Epiphanius uses this word six times in his writings. Four times the word is in the plural and refers to the twenty-seven(two) books of the Old Testament (*Mens.* 3 ln. 93, 4 ln. 106, 10 ln. 303; *Pan.* 55.2.1). The two instances of the singular modify λόγος in theological contexts (*Pan.* 71.3.9, 71.4.3; for the λόγος ἐνδιάθετος ('internal *logos*') and the λόγος προφορικός ('uttered *logos*') as theological terms to illustrate the distinction between the Father and Logos respectively, cf. Lampe 1961: 809). For the use of the two *logoi* in the allegorical interpretation of Philo and the D-Scholia to the *Iliad*, cf. Kamesar 2004. The usage of *endiathetos* in *Pan.* 55.2.1 is illustrative of the meaning of this word when it describes writings: Καὶ γὰρ παρά τισι τοῦ Μελχισεδὲκ ὁ πατήρ τε καὶ ἡ μήτηρ ἐμφέρεται· οὐκ ἔχει δὲ κατὰ τὰς ῥητὰς γραφὰς καὶ ἐνδιαθέτους τοῦτο. Epiphanius reports that other (apocryphal) accounts mention both the father and mother of Melchizedek, but they are not included in the story according to the specified and established scriptures. *Endiathetos* is close to the meaning of *endiathēkos* 'encovenanted' used by Origen and Eusebius, and Epiphanius uses the word to denote an exclusive list of books. His antiquarian and historical sensibilities may have influenced him to use *endiathetos*, since it also has been used to describe something that is 'fixed' and 'long standing' or 'traditional', as opposed to something that is temporary (cf. LSJ ἐνδιάθετος sub II).

[426] Epiphanius's total number of books (twenty-two + seventy-two) agrees with the ninety-four books of 4 Ezra 14:44–8. However, 4 Ezra has twenty-four canonical books, with seventy esoteric books, while Epiphanius appears to use the number twenty-two after Josephus's reckoning of the books. But see p. 7n24.

the Apocalypse of John. It thus corresponds to the twenty-seven-book New Testament, with the possible exceptions of 2 Peter and 2–3 John.

Studies: Dechow 1988; Adler 1990: 472–501; Bregman 1991: 125–38; Jacobs 2013; Kim 2015.

Panarion 8.6.1–4

Date: ca. 376

Introduction: In *Pan.* 8, Epiphanius recounts the history of the Jewish people and he includes a list of their twenty-seven sacred books reckoned as twenty-two according to the letters of the Hebrew alphabet. In the context, Epiphanius describes these books as prophetic oracles concerning the Christ to come (*Pan.* 8.5.6) and in 8.6.5–10, he provides what he calls types (τύποι) in the Law whose truth (ἀλήθεια) is in the Gospel. The prophetic significance of these twenty-seven books contributed to their authoritative, established status among the Jews and the Christians.

Text[427]	Translation
(1) Ἔσχον δὲ οὗτοι οἱ Ἰουδαῖοι ἄχρι τῆς ἀπὸ Βαβυλῶνος τῆς αἰχμαλωσίας ἐπανόδου βίβλους τε καὶ προφήτας τούτους καὶ προφητῶν βίβλους ταύτας· (2) πρώτην μὲν Γένεσιν δευτέραν Ἔξοδον τρίτην Λευιτικὸν τετάρτην Ἀριθμοὺς πέμπτην Δευτερονόμιον ἕκτη βίβλος Ἰησοῦ τοῦ Ναυῆ ἑβδόμη τῶν Κριτῶν ὀγδόη τῆς Ῥοὺθ ἐνάτη τοῦ Ἰὼβ δεκάτη τὸ Ψαλτήριον ἑνδεκάτη Παροιμίαι Σολομῶντος δωδεκάτη Ἐκκλησιαστὴς τρισκαιδεκάτη τὸ ᾆσμα τῶν ᾀσμάτων τεσσαρεσκαιδεκάτη Βασιλειῶν πρώτη πεντεκαιδεκάτη Βασιλειῶν δευτέρα ἑκκαιδεκάτη Βασιλειῶν τρίτη ἑπτακαιδεκάτη Βασιλειῶν τετάρτη ὀκτωκαιδεκάτη Παραλειπομένων πρώτη ἐννεακαιδεκάτη	(1) Now, at the time of the return from the Babylonian captivity, these Jews had books and these (following) prophets and these (following) books of prophets:[428] (2) first Genesis, second Exodus, third Leviticus, fourth Numbers, fifth Deuteronomy, sixth Book of Joshua of Naue, seventh Judges, eighth of Ruth,[429] ninth of Job, tenth the Psalter, eleventh Proverbs of Solomon, twelfth Ecclesiastes, thirteenth the Song of Songs, fourteenth first of Kingdoms, fifteenth second of Kingdoms, sixteenth third of Kingdoms, seventeenth fourth of Kingdoms, eighteenth first of Paralipomenon, nineteenth second of Paralipomenon, twentieth the Twelve Prophets, twenty-first Isaiah the prophet,

[427] Bergermann and Collatz 2013: 191–2, ln. 9–20, 1–9.

[428] The repetition of 'books and prophets' and 'books of prophets' sounds awkward in English and in Greek. It seems many of the titles of the books in the following list include 'book' or 'prophet'. When he comes to Isaiah, for example, he does not call it a book. Rather he refers to the book as 'Isaiah the prophet'. Epiphanius claims that the Jews had all of these books at or by the time of the return from the Babylonian exile. In this claim, he appears to be dependent on Josephus in *Against Apion* 1.39–41, who also organized the established books mainly along historical lines. The report in 4 Ezra 14, with which Epiphanius seems familiar (see above, n. 426), would also suggest the same chronology.

[429] Ruth is not listed with Judges in this list, as in *Mens.* 4 and other patristic lists. This list enumerates the books as twenty-seven, which precludes joining Ruth with Judges.

Text	Translation
Παραλειπομένων δευτέρα εἰκοστὴ τὸ Δωδεκαπρόφητον εἰκοστὴ πρώτη Ἡσαΐας ὁ προφήτης εἰκοστὴ δευτέρα Ἰερεμίας ὁ προφήτης μετὰ τῶν Θρήνων καὶ ἐπιστολῶν αὐτοῦ τε καὶ <τοῦ> Βαροὺχ εἰκοστὴ τρίτη Ἰεζεκιὴλ ὁ προφήτης εἰκοστὴ τετάρτη Δανιὴλ ὁ προφήτης εἰκοστὴ πέμπτη Ἔσδρας ᾱ, εἰκοστὴ ἕκτη Ἔσδρας β̄, εἰκοστὴ ἑβδόμη Ἐσθήρ.	twenty-second Jeremiah the prophet with the Lamentations[430] and Epistles, both his own and Baruch's,[431] twenty-third Ezekiel the prophet, twenty-fourth Daniel the prophet, twenty-fifth Esdras I, twenty-sixth Esdras II, twenty-seventh Esther.[432]
(3) αὗταί εἰσιν αἱ εἴκοσι ἑπτὰ βίβλοι ἐκ θεοῦ δοθεῖσαι τοῖς Ἰουδαίοις· εἴκοσι δύο δέ εἰσιν ὡς τὰ παρ' αὐτοῖς στοιχεῖα τῶν Ἑβραϊκῶν γραμμάτων ἀριθμούμεναι διὰ τὸ διπλοῦσθαι δέκα βίβλους εἰς πέντε λογιζομένας. περὶ τούτου δὲ ἄλλῃ που σαφῶς εἰρήκαμεν.	(3) These are the twenty-seven books given by God to the Jews; now these are numbered twenty-two just as their letters in Hebrew characters because ten books are double, being reckoned as five. Now we have spoken clearly concerning this in another place.[433]
(4) εἰσὶ δὲ καὶ ἄλλαι δύο βίβλοι παρ' αὐτοῖς ἐν ἀμφιλέκτῳ, ἡ Σοφία τοῦ Σιρὰχ καὶ ἡ τοῦ	(4) Now they also have two other books in dispute,[434] the Wisdom of Sirach and the one

[430] The joining of Lamentations to Jeremiah as a double book is also known from Jerome's *Prol. Gal.* (cf. ch. 4 on Jerome, p. 199).

[431] Epiphanius includes the Epistles of Jeremiah and Baruch with the book of Jeremiah as a matter of Jewish custom, but there is little evidence that Jews at this time actually did accept these books, and later we will see that Epiphanius himself provides contrary evidence (cf. *Mens.* 5 below). However, he probably intends that the Epistles of Jeremiah and Baruch are considered to be part of the canon of the church, since they were reckoned to be part of the book of Jeremiah, although he nowhere states this conclusion. Epiphanius's reference to the 'Epistle of Baruch' is intriguing and unique among the lists. What is known today as the Epistle of Baruch is part of 2 Baruch, an apocalyptic work from the first and second centuries (Charlesworth 1983: 615ff, 647). Epiphanius may be referring to this portion of 2 Baruch, or he could be using the expression 'Epistle of Baruch' to refer to the book of Baruch. For the first position, see Beckwith 1985: 190. For the second position, see Assan-Dhôte and Moatti-Fine 2008: 24. In either case, it seems unlikely that Jews were including this work in their canon, and only the book of Baruch was included in some early Christian lists. See the Appendix, pp. 262–3.

[432] Epiphanius includes the disputed Esther in all three of his lists.

[433] Epiphanius comments on the canon of the Jews. He numbers the books as twenty-seven but immediately notes that the same books are reckoned as twenty-two by the Jews, since the ten books that are double correspond to the five double letters in the Hebrew alphabet (Cf. *Mens.* 4 below.). The number twenty-seven is not arbitrary, for it appears to be dependent on an earlier source (Cf. *Mens.* 23 below and the section on the Bryennios List above, pp. 70–8). The number twenty-two depends on a Jewish tradition such as the one recorded in Josephus, who did not list the books, nor show the correspondence to the Hebrew alphabet (*Against Apion* 1.38–41, pp. 57–65 above).

[434] Epiphanius says that the Jews have two other books in dispute (ἐν ἀμφιλέκτῳ): Wisdom of Solomon and Sirach. Epiphanius uses ἀμφίλεκτος on two other occasions not in reference to books of scripture. In *Pan.* 31.2.2, the birthplace of Valentinos is 'in dispute if one must speak truth', even though Epiphanius will not keep silent about the information that has come to him concerning it. In *Pan.* 70.10.1, he reports that 'the Audianoi cite the Constitution of the Apostles as in dispute by many, but it is not discredited'. Epiphanius, therefore, uses this term to show that there is genuine disagreement and dispute over records and information from the past, and therefore he uses the term fittingly to describe books not established nor apocryphal. In actuality, we have little evidence that Jews did dispute the status of these books. The Wisdom of Solomon was almost certainly composed in Greek and did not seem to enjoy as wide a reception among Jews as among Christians. Rabbinic literature preserves some citations and discussions of Sirach or Ben Sira (Ecclesiasticus), but also the explicit statement that the book does not defile the hands, the

Text	Translation
Σολομῶντος, χωρὶς ἄλλων τινῶν βιβλίων ἐναποκρύφων.	of Solomon, separate from some other apocryphal[435] books.

De mensuris et ponderibus 4–5

Date: 392[436]

Introduction: In *Mens.* 4–5, Epiphanius is in the midst of a protracted discussion of the Aristarchian text-critical sign known as the *obelos*, which began in *Mens.* 3. This was the sign Origen used to mark the portions of the LXX absent from the Hebrew.[437] The discussion continues through *Mens.* 6. In *Mens.* 3, ln. 76–95, he explains how the Seventy-two Translators rendered their Hebrew source and he concludes this section with a reference to the twenty-seven (two) specified and established books. In the next section, he then must explain the numbering of the books according to the letters of the Hebrew alphabet and then proceed to list the books.

Mens. 4–5 contains five pentateuchs or five groups of five books with two remaining books. In *Mens.* 4, the Old Testament can be divided into four pentateuchs with two remaining books, while in *Mens.* 5 Epiphanius shows with precision how the Psalter has traditionally been divided into five books, thus making another pentateuch. These pentateuchs in this context illustrate that antiquarian literature is 'the constellation of fragments loosely and contingently united'.[438]

peculiar rabbinic way of saying that the book is not sacred (as briefly discussed in ch. 1, p. 14). Why does Epiphanius mention these two books as in dispute among the Jews? He may be advocating for their inclusion in the Christian canon by claiming that they are on the edges of the Jewish canon. But by claiming that the Jews keep these two books separate from some apocryphal books (χωρὶς ἄλλων τινῶν βιβλίων ἐναποκρύφων), Epiphanius may be saying that Wisdom of Solomon and Sirach belong to a category of writings between canonical and apocryphal, a middle category of useful books attested also by some other patristic authors (cf., e.g., the section on Athanasius above, esp. pp. 128–9, and ch. 4 for the section on Rufinus, esp. p. 219). He includes Wisdom of Solomon and Sirach among the Divine Scriptures elsewhere (cf. *Pan.* 76.22.5 below). However, in his clearest exposition on the matter in *Mens.* 4, he appears to be speaking for Christians when he describes their usefulness but also says that they are not included within the number of specified and established books.

[435] An interesting word, ἐναπόκρυφος (*enapocryphos*) is used only three times according to *TLG* (Acta Thomae 123.3; *Pan.* 8.6; Doctrina Patrum 238.3). The last source is from the seventh to eighth centuries and cites the *Panarion*. The Acts of Thomas in the third century used the word to describe God in a prayer, and it probably has the meaning 'hidden' in order to describe the hidden God. Epiphanius uses ἀπόκρυφος 'apocrypha' (e.g. *Mens.* 5) of esoteric works elsewhere, and he uses ἐναποκρύφων here in a similar way. There is no discernible difference in meaning and unfortunately the evidence is too meagre to probe further.

[436] *Mens.* 20, ln. 581–3. Epiphanius references 'the present, second consulship of Arcadius', which was 392.

[437] Origen, *Comm. Matt.* 15.14.   [438] Jacobs 2013: 457.

Text[439]	Translation
(4) Εἴκοσι γὰρ καὶ δύο ἔχουσι στοιχείων ὀνόματα, πέντε δέ εἰσιν ἐξ αὐτῶν διπλούμεναι. Τὸ γὰρ χὰφ ἔστι διπλοῦν καὶ τὸ μὲμ καὶ τὸ νοῦν καὶ τὸ φὶ καὶ τὸ σαδέ. Διὸ καὶ αἱ βίβλοι κατὰ τοῦτον τὸν τρόπον εἴκοσι δύο μὲν ἀριθμοῦνται, εἴκοσι ἑπτὰ δὲ εὑρίσκονται, διὰ τὸ πέντε ἐξ αὐτῶν διπλοῦσθαι. Συνάπτεται γὰρ ἡ Ῥοὺθ τοῖς Κριταῖς καὶ ἀριθμεῖται παρ᾽ Ἑβραίοις μία βίβλος. Συνάπτεται ἡ πρώτη τῶν Παραλειπομένων τῇ δευτέρᾳ καὶ λέγεται μία βίβλος. Συνάπτεται ἡ πρώτη τῶν Βασιλειῶν τῇ δευτέρᾳ καὶ λέγεται μία βίβλος. Συνάπτεται ἡ τρίτη τῇ τετάρτῃ καὶ λέγεται μία βίβλος. Συνάπτεται ἡ πρώτη τοῦ Ἔσδρα τῇ δευτέρᾳ καὶ γίνεται μία βίβλος. Οὕτως οὖν σύγκεινται αἱ βίβλοι ἐν πεντατεύχοις τέτταρσι καὶ μένουσιν ἄλλαι δύο ὑστερούσαι, ὡς εἶναι τὰς ἐνδιαθέτους βίβλους οὕτως· πέντε μὲν νομικάς, Γένεσιν, Ἔξοδον, Λευιτικόν, Ἀριθμούς, Δευτερονόμιον· αὕτη ἡ πεντάτευχος ἡ καὶ νομοθεσία· πέντε δὲ στιχήρεις· ἡ τοῦ Ἰὼβ βίβλος, εἶτα τὸ Ψαλτήριον, Παροιμίαι Σολομῶντος, Ἐκκλησιαστής, Ἄσμα Ἀσμάτων. Εἶτα ἄλλη πεντάτευχος τὰ καλούμενα Γραφεῖα, παρά τισι δὲ Ἁγιόγραφα λεγόμενα, ἅτινά ἐστιν οὕτως· Ἰησοῦ τοῦ Ναυῆ βίβλος, Κριτῶν μετὰ τῆς Ῥοὺθ, Παραλειπομένων πρώτη μετὰ τῆς	(4) For they [the Jews] have twenty-two names of letters, but five of them are double. For the *Chaph* is double and the *Mem* and the *Nun* and the *Phi* and the *Sade*. Therefore, also the books are numbered twenty-two in this manner, but twenty-seven are found, because five of them are double. For Ruth is joined to the Judges and is numbered as one book by the Hebrews. The first of Paralipomenon[440] is joined to the second and is counted as one book. The first of Kingdoms is joined to the second and is counted as one book. The third is joined to the fourth and is counted as one book. The first of Esdras is joined to the second and becomes one book. Therefore in this way the books lie together in four pentateuchs and two other late ones remain, so that the established books are thus: five pertaining to laws, Genesis, Exodus, Leviticus, Numbers, Deuteronomy; this is the pentateuch which is also legislation.[441] Now five are in verse: the book of Job,[442] then the Psalter, Proverbs of Solomon, Ecclesiastes, Song of Songs. Then there is another pentateuch, those called Writings, but called *Hagiographa* by some, which is thus: book of Joshua of Naue, of Judges with Ruth, first of Paralipomenon with the second, first of Kingdoms with the second,

---

[439] Moutsoulas 1973: 161–3, ln. 96–148.   [440] 1–2 Chronicles in the English Bible.

[441] In the seventh and eighth centuries, John of Damascus had almost the exact same ordering of pentateuchs, except his list transposed the second and third ones: Law, Hagiographa, Poetry, Prophets, and two remaining books. He also affirms that Wisdom and Sirach are not included in the number but that they are virtuous (ἐνάρετοι) and beautiful (καλαί) (PG 94: 1179–80).

[442] The placement of Job after Deuteronomy in this list appears to be deliberate and has ancient precedent. Jerome's *Epistle* 53 also places Job after Deuteronomy. See ch. 4 on Jerome, p. 204. See also Brock 2013. The tradition of identifying Job with Jobab, son of Zerah, one of the sons of Esau, is as old as the longer ending of Greek Job (42:17ba; cf. Gen. 36:33 and 36:13). This identification either placed Job one generation earlier than Moses or made him his contemporary. Olympiodorus ponders both options in his Commentary on Job; cf. Olympiodorus (1984: 396,22–397,6), which then made it probable that Moses would have heard of the trials of Job and the deliberations with his friends and recorded them. The Talmud preserves the claim that Moses wrote the book of Job; cf. b. B. Bat. 14b–15a. This same claim is found in the later Syriac father, Isho'dad of Merv, as well as the Greek authors, such as Methodius and Arian Julian (cf. Brock 2013: 57–60). This alleged connection between Moses and the authorship of Job perhaps accounts for the Job fragments written in the palaeo-Hebrew script found in Cave 4 of Qumran. Only the books of the Pentateuch and Job have been found written in this script, and the reason appears to be that they were all thought to be written by Moses himself (cf. ibid.: 61). Therefore, Epiphanius must have placed Job after Deuteronomy on the basis of ancient sources. (He also thought Job lived during patriarchal times; cf. *Pan.* 4.1.9–10.) When John of Damascus used this list a few centuries later (see previous note), he transposed the second and third pentateuchs to conform to the order of books familiar to him in the Greek manuscripts, and thus severed the connection between Moses and the authorship of Job in the Greek tradition (PG 94: 1180).

Text	Translation
δευτέρας, Βασιλειῶν πρώτη μετὰ τῆς δευτέρας, Βασιλειῶν τρίτη μετὰ τῆς τετάρτης. Αὕτη τρίτη πεντάτευχος. Ἄλλη πεντάτευχος τὸ δωδεκαπρόφητον, Ἡσαΐας, Ἱερεμίας, Ἱεζεκιήλ, Δανιήλ. Καὶ εἶτα ἐπληρώθη ἡ προφητικὴ πεντάτευχος. Ἔμειναν δὲ ἄλλαι δύο, αἵτινές εἰσι τοῦ Ἔσδρα, δύο εἰς μίαν λογιζόμεναι, καὶ ἡ ἄλλη βίβλος ἡ τῆς Ἐσθήρ. Καὶ ἐκπληρώθησαν αἱ εἴκοσι δύο βίβλοι κατὰ τὸν ἀριθμὸν τῶν εἴκοσι δύο στοιχείων παρ᾽ Ἑβραίοις. Αἱ γὰρ στιχήρεις δύο βίβλοι, ἥ τε τοῦ Σολομῶντος, ἡ Πανάρετος λεγομένη, καὶ ἡ τοῦ Ἰησοῦ τοῦ υἱοῦ Σειράχ, ἐκγόνου δὲ τοῦ Ἰησοῦ, (ὁ γὰρ πάππος αὐτοῦ Ἰησοῦς ἐκαλεῖτο), τοῦ καὶ τὴν σοφίαν ἑβραϊστὶ γράψαντος, ἣν ὁ ἔκγονος αὐτοῦ Ἰησοῦς ἑρμηνεύσας ἑλληνιστὶ ἔγραψε. Καὶ αὗται χρήσιμοι μέν εἰσι καὶ ὠφέλιμοι, ἀλλ᾽ εἰς ἀριθμὸν τῶν ῥητῶν οὐκ ἀναφέρονται. Διὸ οὐδὲ ἐν τῷ ἀαρὼν ἐνετέθησαν, τουτέστιν ἐν τῇ τῆς διαθήκης κιβωτῷ.	third of Kingdoms with the fourth. This is the third pentateuch. Another pentateuch is the Twelve Prophets, Isaiah, Jeremiah,[443] Ezekiel, Daniel. And then the prophetic pentateuch was filled. Now two others remained which are of Esdras, two reckoned as one, and the other book which is of Esther. And the twenty-two books were filled according to the number of the twenty-two letters of the Hebrews. For the two books in verse, both the one of Solomon, being called *the Excellent*, and the one of Jesus son of Sirach,[444] and the grandson Jesus (for his grandfather was called Jesus),[445] who wrote the wisdom in Hebrew, which his grandson, Jesus, wrote by translating it into Greek. And these are useful and beneficial, but they are not offered up to the number of the specified books. Therefore neither were they placed in the ark [aarōn], that is, in the ark of the covenant.

[443] In *Mens.* 5, Epiphanius conveys that the Jews have joined only Lamentations to the book of Jeremiah. However, he appears to say that Christians join also the Epistles of Jeremiah and Baruch to Jeremiah and Lamentations. See above, n. 431, for the discussion of the reference to the Epistle of Baruch. Epiphanius restricts his entire usage of Baruch to 3:36–8 from which he supports the doctrine of the incarnation of the Divine Son. He cites the full three verses on one occasion, introducing the citation with 'as the Scripture says' (ὡς λέγει ἡ γραφή) and introducing his inference from it with 'how does the divine Scripture instruct us' (πῶς ἡ θεία γραφὴ ἡμᾶς συνετίζει) (*Pan.* 57.2.3). He cites 3:36 without a citation formula once (*Pan.* 57.9.1) and with the formula 'the scripture also says' (φησιν ἡ γραφὴ καί) (*Pan.* 69.31.6). He combines a citation of the first part of v. 37 with some other material once without citation formula (*Pan.* 69.53.7). Epiphanius cites 3:37–8 in support of the true divinity of the Son in part of his refutation of Arianism (*Pan.* 69.31.6–7). He quotes and interprets key phrases from 3:37–8 commenting that 'the divine scripture cannot be in dispute' (ὡς οὐκ ἀμφιβάλλει ἡ θεία γραφή) (*Pan.* 80.3.5). In *De fide* 16.2, he once again cites 3:38 as a prophecy that was fulfilled in the appearance of the incarnation of the Son (πληρωθῇ τὸ εἰρημένον). In *Pan.* 69.55.6, 3:38 is cited as part of the Scriptures again in support of the Son's equality with the Father, and any notion of inequality results from the incarnation. Finally, in *Ancoratus* 78.8, Epiphanius cites the last part of v. 38 to support the Son's dwelling among humanity 'according to what has been written' (κατὰ τὸ γεγραμμένον).

[444] The books of Wisdom and Sirach are not said to be in dispute as in *Pan.* 8.6, but rather Epiphanius calls them 'useful and beneficial'. Although these books are praiseworthy, they are not offered up to the number of the specified writings, and they were not placed in the ark of the covenant. This mention of ark of the covenant may recall the practice of laying up sacred writings in the ark located in the tabernacle and temple (cf. Exod. 25:16, 40:20; Deut. 10:2 et al.; for Second Temple evidence see, e.g., Josephus's *Jewish War* 7.148–50). His description of these two books agrees with that of Athanasius, who excludes them from the canonized books but appoints them for reading to catechumens who desire instruction in the word of piety (cf. the section on Athanasius above, pp. 124–25, for details).

[445] He reports that Sirach was originally written in Hebrew by a Jesus son of Sirach and was translated into Greek by the grandson who was also named Jesus. The Prologue to Sirach mentions that the grandfather was named Jesus (5), but it nowhere mentions that the name of the grandson is Jesus.

Text	Translation
(5) Ἀλλὰ καὶ ἔτι τοῦτό σε μὴ παρέλθῃ, ὦ φιλόκαλε, ὅτι καὶ τὸ Ψαλτήριον διεῖλον εἰς πέντε βιβλία οἱ Ἑβραῖοι, ὥστε εἶναι καὶ αὐτὸ ἄλλην πεντάτευχον. Ἀπὸ γὰρ πρώτου ψαλμοῦ ἄχρι τεσσαρακοστοῦ μίαν ἐλογίσαντο βίβλον· ἀπὸ δὲ τεσσαρακοστοῦ πρώτου ἄχρι τοῦ ἑβδομηκοστοῦ πρώτου δευτέραν ἡγήσαντο· ἀπὸ ἑβδομηκοστοῦ δευτέρου ἕως ὀγδοηκοστοῦ ὀγδόου τρίτην βίβλον ἐποιήσαντο· ἀπὸ δὲ ὀγδοηκοστοῦ ἐνάτου ἕως ἑκατοστοῦ πέμπτου τετάρτην ἐποίησαν· ἀπὸ δὲ ἑκατοστοῦ ἕκτου ἕως τοῦ ἑκατοστοῦ πεντηκοστοῦ τὴν πέμπτην συνέθηκαν. Ἕκαστον γὰρ ψαλμὸν ἔχοντα ἐν τῷ τέλει τὸ εὐλογητὸς Κύριος, γένοιτο, γένοιτο, τέλος εἶναι βιβλίου ἐδικαίωσαν. Εὑρίσκεται δὲ τοῦτο ἔν τε τῷ τεσσαρακοστῷ καὶ ἐν τῷ ἑβδομηκοστῷ πρώτῳ καὶ ἐν τῷ ὀγδοηκοστῷ ὀγδόῳ καὶ ἐν τῷ ἑκατοστῷ πέμπτῳ. Καὶ ἐπληρώθησαν αἱ τέσσαρες βίβλοι. Ἐν δὲ τῷ τέλει τῆς πέμπτης βίβλου ἀντὶ τοῦ εὐλογητὸς Κύριος γένοιτο γένοιτο τὸ «πᾶσα πνοὴ αἰνεσάτω τὸν Κύριον, ἀλληλούια». Οὕτω γὰρ λογισάμενοι τὴν περὶ τούτου πᾶσαν ὑπόθεσιν ἀνεπλήρωσαν. Αὗται τοίνυν αἱ εἴκοσι καὶ ἑπτὰ εἴκοσι δύο δὲ ἀριθμούμεναι μετὰ καὶ τοῦ Ψαλτηρίου καὶ τῶν ὄντων ἐν τῷ Ἱερεμίᾳ φημὶ δὲ καὶ τῶν Θρήνων καὶ τῶν ἐπιστολῶν Βαρούχ τε καὶ Ἱερεμίου, εἰ καὶ οὐ κεῖνται αἱ ἐπιστολαὶ παρ' Ἑβραίοις, ἢ μόνον ἡ τῶν Θρήνων τῷ Ἱερεμίᾳ συναφθεῖσα, τὸν τρόπον ὃν εἴπομεν ἡρμηνεύθησαν κατὰ περίοδον ἑκάστῃ ζυγῇ ἑρμηνευτῶν ἐπιδιδόμεναι καὶ ἀπὸ τῆς πρώτης ζυγῆς τῇ δευτέρᾳ καὶ πάλιν ἀπὸ τῆς δευτέρας τῇ τρίτῃ καὶ οὕτω παρῆλθον κυκλεύουσαι ἑκάστη τριακοντάκις καὶ ἑξάκις ἑρμηνευθεῖσαι, ὡς δ' ᾄδεται λόγος καὶ αἱ εἴκοσι δύο καὶ ἑβδομήκοντα δύο τῶν ἀποκρύφων.	(5) But still also let this not elude you, O scholar, that also the Hebrews divide the Psalter into five books, so that even it is another pentateuch.[446] For from the first psalm until the fortieth they reckoned as one book, and from the forty-first until the seventy-first they considered a second; from the seventy-second until the eighty-eighth they made a third book; from the eighty-ninth until the one-hundred-and-fifth they made a fourth; from the one-hundred-and-sixth until the one-hundred-and-fiftieth they put together a fifth.[447] For they deem that each psalm having at its end the benediction 'Lord, may it be, may it be' is the end of a book.[448] And this is found in the fortieth and in the seventy-first and in the eighty-eighth and in the one-hundred-and-fifth. And the four books are filled. Now in the end of the fifth book in place of the benediction 'Lord, may it be, may it be' is the phrase 'Let every breath praise the Lord, *alleluia*.' For having reckoned the whole subject in this way, they fill it up. Therefore, these are the twenty and seven (books) but being numbered as twenty-two with both the Psalter and those in Jeremiah—now I speak also of the Lamentations, and of the Epistles of Baruch, and of Jeremiah, although the epistles are not among the Hebrews, rather only Lamentations, which is joined to Jeremiah. With respect to the method, which we said, they were translated, they were given to each pair of translators in a rotation and from the first pair to the second and again from the second to the third and thus they went, each one, going around and translated thirty-six times, as the account runs, both the twenty-two and seventy-two of the apocrypha.

[446] The Psalter was divided into five books so that it is another pentateuch, thus making five pentateuchs. Origen is the earliest father to convey the five-book Psalter. See *Comm. Psa. prol.* (PG 12: 1056). Hilary of Poitiers also knows of this tradition. See *Tract. Psal.* Instr. 1 (CSEL 22.3). The fifth book of the Psalter, according to Epiphanius, ends with Psalm 150 of the LXX Psalter. He, therefore, does not include Psalm 151 in the Psalter. Perhaps he was aware of the superscription to Psalm 151, which notes that it is outside of the number: Οὗτος ὁ ψαλμὸς ἰδιόγραφος εἰς Δαυιδ καὶ ἔξωθεν τοῦ ἀριθμοῦ· ὅτε ἐμονομάχησεν τῷ Γολιαδ.

[447] Epiphanius is employing the enumeration of the LXX Psalter, which for most of the book diverges by one from the Hebrew Psalter and thus from most English Bibles. The five books of the Psalter in the Hebrew numbering are: Book 1: Psalms 1–41; Book 2: Psalms 42–72; Book 3: Psalms 73–89; Book 4: Psalms 90–106; Book 5: Psalms 107–50.

[448] 'May it be' (γένοιτο) is the LXX's translation for the Hebrew 'amen'.

De mensuris et ponderibus 22–3

Date: 392

Introduction: Epiphanius included a third Old Testament list of books, the second one of *Mens*. He used a list of books with both Hebrew and Greek titles as a fitting conclusion of his discussion of the 'just' *modius*,[449] which is precisely twenty-two *xestai*, which he knows because the Hebrews invented it with great precision.[450] The measure of twenty-two *xestai* is then explained by appealing to four significant groupings of twenty-two: twenty-two works of God in the creation week (ln. 635–5), twenty-two heads of generations from Adam to Jacob, who is also Israel (ln. 665–72), twenty-two letters of the Hebrew alphabet (ln. 673–9), and twenty-two books of the Old Testament (ln. 679–96).[451] According to Jacobs, 'Epiphanius has concocted a numerical and figurative interpretation of the *modius* that connects sacred history, divine order, and the form of the Hebrew Bible, a *tour de force* even Origen would likely appreciate.'[452]

Text[453]	Translation
(22) [...] Δι' ὃ καὶ εἴκοσι δύο εἰσὶ τὰ παρὰ τοῖς Ἑβραίοις γράμματα, ἅ ἐστι ταῦτα· ἄλεφ, βήθ, γιμηλ, δελεδ, η, ουαῦ, ζήθ, ἤθ, τήθ, ἰώθ, χάφ, λαμεδ, μήμ, νουν, σαμεχ, αϊν, φη, σαδη, κωφ, ρης, σιν, θαυ. Διόπερ καὶ εἴκοσι δύο βίβλοι εἰσὶ τῆς Παλαιᾶς Διαθήκης ῥηταὶ καὶ παρ' αὐτοῖς τοῖς Ἑβραίοις εἴκοσι ἑπτὰ μὲν οὖσαι εἴκοσι δύο δὲ ἀριθμούμεναι ἐπειδήπερ καὶ πέντε τῶν στοιχείων παρ' αὐτοῖς διπλοῦνται τὸ χὰφ διπλοῦν καὶ τὸ μὲμ καὶ τὸ νοῦν καὶ τὸ φὶ καὶ τὸ σάδι.	(22)...On account of which the letters of the Hebrews are also twenty-two, which are these: *Aleph, Bēth, Gimēl, Deled, Ē, Ouau, Zēth, Ēth, Tēth, Iōth, Chaph, Lamed, Mēm, Noun, Samech, Aïn, Phē, Sadē, Kōph, Rēs, Sin, Thau.* Wherefore also there are twenty-two specified books of the Old Covenant, although on the one hand the Hebrews have twenty-seven (books) but on the other hand they are numbered as twenty-two since five of their letters are double: the *Chaph* is double, and the *Mem*, and the *Noun*, and the *Phi*, and the *Sadi*.
(23) Οὕτως γὰρ αἱ βίβλοι ἀριθμοῦνται α' Βιρσήθ, ἣ καλεῖται Γένεσις κόσμου. Ἐλησιμώθ, ἡ Ἔξοδος τῶν υἱῶν Ἰσραὴλ ἐξ Αἰγύπτου. Οὐαϊεκρά, ἣ ἑρμηνεύεται Λευιτικόν. Οὐαϊδαβήρ, ἥ ἐστιν Ἀριθμῶν. Ἐλλεδεβαρείμ, τὸ Δευτερονόμιον. Διησοῦ, ἡ τοῦ Ἰησοῦ τοῦ Ναυῆ. Διώβ, ἡ τοῦ Ἰώβ. Δεσωφτείμ, ἡ τῶν Κριτῶν. Δερούθ,	(23) For in this way the books are numbered. First, *Birsēth*, which is called Genesis of the World. *Elēsimōth*, the Exodus of the Sons of Israel out of Egypt. *Ouaïekra*, which is translated Leviticus. *Ouaïdabēr*, which is Numbers. *Elledebareim*, Deuteronomy. *Diēsou*, the one of Joshua son of Naue. *Diōb*, the one of Job.[454] *Desōphteim*, the one of the Judges. *Derouth*,

---

[449] Cf. Deut. 25:15.

[450] Jacobs 2013: 455. The *xestēs* was a Roman measure that equalled one pint.

[451] Cf. Epiphanius's own summary of these groupings of twenty-two in *Mens*. ln. 696–703.

[452] Jacobs 2013: 455.

[453] Moutsoulas 1973: 190–1, ln. 673–96. For a discussion of the language and provenance of this list, cf. the section on the Bryennios List above, pp. 72–5.

[454] The placement of Job between Joshua and Judges is intriguing. The Bryennios List also placed Job before Judges (albeit after Ruth, not Joshua). See the section on the Bryennios List above, p. 71. This list from Epiphanius and the Bryennios List probably descend from a common source. This placement of Job perhaps relies on the view attributed to Rabbi Eliezer that Job lived in the

Text	Translation
ἡ τῆς Ῥούθ. Σφερτελείμ, τὸ Ψαλτήριον.	*Derouth*, the one of Ruth.[455] *Spherteleim*, the
Δεβριαμείν, ἡ πρώτη τῶν Παραλειπομένων.	Psalter. *Debriiamein*, the first of the
Δεβριαμείν, Παραλειπομένων δευτέρα.	Paralipomenon. *Debriiamein*, second of
Δεσαμουήλ, Βασιλειῶν πρώτη.	Paralipomenon.[456] *Desamouēl*, first of
Δαδουδεσαμουήλ, Βασιλειῶν δευτέρα.	Kingdoms. *Dadoudesamouēl*, second of
Δμαλαχείμ, Βασιλειῶν τρίτη. Δμαλαχείμ,	Kingdoms. *Dmalacheim*, third of Kingdoms.
Βασιλειῶν τετάρτη. Δμεθαλώθ, ἡ Παροιμιῶν.	*Dmalacheim*, fourth of Kingdoms. *Dmethalōth*,
Δεκωέλεθ, ὁ Ἐκκλησιαστής. Σιραθσιρείν, τὸ	the one of Proverbs. *Dekōeleth*, Ecclesiastes
Ἆσμα τῶν Ἀσμάτων. Δαθαριασαρά, τὸ	*Sirathsirein*, the Song of Songs. *Dathariasara*,
Δωδεκαπρόφητον. Δησαΐου, τοῦ προφήτου	the Twelve Prophets. *Dēsaïou*, of the prophet
Ἡσαΐου. Διερεμίου, ἡ τοῦ Ἱερεμίου. Διεζεκιήλ,	Isaiah. *Dieremiou*, the one of Jeremiah.
ἡ τοῦ Ἱεζεκιήλ. Δεδανιήλ, ἡ τοῦ Δανιήλ.	*Diezekiēl*, the one of Ezekiel. *Dedaniēl*, the one
Δέσδρα, ἡ τοῦ Ἔσδρα πρώτη. Δέσδρα, ἡ τοῦ	of Daniel. *Desdra*, the one of first Esdras.
Ἔσδρα δευτέρα. Δεσθήρ, ἡ τῆς Ἐσθήρ. Αὗται	*Desdra*, the one of second Esdras. *Desthēr*, the
δὲ αἱ εἴκοσι ἑπτὰ βίβλοι εἴκοσι δύο	one of Esther. Now these twenty-seven books
ἀριθμοῦνται κατὰ τὸν ἀριθμὸν τῶν στοιχείων,	are numbered as twenty-two according to the
ἐπειδήπερ καὶ πέντε στοιχεῖα διπλοῦνται,	number of the letters, since also five letters are
καθὼς ἄνω προείπομεν. Ἔστι δὲ καὶ ἄλλη	double, just as we said above. And there is
μικρὰ βίβλος, ἣ καλεῖται Κινώθ, ἥτις	another small book, which is called *Kinōth*,
ἑρμηνεύεται θρῆνοι Ἱερεμίου. Αὕτη δὲ τῷ	which is translated Lamentations of Jeremiah.
Ἱερεμίᾳ συνάπτεται, ἥτις ἐστὶ περισσὴ τοῦ	This one is joined to Jeremiah, which is beyond
ἀριθμοῦ καὶ τῷ Ἱερεμίᾳ συναπτομένη.	the number and joined to Jeremiah.

Panarion 76.22.5

Date: ca. 376

Introduction: Epiphanius addresses the Arian, Aëtius, in this context. If Aëtius had been begotten by the Holy Spirit and instructed by the prophets and apostles, he would have gone through all of the Divine Scriptures and realized that the word ἀγέννητός (unbegotten) never appears in them: the twenty-seven(two) books of the OT canon, the books of the NT canon, and the Wisdom books of Solomon and Sirach.

time of the Judges (B. Bat. 15b; cf. Beckwith 1985: 190), though, as already noted, Epiphanius himself dated Job earlier than this period (*Pan.* 4.1.9–10).

[455] That Ruth comes after Judges and directly before the Psalter in *Mens.* 22–23 combines two known traditions. Patristic lists usually count Ruth as a part of Judges, as Epiphanius does in the two lists we examined previously. After all, the book of Ruth is set during the time of the Judges (Ruth 1:1). In B. Bat. 14b, Ruth precedes Psalms, and the reason given for the order is that her story was one of suffering that concluded in happiness because David issued from her (Ruth 4:18–22) and wrote hymns and praises (cf. ch. 2 on the Babylonian Talmud, pp. 68–9).

[456] Chronicles appear before Kingdoms in this list, as they did in the previous one. In *Pan.* 8.6, Kingdoms come before Chronicles. The vacillation in the ordering of these books may be due to chronological concerns over which books should be placed first. Since Chronicles begin with a reference to Adam, Epiphanius may have considered them more fit to introduce the books of Kingdoms.

Text[457]	Translation[458]
εἰ γὰρ ἦς ἐξ ἁγίου πνεύματος γεγεννημένος	For if you were begotten from the Holy Spirit
καὶ προφήταις καὶ ἀποστόλοις	and instructed in the prophets and apostles, you
μεμαθητευμένος, ἔδει σε διελθόντα ἀπ᾿ ἀρχῆς	must have gone through (the record) from the
γενέσεως κόσμου ἄχρι τῶν τῆς Ἐσθὴρ χρόνων,	beginning of the genesis of the world until
ἐν εἴκοσι καὶ ἑπτὰ βίβλοις παλαιᾶς διαθήκης	the times of Esther in twenty-seven books of
εἴκοσι δύο ἀριθμουμέναις, τέτρασι δὲ ἁγίοις	the Old Covenant,[459] which are numbered as
εὐαγγελίοις καὶ ἐν τεσσαρεσκαίδεκα	twenty-two, and in the four holy gospels, and in
ἐπιστολαῖς τοῦ ἁγίου ἀποστόλου Παύλου καὶ	fourteen epistles of the holy apostle Paul, and
ἐν ταῖς πρὸ τούτων [καὶ] σὺν ταῖς ἐν τοῖς	in the general epistles of James, Peter,[460] John,
αὐτῶν χρόνοις Πράξεσι τῶν ἀποστόλων	and Jude before these [and] with the Acts of the
καθολικαῖς ἐπιστολαῖς Ἰακώβου καὶ Πέτρου	Apostles in their times, and in the Revelation
καὶ Ἰωάννου καὶ Ἰούδα, καὶ ἐν τῇ τοῦ Ἰωάννου	of John,[461] and in the Wisdom books, I mean of
Ἀποκαλύψει, ἔν τε ταῖς Σοφίαις, Σολομῶντός	Solomon and of the son of Sirach,[462] and in
τέ φημι καὶ υἱοῦ Σειράχ, καὶ πάσαις ἁπλῶς	short having gone through all the Divine
γραφαῖς θείαις <ἐρευνᾶν> καὶ ἑαυτοῦ	Scriptures, I say, you should have condemned
καταγνῶναι ὅτι ὄνομα, ὅπερ οὐδαμοῦ	yourself for bringing forward as not unfitting

[457] Dummer 1985: 369, ln. 16–28.   [458] Revised and adapted from Bruce 1988: 213–14.

[459] The canon of the Old Testament is a summary of the three previous lists from *Panarion* and *De mensuris*. The general chronological ordering of the books in those lists is confirmed, since here Epiphanius summarizes the material of the twenty-seven(two) books along chronological lines from the beginning of the world to the times of Esther. As stated above, it appears that Epiphanius, the antiquarian, has followed Josephus, who also organized the first eighteen books of the Old Testament along chronological lines.

[460] Epiphanius does not make clear in this passage how many Petrine epistles he accepts. However, he cites and alludes to 2 Peter many times (cf. *Pan.* 48.12.5; 41.3.6; 38.4.9 et al.). Most clearly in *Pan.* 66.64.5 he cites 2 Peter 1:19 with the attribution 'as Peter says in his epistle'. It seems that Epiphanius held to Petrine authorship of the epistle and therefore accepted two authentic Petrine epistles.

[461] The Apocalypse of John is listed without reservation; likewise, James and Jude. As for the disputed Johannine epistles, whereas Eusebius had considered only 1 John to be universally received, Epiphanius makes clear elsewhere that he accepts 'epistles' (plural) of John. In *Pan.* 51.35.2 he says, 'Among whom (i.e. holy apostles) the holy John communicated to the holy church through the Gospel and the Epistles (ἐπιστολῶν) and the Apocalypse from the same holy gift'. There is no evidence of Epiphanius's use of 2–3 John, but it does seem unlikely that he would accept 2 John without accepting 3 John. In *Pan.* Prooemium I 1.4.5, Epiphanius notes that the Alogoi do not receive the Gospel and Apocalypse of John (cf. *Pan.* 51.3–35 for his treatment of the Alogoi). For the most recent treatment and assessment of the controversy over the Johannine books, the Gospel, and the Apocalypse, in the early church and Epiphanius's contribution to it, see Manor 2016.

[462] The Wisdom books of Solomon and Sirach are not included in the twenty-seven books of the Old Testament and appear at the end of the summary lists of the Old and New Testaments. This placement of Sirach and Wisdom at the end of the NT list coheres with a wider patristic practice of listing the useful non-canonical books after the canons of the Old Testament and the New Testament (see Horbury 1994). That he refers to them collectively as the Wisdom books, fit for instruction of Christians, accords with his previous description of these books as useful and beneficial. They are in dispute, and not established. However, they are separate from the apocryphal books, which may indicate a middle category of useful Scripture, which is between canonical Scripture and apocryphal books. They are useful Scripture for the training and instruction of Christians, but they are not canonical Scripture according to Epiphanius, for they are only mentioned as useful and not as among the number of specified and established books.

Text	Translation
ἐντέτακται, ἦλθες ἡμῖν φέρων, οὐκ ἀπρεπὲς μὲν θεῷ, ἀλλ᾽ εὐσεβὲς εἰς θεόν, τὸ τοῦ ἀγεννήτου ὄνομα, μηδαμοῦ δὲ ἐν θείᾳ γραφῇ ῥηθέν·	for God but actually pious towards God a word which is nowhere listed, the word 'unbegotten'(ἀγεννητός), nowhere mentioned in Divine Scripture.

The Canon Lists of Epiphanius

Panarion 8.6

1. Genesis
2. Exodus
3. Leviticus
4. Numbers
5. Deuteronomy
6. Joshua
7. Judges
8. Ruth
9. Job
10. Psalter
11. Proverbs
12. Ecclesiastes
13. Song of Songs
14. First Kingdoms   (= 1 Samuel)
15. Second Kingdoms   (= 2 Samuel)
16. Third Kingdoms   (= 1 Kings)
17. Fourth Kingdoms   (= 2 Kings)
18. First Paralipomenon   (= 1 Chronicles)
19. Second Paralipomenon   (= 2 Chronicles)
20. Twelve Prophets
21. Isaiah
22. Jeremiah + Lamentations + Epistles of: Jeremiah + Baruch
23. Ezekiel
24. Daniel
25. First Esdras
26. Second Esdras
27. Esther
Disputed Books
  The Wisdom of Sirach
  The Wisdom of Solomon

The ordering of the books differs from Epiphanius's other lists. For example, only in this list does he place Kingdoms before Paralipomenon. In the following two lists, he places Paralipomenon before Kingdoms, probably because the genealogy that begins with Adam chronologically precedes any of the material found in Kingdoms. In general, his lists appear to follow a chronological order.[463] Moreover, the placement of Job differs among his lists. In this list, Job follows Ruth, which still places Job in the period of the Judges. In *Mens.* 23, Job comes before the book of Judges for the same reason.[464] In *Mens.* 4, Job follows Deuteronomy, probably because of the view that Job was authored by Moses and that Job lived in the patriarchal period.

De mensuris et ponderibus 4–5

First Pentateuch – Five Books of Law
  Genesis
  Exodus
  Leviticus
  Numbers
  Deuteronomy
Second Pentateuch – Five Books in Verse
  Job
  Psalter
  Proverbs
  Ecclesiastes
  Song of Songs
Third Pentateuch – Five Books called *Hagiographa*
  Joshua
  Judges + Ruth
  First and Second Paralipomenon   (= 1–2 Chronicles)
  First and Second Kingdoms   (= 1–2 Samuel)
  Third and Fourth Kingdoms   (= 1–2 Kings)
Fourth Pentateuch – Five Books of Prophecy
  Twelve Prophets
  Isaiah
  Jeremiah + Lamentations [+ Epistle of Baruch + Epistle of Jeremiah]
  Ezekiel
  Daniel
Two Remaining Books
  First and Second Esdras
  Esther
Two Useful and Beneficial Books in Verse
  Wisdom of Solomon
  Wisdom of Sirach

---

[463] Cf. *Mens.* 23 and *Pan.* 76.22.5 below.

[464] Cf. *Mens.* 23, where Job comes before Judges for the same reason, even though Epiphanius elsewhere believed that Job belonged to the patriarchal period (*Pan.* 4.1.9–10).

The twenty-two letters of the Hebrew alphabet have names and five of these letters are double letters; that is, they have both a medial and final form.[465] Therefore, the Hebrews have twenty-seven books but because five of them are double (corresponding to the five double letters), they can number them as twenty-two. By joining Ruth with Judges, First Paralipomenon with Second, First Kingdoms with Second, Third Kingdoms with Fourth, and First Esdras with Second, the Jews have twenty-two specified books.

De mensuris et ponderibus 22–3

Twenty-Seven(Two) Specified Books of the Old Covenant

Genesis
Exodus
Leviticus
Numbers
Deuteronomy
Joshua
Job
Judges
Ruth
Psalter

First Paralipomenon	(= 1 Chronicles)
Second Paralipomenon	(= 2 Chronicles)
First Kingdoms	(= 1 Samuel)
Second Kingdoms	(= 2 Samuel)
Third Kingdoms	(= 1 Kings)
Fourth Kingdoms	(= 2 Kings)

Proverbs
Ecclesiastes
Song of Songs
Twelve Prophets
Isaiah
Jeremiah + Lamentations
Ezekiel
Daniel
First Esdras
Second Esdras
Esther

---

[465] *Chaph* (ך כ), *Mem* (ם מ), *Nun* (ן נ), *Phi* (ף פ), and *Sade* (ץ צ) are the five double letters. For a complete listing of the names of the letters, see *Mens.* 22 above.

This third list contains the same books and the same number of books as the previous lists, though in a different order. The first five books are in their normal place, and the Prophets and late history books (Esdras A and B and Esther) again conclude the list. Thus the list unfolds chronologically from the Genesis of the world to the times of Esther. This list has been attested independently in the Bryennios List (for details, see the beginning of this chapter).

Panarion 76.22.5

Old Testament
    From Genesis of the world to the times of Esther in Twenty-Seven(Two) Books
New Testament
    Four Holy Gospels
    Fourteen Epistles of Paul
    Acts of the Apostles
    Catholic Epistles of
        James
        Peter   (= 1–2 Peter)
        John   (= 1–3 John?)
        Jude
    Apocalypse of John
Wisdom Books of
  Solomon
  Son of Sirach

Epiphanius's Scriptures: Epiphanius's antiquarian impulse moved him to use the many sources at his disposal. In reconstructing the history and origins of the heresies that he describes in the *Panarion*, he used Jubilees or more probably a chronicle derived from this work.[466] He does not call Jubilees or this chronicle Scripture. On another occasion, he referred to one of the beatitudes from the Acts of Paul and Thecla (5) as Scripture (*Pan.* 77.27.7).[467] He depends on the Protoevangelium of James in *Pan.* 78–9, in which he treats Marian heresy, but he does not explicitly cite or identify this source as Scripture (*Pan.* 78–9). He cites a parable from an Apocryphon of Ezekiel in order to illustrate the relationship of the body to the soul, but he does not call it Scripture (*Pan.* 64.70.5–17).[468] He thus uses many sources, and on occasion he can refer

---

[466] Adler 1990: 476.

[467] Jacobs 2013: 447. This citation of the Acts of Thecla is interesting, since it is connected to another citation from the book of James (1:27). Both texts are introduced with the formula: 'According to what has been written' (κατὰ τὸ γεγραμμένον).

[468] Bregman 1991; Jacobs 2013: 448. Epiphanius cites the Apocryphon of Ezekiel with the following introduction: 'the things spoken (ῥηθέντα) by Ezekiel, the prophet, in his apocryphon... I will present (παραθήσομαι) them here'. He does not present this work as Scripture, but as helpful instruction on the relationship of the body and soul.

to a work such as the Acts of Thecla as Scripture, even though this is an intriguing example since he cited from the book of James prior.

In *Pan.* 76.22.5, he included the Wisdom books of Solomon and Sirach among the Divine Scriptures (γραφαῖς θείαις) from which a Christian would have learned. Although these are grouped among the Divine Scriptures, Epiphanius also says they are 'in dispute' among the Jews (*Pan.* 8.6) and 'not included in the number of specified and established books', even though they are useful and beneficial (*Mens.* 4). Although they are not included in the number of specified books, he also reports that they are separate from some apocryphal books. He is perhaps in agreement with other church fathers regarding a middle category of books between the canonical works and the apocryphal or esoteric works. Epiphanius considered various works as Scripture, but this observation is held in tension with his conception of a canon of Scripture.

Epiphanius's canon: Although Epiphanius refers to a number of works as Scripture, according to the evidence of the lists and the terms he used to describe the books in these lists he also conceived of a narrow and exclusive type of Scripture. One observes a clearer case for the books of the Old Testament than for the New. Regarding the Old Testament, he numbered the books as twenty-seven or as twenty-two, according to the number of the letters of the Hebrew alphabet. He described these books as the specified and established books of the Old Testament. For the New Testament, he included the disputed books of Hebrews (Paul's epistles are numbered as fourteen), the epistles of Peter, John, Jude, and the Apocalypse of John. His New Testament probably consisted of the twenty-seven books of the traditional New Testament.

4

Latin Christian Lists

INTRODUCTION

Christians from the West were slower than their Eastern counterparts to form lists of the canon of Scripture. The earliest list that is traditionally considered Western, the Muratorian Fragment, is dated to sometime between the end of the second century and as late as the fourth century CE. The Latin of this list is almost certainly translated from Greek, and the provenance of the list (East or West) is currently under debate. We include the list here because it has traditionally been associated with the West, and nothing of its hypothesized original Greek remains, only the Latin.[1] With this possible exception, all of the Western lists date to the fourth century and later. In some cases, we cannot discern the specific author of the list (cf. Mommsen Catalogue, Codex Claromontanus, *Breviarium Hipponense*) or even where and exactly when it was composed (cf. Muratorian Fragment). However, in several cases we know the author of the list, the place where he composed it, when he composed it, and even some of the circumstances in which he crafted it.

Mainly, Christian scholars from North Africa, Gaul (modern-day France), Dalmatia (perhaps close to modern-day Bosnia, Slovenia, or Croatia), and Italy took the responsibility to draft these lists. However, pinpointing the origins of some of these fathers is only the beginning of locating them, since Jerome and Rufinus travelled to Egypt and in and around Palestine extensively. In the case of these last two, their respective lists—especially the OT portions—appear to be influenced by Eastern Christianity, and in the case of Jerome, probably also by the Judaism he encountered in Palestine. With some difference, Hilary's list reflects that of Origen.

The reasons for composing these lists were variegated. Lists could be drafted for ordinary purposes such as a price guide for copying the biblical books (cf. Mommsen Catalogue and perhaps Codex Claromontanus). The Muratorian Fragment perhaps served as an introduction to Christian Scripture. Jerome's most famous canonical list (the *Prologus Galeatus*) serves as the preface to one

---

[1] A good case could also be made to include the Muratorian Fragment in ch. 3.

of his biblical translations. His other lists appear in epistolary correspondence, as also does the list from Pope Innocent I. Hilary includes a list in the introduction to his Psalms commentary. Augustine's list appears in a handbook on biblical interpretation, while Rufinus's appears in a commentary on the Apostles' Creed. Finally, the *Breviarium Hipponense* preserves the decisions of a council in North Africa.

For each list below we have provided introductions to the list and the author of the list when known, summaries of the information pertaining to the canon, the text, and translation (in synoptic columns) of the work in which the list is located, analysis and commentary on the lists themselves, a summary list of books, and, if relevant, any concluding comments on the canon list.

MURATORIAN FRAGMENT

In 1700, Lodovico Antonio Muratori (1672–1750) discovered in the Ambrosian Library at Milan a seventh- or eighth-century codex comprising seventy-six leaves and containing several writings from Ambrose of Milan, Eucherius of Lyon, and John Chrysostom (all fourth- and fifth-century writers), along with several early Christian creeds.[2] Metzger considers the codex to be 'a commonplace book of some monk, who copied a miscellaneous assortment of texts from various sources'.[3] Within this codex (fol. 10^r–11^r), Muratori also found a brief list (eighty-five lines) of NT books, the beginning and (probably) the end of which have not been preserved. Muratori published this 'Muratorian Fragment' in 1740 as an example of barbaric Latin in medieval Italy.[4] The scribe responsible for the manuscript was extremely careless, as may be judged not only by the quality of the Latin of the Fragment itself but also by the fact that the scribe copied twice the same passage (thirty-five lines) from Ambrose (*Abr.* 1.3.15).[5] Excerpts of the Fragment (lines 42–50, 54–7, 63–8, 81–5) were included in a prologue to the Pauline Epistles, found now in four manuscripts of the eleventh and twelfth centuries belonging to the Benedictine monastery on Monte Cassino, southeast of Rome.[6] The Latin in these manuscripts is of higher quality than that in Muratori's codex.

Most aspects of the Muratorian Fragment are subject to debate, including the genre, date, provenance, and the interpretation of most of its lines. About

---

[2] The codex is catalogued as Cod. Ambr. I 101 sup. On its date, see Henne 1990–1. On the contents of the manuscript, see Hahneman 1992: 17–22.

[3] Metzger 1987: 192; cf. Markschies (2015: 204): 'a sort of monastic handbook on the Bible'.

[4] Muratori 1740: cols. 853–6.

[5] The double text of Ambrose, with notes, is presented in Tregelles 1867: 21–8; see also Westcott 1889: 521–38 (Appendix C), esp. 527–31.

[6] The manuscripts are Cod. Cass. 235 (C^2), 349 (C), 535 (C^3), and 552 (C^1). See Harnack 1898; Hahneman 1992: 9–10.

the original language, scholars have tended to agree. From the time that Muratori published the Fragment, almost all scholars have assumed that its original language was Greek, and this consensus shows no signs of eroding.[7] The translation into Latin probably dates to the latter half of the fourth century, a view based not only on a linguistic analysis of the Latin, but also on the borrowings from the Fragment that have been identified in the preface to the *Tractatus in Matthaeum* written by the fourth/fifth-century bishop Chromatius of Aquileia.[8]

The Fragment has traditionally been assigned to late-second-century Rome. This dating especially relies on ln. 73–7, where the unknown author, today called the Fragmentist, explains that the Shepherd of Hermas was written 'very recently, in our times, in the city of Rome, while bishop Pius, his brother, was occupying the [episcopal] chair of the church of the city of Rome'. Pius I served as bishop of Rome in the mid-second century (ca. 140–54 CE). Additionally, the Fragment's references to Marcion (lines 65, 83) and the Montanists ('Cataphrygians', line 84) fit comfortably with such a dating. The idea of a Roman provenance depends on the designation of Rome as simply *urbs* ('city'; ln. 38), the presence of Revelation (more accepted in the West than the East), and the absence of James and Hebrews (more accepted in the East than the West).[9]

The traditional dating and provenance were challenged by Albert Sundberg, who proposed a fourth-century Eastern provenance. The movement to revise the Fragment's date gained momentum due to Geoffrey Mark Hahneman's elaboration of Sundberg's thesis; their arguments have gained a significant following.[10] Against the usual understanding of ln. 74–6, Sundberg interpreted the crucial statement as meaning only that the Shepherd was composed very recently, in our 'times'; that is, during the post-apostolic period. Thus, the Fragmentist would not be saying that he himself lived close to the time of the composition of the Shepherd, which he dates to the period of Pius, but rather that the Shepherd was written in the post-apostolic period. In this sense, the wording has little bearing on the date of the Fragment except to liberate it from a second-century date. Sundberg and Hahneman have emphasized that without this argument for a second-century date, the Fragment itself, with its list of NT books, fits much more comfortably in the fourth century when such lists proliferated, whereas it would be an anomaly in the second century.[11]

---

[7] See Guignard 2015. Harnack (1925) had suggested that Latin was the original language, but he persuaded few. Several retroversions into Greek have been produced; see, e.g., Lightfoot 1885: 1.405–13; Zahn 1888–92: 2.140–3.

[8] On the linguistic evidence, see Guignard 2015: 601–9. On Chromatius's use of the Fragment, see Lemarié 1978; Kaestli 1994: 630–4; Verheyden 2003: 552–3.

[9] Campenhausen 1972: 243–61; Metzger 1987: 191–201.

[10] On the influence of Hahneman 1992, see Schnabel 2014: 244–6.

[11] Many other arguments also enter the discussion; for summaries, see Verheyden 2003; McDonald 2017: 2.274–304.

The debate continues unabated. The traditional dating still commands a significant following, and several scholars have offered detailed critiques of Hahneman's more elaborate defence of the revised dating.[12] Among other matters, some scholars interpret the genre of the Fragment as lending support to the traditional dating. Whereas Sundberg and Hahneman insist that the Fragment has its most exact parallels with the fourth-century canon lists, other scholars have long noted the peculiar form of the Fragment, suggesting that it should be classified not as a canon list but as an introduction to the New Testament, a type of preface similar to the Marcionite prologues.[13] A recent assessment asserts that 'the older consensus (i.e. on an earlier date) has now been widely restored.'[14] Perhaps widely, but not universally. McDonald, for instance, still finds the arguments for the later date compelling, though he recognizes the problems in any dating for the Fragment and considers possible the mediating position of Armstrong, who attributes the Fragment to Victorinus of Pettau in the third century.[15] Clare Rothschild takes another mediating position, arguing that the Fragment is a forgery designed to legitimate later views of the canon by representing them as earlier, second-century views.[16]

New Testament canon: The Fragment describes Luke and John as the third and fourth Gospels, and likely Matthew and Mark preceded these as the first and second Gospels. The letters of Paul include all of the canonical letters (in an unusual order) without Hebrews. The fragment warns against two forged Pauline letters, that to the Laodiceans and another to the Alexandrians. Next comes the Epistle of Jude and two epistles of John, followed by the Wisdom of Solomon and two Apocalypses, that of John and that of Peter, though there is the admission that some do not permit the Apocalypse of Peter to be read publicly. Finally, the Shepherd of Hermas is quite definitely rejected as a work for public reading,[17] though private reading of it is encouraged. The fragment ends with a proscription of the writings of various heretics. There is no mention of the letters of Peter and of James, nor of that to the Hebrews.

[12] See esp. Kaestli 1994; Hill 1995; Verheyden 2003.
[13] Lietzmann 1907: 53–4; Campenhausen 1972: 245–6; Metzger 1987: 194; Kaestli 1994: 615–17; Verheyden 2003: 531; Stanton 2004: 69; Markschies 2015: 203, 205. On the Marcionite Prologues, see Jongkind 2015.
[14] Guignard 2015: 598. See also Gamble (2002: 270), who acknowledges that 'recent opinion has inclined toward the traditional date and provenance'.
[15] See Armstrong 2008; McDonald 2017: 2.274–304; against Armstrong, see Guignard 2015: 600, whose argument is accepted by Houghton 2016: 17. Guignard judges that Victorinus knew the Fragment in Greek (pp. 601–4). McDonald (2017: 2.245n59) signals a 'forthcoming response' to Armstrong's position written by Hahneman.
[16] See Rothschild forthcoming; she previewed her argument in Rothschild 2008.
[17] So the usual interpretation; but see Guignard (2015: 623), who interprets the Fragment as permitting the public reading of the Shepherd.

Studies: Several decades ago Campenhausen noted that the 'literature on the Muratorianum long ago became quite unmanageable'.[18] See the select bibliography in Markschies 2012: 117–18; for references to older literature, see Verheyden 2003: 488–9 nn. 2–3; for editions of the text, see Schnabel 2014: 232. The most important recent discussions of the date and provenance of the fragment include: Sundberg 1973; Ferguson 1982; Hahneman 1992; Henne 1993; Kaestli 1994; Hill 1995; Verheyden 2003; Armstrong 2008; Norelli 2013: 972–81; Schnabel 2014; Markschies 2015: 202–9; McDonald 2017: 2.274–304.

The Text of the Muratorian Fragment

Date: second, third, or fourth century

Text[19]	Translation[20]
quibus tamen interfuit et ita posuit. **Tertium euangelii librum secundum Lucan** Lucas iste medicus post ascensum Christi, cum eum Paulus quasi ut iuris studiosum.[21]	…at which nevertheless he was present, and so he placed [them in his narrative].[22] The third book of the Gospel is that according to Luke. Luke, the well-known physician [cf. Col. 4:14], after the ascension of Christ,
5 secum adsumsisset, nomine suo ex opinione conscripsit: dominum tamen nec ipse uidit in carne, et idem, prout assequi potuit, ita et a natiuitate Iohannis incipit dicere. **Quartum euangeliorum Iohannes ex discipulis,**	when Paul had taken him with him as one zealous for the law, composed it in his own name, according to [the general] belief. Yet he himself had not seen the Lord in the flesh; and therefore, as he was able to ascertain events, so indeed he begins to tell the story from the birth of John. The fourth of the Gospels is that of John, [one] of the disciples.

---

[18] Campenhausen 1972: 243.

[19] Souter 1954: 191–4; departures from Souter's text are noted. Souter presents a corrected text, emending the manuscript's faulty Latin where the solution is relatively obvious. Some lines are certainly faulty but do not allow a definite solution. The text as presented in the manuscript, with all its errors, can be accessed in various sources, e.g., Hahneman 1992: 6–7. Some lines in the manuscript are rubricated, which Hahneman prints in bold, a practice adopted here. A facsimile can be found in Tregelles 1867. See Westcott 1889: Appendix C for a brief presentation of the text in Muratori's manuscript, the extracts from the later manuscripts, discussion of the scribal faults, and a corrected text of the Fragment with notes.

[20] Metzger 1987: 305–7. Metzger translates the corrected text of Lietzmann 1933. Lietzmann's text closely resembles that of Souter.

[21] So the manuscript; Souter prints the conjecture *quasi adiutorem studiosum*. The line has generated several conjectural emendations, a number of them mentioned by Metzger 1987: 305n2. Metzger translates the Latin as it stands, with a reference to Chromatius's use of the Fragment in his similar description of Luke as *eruditissmus legis*.

[22] Scholars typically assume that the first lines of this list would have mentioned the Gospel of Matthew and the Gospel of Mark, and that this first preserved sentence perhaps refers to Mark's absence at the events of Jesus's life but his recording the reminiscences of Peter, a tradition attested since Papias.

Text	Translation
10 cohortantibus condiscipulis et episcopis suis, dixit, 'Conieiunate mihi hodie triduo, et quid cuique fuerit reuelatum, alterutrum nobis enarremus.' Eadem nocte reue- latum Andreae ex apostolis ut recognos-	To his fellow disciples and bishops, who had been urging him [to write], he said, 'Fast with me from today for three days, and what will be revealed to each one let us tell it to one another.' In the same night it was revealed to Andrew, [one] of the apostles,
15 centibus cunctis Iohannes suo nomine cuncta describeret; et ideo licet uaria sin- gulis euangeliorum libris principia doceantur, nihil tam differt creden- tium fidei, cum uno ac principali spiritu de-	that John write down all things in his own name while all of them should review it.[23] And so, though various elements may be taught in the individual books of the Gospels,[24] nevertheless this makes no difference to the faith of believers, since by the one sovereign Spirit all things
20 clarata sint in omnibus omnia de natiui- tate, de passione de resurrectione, de conuersatione cum discipulis suis, ac de gemino eius aduentu. Primo in humilitate despectus quod fu-	have been declared in all [the Gospels]:[25] concerning the nativity, concerning the passion, concerning the resurrection, concerning life with his disciples, and concerning his twofold coming; the first in lowliness when he was despised, which has taken place,
25 it secundo in potestate regali prae claro[26] quod futurum est. Quid ergo mirum si Iohannes tam constanter singula etiam in epistulis suis proferat? dicens in semet ipso 'Quae uidimus oculis	the second glorious in royal power, which is still in the future. What marvel is it, then, if John so consistently mentions these particular points also in his Epistles, saying about himself: 'What we have seen with our eyes
30 nostris et auribus audiuimus et manus nostrae palpauerunt, haec scripsimus uobis.' Sic enim non solum uisorem sed auditorem se et scriptorem omnium mirabilium domini per ordi- nem profitetur. Acta autem omnium apostolorum	and heard with our ears and our hands have handled, these things we have written to you' [1 John 1:1–3]? For in this way he professes [himself] to be not only an eye-witness and hearer, but also a writer of all the marvellous deeds of the Lord, in their order. Moreover, the acts of all the apostles
35 sub uno libro scripta[27] sunt. Lucas 'optime Theofi- lo' conprendit quae sub praesentia eius singula gerebantur, sicuti et semote passione Petri euidenter declarat, et profectione Pauli ab Vr- be ad Hispaniam proficiscentis. Epistulae autem	were written in one book. For 'most excellent Theophilus' [cf. Luke 1:3] Luke compiled the individual events that took place in his presence—as he plainly shows by omitting the martyrdom of Peter as well as the departure of Paul from the city [of Rome] when he journeyed to Spain. As for the Epistles of

[23] A similar legend is found in Clement of Alexandria (*apud* Eusebius, *Hist. eccl.* 6.14.7), Victorinus of Pettau (*Comm. Apoc.* 11:1), and Jerome (*Vir. ill.* 9; *Comm. Matt.* praef.).

[24] Guignard (2015: 620) suggests translating this clause: 'though the beginnings prove to be different for the individual books of the Gospels'.

[25] Similarly, Irenaeus states that the Gospel has four aspects, but it is 'bound together by one Spirit' (*Haer.* 3.11.8).

[26] Lines 25–6 follow Lietzmann 1933. The manuscript has: *secundum potestate regali preclarum quod foturum est*; Souter (1954) prints: *secundum potestatem regalis patris, praeclarum quod futurum est*.

[27] Lietzmann 1933; Souter (1954) prints *scribta*, with the manuscript.

Text	Translation
40 Pauli, quae a quo loco uel qua ex causa directae sint uolentibus intellegere ipsae declarant. Primum omnium Corinthiis scisma heresis in-Terdicens, deinceps Galatis circumcisionem, Romanis autem ordinem scripturarum sed	Paul, they themselves make clear to those desiring to understand, which ones [they are], from what place, or for what reason they were sent. First of all, to the Corinthians, prohibiting their heretical schisms; next, to the Galatians, against circumcision;
45 principium earum esse Christum intimans prolixius scripsit, de quibus singulis [28] neces-se est a nobis disputari. Cum ipse beatus apostolus Paulus, sequens prodecessoris sui Iohannis ordinem non nisi nominatim septem	then to the Romans he wrote at length, explaining the order (or, plan) of the Scriptures, and also that Christ is their principle (or, main theme). It is necessary for us to discuss these one by one, since the blessed apostle Paul himself, following the example of his predecessor
50 ecclesiis scribat, ordine tali: ad Corinthios prima, ad Efesios secunda, ad Philippenses ter-tia, ad Colosenses quarta, ad Galatas quin-ta, ad Tessalonicenses sexta, ad Romanos septima;—uerum Corinthiis et Tessalonicen-	John, writes by name to only seven churches[29] in the following sequence: to the Corinthians first, to the Ephesians second, to the Philippians third, to the Colossians fourth, to the Galatians fifth, to the Thessalonians sixth, to the Romans seventh. It is true that he writes once more to
55 sibus, licet pro correptione, iteratur—, una tamen per omnem orbem terrae ecclesia diffusa esse dinoscitur. Et Iohannes enim in A-pocalypsi, licet septem ecclesiis scribat, tamen omnibus dicit. Verum ad Filemonem una	the Corinthians and to the Thessalonians for the sake of admonition, yet it is clearly recognizable that there is one Church spread throughout the whole extent of the earth. For John also in the Apocalypse, though he writes to seven churches, nevertheless speaks to all. [Paul also wrote]
60 et ad Titum una et ad Timotheum duae pro affect-tu et dilectione, in honorem tamen ecclesiae ca-tholicae in ordinationem ecclesiasticae disciplinae sanctificatae sunt. Fertur etiam ad Laudicenses, alia ad Alexandrinos Pauli no-	out of affection and love one to Philemon, one to Titus, and two to Timothy; and these are held sacred in the esteem of the Church catholic for the regulation of ecclesiastical discipline. There is current also [an epistle] to the Laodiceans,[30] [and] another to the Alexandrians,[31] [both] forged in Paul's

[28] Souter (1954) inserts *non* before *necesse*, which he thinks must have been left out of the manuscript. Metzger's translation follows the manuscript instead of Souter's conjecture.

[29] This tradition is well attested in ancient Christian authors of the West: Dahl 1962; Hahneman 1992: 117 (with n. 97), 123.

[30] Tertullian (*Marc.* 5.11.12; 5.17.1) reports that the followers of Marcion used the title Laodiceans in reference to the canonical epistle to the Ephesians (note that some early and important manuscripts—P[46], Sinaiticus, Vaticanus—omit 'in Ephesus' at Eph. 1:1). There is an apocryphal Latin *Laodiceans* (possibly originally composed in Greek), heavily dependent on the canonical Philippians, the date of which is debated; see Hahneman 1992: 196–200; Pervo 2010: 105–9; Tite 2012. Whether the Fragmentist refers to one of these two compositions, or to a third composition now lost to us, cannot be finally determined, though such a determination may have implications for the date of the Fragment.

[31] Scholars have failed to identify an apocryphal *Epistle to the Alexandrians*; see Pervo 2010: 109–10.

Text	Translation
65 mine finctae ad heresem Marcionis, et alia plura quae in catholica ecclesia recipi non potest: fel enim cum melle misceri non congruit. Epistola sane Iudae et suprascripti Iohannis duae in catholica habentur et Sapi-	name to [further] the heresy of Marcion, and several others which cannot be received into the catholic church—for it is not fitting that gall be mixed with honey. Moreover, the Epistle of Jude and two of the above-mentioned (or, bearing the name of) John are counted (or, used) in the catholic [Church][32]; and [the book of] Wisdom,[33]
70 entia ab amicis Salomonis in honorem ipsius scripta. Apocalypsin etiam Iohannis et Petri tantum recipimus, quam quidam ex nostris legi in ecclesia nolunt. Pastorem uero nuperrime temporibus nostris in urbe	written by the friends of Solomon in his honor.[34] We receive only the apocalypses of John and Peter, though some of us are not willing that the latter be read in church.[35] But Hermas wrote the Shepherd very recently, in our times, in the city of Rome,
75 Roma Herma conscripsit, sedente cathedram urbis Romae ecclesiae Pio episcopo fratre eius, et ideo legi eum quidem oportet, se puplicare uero in ecclesia populo neque inter prophetas conpleto numero, neque inter	while bishop Pius,[36] his brother, was occupying the [episcopal] chair of the church of the city of Rome.[37] And therefore it ought indeed to be read; but it cannot be read publicly to the people in church either among the prophets, whose number is complete, or among

[32] The reference to the 'two' epistles of John (rather than three, or one) is difficult. Perhaps the Fragmentist means 2–3 John, as he had already alluded to 1 John at lines 28–33; see Westcott 1889: 219n1. Peter Katz proposed an emendation such that the original Greek would have read δύο σὺν καθολικῇ, 'two [letters] with the Catholic [epistle]', constituting the three traditional letters of John. According to the conjecture, the Greek phrase was transliterated into Latin as *dua<e> sin catholica*, corrupted to *duas in catholica* (Katz 1957). Moule (1981: 26n2) proposed instead δύο πρὸς καθολικήν. But see Lieu (1986: 18–30; cf. Hahneman 1992: 15) for some evidence that 1–2 John perhaps circulated without 3 John. For other explanations, see Guignard 2015: 611n71.

[33] The presence of the Wisdom of Solomon—usually considered a part of the Old Testament, even if apocryphal or deuterocanonical—in a discussion of NT books is strange and often remarked upon. Zahn (1888–92: 2.66) conjectured that a negative had fallen out of the text. Proponents of a fourth-century date point to the parallels in Eusebius, *Hist. eccl.* 5.8.1–8 (discussing Irenaeus) and Epiphanius, *Pan.* 76.22.5 (see the discussion of Epiphanius in chapter 3). Horbury (1994) has suggested that the Fragment's reference to the Wisdom of Solomon coheres with a wider patristic practice of placing at the end of the entire canon the useful non-canonical books for each Testament.

[34] So says the Latin. Tregelles 1867: 53 long ago suggested that the Fragment's *ab amicis* mistranslates an original Greek ὑπὸ Φίλωνος ('by Philo'), mistaking it for ὑπὸ φίλων ('by the friends'). If this were the case, then *Salomonis* ('of Solomon') would not go with *amicis* ('friends' or, rather, Philo), but instead would go with Wisdom (of Solomon). The idea that Philo was the author of Wisdom was also reported by Jerome (*Praef. lib. Sal.*). Not all scholars are convinced by this emendation; see Horbury 1994; Kaestli 1994: 623–6.

[35] On the Apocalypse of Peter, see Hahneman 1992: 205–8; cf. Eusebius *Hist. eccl.* 3.25.4–5 (spurious), 3.3.2 (rejected). But at *Hist. eccl.* 6.14.1, it is among Clement's *antilegomena*.

[36] Pius I, bishop of Rome ca. 140–54.

[37] Regarding the Fragment's information about the Shepherd, see Verheyden 2003: 501–12.

Text	Translation
80 apostolos in fine temporum potest. Arsinoi autem seu Valentini uel Miltiadis nihil in totum recipimus, qui etiam nouum Psalmorum librum Marcioni conscripse-runt una cum Basilide et Asiano Catafry-gum constitutore.	the apostles, for it is after [their] time. But we accept nothing whatever of Arsinous or Valentinus or Miltiades,[38] who also composed a new book of psalms for Marcion, together with Basilides, the Asian founder of the Cataphrygians....[39]

The Canon List of the Muratorian Fragment

[Matthew]
[Mark]
Luke (= third Gospel)
John (= fourth Gospel)
Epistles of John (including 1 John)
Acts of the Apostles
Epistles of Paul
   Corinthians (two)
   Ephesians
   Philippians
   Colossians
   Galatians
   Thessalonians (two)
   Romans
   Philemon
   Titus
   Timothy (two)
   Laodiceans (forged)
   Alexandrians (forged)
Jude
John (two)
Wisdom of Solomon
Apocalypse of John
Apocalypse of Peter (for private reading only, according to some)
Shepherd of Hermas (for private reading only)

The Fragment makes no mention of some works now included in the New Testament—namely, 1–2 Peter, James, Hebrews. Westcott insists—in a judgement followed by several scholars, including Hahneman—that the 'cause of the

---

[38] Valentinus is a well-known Gnostic leader of the second century. Mi(l)tiades and Arsinous are more obscure.

[39] The Cataphrygians are the Montanists. On this last sentence, see Westcott (1889: 538n2): 'The conclusion is hopelessly corrupt, and evidently was so in the copy from which the Fragment was derived'; Markschies (2015: 207): these lines 'are—from the vantage point of the modern historian—completely chaotic'. But Markschies provides further discussion.

omissions cannot have been ignorance or doubt. It must be sought either in the character of the writing, or in the present condition of the text.'[40]

CODEX CLAROMONTANUS

The sixteenth-century scholar Theodor Beza discovered a sixth-century Greek and Latin codex of the Pauline Epistles (D[P] or 06) in the monastery at Clermont-en-Beauvaisis in northern France, naming the manuscript after the location of its discovery. Within this *Codex Claromontanus*, four pages separate Hebrews from Philemon, which someone has used to copy a Latin catalogue of books.[41] The catalogue contains the Latin names of the OT and NT books, along with their stichometry.[42] The handwriting and ink indicate that the scribe who copied the catalogue was not the scribe of the Pauline codex.[43] This Latin list might be a translation of an earlier Greek list, though scholars have argued for other positions, as well.[44] Scholars have typically dated the list to the fourth century, perhaps even a little earlier,[45] but beyond that general timeframe there is more disagreement. While some scholars emphasize the features of the list that would be unusual in the later fourth century (the inclusion of the Apocalypse of Peter, for instance),[46] thus indicating an earlier date, others emphasize the features that are unusual in the earlier fourth century (the inclusion of all seven Catholic Epistles) and therefore opt for a somewhat later date.[47]

Old Testament canon: The Old Testament matches fairly closely the canon later approved at the Council of Trent. All the books of the Jewish canon are included here, with the exception of Chronicles, one sign of several that the list was carelessly transcribed (see notes below). In addition, this stichometric catalogue includes the deuterocanonical books Wisdom of Solomon, Wisdom of Sirach, Judith, Tobit, and 1–2 Maccabees, as well as 4 Maccabees. Probably 3 Maccabees has been accidentally omitted.[48] The title 'Jeremiah' may contain additional material such as Lamentations and Baruch, though these texts go unmentioned.

---

[40] Westcott 1889: 219: Hahneman 1992: 25–6; cf. Verheyden 2003: 528–30.

[41] The catàlogue takes up only two-and-a-half pages (468v–469v), leaving a further page-and-a-half blank.

[42] On stichometry, see the comments on the Mommsen Catalogue in this chapter, p. 189.

[43] Zahn 1892: 161–2.

[44] Zahn (ibid.: 166–71) favoured a Greek origin. On the other suggestions, see Brandt 2001: 248.

[45] Zahn (1892: 172) allows for a date in the third or beginning of the fourth century.

[46] Harnack 1893–1904: 85; Metzger 1987: 229–30, relying on Zahn 1892: 168–71; Markschies 2012: 124.

[47] Hahneman (1992: 142–3) argues for a date 'some time in the second quarter of the fourth century' because the list appears to him more advanced than that of Eusebius but not so advanced as that of Athanasius.

[48] Zahn 1892: 164.

New Testament canon: The New Testament contains most of the books in the traditional twenty-seven-book New Testament, without Philippians, Thessalonians, and Hebrews. Scholars generally attribute the omission of these books to scribal error.[49] There are also listed some books beyond the traditional New Testament; the list concludes with mention of the Epistle of Barnabas, the Revelation of John, the Acts of the Apostles, the Shepherd of Hermas, the Acts of Paul, and the Revelation of Peter, but the first and last three of these titles are preceded by a horizontal stroke that appears to be an obelus, probably indicating their dubious status.

Studies: Zahn 1892: 157–72; Harnack 1893–1904: 2/2.84–8; Metzger 1987: 229–30; Hahneman 1992: 140–3.

The List Inserted into Codex Claromontanus

Date: first half of the fourth century

Text[50]		Translation	
Uersus scribturarum sanctarum		Lines of the Holy Scriptures	
ita Genesis	uersus $\overline{\overline{IIII}}$D	So Genesis	Lines 4,500
Exodus	uersus $\overline{\overline{III}}$DCC	Exodus	Lines 3,700
Leviticum	uersus $\overline{\overline{II}}$DCCC	Leviticus	Lines 2,800
Numeri	uersus $\overline{\overline{III}}$DCL	Numbers	Lines 3,650
Deuterenomium	uer. $\overline{\overline{III}}$CCC	Deuteronomy	Lines 3,300
Jesu Nauue	uer. $\overline{\overline{II}}$	Joshua	Lines 2,000
Judicum	uer. $\overline{\overline{II}}$	Judges	Lines 2,000
Rud	uer. CCL	Ruth	Lines 250
Regnorum	uer.	Reigns[51]	Lines
primus liber	uer. $\overline{\overline{II}}$D	First book	Lines 2,500
secundus lib.	uer. $\overline{\overline{II}}$	Second book	Lines 2,000
tertius lib.	uer. $\overline{\overline{II}}$DC	Third book	Lines 2,600
quartus lib.	uer. $\overline{\overline{II}}$CCCC	Fourth book	Lines 2,400
Psalmi Dauitici	uer. $\overline{\overline{U}}$	Psalms of David	Lines 5,000
Proverbia	uer. $\overline{\overline{I}}$DC	Proverbs	Lines 1,600
Aeclesiastes	DC	Ecclesiastes	600
Cantica Canticorum	CCC	Songs of Songs	300
Sapientia	uers. $\overline{\overline{I}}$	Wisdom[52]	Lines 1,000
Sapientia IHU	uer. $\overline{\overline{II}}$D	Wisdom of Jesus[53]	Lines 2,500

---

[49] ibid.; Metzger 1987: 230; Hahneman 1992: 142.

[50] Images of the entire manuscript have been made available by the *Bibliothèque nationale de France*, which may be accessed at <http://gallica.bnf.fr/ark:/12148/btv1b84683111>. The list of books starts at <http://gallica.bnf.fr/ark:/12148/btv1b84683111/f868.image>. Cf. Zahn 1892: 158–9.

[51] Reigns is the typical English translation for the Latin title of the books more commonly known in English as Samuel and Kings. (The Greek title is Kingdoms.) The omission of Chronicles is odd, probably accidental.

[52] Wisdom of Solomon   [53] i.e., Ben Sira or Ecclesiasticus, written by Jesus ben Sira.

Text		Translation	
XII Profetae	uer. $\overline{\text{IIICX}}$	Twelve Prophets[54]	Lines 3,110
Ossee[55]	uer. DXXX	Hosea	Lines 530
Amos	uer. CCCCX	Amos	Lines 410
Micheas	uer. CCCX	Micah	Lines 310
Joel	uer. XC	Joel	Lines 90
Abdias	uer. LXX	Obadiah	Lines 70
Jonas	uer. CL	Jonah	Lines 150
Naum	uer. CXL	Nahum	Lines 140
Ambacum	uer. CLX	Habakkuk	Lines 160
Sophonias	uer. CLX	Zephaniah	Lines 160
Aggeus	uers. CX	Haggai	Lines 110
Zacharias	uer. DCLX	Zechariah	Lines 660
Malachiel	uer. CC	Malachi	Lines 200
Eseias	uer. $\overline{\text{IIIDC}}$	Isaiah	Lines 3,600
Jeremias	uer. $\overline{\text{IIIILXX}}$	Jeremiah[56]	Lines 4,070
Ezechiel	uer. $\overline{\text{IIIDC}}$	Ezekiel	Lines 3,600
Daniel	uer. $\overline{\text{IDC}}$	Daniel	Lines 1,600
Maccabeorum sic.		Of the Maccabees, thus:	
lib. primus	uer. $\overline{\text{IICCC}}$	First book	Lines 2,300
lib. secundus	uer. $\overline{\text{IICCC}}$	Second book	Lines 2,300
lib. quartus	uer. $\overline{\text{I}}$	Fourth book	Lines 1,000
— Judit	uer. $\overline{\text{ICCC}}$	Judith	Lines 1,300
Hesdra	ID	Ezra[57]	Lines 1,500
Ester	uer. $\overline{\text{I}}$	Esther	Lines 1,000
Job	uer. $\overline{\text{IDC}}$	Job	Lines 1,600
Tobias	uer. $\overline{\text{I}}$	Tobit	Lines 1,000
Euangelia IIII		Gospels 4[58]	
Mattheum	uer. $\overline{\text{IIDC}}$	Matthew	Lines 2,600
Johannes	uer. $\overline{\text{II}}$	John	Lines 2,000
Marcus	uer. $\overline{\text{IDC}}$	Mark	Lines 1,600
Lucam	uer. $\overline{\text{IIDCCCC}}$	Luke	Lines 2,900
Epistulas Pauli		Letters of Paul[59]	
ad Romanos	uer. $\overline{\text{IXL}}$	To the Romans	Lines 1,040

[54] The list of Minor Prophets follows the Greek order rather than the traditional Hebrew order; see Dines 2015: 439–40.

[55] This line begins a new page in the manuscript (468r), on which the list is written in two columns (not replicated here), such that *Ossee* appears on the same line as *Ester*. This entire page, except for the last line (line 22), is in two columns. Line 21 contains the stichometry for *Judit* and *ad Petrum*. Line 22 has the reference to *Hesdra*. The next page returns to the one-column format of the first page. According to Markschies 2012: 124, the scribe used the two-column format to save space.

[56] Jeremiah probably includes Lamentations, Baruch, and the Epistles of Jeremiah.

[57] It is uncertain whether *Hesdra* here refers to Ezra–Nehemiah or to 1 Esdras.

[58] The more common 'Western' order for the Gospels is Matthew, John, Luke, Mark. The order of the current list is paralleled by the order in the St Gall manuscript of the Mommsen Catalogue.

[59] Several of Paul's letters go unmentioned here. According to Metzger (1987: 230; cf. Zahn 1892: 171–2): 'The absence of Philippians, 1 and 2 Thessalonians, and Hebrews is probably to be accounted for by an error of the scribe (or translator?) whose eye may have jumped from Ἐφεσίους to Ἑβραίους.' Hahneman (1992: 141) agrees that the omission is probably accidental. For a different explanation regarding the omission of Hebrews, see below on the *Epistle of Barnabas*.

Text		Translation	
ad Chorintios I	uer. ĪLX	To the Corinthians I	Lines 1,060
ad Chorintios II	uer. LXX	To the Corinthians II	Lines 70[60]
ad Galatas	uer. CCCL	To the Galatians	Lines 350
ad Efesios	uer. CCCLXXV	To the Ephesians	Lines 375
ad Timotheum I.	uer. CCVIII	To Timothy I	Lines 208[61]
ad Timotheum II.	uer. CCLXXXVIIII	To Timothy II	Lines 289
ad Titum	uer. CXL	To Titus	Lines 140
ad Colosenses	uer. CCLI	To the Colossians	Lines 251
ad Filimonem	uer. L	To Philemon	Lines 50
— ad Petrum prima[62]	CC	To Peter first[63]	200
ad Petrum II	uer. CXL	To Peter II	Lines 140
Jacobi	uer. CCXX[64]	Of James	Lines 220
Pr. Johanni epist.	CCXX	First epistle of John	220
Johanni epistula II.	XX	Epistle of John II	20
Johanni epistula III.	XX	Epistle of John III	20
Judae epistula	uer. LX	Epistle of Jude	Lines 60
— Barnabae epist.[65]	uer. DCCCL	Epistle of Barnabas[66]	Lines 850
Johannis revelatio	ĪCC	Revelation of John	1,200
Actus apostolorum	ĪIDC	Acts of the Apostles	2,600
— Pastoris	uersi ĪIII	Of the Shepherd	Lines 4,000
— Actus Pauli	uer. ĪIIDLX	Acts of Paul	Lines 3,560
— Revelatio Petri	CCLXX	Revelation of Peter	270

The Canon List of Codex Claromontanus

Old Testament
    Genesis
    Exodus

[60] This number is too low; Hahneman (1992: 141) attributes this number to the carelessness of the scribe.

[61] This number is too low; Hahneman (ibid.: 141) attributes this number to the carelessness of the scribe.

[62] A horizontal stroke appears before the reference to 1 Peter, possibly indicating that it should not be counted as one of the Pauline letters. On the similar horizontal stroke appearing before four of the final six books in this catalogue, see below.

[63] The inclusion of letters 'to' Peter is odd, probably due to the inattentiveness of the scribe (Metzger 1987: 229–30).

[64] This is the first line of the final page of the list in the manuscript (468v). This page contains eleven lines in one column.

[65] Beside the references to the Epistle of Barnabas, the Shepherd, the Acts of Paul, and the Revelation of Peter, there is a horizontal stroke extending into the left margin. This mark resembles an obelus, which usually indicated the spurious nature of the words so marked.

[66] Possibly the original compiler of this list intended the title Barnabae epist. as a reference to the (canonical) Epistle to the Hebrews, which otherwise goes unmentioned in this list, and was sometimes attributed to Barnabas in ancient Latin sources. See Zahn 1892: 169; de Boer 2014: 252. The stichometric calculation of 850 lines might lend support for this hypothesis, since a higher calculation would be expected for the longer Epistle of Barnabas. Against this suggestion, see Hahneman 1992: 141.

Leviticus
Numbers
Deuteronomy
Joshua
Judges
Ruth
1–4 Reigns (= 1–2 Samuel and 1–2 Kings)
Psalms
Proverbs
Ecclesiastes
Song of Songs
Wisdom of Solomon
Wisdom of Jesus Sirach
Twelve Prophets
      Hosea
      Amos
      Micah
      Joel
      Obadiah
      Jonah
      Nahum
      Habakkuk
      Zephaniah
      Haggai
      Zechariah
      Malachi
Isaiah
Jeremiah (+ Lamentations? + Baruch? + Epistle of Jeremiah?)
Ezekiel
Daniel
1–2, 4 Maccabees
Judith
Ezra (1 Esdras? Ezra–Nehemiah?)
Esther
Job
Tobit
New Testament
    Gospels, four
      Matthew
      John
      Mark
      Luke
    Paul
      Romans
      1–2 Corinthians
      Galatians
      Ephesians

> 1–2 Timothy
> Titus
> Colossians
> Philemon
1–2 Peter
James
1–3 John
Jude
Epistle of Barnabas (Hebrews?) (obelized)
Revelation
Acts
Shepherd (obelized)
Acts of Paul (obelized)
Revelation of Peter (obelized)

Books traditionally included in the Christian Bible but omitted here: Chronicles, Philippians, Thessalonians, and Hebrews. Very probably the omission of each of these books is due to scribal error, as suggested in the notes above.

MOMMSEN CATALOGUE, OR THE CHELTENHAM LIST

In 1886, the classical scholar Theodor Mommsen published a stichometric list of the biblical books from a tenth-century manuscript at one time in Cheltenham, England, now housed in the Biblioteca Nazionale in Rome.[67] A few years later, Mommsen came upon another copy of the list in an eighth- or ninth-century manuscript at St Gall in Switzerland.[68] This list in both manuscripts appears at the end of a larger work called the *Liber generationis* (The Book of Generation), a type of handbook for biblical study containing lists of 'the sons of Noah and where they lived, with information on the rivers of the Old Testament, and kings and judges reaching to the consulships of Valentinian and Valens in AD 365'.[69] It is probable that the *Liber generationis* was revised in 365 and at that time incorporated the list of biblical books (which is mentioned in the work's preface),[70] along with an immediately following list (again, stichometric) of works of Cyprian.[71] Both manuscripts present the *Liber generationis* as only one part of a larger 'Compendium' of eleven works designed to aid Bible study, and this Compendium likely dates to 427.[72] From the time that Mommsen

---

[67] Mommsen 1886; Sanday 1891. For the history of this manuscript, see Rouse and McNelis 2000: 237–8.

[68] Mommsen 1890.   [69] Rouse and McNelis 2000: 215.   [70] ibid.: 208–9.

[71] For this latter list of books, see Sanday 1891: 224–5.

[72] For a description of the Compendium, see Rouse and McNelis 2000: 211–18; on the date, see ibid.: 225–6. Both manuscripts have added this compendium to still other works. For an overview of the entire contents of the St Gall manuscript, see ibid.: 234–6; for the Roman (Cheltenham) manuscript, see ibid.: 236–8.

discovered the lists (that of the biblical books and that of Cyprian's works), scholars have confidently placed their origins in North Africa, the provenance of the *Liber generationis* itself, as well as the larger Compendium, and there are reasons to associate all of these works with the Donatist church.[73]

The list of biblical books (and the list of Cyprianic works) concluding the *Liber generationis* in these two manuscripts is a stichometry, indicating the number of lines—or 'stichs'—in each book listed. E.M. Thompson explains:

> It was the custom of the Greeks and Romans to compute the length of their literary works by measured lines. In poetry the unit was of course the verse; in prose works an artificial unit had to be found, for no two scribes would naturally write lines of the same length. On the authority of Galen (*De Placit. Hipp. et Plut.* viii. 1) we learn that the unit of measurement among the Greeks was the average Homeric line consisting of about sixteen syllables.[74]

Thompson goes on to explain that a similar system was in use for Latin manuscripts, as we learn from a note appearing between the list of biblical books and the list of Cyprian's works in the two manuscripts we have been discussing. According to the note, Latin scribes employed the average Virgilian line of sixteen syllables as the standard of measurement.[75] By means of this standard measurement for literary works, scribes would be paid for their labour according to the number of lines of the work copied, and one could confirm the accuracy or completeness of a copy. A desire for such confirmation may have led to the inclusion of the stichometries for the biblical books and for Cyprian's works within the revision of the *Liber generationis* completed in 365.[76]

We should probably date the list of biblical books no later than 365, the apparent date for the revision of the *Liber generationis* including this list.[77] While scholars have occasionally dated the list later than the fourth century,[78] most scholars have considered the date of the last consulship mentioned in the *Liber generationis* (i.e., the probable date of the revision) to be also the date of the composition of the list.[79] As Rouse and McNelis point out, the date of the

---

[73] On the North African origins of the list of the biblical books, see ibid.: 204; Bogaert 2003: 164. On the association of the *Liber generationis* with Donatism, see Rouse and McNelis 2000: 209–10; on the association of the Compendium with Donatism, see ibid.: 224–6.

[74] Thompson 1912: 67.

[75] ibid.: 69; Grafton and Williams 2006: 106–7; on the stichometry of the two manuscripts discussed here, see Rouse and McNelis 2000: 201–7. Rouse and McNelis (p. 202) note that these lists are 'the only surviving Latin stichometric lists from late antiquity', seemingly indicating a decline of the use of stichometry at this time in the Latin West. They do also mention (p. 202n64) the stichometry of the Codex Claromantanus (on which see the preceding section in this chapter), and there are later stichometries mentioned by Sanday 1891: 264–5.

[76] See Rouse and McNelis 2000: 210 for further possibilities.

[77] On the date of the revision, see ibid.: 208.

[78] Berger (1893: 319–21) thought the link between the OT books and the elders of John's Apocalypse (see below) depended on Jerome.

[79] See, e.g., Sanday 1891: 219–22; Hahneman 1992: 145–6. Sanday also thinks the content of the list, with its omission of Hebrews (p. 245), James, and Jude (p. 252), indicates a date 'not later than the end of the fourth century' (p. 245).

revision merely provides the *terminus ante quem* for the list, not necessarily the date of composition.[80]

Old Testament canon: All the books of the Jewish canon are included here, with the exception of Ezra. In addition, this stichometry includes two books of Maccabees, Tobit, and Judith, along with (probably) the Wisdom of Solomon and Sirach. The books of Solomon are not individually named, or even numbered, but the stichometric value, if trustworthy, indicates that the list includes more than merely the three Solomonic books contained in the Jewish canon. It is unclear what books may be included with Jeremiah.

New Testament canon: No additional books beyond those included in the traditional New Testament are found here, but some books are omitted: Hebrews, James, and Jude are completely unmentioned, and one of the manuscripts contains a curious note connected to the epistles of John and Peter.

Studies: Mommsen 1886; Zahn 1888–92: 2.143–56, 1007–12; Mommsen 1890; Sanday 1891; Metzger 1987: 231–2; Rouse and McNelis 2000; Bogaert 2003: 164–70; Markschies 2012: 121–4.

The Text of the Mommsen Catalogue

Date: before 365 CE[81]

Text[82]		Translation[83]	
Incipit indiculum ueteris testamenti qui sunt libri canonici sic		So begins the index of the Old Testament which are the canonical books	
Genesis	uersus $\overline{\text{III}}$DCC	Genesis	Lines 3,700
Exodus	uer $\overline{\text{III}}$	Exodus	Lines 3,000
Numeri	uer $\overline{\text{III}}$	Numbers	Lines 3,000
Leuiticus	uer $\overline{\text{II}}$CCC	Leuiticus[84]	Lines 2,300
Deuteronomium	uer $\overline{\text{II}}$DCC	Deuteronomy	Lines 2,700
Hiesu Naue	uer MDCCL	Joshua Naue	Lines 1,750
Iudicum	uer MDCCL	Judges	Lines 1,750
Fiunt libri VII	uer $\overline{\text{XVIII}}$C	7 books total	Lines 18,100
Rut	uer CCL	Ruth[85]	Lines 250
Regnorum liber I	uer $\overline{\text{II}}$CCC	Of Reigns[86] book 1	Lines 2,300
Regnorum liber II	uer $\overline{\text{II}}$CC	Of Reigns book 2	Lines 2,200
Regnorum liber III	uer $\overline{\text{II}}$DL	Of Reigns book 3	Lines 2,550

---

[80] Rouse and McNelis 2000: 209.   [81] See the discussion above.

[82] Preuschen 1893: 138–40.   [83] For the NT portion, see Metzger 1987: 311–12.

[84] This peculiar order for the Pentateuchal books is mirrored in Melito's list, on which see the discussion at p. 80n37.

[85] Ruth is usually grouped with Judges, but here it stands closer to Kings; see also Augustine (p. 227) and Innocent (p. 232n234).

[86] 1–4 Reigns is equivalent to the books known in English as 1–2 Samuel and 1–2 Kings.

Text		Translation	
Regnorum liber IIII	uer $\overline{\text{II}}$CCL	Of Reigns book 4	Lines 2,250
Fiunt	uersus $\overline{\text{VIIII}}$D	They total	Lines 9,500
Paralipomenon liber I	uer $\overline{\text{II}}$XL	Paralipomena[87] book 1	Lines 2,040
liber II	uer $\overline{\text{II}}$C	book 2	Lines 2,100
Machabeorum liber I	uer $\overline{\text{II}}$CCC	Of Maccabees book 1	Lines 2,300
liber II	uer MDCCC	book 2	Lines 1,800
Iob	uer MDCC	Job	Lines 1,700
Tobias	uer DCCCC	Tobit	Lines 900
Hester	uer DCC	Esther	Lines 700
Iudit	uer MC	Judith	Lines 1,100
Psalmi Dauitici CLI	uer $\overline{\text{V}}$	Of David Psalms, 151[88]	Lines 5,000
Salomonis	uer $\overline{\text{VI}}$D	Of Solomon[89]	Lines 6,500
Prophetae maiores	uer $\overline{\text{XV}}$CCCLXX numero $\overline{\text{IIII}}$	Major Prophets[90]	Lines 15,370 four in number
Esaias	uer $\overline{\text{III}}$DLXXX	Isaiah	Lines 3,580
Ieremias	uer $\overline{\text{IIII}}$CCCCL	Jeremiah	Lines 4,450
Daniel	uer MCCCL	Daniel	Lines 1,350
Ezechiel	uer $\overline{\text{III}}$CCCXL	Ezekiel	Lines 3,340
Prophetae XII	uer $\overline{\text{IIII}}$DCCC	Twelve Prophets	Lines 3,800
Erunt omnes uersus numero	$\overline{\text{LXVIIII}}$D	All the lines will be in number	Lines 69,500

Sed ut in apocalypsi Iohannis dictum est: 'uidi XXIIII seniores mittentes coronas suas ante thronum.' maiores nostri probant, hos libros esse canonicos et hoc dixisse seniores.	But as in the Revelation of John it is said: 'I saw twenty-four elders casting their crowns before the throne' [Rev. 4:10].[91] Our predecessors show that these are the canonical books and that the elders have said this.

[87] Paralipomena is the Greek and Latin name for the book of Chronicles.

[88] Specifying a Psalter of 151 psalms is unusual in the canon lists, but manuscripts of the Psalter containing 151 psalms are widespread (Bogaert 2003: 166). While the Roman Catholic Church stands in agreement with Protestants and Jews in having a Psalter containing 150 psalms, the major codices of the LXX (i.e., Vaticanus, etc.) contain an additional psalm, which, according to its heading, is 'outside the number'. This additional psalm (traditionally called Psalm 151) is found in some eastern Christian Bibles, such as that of the Greek Orthodox.

[89] The list does not specify which books of Solomon are included, but the number of lines here (6,500) indicates more than Proverbs, Ecclesiastes, and Song of Songs, and several fourth-century Latin canonical lists (see especially Augustine) suggest that Wisdom of Solomon and Sirach would also be included here.

[90] Augustine is usually cited as the earliest instance of the terminology of major and minor prophets (*City of God* 18.29), but already the present list implies the same distinction with its title 'Major Prophets' before the four longer prophetic books.

[91] The same connection between the twenty-four elders of Revelation and twenty-four books of the Bible is found in Jerome's *Prologus Galeatus*, on which see below, pp. 201–2. But for Jerome, the twenty-four books in question constituted the Old Testament. The Old Testament of the Mommsen Catalogue includes twenty-seven titles, and it is hard to arrange the books in such a way that the total equals twenty-four (but see Turner 1891). On the other hand, the Catalogue has twenty-four book titles in the New Testament. See Bogaert 2003: 168–9.

Text		Translation	
Item indiculum noui testamenti		Likewise the index of the New Testament	
Euangelia IIII		Four Gospels[92]	
Mattheum	ur $\overline{II}$DCC	Matthew	Lines 2,700
Marcum	uer MDCC	Mark	Lines 1,700
Iohannem	ur MDCCC	John	Lines 1,800
Lucam	ur $\overline{III}$CCC	Luke	Lines 3,300
Fiunt omnes	uersus $\overline{X}$	They all total	Lines 10,000
Eplae Pauli	$\overline{n}$ XIII	Epistles of Paul	Thirteen in number[93]
Actus aplorum	uer $\overline{III}$DC	Acts of the Apostles	Lines 3,600
Apocalipsis	uer MDCCC	Revelation	Lines 1,800
Eplae Iohannis III [una sola]	ur CCCL	Epistles of John, 3 [one only][94]	Lines 350
Eplae Petri II [una sola]	uer CCC	Epistles of Peter, 2 [one only]	Lines 300
Quoniam indiculum versuum in urbe Roma non ad liquidum, sed et alibi auaritiae causa non habent integrum, per singulos libros computatis syllabis posui numero XVI uersum Virgilianum omnibus libris numerum adscribsi.		Since the index of lines in the city of Rome is not clearly given, and elsewhere too through avarice for gain they do not preserve it in full, I have gone through the books singly, counting sixteen syllables to the line, and have appended to every book the number of Virgilian hexameters.[95]	

[92] This is the order of the Gospels according to the Roman (Cheltenham) manuscript, an order of the Gospels that is paralleled only in the Curetonian Syriac Gospels and in the commentary of Theophilus of Antioch (Metzger 1987: 231). The St Gall manuscript has the order Matthew–John–Mark–Luke. Cf. Codex Claromontanus in this chapter (p. 185n58), and see Bogaert 1999.

[93] Oddly, this list does not include the stichometry for Paul, but it mentions instead the number of letters—thirteen—which must not include Hebrews. On the meaning of the Latin, see Bogaert 2003: 166n32. It is possible that the number xiii results from scribal error, and xiiii (including Hebrews) was intended, but the omission of Hebrews in a fourth-century Latin list is not surprising. See the appendix, pp. 271–2.

[94] This obscure note appears only in the Roman (Cheltenham) manuscript, not the St Gall manuscript. Since it is connected to the letters of John and of Peter, it perhaps represents a second opinion, that only one Johannine and Petrine epistle should be included; Metzger 1987: 231–2. Or the opposite view may be correct, that the original stichometry contained only one Petrine and one Johannine epistle, and the later scribe corrected this to a higher number (three letters of John and two of Peter) but also wanted to indicate that the stichometric figure was valid for only the major Petrine and Johannine epistles; see Turner 1891: 307–8; Markschies 2012: 221–4.

[95] Thompson 1912: 69: 'The text of the memorandum is imperfect, but the meaning of the writer is clear, namely, that it had become the practice both in Rome and elsewhere, with a view to unfair profits (in the book-trade), to manipulate the records of the length of the contents of literary works; and that therefore he had made calculations of the number of *versus* in the several books under his hand, the average Virgilian hexameter of sixteen syllables being the unit of measurement, and had noted the total in each instance.' But Rouse and McNelis (2000: 205) believe that this note has reference specifically to the stichometry of Cyprian immediately following and not to the preceding biblical stichometry.

The Canon List of the Mommsen Catalogue

Old Testament
    Genesis
    Exodus
    Numbers
    Leviticus
    Deuteronomy
    Joshua Naue
    Judges
    Ruth
    1–4 Reigns (= 1–2 Samuel and 1–2 Kings)
    1–2 Paralipomena (= 1–2 Chronicles)
    1–2 Maccabees
    Job
    Tobit
    Esther
    Judith
    Psalms
    Solomon
    Major Prophets, 4
    Isaiah
    Jeremiah
    Daniel
    Ezekiel
    Twelve Prophets
New Testament
    Matthew
    Mark
    John
    Luke
    Epistles of Paul, 13
    Acts of the Apostles
    Revelation
    Epistles of John, 3 (or 1?)
    Epistles of Peter, 2 (or 1?)

Several books often included in canon lists are unmentioned here: Ezra,[96] Hebrews, James, and Jude.

---

[96] Bogaert (2003: 166; 2014: 47) wonders whether the absence of Ezra was an accident here, even though its absence would not be completely unique, since some manuscripts of Augustine's canon list (in *Doctr. chr.*, see below) omit Ezra, as does the Latin form of the list associated with the Synod of Laodicea, along with a few other sources (Bogaert 2000: 13–14; 2014: 73n74).

HILARY OF POITIERS

Hilary (ca. 310–ca. 367) was born in or near Poitiers in what is today west-central France.[97] According to his own testimony, he was baptized as an adult and served as bishop of Poitiers only briefly before the Synod of Béziers in 356.[98] This pro-Arian synod condemned Hilary's Nicene Christology and exiled him to Phrygia, where he spent the next four years strengthening his understanding of the Greek theological tradition. During this time, he also wrote some of his own theological works, such as *De Trinitate* and *De Synodis*. He returned to Gaul in 360, and he spent the last years of his life defending the Nicene faith. His writings include an early commentary on Matthew and a later incomplete commentary on the Psalter (the *Tractatus super Psalmos*), covering fifty-eight Psalms. The introduction to this Psalms commentary contains Hilary's list of canonical books for the Old Testament.

Old Testament canon: Hilary asserts that the books of the Old Testament number twenty-two. He essentially lists the books of the Jewish canon, except that he includes the Epistle of Jeremiah as a part of Jeremiah, and it is not exactly clear which book of Esdras he intends by his unusual title ('Words of the Days of Esdras'). After naming each of the twenty-two books, he acknowledges that some people add Tobit and Judith, thus arriving at the number twenty-four, in accordance with the letters of the Greek alphabet.

Studies: Howorth 1909–10: 323–5; Hennings 1994: 184–6.

Instructio Psalmorum 15

Date: 364–7

Introduction: Hilary's *Tractatus super Psalmos* begins with an introduction called the *Instructio*, in twenty-four chapters. Since ancient times readers have recognized Hilary's indebtedness to Origen's commentary on the Psalter,[99] and this dependence extends, it seems, even to Hilary's canon list. It was, after all, in a comment to Psalm 1 that Origen listed the books of the Hebrew canon.[100] Accordingly, Hilary's list mirrors Origen's almost exactly, from the order of the books to the inclusion of Lamentations and the Epistle of Jeremiah with Jeremiah. But whereas Origen had mentioned Maccabees as outside the official list, Hilary omits reference to Maccabees and comments instead that some include Tobit and Judith.

---

[97] For a brief survey of the data available for Hilary's biography, see Beckwith 2008: 6–10.
[98] *De Synodis* 91; PL 10.545a.   [99] Cf. Jerome, *Vir ill.* 100; see Burns 2012: 65–77.
[100] See ch. 3 on Origen pp. 84–7.

Text[101]	Translation[102]
Et ea causa est, ut in uiginti duos libros lex Testamenti Veteris deputetur, ut cum litterarum numero conuenirent. Qui ita secundum traditiones ueterum deputantur, ut Moysi sint libri quinque, Iesu Naue sextus, Iudicum et Ruth septimus, primus et secundus Regnorum octauus, tertius et quartus in nonum, Paralipomenon duo in decimum sint, sermones dierum Esdrae in undecimum, liber Psalmorum duodecimus sit, Salomonis Prouerbia, Ecclesiastes, Canticum canticorum in tertium decimum et quartum decimum et quintum decimum, duodecim autem omnes Prophetae in sextum decimum, Esaias deinde et Hieremias cum lamentatione et epistula, sed et Daniel et Ezechiel et Iob et Hester uiginti duum librorum numerum consumment. Quibusdam autem uisum est, additis Tobia et	And therefore the law of the Old Testament is reckoned in twenty-two books, so that they agree with the number of the letters.[103] They are reckoned according to the traditions of our forebears so that there are five books of Moses, a sixth of Joshua Nave, a seventh of Judges and Ruth,[104] first and second of the Kingdoms is eighth,[105] third and fourth in the ninth,[106] two of Paralipomenon are in the tenth,[107] words of the days of Esdras in the eleventh,[108] the book of Psalms is twelfth, Proverbs of Solomon, and his Ecclesiastes and Song of Songs in the thirteenth, fourteenth, and fifteenth, and all the Twelve Prophets in the sixteenth, then Isaiah and Jeremiah with Lamentations and the Epistle,[109] but also Daniel, and Ezekiel, and Job, and Esther complete the number of the twenty-two books. But to some it seems good to add Tobit and Judith[110] in order to enumerate twenty-four

---

[101]   Doignon 1997: 61, 12–13.

[102]   We appreciate the help of Will Dilbeck on this translation.

[103]   This theme—that the OT books number twenty-two in conjunction with the Hebrew alphabet—finds expression in other patristic authors, the earliest being Origen.

[104]   Several patristic authors also combine Judges and Ruth in one volume; cf., e.g., Origen.

[105]   The first two books of Kingdoms are 1–2 Samuel.

[106]   The third and fourth books of Kingdoms are 1–2 Kings.

[107]   Paralipomenon is our Chronicles.

[108]   This is a strange title for the book(s) of Ezra. *Verba Dierum* is a title associated with Chronicles, a literal translation of the Hebrew title *Divrei ha-Yamim*; see Jerome, *Prologus Galeatus*. Origen's list includes references to the Hebrew titles with Greek translations for these titles. Like Hilary, Origen lists Paralipomenon immediately before Ezra, thus: Παραλειπομένων α′ β′ ἐν ἑνί, Δαβρηϊαμειν, ὅπερ ἐστὶν 'λόγοι ἡμερῶν'· Ἔζρας α′ β′ ἐν ἑνί, Εζρα, ὅ ἐστιν 'βοηθός'. (The phrase 'λόγοι ἡμερῶν' is translated by Rufinus as *sermones dierum*.) It seems probable that Hilary has misread Origen's list, taking the Greek translation of Paralipomenon's Hebrew title as if it were a part of the title for the following book, Ezra. Or perhaps Hilary's copy of Origen's Psalms commentary had suffered corruption, a possibility strengthened by the presence of the Hebrew titles transliterated into Greek, which would have appeared strange to many Greek scribes. The omission of the Twelve Prophets in the text of Origen as we have it also suggests that his list suffered early corruption.

[109]   Origen's list also included under the title Jeremiah both Lamentations and the Epistle of Jeremiah. Bogaert (2014: 47–8; cf. Bogaert 2005: 298) thinks that Hilary has in mind a text of Jeremiah containing Baruch along with Lamentations and the Epistle (= Baruch ch. 6), an idea supported by Hilary's twice citing material from Baruch under the name of Jeremiah (*Tract. Psal.* 68.19 [Bar 3:36]; *Trin.* 4.42 [Bar. 3:35–7]).

[110]   Hilary departs from following Origen's list at this point. It is unclear why Hilary specifies Tobit and Judith here, or to whom he refers as including these two books in order to make up the number twenty-four. No other canon list collected in this volume contains only Tobit and Judith without any of the other deuterocanonicals. Tobit and Judith were two popular books in the fourth century (see Gallagher 2015b), and earlier Origen had mentioned them both as books not used by the Jews, though they were used by churches (*Ep. Afr.* 19; see Gallagher 2012a: 57–9).

Text	Translation
Iudith, uiginti quattuor libros secundum numerum graecarum litterarum connumerare, Romana quoque lingua media inter Hebraeos Graecosque conlecta, quia his maxime tribus linguis sacramentum uoluntatis Dei et beati regni expectatio praedicatur; ex quo illud Pilati fuit ut his tribus linguis regem Iudaeorum Dominum Iesum Christum esse praescriberet. Nam quamuis multae barbarae gentes Dei cognitionem secundum apostolorum praedicationem et manentium hodie illic ecclesiarum fidem adeptae sint, tamen specialiter euangelica doctrina in Romano imperio, sub quo Hebraei et Graeci continentur, consistit.	books, in accordance with the number of the Greek letters.[111] The Roman language also was chosen in the middle between Hebrew and Greek, because in these three languages especially the sacrament of the will of God and the anticipation of his blessed kingdom is preached; since it was Pilate's duty that he might dictate that the Lord Jesus Christ was king of the Jews in these three languages [cf. John 19:19–20]. For although many barbarian peoples have obtained the knowledge of God according to the preaching of the apostles and the faith of those churches that remain here today, nevertheless especially the evangelic doctrine exists in the Roman Empire, under which the Hebrews and Greeks are maintained.

The Canon List of Hilary

Old Testament (twenty-two books, or twenty-four)

1–5	Moses, five books
6	Joshua
7	Judges and Ruth
8	1–2 Kingdoms
9	3–4 Kingdoms
10	1–2 Paralipomenon
11	Words of the Days of Esdras
12	Book of Psalms
13	Proverbs of Solomon
14	Ecclesiastes
15	Song of Songs
16	Twelve Prophets
	Isaiah
	Jeremiah with Lamentations and the Epistle

Hilary mentions Tobit for its information about angels at *Tract. Psal.* 129.7 (cf. Tob. 12:15), and he cites Tob. 12:7 without attribution (*Tract. Psal.* 118.2.6). He cites Judith once, without attribution (Jud. 16:3 at *Tract. Psal.* 125.6). Hilary also occasionally cited other deuterocanonical works, such as Wisdom of Solomon, three times as the 'prophet' (*Tract. Psal.* 118.2.8 [Wis. 17:1]; 135.11 [Wis. 1:7]; *Trin.* 1.7 [Wis. 13:5]); Baruch, under the name Jeremiah (see n. 109); Susanna under her name (*Trin.* 4.8 [Sus. 42]); see Howorth 1909–10: 323–5.

[111] The number twenty-four for the books of the Old Testament is attested already in 4 Ezra 14:45 and Gos. Thom. 52, and in a few later Christian writers, e.g., the Mommsen Catalogue; Ps.-Tertullian, *Carmen adv. Marcionem* 4.198–9; Victorinus of Pettau, *Comm. Apoc.* 4:4; Jerome, *Prol. Gal.* (see below). See ch. 1, pp. 6–7, and the brief discussion in Gallagher 2012a: 52–3 with nn. 136–7. Jews since rabbinic times have enumerated their sacred books as twenty-four, as implied in b. B. Bathra 14b (see ch. 2).

Daniel
Ezekiel
Job
Esther
Some add:
Tobit
Judith

JEROME OF STRIDON

Jerome (ca. 347–420) was the greatest biblical scholar writing in Latin during Late Antiquity.[112] He pushed for Christian reliance on the original languages of the Bible for exegesis and theology, not a particularly remarkable campaign in terms of the New Testament—many of his Latin contemporaries knew Greek— but a revolutionary one for the Old Testament. Promotion of the *hebraica veritas*, the Hebrew truth, became his constant refrain, as he established his authority as one of the only Christian exegetes who attempted to learn Hebrew. After his move to Bethlehem in 386, he translated the entire Hebrew Bible into Latin (ca. 391–405), along with revising the Latin text of the Gospels, and this work became the basis for the Latin Vulgate edition of the Bible. In addition to a number of polemical and theological works, Jerome also wrote major commentaries on the OT prophetic literature, as well as Ecclesiastes, some of the Pauline Epistles, and the Gospel of Matthew. There also survive many of his letters written to friends, colleagues, and patrons.

Old Testament canon: Jerome surveys the books of the Old Testament three times in his writings, and each time it is the Jewish canon that he advocates as the Christian Old Testament. In his *Preface to Samuel and Kings* (the *Prologus Galeatus*), he arranges the Old Testament in conformity with the tripartite Hebrew Bible among Jews (i.e., the Tanak), though he follows a more typically Christian order in *Epistle* 53. In *Epistle* 107, his concern is not the order of the canon but the order in which the books should be studied. In none of the lists do the deuterocanonical books appear, except in the *Prologus Galeatus*, where he labels them apocrypha and says that 'they are not in the canon'. Also, in the *Prologus Galeatus* he numbers the canonical books as twenty-two or twenty-four, depending on whether Ruth and Lamentations count independently or only as appendices to Judges and Jeremiah, respectively. He does not mention a particular number in *Epp.* 53 or 107. He does not mention here the deutero-canonical additions to Daniel or to Esther, but in the prefaces to his translations

---

[112] For a basic introduction, see Rebenich 2002. For detailed treatments of his biblical scholarship, see Kamesar 1993; Williams 2006; Graves 2007.

of those works he explains that since they are not found in Hebrew, he prefixes an obelus to his translation of them. As for the book of Baruch—essentially considered an addition to Jeremiah at this time—Jerome never mentions it in the canon lists collected here, but in the preface to his translation of Jeremiah and in the prologue to his Jeremiah commentary Jerome mentions the absence of Baruch among the Jews and his consequent decision to omit it altogether from either his translation or commentary.

New Testament canon: Jerome surveys the books of the New Testament once, in his *Epistle* 53. His list essentially matches the list of NT books advocated by Athanasius in the *Festal Letter* 39. Jerome leaves open in this letter the exact number of Pauline Epistles, and the status of Hebrews, but it becomes clear from statements elsewhere in Jerome's corpus that he accepts thirteen letters of Paul and the canonicity (and anonymity) of Hebrews. Jerome offers a partial list of NT books in his *Epistle* 107.

Studies: Howorth 1908–9; 1909–10; 1911–12; 1913; Skehan 1952; Gallagher 2012b; 2013a; 2015b.

Prologus Galeatus

Date: early 390s (393?)[113]

Introduction: Jerome designed this preface to his translation of Samuel and Kings as a general introduction to his Latin translations from the Hebrew Bible. The dedicatees are left unnamed, though the reference near the end to them as 'maid-servants of Christ' likely points to Paula and Eustochium, as scholars generally assume.[114]

Text[115]	Translation
Viginti et duas esse litteras apud Hebreos, Syrorum quoque et Chaldeorum lingua testatur, quae hebreae magna ex parte confinis est; nam et ipsi viginti duo elementa habent eodem sono, sed diversis caracteribus. Samaritani etiam pentateuchum Mosi totidem litteris scriptitant, figuris tantum et apicibus discrepantes. Certumque est Ezram scribam legisque doctorem post	That there are twenty-two letters among the Hebrews is shown by the language of the Syrians and Chaldeans,[116] which is very close to Hebrew; for they also have twenty-two letters with the same sound but different characters.[117] The Samaritans also write the Pentateuch of Moses with the same letters, differing only in the shapes and tittles.[118] It is certain that Ezra, the scribe and teacher of the law, after the

---

[113] See Jay 1982.   [114] See, e.g., Fürst 2003: 87.   [115] Gasquet 1944: 1–11.

[116] Jerome uses these two names to describe dialects of the Aramaic language; see Gallagher 2012a: 125–7.

[117] He means that Syriac and Aramaic use different formations for the letters of their alphabet, but the alphabet itself, including the sounds that the letters make, is identical to the Hebrew alphabet.

[118] The Latin word for 'tittle' here (*apex*) is the same word that Jerome uses in his translation of Matt. 5:18, where Jesus said that 'not a jot or a tittle' will pass away from the law until it is all

Text	Translation
captam Hierosolymam et instaurationem templi sub Zorobabel, alias litteras repperisse, quibus nunc utimur, cum ad illud usque tempus idem Samaritanorum et Hebreorum caracteres fuerint. In libro quoque Numerorum haec eadem supputatio, sub levitarum ac sacerdotum censu, mystice ostenditur. Et nomen Domini tetragrammaton in quibusdam graecis voluminibus usque hodie antiquis expressum litteris invenimus. Sed et psalmi tricensimus sextus, et centensimus decimus, et centensimus undecimus, et centensimus octavus decimus, et centensimus quadragensimus quartus, quamquam diverso scribantur metro, tamen eiusdem numeri texuntur alfabeto. Et Hieremiae Lamentationes et oratio eius, Salomonis quoque in fine Proverbia ab eo loco in quo ait: 'Mulierem fortem quis inveniet,' hisdem alfabetis vel incisionibus supputantur. Porro quinque litterae duplices apud eos sunt: chaph, mem, nun, phe, sade; aliter enim per has scribunt principia mediatesque verborum, aliter fines. Unde et quinque a plerisque libri duplices aestimantur: Samuhel, Malachim, Dabreiamin, Ezras, Hieremias cum Cinoth, id est Lamentationibus suis. Quomodo igitur	captivity of Jerusalem and the rebuilding of the temple under Zerubbabel, devised different letters, which we now use, since up to that time the letter shapes of the Samaritans and the Hebrews were the same.[119] And in the book of Numbers this same reckoning is shown mystically in the census of the Levites and priests.[120] And the name of the Lord, the Tetragrammaton, in certain Greek scrolls we find still today expressed in the ancient letters.[121] But also Psalm 36, 110, 111, 118, and 144, though they are written in different metre, still they are interwoven with the alphabet of the same number.[122] And the Lamentations of Jeremiah and his prayer, and also at the end of the Proverbs of Solomon from the place where it says, 'A strong woman who will find' [Prov. 31:10], are reckoned with the same letters and clauses. Furthermore, five letters are doubled among them: *chaph, mem, nun, phe, sade*; for with these they write the beginnings and middle parts of words one way, and the ends another way.[123] So also five books are considered by many to be doubled: Samuel, *Malachim, Dabreiamin*, Ezra, Jeremiah with *Cinoth*, that is, his Lamentations.[124] Therefore, just as there are twenty-two letters with which we write in Hebrew everything that we say, and by their

fulfilled. The Samaritans at the time of Jerome—and still today—use a script developed from the paleo-Hebrew script of ancient Israelite times. See in general Yardeni 2002 and on the Samaritans particularly, ibid.: 25.

[119] Jerome is referring to the change from using the paleo-Hebrew form of the alphabet to the Aramaic 'square' script for writing Hebrew. On this change and the ancient traditions associated with it, see Gallagher 2012a: 121–3.

[120] Num. 3:39: 'The total enrollment of the Levites whom Moses and Aaron enrolled at the commandment of the LORD, by their clans, all the males from a month old and upward, was twenty-two thousand.' (NRSV)

[121] A number of Greek biblical manuscripts contain the Tetragrammaton in paleo-Hebrew script. See Gallagher 2013b: 300–4.

[122] Jerome follows the LXX enumeration of the psalms here (as he does also in his Vulgate translation). The MT numbering—followed by most English translations—would be Psalms 37, 111, 112, 119, and 145. Each of these psalms is an alphabetic acrostic in Hebrew. The idea that the psalms were written in metre conforming to Greek and Latin metrics is traced by Kugel 1981: ch. 4.

[123] These five Hebrew letters have medial forms and final forms, somewhat like the lowercase Greek *sigma*.

[124] The italicized names of books are used by Jerome here and explained by him later in the text. These names for the books presumably would have been unfamiliar to his readers. The idea that there are five doubled books that correspond to the five Hebrew letters with medial and final forms is also found in Epiphanius, who, however, mentions Judges–Ruth as one of the doubled books rather than Jeremiah–Lamentations (*Mens.* 4).

Text	Translation
viginti duo elementa sunt, per quae scribimus hebraice omne quod loquimur, et eorum initiis vox humana conprehenditur, ita viginti duo volumina supputantur, quibus quasi litteris et exordiis, in Dei doctrina, tenera adhuc et lactans viri iusti eruditur infantia.	elements the human voice is expressed, so twenty-two scrolls are reckoned, by which, like letters and prefaces, the infancy of a just man—still young and nursing—is instructed in the teaching of God.[125]
Primus apud eos liber vocatur Bresith, quem nos Genesim dicimus; secundus Hellesmoth, qui Exodus appellatur; tertius Vaiecra, id est Leviticus; quartus Vaiedabber, quem Numeros vocamus; quintus Addabarim, qui Deuteronomium praenotatur. Hii sunt quinque libri Mosi, quos proprie Thorath, id est Legem appellant.	The first book is called among them *Bresith*, which we name Genesis; second *Hellesmoth*, which is labelled Exodus; third *Vaiecra*, that is, Leviticus; fourth *Vaiedabber*, which we call Numbers; fifth *Addabarim*, which is titled Deuteronomy.[126] These are the five books of Moses, which they appropriately label *Thorath*, that is, Law.
Secundum Prophetarum ordinem faciunt, et incipiunt ab Iesu filio Nave, qui apud eos Iosue Bennum dicitur. Deinde subtexunt Sopthim, id est Iudicum librum; et in eundem conpingunt Ruth, quia in diebus iudicum facta narratur historia. Tertius sequitur Samuhel, quem nos Regnorum primum et secundum dicimus. Quartus Malachim, id est Regum, qui tertio et quarto Regnorum volumine continetur; meliusque multo est Malachim, id est Regum, quam Malachoth, id est Regnorum dicere, non enim multarum gentium regna describit, sed unius israhelitici populi qui tribubus duodecim continetur. Quintus est Esaias, sextus Hieremias, septimus Hiezecihel, octavus liber duodecim Prophetarum, qui apud illos vocatur Thareasra.	They make the order of the Prophets second,[127] and they begin with Jesus son of Nave, who is called among them Joshua ben Nun. Then they append *Sopthim*, that is, the book of Judges, and to it they join Ruth, because the story is narrated as having happened in the days of the Judges. Third there follows Samuel, which we call the first and second [books] of Kingdoms [Reigns]. Fourth, *Malachim*, that is, of Kings, which is contained in the third and fourth scroll of Kingdoms [Reigns]; but it is much better to say *Malachim*, that is, of Kings, than *Malachoth*, that is, of Kingdoms, for it does not describe the kingdoms of many nations, but of one, the Israelite people, which is contained in twelve tribes. Fifth is Isaiah, sixth Jeremiah, seventh Ezekiel, eighth the book of the Twelve Prophets, which is called among them *Thareasra*.[128]

[125] The reckoning of the OT books as twenty-two was very common among Greek and Latin Fathers; see Gallagher 2012a: 85–92. Such a reckoning is first attested by Josephus, *C. Ap.* 1.37–43. The connection of this number of books to the Hebrew alphabet is first attested in a fragment of Origen preserved in Eusebius, *Hist. eccl.* 6.25 (see ch. 3 above, pp. 84–7).

[126] The Hebrew names given by Jerome for each of these books match the modern Jewish names for the books, except in the case of Numbers, which today is called *Bemidbar* ('in the wilderness'), after the fifth word of the book (in Hebrew). The name Jerome gives this book corresponds to the first word of the book, as do the other names for the books of the Pentateuch, except for *Addabarim* for Deuteronomy, which is the second word of the book. For other patristic lists that give the Hebrew names for the books, see the discussion of Origen, Epiphanius, and the Bryennios List in ch. 3.

[127] Jerome divides the Old Testament according to the tripartite division of the Hebrew Bible (the Tanak), an unprecedented move among the church fathers. Nevertheless, the sequence of the individual books within the Prophets and Hagiographa is not known elsewhere. There is no known Jewish list where Ruth follows Judges or Lamentations follows Jeremiah, or where Esther concludes the whole canon.

[128] The Twelve Prophets is the common patristic designation for the Minor Prophets, nearly always counted as a single book. The Aramaic word reported by Jerome as the title means 'twelve'.

Text	Translation
Tertius ordo αγιογραφα possidet, et primus liber incipit ab Iob, secundus a David, quem quinque incisionibus et uno Psalmorum volumine conprehendunt; tertius est Salomon, tres libros habens: Proverbia, quae illi Parabolas, id est Masaloth appellant, et Ecclesiasten, id est Accoeleth, et Canticum canticorum, quem titulo Sirassirim praenotant; sextus est Danihel, septimus Dabreiamin, id est Verba dierum, quod significantius χρονικον totius divinae historiae possumus appellare, qui liber apud nos Paralipomenon primus et secundus scribitur; octavus Ezras, qui et ipse similiter apud Graecos et Latinos in duos libros divisus est, nonus Hester.	The third order encompasses the αγιογραφα,[129] and the first book begins with Job, the second with David, which they embrace in five divisions and in one book of Psalms.[130] Third is Solomon, who has three books: Proverbs, which they label Parables, that is, *Masaloth*, and Ecclesiastes, that is, *Accoeleth*, and Song of Songs, which they prefix with the title *Sirassirim*. Sixth is Daniel, seventh *Dabreiamin*, that is, Words of the Days, which more meaningfully we can label a χρονικον of all divine history, which book among us is written as the first and second Paralipomenon;[131] eighth Ezra, which is also itself divided into two books similarly among Greeks and Latins,[132] ninth Esther.
Atque ita fiunt pariter veteris legis libri viginti duo, id est Mosi quinque, Prophetarum octo, Agiograforum novem. Quamquam nonnulli Ruth et Cinoth inter Agiografa scriptitent et libros hos in suo putent numero supputandos, ac per hoc esse priscae legis libros viginti quattuor, quos sub	So they make all together twenty-two books of the old law, that is, five of Moses, eight of the Prophets, nine of the Hagiographa. Although some write Ruth and *Cinoth* among the Hagiographa and think that these books should be reckoned with their own number and thus that there are twenty-four books of the ancient

The earliest attestation for the term 'Minor Prophets' is Augustine (*City of God* 18.29). Augustine is also the first author to count the Minor Prophets separately as twelve individual books. Earlier, Gregory of Nazianzus and Amphilochius of Iconium had listed individually each of the Minor Prophets, but Gregory still reckoned twenty-two total books for the Old Testament (Amphilochius reported no total number).

[129] Jerome uses Greek characters for this Greek word meaning 'sacred writings'. The common Hebrew term for this division is *Ketuvim*, 'writings'. Jerome uses the term *Agiografa* (or, more commonly in English, Hagiographa) in Latin only six times: twice more in this preface, twice in his *Preface to Daniel*, and once each in his prefaces to Tobit and Judith, on which see Gallagher 2015b.

[130] The Psalter exhibits a fivefold division, as was recognized already by ancient Jews and Christians; see de Lange 1976: 177n32. For a modern examination of this fivefold structure, see Wilson 1985.

[131] The English title Chronicles reflects the Greek term that Jerome suggests would be a more appropriate title for the book. The Hebrew title of the book, *Divrei Ha-Yamim* (Jerome's *Dabreiamin*), which literally means 'Events [or: Words] of the Days', essentially signifies a chronicle. The Greek title *Paraleipomena* means 'things omitted', and it became the common designiation for the book among the Latin fathers. See Knoppers and Harvey 2002.

[132] Jerome seems to be saying that the book that the Jews call 'Ezra' (= Ezra and Nehemiah in English Bibles) was sometimes divided by Greeks into two books. There is barely any evidence to confirm this assertion. The Greeks certainly did talk about two books of Esdras, but these included a literal Greek translation of our canonical Ezra (2 Esdras) and another Greek book (now considered apocryphal) that combines material from Ezra with material from Nehemiah and the end of Chronicles (1 Esdras). See Janz 2010: 29–33. Jerome surely does not intend to include 1 Esdras in the canon here. He never translated 1 Esdras. He perhaps regarded it as a variant edition of Ezra-Nehemiah. See his *Preface to Ezra* 18–19, and see the Appendix, p. 269. On the confusing enumeration of the books of Ezra, see Bogaert 2000.

Text	Translation
numero viginti quattuor seniorum Apocalypsis Iohannis inducit adorantes Agnum et coronas suas prostratis vultibus offerentes, stantibus coram quattuor animalibus oculatis retro et ante, id est et in praeteritum et in futurum, et indefessa voce clamantibus: 'Sanctus, sanctus, sanctus Dominus Deus omnipotens, qui erat et qui est et qui futurus est.'	law, which books the Apocalypse of John introduces under the number of the twenty-four elders adoring the Lamb and with prostrate face presenting their crowns [Rev. 4:4–10],[133] while the four animals with eyes behind and in front—that is, both into the past and into the future—were standing in the open and calling out with unceasing voice: 'Holy, holy, holy is the Lord God omnipotent, who was and who is and who will be' [Rev. 4:8].
Hic prologus scripturarum quasi galeatum principium omnibus libris, quos de hebreo vertimus in latinum, convenire potest, ut scire valeamus, quicquid extra hos est, inter Apocrifa seponendum. Igitur Sapientia, quae vulgo Salomonis inscribitur, et Iesu filii Sirach liber et Iudith et Tobias et Pastor non sunt in canone. Macchabeorum primum librum hebraicum repperi, secundus graecus est, quod et ex ipsa φρασιν probari potest.	This prologue of the Scriptures can function as a helmeted preface for all the books, which we are converting from Hebrew to Latin, so that we are able to know that whatever is outside of these should be removed into the apocrypha.[134] Therefore, Wisdom, which commonly is inscribed 'of Solomon',[135] and the book of Jesus son of Sirach,[136] and Judith, and Tobit, and the Shepherd[137] are not in the canon. I have found the first book of Maccabees in Hebrew, the second is Greek, which can be demonstrated from the style itself.
Quae cum ita se habeant, obsecro te lector, ne laborem meum reprehensionem aestimes antiquorum. In tabernaculum Dei offert unusquisque quod potest: alii aurum et argentum et lapides pretiosos, alii byssum et purpuram, coccum offerunt et iacinctum; nobiscum bene agetur, si obtulerimus pelles et caprarum pilos. Et tamen Apostolus contemptibiliora nostra magis necessaria iudicat. Unde et tota illa tabernaculi pulchritudo, et per singulas species Ecclesiae praesentis futuraeque distinctio, pellibus tegitur et ciliciis, ardoremque solis et iniuriam imbrium ea, quae viliora sunt, prohibent. Lege ergo primum Samuhel et Malachim meum; meum, inquam, meum: quidquid enim crebrius vertendo et emendando sollicitius et didicimus et	Since these things are so, I ask you, reader, not to consider my work to be a criticism of the ancients. In the tabernacle of God, someone offers what he can: some offer gold, and silver, and precious stones, others flax and purple, scarlet and sapphire [cf. Exod. 25:2–7]; it will go well with us if we offer skins and goats' hair. And the apostle judges our more despised members to be more necessary [1 Cor. 12:22]. So also the entire beauty of the tabernacle and, in individual likenesses, the ornament of the present and future church is covered with skins and hair, and those things that are more vile prevent the heat of the sun and the injury of the rains. So read first my Samuel and *Malachim*, mine, I say, mine: for whatever we learn and hold by translating frequently and by emending carefully is ours. And when you understand

---

[133] Several times Jerome mentions this connection between the books of the Old Testament counted as twenty-four and the twenty-four elders of the Apocalypse; cf. *Praef. Dan.* 47–8; *Comm. Ezech.* 43:13–17; *Praef. Ezra* 20–1. Jerome relies on Victorinus of Pettau, *Comm. Apoc.* 4:4. For other Christian sources using the number twenty-four, see Gos. Thom. 52; Mommsen Catalogue of canonical books. The same number (twenty-four) is common among Jews, attested in 4 Ezra 14:45 and implied in b. B. Bathra 14b.

[134] On this statement, see Gallagher 2012b.   [135] The Wisdom of Solomon.

[136] The book of Jesus son of Sirach is commonly known in English as Ecclesiasticus, a name also attested in Latin; cf. Augustine, *Doctr. chr.* 2.13 (below, pp. 227–8).

[137] The Shepherd of Hermas.

Text	Translation
tenemus, nostrum est. Et cum intellexeris, quod antea nesciebas, vel interpretem me aestimato, si gratus es, vel παραφραστην, si ingratus. Quamquam mihi omnino conscius non sim, mutasse me quippiam de hebraica veritate. Certe si incredulus es, lege graecos codices et latinos et confer cum his opusculis, et ubicumque inter se videris discrepare, interroga quemlibet Hebreorum, cui magis accomodare debeas fidem, et si nostra firmaverit, puto quod eum non aestimes coniectorem, ut in eodem loco mecum similiter divinarit.	what you did not know before, consider me a translator, if you are gracious, or a παραφραστης [paraphraser], if you are ungracious, although for myself I am not at all conscious that I have altered anything from the Hebrew truth. Certainly, if you are incredulous, read Greek codices and Latin ones and compare them with this little volume, and wherever you see among them a discrepancy, ask whomever you like of the Hebrews, to whom you would attach greater fidelity, and if he confirms ours, I think that you would not consider him a soothsayer, so that he would divine similarly to me in the same passage.
Sed et vos famulas Christi rogo, quae Domini discumbentis pretiosissimo fidei myro unguitis caput, quae nequaquam Salvatorem quaeritis in sepulchro, quibus iam ad Patrem Christus ascendit, ut contra latrantes canes, qui adversum me rabido ore deseviunt et circumeunt civitatem, atque in eo se doctos arbitrantur, si aliis detrahant, orationum vestrarum clypeos opponatis. Ego sciens humilitatem meam, illius semper sententiae recordabor: 'Custodiam vias meas, ut non delinquam in lingua mea; posui ori meo custodiam, cum consisteret peccator adversum me; obmutui et humiliatus sum, et silui a bonis.'	But you maid-servants of Christ, you who anoint the head of the reclining Lord with the most precious myrrh of the faith [cf. Matt. 26:7; Mark 14:3], you who in no way seek the Saviour in the tomb [cf. John 20:15–17], for whom now Christ has ascended to the Father, I ask that you place the shields of your prayers against the barking dogs who rage against me with rabid mouth and walk around the city and imagine in it that they are learned, if they drag others down. Knowing my own humble position, I will always remember that sentiment: 'I will guard my ways, so that I do not offend with my tongue; I have placed a guardian for my mouth, since a sinner stands against me; I have become silent and I am humbled, and I have become silent from good things' [Psa. 39:1–2].

Epistle 53

Date: 395.

Introduction: In this letter to Paulinus, later bishop of Nola (near Naples), Jerome encourages close attention to Scripture. He surveys a recommended course in scriptural reading in sections 8–9. This letter served as a preface to the Bible in many manuscripts of the Vulgate, beginning in the ninth century.[138]

---

[138] Marsden 1995: 36.

Text[139]	Translation[140]
8. (1) Uidelicet manifestissima est Genesis, in qua de creatura mundi, de exordio generis humani, de diuisione terrae, de confusione linguarum et de gente \<pergente\> usque ad Aegyptum scribitur Hebraeorum. patet Exodus cum decem plagis, cum decalogo, cum mysticis diuinisque praeceptis. in promptu est Leuiticus liber, in quo singula sacrificia, immo singulae paene syllabae et uestes Aaron et totus ordo Leuiticus spirant caelestia sacramenta.	8. (1) Genesis, we shall be told, needs no explanation; its topics are too simple—the birth of the world, the origin of the human race, the division of the earth, the confusion of tongues, and the descent of the Hebrews into Egypt. Exodus, no doubt, is equally plain, containing as it does merely an account of the ten plagues, the decalogue, and sundry mysterious and divine precepts. The meaning of Leviticus is of course self-evident, although every sacrifice that it describes, nay more, every word that it contains, the description of Aaron's vestments, and all the regulations connected with the Levites are symbols of things heavenly.
(2) Numeri uero nonne totius arithmeticae et prophetiae Balaam et quadraginta duarum per heremum mansionum mysteria continent? Deuteronomium quoque, secunda lex et euangelicae legis praefiguratio, nonne sic ea habet, quae priora sunt, ut tamen noua sint omnia de ueteribus? hucusque Moyses, hucusque πεντάτευχος, quibus quinque uerbis uelle se loqui in ecclesia gloriatur apostolus.	(2) The book of Numbers too—are not its very figures, and Balaam's prophecy [Num. 22–4], and the forty-two camping places in the wilderness [Num. 33] so many mysteries? Deuteronomy also, that is the second law or the foreshadowing of the law of the gospel—does it not, while exhibiting things known before, put old truths in a new light? So far the 'five words' of the Pentateuch, with which the apostle boasts his wish to speak in the church [1 Cor. 14:19].
(3) Iob, exemplar patientiae, quae non mysteria suo sermone conplectitur? prosa incipit, uersu labitur, pedestri sermone finitur; omnisque dialecticae proponit λήμματα, propositione, adsumptione, confirmatione, conclusione determinat. singula in eo uerba plena sunt sensibus et, ut de ceteris sileam, resurrectionem corporum sic prophetat, ut nullus de ea uel manifestius uel cautius scripserit: scio, inquit, QUOD REDEMPTOR MEUS UIUAT ET IN NOUISSIMO DE TERRA RESURRECTURUS SIM. ET RURSUM CIRCUMDABOR PELLE MEA ET IN CARNE MEA UIDEBO DEUM, QUEM UISURUS SUM EGO IPSE ET OCULI MEI CONSPECTURI SUNT ET NON ALIUS. REPOSITA EST HAEC SPES MEA IN SINU MEO.	(3) Then, as for Job, that pattern of patience, what mysteries are there not contained in his discourses? Commencing in prose the book soon glides into verse and at the end once more reverts to prose. By the way in which it lays down propositions, assumes postulates, adduces proofs, and draws inferences, it illustrates all the laws of logic. Single words occurring in the book are full of meaning. To say nothing of other topics, it prophesies the resurrection of men's bodies at once with more clearness and with more caution than any one has yet shown. 'I know', Job says, 'that my redeemer lives, and that at the last day I shall rise again from the earth; and I shall be clothed again with my skin, and in my flesh shall I see God. Whom I shall see for myself, and my eyes shall behold, and not another. This my hope is stored up in my own bosom' [Job 19:25–7].
(4) ueniam ad Iesum Naue, typum domini non solum in gestis, uerum et in nomine:	(4) I will pass on to Jesus the son of Nave[141]—a type of the Lord in name as well as in deed—

[139] Hilberg 1910–18: 1.454–63.   [140] NPNF.
[141] As he is called in Greek and Latin. His more familiar English name—Joshua son of Nun—reflects the Hebrew a little more closely.

Text	Translation
transit Iordanen, hostium regna subuertit, diuidit terram uictori populo et per singulas urbes, uiculos, montes, flumina, torrentes atque confinia ecclesiae caelestisque Hierusalem spiritalia regna discribit. in Iudicum libro quot principes populi, tot figurae sunt. Ruth Moabitis de Moabitide Esaiae explet uaticinium dicentis: EMITTE AGNUM, DOMINE, DOMINATOREM TERRAE DE PETRA DESERTI AD MONTEM FILIAE SION.	who crossed over Jordan, subdued hostile kingdoms, divided the land among the conquering people and who, in every city, village, mountain, river, hill-torrent, and boundary which he dealt with, marked out the spiritual realms of the heavenly Jerusalem, that is, of the church [cf. Gal. 4:26]. In the book of Judges every one of the popular leaders is a type. Ruth the Moabitess fulfils the prophecy of Isaiah: 'Send a lamb, O Lord, as ruler of the land from the rock of the wilderness to the mount of the daughter of Zion' [Isa. 16:1].
(5) Samuhel in Heli mortuo et in occisione Saulis ueterem legem abolitam, porro in Sadoc atque Dauid noui sacerdotii nouique imperii sacramenta testatur. Malachim, id est tertius et quartus Regum liber, a Salomone usque ad Iechoniam et ab Hieroboam, filio Nabat, usque ad Osee, qui ductus est in Assyrios, regnum Iuda et regnum describit Israhel. si historiam respicias, uerba simplicia sunt; si in litteris sensum latentem, ecclesiae paucitas et hereticorum contra ecclesiam bella narrantur.	(5) Under the figures of Eli's death and the slaying of Saul Samuel shows the abolition of the old law. Again in Zadok and in David he bears witness to the mysteries of the new priesthood and of the new royalty. The third and fourth books of Kings called in Hebrew *Malâchim* give the history of the kingdom of Judah from Solomon to Jeconiah, and of that of Israel from Jeroboam the son of Nebat to Hoshea who was carried away into Assyria. If you merely regard the narrative, the words are simple enough, but if you look beneath the surface at the hidden meaning of it, you find a description of the small numbers of the church and of the wars which the heretics wage against it.
(6) duodecim prophetae in unius uoluminis angustias coartati multo aliud, quam sonant in littera, praefigurant. Osee crebro nominat Effraim, Samariam, Ioseph, Iezrahel et uxorem fornicariam et fornicationis filios et adulteram cubiculo clausam mariti multo tempore sedere uiduam et sub ueste lugubri uiri ad se reditum praestolari.	(6) The twelve prophets whose writings are compressed within the narrow limits of a single volume,[142] have typical meanings far different from their literal ones. Hosea speaks many times of Ephraim, of Samaria, of Joseph, of Jezreel, of a wife of whoredoms and of children of whoredoms, of an adulteress shut up within the chamber of her husband, sitting for a long time in widowhood and in the garb of mourning, awaiting the time when her husband will return to her.
(7) Iohel, filius Bathuel, describit terram duodecim tribuum eruca, brucho, locusta, rubigine uastante consumptam et post euersionem prioris populi effusum iri spiritum sanctum super seruos dei et ancillas, id est super centum uiginti credentium nomina, et effusum iri in cenaculo Sion, qui centum uiginti ab uno usque ad quindecim paulatim et per incrementa surgentes	(7) Joel the son of Pethuel describes the land of the twelve tribes as spoiled and devastated by the palmerworm, the canker-worm, the locust, and the blight, and predicts that after the overthrow of the former people the Holy Spirit shall be poured out upon God's servants and handmaids [Joel 2:29]; the same spirit, that is, which was to be poured out in the upper chamber at Zion upon the 120 believers

---

[142] The twelve so-called Minor Prophets often appeared together on a single scroll and were counted as a single book in ancient Christianity, as also in ancient (and modern) Judaism.

Text	Translation
quindecim graduum numerum efficiunt, qui in psalterio mystice continentur.	[Acts 2:1–4; cf. 2:16]. These believers rising by gradual and regular gradations from one to fifteen form the steps to which there is a mystical allusion in the psalms of degrees [Psa. 120–34].
(8) Amos, pastor et rusticus ruborum mora destringens, paucis uerbis explicari non potest. quis enim digne exprimat tria et quattuor scelera Damasci, Gazae, Tyri, Idumeae, filiorum Ammon et Moab et in septimo octauoque gradu Iudae et Israhel? hic loquitur ad uaccas pingues, quae sunt in monte Samariae, et ruituram domum maioremque minoremque testatur.	(8) Amos, although he is only a herdman from the country, a gatherer of sycomore fruit, cannot be explained in a few words. For who can adequately speak of the three transgressions and the four of Damascus, of Gaza, of Tyre, of Idumæa, of Moab, of the children of Ammon, and in the seventh and eighth place of Judah and of Israel [Amos 1–2]? He speaks to the fat cattle that are in the mountain of Samaria [Amos 4:1], and bears witness that the great house and the little house shall fall [6:11].
(9) ipse cernit fictorem locustae et stantem dominum super murum litum uel adamantinum et uncinum pomorum adtrahentem supplicia peccatoribus et famem in terram: non famem panis neque sitim aquae, sed audiendi uerbum domini. Abdias, qui interpretatur seruus domini personat contra Edom et sanguineum terrenumque, fratris quoque Iacob semper aemulum, hasta percutit spiritali.	(9) He sees now the maker of the grasshopper [7:1], now the Lord, standing upon a wall daubed or made of adamant [7:7], now a basket of apples that brings doom to the transgressors [8:1], and now a famine upon the earth not a famine of bread, nor a thirst for water, but of hearing the words of the Lord [8:11]. Obadiah, whose name means the servant of God,[143] thunders against Edom red with blood and against the creature born of earth. He smites him with the spear of the spirit because of his continual rivalry with his brother Jacob.
(10) Ionas, columba pulcherrima, naufragio suo passionem domini praefigurans mundum ad paenitentiam reuocat et sub nomine Nineue salutem gentibus nuntiat. Micheas de Morasthi, coheres Christi, uastationem adnuntiat filiae latronis et obsessionem ponit contra eam, quia maxillam percusserit iudicis Israhel. Naum, consolator orbis, increpat ciuitatem sanguinum et post euersionem illius loquitur: ECCE SUPER MONTES PEDES EUANGELIZANTIS ET ADNUNTIANTIS PACEM.	(10) Jonah, fairest of doves, whose shipwreck shows in a figure the passion of the Lord [cf. Matt. 12:39; 16:4], recalls the world to penitence, and while he preaches to Nineveh, announces salvation to all the heathen. Micah the Morasthite, a joint heir with Christ, announces the spoiling of the daughter of the robber and lays siege against her, because she has smitten the jawbone of the judge of Israel. Nahum, the consoler of the world, rebukes the bloody city and when it is overthrown cries: 'Behold upon the mountains the feet of him that brings good tidings' [Nahum 1:15].
(11) Ambacum, luctator fortis et rigidus, stat super custodiam suam et figit gradum super munitionem, ut Christum in cruce contempletur et dicat: OPERUIT CAELOS UIRTUS EIUS ET LAUDIS EIUS PLENA EST TERRA ET SPLENDOR EIUS UT LUX ERIT; CORNUA IN MANIBUS EIUS, IBI ABSCONDITA EST FORTITUDO EIUS.	(11) Habakkuk, like a strong and unyielding wrestler, stands upon his watch and sets his foot upon the tower [Hab. 2:1–2] that he may contemplate Christ upon the cross and say His glory covered the heavens and the earth was full of his praise. And his brightness was as the light; he had horns coming out of his hand: and there was the hiding of his power [3:3–4].

---

[143] Jerome goes on to propose meanings for the names of each of the Twelve Prophets, except for Micah and Malachi.

Text	Translation
(12) Sophonias, speculator et arcanorum domini cognitor, audit clamorem a porta piscium et eiulatum a secunda et contritionem a collibus. indicit quoque ululatum habitatoribus Pilae, quia conticuit omnis populus Chanaan, disperierunt uniuersi, qui inuoluti erant argento.	(12) Zephaniah, that is the bodyguard and knower of the secrets of the Lord, hears a cry from the fishgate, and an howling from the second, and a great crashing from the hills. He proclaims howling to the inhabitants of the mortar; for all the people of Canaan are undone; all they that were laden with silver are cut off [Zeph. 1:10–11].
(13) Aggeus, festinus et laetus, qui seminauit in lacrimis, ut in gaudio meteret, destructum templum aedificat deumque patrem inducit loquentem: ADHUC UNUM MODICUMQUE, ET EGO COMMOUEBO CAELUM ET TERRAM ET MARE ET ARIDAM ET MOUEBO OMNES GENTES; ET UENIET DESIDERATUS CUNCTIS GENTIBUS.	(13) Haggai, that is he who is glad or joyful, who has sown in tears to reap in joy, is occupied with the rebuilding of the temple. He represents the Lord—the Father, that is—as saying, 'Yet once, it is a little while, and I will shake the heavens, and the earth, and the sea, and the dry land; and I will shake all nations and he who is desired of all nations shall come' [Hag. 2:6–7].
(14) Zacharias, memor domini sui, multiplex in prophetia, Iesum uestibus sordidis indutum et lapidem oculorum septem candelabrumque aureum cum totidem lucernis, quot oculis, duas quoque oliuas a sinistris lampadis cernit et a dextris, ut post equos rufos, uarios, albos et nigros et dissipatas quadrigas ex Effraim et equum de Hierusalem pauperem regem uaticinetur et praedicet sedentem super pullum filium asinae subiugalis.	(14) Zechariah, he that is mindful of his Lord, gives us many prophecies. He sees Jesus, clothed with filthy garments [Zech. 3:3], a stone with seven eyes [3:9], a candle-stick all of gold with lamps as many as the eyes, and two olive trees on the right side of the bowl and on the left [4:2–3]. After he has described the horses, red, black, white, and grisled [6:1–3] and the cutting off of the chariot from Ephraim and of the horse from Jerusalem [9:10], he goes on to prophesy and predict a king who shall be a poor man and who shall sit upon a colt the foal of an ass [9:9].
(15) Malachias aperte et in fine omnium prophetarum de abiectione Israhel et uocatione gentium: NON EST MIHI, ait, UOLUNTAS IN UOBIS, DICIT DOMINUS EXERCITUUM, ET MUNUS NON ACCIPIAM DE MANU UESTRA. AB ORTU ENIM SOLIS USQUE AD OCCASUM MAGNUM EST NOMEN MEUM IN GENTIBUS ET IN OMNI LOCO SACRIFICATUR ET OFFERTUR NOMINI MEO OBLATIO MUNDA.	(15) Malachi, the last of all the prophets, speaks openly of the rejection of Israel and the calling of the nations. 'I have no pleasure in you, says the Lord of hosts, neither will I accept an offering at your hand. For from the rising of the sun even unto the going down of the same, my name is great among the Gentiles: and in every place incense is offered unto my name, and a pure offering' [Mal. 1:10–11].
(16) Esaiam, Hieremiam, Ezechiel, Danihel quis possit uel intellegere uel exponere? quorum primus non prophetiam mihi uidetur texere, sed euangelium; secundus uirgam nuceam et ollam succensam a facie aquilonis et pardum spoliatum suis coloribus et quadruplex diuersis metris nectit alphabetum; tertius principia et finem tantis habet obscuritatibus inuoluta, ut apud Hebraeos ipsae partes cum exordio Geneseos ante annos triginta non legantur; quartus	(16) As for Isaiah, Jeremiah, Ezekiel, and Daniel, who can fully understand or adequately explain them? The first of them seems to compose not a prophecy but a Gospel.[144] The second speaks of a rod of an almond tree [Jer. 1:11] and of a seething pot with its face toward the north [1:13], and of a leopard which has changed its spots [13:23]. He also goes four times through the alphabet in different metres.[145] The beginning and ending of Ezekiel, the third of the four, are involved in so great obscurity that like the commencement of

---

[144] A common patristic description of Isaiah; Sawyer 1996.
[145] Lamentations, commonly attributed to Jeremiah, contains four alphabetic acrostic poems in its first four chapters.

Text	Translation
uero, qui et extremus inter quattuor prophetas, temporum conscius et totius mundi φιλοῖστωρ, lapidem praecisum de monte sine manibus et regna omnia subuertentem claro sermone pronuntiat.	Genesis they are not studied by the Hebrews until they are thirty years old.[146] Daniel, the fourth and last of the four prophets, having knowledge of the times and being interested in the whole world, in clear language proclaims the stone cut out of the mountain without hands that overthrows all kingdoms [Dan. 2:45].
(17) Dauid, Simonides noster, Pindarus et Alcaeus, Flaccus quoque, Catullus et Serenus, Christum lyra personat et in decacordo psalterio ab inferis excitat resurgentem. Salomon, pacificus et amabilis domini, mores corrigit, naturam docet, ecclesiam iungit et Christum sanctarumque nuptiarum dulce canit ἐπιθαλάμιον.	(17) David, who is our Simonides, Pindar, and Alcæus, our Horace, our Catullus, and our Serenus all in one,[147] sings of Christ to his lyre; and on a psaltery with ten strings calls him from the lower world to rise again. Solomon, a lover of peace and of the Lord, corrects morals, teaches nature, unites Christ and the church, and sings a sweet marriage song to celebrate that holy bridal.[148]
(18) Esther in ecclesiae typo populum liberat de periculo et interfecto Aman, qui interpretatur iniquitas, partes conuiuii et diem celebrem mittit in posteros. Paralipomenon liber, id est instrumenti ueteris ἐπιτομή, tantus ac talis est, ut, absque illo si quis scientiam scripturarum sibi uoluerit adrogare, se ipsum inrideat. per singula quippe nomina iuncturasque uerborum et praetermissae in Regum libris tanguntur historiae et innumerae explicantur euangelii quaestiones.	(18) Esther, a type of the church, frees her people from danger and, after having slain Haman whose name means iniquity, hands down to posterity a memorable day and a great feast. The book of *Paralipomena* or epitome of the old dispensation[149] is of such importance and value that without it any one who should claim to himself a knowledge of the Scriptures would make himself a laughing stock in his own eyes. Every name used in it, nay even the conjunction of the words, serves to throw light on narratives passed over in the books of Kings and upon questions suggested by the Gospel.
(19) Esdras et Neemias, adiutor uidelicet et consolator a domino, in unum uolumen artantur: instaurant templum, muros extruunt ciuitatis; omnisque illa turba populi redeuntis in patriam et discriptio sacerdotum, Leuitarum, Israhelis, proselitorum ac per singulas familias murorum et turrium opera diuisa aliud in cortice praeferunt, aliud retinent in medulla.	(19) Ezra and Nehemiah, that is the Lord's helper and His consoler, are united in a single book. They restore the Temple and build up the walls of the city. In their pages we see the throng of the Israelites returning to their native land, we read of priests and Levites, of Israel proper and of proselytes; and we are even told the several families to which the task of building the walls and towers was assigned. These references convey one meaning upon the surface, but another below it.

[146] Jerome mentions this Jewish tradition also in the prologue to his *Commentary on Ezekiel*, where he also adds Song of Songs to the list of books forbidden to readers under age thirty. These same four sections of Scripture also appear as forbidden among young Jews in the prologue to Origen's *Commentary on the Song of Songs*.

[147] Greek and Latin poets.

[148] The name Solomon is related to the Hebrew word for peace (*shalom*). The description of Solomon's activities alludes to his different books: in the Proverbs he corrects morals, in Ecclesiastes he teaches nature, and in the Song of Songs he unites Christ and the church and sings a sweet marriage song.

[149] *Paralipomena* is the Greek title for Chronicles. By calling it also the 'epitome of the old dispensation', Jerome highlights its important role of surveying history from creation (the first word of the book is Adam, the first man, according to Genesis) to the exile.

Text	Translation
9. (1) Cernis me scripturarum amore raptum excessisse modum epistulae et tamen non inplesse, quod uolui. audiuimus tantum, quid nosse, quid cupere debeamus, ut et nos quoque possimus dicere: CONCUPIUIT ANIMA MEA DESIDERARE IUSTIFICATIONES TUAS IN OMNI TEMPORE. ceterum Socraticum illud inpletur in nobis: 'hoc tantum scio, quod nescio.'	9. (1) You see how, carried away by my love of the Scriptures, I have exceeded the limits of a letter yet have not fully accomplished my object. We have heard only what it is that we ought to know and to desire, so that we too may be able to say with the psalmist: My soul breaks out for the very fervent desire that it has always unto your judgements [cf. Psa. 119:20]. But the saying of Socrates about himself—this only I know that I know nothing[150]—is fulfilled in our case also.
(2) tangam et nouum breuiter testamentum: Mattheus, Marcus, Lucas, Iohannes, quadriga domini et uerum cherubin, quod interpretatur 'scientiae multitudo,' per totum corpus oculati sunt, scintillae micant, discurrunt fulgora, pedes habent rectos et in sublime tendentes, terga pennata et ubicumque uolitantia. tenent se mutuo sibique perplexi sunt et quasi rota in rota uoluuntur et pergunt; quocumque eos flatus sancti spiritus duxerit.	(2) The New Testament I will briefly deal with. Matthew, Mark, Luke, and John are the Lord's team of four, the true cherubim or store of knowledge. With them the whole body is full of eyes, they glitter as sparks, they run and return like lightning, their feet are straight feet, and lifted up, their backs also are winged, ready to fly in all directions. They hold together each by each and are interwoven one with another: like wheels within wheels they roll along and go wherever the breath of the Holy Spirit wafts them.[151]
(3) Paulus apostolus ad septem scribit ecclesias—octaua enim ad Hebraeos a plerisque extra numerum ponitur—, Timotheum instruit ac Titum, Philemonem pro fugitiuo famulo deprecatur. super quo tacere melius puto quam pauca dicere.	(3) The apostle Paul writes to seven churches[152]— for an eighth, that to the Hebrews, is not generally counted in with the others.[153] He instructs Timothy and Titus; he intercedes with Philemon for his runaway slave. Of him I think it better to say nothing than to write inadequately.
(4) Actus apostolorum nudam quidem sonare uidentur historiam et nascentis ecclesiae infantiam texere, sed, si nouerimus scriptorem eorum Lucam esse medicum, cuius laus est in euangelio, animaduertimus pariter omnia uerba illius languentis animae esse medicamina.	(4) The Acts of the Apostles seem to relate a mere unvarnished narrative descriptive of the infancy of the newly born church; but when once we realize that their author is Luke the physician whose praise is in the gospel, we shall see that all his words are medicine for the sick soul.

[150] On this statement commonly attributed to Socrates in antiquity, see Fine 2008.

[151] Jerome's description of the Gospels echoes Ezekiel's vision of the four living creatures (Ezek. 1:10; cf. Rev. 4:7), a common patristic representation of the four Evangelists. Cf. Irenaeus, *Against Heresies* 3.11.8–9; Burridge 2014: 25–33.

[152] Rome, Corinth, Galatia, Ephesus, Philippi, Colossae, Thessalonica. It is clear from other sources (e.g. *Vir. ill.* 5) that Jerome includes two letters to Corinth and two to Thessalonica. The tradition that Paul wrote to seven churches is attested also in the Muratorian Fragment (lines 47–50) and several other sources; see p. 180 with n. 29.

[153] Elsewhere (e.g., *Vir. ill.* 5; *Epist.* 129.3) Jerome acknowledges doubts about the Pauline authorship of Hebrews, and in the latter passage he admits that Latin churches generally do not receive it in the canon, though he himself argues against this position (this passage from *Epist.* 129 is quoted below, pp. 214–15). In the present passage in *Epist.* 53, it may be, however, that Jerome is not acknowledging doubts about the Pauline authorship of Hebrews, but rather explaining that Hebrews—whether Paul wrote it or not—does not fit the seven-church scheme into which Jerome's contemporaries often fit Paul's letters: it is not counted with the rest, i.e., as one of the seven letters written to churches.

Text	Translation
(5) Iacobus, Petrus, Iohannes, Iudas septem epistulas ediderunt tam mysticas quam succinctas et breues pariter et longas: breues in uerbis, longas in sententiis, ut rarus non in earum lectione caecutiat.	(5) The apostles James, Peter, John, and Jude, have published seven epistles[154] at once spiritual and to the point, short and long, short that is in words but lengthy in substance so that there are few indeed who do not find themselves in the dark when they read them.
(6) Apocalypsis Iohannis tot habet sacramenta, quot uerba. parum dixi et pro merito uoluminis laus omnis inferior est; in uerbis singulis multiplices latent intellegentiae.	(6) The Apocalypse of John has as many mysteries as words. In saying this I have said less than the book deserves. All praise of it is inadequate; manifold meanings lie hidden in its every word.

Epistle 107

Date: 403

Introduction: Laeta was the daughter-in-law of Paula, Jerome's longtime patroness. Laeta had written to Jerome seeking advice on raising her newborn daughter, also named Paula. Jerome's reply includes a section on what a young woman ought to read. Jerome offers a survey of Scripture in section 12.

Text[155]	Translation[156]
12. (1) Pro gemmis aut serico diuinos codices amet, in quibus non auri et pellis Babyloniae uermiculata pictura, sed ad fidem placeat emendata et erudita distinctio. discat primum Psalterium, his se canticis auocet et in Prouerbiis Salomonis erudiatur ad uitam. in Ecclesiaste consuescat calcare, quae mundi sunt; in Iob uirtutis et patientiae exempla sectetur. ad Euangelia transeat numquam ea positura de manibus; Apostolorum Acta et Epistulas tota cordis inbibat uoluntate.	12. (1) Let her treasures be not silks or gems but manuscripts of the Holy Scriptures; and in these let her think less of gilding, and Babylonian parchment, and arabesque patterns, than of correctness and accurate punctuation. Let her begin by learning the Psalter, and then let her gather rules of life out of the Proverbs of Solomon. In Ecclesiastes let her gain the habit of despising the world and its vanities. Let her follow the example set in Job of virtue and of patience. Then let her pass on to the Gospels never to be laid aside when once they have been taken in hand. Let her also drink in with a willing heart the Acts of the Apostles and the Epistles.
(2) cumque pectoris sui cellarium his opibus locupletarit, mandet memoriae Prophetas et Heptateuchum et Regum ac Paralipomenon libros Hesdraeque et Hester uolumina, ut	(2) As soon as she has enriched the storehouse of her mind with these treasures, let her commit to memory the Prophets, the Heptateuch,[157] the books of Kings and of *Paralipomena*, the rolls

---

[154] These seven epistles must include James, 1–2 Peter, 1–3 John, and Jude.

[155] Hilberg 1910–18: 2.302–3.   [156] NPNF.

[157] The Heptateuch is the first seven books of the Old Testament: Genesis, Exodus, Leviticus, Numbers, Deuteronomy, Joshua, Judges. Jerome may intend to include Ruth as a part of Judges, as he does in the *Prologus Galeatus*.

Text	Translation
ultimum sine periculo discat Canticum canticorum, ne, si in exordio legerit, sub carnalibus uerbis spiritalium nuptiarum epithalamium non intellegens uulneretur.	also of Ezra and Esther.[158] When she has done all these she may safely read the Song of Songs but not before: for, were she to read it at the beginning, she would fail to perceive that, though it is written in fleshly words, it is a marriage song of a spiritual bridal.[159] And not understanding this, she would suffer hurt from it.
(3) caueat omnia apocrypha et, si quando ea non ad dogmatum ueritatem, sed ad signorum reuerentiam legere uoluerit, sciat non eorum esse, quorum titulis praenotantur, multaque his admixta uitiosa et grandis esse prudentiae aurum in luto quaerere. Cypriani opuscula semper in manu teneat, Athanasii epistulas et Hilarii libros inoffenso decurrat pede. illorum tractatibus, illorum delectetur ingeniis, in quorum libris pietas fidei non uacillet; ceteros sic legat, ut magis iudicet, quam sequatur.	(3) Let her avoid all apocryphal writings, and if she is led to read such not by the truth of the doctrines which they contain but out of respect for the miracles contained in them; let her understand that they are not really written by those to whom they are ascribed, that many faulty elements have been introduced into them, and that it requires infinite discretion to look for gold in the midst of dirt.[160] Cyprian's writings let her have always in her hands. The letters of Athanasius and the treatises of Hilary she may go through without fear of stumbling. Let her take pleasure in the works and wits of all in whose books a due regard for the faith is not neglected. But if she reads the works of others let it be rather to judge them than to follow them.

The Canon Lists of Jerome

Prologus Galeatus

Old Testament
  Torah
    Genesis
    Exodus
    Leviticus
    Numbers
    Deuteronomy

[158] In the Greek tradition, the two books of Samuel and the two books of Kings were collectively known as the four books of Kingdoms. Jerome reflects this custom when he omits mention of Samuel and assumes its position as one of the books of Kings. Also according to ancient custom, the book of Ezra included Nehemiah.

[159] Christians commonly allegorized the Song of Songs to make its message not about erotic love between humans but instead about Christ's love for the church. Jews similarly allegorized the book in terms of God's love for Israel. The advice to delay reading Song of Songs until one has gained maturity is also found in the preface to Jerome's *Commentary on Ezekiel*.

[160] It is not clear which books Jerome has in mind; on the identity of the apocrypha in Jerome, see Gallagher 2012b.

> Prophets
> > Joshua
> > Judges-Ruth
> > Samuel
> > Kings
> > Isaiah
> > Jeremiah(–Lamentations)[161]
> > Ezekiel
> > Twelve
> Hagiographa
> > Job
> > Psalms
> > Proverbs
> > Ecclesiastes
> > Song of Songs
> > Daniel
> > Chronicles
> > Ezra(-Nehemiah)
> > Esther
> Apocrypha
> > Wisdom of Solomon
> > Jesus son of Sirach
> > Judith
> > Tobit
> > Shepherd of Hermas
> > 1–2 Maccabees

Jerome also knows a tradition whereby Ruth and Lamentations are reckoned separately among the Hagiographa.

As for the books he labels here 'apocrypha', he groups together the same six OT books (i.e., without the Shepherd of Hermas) in his *Preface to the Books of Solomon*, where he says that they could be read in church but not used to establish doctrine.

> Sicut ergo Iudith et Tobi et Macchabeorum libros legit quidem Ecclesia, sed inter canonicos scripturas non recipit, sic et haec duo volumina legat ad aedificationem plebis, non ad auctoritatem ecclesiastoricorum dogmatum confirmandam.

> Therefore, just as the church reads the books of Judith and Tobit and the Maccabees, but does not receive them among the canonical Scriptures, so also let her read these two volumes [= Wisdom of Solomon and Sirach] for the edification of the people, not for the authoritative confirmation of ecclesiastical doctrines.[162]

---

[161] He does not explicitly mention Lamentations in his list, but earlier he had said that Jeremiah–Lamentations was one of the five doubled books, and later he will say that Lamentations is sometimes counted separately, rather than together with Jeremiah.

[162] Cf. the very similar description of the same books in Rufinus, *Symb.* 36 (see below, p. 219).

Epistle 53

Old Testament
    Genesis
    Exodus
    Leviticus
    Numbers
    Deuteronomy
    Job
    Joshua
    Judges
    Ruth
    1–2 Samuel
    1–2 Kings
    Twelve Prophets
        Hosea
        Joel
        Amos
        Obadiah
        Jonah
        Micah
        Nahum
        Habakkuk
        Zephaniah
        Haggai
        Zechariah
        Malachi
    Isaiah
    Jeremiah (+ Lamentations)[163]
    Ezekiel
    Daniel
    Psalms
    Proverbs
    Ecclesiastes
    Song of Songs
    Esther
    Chronicles
    Ezra–Nehemiah

This list of OT books matches precisely the modern Protestant Old Testament.

New Testament
    Matthew
    Mark

---

[163] Jerome does not name Lamentations, but he does say that in addition to his prophetic book, Jeremiah 'also goes four times through the alphabet in different metres', a reference to the acrostic poems forming the first four chapters of Lamentations.

Luke
John
Paul
    to seven churches, with the eighth (Hebrews) doubted as his
    to Timothy
    to Titus
    to Philemon
Acts of the Apostles
(seven epistles by the following apostles)
James
Peter
John
Jude
Apocalypse of John

This canon list by Jerome closely corresponds to the modern twenty-seven-book New Testament. Aside from the doubt expressed about Hebrews (see below), there is some room for doubt as to how many letters of Paul he includes, but Jerome clarifies elsewhere that Paul wrote nine letters to the seven churches, thus including both Corinthian letters and both Thessalonian letters (*Vir. ill.* 5).

As for Hebrews, Jerome expresses doubts about Pauline authorship elsewhere, though he seems to favour the view that Paul wrote it in Hebrew originally (*Vir. ill.* 5).[164] His discussion of Hebrews in *Epist.* 129.3 'makes it altogether clear that the questions of authenticity and canonicity were understood by St. Jerome to be susceptible of independent treatment.'[165] In this letter he writes as follows:

> Illud nostris dicendum est, hanc epistulam, quae scribitur ad Hebraeos, non solum ab ecclesiis orientis sed ab omnibus retro ecclesiae graeci sermonis scriptoribus quasi Pauli apostoli suscipi, licet plerique eam uel Barnabae uel Clementis arbitrentur, et nihil interesse, cuius sit, cum ecclesiastici uiri sit et cotidie ecclesiarum lectione celebretur. quodsi eam latinorum consuetudo non recipit inter scripturas canonicas, nec graecorum quidem ecclesiae Apocalypsin Iohannis eadem libertate suscipiunt, et tamen nos utramque suscipimus nequaquam huius temporis consuetudinem sed ueterum scriptorum auctoritatem sequentes, qui plerumque utriusque abutuntur testimoniis, non ut interdum de apocryphis facere solent—quippe et gentilium litterarum raro utantur exemplis—, sed quasi canonicis et ecclesiasticis.

> For our own people, let this be said: this Epistle written to the Hebrews is accepted as of the Apostle Paul, not only by the churches of the East, but by all church writers of the past in the Greek language, though many think it to be of Barnabas or of Clement. And it makes no difference whose it is, since it is by a churchman and is honored in the daily reading of the churches. But if Latin usage does not

---

[164] Cf. his *Comm. Isa.* 6.1–3, where he attributes Hebrews to Paul.

[165] Skehan 1952: 268; see Skehan's discussion of Hebrews, ibid.: 269–70. See also Jerome's introduction to a quotation of 2 Peter with the words 'from a letter which is written in the name of the apostle Peter'; cited at ibid.: 269.

receive it among the canonical Scriptures, neither do the churches of the Greeks accept the Apocalypse of John with equal readiness; yet we accept both, following in this not at all the present usage, but the authority of the ancient writers, who for the most part make use of citations from both, not as they are wont to do occasionally for the apocrypha—in fact they use illustrations even from pagan literature, though rarely—but as canonical church texts.[166]

Epistle 107

Jerome provides Laeta what he considers to be an ideal reading sequence for an introduction to scriptural study. He lists the books as follows: Psalter, Proverbs, Ecclesiastes, Job, Gospels, Acts of the Apostles, Epistles, Prophets, Heptateuch, (Samuel-)Kings, Chronicles, Ezra, Esther.

This produces the following Testaments:

Old Testament
      Heptateuch
      Samuel
      Kings
      Chronicles
      Ezra(–Nehemiah)
      Esther
      Job
      Psalter
      Proverbs
      Ecclesiastes
      Song of Songs
      Prophets

Possibly Ruth would be included with Judges as part of the Heptateuch. It would be strange for Jerome to omit mention of Ruth in a reading list for a young girl (unless he understands the events of chapter 3 too well!). The generic title 'Prophets' no doubt includes the same books as in the modern Christian canon, i.e., Isaiah, Jeremiah (with Lamentations), Ezekiel, Daniel, and the Twelve Minor Prophets. This list matches precisely the modern Protestant Old Testament.

New Testament
      Gospels
      Acts of the Apostles
      Epistles

It would have been nice had Jerome more precisely named which epistles he had in mind, but we know fairly well what he includes in this category from his

---

[166] Translation: ibid.: 269–70.

Epist. 53 to Paulinus (cited above). He does not mention here the Apocalypse of John, though Jerome obviously valued this work: he translated the *Commentary on the Apocalypse* by Victorinus of Pettau, and he includes the Apocalypse in his list when addressing Paulinus (*Epist.* 53). Also note his comment on the Apocalypse in *Epist.* 129.3 (quoted above), and his statement that John the apostle wrote the Apocalypse (*Vir. ill.* 9). Possibly its omission here is an oversight, or perhaps Jerome did not want to recommend the Apocalypse to the young Paula, since 'it has as many mysteries as words' (*Epist.* 53.9).

RUFINUS OF AQUILEIA

Rufinus (ca. 345–410) has secured his reputation as a Latin translator of important Greek theological works, some of which now survive only in Rufinus's translation.[167] Born in the north Italian town of Concordia, west of Aquileia, he went east in the early 370s, first to Egypt and then, about 380, to Jerusalem, where he directed a monastery. He returned to Italy in 397, and from that point he produced some original compositions and numerous translations, among them many of Origen's homilies and commentaries and the same author's *De principiis*. During this period he also composed his *Commentary on the Apostles' Creed* (*Commentarius in symbolum Apostolorum*), which contains a passage detailing the books of the biblical canon.

Old Testament canon: Rufinus's Old Testament closely corresponds to the contents of the Jewish canon. He does not specify which books are included within the title 'Jeremiah', though likely he includes here Lamentations and possibly Baruch and the Epistle of Jeremiah. The order in which Rufinus presents the Old Testament matches the modern Christian Old Testament, except that the poetic books follow the prophets in Rufinus. He has a separate category of books called 'ecclesiastical' that are non-canonical but useful to the church. The OT ecclesiastical books include essentially the deuterocanonical books of the modern Catholic Bible, with the absence of Baruch.

New Testament canon: The NT canon list here matches precisely both the content and order of the modern Western New Testament, except that for Rufinus, the letters of Peter precede James, and Jude precedes the letters of John. The NT ecclesiastical books include the Shepherd of Hermas, the Two Ways (the Didache?), and the Judgement of Peter, possibly an alternative name for the Two Ways.

Studies: Stenzel 1942; Kelly 1955: 20–6; Wermelinger 1984: 160–6; Gallagher 2016b.

---

[167] The standard work on Rufinus's life is Murphy 1945. For the era of his literary activity, which he concentrated at the end of his life, see Hammond 1977.

Commentary on the Apostles' Creed

Date: ca. 404[168]

Introduction: Rufinus offers a brief commentary on the entire creed as it was known at Aquileia in northern Italy in the early fifth century. His discussion of the Holy Spirit consists of little more than an assertion of the full divinity of the Spirit and an exposition of the biblical canon, which the Spirit inspired.

Text[169]	Translation[170]
(34) [...] Hic igitur Spiritus Sanctus est, qui in Veteri Testamento legem et prophetas, in Nouo euangelia et apostolos inspirauit. Vnde et apostolus dicit: omnis scriptura diuinitus inspirata utilis est ad docendum. Et ideo quae sint Noui ac Veteris Instrumenti uolumina, quae secundum maiorum traditionem per ipsum Sanctum Spiritum inspirata creduntur et ecclesiis Christi tradita, conpetens uidetur hoc in loco euidenti numero, sicut ex patrum monumentis accepimus, designare.	(34) [...] It was this Holy Spirit, then, who inspired the Law and the Prophets in the Old Testament, and the Gospels and the Apostles in the New. So the Apostle remarks: *All Scripture, inspired of God, is profitable to teach* [2 Tim. 3:16]. Consequently, it seems appropriate at this point, basing myself on the records of the fathers,[171] to enumerate the books of the New and Old Testament which, according to the tradition of our forefathers, are believed to have been inspired by the Holy Spirit Himself and to have been entrusted by Him to the churches of Christ.
(35) Itaque Veteris instrumenti primo omnium Mosi quinque libri sunt traditi: Genesis Exodus Leuiticus Numeri Deuteronomium. Post hos Iesu Naue et Iudicum simul cum Ruth. Quattuor post	(35) In the Old Testament, then, first of all five books by Moses have been handed down— Genesis, Exodus, Leviticus, Numbers, and Deuteronomy; then Joshua, the son of Nun, and Judges, together with Ruth;[172] then four books

---

[168] See Hammond 1977: 388–9, 428; against the much earlier date assumed by Sundberg 1964: 153–5.

[169] Simonetti 1961: 170–1.

[170] Adapted from Kelly 1955: 72–3. In the numbering followed by Kelly, Rufinus's discussion of the canon is found in sections 36–8. We have altered Kelly's section numbers to agree with those of Simonetti.

[171] Rufinus means that he intends to transmit the traditional teaching on the biblical canon which he has inherited from his predecessors. He also says later, at §36, that his list includes 'the writings which the Fathers included in the canon'. By the early fifth century, when Rufinus wrote, the church had achieved substantial harmony on the books of the NT canon, though uncertainty continued on some aspects. The OT canon had long mirrored the Jewish canon, but now in some quarters encompassed additional books (i.e., the deuterocanonical books, which Rufinus calls ecclesiastical; see the section on Augustine in this chapter). Priscillian of Avila had not advocated expanding the canon, but he did encourage the reading of Christian apocrypha. Rufinus perhaps has such practices in mind when he insists that his information on the Scriptures depends on the fathers. For similar language about receiving the biblical canon from the 'fathers' (or 'ancestors'), see Athanasius, *Ep. fest.* 39.16, 20. Given the other links between Rufinus's canon list and that of Athanasius, it is possible that Rufinus emphasizes the origin of his canon list with the fathers because Athanasius had done so.

[172] Several early Christian canonical lists specify that Ruth counts as a part of the book of Judges; see, e.g., the Origen, *Sel. Ps.* 1; Jerome, *Prol. Gal.* The point of not reckoning Ruth separately was to arrive at the number twenty-two for the entire list of OT books, corresponding to the number of letters in the Hebrew alphabet. Rufinus does not mention the total number of books for the Old Testament, but some of his comments make most sense if he had this number in mind.

Text	Translation
haec: Regnorum libri, quos Hebraei duos numerant; Paralipomenon, qui Dierum dicitur liber; et Esdrae duo, qui apud illos singuli conputantur; et Esther. Prophetarum uero Esaias Ieremias Ezechihel Danihel; praeterea Duodecim Prophetarum liber unus. Iob quoque et Psalmi Dauid singuli sunt libri. Solomonis uero tres ecclesiis traditi: Prouerbia Ecclesiastes Cantica canticorum. In his concluserunt librorum numerum Veteris Testamenti.	of Reigns, reckoned by the Jews as two;[173] Paralipomenon, otherwise called the Book of Days;[174] two books of Esdras, which among them are counted as one;[175] and Esther.[176] Of prophets we have Isaiah,[177] Jeremiah,[178] Ezekiel, and Daniel, and in addition, a single book of the Twelve Prophets.[179] Job, also, and the Psalms of David are each of them one book. There are three which Solomon bequeathed to the churches, namely, Proverbs, Ecclesiastes, and the Song of Songs. With these they completed the list of books belonging to the Old Testament.
Noui uero quattuor euangelia: Mathaei Marci Lucae Johannis. Actus Apostolum, quos descripsit Lucas. Pauli apostoli epistulae quattuordecim; Petri apostoli epistulae duae; Iacobi fratris Domini et apostoli una; Iudae una; Iohannis tres; Apocalypsis Iohannis.	In the New there are four Gospels, those of Matthew, Mark, Luke, and John; the Acts of the Apostles, composed by Luke; fourteen epistles by the apostle Paul;[180] two by the apostle Peter; one by James, brother of the Lord and Apostle; one by Jude; three by John;[181] the Apocalypse of John.

[173] The four books of Reigns (or Kingdoms) is the Latin (and Greek) name for the books that correspond to our 1–2 Samuel and 1–2 Kings, which Jewish tradition reckon as simply two books, Samuel and Kings.

[174] Paralipomenon ('things omitted') is the Greek title of Chronicles, known in Hebrew as *Divrei Ha-Yamim*, 'Events [or: Words] of the Days'. See Knoppers and Harvey 2002. Rufinus may depend for this alternative title 'Book of Days' on Jerome, *Prol. Gal.*, though Jerome gave the title there as Words of the Days.

[175] Like Origen, Rufinus understands that Jews have only one book of Ezra, and he knows that really two books are combined under the one title Ezra. As for Origen, so for Rufinus it is not clear whether he thinks these two books are Ezra and Nehemiah—which is actually the case for Jewish tradition—or whether he equates the two books that Jews call Ezra to the books known in English as 1 Esdras and Ezra-Nehemiah (= 2 Esdras in the Greek tradition). If he is dependent on Jerome's *Prol. Gal.*, then Rufinus would certainly know that Jews have only the book of Ezra(-Nehemiah). On problematic names for the books of Ezra (or Esdras) in Latin, see Bogaert 2000 and the Appendix below, p. 269.

[176] Haelewyck (2003: 20–1) tentatively attributes to our Rufinus a preface to Esther found in some Latin manuscripts that describes an edition of the Vetus Latina Esther with the Greek Additions gathered at the end of the book. Bogaert (2014: 49) accepts this attribution as 'very probable'.

[177] Isaiah stands at the head of the prophets in Rufinus's list, which is unusual for lists at this time. More commonly, the Twelve Prophets begin the prophets section, as in Rufinus's translation of Origen's OT canon list (for which, see above, p. 85n58). Isaiah begins the prophets also in Melito and the Codex Sinaiticus, and once in Jerome (the *Prologus Galeatus*, but not *Epist.* 53).

[178] Rufinus makes no mention of Lamentations or any other book commonly associated with Jeremiah (e.g., Baruch, the Letter of Jeremiah); see, e.g., the list of Cyril of Jerusalem and Athanasius of Alexandria. Presumably he would have included at least Lamentations under the heading Jeremiah, probably also Baruch (see Bogaert 2005: 298).

[179] The Twelve Minor Prophets were usually reckoned as a single book in ancient Judaism and Christianity.

[180] The number fourteen implies the inclusion of Hebrews as a Pauline letter, a common idea; see ch. 1, pp. 43–4.

[181] This order for the Catholic Epistles—Peter, James, Jude, John—is unique to Rufinus and Origen's *Hom. Jos.* 7.1, preserved only in Rufinus's Latin translation. See ch. 1, p. 45.

Text	Translation
(36) Haec sunt quae patres intra canonem concluserunt et ex quibus fidei nostrae adsertiones constare uoluerunt. Sciendum tamen est quod et alii libri sunt, qui non canonici sed ecclesiastici a maioribus appellati sunt, ut est: Sapientia, quae dicitur Solomonis, et alia Sapientia, quae dicitur filii Sirach: qui liber apud latinos hoc ipso generali uocabulo Ecclesiasticus appellatur, quo uocabulo non auctor libelli, sed scripturae qualitas cognominata est.	(36) These are the writings which the Fathers included in the canon, and on which they desired the affirmations of our faith to be based. It should also be known that there are other books which were called by our predecessors not 'canonical' but 'ecclesiastical'.[182] Thus, there is Wisdom, which is called 'of Solomon',[183] and another Wisdom, which is called 'of the son of Sirach'. This latter is known by the general title Ecclesiasticus among Latin-speaking people,[184] the description pointing, not to the author of the book, but to the character of the writing.[185]
Eiusdem ordinis est libellus Tobiae et Iudith, et Machabeaorum libri. In Nouo uero Testamento libellus qui dicitur Pastoris siue Hermae, et is qui appellatur Duae Viae, uel Iudicium secundum Petrum.	The Book of Tobit belongs to the same class, as do Judith and the books of the Maccabees.[186] In the New Testament we have the little work known as The Book of the Shepherd or of Hermas, and the book which is named the Two Ways, and The Judgement of Peter.[187]
Quae omnia legi quidem in ecclesiis uoluerunt, non tamen proferri ad auctoritatem ex his fidei confirmandam.	They desired that all these should be read in the churches, but that appeal should not be made to them on points of faith.[188]

[182] Rufinus's distinction between canonical books and other books useful to the church parallels the similar statements made by Athanasius, Jerome, and others. Despite Rufinus's assertion that his predecessors labelled this category 'ecclesiastical', we have no evidence for this designation prior to Rufinus's own canon list. On this middle category, see Gallagher 2013a; 2015b.

[183] Rufinus wants to signal that the Wisdom of Solomon—a Greek composition from the first century BCE—is not actually written by Solomon, despite the title. For other patristic authors who recognized that Solomon did not write the Wisdom of Solomon, see Gallagher 2012a: 42–5.

[184] As Rufinus realizes, the title Ecclesiasticus is peculiar to the Latin tradition; the same work is known in Greek and Hebrew as the Wisdom of Jesus Sirach or Ben Sira. This book had been written in Hebrew in early second-century BCE Palestine by the scribe Jesus ben Sira, and subsequently translated into Greek by the author's grandson, to which the translator attached a preface explaining briefly the origins of the work and its translation. The Hebrew text is no longer wholly extant. D. de Bruyne 1929 argued that the title 'Ecclesiasticus' arose in the Latin tradition likely as a result of an early translation from a Greek text that lacked the grandson's prologue. De Bruyne thus attributes the title to the original Latin translator. Kelly 1955: 139n232 lists Cyprian (*Test.* 3.109–12) as the first to use this title. On the whole question, see Thiele 1987: 153–9.

[185] Perhaps Rufinus here wants to guard against a possible misunderstanding of the significance of the title that could arise on analogy with the canonical Ecclesiastes, *viz.*, that the title refers to the author of the text. Rufinus insists that the title Ecclesiasticus derives from the character of the writing, apparently meaning that the book is ecclesiastical, particularly suited to the church.

[186] Alongside Tobit and Judith, Rufinus includes multiple books of Maccabees, probably the books known today as 1–2 Maccabees. Rufinus's list of OT ecclesiastical books would then match precisely the OT books excluded from the canon by Jerome, *Prol. Gal.*, and which were included in the canon by Augustine, *Doctr. chr.* 2.13.

[187] Rufinus's title 'Two Ways' may point to the Didache or the Epistle of Barnabas, both of which were well respected in the early church. Or it may refer to an independent work constituting the 'two ways' section of the Didache, according to the opinion of Niederwimmer 1998: 6. As for the 'Judgement According to Peter', possibly Rufinus intends this to be an alternative title for 'The Two Ways'; see Aldridge 1999: 242–5. On the other hand, it may simply be a lost work about which little is known; see Stenzel 1942: 58–60. Jerome lists the *Judgement According to Peter* as an apocryphal work (*Vir. ill.* 1); for other Petrine apocrypha see Eusebius, *Hist. eccl.* 3.3.

[188] Rufinus's assertion that the tradition known to him called for the ecclesiastical books to feature in the liturgy but not to confirm points of doctrine finds a close parallel in Jerome's *Preface to the Books of Solomon*, quoted above, p. 212.

Text	Translation
Ceteras uero scripturas apochryphas nominarunt, quas in ecclesia legi noluerunt. Haec nobis a patribus, ut dixi, tradita opportunum uisum est hoc in loco designare ad instructionem eorum, qui prima fidei elementa suscipiunt, ut sciant ex quibus sibi fontibus uerbi dei haurienda sint pocula.	The other writings they designated 'apocryphal', refusing to allow them to be read out in church.[189] Such, then, is the traditional canon handed down to us by the Fathers. As I remarked above, I have thought this the proper place to draw attention to it for the information of catechumens receiving their first lessons in the church and its faith, so that they may be in no doubt about the wellsprings from which their draughts of the word of God must be taken.[190]

The Canon List of Rufinus

Old Testament
      Genesis
      Exodus
      Leviticus
      Numbers
      Deuteronomy
      Joshua
      Judges
      Ruth
      1–4 Kings
      1–2 Paralipomenon
      1–2 Esdras
      Esther
      Isaiah
      Jeremiah   (+ Lamentations? Baruch? Letter of Jeremiah?)
      Ezekiel
      Daniel
      Twelve Prophets
      Job
      Psalms
      Proverbs
      Ecclesiastes
      Song of Songs
New Testament
      Matthew
      Mark
      Luke

[189] On Rufinus's statements concerning apocrypha, see Gallagher 2014a: 6–8.
[190] For a similar description of Scripture, see Athanasius, *Ep. fest.* 39.19 (p. 124).

John
Acts of the Apostles
Paul (fourteen)
Peter (two)
James
Jude
John (three)
Apocalypse of John
Ecclesiastical Books
    Old Testament:
        Wisdom of Solomon
        Wisdom of Sirach = Ecclesiasticus
        Tobit
        Judith
        Books of Maccabees
    New Testament:
        Shepherd of Hermas
        Two Ways
        Judgement of Peter

The Old Testament corresponds to the Protestant Old Testament, assuming that Lamentations is considered a part of Jeremiah, and aside from one feature of the order: in Rufinus's list the poetic books follow the prophetic books. In terms of content, the canon of Rufinus is identical to the canon of Jerome, his erstwhile friend and now opponent. It is not correct to say, as Kelly does, that Rufinus 'was acquainted with, and strongly disapproved of, St. Jerome's theories about the canon'.[191] Their canons are the same, so much so that even the non-canonical books that they approve for liturgical use closely cohere. The disagreement Kelly intends to highlight concerns not the biblical canon but the biblical text. Rufinus argues strongly in favour of adhering to the LXX's Greek text (in Latin translation, of course) that had become traditional in the church and which Jerome had challenged through his own Latin translation from the Hebrew text, a translation that would (much later) receive the name Vulgate. The issue of the two texts became especially acute when dealing with biblical books that existed in quite divergent forms in Greek and Hebrew—for instance, the longer Greek form of Daniel with its additional stories (Susanna, Bel and the Dragon, Song of the Three Youths). Jerome disapproved of these additions because the Hebrew text did not contain them, but Rufinus insists that the Greek form of these books is inspired Scripture for the church.[192] Their disagreement revolved around which textual form of the canonical books the church should receive, but they agreed completely on which books were canonical.

The New Testament corresponds to the current twenty-seven-book New Testament, aside from the order of the Catholic Epistles.

---

[191] Kelly 1955: 21.   [192] On this issue, see Gallagher 2012a: 197–208.

The 'ecclesiastical' books for the Old Testament—Wisdom of Solomon, Ecclesiasticus, Tobit, Judith, books of Maccabees—correspond precisely to the deuterocanonical books of the Roman Catholic biblical canon, except that the Roman Catholic Bible also counts Baruch as its own separate work. The 'ecclesiastical' books of the New Testament include the Shepherd of Hermas, the Two Ways, and the Judgement of Peter, which may be an alternative name for the Two Ways. If the Two Ways refers to the Didache, and if the Judgement of Peter is an alternative name for the Two Ways, then Rufinus's NT ecclesiastical books would correspond to those of Athanasius, who lists the Shepherd and the Didache.

BREVIARIUM HIPPONENSE

In October 393, the first plenary council of the African provinces met in the North African city of Hippo. Augustine was serving as a priest in Hippo at the time, and he may have been involved in planning the Council, as Cross speculates: 'It was an event of the first importance, and the choice of place is a sufficient proof that Augustine was the motive power behind it. The remarkable respect in which he was already held is shown by the circumstance that he—a mere presbyter—should have been asked to preach the sermon.'[193] The acts of this Council of Hippo no longer survive, but a summary of the Council's decisions was prepared by the bishops of Byzacena (Tunisia) for submission to the Council of Carthage in August 397. This summary, the *Breviarium Hipponense*, was accepted by the Council of Carthage and reaffirmed at later councils, including a subsequent Council of Carthage in 419.[194] The canons cover a range of topics, especially the status of clergy, the process of ordination, and various liturgical matters. Canon 36 lists the books of the biblical canon.

Old Testament canon: The OT canon includes all of the books of the Jewish canon plus the deuterocanonical books, along with 1 Esdras. In this way, the Old Testament matches precisely the Old Testament promoted by Augustine, with the exception of some differences in order, especially the placement of the group Tobit, Judith, Esther, Ezra, and Maccabees, which concludes the canon here but stands between Job and Psalms in Augustine's list.[195] Jeremiah is mentioned without any additions, but it probably included Lamentations, Baruch, and the Letter of Jeremiah.

---

[193] Cross 1961: 229–30. According to Augustine, *Retract.* 1.17, the content of his sermon on this occasion is preserved in his *De fide et symbolo*.

[194] On the complicated transmission history of the *Breviarium Hipponense*, see Munier 1972–3.

[195] These books also feature a slightly divergent internal order in the two lists: Augustine has Esther before Judith and Maccabees before Ezra. Aside from this group of books and the relative order of Ezekiel and Daniel, the *Breviarium* and Augustine correspond precisely in sequence.

New Testament canon: The New Testament corresponds precisely to the twenty-seven-book canon of Athanasius. The *Breviarium* does not name the individual Gospels, but asserts that there are four, nor the individual letters of Paul, though it attributes to him fourteen (thus including Hebrews).

Studies: Bardy 1955; La Bonnardière 1970: 44–57; 1999: 30–2; Moreau, Bochet, and Madec 1997: 507–14.

Breviarium Hipponense 36

Date: 393[196]

Text[197]	Translation
a) Vt praeter scripturas canonicas nihil in ecclesia legatur sub nomine diuinarum scripturarum.	a) That beyond the canonical Scriptures nothing should be read in church under the name of the Divine Scriptures.[198]
b) Sunt autem canonicae scripturae: genesis. exodus. leuiticus. numeri. deuteronomium. iesu naue. iudicum. ruth. regnorum libri iiii. paralipomenon libri ii. iob. psalterium. salomonis libri v. liber xii prophetarum minorum. item isaias. hieremias. ezechiel. danihel. tobias. iudith. esther. esdrae libri ii. machabeorum libri ii. Noui autem testamenti: euangelia libri iiii. actus apostolorum liber i. pauli apostoli	b) The canonical Scriptures are: Genesis. Exodus. Leviticus. Numbers. Deuteronomy. Joshua. Judges. Ruth. Of Reigns, four books.[199] Of Paralipomenon, two books.[200] Job. Psalter. Of Solomon, five books.[201] Book of Twelve Minor Prophets. Also Isaiah. Jeremiah.[202] Ezekiel. Daniel. Tobit. Judith. Esther. Of Ezra, two books.[203] Of Maccabees, two books. And of the New Testament: Gospels, four books. Of the Acts of the Apostles, one book.

[196] See the opening comments in this section. The *Breviarium Hipponense* was prepared in 397, but it is supposed to represent the conciliar decisions from Hippo in 393.

[197] Munier 1974: 43.

[198] Such a statement appears to be intended to exclude other potential liturgical texts that might be confused with the canonical texts. It is likely that Priscillian of Avila and his followers, who advocated the use of apocryphal texts, are in view.

[199] 1–2 Samuel and 1–2 Kings.

[200] Paralipomenon is the Greek and Latin name for Chronicles.

[201] The five books of Solomon include Proverbs, Ecclesiastes, and Song of Songs (or Song of Solomon), Wisdom of Solomon, and Ecclesiasticus (= Sirach). Augustine recognized that although these five books were often classified as Solomonic, the last two books (Wisdom of Solomon and Ecclesiasticus) were not actually written by Solomon. In his canon list, Augustine reported that Jesus Sirach wrote both of these books, but he later corrected his mistake, noting that Jesus Sirach did not write Wisdom of Solomon (*Retract.* 2.30.2). For further confusion regarding the authorship of these books, see the canon list in the Apostolic Canons, p. 137.

[202] Jeremiah probably includes Lamentations, Baruch, and the Letter of Jeremiah; see Bogaert 2005.

[203] Stuckenbruck (2011: 188) has the idea that 1 and 2 Esdras here refers to Ezra and Nehemiah. Bogaert (2000: 17–20) argues persuasively that Ezra and Nehemiah were considered a single book and were so represented in Old Latin manuscripts at this time. According to Bogaert (ibid.: 11–12), the books of Ezra and Nehemiah did not appear as two books in Latin manuscripts until the late eighth century. The reference to two books of Ezra here must include 1 Esdras and Ezra–Nehemiah, known in LXX manuscripts as Esdras A and Esdras B.

Text	Translation
epistolae xiiii.[204] petri ii. iohannis iii. iude i. iacobi i. apocalipsis iohannis.	Of the apostle Paul, fourteen epistles.[205] Of Peter, two. Of John, three. Of Jude, one. Of James, one. The Apocalypse of John.
c) Ita ut de confirmando isto canone transmarina ecclesia consulatur.	c) That the church across the sea should be consulted to confirm this canon.[206]
d) Liceat etiam legi passiones martyrum, cum anniuersarii dies eorum celebrantur.	d) It is also permissible to read the passions of the martyrs, when their anniversary days are celebrated.[207]

The Canon List of the *Breviarium Hipponense*

Old Testament
       Genesis
       Exodus
       Leviticus
       Numbers
       Deuteronomy
       Joshua
       Judges
       Ruth
       1–4 Reigns
       1–2 Paralipomenon
       Job
       Psalter
       Solomon, five
       Twelve Minor Prophets
       Isaiah
       Jeremiah
       Ezekiel
       Daniel
       Tobit
       Judith
       Esther
       1–2 Ezra
       1–2 Maccabees
New Testament
       Gospels, four
       Acts of the Apostles

[204] Other witnesses have *xiii eiusdem ad hebraeos* ('thirteen, of the same [i.e., Paul] to the Hebrews').

[205] The number fourteen must include Hebrews.

[206] The church across the sea would be Rome, and perhaps Milan; see Cross 1961: 232n1.

[207] On the Acts of the Martyrs, see Musurillo 1972.

Paul, fourteen
1–2 Peter
1–3 John
Jude
James
Apocalypse of John

AUGUSTINE OF HIPPO

Augustine (354–430) is generally recognized as the most important theologian in the Western church after the New Testament.[208] His early career as a teacher of rhetoric prepared him to grapple with Scripture throughout his career as bishop of Hippo in North Africa from 395 until his death. He published many significant biblical commentaries and theological works, and many of his sermons have been preserved. In 396, he began composing his handbook on biblical interpretation, which he called *On Christian Teaching* (*De Doctrina Christiana*), but it lay unfinished for several decades until he finally wrote the last book-and-a-half near the end of his life. In the early portion of this work, Augustine included a list of books in the biblical canon.

Old Testament canon: Augustine included all of the books of the canon later approved by the Council of Trent (i.e., the Roman Catholic biblical canon), except that Augustine did not name explicitly Lamentations, Baruch, or the Epistle of Jeremiah—it is likely that he assumed all of these books under the title 'Jeremiah'—and his reference to two books of Ezra probably intended the books known in the Greek tradition as Esdras A and Esdras B, rather than the Ezra–Nehemiah of the Jewish canon, as at Trent. His biblical canon thus included all the books of the Jewish canon along with the deuterocanonical books Tobit, Judith, 1–2 Maccabees, Wisdom of Solomon, and Sirach, and, additionally, 1 Esdras (i.e. Esdras A). He makes no distinctions among these books, and they are not grouped together, but mixed with the other books. His OT canon corresponds to the contemporary list approved at Hippo and the list issued by Innocent I. Augustine numbered the Old Testament as forty-four books.

New Testament canon: Augustine's NT canon is identical in content to the one promulgated by Athanasius—that is, the traditional twenty-seven-book New Testament. He expresses here no hesitation about any of these books, though the criteria for determining the canon, given just before his list, indicate that there did exist some controversy regarding the biblical canon.

---

[208] For an authoritative and accessible reference work on Augustine, see Fitzgerald 1999. For a brief survey of Augustine's relationship to the Bible, see Harrison 2013.

Studies: Costello 1930; Polman 1961: 63–6, 177–82; Taylor 1978; Wermelinger 1984: 174–84; Moreau, Bochet, and Madec 1997: 506–14; La Bonnardière 1999; Bogaert 2006.

On Christian Teaching 2.8.12.24–13.29

Date: 397

Introduction: Within book two of this treatise on biblical interpretation, Augustine comes to the topic of the biblical canon. He first explains the criteria for establishing the biblical canon, which all have to do with ecclesiastical reception: one should prefer those writings accepted by the consensus of the church, or at least by the majority, and those writings accepted by the more authoritative churches, such as churches that boast an apostolic connection. Augustine then lists the books of both testaments without referencing disputes about any of the books.

Text[209]	Translation[210]
(24) Sed nos ad tertium illum gradum considerationem referamus, de quo disserere quod dominus suggesserit atque tractare instituimus. Erit igitur divinarum scripturarum solertissimus indagator qui primo totas legerit notasque habuerit, etsi nondum intellectu, iam tamen lectione, dumtaxat eas quae appellantur canonicae. Nam ceteras securius leget fide veritatis instructus, ne praeoccupent inbecillum animum et periculosis mendaciis atque phantasmatis eludentes praeiudicent aliquid contra sanam intellegentiam. In canonicis autem scripturis ecclesiarum catholicarum quam plurium auctoritatem sequatur, inter quas sane illae sint quae apostolicas sedes habere et epistolas accipere meruerunt.	(24) But let us take our thoughts back to the third stage.[211] Here I propose to discuss and consider whatever ideas the Lord may provide. The most expert investigator of the Divine Scriptures will be the person who, first, has read them all and has a good knowledge—a reading knowledge, at least, if not yet a complete understanding—of those pronounced canonical.[212] He will read the others more confidently when equipped with a belief in the truth; they will then be unable to take possession of his unprotected mind and prejudice him by their dangerous falsehoods and fantasies.[213] In the matter of canonical Scriptures he should follow the authority of the great majority of catholic churches, including of course those that were found worthy to have apostolic seats and receive apostolic letters.[214]

[209] Green 1963: 39–41.   [210] Slightly adapted from Green 1997.

[211] Immediately prior to this passage, Augustine had expounded on seven stages of Christian maturity: fear, holiness, knowledge, fortitude, resolve of compassion, purity of heart, and wisdom.

[212] Cf. *Civ.* 11.3: 'the Scriptures which are called canonical . . . have the most eminent authority, and we trust them in all matters of which it is not expedient for us to be ignorant but which we are not capable of knowing for ourselves' (trans. Dyson 1998: 451).

[213] Augustine does not counsel abstinence from non-canonical literature, but rather a critical reading by those well grounded in the truth of the canonical Scriptures.

[214] The criteria of canonicity explicated by Augustine are similar to those mentioned by other authors collected in this volume (cf., e.g., ch. 3 on Eusebius), though Augustine is more explicit in his presentation of the ideas, and less explicit in how these principles apply to individual books.

Text	Translation
(25) Tenebit igitur hunc modum in scripturis canonicis, ut eas quae ab omnibus accipiuntur ecclesiis catholicis praeponat eis quas quidam non accipiunt. In eis vero quae non accipiuntur ab omnibus, praeponat eas quas plures gravioresque accipiunt, eis quas pauciores minorisque auctoritatis ecclesiae tenent. Si autem alias invenerit a pluribus, alias a gravioribus haberi, quamquam hoc invenire non possit, aequalis tamen auctoritatis eas habendas puto.	(25) He will apply this principle to the canonical Scriptures: to prefer those accepted by all catholic churches to those which some do not accept. As for those not universally accepted, he should prefer those accepted by a majority of churches, and by the more authoritative ones, to those supported by fewer churches, or by churches of lesser authority. Should he find that some Scriptures are accepted by the majority of churches, but others by the more authoritative ones (though in fact he could not possibly find this situation), I think that they should be considered to have equal authority.
(13.26) Totus autem canon scripturarum, in quo istam considerationem versandam dicimus, his libris continetur: Quinque Moyseos, id est Genesi, Exodo, Levitico, Numeris, Deuteronomio, et uno libro Iesu Nave, uno Iudicum, uno libello qui appellatur Ruth, qui magis ad Regnorum principium videtur pertinere; deinde quattuor Regnorum et duobus Paralipomenon, non consequentibus sed quasi a latere adiunctis simulque pergentibus.	(13.26) The complete canon of Scripture, on which I say that our attention should be concentrated, includes the following books: the five books of Moses (Genesis, Exodus, Leviticus, Numbers, Deuteronomy), and the single books of Joshua, son of Nave, and of Judges, and the little book known as Ruth, which seems to relate more to the beginning of Reigns,[215] and then the four books of Reigns and the two of Paralipomenon,[216] which do not follow chronologically but proceed, as it were, side by side with Reigns.
(27) Haec est historia, quae sibimet annexa tempora continet atque ordinem rerum. Sunt aliae tamquam ex diverso ordine, quae neque huic ordini neque inter se conectuntur, sicut est Iob et Tobias et Esther et Iudith et Machabeorum libri duo et Esdrae duo, qui magis subsequi videntur ordinatam illam historiam usque ad Regnorum vel Paralipomenon terminatam. Deinde prophetae, in quibus David unus liber Psalmorum, et Salomonis tres, Proverbiorum, Cantici canticorum et Ecclesiastes. Nam illi duo libri, unus qui Sapientia et alius qui Ecclesiasticus inscribitur, de quadam similitudine Salomonis esse dicuntur. Nam Iesus Sirach	(27) All this is historiography, which covers continuous periods of time and gives a chronological sequence of events. There are others, forming another sequence, not connected with either this class or each other, like Job, Tobit, Esther, Judith, and the two books of Maccabees, and the two of Ezra,[217] which rather seem to follow on from the chronologically ordered account which ends with Reigns and Paralipomenon. Then come the prophets, including David's single book of Psalms, and three books of Solomon, namely Proverbs, Song of Songs, and Ecclesiastes. The two books entitled Wisdom and Ecclesiasticus are also said to be by Solomon, on the strength of a general similarity; but there is

[215] Reigns is the typical English translation of the Latin title for the books known in English as Samuel and Kings (Kingdoms in Greek).

[216] Paralipomenon (or Paralipomena) is the Greek and Latin title for Chronicles.

[217] Green (1997: 150) suggests that the two books of Ezra are Ezra and Nehemiah, but Bogaert 2000 shows that the reference in all probability would be to the books known in the Greek tradition as Esdras A and Esdras B. Augustine (*Civ.* 18.36) cites a passage peculiar to 1 Esdras (The Tale of the Three Bodyguards, 1 Esdr. 3:1–5:6) as part of the book of Ezra and a potential prophecy of Christ.

Text	Translation
eos conscripsisse constantissime perhibetur; qui tamen quoniam in auctoritatem recipi meruerunt, inter propheticos numerandi sunt.	a strong tradition that Jesus Sirach wrote them,[218] and, in any case, because they have been found worthy of inclusion among authoritative texts, they should be numbered with the prophetic books.
(28) Reliqui sunt eorum libri qui proprie prophetae appellantur, duodecim prophetarum libri singuli, qui connexi sibimet, quoniam numquam seiuncti sunt, pro uno habentur; quorum prophetarum nomina sunt haec: Osee, Ioel, Amos, Abdias, Ionas, Micha, Naum, Abacuc, Sophonias, Aggaeus, Zacharias, Malachi. Deinde quattuor prophetae sunt maiorum voluminum: Esaias, Hieremias, Daniel, Hiezechiel.	(28) There remain the books of the prophets properly so called, the individual books of the Twelve Prophets who, because they are joined together and never separated, are counted as one.[219] Their names are these: Hosea, Joel, Amos, Obadiah, Jonah, Micah, Nahum, Habakkuk, Zephaniah, Haggai, Zechariah, and Malachi.[220] Then there are the four prophets in larger books: Isaiah, Jeremiah,[221] Daniel, Ezekiel.
(29) His quadraginta quattuor libris Testamenti Veteris terminatur auctoritas; Novi autem quattuor librorum evangelio:	(29) These forty-four books form the authoritative Old Testament;[222] the authoritative New Testament consists of the

[218] Augustine has misunderstood the issue of authorship for these Wisdom books. The book known in Latin as Ecclesiasticus is otherwise known as the Wisdom of Jesus Sirach, an indication of its authorship. The book known as Wisdom of Solomon was composed by an unknown author, and there is no known tradition before Augustine attributing its authorship to Jesus Sirach. Augustine acknowledges this error some decades later in his *Retract.* 2.30.2. Both of these books are included implicitly among the Solomonic Books in the *Breviarium Hipponense*.

[219] It was customary to count the Minor Prophets as one book, not only in Christianity but also in Judaism.

[220] The sequence of the Minor Prophets recorded by Augustine differs from the sequence found in many LXX manuscripts, which have the first six books in the order Hosea, Amos, Micah, Joel, Obadiah, Jonah; cf. Dines 2015: 439–40. One would expect Augustine to follow this LXX sequence, since he elsewhere so strongly advocates continued adherence to the LXX within the church; see Gallagher 2016a. Instead, here he follows the sequence found in Hebrew sources, which Jerome stressed in his Vulgate translation; cf. *Praef. XII Proph.*

[221] Augustine does not name Lamentations, which in itself is not unprecedented for patristic canon lists. Lamentations was often explicitly named as a part of the book of Jeremiah, and the two books were counted jointly as a result. Sometimes Lamentations could be left completely unmentioned because it was assumed under the name Jeremiah; see the discussion of Gregory of Nazianzus and Amphilochius in ch. 3, and Rufinus in the current chapter. Augustine apparently follows this practice. Moreover, Baruch is likely included within Jeremiah, as well. Note Augustine's comment on Baruch at *Civ.* 18.33, in regard to Bar. 3:36: 'Some authorities attribute this testimony not to Jeremiah but to his scribe, who was called Baruch; but it is more generally attributed to Jeremiah.' Cf. also *Contra Faustum* 12.43, and see Bogaert 2005: 293.

[222] Augustine's total of forty-four books for the Old Testament is unusual. Normally, patristic authors have twenty-two books in their Old Testament. Augustine's total increases because he includes the deuterocanonical books within his canon, but also because he counts separately several books that are usually counted jointly (i.e., Judges–Ruth, Samuel, Kings, Chronicles, two books of Ezra, Minor Prophets). Only in the case of the Minor Prophets does he acknowledge the tradition of counting these books jointly, for he speaks of 'the individual books of the twelve prophets who because they are joined together and never separated are counted as one'. But Augustine's total forty-four for the entire Old Testament requires that one count the Minor Prophets individually, despite Augustine's comment to the contrary.

Text	Translation
secundum Matthaeum, secundum Marcum, secundum Lucam, secundum Iohannem; quattuordecim epistolis apostoli Pauli: ad Romanos, ad Corinthios duabus, ad Galatas, ad Ephesios, ad Philippenses, ad Thessalonicenses duabus, ad Colossenses, ad Timotheum duabus, ad Titum, ad Philemonem, ad Hebraeos; Petri duabus; tribus Iohannis; una Iudae et una Iacobi; Actibus Apostolorum libro uno et Apocalypsi Iohannis libro uno.	gospel in four books (Matthew, Mark, Luke, John),[223] fourteen letters of the apostle Paul (Romans, Corinthians (two), Galatians, Ephesians, Philippians, Thessalonians (two), Colossians, Timothy (two), Titus, Philemon, Hebrews), two of Peter, three of John, one of Jude, and one of James; the single book of the Acts of the Apostles, and the single book of the Revelation of John.

The Canon List of Augustine

Old Testament
    Five books of Moses
        Genesis
        Exodus
        Leviticus
        Numbers
        Deuteronomy
    Historiography
        Joshua
        Judges
        Ruth
        1–4 Reigns (= 1–2 Samuel and 1–2 Kings)
        1–2 Paralipomenon (= 1–2 Chronicles)
        Job
        Tobit
        Esther
        Judith
        1–2 Maccabees
        1–2 Ezra
    Prophets
        Psalms
        Solomon, three
            Proverbs

---

[223] This Greek order for the Gospels was adopted by Jerome for his revision of the Gospels, but Augustine probably did not yet have access to this work by Jerome. The more common order in Old Latin manuscripts is Matthew, John, Luke, Mark. Augustine discusses the order of the Gospels at *Cons.* 1.2.3. See Houghton 2008: 13–15.

Song of Songs
Ecclesiastes
Wisdom
Ecclesiasticus
Twelve Prophets
   Hosea
   Joel
   Amos
   Obadiah
   Jonah
   Micah
   Nahum
   Habakkuk
   Zephaniah
   Haggai
   Zechariah
   Malachi
Isaiah
Jeremiah
Daniel
Ezekiel

New Testament
Gospels, four
   Matthew
   Mark
   Luke
   John
Paul, fourteen letters
   Romans
   1–2 Corinthians
   Galatians
   Ephesians
   Philippians
   1–2 Thessalonians
   Colossians
   1–2 Timothy
   Titus
   Philemon
   Hebrews
1–2 Peter
1–3 John
Jude
James
Acts of the Apostles
Revelation of John

POPE INNOCENT I

Innocent served as bishop of Rome (402–17) at a critical period in the history of the city and in the development of the Roman church. During his episcopate, the visigothic leader Alaric besieged and eventually sacked Rome (410).[224] Theological controversy continued to plague the church, with the ideas of Pelagius, Priscillian, Vigilantius, and others inciting passions. Through it all, Innocent endeavoured to augment the prestige and authority of the Roman see, a project in which he enjoyed some success. He wrote a number of letters, only a handful of which survive, thanks to later compilers of papal letters who created collections of decretals.[225] Through his letters, Innocent disseminated the positions of the Roman church and promoted it as a bulwark of apostolic truth and an arbiter in ecclesiastical disputes.[226] In one of these letters, addressed to bishop Exsuperius of Toulouse, Innocent included a list of canonical Scripture (*Ep.* 6.7).

Old Testament canon: The Old Testament affirmed by Innocent in *Ep.* 6.7 includes essentially the same books later canonized at the Council of Trent (1546); that is, the books of the Jewish canon together with the deuterocanonical books, without any distinction among the books. There is some room for doubt as to the identity of the two books of Esdras that Innocent mentions, and he does not make explicit which books he might include under the umbrella term 'Jeremiah'. Innocent makes no point about the total number of books included in the Old Testament, but he does sometimes mention that particular titles include one book (e.g., Judges, Tobit, etc.), or two, four, five, or sixteen books. He prefixes to the title Ruth the words *simul et*, which would seem to indicate that Ruth counts with another book.[227] If one counts simply the titles in the list, taking into account the number of books assigned to each title (and counting Ruth as a separate book), one arrives at the number forty-four, the same number of books Augustine says his Old Testament encompasses.

New Testament canon: Innocent's list matches precisely the twenty-seven books declared canonical by Athanasius in 367 and forming the traditional NT canon. Following this list of books, Innocent condemns any non-canonical writing that circulates under the name of an apostle.

---

[224] On Innocent's response to the threat of Alaric, see Dunn 2010.

[225] On the early history of papal decretals, see Jasper and Fuhrmann 2001: 3–40; Dunn, 2015a; 2015b.

[226] For example, Innocent was one of three bishops to whom John Chrysostom made appeal for support immediately prior to his final deposition and exile; see Dunn 2005.

[227] See below on this passage.

Epistle 6 *ad Exsuperium Tolosanum*

Date: 405

Introduction: As bishop of Rome, Innocent had received a letter from Exsuperius, Bishop of Toulouse in southwestern Gaul, containing several questions about ecclesiastical discipline.[228] Innocent's response affirmed the necessity of clerical celibacy, granted penance and communion to a lapsed Christian at the approach of death, determined that adultery was equally sinful whether committed by a husband or a wife, allowed Christian magistrates to impose capital punishment, and presented a list of canonical books. Possibly such a list was requested because of uncertainty arising from the teachings of Priscillian of Avila in nearby Spain.[229] Innocent concludes his list by condemning any other writing that bears the name of an apostle.

Text[230]			Translation	
VII. Qui uero libri recipiantur in canone [scripturarum] breuis adnexus ostendit. Haec sunt [ergo] quae desiderata moneri uoce uoluisti:			(7) But which books should be received in the canon [of the Scriptures], a brief appendix shows. These[, then,] are what you wished with eager voice to be taught:	
Moysi libri V, id est			five books of Moses, that is	
Genesis			Genesis	
Exodi			Exodus	
Leuitici			Leviticus	
Numeri[231]			Numbers	
Deuteronomii			Deuteronomy	
et Iesu Naue	I		and of Jesus Nave[232]	one
Iudicum	I		of Judges	one
Regnorum		libri IIII	of Reigns[233]	four books
simul et Ruth.			together also Ruth[234]	

---

[228] On Exsuperius, see Dunn 2014.

[229] On Priscillian's use of writings condemned by Innocent, see Gallagher 2014a: 9–11. Priscillian did not seek to expand the canon beyond the limits advocated by Innocent (see Jacobs 2000), but he did promote the reading of literature condemned here by Innocent, especially the apocryphal Acts; see Conti 2010: 275–6.

[230] Wurm 1939: 74–8. The formatting has not been preserved.

[231] The usual Latin name for the fourth book of the Pentateuch is *Numeri* (cf. Gk, Ἀριθμοί), a nominative plural form. The other names here are genitive (e.g., book 'of Leviticus', book 'of Deuteronomy'), so the form should have been *Numerorum* (a form unattested in the manuscripts). Wurm's apparatus shows that some witnesses attest the nominative singular (*Numerus*), just as they do for the other books of the Pentateuch.

[232] I.e., Joshua son of Nun.

[233] 'Reigns' is the Latin name for the books more commonly known in English as 1–2 Samuel and 1–2 Kings.

[234] This is an odd placement for Ruth, and Innocent seems to be saying that Ruth counts with Kings, rather than with Judges (the more usual combination). Similarly, Augustine comments in his canon list that Ruth pertains more to the beginning of Kings, though he actually places Ruth after Judges and before Kings. For another iteration of Ruth after Kings, cf. Syriac MS 10 from the Monastery of St Catherine.

Text		Translation	
Prophetarum	libri XVI	of Prophets[235]	sixteen books
Salomonis	libri V	of Solomon[236]	five books
Psalterium.		the Psalter	
Item historiarum		And of the histories	
Iob	liber I	of Job	one book
Tobiae	liber I	of Tobit	one book
Hester	liber I	of Esther	one book
Iudith	liber I	of Judith	one book
Machabeorum	libri II	of the Maccabees	two books
Hesdrae	libri II	of Esdras	two books[237]
Paralypomenon	libri II	of Paralipomenon[238]	two books

Item noui testamenti		And of the New Testament	
euangeliorum	libri IIII	of the Gospels	four books
apostoli Pauli epistulae	XIIII[239]	epistles of the apostle Paul	fourteen[240]
epistulae Iohannis	III	epistles of John	three
epistulae Petri	II	epistles of Peter	two
epistula Iudae	I	epistle of Jude	one
epistula Iacobi	I	epistle of James	one
actus apostolorum		Acts of the Apostles	
apocalypsis Iohannis		Revelation of John	

Cetera autem quae uel sub nomine Matthiae siue Iacobi minoris, uel sub nomine Petri et Iohannis, quae a quodam Leucio scripta sunt	But others, which exist either under the name of Matthias[241] or James the less,[242] or under the name of Peter[243] and John,[244] which were

[235] The sixteen unnamed prophets would include the Twelve Minor Prophets along with Isaiah, Jeremiah—with the usual other books: Lamentations, and perhaps Baruch and the Epistle of Jeremiah—Ezekiel, and Daniel.

[236] The five unnamed books of Solomon would include Proverbs, Ecclesiastes, Song of Songs, Wisdom of Solomon, and Sirach (= Ecclesiasticus).

[237] Bogaert (2014: 53) asserts that the two books of Esdras in Innocent's list must refer to the writings known in the LXX manuscript tradition as Esdras A (i.e., 1 Esdras) and Esdras B (= Ezra–Nehemiah).

[238] Paralipomenon is the Greek and Latin name for the books more commonly known in English as 1–2 Chronicles. The ending of Innocent's Old Testament—Esdras, Paralipomenon— oddly mirrors the Talmudic list.

[239] A few witnesses attest XIII.

[240] The number fourteen must include Hebrews.

[241] Here, Innocent condemns any non-canonical text circulating under the name of an apostle; for English translations and introductions, see Elliott 1993. The Gospel associated with Matthias (see Acts 1:23) is also mentioned by Origen (*Hom. Luc.* 1.2) and Eusebius (*Hist. eccl.* 3.25.6), in both cases as heretical. See ibid.: 19–20.

[242] For the title James the Less (*Iacob minor*), see Mark 15:40. Christian tradition sometimes equated James the Less with James the Lord's Brother (Gal. 1:19) and James the son of Alphaeus (Mark 3:18); see, e.g., Jerome, *Helv.* 15. Innocent surely has in mind the popular second-century infancy Gospel now called *The Protevangelium of James* (English translation in Elliott 1993: 48–67), whose author identifies himself as James (25.1), and whom the *Decretum Gelasianum* 5.2 identifies with James the Less. Cf. Origen, *Comm. Matt.* 10.17.

[243] Several Petrine apocrypha trace their origin probably to the second century: The Preaching of Peter (Elliott 1993: 20–4); The Gospel of Peter (ibid.: 150–8); The Acts of Peter (ibid.: 390–426); and The Apocalypse of Peter (ibid.: 593–612).

[244] The Acts of John was denounced nearly a century earlier by Eusebius (*Hist. eccl.* 3.25.6), our earliest extant reference to the work. See Elliott 1993: 303–47.

Text	Translation
[uel sub nomine Andreae, quae a Xenocaride et Leonida philosophis], uel sub nomine Thomae, et si qua sunt alia; non solum repudianda uerum etiam noueris esse damnanda.	written by a certain Leucius,[245] [or under the name of Andrew,[246] which were written by the philosophers Xenocharides and Leonidas,[247]] or under the name of Thomas,[248] and if there are any others, you should know that they must not only be repudiated but also condemned.

The Canon List of Innocent

Old Testament
    Moses
        Genesis
        Exodus
        Leviticus
        Numbers
        Deuteronomy
    Joshua (Jesus Nave)
    Judges
    1–4 Kingdoms (= 1–2 Samuel and 1–2 Kings)
    Ruth
    Prophets (16 books)
    Solomon (5 books)
    Psalter
    History
        Job
        Tobit
        Esther
        Judith
        1–2 Maccabees
        1–2 Esdras
        1–2 Paralipomenon (= 1–2 Chronicles)

[245] Epiphanius, *Pan.* 51, names Leucius as an apostate follower of the apostle John. On the historicity of this claim, see Baldwin 2005: 102–3.

[246] The Acts of Andrew were denounced nearly a century earlier by Eusebius (*Hist. eccl.* 3.25.6), our earliest extant reference to the work. See Elliott 1993: 230–302.

[247] The claim that the Acts of Andrew were composed by the philosophers Xenocharides and Leonidas is otherwise unattested, and no other source mentions these philosophers. MacDonald (1990: 47–51) seeks to preserve the accuracy of Innocent's statement. Several manuscripts omit the statement about Andrew (as indicated by Wurm's brackets), possibly indicating that it is an interpolation. In any case, scholars generally consider the author of these *Acts* to be well versed in platonist philosophy and to achieve a high Greek style; besides MacDonald, see Warren 1999.

[248] Several works circulated under the name of Thomas: The Gospel of Thomas, early second century (Elliott 1993: 123–47), but apparently never translated into Latin; Infancy Gospel of Thomas, possibly second century in some form (ibid.: 68–83); Acts of Thomas, third century (ibid.: 439–511); and The Apocalypse of Thomas, the shorter recension of which probably dates to the fourth century (ibid.: 645–51).

New Testament
    Gospels (4 books)
    Paul (14 epistles)
    John (3 epistles)
    Peter (2 epistles)
    Jude
    James
    Acts of the Apostles
    Apocalypse of John
Condemned Writings
    Any other book going under the name of:
        Matthew
        James the less
        Peter
        John
        Andrew
        Thomas

5

The Syriac Christian List

INTRODUCTION

In the preceding chapters, we have focused on the early Jewish canon lists and the early Christian Greek and Latin canon lists. In this chapter, we turn to the extant canon lists in the Christian Syriac tradition.

Many Syriac canon lists originated due to contact with Greek Christianity. The Syriac translations of some of the lists that appear in this work such as Athanasius's 39th *Festal Letter* or Epiphanius's canon lists in his *On Weights and Measures* bear testimony to this influence.[1] These works were probably translated into Syriac sometime in the seventh century and were known among both West- and East-Syriac Christians. They appear to be conservative translations of the Greek canon lists.[2] The Syriac versions of the canon lists of Athanasius and Epiphanius maintained the distinction in religious literature between 'canonical' (the twenty-two books) and other books 'useful for reading' (most of the deuterocanonical books) and, according to Van Rompay, this distinction 'served as a guiding principle for Syriac discussions on the canon'.[3]

In chapter 3 in this volume, under the Apostolic Canons, we included a few Syriac versions of the final canon of the Apostolic Canons, which includes a canon list of Scripture, and compared them with the Greek versions of the same list. It appears that the Syriac version of that canon list was written for the Syriac church, since it contains different books (e.g., Tobit is included in the Syriac version, while it is absent from the Greek).

Finally, the canon list in Syriac MS 10 from St Catherine's Monastery appears to be the earliest genuine canon list written in Syriac, and it includes a list of OT and NT books. Its provenance and date continue to be discussed, but we include the list here as a representative of the Syriac canon list tradition.

---

[1] Van Rompay, Forthcoming. See also the sections on Athanasius and Epiphanius in ch. 3.
[2] Van Rompay Forthcoming.   [3] ibid.

ST CATHERINE'S MONASTERY SYRIAC LIST

Syriac MS 10 from the monastery of St Catherine's on the Sinai Peninsula may be attributed to the eighth or ninth century.[4] The manuscript contains 224 leaves, with one column per leaf, with twenty-one lines per column. The contents of the manuscript include homilies and extracts from the following church fathers: Ambrose of Milan, Jacob of Serug, Theophilus of Alexandria, Chrysostom, Proclus, Ephrem, Cyril of Alexandria, Anastasius of Antioch, Isaac, Timotheus, Epiphanius, and Cornelius (all pre-Chalcedonian fathers). At the end of the manuscript are brief notices of the Seventy Apostles and a list of the holy books ascribed to Irenaeus of Lyons.[5]

Syriac was the original language of the list, even if some researchers remain uncertain about its precise geographic provenance.[6] In the general contents, and even the names of some of the books, this list contrasts with other Syriac canon lists translated from Greek sources, perhaps adding to the evidence that it comes from Syria originally.[7]

Regarding the provenance of the list, Harris noted, 'The whole document is suspiciously Syrian in origin. The ascription to Irenaeus may perhaps be due to the insertion of the document on blank leaves at the end of some copy of the works of Irenaeus.'[8] Nevertheless, Haelewyck states that no one knows its geographical origination.[9] He notes that the list's clear distinction between the books belonging to the Hebrew canon (Genesis to Ezra–Nehemiah) and the books added to the Septuagint (1–2 Maccabees, Judith, Wisdom, Sirach) furnishes a 'certain suspicious order'. Furthermore, looking at the Hebrew is not a decisive criterion in Syriac, since 'among the Syriac canonical books one finds books that do not belong to the Jewish canon (Epistle of Jeremiah, Bel, for example), and conversely, canonical books in Hebrew that are not canonical in Syriac (Chronicles, Ezra–Nehemiah, and even Esther)'.[10]

---

[4] The initial description in Harris (1894) records a ninth-century date for the manuscript (p. 4), but Markschies (2012) lists the manuscript as from the eighth or ninth century (p. 131).

[5] Page 1 of this section begins with the following: 'The Names of the Seventy Apostles which were laid down by Irenaeus of Logodonos.' The catalogue of books begins on fol. 216r of this final section of the manuscript.

[6] Haelewyck (2008: 164) notes that one does not know the exact milieu of origin for this list, but neither he nor others register disputes about the original language of the list.

[7] Cp. the Syriac lists in ch. 3 on the Apostolic Canons.

[8] Harris 1894: 16. Harris also notes that the list of seventy names is 'Edessan at all events in its arrangement' (p. 15). The first name is *Adar* who died in *Urhai*, and this apostle must be the Edessan apostle, *Addai* (i.e., Thaddeus of Edessa). Furthermore, several of the seventy names depend on Syriac spellings from the Peshitta (e.g. the names from Rom. 16 are from a source close to the Peshitta).

[9] Haelewyck 2008: 149 and 164.

[10] ibid.: 164. This comment comes in the context where he expresses doubt that one can use this canon list as a solid foundation for the primitive Syriac canon, since one does not know either the milieu of origin or the exact date.

Researchers mainly agree on a later fourth-century date (ca. 350–400) for the list, noting that the date must not be pushed too late due to the absence of the Catholic Epistles, the Apocalypse, and the order of Galatians as the first letter among the Pauline letters.[11] Furthermore, the distinction made between the protocanonical books and the deuterocanonical books in the OT section would support a late fourth-century date for the list.[12]

Old Testament canon: The Old Testament section contains an unmixed listing of protocanonical (Genesis to Ezra–Nehemiah) and deuterocanonical books (1–2 Maccabees, Judith, Wisdom, Sirach). The protocanonical books number twenty-two books implicitly by omitting Ecclesiastes and Song of Songs and by listing Ruth and Lamentations separately from Judges and Jeremiah, respectively. The deuterocanonical books of 3–4 Maccabees, 3 Ezra (= Esdras A in Greek tradition), and Tobit are also lacking from the list, but are found in later Syriac MSS. Tobit and 3 Ezra are not included in the earliest Syriac MSS (7a1 and 8a1, first half of seventh- and eighth-century MSS, respectively), while 3–4 Maccabees are included in 7a1 and 3 Maccabees is included in 8a1.[13]

New Testament canon: The NT section includes the four Gospels, Acts, and the fourteen Epistles of Paul (after restoring the errors of copying in the manuscript)—only nineteen books of the traditional twenty-seven books of the New Testament. The omission of the Catholic Epistles and Revelation reflects ongoing disputes over these books in the fourth century in the East. The Peshitta version in the fifth century only included the three longer Catholic Epistles (James, 1 Peter, 1 John) and excluded the four shorter ones and the Apocalypse, resulting in a twenty-two-book NT canon.[14]

Studies: Harris 1894: 4–16; Zahn 1900: 788–806; Bauer 1903: 33–8; Haelewyck 2008: 149–50, 164; Markschies 2012: 131–3.

[11] Zahn (1900: 805) concluded a date range of 350–400, and Markschies (2012: 131) follows him. Markschies (ibid.: 131) also notes that Bauer (1903) votes for a date in the latter part of the fourth century (p. 33).

[12] Haelewyck 2008: 149 and 164. Haelewyck is not fully convinced of the fourth-century date for the list, but only cites that one must remain uncertain (p. 164). His comments are mainly reserved for the OT portion of the list. However, once one considers the entire list in the light of the canon disputes in the fourth century, one sees that this list of books of the Old and New Testaments belongs there.

[13] Cf. Forness (2014: 45–6) for further defence of the consensus date (between late sixth and early seventh century) for MS 7a1.

[14] Sebastian Brock (2006) says that the rest of the Catholic Epistles and Revelation were not translated into Syriac until the sixth century (pp. 34–5).

St Catherine's Monastery Syriac MS 10

Date: 350–400

Text[15]	Translation
	Concerning the number of the holy books,
	(and) concerning the number of verses
	[litter. how many verses] there are
	in each one of them.
	Creation:[16] 4,516 verses.
	Exodus: 3,378 verses.
	Of Priests:[17] 2,684 verses.
	Numbers: 3,481 verses.
	Deuteronomy: 2,982 verses.
	The total of the Pentateuch: 17,041 verses.[18]
	Yeshu' son of Nun: 1,953 verses.
	Judges:[20] 2,088 verses.
	Samuel:[21] 3,436 verses.
	Book of Kings:[22] 6,113 verses.[23]

[15] Harris 1894: 11–14; for online images of the manuscript, go to https://www.loc.gov/resource/amedmonastery.00279386267-ms/?sp=224;.

[16] Cf. ch. 3 on Amphilochius, who also used 'Creation' as a title for Genesis.

[17] That is, Leviticus.

[18] Haelewyck (2008: 149n32) notes that the number 17,041 after the Pentateuch is the only correct one in the list.

[19] Per the manuscript. The scribe intended ܐܠܦܝܢ 'thousands'.

[20] *šbṭ*. 'Judges'. The colophon to the book of Judges in the Peshitta Codex Ambrosianus B 21 (fol. 81v, p. 170; early seventh century) offers later commentary on the title of this book: finished transcribing Joshua son of Nun and the book of the Judges [ܕܝܢ; *dyn*'] of the sons of Israel, which is called in Hebrew 'Judges' [ܫܒܛ; *šbṭ*']. The title for this book in Syriac is ܕܝܢ (*dyn*'; 'Judges'), taken from the Peshitta version of Judges 2:16–18 (also cp. the Syriac title of this book in ch. 3 on the Apostolic Canons). The Syriac/Aramaic title in this list is the result of *p/b* interchange in Semitic languages (cp. Hebrew *špṭim* 'Judges' from Judges 2:16–18; cf. also Sokoloff (2009: 1586b) contains instances with *p*, that is, *špṭ* 'judge'). For Greek transliterations of this Hebrew title, cf. ch. 3 on the Bryennios List, Origen, Epiphanius, and ch. 4 on Jerome in the present work. Evidently, the book could be called by either its Syriac or Hebrew title.

[21] 'Samuel' with the large number of verses implies First and Second Samuel in the Jewish tradition. These books are First and Second Kingdoms in the Greek tradition.

[22] 'Book of Kings' combined with the large number of verses implies First and Second Kings in the Jewish tradition. These books are Third and Fourth Kingdoms in the Greek tradition.

[23] The colophon at the end of this book in Syriac Codex Ambrosianus reports that it has 7,113 verses (fol. 132v). 'Seven' (ܫܒܥ) and 'six' (ܫܬ) begin with the same letter and a scribal error resulted in the traditional number of verses for this book.

Text	Translation
ܘܬܠܬܚܡܫ: ܪܥܘܬ: ܡܐ̈ܬܝܢ	Ruth:[24] 246 verses.
ܘܐܪ̈ܒܥܝܢ ܘܫܬܐ ܦܬܓ̈ܡܐ ܕܘܝܕ	David:[25] 4,830 verses.
ܦܬܓܡܐ ܐܪ̈ܒܥܐ ܐܠܦܝܢ ܘܬ̈ܡܢܡܐܐ	
ܘܬܠܬܝܢ ܣܦܪ ܕܒܪܝܡܝܢ ܦܬܓ̈ܡܐ	Book of Chronicles:[26] 3,553 verses.
ܬܠܬܐ ܐܠ̈ܦܝܢ ܘܚܡܫܡܐܐ ܘܚ̈ܡܫܝܢ	
ܘܬܠܬܐ: ܐܝܘܒ: ܦܬܓ̈ܡܐ ܐܠܦ	Job:[27] 1,548 verses.
ܘܚ̈ܡܫܡܐܐ ܘܐܪ̈ܒܥܝܢ ܘܬܡܢܝܐ	
ܚܟܡܬܐ ܕܡ̈ܬܠܬܐ[28] ܦ̈ܬܓܡܐ	Wisdom of the Proverbs: 1,762 verses.[29]
ܐܠܦ ܘܫ̈ܒܥܡܐܐ ܫ̈ܬܝܢ ܘܬܪ̈ܝܢ	
ܬܪܥܣܪ ܦ̈ܬܓܡܐ ܬܠܬܐ ܐܠܦܝܢ	Twelve [Prophets]: 3,643 verses.
ܘܫ̈ܬܡܐܐ ܘܐܪܒܥܝܢ ܘܬܠܬܐ	
ܐܫܥܝܐ ܦ̈ܬܓܡܐ ܬܠܬܐ ܐܠܦܝܢ	Isaiah: 3,656 verses.
ܘܫܬܡܐܐ ܘܚܡܫܝܢ ܘܫܬܐ ܐܪܡܝܐ:	Jeremiah:[30] 4,252 verses.
ܦ̈ܬܓܡܐ ܐܪ̈ܒܥܐ ܐܠܦܝܢ ܘܡܐ̈ܬܝܢ	
ܘܚܡܫܝܢ ܘܬܪ̈ܝܢ ܐܘܠܝܬܗ ܦܬܓ̈ܡܐ	His Lamentations: 433 verses.
ܐܪܒܥܡܐܐ ܘܬܠܬܝܢ ܘܬܠܬܐ	
ܦܬܓܡܝܢ: ܕܢܝܐܠ ܦܬܓ̈ܡܐ ܐܠܦ	Daniel:[31] 1,555 verses.

[24] Ruth is not combined with Judges in this list as it is in many of the lists. Rather, it comes before Psalms as in the Babylonian Talmud. In Epiphanius's *Mens.* 22–3, Ruth comes after Judges and before Psalms. Ruth after Kings is only attested elsewhere in Innocent I's list, and he appears to join it with Kings (cf. ch. 4 on Innocent I, p. 232n234).

[25] Gregory of Nazianzus also used the title 'David' for the Psalter in his canon list (cf. ch. 3 on Gregory, p. 144n366). Haelewyck 2008: 150 notes that the order Psalms–1–2 Chronicles–Job–Proverbs is unique. He also notes that Psalms grouped with the historical books, after the book of Samuel, is similar to the Bible of Buchanan, 12a1 in the catalogue of the Leiden Peshitta. 12a1 has the order of 1–2 Samuel–Psalms–1–2 Kings–1–2 Chronicles (cf. Brock 2013: 56).

[26] The book of Chronicles is reckoned as one book, as it is in Jewish tradition. The Syriac title *dbrymyn* is a Syriac translation from the Hebrew title of the book 'The Matters of the Days' (cf. Payne Smith 1879a: 814). The two books known as Paralipomenon in the Greek tradition are reckoned as one book in many of the canon lists.

[27] Job appears with Proverbs between the history books and the prophetical books (cf. Haelewyck 2008: 149). In the early Syriac MSS, Job usually appears after the Pentateuch (cf. Brock 2013: 55–7).

[28] Per the facsimile; the scribe intended ܕܡ̈ܬܠܐ.

[29] The books of Qoheleth/Ecclesiastes and Song of Songs are omitted from the list. Zahn 1900: 197 suggests that the omission is due to a copy error. The manuscript certainly evinces errors in the NT part of the list. Furthermore, some of the numbers of verses of the books are too large; 2 Maccabees (5,600 lines in the list) is not more than twice the length of 1 Maccabees (2,766 verses according to the list) (cf. Haelewyck 2008: 150n41). Haelewyck notes that Ecclesiastes and Song of Songs were omitted from a complete Syriac Bible (17a9) (ibid.: 150). However, both books are included in MS 7a1 (fols. 142v–145v). These books were disputed by the Jews at the turn of the second century (cf., e.g., Leiman 1991: 105ff), but they are included in every early Christian canon list. Perhaps, there were still disputes over these two books at the church in Edessa. However, Haelewyck notes that in Syriac circles it is strange for there to be disputes over these books in this list, while there is no dispute over 1–2 Chronicles, Ezra–Nehemiah, and Esther, which were subject to disputes in the Syriac church (Haelewyck 2008: 150).

[30] Baruch and the Epistles of Jeremiah are not listed, while Jeremiah's Lamentations is. Haelewyck imagines that these three works have been joined to Jeremiah (ibid.: 150n40). However, if the list is more dependent on the Jewish canon (as Haelewyck infers), then one should imagine that these other works were not considered to be canonical, though they were joined to Jeremiah in the manuscripts. Cf. ch. 3 on Epiphanius (p. 165; also p. 161n431) for the Jewish view, which did not include Baruch and the Epistle of Jeremiah with Jeremiah.

[31] Haelewyck (ibid.: 150n40) imagines that Bel and Susannah have been joined to Daniel.

Text	Translation
ܚܡܫܡܐܐ ܘܫܒܥܝܢ ܘܫܒܥܐ	
ܚܙܩܝܐܝܠ ܦܬܓܡ̈ܐ ܐܪܒܥܐ ܐܠܦܝܢ	Ezekiel: 4,376 verses.
ܘܬܠܬܡܐܐ ܘܫܒ̈ܥܝܢ ܘܫܬܐ:	
ܐܣܬܝܪ: ܦܬܓܡ̈ܐ ܫܬܡܐܐ	Esther: 650 verses.
ܘܚܡܫܝܢ: ܥܙܪܐ ܦܬܓܡ̈ܐ ܬܪ̈ܝܢ	Ezra:[32] 2,308 verses.
ܐܠܦܝܢ ܘܬܠܬܡܐܐ ܘܬܡܢܝܐ	
ܣܦܪܐ ܩܕܡܝܐ ܕܡܟܒܝܐ:	First Book of Maccabees: 2,766 verses.
ܦܬܓܡ̈ܐ ܬܪ̈ܝܢ ܐ̈ܠܦܝܢ ܘܫܒܥܡܐܐ	
ܘܫ̈ܬܝܢ ܘܫܬܐ: ܣܦܪܐ ܕܬܪ̈ܝܢ	
ܕܡܟܒܝܐ: ܦܬܓܡ̈ܐ ܚܡܫܐ ܐܠܦܝܢ	Second Book of Maccabees: 5,600 verses.[33]
ܘܫ̈ܬܡܐܐ: ܝܗܘܕܝܬ ܦܬܓܡ̈ܐ	Judith:[34] 1,268 verses.
ܐܠܦ ܘܡܐ̈ܬܝܢ ܘܫ̈ܬܝܢ ܘܬܡܢܝܐ:	
ܚܟܡܬܐ ܪܒܬܐ ܦܬܓܡ̈ܐ ܐܠܦ	The Great Wisdom:[35] 1,550 verses.
ܘܚ̈ܡܫܡܐܐ ܘܚ̈ܡܫܝܢ: ܒܪ ܐܣܝܪܐ:	Bar Sira: 2,550 verses.
ܦܬܓܡ̈ܐ ܬܪ̈ܝܢ ܐ̈ܠܦܝܢ ܘܚ̈ܡܫܡܐܐ:	
ܘܚ̈ܡܫܝܢ: ܟܠܗ̇ ܕܥܬܝܩܬܐ ܕܝܬܝܩܬܐ	The total of the Old Testament: 71,574 verses.[36]
ܐ̈ܠܦܐ ܫ̈ܒܥܝܢ ܘܚܕ ܘܚ̈ܡܫܡܐܐ	
ܘܫܒܥܝܢ ܘܐܪܒܥܐ ܦܬܓ̈ܡܝܢ: ܐܘܢܓܠܝܘܢ	
ܕܡܬܝ، ܦܬܓܡ̈ܐ ܬܪ̈ܝܢ ܐ̈ܠܦܝܢ	Gospel of Matthew: 2,522 verses.
ܘܚ̈ܡܫܡܐܐ ܘܥܣ̈ܪܝܢ ܘܬܪ̈ܝܢ܀	
ܐܘܢܓܠܝܘܢ ܕܡܪܩܘܣ: ܦܬ̈ܓܡܐ	Gospel of Mark: 1,675 verses.
ܐܠܦ ܘܫ̈ܬܡܐܐ ܘܫ̈ܒܥܝܢ ܘܚܡܫܐ:	
ܐܘܢܓܠܝܘܢ ܕܠܘܩܐ: ܦܬ̈ܓܡܐ ܬܠܬܐ	Gospel of Luke: 3,083 verses.
ܐܠܦܝܢ ܘܬܡܢܝܢ ܘܬܠܬܐ: ܐܘܢܓܠܝܘܢ	
ܕܝܘܚܢܢ ܦܬܓܡ̈ܐ ܐܠܦ ܘܫܒܥܡܐܐ	Gospel of John: 1,737 verses.
ܘܬ̈ܠܬܝܢ ܘܫܒܥܐ: ܟܠܗ ܐܘܢܓܠܝܘܢ:	The total of the Gospels: 9,218 verses.[37]
ܦܬܓܡ̈ܐ ܬܫܥܐ ܐܠܦܝܢ ܘܡܐ̈ܬܝܢ	
ܘܬܡܢܬܥܣܪ: ܦܪܟܣܝܣ ܕܫܠܝ̈ܚܐ	Acts of the Apostles: 2,720 verses.
ܦܬܓܡ̈ܐ ܬܪ̈ܝܢ ܐܠܦܝܢ ܘܫܒܥܡܐܐ:	
ܘܥܣ̈ܪܝܢ ܕܦܘܠܘܣ ܫܠܝܚܐ ܐ ܓܪ̈ܬܐ	Of Paul the Apostle
ܕ ܓܠܛܝܐ ܦܬܓܡ̈ܐ ܡܐ̈ܬܝܢ ܘܫ̈ܬܝܢ	Letter of the Galatians:[38] 265 verses.
ܚܡܫܐ: ܕܩܘܪܢܬܝܐ ܩܕܡܝܬܐ	Of the Corinthians, first: 946 verses.
ܦܬܓܡ̈ܐ ܬܫܥܡܐܐ ܘܐܪ̈ܒܥܝܢ ܘܫܬܐ:	

[32] This book is probably Ezra–Nehemiah, as the larger number of verses in this list may indicate the combined work. Furthermore, MS 7a1 contains no break between Ezra and Nehemiah (280v) and the colophon at the end of Ezra–Nehemiah calls the work 'the book of Ezra the scribe' (286v). Cf. the manuscript contents of Codex Ambrosianus in ch. 6.

[33] For the discrepancy in verse numbers between the books of Maccabees, cf. n. 29 above.

[34] Although Judith appears in all complete Syriac Bible manuscripts, the sixth-century 'Book of Women' (i.e., texts of Ruth, Esther, Susanna, Judith, Thecla; MS BL, Add. 14,652 (6f1)), and a popular revision of the book was made, it was very rarely quoted or commented on in Syriac literature, and it was probably not part of the liturgy (cf. Van Rompay 2006: 205, 230n82–3). Furthermore, Isho' bar Nun (d. 828) and Isho'dad of Merv (ca. 850) showed disdain for the book and reckoned it extra-canonical (cf. ibid.: 228, 230). Therefore, its appearance among the deuterocanonical books in this list seems appropriate.

[35] That is, The Wisdom of Solomon.

[36] The protocanonical and the deuterocanonical books comprise the whole Old Testament.

[37] Markschies 2012 notes that this is a classic miscalculation, for the total is 9,017 verses (p. 132n449).

[38] Ephrem (fourth-century Syriac father) commented on the Epistles of Paul in this order. Furthermore, the first four (Galatians–1–2 Corinthians–Romans) is the order in which they appeared in Marcion's canon (cf. Metzger 1987: 221).

Text	Translation
ܩܘܪܝܢܬܝܐ ܕܬܪ̈ܬܝܢ ܦܬ̈ܓܡܐ	Of the Corinthians, second: 653 verses.
ܫ̈ܬ ܡܐܐ ܘܚܡܫܝܢ ܘܬܠܬܐ	
ܪ̈ܗܘܡܝܐ ܦܬ̈ܓܡܐ ܬܡܢܡܐܐ ܘܥܣܪܝܢ ܘܚܡܫܐ	Of the Romans: 825 verses.
ܘܐܣܪ̈ܒܝܐ ܚܬܝ̈ܬܐ ܦܬ̈ܓܡܐ ܬܡܢܡܐܐ	Of the Hebrews: 837 verses.
ܘܕܩܘܠܘܣܝܐ ܦܬ̈ܓܡܐ ܡܐܬܝܢ ܘܫܒܥܝܢ ܘܚܡܫܐ	Of the Colossians: 275 verses.
ܘܕܐܦܣܝܐ ܦܬ̈ܓܡܐ ܬܠܬܡܐܐ	
ܘܬܡܢܬܥܣܪ ܦܬ̈ܓܡܐ	Of the Ephesians: 318 verses.
ܘܕܦܝܠܝܦ̈ܣܝܐ ܦܬ̈ܓܡܐ	Of the Philippians: 318 verses.
ܬܠܬܡܐܐ ܘܬܡܢܬܥܣܪ ܕܦܝܠܝܦ̈ܣܝܐ	Of the Philippians:[39] 235 verses.
ܦܬ̈ܓܡܐ ܡܐܬܝܢ ܘܬܠܬܝܢ ܘܚܡܫܐ	
ܘܕܬܣ̈ܠܘܢܝܩܝܐ ܩܕܡܝܐ ܦܬ̈ܓܡܐ	Of the Thessalonians, first: 417 verses.
ܐܪܒܥܡܐܐ ܘܫܒܥܣܪ ܕܬܣ̈ܠܘܢܝܩܝܐ	
ܕܬܪ̈ܬܝܢ ܦܬ̈ܓܡܐ ܡܐܐ ܘܬܡܢܬܥܣܪ	Of the Thessalonians, second: 118 verses.[40]
ܠܛܝܡܬܐܘܣ ܕܬܪ̈ܬܝܢ ܦܬ̈ܓܡܐ	To Timothy, second: 114 verses.
ܘܕܛܝܛܘܣ ܦܬ̈ܓܡܐ ܡܐܐ ܘܫܬܬܥܣܪ	Of Titus: 116 verses.
ܘܕܦܝܠܝܡܘܢ ܦܬ̈ܓܡܐ ܚܡܫܝܢ ܘܬܠܬܐ	Of Philemon: 53 verses
ܘܟܠܗ ܕܫܠܝܚܐ ܦܬ̈ܓܡܐ ܚܡܫܐ	The total of the Apostle: 5,076 verses.[41]
ܐܠܦ̈ܝܢ ܘܫܒܥܝܢ ܘܫܬܐ ܟܠܗܘܢ[42]	
ܦܬ̈ܓܡܐ ܕܣܦܪ̈ܐ ܩ̈ܕܝܫܐ ܕܩܒܠܐ	The total of the holy books which the
ܥܕܬܐ ܩܕܝܫܬܐ ܬܫܥܝܢ ܐܠܦ̈ܝܢ ܦܬ̈ܓܡܐ	Holy church accepts: 90,000 verses.[43]

The Canon List of Syriac MS 10

The Number of the Holy Books
 Genesis
 Exodus
 Leviticus
 Numbers
 Deuteronomy
Whole Pentateuch

[39] Zahn (1900: 799ff) suggested the second instance of Philippians is a mistake for *3 Corinthians*, an apocryphal correspondence between Paul and the Corinthian church written in Greek in the late second century or early third, which became highly regarded and perhaps considered canonical in the fourth-century Syrian church. (Aphrahat and Ephrem cite the work as Scripture and the latter wrote a commentary on it; cf. Metzger 1987: 176, 182, 219; Epp 2002: 492). It was rejected by the Syrian church in the fifth century, but through the Syriac tradition it became highly regarded in the Armenian church from the fourth century, and for several centuries thereafter. However, scholars after Zahn did not follow him in this interpretation, but rather evaluated the second instance of Philippians as a copyist error. Thus the repetition of Philippians is also probably not an unattested, extra-canonical second Philippians (Markschies 2012, 131). Metzger (1987) notes that 'the fact that the first mention of Philippians is assigned the same number of stichoi as is Ephesians, immediately preceding, seems to be proof of parablepsis resulting in dittography' (p. 221n27).

[40] Either 1 Timothy was omitted due to parablepsis resulting in haplography (cf. Markschies 2012: 131) or the mistake of writing Philippians twice influenced the omission of 1 Timothy (cf. Metzger 1987: 221).

[41] The actual total is 5,590 verses. Romans and 2 Timothy are calculated too low (cf. Markschies 2012: 133n450).

[42] The form with a double set of seyame is curious and may be an error in the Harris/Smith Lewis transcription.

[43] Ninety thousand verses appears to be a round number, since the actual total of verses from the end of each book is 94,404 (cf. Haelewyck 2008: 149n32).

Joshua
Judges
Samuel
Book of Kings
Ruth
David   (= Psalms)
Book of Chronicles
Job
Proverbs
The Twelve
Isaiah
Jeremiah
Lamentations
Daniel
Ezekiel
Esther
Ezra   (= Ezra–Nehemiah)
1 Maccabees
2 Maccabees
Judith
Wisdom of Solomon
Son of Sirach
The Whole Old Testament
    Gospel of Matthew
    Gospel of Mark
    Gospel of Luke
    Gospel of John
Total Gospels
Acts of the Apostles
Of Paul the Apostle
    Letter of Galatians
    Of the Corinthians, first
    Of the Corinthians, second
    Of the Romans
    Of the Hebrews
    Of the Colossians
    Of the Ephesians
    Of the Philippians
    [Of the Philippians]
    Of the Thessalonians, first
    Of the Thessalonians, second
    [Of Timothy, first]
    Of Timothy, second
    Of Titus
    Of Philemon
Total of the Apostle
Total of the Holy Books which the Church Accepts

6

Selected Greek, Syriac, Latin, and Hebrew Manuscripts

INTRODUCTION

A full artefactual study of all of the relevant manuscripts is outside of the purview of the present volume.[1] Rather, we supply summaries of the manuscript situations in Greek, Syriac, Latin, and Hebrew, along with the following relatively few lists of manuscript contents for the purpose of further contextualizing the canon lists in the present volume. When relevant, we point the reader to closer studies of the MSS. These ancient manuscripts provide specific contents of Scripture, which largely overlap with the contents of the canon lists. They also provide more titles of the books and specific contents of the books under these titles (e.g. the relationship of Susanna to Daniel can be further visualized by looking at the MSS), further contributing to knowledge of the reception history of each book.[2] We do not attempt to aggregate all of the contents of all the biblical manuscripts here. Instead, only the contents of Greek whole Bible, whole Old Testament, and whole New Testament manuscripts before 1000 CE have been included. Early representative manuscripts from the Latin and Syriac traditions are included as well. The Hebrew Codex Leningrad has been included as a representative of a complete Hebrew Bible. Since the present work treats the early Christian canon lists, only the earliest complete manuscripts are germane to this study.

GREEK MANUSCRIPTS

Whole Bible: There are seven manuscripts that contain—at least, approximately—the whole Bible, Old and New Testaments:

---

[1] For an example of this type of study with reference to early Gospel MSS, see Hill 2013a.
[2] In the Introduction to this volume, we provide an example of how the wider scriptural contents of the manuscripts put the narrower contents of many of the canon lists into relief.

Codex Vaticanus (IV; B/B03).
Codex Sinaiticus (IV; S/א01).
Codex Alexandrinus (V; A/A02).
Ra 68 (XV).
Ra 106 (XIV; without Psalms).
Ra 122 (XV).
Ra 130 (XII/XIII; without Psalms).[3]
Old Testament: There are two Greek manuscripts which contain the whole Old Testament:
Codex Venetus (VIII; V; without Psalms).[4]
Ra 46 (XIII/XIV; without Psalms).
New Testament: There are fifty-seven complete manuscripts of the New Testament (three majuscules and fifty-four minuscules).[5] There are seventy-two NT MSS that do not contain the Gospels and one minuscule (886) that contains everything except the Catholic Epistles.[6] In addition to א01, A02, and B03, only two complete NT MSS from the first millennium CE survive:
Codex Ephraemi Rescriptus (V; C/C04).[7]
Minuscule 1424 (IX/X).

Whole Greek Bible

We include these codices under whole bibles since they were designed to be such, even if that label no longer applies.

---

[3] See *Offizielles Verzeichnis der Rahlfs-Sigeln: Herausgegeben vom Septuaginta-Unternehmen der Akademie der Wissenschaften zu Göttingen* (2012), <http://rep.adw-goe.de/bitstream/handle/11858/00-001S-0000-0022-A30C-8/Rahlfs-Sigeln_Stand_Dezember_2012.pdf?sequence=1>.

[4] Codex V is actually composed of two separate manuscripts believed to have originally been one copy of the whole Old Testament: Bibl. Vat., Vat. gr. 2,106 and Bibl. Marc., Gr. 1. Cf. Rahlfs 1915: 339; 270–2. Because the current form of the MS ends with Gospel canon tables, scholars believe that the MS originally contained the New Testament but that part of the MS was lost when the larger work was divided into smaller sections.

[5] Elliott 2015: 576. He does not include B03 in this number. There were fifty-eight complete minuscule NT manuscripts, but four of these were removed from the *Liste* when the sections containing Revelation were renumbered (180 = 2918, 209 = 2920, 1668 = 2909, and 1040 = 2041).

[6] ibid.: 577.

[7] This manuscript is a palimpsest; the fifth-century NT text was 'erased in the twelfth century and was reused for a Greek translation of thirty-eight tractates by Ephraem' (Aland and Aland 1995: 109). The original order of the books appears to have been Gospels, Acts–Catholic Epistles, Paul, and Revelation (ibid.: 1995: 109). The manuscript contains parts of the following OT books: Job, Proverbs, Ecclesiastes, Song of Songs, Wisdom, and Sirach.

Codex Vaticanus	Codex Sinaiticus[8]	Codex Alexandrinus
Genesis According to the Seventy		Genesis of the *Kosmos*
Exodus		Exodus from Egypt/Exodus of the Sons of Israel out of Egypt
Leviticus		Leviticus
Numbers		Numbers
Deuteronomy		Deuteronomy
Joshua son of Naue		Joshua son of Naue
Judges		Judges
Ruth		Ruth
Of Kingdoms 1		Of Kingdoms 1
Of Kingdoms 2		Of Kingdoms 2
Of Kingdoms 3		Of Kingdoms 3
Of Kingdoms 4		Of Kingdoms 4
Paraleipomenon 1	Paraleipomenon 1[9]	Paraleipomenon of the Kings/
	Esdras B Esther	Kingdoms of Judah 1[10]
Paraleipomenon 2	Tobit[11]	Paraleipomenon of the Kingdoms of Judah 2
Esdras A	Judith[12]	Hosea (1)[13]
Esdras B[14]	Maccabees 1	Amos (2)
Psalms/Book of 150 Psalms[15]	Maccabees 4	Micah (3)
Proverbs	Isaiah	Joel (4)
Ecclesiastes	Jeremiah[16]	Obadiah (5)
Song	Joel (4)[17]	Jonah (6)
Job	Obadiah (5)	Nahum (7)
Wisdom of Solomon	Jonah (6)	Habakkuk (8)
Wisdom of Sirach/Wisdom of Jesus son of Sirach[18]	Nahum (7)	Zephaniah (9)
Esther	Habakkuk (8)	Haggai (10)

[8] The beginning of the manuscript is defective, missing more than thirty-three quires. Parts of the middle of the manuscript are missing also. Cf. Jongkind 2007 for analysis of the MS and its scribes. For the story of the MS, see Parker 2010, and for differing perspectives on the MS, see the recent collection of essays in McKendrick, Parker, Myshrall, O'Hogan 2015.

[9] 9:27–11:22. No title of the book is extant in the manuscript. The missing contents before and after this short section are not clear.

[10] Page 241 has 'Of Kings'. Page 256 has 'Of Kingdoms'.

[11] 2:2–14:15. Fol. 7r contains the title 'Tobeith'. The concluding title, Tobeith, appears on fol. 8r.

[12] 1:1–9:13, 13:9–16:25.

[13] The MS numbers all sixteen prophets (Hosea–Daniel).

[14] Esdras B is Ezra–Nehemiah, counted as a single book. There is no paratextual marker or separate column or division for the start of Nehemiah on p. 607 of the MS. This situation in the MS confirms the references in our lists to a single Esdras B without internal divisions.

[15] At the beginning of the book is the simple title 'Psalms' (p. 625), while on p. 713 after Psalm 150 in a half-empty column is the fuller title 'Book of 150 Psalms' (p. 713). Psalm 151 appears on the top of p. 714 before the book of Proverbs.

[16] 1:1–10:25. Lamentations follows Jeremiah (Quire 49 fol. 7v). The placement of Baruch and the Epistle cannot be determined.

[17] As with Vaticanus, the scribe numbered the Twelve Prophets. Hosea, Amos, and Micah have fallen out of the manuscript.

[18] The fuller title occurs at the end of the book in the manuscript (p. 832).

Codex Vaticanus	Codex Sinaiticus	Codex Alexandrinus
Judith	Zephaniah (9)	Zechariah (11)
Tobit	Haggai (10)	Malachi (12)
Hosea (1)[19]	Zechariah (11)	Isaiah (13)
Amos (2)	Malachi (12)[20]	Jeremiah (14)[21]
Micha (3)	151 Psalms of David[22]	Baruch[23]
Joel (4)	Proverbs/Proverbs of	Lamentations[24]
Obadiah (5)	Solomon	Epistle of Jeremiah[25]
Jonah (6)	Ecclesiastes	Ezekiel (15)
Nahum (7)	Song of Songs	Daniel (16)[26]
Habakkuk (8)	Wisdom of Solomon	Esther
Zephaniah (9)	Wisdom of Jesus son of Sirach	Tobit
Haggai (10)	Job	Judith
Zechariah (11)		Esdras A[27]
Malachi (12)		Esdras B[28]
Isaiah		Maccabees 1
Jeremiah		Maccabees 2
Baruch[29]		Maccabees 3
Lamentations of Jeremiah[30]		Maccabees 4

[19] The scribe numbered the Twelve Prophets. The canon lists of Gregory of Nazianzus and Amphilochius of Iconium preserve the same order of the Twelve Prophets.

[20] At the end of the book, the manuscript has 'Prophet, Angel/Messenger, Malachi (12)' (fol. 87v). For the debate among the ancients over the identity of Malachi, see the section on Amphilochius in ch. 3, p. 152n400.

[21] Though the beginnings of the books of Baruch, Lamentations, and the Epistle are placed in distinct columns and these works are assigned their own titles, they are not given additional numbers among the sixteen prophets. Implicitly, therefore, the three books are grouped with Jeremiah as some of the canon lists also present them.

[22] See the Apostolic Canons for a reference to the 151 Psalms of David.

[23] Baruch is placed in a new, separate column from Jeremiah, with its own title.

[24] Lamentations begins in a separate column from Baruch and is given its own title.

[25] The Epistle begins in a separate column from Lamentations and is given its own title.

[26] On p. 128, the book bears the title 'Daniel' and begins with what we know to be 'Susanna' (ch. 1 according to the MS). On p. 129, the book we know as 'Daniel' begins with ch. 2. Bel and the Dragon is assigned ch. 12 and begins a new column of the work of Daniel (p. 141). On p. 142, at the end of Bel, the MS has 'End of Daniel the Prophet'. The manuscript contains one work, 'Daniel the Prophet'. The three works—Susanna, Bel and the Dragon, and Daniel—are an integrated whole in the MS.

[27] On p. 168, the beginning of this work is called ὁ ἱερεύς, 'the priest'. But at the end of the work, it is called 'Ezras'.

[28] The beginning of Esdras B is called ἱερεύς, 'priest' (perhaps the definite article 'the' has been accidentally omitted). The title at the end of the book is Esdras B. Esdras B is the literal translation of Ezra–Nehemiah, and the start of Nehemiah is signalled in the MS by placing 'The words of Nehemiah, son of Achalia' on two lines shorter than all the others, indicating a division (p. 178). This approach contrasts with the earlier one noted in Vaticanus (n. 14 above), where no division between Ezra and Nehemiah was indicated. Since the division between Ezra and Nehemiah in Alexandrinus is minor and the title at the beginning and the end of the work assumes one work, the scribe still intended to convey that Esdras B is one book.

[29] On p. 1127 of the MS, there is a clear ending to Jeremiah and Baruch begins on a new column with a separate title.

[30] On p. 1133 of the MS, there is a mostly empty column where Baruch ends and Lamentations begins on the next column.

Codex Vaticanus	Codex Sinaiticus	Codex Alexandrinus
Epistle of Jeremiah[31]		Athanasius, Epistle to
Ezekiel		Marcellinus
Daniel[32]		Eusebius, Hypothesis of Psalms
		Psalms 150 and
		Autobiographical Psalm 1[33]
		Odes
		Job
		Proverbs
		Ecclesiastes
		Song of Songs
		Wisdom of Solomon
		Wisdom of Jesus son of Sirach
According to Matthew	According to Matthew	Gospel According to Matthew
According to Mark	According to Mark/Gospel According to Mark	Gospel According to Mark
According to Luke	According to Luke/Gospel According to Luke	Gospel According to Luke
According to John	According to John/Gospel According to John	Gospel According to John
Acts of the Apostles	Romans/To the Romans	Acts of the Holy Apostles
James	To the Corinthians 1	Epistle of James
1 Peter	To the Corinthians 2	Of Peter 1
2 Peter	To the Galatians	Of Peter 2
1 John	To the Ephesians	Of John 1
2 John	To the Philippians	Of John 2
3 John	To the Colossians	Of John 3
Jude	To the Thessalonians 1	Epistle of Jude[34]
To the Romans	To the Thessalonians 2	To the Romans
To the Corinthians 1	To the Hebrews	To the Corinthians 1
To the Corinthians 2	To Timothy 1	To the Corinthians 2
Galatians	To Timothy 2	To the Galatians
Ephesians	To Titus	To the Ephesians
Philippians	To Philemon	To the Philippians
Colossians	Acts/Acts of the Apostles	To the Colossians
1 Thessalonians	Epistle of James	To the Thessalonians 1
2 Thessalonians	Epistle of Peter 1 / Of Peter 1	To the Thessalonians 2

[31] On p. 1139 of the MS, there is a break at the end of Lamentations. The Epistle begins on the top of p. 1140.

[32] Daniel begins on p. 1206 with Susanna. On p. 1209, the book of Daniel begins without break between Susanna and itself. There is no superscription for Bel and the Dragon on p. 1232 of the MS that would set it apart from the work of Daniel. Rather, the book is an integrated unity according to the MS.

[33] The title at the beginning of the work is 'Psalter'. The end of the book of Psalms has this extended title 'Psalms 150 and the Autobiographical Psalm 1'. The superscription of Psalm 151 says that 'this Psalm is autobiographical' (οὗτος ὁ ψαλμὸς ἰδιόγραφος), so the title of the book at the end of the book includes a reference to the one autobiographical psalm. Preceding the book of Psalms there are canons/lists for morning and evening Psalms. The book is followed by the collection known as the Odes.

[34] After Jude, the note in the MS says, 'Acts of the Holy Epistles and Catholic [Epistles]' (fol. 84v). The scribe or compiler of these books considered them a unit.

Codex Vaticanus	Codex Sinaiticus	Codex Alexandrinus
Hebrews[35]	Of Peter 2	To the Hebrews
	Epistle of John 1/Of John 1	To Timothy 1
	Of John 2	To Timothy 2
	Of John 3	To Titus
	Jude	To Philemon
	Revelation of John	Revelation of John
	Epistle of Barnabas	Epistle of Clement to the
	Shepherd of Hermas[36]	Corinthians (1 Clement)
		Epistle of Clement 2[37]
		[Psalms of Solomon][38]

Whole Greek Old Testament

Codex Venetus
[Genesis]
[Exodus]
Leviticus
Numbers
Deuteronomy
Joshua/Joshua of Naue
Judges
Ruth
Of Kingdoms 1
Of Kingdoms 2
Of Kingdoms 3
Of Kingdoms 4
Paraleipomenon 1
Paraleipomenon 2
Esther
Esdras A
Esdras B[39]
Book of Job
Proverbs of Solomon

[35] The manuscript breaks off at Hebrews 9:14 ($\kappa a \theta a$), and a much later scribe added $-\rho\iota\epsilon\iota$ (completing the previous word) all the way to the end of Hebrews. The manuscript probably also originally contained 1–2 Timothy, Titus, and Philemon (cp. Sinaiticus), but these books are no longer extant. Revelation now appears in the manuscript in a later hand, perhaps added by the same fifteenth-century scribe who finished Hebrews. Whether the manuscript originally contained Revelation is an open question, given the nature of the disputes over this book in the fourth century.

[36] 1:1–27:6; 28:5–30:3.

[37] This title is not found on fol. 143r where the book begins, but in the table of contents of the manuscript at the front of Royal MS 1.v

[38] The book is not extant in the manuscript itself, but the initial table of contents of the manuscript lists Psalms of Solomon as the last book of the codex. Either it has fallen out or the compiler of the book never included it as originally planned.

[39] On fol. 131a, there is a minor border between Ezra and Nehemiah in the book of Esdras B, and the title 'The Words of Nehemiah son of Achalia' appears.

Codex Venetus

Ecclesiastes
Songs of Songs which is by Solomon/Song of Songs
Wisdom of Solomon
Wisdom of Jesus, son of Sirach
Hosea
Amos
Joel
Obadiah
Jonah
Micah
Nahum
Habakkuk
Zephaniah
Haggai
Zechariah
Malachi
Isaiah
Jeremiah
Baruch[40]
Lamentations of Jeremiah
Epistle of Jeremiah
Ezekiel
Daniel
Daniel (Susanna-Bel and the Dragon)[41]
Tobit
Judith
Maccabees 1
Maccabees 2
Maccabees 3
Maccabees 4
Chronographion from Adam to Justinian
Letter of Eusebius to Carpianus and Gospel Canons

Whole Greek New Testament

Codex Ephraemi Rescriptus[42]	Minuscule 1424[43]
Gospel According to Matthew	Gospel According to Mathew. Amen.[44]
Gospel According to Mark	Gospel According to Mark/End of the Gospel According to Mark[45]

---

[40] On p. 94 of the MS, there is a clear break between the end of Jeremiah and the beginning of Baruch.

[41] The title of Susanna is Daniel in the MS. There is no division between Susanna and Bel on fol. 125. Thus they appear as one integrated work in the MS.

[42] For images of the manuscript, see <http://www.csntm.org/Manuscript/View/GA_04>.

[43] For images of the manuscript, see <http://www.csntm.org/Manuscript/View/GA_1424>.

[44] Fol. 54v.   [45] Fol. 56r; fol. 83r.

Codex Ephraemi Rescriptus	Minuscule 1424
Gospel According to Luke	Gospel According to Luke/End of the Gospel According to Luke[46]
Gospel According to John	Gospel According to John/End of the Gospel According to John[47]
Acts of the Apostles	Acts of the Apostles of Luke the Evangelist/Acts of the Holy Apostles[48]
James	Catholic Epistle of the Holy Apostle James/Epistle of the Holy Apostle James[49]
1 Peter	Catholic Epistle of Peter 1/Catholic Epistle of Apostle Peter 1[50]
2 Peter	Catholic Epistle of the Holy Peter 2/Epistle of Holy Apostle Peter 2[51]
1 John	Epistle of John 1/Epistle of John the Evangelist[52]
[2 John][53]	Catholic Epistle of John 2/Catholic Epistle of Holy John, the Theologian, 2[54]
3 John	Catholic Epistle of John 3/Catholic Epistle of Holy Apostle John[55]
Jude	Catholic Epistle of Jude/Epistle of the Holy Apostle Jude[56]
To the Romans	Revelation of John/Revelation of the Holy John, the Theologian[57]
1 Corinthians	To the Romans[58]
2 Corinthians	To the Corinthians 1[59]
Galatians	To the Corinthians 2[60]
Ephesians	To the Galatians[61]
Philippians	To the Ephesians[62]
Colossians	To the Philippians[63]
1 Thessalonians	To the Colossians[64]
[2 Thessalonians][65]	To the Thessalonians 1[66]
1 Timothy	To the Thessalonians 2[67]
2 Timothy	To Timothy 1/First [letter] to Timothy[68]
To Titus	To Timothy 2[69]
To Philemon	To Titus[70]
To the Hebrews	To Philemon[71]
Revelation	To the Hebrews[72]

[46] Fol. 85r; fol. 130r. [47] Fol. 131r; fol. 164r. [48] Fol. 165r; fol. 206r.
[49] Fol. 206v; fol. 210r. [50] Fol. 210v; fol. 214v. [51] Fol. 214v; fol. 217r.
[52] Fol. 217v; fol. 221v.
[53] This book is not among the fragments of the codex, though surely it was originally.
[54] Fol. 221v; fol. 222r. [55] Fol. 222r; fol. 222v. [56] Fol. 222v; fol. 224r.
[57] Fol. 224r; fol. 248r. [58] Fol. 249r; fol. 265r. [59] Fol. 265v; fol. 281r.
[60] Fol. 281r; fol. 292r. [61] Fol. 292r; fol. 297r. [62] Fol. 297v; fol. 303r.
[63] Fol. 303r; fol. 305v. [64] Fol. 305v; fol. 310r.
[65] This book was not found among the fragments of the codex, but it was probably among the original contents of the manuscript.
[66] Fol. 310r; fol. 313v. [67] Fol. 313v; fol. 315r. [68] Fol. 315v; fol. 319r.
[69] Fol. 319r; fol. 322r. [70] Fol. 322r; fol. 323v.
[71] Fol. 324r; fol. 324v. [72] Fol. 324v; fol. 336r.

SYRIAC MANUSCRIPTS

Whole Bible: The so-called 'Buchanan Bible' (twelfth century; Cambridge, University Library, MS Oo. I. 1,2; 12a1 according to Peshitta Institute), named after Claudius Buchanan, who obtained it while serving as a missionary in India and brought it back to Cambridge in the nineteenth century, contains both the Old and New Testaments (Peshitta for the Old Testament and Peshitta and Philoxenian for the New Testament).[73] The OT section contains the twenty-two books of the Jewish canon plus Wisdom of Solomon, Letter of Baruch, Baruch and the Epistle of Jeremiah, Bel and the Dragon, Susanna and Judith (as parts of the Syriac book of Women), 1–4 Maccabees, Tobit, and 3 Ezra. The NT section contains the twenty-two books of the Peshitta canon (Gospels, fourteen Epistles of Paul, Acts, James, 1 Peter, and 1 John) as well as the four shorter General Epistles (2 Peter, 2–3 John, Jude) in the Philoxenian version of the sixth century and also the Harklean version of the seventh.[74] The codex ends with the Syriac six books of Clement; that is, documents mainly from the Syrian Octateuch (Gwynn 1909: xliv).[75]

Old Testament: Complete Syriac OT MSS are extremely rare due to their cumbersome nature. Normally, only one book or blocks of books were transmitted. However, there are at least eleven complete OT MSS from the seventeenth century.[76] Before the seventeenth century, there are only six complete OT MSS from the seventh century to the fifteenth century, as follows (according to the Peshitta Institute's numbering system):

7a1 (seventh century).
8a1 (eighth century).
9a1 (ninth century).
13a1 (thirteenth century; extracts only).
15a1 (fifteenth century; incomplete).
15a2 (fifteenth century; incomplete).[77]

New Testament (incomplete list): The British Museum houses the following whole New Testaments:[78]

---

[73] Hunt 1991 argues the manuscript originated in Edessa (Syria) in the early 1190s.

[74] For a description of the NT portion of the MS, see Gwynn 1909: xliv–xlv. According to Gwynn, the MS places these four epistles not in their usual order but subjoined to the three major epistles of the Peshitta. Significantly, the MS adds the following note according to Gwynn, 'The Seven Catholic Epistles of the Apostles'. On the relationship between the seventh-century Harklean to the sixth-century Philoxenian, see Brock 1981.

[75] Books 1 and 2 are the *Testament of our Lord*; book 3 is the *Apostolic Church Order*; book 4 is a short work entitled 'concerning gifts' (cp. Apos. Con. VIII. 1,2); book 5 'concerning appointments/laying on of hands' (Apos. Con. VIII.4–27); the sixth and seventh contain the 'concerning the canons'; the eighth consists of the Apostolic Canons (Wordsworth 1901: 47–8). For an English translation of the Syriac version of book 3, see Arendzen 1902.

[76] Brock 2013: 52. See p. 54 for the contents of some of these MSS.

[77] ibid.: 55. For a listing of the contents of some of these MSS, see ibid.: 56–7.

[78] See Wright 1870 1871 1872 *ad loc.*

Add. 14,470 (fifth/sixth century; Peshitta).
Add. 14,448 (1012; Peshitta).
Add. 17,124 (1234; Harklean Gospels, Peshitta elsewhere).

All three of these MSS have twenty-two books of the traditional twenty-seven books of the New Testament, omitting 2 Peter, 2–3 John, Jude, and the Apocalypse.

The Bodleian Library at Oxford houses MS New College 333, an eleventh-century complete (Revelation?) Harklean New Testament: Matthew, Mark, Luke, John, Acts, James, 1 Peter, 2 Peter, 1 John, 2 John, 3 John, Jude, Paul's Letters (up to Hebrews 11:27).[79] Because the text of the MS ends at Hebrews 11:27 (the last of Paul's letters), we cannot be certain whether the manuscript contained Revelation or not.

Whole Syriac Old Testament

Codex Ambrosianus (7a1)[80]
Genesis
Exodus
Leviticus
Numbers
Deuteronomy
Job
Joshua[81]
Judges
Book of the Prophecy of Samuel (= 1–2 Samuel)[82]
Psalms of David
Book of Kings, also Kingdoms (= 1–2 Kings)[83]
Proverbs
Wisdom of Solomon
Ecclesiastes
Songs of Songs of Solomon
Isaiah

[79] Aland 1986: 32–3.

[80] For a complete study of this manuscript, cf. Forness 2014: 41–76.

[81] Added to this title is a formula 'Again, another writing of'. The scribe used this formula for each historical book to group the books of Joshua, Judges, Samuel, and Kings as a collection even though other books such as Psalms come between them. Cf. ibid.: 52.

[82] There is no new title for 2 Samuel on fol. 91r. On fol. 98v, after the end of 2 Samuel, the final title reads 'The book of the prophecy of Samuel is ended'.

[83] There is no new title for 2 Kings on fol. 123v. The full title at the end of the book is 'Book of Kings of Israel and of Judah' (fol. 132v).

Codex Ambrosianus (7a1)
Jeremiah
Lamentations[84]
Epistle of Jeremiah[85]
Epistle of Baruch[86]
Baruch[87]
Ezekiel
The Twelve Prophets[88]
Daniel
Bel[89]
The Dragon[90]
Ruth
Susanna
Esther
Judith
Wisdom of Bar Sira
Book of the Words of the Days (= 1–2 Chronicles)[91]
Apocalypse of Baruch[92]
4 Ezra
Ezra–Nehemiah[93]
Maccabees 1
Maccabees 2
Maccabees 3
Maccabees 4
Josephus, *War* VI

[84] There is no new title for Lamentations on fol. 74v. The work is integrated with Jeremiah. Compare Latin Codex Amiatinus below.

[85] The Epistle appears on fol. 176r after a major division consisting of blank lines and three dividing borders on fol. 175v. There are five pages between Lamentations and the Epistle.

[86] Appears after a blank line and a dividing border on 176v. Baruch's Epistle forms the last ten chapters of 2 Baruch.

[87] Appears after a dividing border on 177v.

[88] The MS has the title the Twelve Prophets (fol. 194v) and it signals the divisions between them with blank spaces and decorative borders. In the following order: Hosea ('The first prophecy of Hosea'; fol. 194v), Joel ('prophecy of Joel'; fol. 196v), Amos ('prophecy of Amos'; fol. 197v), Obadiah ('prophecy of Obadiah'; fol. 199r), Jonah ('prophecy of Jonah'; fol. 199v), Micah ('prophecy of Micah'; fol. 200r), Nahum ('prophecy of Nahum'; fol. 201r), Habakkuk ('prophecy of Habakkuk'; fol. 201v), Zephaniah ('prophecy of Zephaniah'; fol. 202r), Haggai ('prophecy of Haggai'; fol. 203r), Zechariah ('prophecy of Zechariah'; fol. 203v), and Malachi ('prophecy of Malachi'; fol. 206r).

[89] On fol. 212r, six blank lines and a new title separate Bel from Daniel.

[90] On fol. 212v, three blank lines and new title separate Bel from the Dragon.

[91] There is no new title or blank space indicating a separate work for 2 Chronicles on fol. 246r.

[92] Forness 2014 has shown that the books from Chronicles to Josephus's *War* VI proceed chronologically from the return of the Babylonian exile to the destruction of the city and should not be interpreted as an appendix of disputed books as Beckwith (1985: 195–6) and others have done (p. 59; cf. esp. pp. 55–6).

[93] There is no break between Ezra and Nehemiah on fol. 280v. The colophon at the end of Ezra–Nehemiah says, 'the writing of the book of Ezra the scribe is ended' (fol. 286v). The title of the beginning of the work is 'the second speech of the very same Ezra' (fol. 277r). Presumably, this title links this work with the preceding 4 Ezra ('The first speech of Ezra' according to its colophon). 1 Esdras or Esdras A does not appear in the MS.

Whole Syriac New Testament

BL Add. 14,470[94]
Matthew
Mark
Luke
John
Romans
1 Corinthians
2 Corinthians
Galatians
Ephesians
Philippians
Colossians
1 Thessalonians
2 Thessalonians
1 Timothy
2 Timothy
Titus
Philemon
Hebrews
Acts of the Apostles
James
1 Peter
1 John

LATIN MANUSCRIPTS

Whole Bible: The following list of whole Latin Bibles comes from Houghton 2016.[95] It does not include those entries that consist of 'Parts' of multi-volume Bibles. Only complete MSS are listed here. Whole Bibles containing the Vetus Latina (i.e. Old Latin) tradition (in all cases these VL MSS contain some Vulgate tradition for some books) are as follows:

Codex Sangermanensis (primus) (ca. 810; second volume of Latin Bible containing Odes, Wisdom Literature, Old Testament Apocrypha, New Testament, and beginning of the Shepherd of Hermas).[96]

Codex Gigas or Gigas librorum (ca. 1204–27; Bible and other texts, New Testament; includes Laodiceans).[97]

Biblia de Rosas, Bible de Roda (ca. 1050; Old and New Testaments; includes Laodiceans).[98]

---

[94] In lieu of seeing the manuscript, the contents are from Wright 1870: 40.
[95] For information specific to Anglo-Saxon England, see Marsden 1998.
[96] Houghton 2016: 213–14.   [97] ibid.: 233.   [98] ibid.: 237.

Palimpsestus Legionensis (seventh century; palimpsested tenth century; remains of a Latin Bible).[99]

Codex Gothicus Legionensis or Codex Biblicus Legionensis (960; Old and New Testaments; including Laodiceans).[100]

Three-volume Bible with Old and New Testaments (1162).[101]

Two-volume Bible with Old and New Testaments (twelfth century).[102]

Codex Complutensis primus, First Bible of Alcala (927; Old and New Testaments; includes Laodiceans).[103]

Whole Bibles containing the Vulgate tradition are as follows:

Codex Amiatinus (beginning of eighth century; Old and New Testaments; see specific contents and more bibliography below).[104]

Codex Cavensis or Biblia de Danila (ninth century, as early as 810, but usually dated to after 850; Old and New Testaments [Baruch is in the Old Latin tradition]; includes Laodiceans).[105]

Bible (beginning of ninth century; Old and New Testaments; Revelation is missing).[106]

Codex Grandivallensis, Moutier-Grandval Bible, Codex Carolinus (Bible of Charlemagne) (first half of ninth century; Old and New Testaments).[107]

Bible (ca. 800; Old and New Testaments; oldest complete pandect from Tours).[108]

Codex Vallicellianus (ca. 850; Old and New Testaments).[109]

Codex Hubertianus (ninth or tenth century; Old and New Testaments).[110]

Codex Toletanus (ca. 950; Old and New Testaments; includes Laodiceans).[111]

Codex Sarisburiensis, Bible of William of Hales (1254; Old and New Testaments).[112]

Codex Theodulfianus, Codex Mesmianus, Mesmes Bible (ca. 800; Old and New Testaments).[113]

New Testament: The following list of whole Latin New Testaments comes from Houghton 2016. Whole New Testaments containing the Vetus Latina (i.e. Old Latin) tradition (in all cases these VL MSS contain some Vulgate tradition for some books) are as follows:

Codex Colbertinus (twelfth century; Gospels, Acts, Catholic Epistles, Revelation, Paul; includes Laodiceans).[114]

---

[99] ibid.: 240. [100] ibid.: 249. [101] ibid.: 249. [102] ibid.: 250.
[103] ibid.: 251. [104] ibid.: 254–5. [105] ibid.: 255. [106] ibid.: 262.
[107] ibid.: 263. [108] ibid.: 263. [109] ibid.: 264. [110] ibid.: 269.
[111] ibid.: 277. [112] ibid.: 278. [113] ibid.: 280. [114] ibid.: 213.

Codex Perpinianensis (latter twelfth century; Gospels, Acts, Paul, Catholic, and Revelation).[115]

Codex Wernigerodensis (latter fourteenth century; Gospels, Paul, Acts, Catholic, Revelation; includes Laodiceans).[116]

Liber Ardmachanus; Book of Armagh (ca. 807/8; Gospels, Paul, Catholic, Revelation, and Acts; includes Laodiceans and other hagiographical material).[117]

Whole New Testaments containing the Vulgate tradition are as follows:

Codex Fuldensis or Victor Codex (546; Gospel harmony, rest of New Testament; includes Laodiceans).[118]

Whole Latin Bible

Codex Amiatinus[119]

Old Testament
Genesis
Exodus
Leviticus
Numbers
Deuteronomy
Joshua Naue
Judges
Ruth
Kings 1–2[120]
Kings 3–4[121]
Paralipomenon 1–2[122]
Psalms[123]
Proverbs
Ecclesiastes
Song of Songs
Wisdom of Solomon
Ecclesiasticus of Solomon[124]
Isaiah

---

[115] ibid.: 234.   [116] ibid.: 236.   [117] ibid.: 237.   [118] ibid.: 256–7.

[119] Images of the MS were accessed online here: <http://mss.bmlonline.it/s.aspx?Id=AVTm-15y8phJAZQc8z_X#/book>. For a study of the history of the MS, see Meyvaert 1996.

[120] The second book of Kings is not mentioned explicitly on fol. 221r, but 2 Kings is included. The incipit also includes the note that this book 'is named Samuel in the Hebrew'.

[121] The book of Third and Fourth Kings (fol. 276v). These books are called Malachim 'Kings' in the Hebrew. Third Kings ends on fol. 303v with '*finit*', and Fourth Kings begins on the following folio (304r).

[122] Paralipomenon (1–2 Chronicles) is treated as one book (fol. 329v).

[123] Psalm 151 is included with the superscription that notes that it is 'outside of the number' (fol. 418r).

[124] Title according to fol. 460v.

Codex Amiatinus

Jeremiah–Lamentations[125]
Ezekiel
Daniel[126]
The Twelve Prophets[127]
Job
Tobit
Judith
Esther[128]
Ezra–Nehemiah[129]
1 Maccabees
2 Maccabees
New Testament
Matthew
Mark
Luke
John
Acts of the Apostles
Romans
1 Corinthians
2 Corinthians
Galatians
Ephesians
Philippians
Colossians
1 Thessalonians
2 Thessalonians
1 Timothy
2 Timothy

[125] On fol. 538r, the chapter titles list Lamentations as part of the chapters of Jeremiah. On fol. 586r, Lamentations is integrated with Jeremiah with the first part of verse 1 coloured in red. Baruch and the Epistle of Jeremiah are not incorporated into Jeremiah, or included in the MS.

[126] On fol. 637v, the MS notes in red ink that the following text (Daniel 3:24–90 with the Hymn of the Three Young Men) is not found in the Hebrew books, and on fol. 639r, the text is noted to have come from the version of Theodotion. On fol. 648r, the MS indicates with a heading in red ink that up to this point the text has been from the Hebrew version, but the rest of the book from here to the end is translated from the version of Theodotion. The rest of the book contains what are called Susanna and Bel and the Dragon (i.e. Daniel 13–14 in the Catholic Bible).

[127] The Twelve Prophets are introduced on fol. 650v. They each have their own heading in the following order: Hosea, Joel, Amos, Obadiah, Jonah, Micah, Nahum, Habakkuk, Zephaniah, Haggai, Zechariah, and Malachi.

[128] The MS includes the additions to Esther that are not found in the Hebrew at the end of the protocanonical version of the book, thus following Jerome's procedure of gathering the additions and placing them after Esther 10. Jerome prefixed a note to these additions, signalling that the Hebrew book does not include them, and explaining that he marks them with an obelus (indicating misplaced text). This note can be read in the edition of the Vulgate edited by Weber and Gryson (2007: 724), and the same edition prints the obeli before each line of this additional material. Codex Amiatinus contains this same note from Jerome, preceding the additions, at fol. 726v. However, the MS contains no obeli in this section.

[129] The MS does not contain Esdras A and Esdras B of the Old Latin (= Septuagint) tradition, only Ezra and Nehemiah, as one book, of the Hebrew tradition.

Codex Amiatinus
Titus
Philemon
Hebrews
James
1 Peter
2 Peter
1 John
2 John
3 John
Jude
Revelation of John

HEBREW BIBLE MANUSCRIPT

Codex Leningrad[130]
Torah–Law
Genesis[131]
Exodus
Leviticus
Numbers
Deuteronomy
Neviim–Prophets
Joshua
Judges
Samuel[132]
Kings[133]
Isaiah
Jeremiah
Ezekiel
Hosea[134]
Joel
Amos
Obadiah
Jonah
Micah
Nahum
Habakkuk

[130] The MS can be accessed online here: <https://archive.org/details/Leningrad_Codex>. The colophon of the MS dates the MS to 1008 CE.

[131] The titles for each book are the traditional ones. There are no titles at the heads of these books within the manuscript. Rather, the Hebrew titles of each book are listed at the end of each of the three sections of the Hebrew Bible: Torah (fols 120r–121r), Neviim (fols 326r–327r), and Ketuvim (fols 463r–464r).

[132] There is no new title or Masoretic note between 1 Samuel and 2 Samuel on fol. 168r. Samuel ends on fol. 184r. The same is true for 1 Kings and 2 Kings.

[133] Kings ends on fol. 221v.

[134] They are referred to as תרי עשר 'The Twelve' at the end of the Neviim section.

Codex Leningrad
Zephaniah
Haggai
Zechariah
Malachi
Ketuvim–Writings
Chronicles
Psalms
Job
Proverbs
Ruth
Song of Songs
Ecclesiastes
Lamentations
Esther[135]
Daniel
Ezra[136]

---

[135] 'The Scroll of Esther' on fol. 464r.

[136] There is no division between Ezra and Nehemiah on fol. 454r. In the Hebrew tradition, there is only one book: Ezra.

Antilegomena and the More Prominent Apocrypha

This appendix contains basic information regarding certain disputed writings, whether writings that eventually did become canonical (e.g., Ecclesiastes, Esther, Hebrews) or writings that did not (e.g., the Epistle of Barnabas, the Apocalypse of Peter), or writings that became canonical for only some Christian traditions (e.g., Tobit, Jubilees). The term 'antilegomena' was used by some ancient authors—Eusebius, for example—to describe writings that had a 'disputed' reception. We use the term here in the same sense, though we include within the category more writings than Eusebius mentioned. We also use the term 'apocrypha'—another ancient descriptor of certain writings[1]—to encompass those works that did not enjoy the type of reception that may have led to their inclusion within the mainstream ('catholic') Christian biblical canon, but they enjoyed enough popularity that some church fathers felt the need to point out that the writing in question was not genuine or canonical (e.g., the Gospel of Thomas, the Acts of Paul). There are many early Christian apocrypha, and so here we take note of only the most prominent examples (i.e., those most often discussed, whether in antiquity or modern times).

The works appear below in alphabetical order. We give a basic description of each work and point readers to translations and more extensive discussions. In some cases, we also provide more detail about the reception of the work in Antiquity, including the authors who cited the work and its manuscript attestation. The coverage here is admittedly uneven. In regard to those books that have been accepted by Jews, Protestants, and Catholics, the reader will often find additional relevant discussion in chapter 1.

Barnabas, Epistle of

The Epistle of Barnabas is an early Christian text largely concerned with the allegorical interpretation of the Jewish Torah.[2] Scholars commonly locate its origins in Egypt around the year 130. The first writer to mention Barnabas was Clement of Alexandria, who wrote a commentary on it in his lost *Hypotyposies* (according to Eusebius, *Hist. eccl.* 6.14.1). Clement cites 'the apostle Barnabas' in his *Stromata* several times.[3] Origen included Barnabas within a series of scriptural citations at *Princ.* 3.2.4, and he calls it a 'catholic epistle' at *Cels.* 1.63.[4] Eusebius located Barnabas among the *antilegomena* and

---

[1] Some ancient writings presented themselves as 'secret teachings', using the word *apocrypha* ('secret', 'hidden') in a positive sense (cf. Hill 2013a: 313–16); detractors of such writings often used the term *apocrypha* in a negative sense (Brakke 1994: 413–14; Gallagher 2014a).

[2] For basic orientation, see Carleton Paget 2007. For text and English translation, see Holmes 2007: 370–441. On the reception, see Carleton Paget 1994: 248–58.

[3] *Strom.* 2.6.31.2 (cf. Barn. 1.5; 2.2); 2.7.35.5 (cf. Barn. 4.11); 2.20.116.3–117.4 (cf. Barn. 16.7–9); cf. Eusebius, *Hist. eccl.* 6.13.6; and see Carleton Paget 1994: 3n1.

[4] See further allusions in *Hom. Luc.* 35; *Comm. Rom.* 1.6.1:18.

notha (*Hist. eccl.* 3.25.4; similar at 6.13.6; 6.14.1). Didymus the Blind mentioned Barnabas four times.[5] Jerome considered the attribution to Barnabas, the companion of Paul, to be authentic, but he also labelled the work an *apocryphon* (*Vir. ill.* 6; *Comm. Ezech.* 43:19). He includes Barnabas's Hebrew names in his *Onomastica sacra*, a collection of scriptural names and their meanings. Barnabas appears in the list in Codex Claromontanus under obelus. The earliest extant manuscripts of Barnabas include Codex Sinaiticus—where Barnabas appears after John's Revelation and before the Shepherd of Hermas—and a fourth- or fifth-century Greek fragment of Barn. 9:1–6.[6] The text is also extant in Codex Hierosolymitanus (dated 1056 CE),[7] a group of nine incomplete Greek manuscripts from the eleventh to thirteenth centuries, and a Latin translation (third century?) of the first seventeen chapters.[8]

Baruch, Books of

Several books circulated in Antiquity under the name of Baruch, Jeremiah's scribe (see, e.g., Jer. 36:4): the deuterocanonical book of Baruch (1 Baruch);[9] 2 Baruch, an apocalypse preserved only in Syriac and written to encourage Jews to obey the Torah in the wake of the destruction of Jerusalem by the Romans;[10] 3 Baruch, a second-century CE apocalypse preserved in Greek and Slavonic, in which Baruch tours the heavenly realms;[11] and 4 Baruch, also known as the *Paraleipomena Jeremiou*, a second-century composition, possibly originally Greek, preserved in Greek (dozens of manuscripts, tenth century and later),[12] Ge'ez, Armenian, Slavonic, and Romanian.[13] While each of these writings exerted some influence in early Christianity, the first one continues to be a part of the biblical canon of many Christian groups.

The Book of Baruch, as received in the canon by the Roman Catholic Church, consists of six chapters, but the sixth chapter is actually an independent work, the Epistle of Jeremiah. In Antiquity, these two writings—Baruch and the Epistle of Jeremiah—were regarded as separate works, though in the Greek and Latin traditions they both often appeared as supplements to the canonical book of Jeremiah (see below on 'Jeremiah, Letter of'). The date of Baruch's composition cannot be precisely determined; it was likely written in the second or first century BCE, perhaps in Palestine.[14] The content of Baruch consists of a confession of sin in light of the Babylonian exile (1:1–3:8) and two poems, one in praise of Wisdom (3:9–4:4) and the other expressing hope for Jerusalem's future (4:5–5:9).

---

[5] *Zech.* 234:21–2; 259:21–4; 355:20–4; *Ps.* 300:12–13. Ehrman (1983: 13–14) argues that Didymus the Blind accepted Barnabas as canonical.

[6] On the latter, see Wayment 2013: 37–9.

[7] On this codex, see the section on the Bryennios List in ch. 3, pp. 70–1.

[8] Carleton Paget 2007: 73; Holmes 2007: 375–6.

[9] For basic orientation, see Mendels 1992.

[10] For basic orientation, see Charlesworth 1992a; Collins 2016: 264–80. Second Baruch appears in the Syriac Codex Ambrosianus; see ch. 6, p. 254.

[11] For basic orientation, see Charlesworth 1992b; Collins 2016: 311–15.

[12] See Kraft and Purintun 1972: 3–5; Herzer 2005: xxxvi–xlii.

[13] For basic orientation, see Robinson 1992.

[14] Adams 2014: 4–6; Ryan 2015: 488–90.

Baruch is not extant in Hebrew, and scholars debate whether a Hebrew text ever existed, with recent discussion tending towards a negative conclusion.[15] Four Greek uncial codices preserve the book: Vaticanus (fourth century), Alexandrinus (fifth century), Marchalianus (sixth century), and Venetus (eighth century).[16] It is also attested by a number of Greek minuscules. As for the later Greek translations ('the Three'), there are six Theodotion fragments of Baruch and one fragment attributed to Aquila. Jerome did not translate Baruch into Latin—he explains in the preface to his Jeremiah translation and in the prologue to his Jeremiah commentary that Baruch is not accepted among the Jews[17]—but an Old Latin edition entered the Vulgate. The text is also known in Coptic, Syriac, Geʻez, Arabic, and Armenian.

Early Christians often found Baruch to be valuable. The earliest citation is in Athenagoras of Athens (second century), *Legatio pro Christianis* 9, citing Bar. 3:36 under the title 'Jeremiah'. Irenaeus provides an extensive citation of Bar. 4:36–5:9 at *Haer.* 5.35.1, again, under the title 'Jeremiah'. Many other writers cite material from Baruch as from Jeremiah (see esp. *Civ.* 18.33, citing Bar. 3:36–8), showing that they considered Baruch to be a part of Jeremiah. We can thus assume that for many of the canon lists collected in this volume, the title 'Jeremiah' includes Baruch. The lists that name Baruch as a part of Jeremiah include those from Cyril of Jerusalem, Athanasius, Epiphanius (*Pan.* 8.6.2; *Mens.* 5), and the list associated with the Synod of Laodicea.[18] Latin sources before Jerome always cite Baruch under the title Jeremiah, but since Jerome did not translate Baruch, this material disappeared from Latin manuscripts for several centuries, becoming customary in manuscripts only from the thirteenth century.[19]

Ben Sira

See Sirach below.

Clement, Epistles of

1 Clement: This letter written from the Roman church addresses certain problems in the Corinthian church.[20] The letter includes no reference to its author, but most manuscripts identify the author as a certain Clement,[21] traditionally considered the third bishop of Rome. The letter seems to date to the late first or early second century, as indicated by the fact that some of the leaders appointed by the apostles are still alive (44:3–5). It was a very important text in ancient Christianity, cited by many authors, including Irenaeus (*Haer.* 3.3.3) and Clement of Alexandria, who calls its author the

---

[15] Cf. Adams 2014: 11–12; Ryan 2015: 488.
[16] A lacuna in Sinaiticus prevents us from knowing whether Baruch would have appeared in this manuscript.
[17] Jerome thus treats the additions to Jeremiah (Baruch and the Letter of Jeremiah) differently from his treatment of the additions to Daniel and to Esther, which he did translate, though under obelus.
[18] For all of these lists, see ch. 3. See also in the same chapter the list of Origen, who does not name Baruch but does list the Epistle of Jeremiah as following Jeremiah.
[19] For a summary, see Assan-Dhôte and Moatti-Fine 2008: 22–3; for much more, see Bogaert 2005.
[20] For text and translation, see Holmes 2007: 33–131.
[21] See also Eusebius, *Hist. eccl.* 4.23.11.

'apostle Clement' (*Strom.* 4.17). Eusebius valued the writing highly and testified to its occasional liturgical use in churches (*Hist. eccl.* 3.16), though in his discussion of the NT canon (*Hist. eccl.* 3.25) he did not mention it at all, not even as a disputed book. The use of 1 Clement by Didymus the Blind has been taken as evidence that he received the writing as canonical.[22] Markschies suggests that because the gnostic tractate The Exegesis of the Soul quotes from 1 Clement with an introduction attributing the words to God, 'one can therefore hypothesize that *1 Clement* was part of the biblical "canon" of the author of the tractate from Nag Hammadi'.[23] The text of 1 Clement is completely extant in Greek only in a single manuscript: Codex Hierosolymitanus (1056 CE), the famous manuscript discovered by Bryennios in 1873 that also contains 2 Clement, the Didache, the Epistle of Barnabas, and the letters of Ignatius.[24] Other manuscripts used for the establishment of the text include Codex Alexandrinus (lacking 57:7–63:4), an eleventh-century manuscript of the Latin translation, a twelfth-century manuscript of the Syriac New Testament, and two incomplete Coptic manuscripts.

2 Clement: This anonymous sermon came to circulate under Clement's name in Antiquity. We have no information about its author, date, or provenance, though scholars typically date it to the middle of the second century.[25] Eusebius mentions this 'second letter ascribed to Clement', but he says that it did not enjoy the same reception as 1 Clement (*Hist. eccl.* 3.38.4). The text is preserved in only three manuscripts: Codex Alexandrinus (through 12:5a), Codex Hierosolymitanus (1056 CE), and a twelfth-century Syriac manuscript.[26] In each of these manuscripts, 2 Clement follows 1 Clement.

The canon lists collected in this book uniformly omit the writings of Clement, except for the Apostolic Canons, which includes 1–2 Clement at the end of the New Testament but before the Acts of the Apostles.[27] Codex Alexandrinus includes both 1–2 Clement at the very end of the manuscript, following Revelation, interpreted by some scholars as indicating the canonicity of these writings.[28] These Clementine works form a more integral part of the New Testament in the twelfth-century Syriac manuscript featuring them, where they appear between the Catholic Epistles and the Pauline Epistles.

Corinthians, Third Epistle to the

See Paul, Acts of.

Daniel

The book of Daniel has been received in different versions. The Jewish and Protestant version of the book as represented in the Leningrad Codex (1008 CE) contains only twelve chapters and a relatively short chapter 3 (thirty verses, omitting 'The Prayer of Azariah' and 'The Hymn of the Three Young Men', together comprising sixty-seven verses). The Roman Catholic Bible contains chapters 13 and 14, Susanna and Bel and the Dragon, respectively and the longer chapter 3. The book of Daniel was transmitted in two Greek

---

[22] Ehrman 1983: 17.   [23] Markschies 2015: 259.
[24] See ch. 3 on the Bryennios List (pp. 70–1) for more on this manuscript. Photographs of 1 Clement and 2 Clement may be seen in Lightfoot 1885: 1.1.425–74.
[25] See the commentary by Tuckett 2012.
[26] For descriptions of these manuscripts, see ibid.: 3–6.
[27] See ch. 3 above, p. 137.
[28] Gregory and Tuckett 2005b: 251. For the contents of Alexandrinus, see ch. 6, esp. p. 249.

versions: (1) the earlier Old Greek version (second century BCE); and (2) another version traditionally attributed to Theodotion (first or second century CE). The church used the latter more than the former, so that most of the Greek manuscripts preserve only the version by Theodotion. Both Greek versions contain the additions. Debate over the original language of these additions, Hebrew or Greek, goes back at least as far as Origen's *Letter to Africanus*. Origen affirmed that Susanna was written in Hebrew and then translated into Greek, while Africanus asserted that the book was originally written in Greek.[29] The canonicity of Daniel never seemed to be in doubt, but the Jews probably by the time of Aquila (ca. 130 CE) had already rejected the additions, since there is no evidence of them in Aquila, and Africanus reminds Origen that the version of Daniel received from the Jews does not circulate with the additions of Susanna or Bel and the Dragon.[30]

According to *Biblia Patristica* there is no known Christian use of Daniel 13 and 14 in the second century (perhaps some usage of 14:5 and 14:36 from anonymous sources). That silence changes drastically from 200 to 300, when the two chapters are used some 240 times (many of these are from Origen's *Letter to Africanus*), and again from 300 to 400, when the two chapters are used some 300 times.

Early Greek Uncial MSS include all three works under the one title, Daniel, usually in one of the two following orders: Sus–Dan–Bel and Dragon (Codex Vaticanus and Codex Alexandrinus of the fourth and fifth centuries, respectively) or Dan–Sus–Bel and Dragon (Codex Venetus, eighth century). The three works also appear in Codex Marchalianus of the sixth century. The Greek manuscript tradition, therefore, treats these works as an integrated whole. Syriac Codex Ambrosianus (early seventh century) treats these books individually, separating them with blank spaces and new titles: Daniel–Bel–Dragon (Susanna is removed from Daniel entirely and placed within the Syriac collection of Women: Ruth–Susanna–Esther–Judith). Latin Codex Amiatinus includes the additions to Daniel with Jerome's headings reporting that they are not contained in Hebrew but have been translated from Theodotion.

All of the canon lists in this volume list simply 'Daniel', and at this early period, the additions are almost certainly subsumed under this title. This pattern continues through the lists of the *Dialogue of Timothy and Aquila* (sixth century) and John of Damascus, *De Fide Orthodoxa* 4.17 (PG 94: 1180; ca. 754 CE). The ninth-century canon list of Nicephorus I (d. 811), *Chronographia Brevis*, includes Susanna among disputed (*antilegomena*) books—not canonical books as it lists Daniel (PG 100: 1057)—but it contains no reference to Bel and the Dragon, presumably still including these works under 'Daniel'. Nicephorus also includes a pseudepigraphical book of Daniel among the OT apocryphal books (PG 100: 1060).

The Diatessaron

The *Diatessaron* has traditionally been described as a Gospel-harmony produced by Tatian in the second century, about 170; recent scholarship suggests that Tatian intended his work to be a Gospel (not a Gospel-harmony) and that it was received as such in the Syrian church for some centuries.[31] Tatian used almost exclusively the four canonical Gospels as his sources. It is not clear that he himself called his work the *Diatessaron*; Crawford has argued that he called it simply his Gospel as part of his campaign to

---

[29] Gallagher 2012a: 63–78.   [30] ibid.: 68.   [31] M. Crawford 2013; Watson 2016b.

replace the fourfold Gospel.[32] He did not mention his own name in the text. Eusebius (*Hist. eccl.* 4.29.6) is the one who says that Tatian called his work the *Dia Tessarōn* ('through four,' or 'in fourfold form'). It was known in Syriac as the 'Gospel of the Connected' (i.e., a single, unified text) while the individual canonical Gospels were called collectively the 'Gospel of the Separated'. Ephrem and Aphrahat accepted the *Diatessaron* as the Gospel and label the text's narrator the Evangelist without connecting it to Tatian.[33] It is debated as to whether Tatian composed his Gospel in Syriac or Greek.[34] The text is no longer completely extant; we rely on quotations in Syriac authors (esp. Ephrem and Aphrahat), daughter versions (esp. Latin and Arabic), and a Greek fragment from Dura-Europos dating to the second or third century and containing fourteen lines.[35] In an attempt to establish the supremacy of the fourfold Gospel in Syria, Theodoret tells us that he confiscated more than 200 copies of the *Diatessaron*.[36]

The Didache

The Didache (Greek for 'teaching') is a church manual, the first half of which contains general moral instruction—especially on the two ways: the way of life and the way of death—while the second half prescribes procedures for conducting various ecclesiastical rituals, such as baptism, the Lord's supper, fasting, and prayer.[37] Many scholars date the document to the first century and locate it in Syria, perhaps Antioch specifically. The Didache was long considered lost until Bryennios uncovered a copy in Codex Hierosolymitanus.[38] This discovery allowed for the recognition that the text of the Didache had been incorporated into the Apostolic Constitutions, book 7.[39] The text is now known also in a fourth-century Greek papyrus fragment, a Coptic papyrus fragment, and a partially extant Geʿez translation.[40] Some ancient canonical lists include the Didache, but not as part of the canon proper: Eusebius mentions it as an *antilegomenon* (*Hist. eccl.* 3.25.4), Athanasius includes it among the non-canonical books to be read, and Rufinus lists within his 'ecclesiastical' category a book called the Two Ways, which likely bears some relationship to the Didache.[41] While the work seems to have been well known in early Christianity, it is often difficult to determine in which cases early Christian writers are drawing specifically from the Didache.[42]

---

[32] M. Crawford 2013.   [33] ibid.
[34] See bibliography in M. Crawford 2016: 256n9. Baarda (2012: 337–8) and Schmid (2013: 115–16n5) favour Greek.
[35] For a recent analysis of this fragment, see M. Crawford 2016. For a brief survey of the textual evidence, see Watson 2016b: 97–9. Moreover, medieval translations have often been used in *Diatessaron* research; see Petersen 1994; for an evaluation of this approach, see Schmid 2013.
[36] *Haereticarum fabularum compendium* 1.20, PG 83.372; see further Petersen 1994: 41–5.
[37] For the text and English translation, see Holmes 2007: 334–69.
[38] For more on this MS and its discovery, see the introduction to the section on the Bryennios List in ch. 3, pp. 70–1.
[39] See Niederwimmer 1998: 28–9.   [40] ibid.: 21–7.
[41] For the lists by Eusebius and Athanasius, see ch. 3, p. 102 and p. 125, respectively; for Rufinus, see ch. 4, p. 219. See also Niederwimmer 1998: 4–6.
[42] See ibid.: 6–13. Ehrman (1983: 16–17) thought the evidence was strong enough to suggest that Didymus the Blind accepted the Didache as canonical.

Ecclesiastes/Qoheleth

The Mishnah reports a debate about the status of Song of Songs and Ecclesiastes.

> The Song of Songs and Ecclesiastes render the hands unclean. R. Judah says: The Song of Songs renders the hands unclean, but about Ecclesiastes there is dissension. R. Jose says: Ecclesiastes does not render the hands unclean, and about the Song of Songs there is dissension. R. Simeon says: Ecclesiastes is one of the things about which the School of Shammai adopted the more lenient, and the School of Hillel the more stringent ruling.[43] R. Simeon b. Azzai said: I have heard a tradition from the seventy-two elders on the day when they made R. Eleazar b. Azariah head of the college [of Sages], that the Song of Songs and Ecclesiastes both render the hands unclean. R. Akiba said: God forbid!—no man in Israel ever disputed about the Song of Songs [that he should say] that it does not render the hands unclean, for all the ages are not worth the day on which the Song of Songs was given to Israel; for all the Writings are holy, but the Song of Songs is the Holy of Holies. And if aught was in dispute the dispute was about Ecclesiastes alone. R. Johanan b. Joshua, the son of R. Akiba's father-in-law, said: According to the words of Ben Azzai so did they dispute and so did they decide.
>
> (m. Yad. 3.5)[44]

According to Alexander, this dispute concerned 'the residual area of doubt within the third division' (of the Tanak, i.e., the Ketuvim).[45] But Pope maintains that the 'issue was not whether the book was included in the Canon, but whether it should have been'.[46] That some Rabbis did doubt the inspiration of Ecclesiastes is also suggested by a Tosefta passage:

> R. Simeon b. Menassia' says, "The Song of Songs imparts uncleanness to hands, because it was said by the Holy Spirit. Qoheleth does not impart uncleanness of hands, because it is [merely] the wisdom of Solomon."
>
> (t. Yad. 2.14)[47]

A Talmudic passage is also relevant:

> Rab Judah son of R. Samuel b. Shilath said in Rab's name: The Sages wished to hide the Book of Ecclesiastes, because its words are self-contradictory; yet why did they not hide it? Because its beginning is religious teaching and its end is religious teaching.
>
> (b. Meg. 7a)[48]

The passage then demonstrates that the beginning and ending are religious by citing Eccl. 1:3 and 12:13, and it exhibits the book's contradictions by contrasting 7:3 with 2:2; 8:15 with 2:2, but the Talmudic passage also explores ways of harmonizing these verses.

---

[43] Cf. m. Ed. 5.3.

[44] Translation by Danby 1933: 781–2. Cf. a similar passage at b. Meg. 7a. For discussion of the Mishnah passage, see Barton 1997: 106–30; Lightstone 2002: 175–8; Alexander 2007: 58–64; Lim 2013: 50–2.

[45] Alexander 2007: 62 (italics removed).

[46] Pope 1977: 19. Pope's statement refers particularly to Song of Songs, but, as he goes on to note, the same could be said for Ecclesiastes.

[47] Translation by Neusner 2002: 2.1908. There is a similar passage at b. Meg. 7a.

[48] On the rabbinic terminology of hiding away a book, see Leiman 1976: 72–86; Beckwith 1985: 278–83.

Aside from these rabbinic passages, further evidence for the questionable status of Ecclesiastes might be sought from the fact that it perhaps was translated into Greek only at the end of the first century CE (though this dating is disputed), and was not widely used before the third century.[49]

Some scholars guess that Josephus may have omitted Ecclesiastes from his canon list.[50] It appears in every other canon list collected here except the Syriac list in ch. 5.

Ecclesiasticus

See Sirach below.

Enoch, Books of

The 'book of Enoch' refers to a long, composite, apocalyptic work,[51] preserved primarily in Ethiopian manuscripts and often labelled 1 Enoch to distinguish it from 2 Enoch (preserved mostly in Slavonic)[52] and 3 Enoch (= *Sefer Hekalot*, in Hebrew).[53] All of these works take as their point of departure the brief comments about Enoch in Gen. 5:18–24. First Enoch forms a part of the Ethiopian Bible and it was very important in some ancient Jewish and Christian communities. The book has a complicated history of composition. It survives in more than 120 Ge'ez manuscripts (not all preserving a complete text)[54] in an edition comprising 108 chapters combining various independent works. Scholars debate the dating of these separate works.

Book of Watchers, chs 1–36 (mid- or late-third century BCE)

Parables (or Similitudes), chs 37–71 (around the turn of the Era)

Astronomical Book, chs 72–82 (third century BCE)

Book of Dream Visions, chs 83–90 (160–164 BCE)

Epistle of Enoch, chs 91–108 (early second century BCE)[55]

The Enoch traditions were obviously very popular at Qumran, which yielded fragments of eleven Aramaic manuscripts, attesting every section of the book except the Parables.[56]

As for early Christianity, the canonical book of Jude quoted 1 Enoch 1:9,[57] and Tertullian (*Cult. fem.* 1.3) used this quotation to argue for the canonicity of the book of Enoch. But it seems to have largely fallen out of favour by the end of the fourth century.[58] Augustine

---

[49] Aitken 2015b: 357–8 (on the date), 366 (on reception). For an earlier dating of Greek Ecclesiastes, see Meade and Gentry 2012: 211–12.

[50] Beckwith 1985: 80; Hengel 2002: 101.

[51] For basic orientation to 1 Enoch and a translation, see Nickelsburg and VanderKam 2004. See also Collins 2016: 53–99.

[52] For introduction and translation, see Andersen 1983. More recently, some Coptic fragments were brought to light; see Hagen 2012. See also Collins 2016: 301–10.

[53] For introduction and translation, see Alexander 1983.

[54] Stuckenbruck 2013: 11n23.

[55] Chapter 108 forms an additional book dating to the first century CE.

[56] Moreover, no fragment of ch. 108 survives. See Nickelsburg 2000.

[57] On this quotation, see Bauckham 1990: 225–33; Hultin 2010; Moore 2013.

[58] On reception, see VanderKam 1996; Reed 2005; Stuckenbruck 2013.

acknowledged the quotation of Enoch in Jude, but still placed Enoch among the apocrypha (*Civ.* 15.23; 18.38). As we have seen, 1 Enoch survived by virtue of its inclusion in the Ethiopian Bible.[59] There are also fragments in Greek, Latin, Coptic, and Syriac.[60]

Esdras

There are four books of Ezra, or Esdras, featured in some biblical manuscripts. In later Vulgate manuscripts, the books appeared under these titles: 1 Esdras (= Hebrew Ezra),[61] 2 Esdras (= Nehemiah), 3 Esdras (= LXX Esdras A), 4 Esdras (= Latin Apocalypse of Ezra). Septuagint manuscripts from the fourth century, such as Sinaiticus and Vaticanus, referred to two books of Esdras, Esdras A and Esdras B, this latter being a literal translation of Hebrew Ezra–Nehemiah in one book. Esdras A, on the other hand, is related closely to Ezra–Nehemiah, but contains many differences, so that it constitutes a divergent edition of the book, though scholars debate whether it is earlier or later than Hebrew Ezra–Nehemiah.[62] Its relationship to Hebrew Ezra–Nehemiah may be charted as follows:[63]

2 Chronicles chs 35–6	//	Esdras A ch. 1
Ezra ch. 1	//	Esdras A 2:1–14
Ezra 4:7–24	//	Esdras A 2:15–25
Story of the Three Pages only in Esdras A 3:1–5:6		
Ezra 2:1–4:5	//	Esdras A 5:7–70
Ezra chs 5–10	//	Esdras A chs 6–9:36
Nehemiah 7:73–8:13a	//	Esdras A 9:37–55

The first Hebrew Bible to divide Ezra from Nehemiah so that there are two books rather than one is the first Rabbinic Bible (Venice 1516–17), printed by Daniel Bomberg and edited by Felix Pratensis.[64] The LXX manuscript tradition occasionally attests Ezra and Nehemiah as two separate books.[65] In the Latin tradition, the VL (Vercelli manuscript)[66] and the Vulgate have Ezra–Nehemiah as one book. Latin manuscripts divide Ezra–Nehemiah into two books only from the tenth century, first in Spain, and then this practice was adopted in the Paris Bible of the thirteenth century.[67] The Story of the Three Pages, found only in 1 Esdras (= Esdras A of the LXX), is well known to Latin fathers.[68] Bogaert has emphasized that when the ancient canon lists, whether Greek or Latin, mention two books of Esdras, they must have in mind the books known in the LXX and VL as Esdras A and Esdras B, i.e., our 1 Esdras and Ezra–Nehemiah.[69] Possibly the Bryennios List could be an exception, depending on the extent to which it was influenced by the LXX tradition.

---

[59] On its reception in Ethiopia, see Stuckenbruck 2013: 21–39.

[60] See the discussion of the text in Nickelsburg 2001: 9–20. The major critical commentary is Nickelsburg (ibid.) together with Nickelsburg and VanderKam 2012.

[61] There are also some passages in Aramaic, but the majority of the book is Hebrew.

[62] See, e.g., Fried 2011.   [63] This table is adapted from Bogaert 2000: 6.

[64] See Ginsburg 1897: 925–48, esp. 933–4.   [65] Hanhart 1993: 144, 249.

[66] Bogaert 2000: 17–20.   [67] ibid.: 11.

[68] Denter 1962: 53–67.   [69] Bogaert 2014: 47.

Esther

The Book of Esther is transmitted in two different forms: the shorter version found in the Hebrew text and accepted into the biblical canon of Jews and Protestants, and an expanded version found in the Greek text accepted as scriptural by several Christian groups (e.g., Roman Catholic, Greek Orthodox, etc.). Whereas the Hebrew story never refers to God, nor does it ever say that the characters in the story pray, the Greek version refers to God frequently and records two substantial prayers of Mordecai and Esther. The other expansions provide more detail or background information about the story. The six major additions in Greek Esther comprise 107 verses, constituting about a fifty-per-cent expansion of the text, and appear at various points throughout the book. Some of the additions may have been composed in Hebrew.

The reception of Esther presents many complexities. It is now considered canonical among Jews and all Christian groups, but a few early Christian canon lists omit the book, no Esther scroll has turned up at Qumran, and the Rabbis discussed the status of the book, or at least the scroll containing the book. The reception of Esther is bound up with the reception of the holiday promoted in the book, Purim. The first mention of Purim in external literature appears in 2 Macc. 15:36, where it is called the 'Day of Mordecai' in a way that indicates that the author expected his readers to be familiar with the holiday. Purim is apparently not one of the holidays celebrated by the Qumran community; it does not appear alongside other holidays in their calendar texts, which fact, together with the book's absence among the modern finds in the Qumran caves, suggests that the sectarian group may not have considered Esther authoritative. However, some scholars consider the lack of an Esther scroll among the Dead Sea Scrolls to be a mere accident, and there is some language in some of the scrolls that is reminiscent of language in Esther, suggesting that some Qumran scribes were deeply familiar with Esther.[70]

Other signs of concern about Esther in Antiquity possibly include the Greek expansions, the rabbinic discussions about the book, and the Christian lists omitting it. The expansions of the Greek text indicate that people were reading the book of Esther, but they also seem to show that some readers found the book wanting and desired to improve it.[71] The Talmud cites rabbinic authorities questioning whether the scroll of Esther 'defiles the hands', and whether it was authorized to be written down.

> Rab Judah said in the name of Samuel; [The scroll] of Esther does not make the hands unclean. Are we to infer from this that Samuel was of opinion that Esther was not composed under the inspiration of the holy spirit? How can this be, seeing that Samuel has said that Esther was composed under the inspiration of the holy spirit?—It was composed to be recited [by heart], but not to be written.
>
> (b. Meg. 7a)[72]

The Christian lists completely omitting Esther include Melito of Sardis and Gregory of Nazianzus. Amphilochius of Iconium acknowledges that 'some include Esther', and

---

[70] See Lange 2009: 497–502.
[71] Koller 2014: 119–23. On Greek Esther, see ibid.: 113–23; Boyd-Taylor 2015.
[72] Cf. Yoma 29a; see Leiman 1976: 200–1n634; Beckwith 1985: 291–7, 314–15; Cavalier 2004; 2012: 117–20.

Athanasius positions Esther outside the canon and within the books to be read to catechumens.[73]

Ezekiel

There is no real question that Ezekiel was accepted as of binding authority fairly early within Judaism. Ben Sira mentions the prophet within his praise of famous men (Sir. 49:8), and Josephus clearly included Ezekiel as one of the thirteen prophets that wrote the history of their own times prior to Artaxerxes (*C. Ap.* 1.37–43; see ch. 2). Along with six manuscripts discovered at Qumran, there are also quotations of Ezekiel in the Dead Sea Scrolls.[74] There is a rabbinic tradition, however, that suggests the Rabbis were tempted to 'hide away' the book because of its problematic passages.[75]

> Rab Judah said in Rab's name: In truth, that man, Hananiah son of Hezekiah by name, is to be remembered for blessing: but for him, the Book of Ezekiel would have been hidden, for its words contradicted Torah. What did he do? Three hundred barrels of oil were taken up to him and he sat in an upper chamber and reconciled them.
>
> (b. Šabb. 13b)[76]

'These warnings were not concerning the book's canonicity, but rather its public study and liturgical use.'[77] An examination of rabbinic interaction with Ezekiel leads Sweeney to conclude 'that the rabbinic sages regarded Ezekiel not only as a true book worthy of inclusion in the Jewish Bible, but also as a profound book that must be probed by a qualified sage in order to uncover its profound teachings concerning the character and teachings of the divine presence of G-d'.[78]

Hebrews

Because the Epistle to the Hebrews was anonymous, early Christians had doubts about its authorship and, thus, about its suitability for the biblical canon.[79] Such doubts are especially characteristic of the Western church, though they are not unknown in the East. Christians in the East did recognize the authorship problem; some of them dealt with that issue by supposing that Paul had written the letter in Hebrew to his fellow countrymen, without signing his own name because of the animosity felt by the Jews towards him, and the letter was subsequently translated into Greek by Luke (the view of Clement of Alexandria) or, perhaps, by Clement of Rome (a proposal by Eusebius).[80]

---

[73] For each of these lists, see ch. 3.

[74] See Popović 2014. On the quotations of Ezekiel, see col. 593. Popović cites CD 3.20–4.2 (Ezek. 44:15), introduced with 'as God swore to them through Ezekiel, the prophet, saying'; CD 19.11–12 (Ezek. 9:4); 4Q174 1.16–17 (Ezek. 37:23); 4Q177 2.13–14 (Ezek. 25:8).

[75] On hiding away books, see above on Ecclesiastes, with references to discussion.

[76] The same tradition is found in b. Menaḥ 45a; b. Ḥag 13b. See in general Beckwith 1985: ch. 7; Sweeney 2011.

[77] Stemberger 2014, col. 596.   [78] Sweeney 2011: 23.

[79] We summarized the reception of Hebrews in ch. 1, at the end of the section on 'The Pauline Letter Collection'. The material here will supplement the discussion there.

[80] These opinions are collected by Eusebius, *Hist. eccl.* 3.38.2–3; 6.14.2–3. See also Jerome, *Vir. ill.* 5; 15.

Christians in the West often simply omitted Hebrews.[81] Tertullian's opinion that Barnabas wrote the letter (*De pud.* 10; 20) is possibly echoed in other sources.[82] The Muratorian Fragment does not mention Hebrews. Amphilochius reports that some regard Hebrews as 'spurious' (νόθος; *Iambi* 308–9),[83] and Eusebius seems to class it among the disputed books at *Hist. eccl.* 6.13.6. But by the late fourth century Latin writers seem to generally receive the epistle as Pauline, as evidenced by the canon lists put forward by Jerome, Rufinus, Augustine, Innocent, and the *Breviarium Hipponense*.[84]

James

Eusebius listed James as one of the *antilegomena* (*Hist. eccl.* 3.25.3). Elsewhere he narrates the legend of James's death and then says:

> Such is the story of James, whose is said to be the first of the Epistles called Catholic. It is to be observed that its authenticity is denied (νοθεύεται), since few of the ancients quote it, as is also the case with the Epistle called Jude's, which is itself one of the seven called Catholic; nevertheless we know that these letters have been used publicly (δεδημοσιευμένας) with the rest in most churches.
>
> (*Hist. eccl.* 2.23.24–5)[85]

There is little evidence for the use of James in the second century.[86] 'Origen is the first early theologian to make clear use of the letter of James.'[87]

Jeremiah, Letter of

This short work is a polemic against idolatry in the voice of Jeremiah.[88] At first it probably circulated independently as its own work, but several MSS preserve it after Baruch and in some translations the Epistle is the sixth chapter of Baruch.

Biblia Patristica records only six uses of the Epistle of Jeremiah (Baruch 6) from 100 to 400 CE: Tertullian, Cyprian of Carthage, Eusebius of Caesarea, and Ambrosiaster.

The Epistle is found in four uncials: Alexandrinus, Vaticanus, Marchalianus, and Venetus. In Sinaiticus, there were fifty-six pages that fell out of the prophetic section, and the text of the Epistle was lost as a result (assuming its original presence). Some thirty-five minuscules preserve the Epistle. Furthermore, the book was preserved in the following ancient versions: Old Latin, Bohairic, Sahidic, Fajumic, Syro-hexapla, Christian Palestinian Aramaic, Ge'ez, Arabic, and Armenian.

---

[81] Eusebius acknowledges this geographical divide in the reception of the letter: *Hist. eccl.* 3.3.4; 6.20.3.

[82] See de Boer 2014: 251–3. Philaster of Brescia is familiar with the view that Barnabas wrote it (*Liber de haeresibus* 99). De Boer proposes that Tertullian had access to manuscripts, whether Greek or Latin, ascribing the letter to Barnabas (ibid.: 247–50).

[83] See the section on Amphilochius in ch. 3, esp. p. 154.

[84] See ch. 4 for all of these lists. Elsewhere, Jerome expressed some doubts about authorship (*Comm. Am.* 8:7; *Comm. Jer.* 31:31), as did Augustine (*Inchoat. Expos. Ep. ad Rom.* 11; *Pecc. merit. et Remiss.* 1.27, 50; *Serm.* 55.5).

[85] Translation by Lake 1926.

[86] L. Johnson 1995: 66–79; 2004: 45–60; Allison 2013: 99–109.

[87] Nienhuis 2007: 55.   [88] See deSilva 2002: 214.

The book appears for the first time in our canon lists in the list drafted by Origen, and then was included explicitly in several fourth-century lists (Cyril of Jerusalem, Synod of Laodicea, Athanasius, and Epiphanius; cf. the relevant sections in chapter 3). This book (along with Lamentations and Baruch) is almost certainly subsumed under the title of 'Jeremiah' in all canon lists in this book with the probable exception of Jerome (see ch. 4) and perhaps the Syriac list in ch. 5.

John, Epistles of

The Epistles of John were not received as a unit due to disputes over their authorship: the anonymous 1 John quickly became associated with the Fourth Gospel and therefore John the Apostle, while 2–3 John, written under the name of 'the Elder', generated doubt. Papias (early second century), reputed disciple of John the Apostle and companion of Polycarp, apparently differentiated John the Apostle from another John, called 'the Elder' (cf. Eusebius, *Hist. eccl.* 3.39.5–6).[89] Dionysius of Alexandria in the third century attributed 2–3 John to the apostle, but he refers to 1 John as 'the catholic epistle' and does not attribute this catholicity to the other two (*apud* Eusebius, *Hist. eccl.* 7.24–5). Christian writers used 1 John frequently, 2–3 John less often. Polycarp cites 1 John 4:2–3 (*Phil.* 7.1). Justin Martyr uses 1 John 3:8 (*Dial.* 45.4). Didymus the Blind does not cite 2–3 John and refers to 1 John as the epistle of John; still, one cannot be certain about the status of these two letters in his writings, since they are short and he simply may not have needed to cite them.[90]

Some early papyri preserve these books: P⁹ in the third century (1 John), P⁷⁴ in the seventh century (2–3 John). Sinaiticus and Alexandrinus contain all three epistles of John. Uncial *048 (fifth century) also contains the entirety of 2–3 John, but only portions of 1 John. Early Syriac Peshitta MSS do not include 2–3 John. They eventually appear in some Peshitta MSS in a version known as the Philoxenian, dated to the early part of the sixth century.[91]

The lists in the current volume range from including in the canon all three epistles of John (e.g. Athanasius), only 1 John (Eusebius), or none of them (St Catherine's Monastery Syriac List). By the later part of the fourth century, disputes over 2–3 John appear to wane (though they are sometimes still noted; cf. section on Amphilochius in chapter 3) and the practice is to accept all three of these letters. The later Eastern lists of John of Damascus, *De Fide Orthodoxa* 4.17 (PG 94: 1180; ca. 754 CE), and Nicephorus I (d. 811), *Chronographia Brevis* (PG 100: 1057), include three epistles of John in the canon without mention of any dispute. In the West there is no dispute over 2–3 John with the possible exceptions of the Muratorian Fragment and the Mommsen Catalogue (cf. the relevant sections in chapter 4).

Jubilees

The preface to the book of Jubilees presents the work as the literary product of Moses on Mount Sinai when the Lord gave him the Law and the commandment. This prologue ensured that this work would be influential on some of its earliest readers.[92]

---

[89] The fragments of Papias are collected in Holmes 2007: 722–73. On the two separate Johns, see also Fragment 5 (excerpted from the fifth-century historian Philip of Side).

[90] Ehrman 1983: 7.   [91] Gwynn 1909: xxii–xxiv; cf. ch. 6.

[92] VanderKam 2010; Mroczek 2016: 141–2.

The complete work was known only in a Ge'ez translation before some fifteen Hebrew MSS were found at Qumran.[93] Those discoveries have settled the debates over the original language of composition, and scholars are now certain that the book was originally composed in Hebrew.

The Damascus Document from Qumran refers to Jubilees authoritatively, placing it in parallel with the Law of Moses itself (CD 16:2–4).[94] The book was important enough at Qumran to spawn various re-workings that scholars call Pseudo Jubilees (4Q225–8).[95] Rabbinic literature shows no use of the book, but its influence is felt in a few midrashic texts that extend to the Middle Ages.[96] Early Christian chronographers (e.g. Julius Africanus and Epiphanius of Salamis) made extensive use of Jubilees or a work derived from it.[97]

The canon lists collected in this volume never mention Jubilees, except the Ge'ez version of the canon list in the Apostolic Canons, where the book appears as an 'outside book' to be read to children (cf. the relevant section in chapter 3, p. 138n338). Jubilees may have been known by the title 'Apocalypse of Moses' (so Syncellus) or 'Testament of Moses' (so Nicephorus). It is generally assumed today that these works are not Jubilees as we have it now, but either earlier sources incorporated into Jubilees or later excerpts from the work. Today, the Ethiopian church recognizes Jubilees as part of its Scriptures.[98]

Jude

Jude was listed by Eusebius as one of the *antilegomena* (*Hist. eccl.* 3.25.3). The earliest use of Jude is by the author of 2 Peter, assuming with the majority of scholars that Jude preceded 2 Peter. Tertullian clearly regarded the authority of Jude to be widely accepted, since he used Jude's quotation of Enoch as the basis for his claim that Enoch also should be received as authoritative (*Cult. fem.* 1.3). Jude finds a place in the Muratorian Fragment, and Clement of Alexandria mentions Jude and uses the letter (*Strom.* 3.2.11.2; cf. *Paed.* 3.8.44.3–45.1). Origen uses Jude frequently.[99]

Judith

The book of Judith is accepted as canonical in the Roman Catholic Church and several other Christian traditions, but it is not in the Jewish or Protestant Bibles. The book tells the story of a pious Jewish widow who saves her city from an invading army. While scholars have usually assumed a Hebrew original for Judith, nothing of this hypothesized original survives, and some scholars have argued for a Greek composition.[100]

Biblia Patristica catalogues no second-century instances of the use of Judith but twenty-three instances in the third century, only from chapters 8–14 (Tertullian; Origen; Julius Africanus). In the fourth century, there are some eighty uses of the book.[101] The

---

[93] ibid.: 139.   [94] See VanderKam 1998: 399; Mroczek 2016: 140.

[95] See VanderKam 2010: 43; Mroczek 2016: 140.   [96] VanderKam 2010: 43.

[97] Adler 1990: 476; VanderKam 2010: 44.   [98] Mroczek 2016: 156–8.

[99] See, e.g., Origen, *Comm. Matt.* 10.17.40. For further discussion of the reception of Jude, see Nienhuis and Wall 2013: 223–5.

[100] See Joosten 2008.

[101] Authors include Ambrose of Milan; Didymus of Alexandria; Athanasius of Alexandria (cf. n. 260 in ch. 3); Basil of Caesarea; Gregory of Nyssa; Gregory of Nazianzus; Ambrosiaster; Hilary of Poitiers (cf. n. 110 in ch. 4).

ancients generally seem to have considered Judith to be historical.[102] Still in the eleventh century, Hugh of St Victor assumed the historical character of Judith (*Diligent Examiner* 4.1). Ancient Syriac scholars were divided on this question.[103]

The text is known from many Greek manuscripts (in various recensions), including two fragmentary Greek papyri (823, fifth–sixth century; 999, third century) and four uncials (Vaticanus, Sinaiticus, Alexandrinus, and Venetus), along with a number of ancient versions (Old Latin, Peshitta, Syro-hexapla, Sahidic, Ge'ez, Armenian).

The lists in the current volume catalogue Judith in various ways. Some include it among the canonical books (e.g. Augustine), others do not list it (e.g. Gregory of Nazianzus), and others list it among the intermediate books (e.g. Athanasius). Later in Eastern tradition the *Dialogue of Timothy and Aquila* (sixth century) listed Judith as the twenty-first canonical book upon which Jews and Christians agree. John of Damascus, *De Fide Orthodoxa* 4.17 (PG 94: 1180; ca. 754 CE), does not include the book in the canon. The ninth-century canon list of Nicephorus I (d. 811), *Chronographia Brevis*, includes Judith among the disputed (*antilegomena*) books—not canonical books (PG 100: 1057). In the West, the church generally recognized the canonicity of Judith from the fourth century.

Laodiceans, Epistle of

The canonical Epistle to the Colossians mentions at 4:16 a Pauline letter to the church at Laodicea, though no such letter formed a part of the Pauline letter collection in Antiquity. According to Tertullian (*Marc.* 5.17.1), Marcion referred to canonical Ephesians as Laodiceans. But there also exists an apocryphal letter to the Laodiceans, extant in Latin, though the original text was probably Greek.[104] The earliest manuscript containing the Latin text is the sixth-century Codex Fuldensis, but the Greek text may go back to the late second century. The text was not well received in the East, but in the West it was often accepted as genuinely Pauline, despite Jerome's assurance that everyone rejected it (*Vir. ill.* 5). Even Gregory the Great in the sixth century seems to have accepted the letter's authenticity, though he still excluded it from the canon, limiting the canonical Pauline letters to fourteen.[105] *Laodiceans* is frequently found in medieval Latin copies of the New Testament.[106] A Pauline letter to the Laodiceans is cited as a forgery in the Muratorian Fragment.

Maccabees, 1–4

The four books of Maccabees had a varied reception within Jewish and Christian circles and rarely were they received together. First and Second Maccabees are historiography, 3 Maccabees is a 'historical romance', and 4 Maccabees is a work of rhetorical demonstration.[107] Josephus says that the line of prophets was broken after Artaxerxes and the later records are not worthy of the same trust as the earlier (cf. section on Josephus in

---

[102] Gallagher 2015b: 368–9.   [103] Van Rompay 2006: 226–9.

[104] For discussion and a reconstruction of a Greek text, see Lightfoot 1884: 274–300. More recent summary in Tite 2012: 1–4.

[105] *Moralia in Job* 35.48; see discussion in Lightfoot 1884: 295.

[106] Bogaert 2012: 90. According to Houghton (2016: 194–5), *Laodiceans* is widely attested (e.g. Vg F, VL 6, 51, 58, 61, 62, 91, 109). For a brief survey of its reception, see Hahneman 1992: 199.

[107] See deSilva 2002: *ad loc.* for discussion of these genres.

chapter 2), showing that 1–2 Maccabees were not received in the same way as, for example, 1–2 Kings. There is no evidence of 1–4 Maccabees found in the later Jewish revisers of the first and second centuries (Aquila, Symmachus, and Theodotion), indicating that these books fell into disuse among the Jews.[108]

The evidence in *Biblia Patristica* demonstrates frequent early Christian use of 1–2 Maccabees. Fourth Maccabees had a profound impact on Origen, Gregory of Nazianzus, and John Chrysostom.[109] Earlier, it probably influenced the views of martyrdom found in the second-century writings of Ignatius and Polycarp.[110]

Two uncials, Alexandrinus (fifth century) and Venetus (eighth century), preserve all four books of Maccabees. Codex Sinaiticus (fourth century) contains 1 Maccabees and 4 Maccabees. Many other Greek manuscripts contain some or all of these books, along with some ancient translations.[111]

The lists in the current volume catalogue these books differently. In Greek lists, only the Apostolic Canons accepts 1–4 Maccabees as canonical. The rest of the Greek lists do not include any of these books in the canon. Hilary, Jerome, and Rufinus follow this latter tradition. This practice persists through the *Dialogue of Timothy and Aquila* (sixth century), John of Damascus, *De Fide Orthodoxa* 4.17 (PG 94: 1180; ca. 754 CE), and Nicephorus I (d. 811), *Chronographia Brevis* (PG 100: 1057). Nicephorus catalogues 1–3 Maccabees under 'disputed' (*antilegomena*) books. The practice is different elsewhere. The list in Codex Claromontanus includes 1–2, 4 Maccabees in the canon, while the Mommsen Catalogue, Augustine, the *Breviarium Hipponense*, and Pope Innocent I include 1–2 Maccabees, which books were eventually included in the canon established by the Council of Trent.

Pastoral Epistles

Biblical scholars generally doubt the authenticity of the 'Pauline' letters to Timothy and Titus.[112] Regardless of one's views on that issue, the early Christian reception of the Pastorals does not exhibit as smooth of a path toward acceptance as for the other Pauline letters, even those others also often now doubted as authentic (e.g., Ephesians, 2 Thessalonians, etc.). Tertullian reports that Marcion rejected the Pastoral Epistles because he did not like their teachings (*Marc.* 5.21); whatever the reason, Marcion did not include the Pastorals in his collection of Pauline letters. The earliest manuscript of Paul's letters (P[46], 200 CE) features ten epistles, though originally it certainly contained others. The current form of the manuscript contains no trace of 2 Thessalonians or the Pastorals (though it does have Hebrews), but the interpretation of this manuscript and its relevance to the reception of the Pastorals has been debated by scholars.[113] As we saw in chapter 1, the Pastoral Epistles do feature in every other form of the Pauline letter collection for which we have evidence, and the standard thirteen- or fourteen-letter collection (depending on the presence of Hebrews) was formed by the end of the second

---

[108] Gentry 2016: 229.   [109] deSilva 2002: 379.   [110] ibid.: 378.

[111] The first three books of Maccabees have been published in critical editions by the Septuaginta Unternehmen in Göttingen, and information about manuscripts can be found in these volumes. We still await a critical edition of 4 Maccabees, but the *Offizielles Verzeichnis der Rahlfs-Sigeln* cites many minuscules containing the book, e.g., 44 46 52 55 58 62 71 74 107 120 125 236 312 316 317 322 325 332 335 340 366 367 380 385 387 388 391 397 427 446 448 452 455 457 467 472 473 491 498 524 534 542 577 585 586.

[112] See, e.g., Ehrman 2013: ch. 8.   [113] See ch. 1, p. 41.

century. Moreover, as for the Pastoral Epistles individually, there is attestation for their use as early as the Apostolic Fathers.[114]

Paul, Acts of

The Acts of Paul is a composite work incorporating three writings that also circulated independently: (1) the Acts of Paul and Thecla (= Acts of Paul 3–4); (2) a correspondence between Paul and the Corinthian church, with Paul's letter known as 3 Corinthians (the correspondence forms chapter 8 of Acts of Paul in some translations, chapter 10 in others); and (3) the Martyrdom of Paul (= either chapter 11 or chapter 14 of Acts of Paul, depending on the translation).[115] It was written in the second half of the second century, probably in Asia Minor, as Tertullian attests (*Bapt.* 17.5).[116] Sometimes 3 Corinthians was excerpted from the other material and printed among Paul's letters, though, according to Houghton, it is not well attested in Latin.[117] The Acts of Paul is mentioned by Eusebius as an *antilegomenon* (*Hist. eccl.* 3.25.4), and it is included under obelus near the end of the list in the Codex Claromontanus.

Peter, Apocalypse of

Two independent Apocalypses of Peter circulated in antiquity, one preserved in Greek and Ge'ez and generally considered orthodox, the other discovered in Coptic among the Nag Hammadi finds and associated with a gnostic outlook. The references in this volume to the Apocalypse of Peter concern the first of these works, a Jewish-Christian composition in which Peter takes a tour of hell.[118] Some scholars believe it was written in Palestine at the time of the Bar Kokhba War, 132–5.[119] The Muratorian Fragment (ln. 71–2) mentions the Apocalypse of Peter, explaining that despite its general acceptance some do not permit it to be read in church. Clement of Alexandria quotes from it by name ('Peter in his Apocalypse'),[120] and some other ancient writers (Christian and otherwise) also knew the work.[121] Eusebius of Caesarea (*Hist. eccl.* 3.3.2) claims that no ecclesiastical writer ever made use of the Petrine apocrypha, and in his canon list he classifies the Apocalypse of Peter as a spurious *antilegomenon*, but not a heretical work (*Hist. eccl.* 3.25.4).[122] Sozomen still attests both its ancient classification as spurious and

---

[114] On the reception of the Pastoral Epistles, see Marshall 1999: 2–8.

[115] For an English translation, see Elliott 1993: 350–89.

[116] Barrier 2009: 23–4.

[117] Houghton 2016: 194–5; see also Bogaert 2012: 90.

[118] For an English translation, see Elliott 1993: 593–612; on the reception of the Apocalypse, see Jakab 2003. See also Kraus and Nicklas 2004.

[119] Bauckham 1998: ch. 8; for an evaluation of this hypothesis, see Tigchelaar 2003.

[120] Clement, *Eclogae propheticae* 41; cf. Apoc. Pet. 8.4. Also *Ecl. proph.* 48 (Peter in the Apocalypse says; cf. Apoc. Pet. 8.10); 49 (Peter in the Apocalypse; cf. Apoc. Pet. 8.8–9).

[121] Methodius, *Symposium* 2.6 (quoting without attribution; cf. Apoc. Pet. 8.7); the pagan writer (Porphyry?) cited by Macarius of Magnesia, *Apocriticus* 4.6–7; Cyril of Jerusalem, *Cat.*, 15.20–1 (cf. Apoc. Pet. 6.1–2); Jerome, *Vir. ill.* 5 (labelling it apocryphal); *Homily on the Parable of the Ten Virgins*, ln. 58–60, 77–8 (quoting the Apocalypse by name; cf. Apoc. Pet. 5.8–6.5; 12.4–7). See Bauckham 1998: 256. It may have been used in the second century in the *Sibylline Oracles*; see Buchholz 1988: 45.

[122] As also in the stichometry of Nicephorus (Markschies 2012: 142); but it is considered apocryphal in the *List of Sixty Books* (ibid.: 146). See also Eusebius, *Hist. eccl.* 6.14.1.

its continuing use in some churches (*Hist. eccl.* 7.19). The work appears under obelus in the list included in Codex Claromontanus. The complete text of the Apocalypse of Peter is available only in Ge'ez (in only two manuscripts).[123] In Greek, there exist two fourth-century fragments (the Bodleian fragment and the Rainer fragment),[124] as well as the Akhmim Codex from the sixth century, which contains about half of the original work (but in a secondary edition), along with the Gospel of Peter and 1 Enoch.[125]

Peter, Epistles of

Two epistles associated with Peter are accepted in the biblical canon of most Christian groups. The shorter of these epistles refers to itself as the second (2 Pet. 3:1). This second epistle experienced a difficult and uncertain reception in early Christian circles, while 1 Peter was received very early on. Eusebius characterizes their reception this way:

> Of Peter, one epistle, that which is called his first, is admitted (ἀνωμολόγηται), and the ancient presbyters used this in their own writings as unquestioned, but the so-called second Epistle we have not received as encovenanted (οὐκ ἐνδιάθηκον μὲν εἶναι παρειλήφαμεν), but nevertheless it has appeared useful to many, and has been studied with other Scriptures.
>
> (*Hist. eccl.* 3.3.1)[126]

The history of reception causes Eusebius in his canon list to classify 1 Peter as universally acknowledged and 2 Peter among the *antilegomena* (*Hist. eccl.* 3.25). Echoes or quotations of 1 Peter have been identified in several early sources, such as Polycarp[127] and Irenaeus, who mentions Peter's epistle (*Haer.* 4.9.2; cf. 4.16.5; 5.7.2). Origen is the first extant author to mention Peter's second epistle,[128] though perhaps some earlier Christians exhibit familiarity with the letter.[129]

Peter, Gospel of

This Gospel was first mentioned by Origen (*Comm. Matt.* 10.17),[130] then by Eusebius, who considers it not an *antilegomenon* but a heretical writing (*Hist. eccl.* 3.25.6; cf. 3.3.2).[131] Eusebius (*Hist. eccl.* 6.12) also quotes a letter written by the late-second-century bishop Serapion, who granted the request of the church in Rhossus to use the Gospel of Peter in their worship services, but later changed his mind once he had read the text and

---

[123] For the text, see Buchholz 1988; see also Kraus and Nicklas 2004: 55–63; for a brief summary, see Bauckham 1998: 254–5.

[124] These two fragments possibly (definitely, according to Van Minnen 2003: 35) derive from the same manuscript; see Bauckham 1998: 257.

[125] Bauckham 1998: 257–8; Van Minnen 2003.

[126] Translation adapted from Lake 1926. See similarly Jerome, *Vir. ill.* 1.

[127] See *Phil.* 1.3; 2.1–2; 5.3; 7.2; 8.1–2; 10.2; see Holmes 2005: 220–3.

[128] See Eusebius, *Hist. eccl.* 6.25.8. See further, ch. 1, pp. 44–8.

[129] See Bauckham 1983: 162–3.

[130] For text, translation, and introduction, see Ehrman and Pleše 2011: 371–87. For much more, see Kraus and Nicklas 2004; Foster 2010.

[131] On early Christian use of the Gospel of Peter, see Kraus and Nicklas 2004: 11–19; Foster 2010: 97–115.

found that while it largely agrees with the orthodox faith, certain additions could support a heterodox viewpoint. This Gospel was lost for many centuries before the discovery of the Akhmim Codex (P.Cair. 10759) at the end of the nineteenth century. This codex contains an incomplete copy of the Gospel of Peter.[132] We cannot know for certain whether the text known in the Akhmim Codex as the Gospel of Peter is the same work familiar to Serapion and other early Christians. Most scholars accept this identification, and date the composition of the Gospel to the second century.[133] The Gospel provides an alternative account for the death and resurrection of Jesus.

Revelation

As we noted in chapter 1, the book of Revelation was not fully accepted into the Greek Orthodox biblical canon until the seventeenth century, and it has never formed a part of the Orthodox liturgy. On the other hand, the Western church has usually received Revelation as fully canonical. The earliest references to the book, in both East and West, confirm its apostolic authorship and authority.[134] The book's reception became problematic in the third century as some church leaders endeavoured to diminish the appeal of millenarian speculation based on the book by questioning its authorship. These questions led to concerns about the authority of the book, as reflected both in the canon lists collected in this volume and in the book's transmission history. Eusebius strangely places the book both among the accepted books (reflecting its early and widespread attestation) and among the spurious books (reflecting the more recent concerns). Amphilochius of Iconium notes that the majority do not accept the book, and several lists omit any reference to it.[135] Western lists routinely include it. The Apocalypse frequently circulated by itself in the Greek world, as many manuscripts containing it feature no other portion of the New Testament.[136]

The Shepherd of Hermas

The Shepherd of Hermas is a long apocalyptic work written in Rome, probably during the first half of the second century,[137] more toward the middle of that century if the Muratorian Fragment is to be believed.[138] The Shepherd was a very popular work in early Christianity, as we can tell from both its manuscript attestation and the citations in patristic literature. As for the former, '[e]ighteen separate manuscripts of Hermas

---

[132] For photographs and a transcription, see Foster 2010: 178–95. Photographs are also available at <http://ipap.csad.ox.ac.uk/GP/GP.html>. For discussion of the text, see Kraus and Nicklas 2004: 25–31. Foster (2010: 1) reports that the Akhmim Codex is now missing.

[133] Foster 2010: 169–72.

[134] Examples include Justin Martyr, *Dial.* 81; Irenaeus, *Haer.* 5.26.1; 35.2; Tertullian, *Marc.* 4.5; Origen, *Comm. John* 5 (*apud* Eusebius, *Hist. eccl.* 6.25.9). These same examples are listed in ch. 1 (p. 50n306), which provides a more extensive discussion.

[135] Cyril of Jerusalem, Synod of Laodicea, Apostolic Canons, the Syriac list from St Catherine's Monastery. The list of Gregory of Nazianzus is somewhat more complex; see p. 146n377.

[136] For more detail, see the discussion in ch. 1, pp. 49–52; see also Elliott 2015; Schmid 2015.

[137] For basic orientation to the work, see Verheyden 2007. For text and English translation, see Holmes 2007: 442–685.

[138] See the section on the Muratorian Fragment (ln. 73–80) in ch. 4, pp. 181–2, for its comment on the Shepherd. On different scholarly opinions regarding the date of composition, see Osiek 1999: 18–20.

have survived from the first five centuries CE ranging in size from a tiny parchment scrap to the extensive 62-page Michigan papyrus'.[139] This total does not include the Codex Sinaiticus, which includes the Shepherd as the final writing, after the Epistle of Barnabas.[140] The Shepherd is thus the best attested Christian writing in early Greek manuscripts, after the Gospels of Matthew and John.[141] It was also translated into a variety of languages (Latin, Coptic, Ge'ez, Persian, Georgian).[142] Irenaeus cited the work as a γραφή, usually translated 'Scripture' (*Haer.* 4.20.2).[143] Clement of Alexandria cited it a few times (*Strom.* 1.17.29; 2.1.9, 12),[144] and Tertullian early on seemed to value the Shepherd (*Or.* 16) before turning against it after his acceptance of Montanism (*De pudic.* 10; 20). Origen cited the work several times and believed it to be 'divinely inspired' (*Comm. Rom.* 16.14). Ehrman insists, based on five quotations of the Shepherd 'as Scripture', that Didymus the Blind accepted the Shepherd as canonical.[145] But the Shepherd seems never to appear in early Christian canon lists as fully canonical. The Muratorian Fragment permits only private reading, Athanasius includes the Shepherd among the books to be read by catechumens, Rufinus and Jerome both explicitly exclude the Shepherd from the canon, though Rufinus also says that it should be read for its edifying value, and the list in Codex Claromontanus lists the Shepherd near the end, but a mark—apparently an obelus—stands next to it.

Sirach/Ben Sira/Ecclesiasticus

Sirach is accepted as canonical in the Roman Catholic Church and several other Christian traditions, but it is not in the Jewish or Protestant Bibles. The book is a lengthy collection of wisdom sayings, composed in Hebrew in the early second century BCE by the scribal teacher Jesus Ben Sira, who identifies himself within the book (Sir. 50:27). This Hebrew book was translated into Greek by the author's grandson, who also pre-fixed to the translation a preface. For many centuries only this Greek version, and trans-lations from it, survived, but in modern times substantial fragments of the Hebrew

---

[139] Wayment 2013: 81. Wayment transcribes these texts on pp. 82–169 and publishes photo-graphs of the papyri on pp. 286–390.

[140] See Batovici (2014), who does not think that the inclusion of the Shepherd within Sinaiticus indicates its canonical status.

[141] Hurtado 2006: 32–3.

[142] Osiek 1999: 1–7. The Shepherd appears after the New Testament in a ninth-century Latin Bible from Paris (VL 7); see Bogaert 2012: 90; Houghton 2016: 194–5, 213–14. For the Latin ver-sion, see Tornau and Cecconi 2014. But note Jerome's statement that Latin readers hardly know the work (*Vir. ill.* 10). On the Ge'ez version, see Erho 2015, who dates the translation to the fifth century, surveys the three surviving manuscripts, and explores its canonical status, concluding that it has probably not been considered canonical in Ethiopia since at least the late fourteenth century (perhaps earlier).

[143] But see Hill 2013b.

[144] See Batovici (2013: 51): 'In the light of this [preceding analysis], it becomes clear that, put bluntly, Clement believed Hermas' visions to be genuine. Not a literary genre, not the book of a venerable man, or gnostic or saint, but an account of a genuine revelation, where Hermas is tech-nically a prophet.'

[145] Ehrman 1983: 11–13.

book were recovered, first in the Cairo Genizah, and then among the Dead Sea Scrolls (2Q18) and at Masada.[146] Still, the earliest complete text is in Greek.[147]

The Hebrew fragments at Qumran and Masada show that Jews read the book, and the texts from the Cairo Genizah demonstrate its continuing popularity into medieval times, after the Jewish canon had been defined. This high status is also signalled by the citations of Ben Sira in rabbinic literature, sometimes even with introductory formulas as if it were Scripture.[148]

Christians used the book of Sirach extensively, as attested by the citations in *Biblia Patristica*. The lists in the current volume catalogue Sirach in various ways. Some include it among the canonical books (e.g. Augustine), others do not list it (e.g. Gregory of Nazianzus), and others list it among the intermediate books (e.g. Athanasius). Later in Eastern tradition the *Dialogue of Timothy and Aquila* (sixth century) listed the Wisdom of Jesus son of Sirach among the apocrypha that the Seventy-Two Interpreters handed down to Jews and Christians. Although John of Damascus, *De Fide Orthodoxa* 4.17 (PG 94: 1180; ca. 754 CE), does not include the book in the canon, he describes it as virtuous (ἐνάρετος) and beautiful (καλή). The ninth-century canon list of Nicephorus I (d. 811), *Chronographia Brevis*, includes the Wisdom of the son of Sirach among the disputed (*antilegomena*) books—not canonical books (PG 100: 1057). In the West, the church recognized the canonicity of Ecclesiasticus/Sirach from the fourth century.

Song of Songs

The Song of Songs was discussed in rabbinic literature often in relation to Ecclesiastes.[149] Like Ecclesiastes, the Song might have been translated into Greek very late, perhaps in the first century CE.[150] One rabbinic passage in which the Song appears by itself is the following:

> Our Rabbis taught: He who recites a verse of the Song of Songs and treats it as a [secular] air, and one who recites a verse at the banqueting table unseasonably, brings evil upon the world.

> (b. Sanh. 101a; cf. t. Sanh. 12.10)

This passage suggests some concern to emphasize a pious reading of the Song of Songs. The allegorical approach to the Song developed early and has dominated the reading of

---

[146] For the Masada manuscript (Mas1h), preserving Sir. 39:27–44:17, see Talmon and Yadin 1999. On the Dead Sea Scrolls, see Wright 2000. The scroll of Sirach preserves only a few words from ch. 6, but the Great Psalms Scroll (11Q5) also contains the Hebrew text of Sir. 51:13–19, 30. On the Hebrew manuscripts of Sirach, see also www.bensira.org.

[147] See Ziegler 1980, who mentions four fragmentary papyri (928, 929, 938, 964)—dated to the third, sixth–seventh, fifth, fourth centuries, respectively—five uncials (Alexandrinus, Vaticanus, Ephraemi, Sinaiticus, Venetus), fifty-seven minuscules, and many ancient versions (Latin, Coptic, Syriac, etc.). There is no evidence of the Jewish Greek revisions of Theodotion, Aquila, and Symmachus (Gentry 2016: 229).

[148] For citations with introductory formulas, see b. Ḥag. 13a; Yebam. 63b; Erub. 54a. See also m. 'Abot 4.4; b. Pesaḥ 113b; b. B. Meṣi'a 112a; Tanḥ Mikkeṣ 10; Exod. Rab. 21:7; b. B. Qam. 92b. For the role of Ben Sira in rabbinic literature, see Labendz 2006; T. Ellis 2014.

[149] See above on Ecclesiastes for some of the rabbinic passages relating to the Song of Songs.

[150] See Auwers 2015: 371.

the text, both in Judaism and Christianity, assuring the book an important role in theological reflection in synagogue and church.[151]

Thomas, Gospel of

The Gospel of Thomas is a collection of sayings ascribed to Jesus,[152] probably written in Greek in the latter half of the second century.[153] These sayings are divided by scholars into 114 different units. Many of the sayings have parallels in the Synoptic Gospels; scholars debate the relationship between Thomas and the Synoptics.[154] The Greek text does not survive intact, but only in small papyrus fragments dating to the third century (P.Oxy 1, 654, 655).[155] The finds at Nag Hammadi included a Coptic copy of Thomas in what became known as Codex 2, dating to the first half of the fourth century. In this codex, Thomas follows the Apocryphon of John and precedes the Gospel of Philip and several other works.[156] We have no evidence for an ancient translation into Latin or other languages (besides Coptic). Several early Christian writers mention the (or, a) Gospel of Thomas and consider it heretical,[157] the earliest reference appearing in Hippolytus, *Haer.* 5.7.20.[158] Though Origen classifies this Gospel as heretical (*Hom. Luc.* 1.2), he also seems to think that it might preserve authentic sayings of Jesus.[159] In their respective discussions of the canon, Eusebius (*Hist. eccl.* 3.25.6) and Cyril of Jerusalem (*Catech.* 4.36) name Thomas as the work of heretics (specifically, Manicheans, in the case of Cyril).[160]

Tobit

Tobit is accepted as canonical in the Roman Catholic Church and several other Christian traditions, but it is not in the Jewish or Protestant Bibles.[161] The book tells the story of a pious Israelite exile who experiences difficult circumstances, but whose faithfulness is rewarded in the end. It was composed in Aramaic probably around the turn of the second century BCE.[162]

---

[151] On Christian interpretation of the Song, see Norris 2003; Shuve 2016; on rabbinic interpretation, see Fishbane 2015: 245–310; Kaplan 2015.

[152] For text and translation, along with brief introduction, see Ehrman and Pleše 2011: 303–49.

[153] Gathercole (2014: 124) dates it between 135 and 200.

[154] For a summary, see Ehrman and Pleše 2011: 307–8; Foster 2013: 296–300.

[155] See Luijendijk, 2011. Luijendijk discusses the physical form of these fragments, especially the roll format of P.Oxy 654 (with some reader's aids) and 655 as opposed to the codex format of P.Oxy 1. She believes these manuscripts indicate that Thomas was 'studied in private settings and also may have been recited in worship from a codex' (ibid.: 266).

[156] These other works include the Hypostases of the Archons, on the Origin of the World, Exegesis of the Soul, and the book of Thomas the Contender.

[157] See Gathercole 2012.

[158] Hippolytus quotes a saying somewhat resembling what is now numbered as saying 4. However, see S. Johnson 2010; Gathercole 2012: 54–6.

[159] See Carlson 2014, who discusses *Hom. Jer.* 27.3.7 (cf. *Hom. Jos.* 4.3), probably quoting Gos. Thom. 82. On the other hand, see *Cels.* 8.15–16 (cf. Gos. Thom. 74); *Peri Pascha* (cf. Gos. Thom. 23). See also Luijendijk 2011: 257–61.

[160] See ch. 3, for both of these lists.

[161] On recent scholarship, see A. Perrin 2014.   [162] See Fitzmyer 2003: 50–2.

Early Christians made extensive use of Tobit, as attested by the citations in *Biblia Patristica*. The earliest usage of the book is 2 Clement's dependence on Tobit 12:8–9 for its teaching on charitable giving in 16.4.

The Dead Sea Scrolls included four fragmentary scrolls of Tobit in Aramaic, and one in Hebrew.[163] But the text survives complete only in translation, especially the Greek text usually included among the Septuagint texts.[164] Greek Tobit is found in two fragmentary papyri (910, sixth century; 990, third century); three uncials (Vaticanus, Alexandrinus, Venetus); several minuscules in different recensions; and several versions (Old Latin, Peshitta, Sahidic, Geʻez, Armenian). Jerome produced a Latin translation, claiming to have used as his basic text a Chaldean (i.e., Aramaic) copy.[165]

The lists in the current volume catalogue Tobit in various ways. Some include the book among the canonical books (e.g. Augustine), others do not list it (e.g. Gregory of Nazianzus), and others list it among the intermediate books (e.g. Athanasius). Later in Eastern tradition, the *Dialogue of Timothy and Aquila* (sixth century) listed Tobit among the apocrypha that the Seventy-Two Interpreters handed down to Jews and Christians. John of Damascus, *De Fide Orthodoxa* 4.17 (PG 94: 1180; ca. 754 CE), does not include the book in the canon. The ninth-century canon list of Nicephorus I (d. 811), *Chronographia Brevis*, includes Tobit and Tobias among the disputed (*antilegomena*) books—not canonical books (PG 100: 1057). In the West, the church recognized the canonicity of Tobit from the late fourth century.

Wisdom of Solomon

The Wisdom of Solomon is accepted as canonical in the Roman Catholic Church and several other Christian traditions, but it is not in the Jewish or Protestant Bibles. It is a wisdom work composed in Greek during the first century (BCE or CE), probably in Alexandria.[166] While we have little evidence for its influence within Judaism,[167] it became a very important text in early Christianity, as Christian authors often found in it material ripe for Christological appropriation.[168] According to *Biblia Patristica*, second-century authors use Wisdom of Solomon some fifteen times, third-century authors use it some 340 times,[169] and fourth-century authors use it some 930 times.[170]

There are two fragmentary papyri (928, third century; 950, fourth–fifth century). Five uncials contain the work (Alexandrinus; Vaticanus; Ephraemi; Sinaiticus; Venetus), as well as forty-five minuscules. The following versions also preserve the book: Old Latin, Vulgate, Bohairic, Sahidic, Peshitta, Christian Palestinian Aramaic, Syro-hexapla, Geʻez, Arabic, and Armenian. Jerome did not translate the book, and he recognized that it was composed in Greek, by Philo Judaeus, he thought (*Praef. lib. Sal.*).

---

[163]   See Fitzmyer 2000.

[164]   For a synopsis of Tobit texts, see Weeks, Gathercole, and Stuckenbruck 2004.

[165]   See Gallagher 2015b.

[166]   Aitken 2015c: 402–4.

[167]   According to Gentry (2016: 229), there is no evidence of the Jewish Greek revisions of Theodotion, Aquila, and Symmachus for this book.

[168]   See the discussion in Gallagher 2012a: 38–46 (on Origen).

[169]   Tertullian; Origen; Cyprian of Carthage; Novatian of Roma; Hippolytus of Rome; Theognostus of Alexandria; Dionysius of Alexandria; Gregory Thaumaturgus; Victorinus of Pettau.

[170]   Didymus of Alexandria; Eusebius of Caesarea; Basil of Caesarea; Athanasius; Gregory of Nazianzus; Ambrosiaster; Gregory of Nyssa; Ambrose of Milan; Epiphanius; Hilary of Poitiers; John Chrysostom; Cyril of Jerusalem; Lactantius; Amphilochius of Iconium.

The lists in the current volume catalogue Wisdom of Solomon in various ways. Some include it among the canonical books (e.g. Augustine), others do not list it (e.g. Gregory of Nazianzus), and others list it among the intermediate books (e.g. Athanasius). Later in Eastern tradition the *Dialogue of Timothy and Aquila* (sixth century) listed Wisdom of Solomon among the apocrypha that the Seventy-Two Interpreters handed down to Jews and Christians. Although John of Damascus, *De Fide Orthodoxa* 4.17 (PG 94: 1180; ca. 754 CE), does not include the book in the canon, he describes it as virtuous ($\dot{\epsilon}\nu\dot{\alpha}\rho\epsilon\tau$os) and beautiful ($\kappa\alpha\lambda\dot{\eta}$). The ninth-century canon list of Nicephorus I (d. 811), *Chronographia Brevis*, includes the Wisdom of Solomon among the disputed (*antilegomena*) books—not canonical books (PG 100: 1057). In the West, the church recognized the canonicity of Wisdom of Solomon from the late fourth century.

Bibliography

Primary Sources

Amphilochius of Iconium: Oberg, Eberhard, ed. 1969. *Amphilochii Iconiensis iambi ad Seleucum*. Patristische Texte und Studien 9. Berlin: De Gruyter.

Apostolic Canons: Metzger, M, ed. 1985, 1986, 1987. *Les Constitutions Apostolique*. Sources chrétiennes 320, 329, 336. Paris: Cerf.

Athanasius of Alexandria: Joannou, Périclès-Pierre, ed. 1963. *Fonti: Discipline générale antique (IVe–IXe s.)*. Rome: Grottaferrata.

Augustine of Hippo: Green, Guilelmus M., ed. 1963. *Sancti Aureli Augustini Opera* 6.4: *De Doctrina Christiana libri quattuor*. Corpus Scriptorum Ecclesiasticorum Latinorum 80. Vienna: Hoelder-Pichler-Tempsky.

Babylonian Talmud: Epstein, Isidore, ed., Maurice Simon, trans. 1960. *Hebrew–English Edition of the Babylonian Talmud*, 30 vols. London: Soncino.

Breviarium Hipponense: Munier, C., ed. 1974. *Concilia Africae a. 345–525*. CCSL 149. Turnhout: Brepols.

Bryennios List: Harris, J. Rendel. 1885. *Three Pages of the Bryennios Manuscript*. Baltimore, MD: Johns Hopkins University.

Codex Claromontanus: Zahn, Theodor. 1892. *Geschichte des neutestamentlichen Kanons*. Erlangen: A. Dichert.

Cyril of Jerusalem: Reischl, W.C. and J. Rupp, eds. 1848–60. *Cyrilli Hierosolymorum archiepiscopi opera quae supersunt omnia*, 2 vols. Munich: Lentner; repr., Hildesheim: Georg Olms Verlagsbuchhandlung, 1967a and 1967b.

Epiphanius of Salamis: Bergermann, Marc and Christian-Friedrich Collatz, eds. 2013. *Epiphanius I: Ancoratus und Panarion Haer. 1–33*. GCS N.F. 10. Berlin: De Gruyter.

Epiphanius of Salamis: Dummer, Jürgen, ed. 1985. *Epiphanius III: Panarion haer. 65–80 De fide*. GCS 37. Leipzig: Hinrichs.

Epiphanius of Salamis: Moutsoulas, Elia D., ed. 1973. 'Τὸ Περὶ μέτρων καὶ σταθμῶν' ἔργον Ἐπιφανίου τοῦ Σαλαμῖνος'. Θεολογία 44: 157–98.

Eusebius of Caesarea: Schwartz, Eduard, ed. 1908. *Eusebius Werke* 2.1: *Die Kirchengeschichte*, Books I–V. GCS 9.1. Leipzig: Hinrichs.

Gregory of Nazianzus: Migne, J.-P, ed. 1862. *Carmina Theologica, Book I, Section I, Carmen XII*. PG 37. Paris: Imprimerie Catholique.

Hilary of Poitiers: Doignon, J., ed. 1997. *Tractatus super Psalms*. CCSL 61. Turnhout: Brepols.

Innocent I of Rome: Wurm, Hubert, ed. 1939. 'Decretales selectae ex antiquissimis Romanorum pontificum epistulis decretalibus'. *Apollinaris* 12: 40–93.

Jerome of Stridon: Gasquet, Aidano, ed. 1944. *Biblia Sacra iuxta latinam vulgatam versionem ad codicum fidem: Liber Samuehlis*. Rome: Vatican.

Jerome of Stridon: Hilberg, Isidorus, ed. 1910–1918. *Hieronymus, Epistulae*, 3 vols. CSEL 54–56. Vienna: Tempsky.

Josephus: Niese, Benedictus, ed. 1889 (repr. 1955). *Flavii Iosephi Opera*, vol. 5: *De Iudaeorum Vetustate Sive Contra Apionem Libri II*. Berlin: Weidmann.

Melito of Sardis: Schwartz, Eduard, ed. 1903. *Eusebius Werke* 2.1: *Die Kirchengeschichte*, Books I–V. GCS 9.1. Leipzig: Hinrichs.

Mommsen Catalogue: Preuschen, Erwin. 1893. *Analecta: kürzere Texte zur Geschichte der alten Kirche und des Kanons*. Freiburg/Leipzig: Mohr Siebeck.

Muratorian Fragment: Souter, Alexander. 1954. *The Text and Canon of the New Testament*, 2nd edn. London: Duckworth.

Origen of Alexandria: Baehrens, W.A., ed. 1921. *Origenes Werke VII: Homilien zum Hexateuch in Rufins Übersetzung*. GCS 30. Leipzig: Hinrichs.

Origen of Alexandria: Schwartz, Eduard, ed. 1908. *Eusebius Werke* 2.2: *Die Kirchengeschichte*, Books VI–X. GCS 9.2. Leipzig: Hinrichs.

Rufinus of Aquileia: Simonetti, M., ed. 1961. CCSL 20. Turnhout: Brepols.

St Catherine's Monastery Syriac List: Harris, J.R. 1894. *Catalogue of the Syriac MSS. in the Convent of S. Catharine on Mount Sinai*, compiled by Agnes Smith Lewis. *Studia Sinaitica* 1. London: Cambridge University Press.

Synod of Laodicea: Joannou, Périclès-Pierre, ed. 1962. *Fonti: Discipline générale antique (IVe–IXe s.)*. Rome: Grottaferrata.

Secondary Literature

Adams, Sean A. 2014. *Baruch and the Epistle of Jeremiah: A Commentary on the Texts in Codex Vaticanus*. Septuagint Commentary Series. Leiden: Brill.

Adler, William. 1990. 'The Origins of the Proto-Heresies: Fragments from a Chronicle in the First Book of Epiphanius' *Panarion*'. *Journal of Theological Studies* 41: 472–501.

Aitken, James K, ed. 2015a. *T&T Clark Companion to the Septuagint*. London: Bloomsbury.

Aitken, James K. 2015b. 'Ecclesiastes', in *T&T Clark Companion to the Septuagint*, ed. James K. Aitken, pp. 356–69. London: Bloomsbury.

Aitken, James K. 2015c. 'Wisdom of Solomon', in *T&T Clark Companion to the Septuagint*, ed. James K. Aitken, pp. 356–69. London: Bloomsbury.

Aland, Barbara. 1986. *Das Neue Testament in syrischer Überlieferung: I. Die großen katholischen Briefe*. ANTF 7. Berlin: De Gruyter.

Aland, Kurt and Barbara Aland. 1995. *The Text of the New Testament: An Introduction to the Critical Editions and to the Theory and Practice of Modern Textual Criticism*. 2nd edn, rev. and enl; trans. Erroll F. Rhodes. Grand Rapids, MI: Eerdmans.

Aldridge, Robert E. 1999. 'Peter and the "Two Ways"'. *Vigiliae Christianae* 53: 233–64.

Alexander, P. 1983. '3 (Hebrew Apocalypse of) Enoch', in *The Old Testament Pseudepigrapha*, vol. 1: *Apocalyptic Literature and Testaments*, ed. James H. Charlesworth, pp. 223–315. Garden City, NY: Doubleday.

Alexander, Philip S. 2007. 'The Formation of the Biblical Canon in Rabbinic Judaism', in *The Canon of Scripture in Jewish and Christian Tradition*, eds Philip S. Alexander and Jean-Daniel Kaestli, pp. 57–80. Prahins: Éditions du Zèbre.

Allison, Dale C. 2013. *A Critical and Exegetical Commentary on the Epistle of James*. ICC. New York: Bloomsbury.

Andersen, F.I. 1983. '2 (Slavonic Apocalypse of) Enoch', in *The Old Testament Pseudepigrapha*, vol. 1: *Apocalyptic Literature and Testaments*, ed. James H. Charlesworth, pp. 92–221. Garden City, NY: Doubleday.

Aragione, Gabriella. 2005. 'La *Lettre festale* 39 d'Athanase. Présentation et traduction de la version copte et de l'extrait grec', in *Le canon du Nouveau Testament: Regards nouveaux sur l'histoire de sa formation*, eds Gabrielle Aragione, Éric Junod, and Enrico Norelli. Le Monde de la Bible 54, pp. 197–219. Genève: Labor et Fides.

Arendzen, J.P. 1902. 'An Entire Syriac Text of the "Apostolic Church Order"'. *Journal of Theological Studies* 3: 59–80.

Armstrong, Jonathan J. 2006. 'The Role of the Rule of Faith in the Formation of the New Testament Canon according to Eusebius of Caesarea'. Ph.D. thesis, Fordham University. Published form: Lewiston, NY: Edwin Mellen, 2014 (*non vidimus*).

Armstrong, Jonathan J. 2008. 'Victorinus of Pettau as the Author of the Canon Muratori'. *Vigiliae Christianae* 62: 1–34.

Assan-Dhôte, Isabelle and Jacqeline Moatti-Fine. 2008. *La Bible D'Alexandrie: Baruch, Lamentations, Lettre de Jérémie: Traduction du texte grec de la Septante Introduction et notes*. Paris: Cerf.

Audet, Jean-Paul. 1950. 'A Hebrew-Aramaic List of Books of the Old Testament in Greek Transcription'. *Journal of Theological Studies* n.s. 1: 135–54; repr. in *The Canon and Masorah of the Hebrew Bible: An Introductory Reader*, ed. Sid Z. Leiman, pp. 52–71. New York: Ktav, 1974.

Aune, David E. 1997. *Revelation 1–5*. Word Biblical Commentary 52a. Dallas, TX: Word Books.

Auwers, Jean-Marie. 2015. 'Canticles (Song of Songs)', in *T&T Clark Companion to the Septuagint*, ed. James K. Aitken, pp. 370–84. London: Bloomsbury.

Baarda, Tjitze. 2012. 'Tatian's Diatessaron and the Greek Text of the Gospels', in *The Early Text of the New Testament*, eds Charles E. Hill and Michael J. Kruger, pp. 336–49. Oxford: Oxford University Press.

Backus, Irena. 2000. *Reformation Readings of the Apocalypse: Geneva, Zurich, and Wittenberg*. Oxford: Oxford University Press.

Baldwin, Matthew C. 2005. *Whose Acts of Peter? Text and Historical Context of the Actus Vercellenses*. Tübingen: Mohr Siebeck.

Barclay, John M.G. 2007. *Against Apion*, vol. 10: *Flavius Josephus: Translation and Commentary*, ed. Steve Mason. Leiden: Brill.

Bardy, Gustave. 1955. 'Conciles d'Hippone au temps de saint Augustin'. *Augustiniana* 5: 441–58.

Barkhuizen, J.H. 2001. 'Amphilochius of Iconium: Homily 1 "On the Nativity"'. *Acta Patristica et Byzantina* 12: 1–23.

Barr, James. 1983. *Holy Scripture: Canon, Authority and Criticism*. Philadelphia, PA: Westminster.

Barrier, Jeremy W. 2009. *The Acts of Paul and Thecla*. Tübingen: Mohr Siebeck.

Barthélemy, Dominique. 1963. *Les devanciers d'Aquila: première publication intégrale du texte des fragments du Dodécaprophéton*. Leiden: Brill.

Barthélemy, Dominique. 1984. 'L'État de la Bible juive depuis le début de notre ère jusqu'à la deuxième révolte contre Rome (131–135)', in *Le canon de l'Ancien Testament: sa formation et son histoire*, eds Jean-Daniel Kaestli and Otto Wermelinger, La Monde de la Bible 10, pp. 9–45. Geneva: Labor et Fides.

Barton, John. 1986. *Oracles of God: Perceptions of Ancient Prophecy in Israel after the Exile*. New York: Oxford University Press.

Barton, John. 1997. *Holy Writings, Sacred Text: The Canon in Early Christianity*. Louisville, KY: Westminster John Knox.

Barton, John. 2013. 'The Old Testament Canons', in *The New Cambridge History of the Bible*, vol. 1: *From the Beginnings to 600*, eds James Carleton Paget and Joachim Schaper, pp. 145–64. Cambridge: Cambridge University Press.

Batovici, Dan. 2013. 'Hermas in Clement of Alexandria', in *Studia Patristica* 66, ed. Markus Vinzent, pp. 41–51. Leuven: Peeters.

Batovici, Dan. 2014. 'Textual Revisions of the *Shepherd of Hermas* in Codex Sinaiticus'. *Zeitschrift für Antikes Christentum* 18: 443–70.

Bauckham, Richard J. 1983. *Jude, 2 Peter*. Word Biblical Commentary. Waco, TX: Word Books.

Bauckham, Richard. 1990. *Jude and the Relatives of Jesus in the Early Church*. London: T&T Clark.

Bauckham, Richard. 1998. *The Fate of the Dead: Studies on the Jewish and Christian Apocalypses*. Leiden: Brill.

Bauckham, Richard. 2017. *Jesus and the Eyewitnesses: The Gospels as Eyewitness Testimony*, 2nd edn. Grand Rapids, MI: Eerdmans.

Bauer, Walter. 1903. *Der Apostolos der Syrer in der Zeit von der Mitte des vierten Jahrhunderts bis zur Spaltung der syrischen Kirche*. Gieszen: J. Ricker'sche.

Baum, Armin D. 1997. 'Der neutestamentliche Kanon bei Eusebios (*Hist. eccl.* III, 25, 1–7) im Kontext seiner literaturgeschichtlichen Arbeit'. *Ephemerides Theologicae Lovanienses* 73: 307–48.

Baynes, Leslie. 2012 '*Enoch* and *Jubilees* in the Canon of the Ethiopian Orthodox Church', in vol. 2 of *A Teacher for All Generations: Essays in Honor of James C. VanderKam*, eds Eric F. Mason, Kelley Coblentz Bautch, Angela Kim Harkins, and Daniel A. Machiela, pp. 799–818. Leiden: Brill.

Beckwith, Carl L. 2008. *Hilary of Poitiers on the Trinity: From De Fide to De Trinitate*. Oxford: Oxford University Press.

Beckwith, Roger. 1985. *The Old Testament Canon of the New Testament Church*. Grand Rapids, MI: Eerdmans.

Beckwith, Roger. 1991. 'A Modern Theory of the Old Testament Canon'. *Vetus Testamentum* 41: 385–95.

BeDuhn, Jason D. 2013. *The First New Testament: Marcion's Scriptural Canon*. Salem, OR: Polebridge.

Ben-Eliyahu, Eyal, Yehudah Cohn, and Fergus Millar. 2012. *Handbook of Jewish Literature from Late Antiquity, 135–700 CE*. Oxford: Oxford University Press.

Ben Zvi, Ehud and James D. Nogalski. 2009. *Two Sides of a Coin: Juxtaposing Views on Interpreting the Book of the Twelve/the Twelve Prophetic Books*. Piscataway, NJ: Gorgias.

Berger, Samuel. 1893. *Histoire de la Vulgate pendant les premiers siècles du moyen âge*. Paris: Hachette.

Bird, Michael F. 2011. 'The Reception of Paul in the *Epistle to Diognetus*', in *Paul and the Second Century*, eds Michael F. Bird and Joseph R. Dodson, pp. 70–90. New York: Bloomsbury.

Blackwell, Ben C. 2011. 'Paul and Irenaeus', in *Paul and the Second Century*, eds Michael F. Bird and Joseph R. Dodson, pp. 190–206. New York: Bloomsbury.

Blenkinsopp, Joseph. 1977. *Prophecy and Canon: A Contribution to the Study of Jewish Origins*. Notre Dame, IN: University of Notre Dame Press.

Bogaert, Pierre-Maurice. 1999. 'Ordres anciens des évangiles et tétraévangile en un seul codex'. *Revue théologique de Louvain* 30: 297–314.

Bogaert, Pierre-Maurice. 2000. 'Les livres d'Esdras et leur numérotation dans l'histoire du canon de la Bible latine'. *Revue bénédictine* 110: 5–26.

Bogaert, Pierre-Maurice. 2003. 'Aux origines de la fixation du canon: Scriptoria, listes et titres. Le *Vaticanus* et la stichométrie de Mommsen', in *The Biblical Canons*, eds J.-M. Auwers and H.J. de Jonge, pp. 153–76. Leuven: Leuven University Press.

Bogaert, Pierre-Maurice. 2005. 'Le livre de Baruch dans les manuscrits de la Bible latine. Disparition et reintegration'. *Revue bénédictine* 115: 286–342.

Bogaert, Pierre-Maurice. 2006. 'Les bibles d'Augustin'. *Revue théologique de Louvain* 37: 513–31.

Bogaert, Pierre-Maurice. 2012. 'The Latin Bible, c. 600 to c. 900', in *The New Cambridge History of the Bible*, vol. 2: *From 600 to 1450*, eds Richard Marsden and Ann E. Matter, pp. 69–92. Cambridge: Cambridge University Press.

Bogaert, Pierre-Maurice. 2014. 'Les frontièrs du canon de l'Ancien Testament dans l'Occident latin', in *La Bible juive dans l'Antiquité*, eds Rémi Gounelle and Jan Joosten, pp. 41–95. Lausanne: Éditions du Zèbre.

Bokedal, Tomas. 2014. *The Formation and Significance of the Christian Biblical Canon: A Study in Text, Ritual and Interpretation*. New York: Bloomsbury.

Bond, Helen K. 2015. 'Was Peter Behind Mark's Gospel?', in *Peter in Early Christianity*, eds Helen K. Bond and Larry W. Hurtado, pp. 46–61. Grand Rapids, MI: Eerdmans.

Bonis, Constantine G. 1959. 'Problem Concerning Faith and Knowledge, or Reason and Revelation, as Expounded in Letters of St. Basil the Great to Amphilochius of Iconium'. *The Greek Orthodox Theological Review* 5.1: 27–44.

Bovon, François. 2012. 'Beyond the Canonical and the Apocryphal Books, the Presence of a Third Category: The Books Useful for the Soul'. *Harvard Theological Review* 105: 125–37.

Boyd-Taylor, Cameron. 2015. 'Esther and Additions to Esther', in *T&T Clark Companion to the Septuagint*, ed. James K. Aitken, pp. 203–21. London: Bloomsbury.

Bradshaw, Paul F. 2002. *The Search of the Origins of Christian Worship*, 2nd edn. Oxford: Oxford University Press.

Brakke, David. 1994. 'Canon Formation and Social Conflict in Fourth-Century Egypt: Athanasius of Alexandria's Thirty-Ninth *Festal Letter*'. *Harvard Theological Review* 87: 395–419.

Brakke, David. 2010. 'A New Fragment of Athanasius' Thirty-Ninth *Festal Letter*: Heresy, Apocrypha, and the Canon'. *Harvard Theological Review* 103: 47–66.

Brandt, Peter. 2001. *Endgestalten Des Kanons: Das Arrangement Der Schriften Israels in Der Jüdischen und Christlichen Bibel*. Berlin: Philo.

Braude, William G. trans. 1959. *The Midrash on Psalms*, 2 vols. New Haven, CT: Yale University Press.

Bregman, Marc. 1991. 'The Parable of the Lame and the Blind: Epiphanius' Quotation from an Apocryphon of Ezekiel'. *Journal of Theological Studies* 42: 125–38.

Brock, Sebastian P. 1981. 'The Resolution of the Philoxenian/Harclean Problem', in *New Testament Textual Criticism: Essays in Honour of Bruce M. Metzger*, eds Eldon J. Epp and Gordon D. Fee, pp. 325–43. Oxford: Clarendon Press.

Brock, Sebastian. 2006. *The Bible in the Syriac Tradition*, 2nd rev. edn. Piscataway, NJ: Gorgias Press.

Brock, Sebastian P. 2013. 'The Position of Job in Syriac Biblical Manuscripts: The Survival of an Ancient Tradition', in *Graeco-Latina et Orientalia: Studia in honorem Angeli Urbani heptagenarii*, eds Samir Khalil Samir and Juan Pedro Monferrer-Sala. Series Syro-Arabica 2, pp. 49–62. Cordoba, Spain: CNERU-CDEAC.

Brock, Sebastian P. and Lucas Van Rompay. 2014. *Catalogue of the Syriac Manuscripts and Fragments in the Library of Deir Al-Surian, Wadi Al-Natrun (Egypt)*. Leuven: Peeters.

Brooke, George J. 2007. ' "Canon" in the Light of the Qumran Scrolls', in *The Canon of Scripture in Jewish and Christian Tradition*, eds Philip S. Alexander and Jean-Daniel Kaestli, pp. 81–98. Prahins: Éditions du Zèbre.

Brooks, James A. 1992. 'Clement of Alexandria as a Witness to the Development of the New Testament Canon'. *Second Century* 9: 41–55.

Bruce, Barbara J. 2002. *Origen: Homilies on Joshua*. Fathers of the Church 105. Washington, D.C.: Catholic University of America Press.

Bruce, F.F. 1988. *The Canon of Scripture*. Downers Grove, IL: Intervarsity.

Bruk A. Asale. 2016. 'The Ethiopian Orthodox Tewahedo Church Canon of the Scriptures: Neither Open nor Closed'. *The Bible Translator* 67: 202–22.

Bryennios, Philotheos. 1883. Διδαχη των Δωδεκα Αποστολων εκ του ιεροσολυμιτικου χειρογραφου. Constantinople: ΤΥΠΟΙΣ Σ. Ι. ΒΟΥΤΥΡΑ.

Buchholz, D.D. 1988. *Your Eyes Will Be Opened: A Study of the Greek (Ethiopic) Apocalypse of Peter*. Atlanta, GA: Scholars Press.

Buhl, Frants. 1892. *Canon and Text of the Old Testament*. Edinburgh: T&T Clark.

Burns, Paul C. 2012. *A Model for the Christian Life: Hilary of Poitiers' Commentary on the Psalms*. Washington, D.C.: Catholic University of America Press.

Burridge, Richard A. 2014. *Four Gospels, One Jesus? A Symbolic Reading*, 3rd edn. Grand Rapids, MI: Eerdmans.

Campbell, J.G. 2000. '4QMMT^d and the Tripartite Canon'. *Journal for the Study of Judaism* 51: 181–90.

Campenhausen, Hans von. 1972. *The Formation of the Christian Bible*. Philadelphia, PA: Fortress.

Camplani, Alberto. 2003. *Atanasio di Alessandria. Lettere festali; Anonimo. Indice delle lettere festali*. Milan: Paoline.

Camplani, A. 2014. 'Athanasius of Alexandria', in *Encyclopedia of Ancient Christianity* vol. 1, ed. Angelo Di Berardino. Downers Grove, IL: Intervarsity.

Canessa, André. 1997. 'Études sur la Bible grecque des Septante: 1 Esdras', 2 vols. Ph.D. thesis, Université de Provence.

Carleton Paget, James. 1994. *The Epistle of Barnabas: Outlook and Background*. Tübingen: Mohr Siebeck.

Carleton Paget, James. 2005. 'The *Epistle of Barnabas* and the Writings that Later Formed the New Testament', in *The Reception of the New Testament in the Apostolic Fathers*, eds Andrew F. Gregory and Christopher M. Tuckett, pp. 229–49. Oxford: Oxford University Press.

Carleton Paget, James. 2007. 'The *Epistle of Barnabas*', in *The Writings of the Apostolic Fathers*, ed. Paul Foster, pp. 72–80. London: T&T Clark.

Carlson, Stephen C. 2014. 'Origen's Use of the *Gospel of Thomas*', in *Sacra Scriptura: How 'Non-Canonical' Texts Functioned in Early Judaism and Early Christianity*, eds James H. Charlesworth and Lee Martin McDonald, pp. 137–51. New York: Bloomsbury.

Carr, David M. 1996. 'Canonization in the Context of Community: An Outline of the Formation of the Tanakh and the Christian Bible', in *A Gift of God in Due Season: Essays on Scripture and Community in Honor of James A. Sanders*, eds Richard D. Weis and David M. Carr, pp. 22–64. Sheffield: Sheffield Academic Press.

Carr, David M. 2005. *Writing on the Tablet of the Heart: Origins of Scripture and Literature*. Oxford: Oxford University Press.

Carr, David M. 2011. *The Formation of the Hebrew Bible: A New Reconstruction*. Oxford: Oxford University Press.

Cavalier, Claudine. 2004. 'La canonicité d'Esther dans le Judaïsme rabbinique: Les documents talmudiques'. *Revue des études juives* 163.1–2: 5–23.

Cavalier, Claudine. 2012. *Esther*. La Bible d'Alexandrie 12. Paris: Cerf.

Ceriani, A.M. 1876–83. *Translatio syra pescitto Veteris Testamenti ex Codice Ambrosiano sec. fere VI photolithographice edita curante et adnotante* Mediolani: In officinis photolithographica Angeli della Croce et typographica J.B. Pogliani et sociorum; London: Apud Williams et Norgate.

Chapa, Juan. 2016. 'Textual Transmission of "Canonical" and "Apocryphal" Writings within the Development of the New Testament Canon: Limits and Possibilities'. *Early Christianity* 7: 113–33.

Chapman, Stephen B. 2000. *The Law and the Prophets: A Study in Old Testament Canon Formation*. Tübingen: Mohr Siebeck.

Chapman, Stephen B. 2010. 'The Canon Debate: What It Is and Why It Matters'. *Journal of Theological Interpretation* 4: 273–94.

Chapman, Stephen B. 2013. 'Modernity's Canonical Crisis: Historiography and Theology in Collision', in *Hebrew Bible/Old Testament: The History of Its Interpretation*, vol. 3: *From Modernism to Post-Modernism (The Nineteenth and Twentieth Centuries)*, part 1: *The Nineteenth Century—a Century of Modernism and Historicism*, ed. Magne Sæbø, pp. 651–87. Göttingen: Vandenhoeck & Ruprecht.

Chapman, Stephen B. 2016. 'Collections, Canons, and Communities', in *The Cambridge Companion to the Hebrew Bible/Old Testament*, eds Stephen B. Chapman and Marvin A. Sweeney, pp. 28–54. Cambridge: Cambridge University Press.

Charlesworth, James H., ed. 1983–5. *Old Testament Pseudepigrapha*, 2 vols. New York: Doubleday.

Charlesworth, James H. 1992a. 'Baruch, Book of 2 (Syriac)', in *Anchor Bible Dictionary*, vol. 1, ed. David Noel Freedman, pp. 620–1. New York: Doubleday.

Charlesworth, James H. 1992b. 'Baruch, Book of 3 (Greek)', in *Anchor Bible Dictionary*, vol. 1, ed. David Noel Freedman, pp. 621–2. New York: Doubleday.

Charlesworth, James H. 2008. 'Writings Ostensibly Outside the Canon', in *Exploring the Origins of the Bible: Canon Formation in Historical, Literary, and Theological Perspective*, eds Craig A. Evans and Emanuel Tov, pp. 57–85. Grand Rapids, MI: Baker.

Charlesworth, Scott D. 2007. 'T. C. Skeat, P^{64}, P^{67} and P^4, and the Problem of Fibre Orientation in Codicological Reconstruction'. *New Testament Studies* 53: 582–604.

Childs, Brevard. 1979. *An Introduction to the Old Testament as Scripture*. Philadelphia, PA: Fortress.

Cirafesi, Wally V. and Gregory Peter Fewster. 2016. 'Justin's ἀπομνημονεύματα and Ancient Greco-Roman Memoirs'. *Early Christianity* 7: 186–212.

Cohen, Shaye J.D. 2010. *The Significance of Yavneh and Other Essays in Jewish Hellenism*. Tübingen: Mohr Siebeck.

Collins, John J. 2013. *The Dead Sea Scrolls: A Biography*. Princeton, IL: Princeton University Press.

Collins, John J. 2016. *The Apocalyptic Imagination: An Introduction to Jewish Apocalyptic Literature*, 3rd edn. Grand Rapids, MI: Eerdmans.

Colson, F.H. ed. 1941. *Philo*, vol. 9. Loeb Classical Library 363. Cambridge, MA: Harvard University Press.

Constantinou, Eugenia Scarvelis, trans. 2011. *Andrew of Caesarea: Commentary on the Apocalypse*. Fathers of the Church 123. Washington, D.C.: Catholic University of America Press.

Constantinou, Eugenia Scarvelis. 2012. 'Banned from the Lectionary: Excluding the Apocalypse of John from the Orthodox New Testament Canon', in *The Canon of the Bible and the Apocrypha in the Churches of the East*, ed. Vahan S. Hovhanessian, pp. 51–61. New York: Peter Lang.

Constantinou, Eugenia Scarvelis. 2013. *Guiding to a Blessed End: Andrew of Caesarea and His Apocalypse Commentary in the Ancient Church*. Washington, D.C.: Catholic University of America Press.

Conti, Marco. 2010. *Priscillian of Avila: Complete Works*. Oxford Early Christian Texts. Oxford: Oxford University Press.

Cook, L. Stephen. 2011. *On the Question of the 'Cessation of Prophecy' in Ancient Judaism*. Tübingen: Mohr Siebeck.

Cooper, Stephen Andrew. 2005. *Marius Victorinus' Commentary on Galatians: Introduction, Translation, and Notes*. Oxford: Oxford University Press.

Costello, Charles Joseph. 1930. *St. Augustine's Doctrine on the Inspiration and Canonicity of Scripture*. Washington, D.C.: The Catholic University of America.

Crawford, Matthew R. 2013. 'Diatessaron, a Misnomer? The Evidence from Ephrem's Commentary'. *Early Christianity* 4: 362–85.

Crawford, Matthew R. 2015. ' "Reordering the Confusion": Tatian, the Second Sophistic, and the so-called *Diatessaron*'. *Zeitschrift für Antikes Christentum* 19: 209–36.

Crawford, Matthew R. 2016. 'The Diatessaron, Canonical or Non-Canonical? Rereading the Dura Fragment'. *New Testament Studies* 62: 253–77.

Crawford, Sidnie White. 2008. *Rewriting Scripture in Second Temple Times*. Grand Rapids, MI: Eerdmans.

Cross, F.L. 1961. 'History and Fiction in the African Canons'. *Journal of Theological Studies* 12: 227–47.

Cross, Frank Moore. 1998. *From Epic to Canon: History and Literature in Ancient Israel*. Baltimore, MD: The Johns Hopkins University Press.

Dahl, Nils Alstrup. 1962. 'The Particularity of the Pauline Epistles as a Problem in the Ancient Church', in *Neotestamentica et Patristica: eine Freundesgabe, Herrn Professor Dr. Oscor Cullmann zu seinem 60. Geburtstag überreicht*, pp. 261–71. Leiden: Brill.

Dahl, Nils A. 1978. 'The Origin of the Earliest Prologues to the Pauline Letters'. *Semeia* 12: 233–77.

Danby, Herbert, trans. 1933. *The Mishnah: Translated from the Hebrew with Introduction and Brief Explanatory Notes*. Oxford: Oxford Univesity Press.

Darshan, Guy. 2012. 'The Twenty-Four Books of the Hebrew Bible and Alexandrian Scribal Methods', in *Homer and the Bible in the Eyes of Ancient Interpreters*, ed. Maren R. Niehoff, pp. 221–44. Leiden: Brill.

Datema, Cornelis. 1978. *Amphilochii Iconiensis Opera: Orationes, Pluraque Alia Quae Supersunt, Nonnulla etiam Spuria*. CCG 3. Turnhout: Brepols.

De Boer, E.A. 2014. 'Tertullian on "Barnabas' Letter to the Hebrews" in *De Pudicitia* 20.1–5'. *Vigiliae Christianae* 68: 243–63.

De Bruyne, D. 1929. 'Le prologue, le titre et la finale de l'Ecclésiastique'. *Zeitschrift für die alttestamentliche Wissenschaft* 47: 257–63.

De Lange, N.R.M. 1976. *Origen and the Jews: Studies in Jewish–Christian Relations in Third-Century Palestine*. Cambridge: Cambridge University Press.

De Regt, Lénart J. 2016. 'Canon and Biblical Text in the Slavonic Tradition in Russia'. *The Bible Translator* 67: 223–39.

Dean, James Elmer. 1935. *Epiphanius' Treatise on Weights and Measures: The Syriac Version*. SAOC 11. Chicago, IL: University of Chicago Press.

Dechow, Jon F. 1988. *Dogma and Mysticism in Early Christianity: Epiphanius of Cyprus and the Legacy of Origen*. Patristic Monograph Series 13. Louvain: Peeters.

Dempster, Stephen G. 2008. 'Torah, Torah, Torah: The Emergence of the Tripartite Canon', in *Exploring the Origins of the Bible: Canon Formation in Historical, Literary, and Theological Perspective*, eds Craig A. Evans and Emanuel Tov, pp. 87–127. Grand Rapids, MI: Baker.

Dempster, Stephen G. 2016. 'The Old Testament Canon, Josephus, and Cognitive Environment', in *The Enduring Authority of the Christian Scriptures*, ed. D.A. Carson, pp. 321–61. Grand Rapids, MI: Eerdmans.

Denter, Thomas. 1962. *Die Stellung der Bücher Esdras im Kanon des Alten Testaments: eine kanongeschichtliche Untersuchung*. Marienstatt: Buch- und Kunsthandlung.

deSilva, David A. 2002. *Introducing the Apocrypha: Message, Context, and Significance*. Grand Rapids, MI: Baker.

Dines, Jennifer M. 2015. 'The Minor Prophets', in *T&T Clark Companion to the Septuagint*, ed. James K. Aitken, pp. 438–55. London: Bloomsbury.

Doran, Robert. 2012. *2 Maccabees*. Hermeneia. Minneapolis, MN: Fortress.

Dorival, Gilles. 2003. 'L'apport des Pères de l'Église à la question de la clôture du canon de l'Ancien Testament', in *The Biblical Canons*, eds J.-M. Auwers and H.J. de Jonge, pp. 81–110. Leuven: Leuven University Press.

Dorival, Gilles. 2004. 'La formation du canon biblique de l'Ancien Testament: Position actuelle et problems', in *Recueils normatifs et canons dans l'Antiquité: Perspectives nouvelles sur la formation des canons juif et chrétien dans leur contexte culturel*, ed. Enrico Norelli, pp. 83–112. Prahins: Zèbre.

Dorival, Gilles. 2013. 'Origen', in *The New Cambridge History of the Bible*, vol. 1: *From the Beginnings to 600*, eds James Carleton Paget and Joachim Schaper, pp. 605–29. Cambridge: Cambridge University Press.

Dorival, Gilles. 2014. 'La formation du canon des Écritures juives. Histoire de la recherché et perspectives nouvelles', in *La Bible juive dans l'Antiquité*, eds Rémi Geounelle and Jan Joosten, pp. 9–40. Lausanne: Zèbre.

Dozeman, Thomas B., Konrad Schmid, and Baruch J. Schwartz, eds. 2011. *The Pentateuch: International Perspectives on Current Research*. Tübingen: Mohr Siebeck.

Duff, Jeremy. 1998. 'P46 and the Pastorals: A Misleading Consensus?'. *New Testament Studies* 44: 578–90.

Dulaey, Martine, ed. 1997. *Victorin de Poetovio: Sur L'Apocalypse et autre écrits*. Sources chrétiennes 423. Paris: Cerf.

Dummer, Jürgen. 1968. 'Die Sprachkenntnisse des Epiphanius', in *Die Araber in der alten Welt*. Vol. 5, part 1, eds F. Altheim and R. Stiehl, pp. 392–435. Berlin: De Gruyter; repr. in Dummer, Jürgen. 2006. *Philologia Sacra et Profana: ausgewählte Beiträge zur Antike und zu ihrer Wirkungsgeschichte*, pp. 29–72. Stuttgart: Steiner.

Dungan, David L. 2007. *Constantine's Bible: Politics and the Making of the New Testament*. Minneapolis, MN: Fortress.

Dunkle, Brian P. 2009. 'Gregory Nazianzen's Poems on Scripture: Introduction, Translation, and Commentary'. Thesis, Boston College, 2009, available online at <http://dlib.bc.edu/islandora/object/bc-ir:101189>.

Dunn, Geoffrey D. 2005. 'Roman Primacy in the Correspondence between Innocent I and John Chrysostom', in *Giovanni Crisostomo: Oriente e Occidente tra IV e V secolo; XXXIII Incontro di studiosi dell'antichità cristiana, Roma, 6–8 maggio 2004*, pp. 687–98. Rome: Institutum Patristicum Augustinianum.

Dunn, Geoffrey D. 2010. 'Innocent I, Alaric, and Honorius: Church and State in Early Fifth-Century Rome', in *Studies of Religion and Politics in the Early Christian Centuries*, eds David Luckensmeyer and Pauline Allen, Early Christian Studies 13, pp. 243–61. Strathfield, Australia: St Pauls.

Dunn, Geoffrey D. 2014. 'Episcopal Crisis Management in Late Antique Gaul: The Example of Exsuperius of Toulouse'. *Antichthon* 48: 126–43.

Dunn, Geoffrey D. 2015a. 'Collectio Corbeiensis, Collectio Pithouensis, and the Earliest Collections of Papal Letters', in *Collecting Early Christian Letters: From the Apostle Paul to Late Antiquity*, eds Bronwen Neil and Pauline Allen, pp. 175–205. Cambridge: Cambridge University Press.

Dunn, Geoffrey D. 2015b. 'The Emergence of Papal Decretals: The Evidence of Zosimus of Rome', in *Shifting Genres in Late Antiquity*, eds Geoffrey Greatrex and Hugh Elton, pp. 81–92. Burlington, VT: Ashgate.

Dyson, R.W., trans. 1998. *Augustine: The City of God Against the Pagans*. Cambridge: Cambridge University Press.

Edwards, James R. 2009. *The Hebrew Gospel and the Development of the Synoptic Tradition*. Grand Rapids, MI: Eerdmans.

Ehrman, Bart D. 1983. 'The New Testament Canon of Didymus the Blind'. *Vigiliae Christianae* 37: 1–21.

Ehrman, Bart D. 2013. *Forgery and Counterforgery: The Use of Literary Deceit in Early Christian Polemics*. Oxford: Oxford University Press.

Ehrman, Bart D. and Zlatko Pleše. 2011. *The Apocryphal Gospels: Texts and Translations*. Oxford: Oxford University Press.

Elliott, J.K. 1993. *The Apocryphal New Testament: A Collection of Apocryphal Christian Literature in an English Translation Based on M.R. James*. Oxford: Oxford University Press.

Elliott, J.K. 1996. 'Manuscripts, the Codex and the Canon'. *Journal for the Study of the New Testament* 63: 105–23.

Elliott, J.K. 2015. 'Recent Work on the Greek Manuscripts of Revelation and the Consequences for the *Kurzgefasste Liste'. Journal of Theological Studies* 66.2: 574–84.

Ellis, E. Earle. 1991. *The Old Testament in Early Christianity: Canon and Interpretation in the Light of Modern Research*. Tübingen: Mohr-Siebeck; repr. Eugene, OR: Wipf and Stock, 2003.

Ellis, Teresa Ann. 2014. 'Negotiating the Boundaries of Tradition: The Rehabilitation of the Book of Ben Sira (Sirach) in *b. Sanhedren* 100b', in *Sacra Scriptura: How 'Non-Canonical' Texts Functioned in Early Judaism and Early Christianity*, eds James H. Charlesworth and Lee Martin McDonald, pp. 46–63. London: Bloomsbury.

Elman, Yaakov. 2004. 'Classical Rabbinic Interpretation', in *The Jewish Study Bible*, eds Adele Berlin and Marc Zvi Brettler, pp. 1844–63. Oxford: Oxford University Press.

Epp, Jay Eldon. 2002. 'Issues in the Interrelation of New Testament Textual Criticism and Canon', in *The Canon Debate*, eds Lee Martin McDonald and James A. Sanders, pp. 485–515. Peabody, MA: Hendrickson.

Erho, Ted. 2015. 'The Shepherd of Hermas in Ethiopia', in *L'Africa, l'Oriente Mediterraneo e l'Europa: Tradizione e Culture a Confronto*, ed. Paolo Nicelli, pp. 97–117. Milan: Biblioteca Ambrosiana.

Ernest, James D. 2004. *The Bible in Athanasius of Alexandria*. The Bible in Ancient Christianity 2. Leiden: Brill.

Evans, Craig A. 2007. 'The Jewish Christian Gospel Tradition', in *Jewish Believers in Jesus: The Early Centuries*, eds Oskar Skarsaune and Reidar Hvalvik, pp. 241–77. Peabody, MA: Hendrickson.

Ferguson, Everett. 1982. 'Canon Muratori: Date and Provenance', in *Studia Patristica* 17/2, ed. E.A. Livingstone, pp. 677–83. Oxford: Pergamon.

Ferguson, Everett. 2002. *Early Christians Speak: Faith and Life in the First Three Centuries*. vol. 2. Abilene, TX: ACU Press.

Fernández Marcos, Natalio. 2000. *The Septuagint in Context: Introduction to the Greek Version of the Bible*. Leiden: Brill.

Field, Frederick. 1875. *Origenis Hexaplorum quae supersunt sive veterum interpretum graecorum in totum Vetus Testamentum fragmenta*, 2 vols. Oxford: Oxford University Press; repr. Hildesheim: Georg Olms Verlagsbuchhandlung, 1964.

Fine, Gail. 2008. 'Does Socrates Claim to Know that He Knows Nothing?'. *Oxford Studies in Ancient Philosophy* 35: 49–85.

Fishbane, Michael A. 2002. *Haftarot: The Traditional Hebrew Text with the New JPS Translation*. Philadelphia, PA: Jewish Publication Society.

Fishbane, Michael. 2015. *Song of Songs: The Traditional Hebrew Text with the New JPS Translation*. The JPS Bible Commentary. Philadelphia, PA: Jewish Publication Society.

Fitzgerald, Allan D. 1999. *Augustine through the Ages: An Encyclopedia*. Grand Rapids, MI: Eerdmans.

Fitzmyer, Joseph A. 2000. 'Tobit, Book of', in *Encyclopedia of the Dead Sea Scrolls*, vol. 2, eds Lawrence H. Schiffman and James C. VanderKam, pp. 948–50. Oxford: Oxford University Press.

Fitzmyer, Joseph A. 2003. *Tobit*. New York: De Gruyter.

Forness, Philip Michael. 2014. 'Narrating History Through the Bible in Late Antiquity'. *Le Muséon* 127: 41–76.

Foster, Paul. 2005. 'The Epistles of Ignatius of Antioch and the Writings that Later Formed the New Testament', in *The Reception of the New Testament in the Apostolic*

Fathers, eds Andrew F. Gregory and Christopher M. Tuckett, pp. 159–86. Oxford: Oxford University Press.

Foster, Paul. 2010. *The Gospel of Peter: Introduction, Critical Edition and Commentary*. Leiden: Brill.

Foster, Paul. 2011. 'Justin and Paul', in *Paul and the Second Century*, eds Michael F. Bird and Joseph R. Dodson, pp. 108–25. New York: Bloomsbury.

Foster, Paul. 2013. 'The Reception of the Canonical Gospels in the Non-Canonical Gospels'. *Early Christianity* 4: 281–309.

Frey, Jörg. 2015. 'Texts about Jesus: Non-canonical Gospels and Related Literature', in *The Oxford Handbook of Early Christian Apocrypha*, eds Andrew Gregory and Christopher Tuckett, pp. 13–47. Oxford: Oxford University Press.

Fricke, Klaus Dietrich. 1991. 'The Apocrypha in the Luther Bible', in *The Apocrypha in Ecumenical Perspective: The Place of the Late Writings of the Old Testament among the Biblical Writings and Their Significance in the Eastern and Western Church Traditions*, ed. Siegfried Meurer, pp. 46–87. New York: United Bible Societies.

Fried, Lisbeth S, ed. 2011. *Was 1 Esdras First? An Investigation into the Priority and Nature of 1 Esdras*. Ancient Israel and Its Literature 7. Atlanta, GA: SBL.

Fried, Lisbeth S. 2014. *Ezra and the Law in History and Tradition*. Columbia, SC: University of South Carolina Press.

Fürst, Alfons. 2003. *Hieronymus: Askese und Wissenschaft in der Spätantike*. Freiburg: Herder.

Füssel, Stephan, ed. 2002. *Biblia, das ist, Die gantze Heilige Schrifft deudsch*. Cologne: Taschen. Facsimile of the *Biblia* translated into German by Martin Luther, 1534.

Gallagher, Edmon L. 2012a. *Hebrew Scripture in Patristic Biblical Theory: Canon, Language, Text*. Leiden: Brill.

Gallagher, Edmon L. 2012b. 'The Old Testament *Apocrypha* in Jerome's Canonical Theory'. *Journal of Early Christian Studies* 20: 213–33.

Gallagher, Edmon L. 2013a. 'Jerome's *Prologus Galeatus* and the OT Canon of North Africa', in *Studia Patristica* 69, ed. Markus Vinzent, pp. 99–106. Leuven: Peeters.

Gallagher, Edmon L. 2013b. 'The Religious Provenance of the Aquila Manuscripts from the Cairo Genizah'. *Journal of Jewish Studies* 64: 283–305.

Gallagher, Edmon L. 2014a. 'Writings Labeled "Apocrypha" in Latin Patristic Sources', in *Sacra Scriptura: How 'Non-Canonical' Texts Functioned in Early Judaism and Early Christianity*, eds James H. Charlesworth and Lee Martin McDonald, pp. 1–14. London: Bloomsbury.

Gallagher, Edmon L. 2014b. 'The Blood from Abel to Zechariah in the History of Interpretation'. *New Testament Studies* 60: 121–38.

Gallagher, Edmon L. 2014c. 'The End of the Bible? The Position of Chronicles in the Canon'. *Tyndale Bulletin* 65: 181–99.

Gallagher, Edmon L. 2015a 'The Jerusalem Temple Library and Its Implications for the Canon of Scripture'. *Restoration Quarterly* 57: 39–52.

Gallagher, Edmon L. 2015b. 'Why Did Jerome Translate Tobit and Judith?'. *Harvard Theological Review* 108: 356–75.

Gallagher, Edmon L. 2016a. 'Augustine on the Hebrew Bible'. *Journal of Theological Studies* 67: 97–114.

Gallagher, Edmon L. 2016b. 'Origen *via* Rufinus on the New Testament Canon'. *New Testament Studies* 62: 461–76.

Gallay, Paul, ed. 1978. *Gregoire de Nazianze Discours 27–31: Discours théologiques.* Sources chrétiennes 250. Paris: Cerf.

Gamble, Harry Y. 1985. *The New Testament Canon: Its Making and Meaning.* Philadelphia, PA: Fortress.

Gamble, Harry Y. 1995. *Books and Readers in the Early Church: A History of Early Christian Texts.* New Haven, CT: Yale University Press.

Gamble, Harry Y. 2002. 'The New Testament Canon: Recent Research and the Status Quaestionis', in *The Canon Debate*, eds Lee Martin McDonald and James A. Sanders, pp. 267–94. Peabody, MA: Hendrickson.

Gamble, Harry Y. 2006. 'Marcion and the "Canon"', in *The Cambridge History of Christianity*, vol. 1: *Origins to Constantine*, eds Margaret M. Mitchell and Frances M. Young, pp. 195–213. Cambridge: Cambridge University Press.

García Martínez, Florentino. 2012. 'Parabiblical Literature from Qumran and the Canonical Process'. *Revue de Qumran* 25: 525–56.

Gathercole, Simon. 2012. 'Named Testimonia to the *Gospel of Thomas*: An Expanded Inventory and Analysis'. *Harvard Theological Review* 105: 53–89.

Gathercole, Simon. 2014. *The Gospel of Thomas: Introduction and Commentary.* Leiden: Brill.

Gentry, Peter J. 1995. *The Asterisked Materials in the Greek Job.* Atlanta, GA: Scholars Press.

Gentry, Peter J. 2016. 'Pre-Hexaplaric Translations, Hexapla, post-Hexaplaric Translations', in *Textual History of the Bible: The Hebrew Bible, Vol. 1A: Overview Articles*, eds Armin Lange and Emanuel Tov, pp. 211–35. Leiden: Brill.

Gilbert, Peter. 2001. *On God and Man: The Theological Poetry of St. Gregory of Nazianzus.* Crestwood, NY: St Vladimir's Seminary.

Ginsburg, Christian D. 1867. *The Massoreth Ha-Massoreth of Elias Levita.* London: Longmans, Green, Reader & Dyer.

Ginsburg, Christian D. 1897. *Introduction to the Massoretico-Critical Edition of the Hebrew Bible*; repr. New York: Ktav, 1966.

Goodblatt, David. 1982. 'Audet's "Hebrew-Aramaic" List of the Books of the OT Revisited'. *Journal of Biblical Literature* 101: 75–84.

Goodblatt, David. 2006. *Elements of Ancient Jewish Nationalism.* Cambridge: Cambridge University Press.

Goodman, Martin. 1994. 'Sadducees and Essenes after 70 CE', in *Crossing the Boundaries: Essays in Biblical Interpretation in Honour of Michael D. Goulder*, eds Stanley E. Porter, Paul Joyce, and David E. Orton, pp. 347–56. Leiden: Brill.

Goodman, Martin. 2009. 'Religious Variety and the Temple in the Late Second Temple Period and Its Aftermath'. *Journal of Jewish Studies* 60: 202–13.

Grafton, Anthony and Megan Hale Williams. 2006. *Christianity and the Transformation of the Book: Origen, Eusebius, and the Library of Caesarea.* Cambridge, MA: Harvard University Press.

Grant, Robert. 1993. *Heresy and Criticism: The Search for Authenticity in Early Christian Literature.* Louisville, KY: John Knox.

Grant, Robert M. 1980. *Eusebius as Church Historian.* Oxford: Oxford University Press.

Graves, Michael. 2007. *Jerome's Hebrew Philology: A Study Based on His Commentary on Jeremiah.* Leiden: Brill.

Green, R.P.H., trans. 1997. *Saint Augustine, On Christian Teaching.* Oxford: Oxford University Press.

Gregory, Andrew. 2003. *The Reception of Luke and Acts in the Period before Irenaeus*. Tübingen: Mohr Siebeck.

Gregory, Andrew F. 2005. '*1 Clement* and the Writings that Later Formed the New Testament', in *The Reception of the New Testament in the Apostolic Fathers*, eds Andrew F. Gregory and Christopher M. Tuckett, pp. 129–57. Oxford: Oxford University Press.

Gregory, Andrew F. 2010. 'The Reception of Luke and Acts and the Unity of Luke-Acts', in *Rethinking the Unity and Reception of Luke and Acts*, eds Andrew F. Gregory and C. Kavin Rowe, pp. 82–93. Columbia, SC: University of South Carolina Press.

Gregory, Andrew F. and Christopher M. Tuckett, eds. 2005a. *The Reception of the New Testament in the Apostolic Fathers*. Oxford: Oxford University Press.

Gregory, Andrew F. and Christopher M. Tuckett. 2005b. '*2 Clement* and the Writings that Later Formed the New Testament', in *The Reception of the New Testament in the Apostolic Fathers*, eds Andrew F. Gregory and Christopher M. Tuckett, pp. 251–92. Oxford: Oxford University Press.

Gregory, Andrew F. and Christopher M. Tuckett. 2005c. *Trajectories through the New Testament and the Apostolic Fathers*. Oxford: Oxford University Press.

Grosheide, F.W., ed. 1948. *Some Early Lists of the Books of the New Testament*. Leiden: Brill.

Gryson, Roger. 1997. 'Les Commentaires patristiques latins de l'Apocalypse'. *Revue théologique de Louvain* 28: 305–37, 484–502.

Guignard, Christophe. 2015. 'The Original Language of the Muratorian Fragment'. *Journal of Theological Studies* 66: 596–624.

Guillaume, Philippe. 2004. 'New Light on the Nebiim from Alexandria: A Chronography to Replace the Deuteronomistic History'. *Journal of Hebrew Scriptures* 5.

Gustafsson, B. 1961. 'Eusebius' Principles in Handling His Sources, as Found in His Church History, Books I–VII', in *Studia Patristica* 4, ed. F.L. Cross, pp. 429–41. Berlin: Akademie.

Gwynn, John. 1909. *Remnants of the Later Syriac Versions of the Bible In Two Parts: Part I: New Testament Part II: Old Testament*. London: Williams and Norgate.

Haelewyck, Jean-Claude. 2003. *Hester*. Vetus Latina 7/3. Fascicule 1: *Introduction*. Freiburg: Herder.

Haelewyck, Jean-Claude. 2008. 'Le Canon de L'Ancien Testament dans la Tradition Syriaque (Manuscrits Bibliques, Listes Canoniques, Auteurs)', in *L'Ancien Testament en syriaque*, eds F. Briquel Chatonnet and Ph. Le Moigne, Etudes syriaques 5, pp. 141–71. Paris: Geuthner.

Hagen, Joost L. 2012. 'No Longer "Slavonic" Only: 2 Enoch Attested in Coptic from Nubia', in *New Perspectives on 2 Enoch: No Longer Slavonic Only*, eds Andrei A. Orlov and Gabriele Boccaccini, pp. 7–34. Leiden: Brill.

Hahneman, Geoffrey Mark. 1992. *The Muratorian Fragment and the Development of the Canon*. Oxford Theological Monographs. Oxford: Oxford University Press.

Hahneman, Geoffrey Mark. 2002. 'The Muratorian Fragment and the Origins of the New Testament Canon', in *The Canon Debate*, eds Lee Martin McDonald and James A. Sanders, pp. 405–15. Peabody, MA: Hendrickson.

Hall, Stuart George. 1979. *Melito of Sardis: On Pascha and Fragments*. Oxford: Oxford University Press.

Hammond, C. P. 1977. 'The Last Ten Years of Rufinus' Life and the Date of His Move South from Aquileia'. *Journal of Theological Studies* 28: 372–429.

Hanhart, Robert. 1993. *Esdrae liber II*. Septuaginta Vetus Testamentum Graecum, vol. VIII/2. Göttingen: Vandenhoeck & Ruprecht.

Hanson, R.P.C. 1954. *Origen's Doctrine of Tradition*. London: SPCK.

Harl, Marguerite, ed. 1983. *Origène, Sur les Écritures: Philocalie, 1–20 et la Lettre à Africanus sur l'Histoire de Suzanne*. Sources chrétiennes 302. Paris: Cerf.

Harnack, Adolf. 1893–1904. *Geschichte der altchristlichen Litteratur bis Eusebius*. 2 parts, 2 vols. each. Leipzig: Hinrichs.

Harnack, Adolf. 1898. 'Excerpts aus dem Muratorischen Fragment (saec. xi et xii)'. *Theologische Literaturzeitung* 23: 131–4.

Harnack, Adolf. 1925. 'Über den Verfasser und den literarischen Charakter des Muratorischen Fragmentes'. *Zeitschrift für die neutestamentliche Wissenschaft* 24: 1–16.

Harrison, Carol. 2013. 'Augustine', in *The New Cambridge History of the Bible*, vol. 1: *From the Beginnings to 600*, eds James Carleton Paget and Joachim Schaper, pp. 676–96. Cambridge: Cambridge University Press.

Head, Peter M. 2005. 'Is P⁴, P⁶⁴, and P⁶⁷ the Old Manuscript of the Four Gospels? A Response to T.C. Skeat'. *New Testament Studies* 51: 450–7.

Heine, Ronald E. 2010. *Origen: Scholarship in the Service of the Church*. Oxford: Oxford University Press.

Heine, Ronald E. 2011. 'Origen and the Eternal Boundaries', in *Die Septuaginta und das frühe Christentum/The Septuagint and Christian Origins*, eds Thomas Scott Caulley and Hermann Lichtenberger, pp. 393–409. Tübingen: Mohr Siebeck.

Heller, Marvin J. 1995. 'Designing the Talmud: The Origins of the Printed Talmudic Page'. *Tradition* 29: 40–51.

Hengel, Martin. 1989. *The Johannine Question*. Philadelphia, PA: Trinity Press.

Hengel, Martin. 2000. *The Four Gospels and the One Gospel of Jesus Christ*. Harrisburg, PA: Trinity Press International.

Hengel, Martin. 2002. *The Septuagint as Christian Scripture: Its Prehistory and the Problem of Its Canon*. Grand Rapids, MI: Baker.

Hengel, Martin. 2007. 'Die Evangelienüberschriften', in *Kleine Schriften*, vol. 5: *Jesus und die Evangelien*, pp. 526–67. Tübingen: Mohr Siebeck.

Henne, Philippe. 1990–1. 'Le Canon de Muratori: Orthographe et datation'. *Archivum Bobiense* 12–13: 289–304.

Henne, Philippe. 1993. 'La datation du canon de Muratori'. *Revue biblique* 100: 54–75.

Hennings, Ralph. 1994. *Der Briefwechsel zwischen Augustinus und Hieronymus und ihr Streit um den Kanon des Alten Testaments und die Auslegung von Gal. 2,11–14*. Leiden: Brill.

Henry, Jonathan K. 2014. 'The *Acts of Thomas* as Sacred Text', in *Sacra Scriptura: How 'Non-Canonical' Texts Functioned in Early Judaism and Early Christianity*, eds James H. Charlesworth and Lee Martin McDonald, pp. 152–70. London: Bloomsbury.

Herzer, Jens, trans. 2005. *4 Baruch (Paraleipomena Jeremiou)*. Atlanta, GA: SBL.

Hess, Hamilton. 2002. *The Early Development of Canon Law and the Council of Serdica*. Oxford: Oxford University Press.

Hill, Charles E. 1995. 'The Debate over the Muratorian Fragment and the Development of the Canon'. *Westminster Theological Journal* 57: 437–52.

Hill, Charles E. 1998. 'What Papias Said about John (and Luke): A "New" Papian Fragment'. *Journal of Theological Studies* 49: 582–629.

Hill, Charles E. 2001. *Regnum Caelorum: Patterns of Millennial Thought in Early Christianity*, 2nd edn. Grand Rapids, MI: Eerdmans.

Hill, Charles E. 2004. *The Johannine Corpus in the Early Church*. Oxford: Oxford University Press.

Hill, Charles E. 2011. 'Intersections of Jewish and Christian Scribal Culture: The Original Codex containing P4, P64 and P67, and Its Implications', in *Among Jews, Gentiles, and Christians in Antiquity and the Middle Ages: Studies in Honour of Professor Oskar Skarsaune on His 65th Birthday*, eds Reidar Hvalvik and John Kaufman, pp. 75–91. Trondheim: Tapir.

Hill, Charles E. 2013a. 'A Four-Gospel Canon in the Second Century? Artifact and Artifiction'. *Early Christianity* 4: 310–34.

Hill, Charles E. 2013b. ' "The Writing which Says…" ': *The Shepherd of Hermas* in the Writings of Irenaeus', in *Studia Patristica* 65, ed. M. Vinzent, pp. 127–38. Leuven: Peeters.

Höffken, Peter. 2001. 'Zum Kanonsbewusstsein des Josephus Flavius in *Contra Apionem* und in den *Antiquitates*'. *Journal for the Study of Judaism* 32: 159–77.

Holl, Karl. 1904. *Amphilochius von Ikonium in seinem Verhältnis zu den grossen Kappadoziern*. Tübingen: Mohr Siebeck.

Holmes, Michael. 2007. *Apostolic Fathers: Greek Texts and English Translations*, 3rd edn. Grand Rapids, MI: Baker.

Holmes, Michael W. 2005. 'Polycarp's *Letter to the Philippians* and the Writings that Later Formed the New Testament', in *The Reception of the New Testament in the Apostolic Fathers*, eds Andrew F. Gregory and Christopher M. Tuckett, pp. 187–227. Oxford: Oxford University Press.

Horbury, William. 1994. 'The Wisdom of Solomon in the Muratorian Fragment'. *Journal of Theological Studies* 45: 149–59.

Horbury, William. 1995. 'The Christian Use and the Jewish Origins of the Wisdom of Solomon', in *Wisdom in Ancient Israel: Essays in Honour of J.A. Emerton*, eds J. Day, R.P. Gordon, and H.G.M. Williamson, pp. 182–96. Cambridge: Cambridge University Press.

Houghton, H.A.G. 2008. *Augustine's Text of John: Patristic Citations and Latin Gospel Manuscripts*. Oxford: Oxford University Press.

Houghton, H.A.G. 2016. *The Latin New Testament: A Guide to Its Early History, Texts, and Manuscripts*. Oxford: Oxford University Press.

Howorth, H.H. 1908–9. 'The Influence of St. Jerome on the Canon of Western Christianity, I'. *Journal of Theological Studies* 10: 481–96.

Howorth, H.H. 1909–10. 'The Influence of St. Jerome on the Canon of Western Christianity, II'. *Journal of Theological Studies* 11: 321–47.

Howorth, H.H. 1911–12. 'The Influence of St. Jerome on the Canon of Western Christianity, III'. *Journal of Theological Studies* 13: 1–18.

Howorth, H.H. 1913. 'The Decretal of Damasus'. *Journal of Theological Studies* 14: 321–37.

Hultin, Jeremy. 2010. 'Jude's Citation of 1 Enoch', in *Jewish and Christian Scriptures: The Function of 'Canonical' and 'Non Canonical' Religious Texts*, eds James H. Charlesworth and Lee Martin McDonald, pp. 113–28. London: Bloomsbury.

Hunt, Lucy-Anne. 1991. 'The Syriac Buchanan Bible in Cambridge: Book Illumination in Syria, Cilicia and Jerusalem of the Later Twelfth Century'. *Orientalia Christiana Periodica* 57: 331–69.

Hurtado, Larry W. 2006. *The Earliest Christian Artifacts: Manuscripts and Christian Origins*. Grand Rapids: Eerdmans.

Ilan, Tal. 2012. 'The Term and Concept of TaNaKh', in *What Is Bible?*, eds Karin Finsterbusch and Armin Lange, pp. 219–34. Leuven: Peeters.

Inowlocki, Sabrina. 2005. '"Neither Adding nor Omitting Anything": Josephus' Promise not to Modify the Scriptures in Greek and Latin Context'. *Journal of Jewish Studies* 56: 48–65.

Jacobs, Andrew S. 2000. 'The Disorder of Books: Priscillian's Canonical Defense of Apocrypha'. *Harvard Theological Review* 93: 135–59.

Jacobs, Andrew S. 2013. 'Epiphanius of Salamis and the Antiquarian's Bible'. *Journal of Early Christian Studies* 21:3: 437–64.

Jacobs, Louis. 1991. *Structure and Form in the Babylonian Talmud*. Cambridge: Cambridge University Press.

Jakab, Attila. 2003. 'The Reception of the *Apocalypse of Peter* in Ancient Christianity', in *The Apocalypse of Peter*, eds J. N. Bremmer and István Czachesz, pp. 174–85. Leuven: Peeters.

Janz, Timothy. 2010. *Deuxième livre d'Esdras*. La Bible d'Alexandrie 11.2. Paris: Cerf.

Jasper, Detlev and Horst Fuhrmann. 2001. *Papal Letters in the Early Middle Ages*. History of Medieval Canon Law. Washington, D.C.: Catholic University of America Press.

Jay, Pierre. 1982. 'La Datation des premières traductions de l'Ancien Testament sur l'hébreu par saint Jérôme'. *Revue d'études augustiniennes* 28: 208–12.

Jenkins, Philip. 2015. *The Many Faces of Christ: The Thousand-Year Story of the Survival and Influence of the Lost Gospels*. New York: Basic Books.

Jepsen, A. 1959. 'Zur Kanongeschichte des Alten Testaments'. *Zeitschrift für die alttestamentliche Wissenschaft* 71: 114–36.

Joannou, Périclès-Pierre. 1962–3. *Fonti: Discipline générale antique (IVe–IXe s.)*, 2 vols. Rome: Grottaferrata.

Jobes, Karen H. and Moisés Silva. 2015. *Invitation to the Septuagint*, 2nd edn. Grand Rapids, MI: Baker.

Johnson, Aaron P. 2014. *Eusebius*. Understanding Classics. London: I.B. Tauris.

Johnson, Luke Timothy. 1995. *The Letter of James: A New Translation with Introduction and Commentary*. Anchor Bible. New York: Doubleday.

Johnson, Luke Timothy. 2004. *Brother of Jesus, Friend of God: Studies in the Letter of James*. Grand Rapids, MI: Eerdmans.

Johnson, Steven R. 2010. 'Hippolytus's *Refutatio* and the Gospel of Thomas'. *Journal of Early Christian Studies* 18: 305–26.

Jongkind, Dirk. 2007. *Scribal Habits of Codex Sinaiticus*. Texts and Studies, Third Series, vol. 5. Piscataway, NJ: Gorgias Press.

Jongkind, Dirk. 2015. 'On the Marcionite Prologues to the Letters of Paul', in *Studies on the Text of the New Testament and Early Christianity: Essays in Honor of Michael W. Holmes*, eds Daniel M. Gurtner, Juan Hernández Jr, and Paul Foster, pp. 389–407. Leiden: Brill.

Jonkers, E.J. 1954. *Acta et Symbola Conciliorum Quae Saeculo Quarto Habita Sunt*. Leiden: Brill.

Joosten, Jan. 2008. 'The Original Language and Historical Milieu of the Book of Judith'. *Meghillot* 5–6: *159–*76.

Joosten, Jan. 2016. 'The Origin of the Septuagint Canon', in *Die Septuaginta—Orte und Intentionen: 5. Internationale Fachtagung veranstaltet von Septuaginta Deutsch*

(*LXX.D*), *Wuppertal 24.–27. Juli 2014*, eds Siegfried Kreuzer, Martin Meiser, and Marcus Sigismund, pp. 688–99. Tübingen: Mohr Siebeck.

Junod, Éric. 1984. 'La formation et la composition de l'Ancien Testament dans l'Église grecque des quatre premiers siècles', in *Le Canon de l'Ancien Testament: Sa formation et son histoire*, eds Jean-Daniel Kaestli and Otto Wermelinger, La Monde de la Bible 10, pp. 105–34. Geneva: Labor et Fides.

Junod, Éric. 2003. 'Quand l'évêque Athanase se prend pour l'évangéliste Luc (*Lettre festale XXXIX* sur le canon des Écritures)', in *Early Christian Voices in Texts, Traditions and Symbols: Essays in Honor of François Bovon*, eds David Warren, Ann Graham Brock, and David W. Pao, Biblical Interpretation Series 66, pp. 197–208. Boston, MA: Brill.

Junod, Éric. 2005. 'D'Eusèbe de Césarée à Athanase d'Alexandrie en passant par Cyrille de Jérusalem: de la construction savante du Nouveau Testament à la clôture ecclésiastique du canon', in *Le canon du Nouveau Testament: Regards nouveaux sur l'histoire de sa formation*, eds Gabriella Aragione, Éric Junod, and Enrico Norelli, Le Monde de la Bible 54, pp. 169–95. Paris: Labor et Fides.

Junod, Éric. 2011. 'Les mots d'Eusèbe de Césarée pour désigner les livres du Nouveau Testament et ceux qui n'en font pas partie', in *Eukarpa. Études sur la Bible et ses exégètes en hommage à Gilles Dorival*, eds M. Loubet and D. Pralon, pp. 341–53. Paris: Cerf.

Kaestli, J.-D. 1994. 'La place du *Fragment de Muratori* dans l'histoire du canon. À propos de la thèse de Sundberg et Hahneman'. *Cristianesimo nelle Storia* 15: 609–34.

Kaestli, Jean-Daniel. 2007. 'La formation et la structure du canon biblique: que peut apporter l'étude de la Septante?', in *The Canon of Scripture in Jewish and Christian Tradition*, eds Philip S. Alexander and Jean-Daniel Kaestli, pp. 99–113. Prahins: Zèbre.

Kaestli, Jean-Daniel and Otto Wermelinger, eds. 1984. *Le Canon de l'Ancien Testament: Sa formation et son histoire*. La Monde de la Bible 10. Geneva: Labor et Fides.

Kalin, Everett R. 1990. 'Re-examining New Testament Canon History: 1. The Canon of Origen'. *Currents in Theology and Mission* 17: 274–82.

Kalin, Everett R. 2002. 'The New Testament Canon of Eusebius', in *The Canon Debate*, eds Lee Martin McDonald and James A. Sanders, pp. 386–404. Peabody, MA: Hendrickson.

Kamesar, Adam. 1993. *Jerome, Greek Scholarship, and the Hebrew Bible: A Study of the Quaestiones in Genesim*. Oxford: Oxford University Press.

Kamesar, Adam. 2004. 'The *Logos Endiathetos* and the *Logos Prophorikos* in Allegorical Interpretation: Philo and the D-Scholia to the *Iliad*'. *Greek, Roman, and Byzantine Studies* 44: 163–81.

Kamesar, Adam. 2009. 'Biblical Interpretation in Philo', in *The Cambridge Companion to Philo*, ed. A. Kamesar, pp. 65–91. Cambridge: Cambridge University Press.

Kaplan, Jonathan. 2015. *My Perfect One: Typology and Early Rabbinic Interpretation of Song of Songs*. Oxford: Oxford University Press.

Katz, Peter. 1956. 'The Old Testament Canon in Palestine and Alexandria'. *Zeitschrift für die neutestamentliche Wissenschaft* 47: 191–217; repr. in *The Canon and Masorah of the Hebrew Bible: An Introductory Reader*, ed. Sid Z. Leiman, pp. 72–98. New York: Ktav, 1974.

Katz, Peter. 1957. 'The Johannine Epistles in the Muratorian Canon'. *Journal of Theological Studies* 8: 273–4.

Katz, Steven T., ed. 2006. *The Cambridge History of Judaism*, vol. 4: *The Late Roman-Rabbinic Period*. Cambridge: Cambridge University Press.

Kelly, J.N.D. 1955. *Rufinus: A Commentary on the Apostle's Creed*. Ancient Christian Writers 20. New York: Newman.

Kim, Young Richard. 2015. *Epiphanius of Cyprus: Imagining an Orthodox World*. Ann Arbor, MI: University of Michigan Press.

Klauck, Hans-Josef. 2008. *The Apocryphal Acts of the Apostles: An Introduction*. Waco, TX: Baylor University Press.

Knecht, Andreas, ed. 1972. *Gregor von Nazianz, Gegen die Putzucht der Frauen*. Heidelberg: Universitätsverlag Winter.

Knoppers, Gary N. 2013. *Jews and Samaritans: The Origins of Their Early Relations*. Oxford: Oxford University Press.

Knoppers, Gary N. and Paul B. Harvey Jr. 2002. 'Omitted and Remaining Matters: On the Names Given to the Book of Chronicles in Antiquity'. *Journal of Biblical Literature* 121: 227–43.

Koester, Helmut. 1990. *Ancient Christian Gospels: Their History and Development*. Philadelphia, PA: TPI.

Koller, Aaron. 2014. *Esther in Ancient Jewish Thought*. Cambridge: Cambridge University Press.

Kooij, Arie van der. 2003. 'Canonization of Ancient Hebrew Books and Hasmonean Politics', in *The Biblical Canons*, eds J.-M. Auwers and H. J. De Jonge, pp. 27–38. Leuven: Peeters.

Kooij, Arie van der. 2012. 'Preservation and Promulgation: The Dead Sea Scrolls and the Textual History of the Hebrew Bible', in *The Hebrew Bible in Light of the Dead Sea Scrolls*, eds Nóra Dávid, Armin Lange, Kristin De Troyer, and Shani Tzoref. Forschungen zur Religion und Literatur des Alten und Neuen Testaments 239, pp. 29–40. Göttingen: Vandenhoeck & Ruprecht.

Kraft, Robert A. 2007. 'Para-mania: Beside, Before and Beyond Bible Studies'. *Journal of Biblical Literature* 126: 5–27.

Kraft, Robert A. and Ann-Elizabeth Purintun. 1972. *Paraleipomena Jeremiou*. Missoula, MT: SBL.

Kraus, Thomas J. and Tobias Nicklas, eds. 2004. *Das Petrusevangelium und die Petrusapokalypse: Die griechischen Fragmente mit deutscher und englischer Übersetzung*. GCS. Berlin: De Gruyter.

Kruger, Michael J. 2015. 'Origen's List of New Testament Books in *Homiliae in Josuam* 7.1: A Fresh Look', in *Mark, Manuscripts, and Monotheism: Essays in Honor of Larry W. Hurtado*, eds Chris Keith and Dieter T. Roth, pp. 99–117. New York: Bloomsbury.

Kruger, Michael J. 2016. 'The Reception of the Book of Revelation in the Early Church', in *Book of Seven Seals: The Peculiarity of Revelation, Its Manuscripts, Attestation, and Transmission*, eds Thomas J. Kraus and Michael Sommer, pp. 159–74. Tübingen: Mohr Siebeck.

Kugel, James L. 1981. *The Idea of Biblical Poetry: Parallelism and Its History*. Baltimore, MD: Johns Hopkins University Press.

La Bonnardière, Anne-Marie. 1970. *Le Livre de la Sagesse*. Biblia Augustiniana, A.T. 4. Paris: Études Augustiniennes.

La Bonnardière, Anne-Marie. 1999. 'The Canon of Sacred Scripture', in *Augustine and the Bible*, ed. Pamela Bright, pp. 26–41. Notre Dame, IN: University of Notre Dame Press.

Labendz, Jenny R. 2006. 'The Book of Ben Sira in Rabbinic Literature'. *AJS Review* 30: 347–92.

Lagarde, Paul Anton de. 1856. *Reliquiae Juris Ecclesiastici Antiquissimae: Syriace.* Leipzig: B. G. Teubner.

Lake, Kirsopp, trans. 1926. *Eusebius: The Ecclesiastical History.* Vol. 1. Cambridge, MA: Harvard University Press.

Lampe, G.W.H. 1961. *A Patristic Greek Lexicon.* Oxford: Clarendon Press.

Lange, Armin. 2004. 'From Literature to Scripture: The Unity and Plurality of the Hebrew Scriptures in Light of the Qumran Library', in *One Scripture or Many? Canon from Biblical, Theological, and Philosophical Perspectives*, eds Christine Helmer and Christof Landmesser, pp. 51–107. Oxford: Oxford University Press.

Lange, Armin. 2007a. ' "Nobody Dared to Add to Them, to Take from Them, or to Make Changes" (Josephus, AG. AP. 1.42): The Textual Standardization of Jewish Scriptures in Light of the Dead Sea Scrolls', in *Flores Florentino: Dead Sea Scrolls and Other Early Jewish Studies in Honour of Florentino García Martínez*, eds A. Hilhorst, Émile Puech, and Eibert Tigchelaar, pp. 105–26. Leiden: Brill.

Lange, Armin. 2008b. ' "The Law, the Prophets, and the Other Books of the Fathers" (Sir, Prologue): Canonical Lists in Ben Sira and Elsewhere?', in *Studies in the Book of Ben Sira: Papers of the Third International Conference on the Deuterocanonical Books, Shime'on Centre, Papa, Hungary, 18–20 May, 2006*, eds Géza G. Xeravits and József Zsengellér, pp. 55–80. Leiden: Brill.

Lange, Armin. 2009. *Handbuch der Textfunde vom Toten Meer*, vol. 1: *Die Handschriften biblischer Bücher von Qumran und den anderen Fundorten*. Tübingen: Mohr Siebeck.

Lange, Armin. 2014. 'The Canonical History of the Hebrew Bible and the Christian Old Testament in Light of Egyptian Judaism', in *Die Septuaginta—Text, Wirkung, Rezeption*, eds Wolfgang Kraus and Siegfried Kreuzer, pp. 660–80. Tübingen: Mohr Siebeck.

Lapham, F. 2003. *Peter: The Myth, the Man and the Writings: A Study of Early Petrine Text and Tradition.* Sheffield: Sheffield Academic Press.

Lapin, Hayim. 2012. *Rabbis as Romans: The Rabbinic Movement in Palestine, 100–400 CE.* Oxford: Oxford University Press.

Larcher, C. 1969. *Études sur le Livre de la Sagesse.* Paris: J. Gabalda.

Lash, Ephrem. 2007. 'The Canon of Scripture in the Orthodox Church', in *The Canon of Scripture in Jewish and Christian Tradition*, eds Philip S. Alexander and Jean-Daniel Kaestli, pp. 217–32. Prahins: Zèbre.

Law, Timothy Michael. 2013. *When God Spoke Greek: The Septuagint and the Making of the Christian Bible.* Oxford: Oxford University Press.

Leemans, Johan. 1997. 'Athanasius and the Book of Wisdom'. *Ephemerides Theologicae Lovanienses* 73: 349–68.

Leemans, Johan. 2003. 'Canon and Quotation: Athanasius' Use of Jesus Sirach', in *The Biblical Canons*, eds J.-M. Auwers and H.J. de Jonge, pp. 265–77. Leuven: Leuven University Press.

Lefort, Louis-Théophile. 1943. *Les vies coptes de saint Pachôme et de ses premiers successeurs: traduction français.* Louvain: Bibliothèque du Muséon.

Lefort, Louis-Théophile. 1953. *S. Pachomii Vita Bohairice Scripta.* Corpus Scriptorum Christianorum Orientalium 89. Scriptores Coptici 7. Louvain: Peeters.

Leiman, Sid Z. 1976. *The Canonization of Hebrew Scripture: The Talmudic and Midrashic Evidence.* Hamden, CT: Transactions of the Connecticut Academy of Arts and Sciences.

Leiman, Sid Z. 1991. *The Canonization of Hebrew Scripture: The Talmudic and Midrashic Evidence*, 2nd edn. New Haven, CT: Transactions.

Lemarié, Joseph. 1978. 'Saint Chromace d'Aquilée, témoin du Canon de Muratori'. *Revue d'études augustiniennes* 24: 101–2.

Lewis, Jack P. 1964. 'What Do We Mean by Jabneh?'. *Journal of Bible and Religion* 32: 125–32; repr. in *The Canon and Masorah of the Hebrew Bible: An Introductory Reader*, ed. Sid Z. Leiman, pp. 254–61. New York: Ktav, 1974.

Lewis, Jack P. 2002. 'Jamnia Revisited', in *The Canon Debate*, eds Lee Martin McDonald and James A. Sanders, pp. 146–62. Peabody, MA: Hendrickson.

Lietzmann, Hans. 1907. *Wie wurden die Bücher des Neuen Testaments heilige Schrift? Fünf Vorträge*. Tübingen: Mohr.

Lietzmann, Hans. 1933. *Das Muratorische Fragment und die Monarchianischen Prologe zu den Evangelien*, 2nd edn. Bonn: A. Marcus and E. Weber.

Lieu, Judith. 1986. *The Second and Third Epistles of John: History and Background*. Edinburgh: T&T Clark.

Lightfoot, J.B. 1884. *Saint Paul's Epistles to the Colossians and to Philemon*, 7th edn. London: Macmillan.

Lightfoot, J.B. 1885. *The Apostolic Fathers*, 2nd edn, 5 vols. Cambridge: Macmillan.

Lightstone, Jack N. 2002. 'The Rabbis' Bible: The Canon of the Hebrew Bible and the Early Rabbinic Guild', in *The Canon Debate*, eds Lee Martin McDonald and James A. Sanders, pp. 163–84. Peabody, MA: Hendrickson.

Lim, Timothy H. 2001. 'The Alleged Reference to the Tripartite Division of the Hebrew Bible'. *Revue de Qumran* 20: 23–37.

Lim, Timothy H. 2010. 'The Defilement of the Hands as a Principle Determining the Holiness of Scriptures'. *Journal of Theological Studies* 61: 501–15.

Lim, Timothy H. 2013. *The Formation of the Jewish Canon*. New Haven, CT: Yale University Press.

Lincicum, David. 2015. 'The Paratextual Invention of the Term "Apostolic Fathers"'. *Journal of Theological Studies* 66: 139–48.

Lindemann, Andreas. 1990. 'Paul in the Writings of the Apostolic Fathers', in *Paul and the Legacies of Paul*, ed. William S. Babock, pp. 25–45. Dallas, TX: SMU Press.

Lindemann, Andreas. 2003. 'Die Sammlung der Paulusbriefe im 1. und 2. Jahrhundert', in *The Biblical Canons*, eds J.-M. Auwers and H.J. de Jonge, pp. 321–51. Leuven: Leuven University Press.

Lockett, Darian R. 2015. 'Are the Catholic Epistles a Canonically Significant Collection? A *Status Quaestionis*'. *Currents in Biblical Research* 14: 62–80.

Lorenz, R. 1986. *Der zehnte Osterfestbrief des Athanasius von Alexandrien*. Berlin: De Gruyter.

Luijendijk, AnneMarie. 2011. 'Reading the *Gospel of Thomas* in the Third Century: Three Oxyrhynchus Papyri and Origen's *Homilies*', in *Reading New Testament Papyri in Context*, eds Claire Clivaz and Jean Zumstein, pp. 241–67. Leuven: Peeters.

MacDonald, Dennis R. 1990. *The Acts of Andrew and The Acts of Andrew and Matthias in the City of the Cannibals*. Atlanta, GA: Scholars Press.

Manor, T. Scott. 2013. 'Papias, Origen, and Eusebius: The Criticisms and Defense of the Gospel of John'. *Vigiliae Christianae* 67: 1–21.

Manor, T. Scott. 2016. *Epiphanius' Alogi and the Johannine Controversy: A Reassessment of Early Ecclesial Opposition to the Johannine Corpus*. Leiden: Brill.

Markschies, Christoph. 2012. 'Haupteinleitung', in *Antike christliche Apokryphen in deutscher Übersetzung*, Band I: *Evangelien und Verwandtes*, Teilband 1, eds C. Markschies and J. Schröter, pp. 1–180. Tübingen: Mohr Siebeck.

Markschies, Christoph. 2015. *Christian Theology and Its Institutions in the Early Roman Empire: Prolegomena to a History of Early Christian Theology*. Waco, TX: Baylor University Press; Tübingen: Mohr Siebeck.

Markschies, Christoph, and Jens Schröter, eds. 2012. *Antike christliche Apokryphen in deutscher Übersetzung*, Band I: *Evangelien und Verwandtes*. Tübingen: Mohr Siebeck.

Marsden, Richard. 1995. *The Text of the Old Testament in Anglo-Saxon England*. Cambridge: Cambridge University Press.

Marsden, Richard. 1998. ' "Ask What I am Called": the Anglo-Saxons and their Bibles', in *The Bible as Book: The Manuscript Tradition*, eds John Sharpe and Kimberly Van Kampen, pp. 145–76. London: The British Library and Oak Knoll Press.

Marshall, I. Howard. 1999. *A Critical and Exegetical Commentary on the Pastoral Epistles*. Edinburgh: T&T Clark.

Martens, Peter W. 2012. *Origen and Scripture: The Contours of an Exegetical Life*. Oxford: Oxford University Press.

Mason, Steve. 1991. *Flavius Josephus on the Pharisees: A Composition-Critical Study*. Leiden: Brill.

Mason, Steve. 2002. 'Josephus and His Twenty-Two Book Canon', in *The Canon Debate*, eds Lee Martin McDonald and James A. Sanders, pp. 110–27. Peabody, MA: Hendrickson.

Mason, Steve. 2010. 'Josephus', in *The Eerdmans Dictionary of Early Judaism*, eds John J. Collins and Daniel C. Harlow, pp. 828–32. Grand Rapids, MI: Eerdmans.

Mazzucco, Clementina. 1982. 'Eusèbe de Césarée et l'Apocalypse de Jean', in *Studia Patristica* 17/1, ed. E.A. Livingstone, pp. 317–24. Oxford: Pergamon.

McDonald, Lee Martin. 2007. *The Biblical Canon: Its Origin, Transmission, and Authority*. Peabody, MA: Hendrickson.

McDonald, Lee Martin. 2017. *The Formation of the Biblical Canon*, 2 vols. London: Bloomsbury.

McDonald, Lee Martin and James A. Sanders, eds. 2002. *The Canon Debate*. Peabody, MA: Hendrickson.

McGinn, Bernard. 2009. 'Turning Points in Early Christian Apocalypse Exegesis', in *Apocalyptic Thought in Early Christianity*, ed. Robert J. Daly, pp. 81–105. Grand Rapids, MI: Baker.

McGuckin, John A. 2001. *St. Gregory of Nazianzus: An Intellectual Biography*. Crestwood, NY: St Vladimir's Seminary.

McGuckin, John Anthony, ed. 2004. *The Westminster Handbook to Origen*. Louisville, KY: WJK.

McKendrick, Scot, David Parker, Amy Myshrall, and Cillian O'Hogan. 2015. *Codex Sinaiticus: New Perspectives on the Ancient Biblical Manuscript*. London: The British Library.

Meade, John D. and Peter J. Gentry. 2012. 'Evaluating Evaluations: The Commentary of *BHQ* and the Problem of הוֹלֵלוֹת in Ecclesiastes in 1:17', in *Sophia-Paideia. Sapienza e educazione (Sir 1,27)—Miscellanea di studi offerti in onore del prof. Don Mario Cimosa*, pp. 197–217. Rome: LAS Editrice.

Mendels, Doron. 1992. 'Baruch, Book of', in *Anchor Bible Dictionary*, vol. 1, ed. David Noel Freedman, pp. 618–20. New York: Doubleday.

Metzger, Bruce M. 1987. *The Canon of the New Testament: Its Origin, Development, and Significance*. Oxford: Oxford University Press.

Metzger, Bruce M. 2003. 'The Future of New Testament Textual Studies', in *The Bible as Book: The Transmission of the Greek Text*, eds S. McKendrick and O. O'Sullivan, pp. 201–8. New Castle, DE: Oak Knoll Press.

Metzger, Bruce M. and Bart D. Ehrman. 2005. *The Text of the New Testament: Its Transmission, Corruption, and Restoration*, 4th edn. Oxford: Oxford University Press.

Meyvaert, Paul. 1996. 'Bede, Cassiodorus, and the Codex Amiatinus'. *Speculum* 71.4: 827–83.

Moberly, R.W.L. 2009. 'Pentateuch', in *The New Interpreter's Dictionary of the Bible*, vol. 4, ed. Katherine Doob Sakenfeld, pp. 430–8. Nashville, TN: Abingdon.

Mommsen, Theodor. 1886. 'Zur lateinischen Stichometrie'. *Hermes: Zeitschrift für klassische Philogie* 21: 142–56.

Mommsen, Theodor. 1890. 'Zur lateinischen Stichometrie'. *Hermes: Zeitschrift für klassische Philogie* 25: 636–8.

Moore, Nicholas J. 2013. 'Is Enoch Also Among the Prophets? The Impact of Jude's Citation of *I Enoch* on the Reception of Both Texts in the Early Church'. *Journal of Theological Studies* 64: 498–515.

Moreau, Madeleine, Isabelle Bochet, and Goulven Madec. 1997. *La doctrine chrétienne*. Bibliothèque augustinienne, Oeuvres de saint Augustin 11/2. Paris: Institut d'Études Augustiniennes.

Moss, Cyril. 1930. 'S. Amphilochius of Iconium on John 14,28: "The Father who sent me, is greater than I"'. *Le Muséon: Revue d'Études Orientales* 43: 317–64.

Moule, Charles F.D. 1981. *Birth of the New Testament*, 3rd edn. London: Black.

Mount, Christopher. 2002. *Pauline Christianity: Luke-Acts and the Legacy of Paul*. Leiden: Brill.

Moyise, Steve. 2015. *The Old Testament in the New*, 2nd edn. London: Bloomsbury.

Mroczek, Eva. 2015. 'The Hegemony of the Biblical in the Study of Second Temple Literature'. *Journal of Ancient Judaism* 6: 2–35.

Mroczek, Eva. 2016. *The Literary Imagination in Jewish Antiquity*. Oxford: Oxford University Press.

Mullen, Roderic L. 1997. *The New Testament Text of Cyril of Jerusalem*. The New Testament in the Greek Fathers 7. Atlanta, GA: Society of Biblical Literature.

Müller, Mogens. 2008. 'Die Septuaginta als Teil des christlichen Kanons', in *Die Septuaginta—Texte, Kontexte, Lebenswelten: International Fachtagung veranstaltet von Septuaginta Deutsch (LXX.D), Wuppertal 20.–23. Juli 2006*, eds Martin Karrer and Wolfgang Kraus, pp. 708–27. Tübingen: Mohr Siebeck.

Munier, Charles. 1972–3. 'La tradition manuscrite de l'Abrégé d'Hippone et le canon des Écritures des églises africaines'. *Sacris Erudiri* 21: 43–55.

Muratori, Ludovico Antonio. 1740. *Antiquitates Italicae Medii Ævi*, vol. 3. Milan: Ex Typographia Societatis Palatinae.

Murphy, F.X. 1945. *Rufinus of Aquileia (345–411): His Life and Works*. Washington, D.C.: The Catholic University of America Press.

Musurillo, Herbert, ed. and trans. 1972. *The Acts of the Christian Martyrs: Introduction, Texts and Translations*. Oxford: Oxford University Press.

Myers, Jacob M. 1974. *I and II Esdras*. Anchor Bible. Garden City, NY: Doubleday.

Nautin, Pierre. 1977. *Origène: Sa vie et son œuvre*. Paris: Beauchesne.

Neusner, Jacob, trans. 1988. *The Mishnah: A New Translation*. New Haven, CT: Yale University Press.

Neusner, Jacob, trans. 2002. *The Tosefta: Translated from the Hebrew with a New Introduction*. Peabody, MA: Hendrickson.

Nickelsburg, George W.E. 2000. 'Enoch, Books of', in *Encyclopedia of the Dead Sea Scrolls*, vol. 1, eds Lawrence H. Schiffman and James C. VanderKam, pp. 249–53. Oxford: Oxford University Press.

Nickelsburg, George W.E. 2001. *1 Enoch 1: A Commentary on the Book of 1 Enoch, Chapters 1–36; 81–108*. Hermeneia. Minneapolis, MN: Fortress.

Nickelsburg, George W.E. and James C. VanderKam. 2004. *1 Enoch: A New Translation*. Minneapolis, MN: Fortress.

Nickelsburg, George W.E. and James C. VanderKam. 2012. *1 Enoch 2: A Commentary on the Book of 1 Enoch Chapters 37–82*. Hermeneia. Minneapolis, MN: Fortress.

Nicklas, Tobias. 2016. 'New Testament Canon and Ancient Christian "Landscapes of Memory"'. *Early Christianity* 7: 5–23.

Niederwimmer, Kurt. 1998. *The Didache*. Hermeneia. Minneapolis, MN: Fortress.

Nienhuis, David R. 2007. *Not by Paul Alone: The Formation of the Catholic Epistle Collection and the Christian Canon*. Waco, TX: Baylor University Press.

Nienhuis, David R. and Robert W. Wall. 2013. *Reading the Epistles of James, Peter, John and Jude as Scripture: The Shaping and Shape of a Canonical Collection*. Grand Rapids, MI: Eerdmans.

Norelli, Enrico. 1995. *Ascensio Isaiae: Commentarius*. Corpus Christianorum Series Apocryphorum 8. Turnhout: Brepols.

Norelli, Enrico. 2010. 'Of Books and Bishops: The Second Century as a Key to the Processes that Led to a New Testament Canon'. *Zeitschrift für Religionswissenschaft* 18: 179–98.

Norelli, Enrico. 2013. 'Les bases de la formation du canon du Nouveau Testament', in *Histoire de la littérature grecque chrétienne*, vol. 2: *De Paul apôtre à Irénée de Lyon*, eds Enrico Norelli and Bernard Pouderon, pp. 915–91. Paris: Cerf.

Norris, Frederick. 1997. 'Gregory Nazianzen: Constructing and Constructed by Scripture', in *The Bible in Greek Christian Antiquity*, ed. Paul Blowers, pp. 149–62. Notre Dame, IN: Notre Dame University Press.

Norris, Richard A. 2003. *The Song of Songs: Interpreted by Early Christian and Medieval Commentators*. Grand Rapids, MI: Eerdmans.

Nuffelen, Peter van. 2007. 'The Career of Cyril of Jerusalem (c. 348–87): A Reassessment'. *Journal of Theological Studies* 58.1: 134–46.

O'Connell, Kevin G. 1972. *The Theodotionic Revision of the Book of Exodus: A Contribution to the Study of the Early History of the Transmission of the Old Testament in Greek*. Cambridge, MA: Harvard University Press.

O'Malley, John W. 2013. *Trent: What Happened at the Council*. Cambridge, MA: Harvard University Press.

Olympiodorus. 1984. *Kommentar zu Hiob*, eds Ursula Hagedorn and Dieter Hagedorn. Patristische Texte und Studien 24. Berlin: De Gruyter.

Opitz, H.G. 1938. *Athanasius Werke* 2.3. Berlin: De Gruyter.

Orthodox Study Bible. 2008. Nashville, TN: Thomas Nelson.

Osiek, Carolyn. 1999. *The Shepherd of Hermas: A Commentary*. Hermeneia. Minneapolis, MN: Fortress.

Oulton, J.E.L., trans. 1932. *Eusebius: The Ecclesiastical History*. Vol. 2. Cambridge, MA: Harvard University Press.

Pagels, Elaine. 2012. *Revelations: Visions, Prophecy, & Politics in the Book of Revelation*. New York: Viking.

Pajunen, Mika S. 2014. 'Perspectives on the Existence of a Particular Authoritative Book of Psalms in the Late Second Temple Period'. *Journal for the Study of the Old Testament* 39: 139–63.

Parker, D.C. 2008. *An Introduction to the New Testament Manuscripts and Their Texts*. Cambridge: Cambridge University Press.

Parker, D.C. 2010. *Codex Sinaiticus: The Story of the World's Oldest Bible*. London: British Library.

Patmore, Hector M. 2015. '1 Esdras', in *The T&T Clark Companion to the Septuagint*, ed. James K. Aitken, pp. 178–94. New York: Bloomsbury.

Payne Smith, Robert. 1879a and 1879b. *Thesaurus Syriacus*. Oxford: Clarendon Press.

Pennington, Kenneth. 2007. 'The Growth of Church Law', in *The Cambridge History of Christianity vol. 2: Constantine to c. 600*, eds Augustine Casiday and Frederick W. Norris, pp. 386–402. Cambridge: Cambridge University Press.

Pentiuc, Eugen J. 2014. *The Old Testament in Eastern Orthodox Tradition*. Oxford: Oxford Univesity Press.

Perler, Othmar, ed. and trans. 1966. *Méliton de Sardes: Sur la Pâque et fragments*. Sources chrétiennes 123. Paris: Cerf.

Perrin, Andrew B. 2014. 'An Almanac of Tobit Studies: 2000–2014'. *Currents in Biblical Research* 13: 107–42.

Perrin, Nicholas. 2003. 'Hermeneutical Factors in the Harmonization of the Gospels and the Question of Textual Authority', in *The Biblical Canons*, eds J.-M. Auwers and H.J. de Jonge, pp. 599–605. Leuven: Leuven University Press.

Perrin, Nicholas. 2011. 'Paul and Valentinian Interpretation', in *Paul and the Second Century*, eds Michael F. Bird and Joseph R. Dodson, pp. 126–39. New York: Bloomsbury.

Pervo, Richard I. 2010. *The Making of Paul: Constructions of the Apostle in Early Christianity*. Minneapolis, MN: Fortress.

Pervo, Richard I. 2013. *The Acts of Paul: A New Translation with Introduction and Commentary*. Eugene, OR: Cascade.

Petersen, William L. 1994. *Tatian's Diatessaron: Its Creation, Dissemination, Significance, and History in Scholarship*. Leiden: Brill.

Polman, A.D.R. 1961. *The Word of God According to St. Augustine*. Grand Rapids, MI: Eerdmans.

Pope, Marvin H. 1977. *Song of Songs: A New Translation with Introduction and Commentary*. Anchor Bible. New York: Doubleday.

Popović, Mladen. 2014. 'Ezekiel (Book and Person). III. Judaism. A. Second Temple and Hellenistic Judaism', in *Encyclopedia of the Bible and Its Reception*, vol. 8: *Essenes-Fideism*, cols 592–5. Berlin: De Gruyter.

Porter, Stanley E. 2004. 'When and How Was the Pauline Canon Compiled? An Assessment of Theories', in *The Pauline Canon*, ed. Stanley E. Porter, pp. 95–127. Leiden: Brill.

Porter, Stanley E. 2008. 'Paul and the Process of Canonization', in *Exploring the Origins of the Bible: Canon Formation in Historical, Literary, and Theological Perspective*, eds Craig A. Evans and Emanuel Tov, pp. 173–202. Grand Rapids, MI: Baker.

Porter, Stanley E. 2011. 'Paul and the Pauline Letter Collection', in *Paul and the Second Century*, eds Michael F. Bird and Joseph R. Dodson, pp. 19–36. New York: Bloomsbury.

Pummer, Reinhard. 2002. *Early Christian Authors on Samaritans and Samaritanism*. Tübingen: Mohr Siebeck.

Pummer, Reinhard. 2016. *The Samaritans: A Profile*. Grand Rapids, MI: Eerdmans.

Qimron, Elisha and John Strugnell, eds. 1994. *Qumran Cave 4, V: Miqṣat Maʿaśe Ha-Torah*. Discoveries in the Judean Desert 10. Oxford: Oxford University Press.

Rahlfs, Alfred. 1915. *Verzeichnis der griechischen Handschriften des Alten Testament*. Mitteilungen des Septuaginta-Unternehmens der Königlichen Gesellschaft der Wissenchaften, no. 2. Berlin: Weidmannsche Buchhandlung.

Rebenich, Stefan. 2002. *Jerome*. Early Church Fathers. New York: Routledge.

Reed, Annette Yoshiko. 2005. *Fallen Angels and the History of Judaism and Christianity: The Reception of Enochic Literature*. Cambridge: Cambridge University Press.

Reed, Annette Yoshiko. 2015. 'The Afterlives of New Testament Apocrypha'. *Journal of Biblical Literature* 134: 401–25.

Robbins, Gregory Allen. 1986. '*Peri Tōn Endiathēkōn Graphōn*: Eusebius and the Formation of the Christian Bible'. Ph.D. thesis, Duke University.

Robbins, Gregory Allen. 1993. 'Eusebius' Lexicon of Canonicity', in *Studia Patristica* 25, ed. E. A. Livingstone, pp. 134–41. Leuven: Peeters.

Robinson, Stephen E. 1992. 'Baruch, Book of 4', *Anchor Bible Dictionary*, vol. 1, ed. David Noel Freedman, p. 622. New York: Doubleday.

Rompay, Lucas Van. 2006. '*No Evil Word about Her*. The Two Syriac Versions of the Book of Judith', in *Text, Translation, and Tradition. Studies on the Peshitta and its Use in the Syriac Tradition Presented to Konrad D. Jenner on the Occasion of his Sixty-Fifth Birthday*, eds W.Th. van Peursen and R.B. ter Haar Romeny, Monographs of the Peshitta Institute Leiden, 14, pp. 205–30. Leiden: Brill.

Rompay, Lucas Van. Forthcoming. '1.1 The Canonical History of the Deutero-Canonical Texts 1.1.3 The Syriac Canon', in *The Textual History of the Bible*, vol. 2, eds Armin Lange and Matthias Henze, np. Leiden: Brill.

Roth, Dieter T. 2015. *The Text of Marcion's Gospel*. Leiden: Brill.

Rothschild, Clare K. 2008. 'Muratorian Canon as Fraud'. Unpublished paper presented at the annual meeting of the Society of Biblical Literature. Boston, MA.

Rothschild, Clare K. Forthcoming. *The Muratorian Fragment*. Tübingen. Mohr Siebeck.

Rouse, Richard and Charles McNelis. 2000. 'North African Literary Activity: A Cyprian Fragment, the Stichometric Lists and a Donatist Compendium'. *Revue d'histoire des textes* 30: 189–238.

Rowe, C. Kavin. 2010. 'Literary Unity and Reception History: Reading Luke-Acts as Luke and Acts', in *Rethinking the Unity and Reception of Luke and Acts*, eds Andrew F. Gregory and C. Kavin Rowe, pp. 74–81. Columbia, SC: University of South Carolina Press.

Ruwet, Jean. 1942. 'Les "Antilegomena" dans les œuvres d'Origène'. *Biblica* 23: 18–42.

Ruwet, Jean. 1943. 'Les "Antilegomena" dans les œuvres d'Origène: les antilegomena de l'Ancien Testament'. *Biblica* 24: 18–58.

Ruwet, Jean. 1944. 'Les apocryphes dans les œuvres d'Origène'. *Biblica* 25: 143–66, 311–34.

Ruwet, Jean. 1952. 'Le canon alexandrin des Écritures. Saint Athanase'. *Biblica* 33: 1–29.

Ryan, Daniel. 2015. 'Baruch', in *T&T Clark Companion to the Septuagint*, ed. James K. Aitken, pp. 487–99. London: Bloomsbury.

Ryle, Herbert Edward. 1892. *The Canon of the Old Testament: An Essay on the Gradual Growth and Formation of the Hebrew Canon of Scripture*. London: Macmillan.

Sanday, W. 1891. 'The Cheltenham List of the Canonical Books of the Old and New Testament and of the Writings of Cyprian', in *Studia Biblica et Ecclesiastica*, vol. 3, pp. 217–303. Oxford: Oxford University Press.

Sanders, James A. 2005 [1972]. *Torah and Canon*, 2nd edn. Eugene, OR: Cascade.

Sarna, N.M. 2000. 'Ancient Libraries and the Ordering of the Biblical Books', in *Studies in Biblical Interpretation*, pp. 35–66. Philadelphia, PA: Jewish Publication Society.

Satlow, Michael L. 2014. *How the Bible Became Holy*. New Haven, CT: Yale University Press.

Sawyer, John F.A. 1996. *The Fifth Gospel: Isaiah in the History of Christianity*. Cambridge: Cambridge University Press.

Scheck, Thomas P. 2002. *Origen: Commentary on Romans*. Fathers of the Church 104. Washington, D.C.: Catholic University of America Press.

Scherbenske, Eric W. 2013. *Canonizing Paul: Ancient Editorial Practice and the Corpus Paulinum*. Oxford: Oxford University Press.

Schmid, Ulrich. 1995. *Marcion und sein Apostolos: Rekonstruktion und historische Einordnung der marcionitischen Paulusbriefausgabe*. Berlin: De Gruyter.

Schmid, Ulrich. 2013. 'The Diatessaron of Tatian', in *The Text of the New Testament in Contemporary Research: Essays on the Status Quaestionis*, 2nd edn, eds Bart D. Ehrman and Michael W. Holmes, pp. 115–42. Leiden: Brill.

Schmid, Ulrich. 2015. 'Die Apokalypse, überliefert mit anderen neutestamentlichen Schriften—eapr-Handschriften', in *Studien zum Text der Apokalypse*, eds Marcus Sigismund, Martin Karrer, and Ulrich Schmid, pp. 421–41. Berlin: De Gruyter.

Schnabel, Eckhard J. 2014. 'The Muratorian Fragment: The State of Research'. *Journal of the Evangelical Theological Society* 57: 231–64.

Schodde, George H. 1885. 'The Apostolic Canons, Translated from the Ethiopic'. *Journal of Biblical Literature* 5: 61–72.

Schröter, Jens. 2013. *From Jesus to the New Testament: Early Christian Theology and the Origin of the New Testament Canon*. Waco, TX: Baylor University Press; Tübingen: Mohr Siebeck.

Schröter, Jens. 2015. 'The Formation of the New Testament Canon and Early Christian Apocrypha', in *The Oxford Handbook of Early Christian Apocrypha*, eds Andrew Gregory and Christopher Tuckett, pp. 167–84. Oxford: Oxford University Press.

Schröter, Jens. 2016. 'Apocryphal and Canonical Gospels within the Development of the New Testament Canon'. *Early Christianity* 7: 24–46.

Schürer, Emil. 1973–1987. *The History of the Jewish People in the Age of Jesus Christ (175 BC–AD 135)*, rev. Geza Vermes and Fergus Millar, 3 vols in 4. Edinburgh: T&T Clark.

Schwartz, Seth. 2011. 'How Many Judaisms Were There? A Critique of Neusner and Smith on Definition and Mason and Boyarin on Categorization'. *Journal of Ancient Judaism* 2: 208–38.

Shuve, Karl. 2016. *The Song of Songs and the Fashioning of Identity in Early Latin Christianity*. Oxford: Oxford University Press.

Simonetti, M. 2014. 'Cyril of Jerusalem', in *Encyclopedia of Ancient Christianity*, vol. 1, ed. Angelo Di Berardino, pp. 654–5. Downers Grove, IL: InterVarsity.

Simonetti, Manlio. 1994. *Biblical Interpretation in the Early Church: An Introduction to Patristic Exegesis*. Edinburgh: T&T Clark.

Skarsaune, Oskar. 1996. 'The Question of Old Testament Canon and Text in the Early Greek Church', in *Hebrew Bible/Old Testament: The History of Its Interpretation*, vol. 1: *From the Beginnings to the Middle Ages (Until 1300)*, part 1: *Antiquity*, ed. Magne Sæbø, pp. 443–50. Göttingen: Vandenhoeck & Ruprecht.

Skeat, T.C. 1992. 'Irenaeus and the Four-Gospel Canon'. *Novum Testamentum* 34: 194–9.

Skeat, T.C. 1997. 'The Oldest Manuscript of the Four Gospels?'. *New Testament Studies* 43: 1–31.

Skehan, Patrick W. 1952. 'St. Jerome and the Canon of the Holy Scriptures', in *A Monument to Saint Jerome: Essays on Some Aspects of His Life, Works and Influence*, ed. Francis X. Murphy, pp. 259–87. New York: Sheed & Ward.

Sokoloff, Michael. 2009. *A Syriac Lexicon: A Translation from the Latin, Correction, Expansion, and Update of C. Brockelmann's Lexicon Syriacum*. Winona Lake, IN: Eisenbrauns and Piscataway, NJ: Gorgias Press.

Spellman, Ched. 2014. *Toward a Canon-Conscious Reading of the Bible: Exploring the History and Hermeneutics of the Canon*. Sheffield: Sheffield Phoenix.

Stanton, Graham. 2003. 'Jesus Traditions and Gospels in Justin Martyr and Irenaeus', in *The Biblical Canons*, eds J.-M. Auwers and H.J. de Jonge, pp. 353–70. Leuven: Leuven University Press.

Stanton, Graham N. 2004. *Jesus and Gospel*. Cambridge: Cambridge University Press.

Steinberg, Julius. 2006. *Die Ketuvim: Ihr Aufbau und ihre Botschaft*. Hamburg: Philo.

Steinberg, Julius and Timothy J. Stone. 2015. 'The Historical Formation of the Writings in Antiquity', in *The Shape of the Writings*, eds Julius Steinberg and Timothy J. Stone, pp. 1–58. Winona Lake, IN: Eisenbrauns.

Steins, Georg. 1995. *Die Chronik als kanonisches Abschlussphänomen: Studien zur Entstehung und Theologie von 1/2 Chronik*. Weinheim: Beltz.

Stemberger, Günter. 2014. 'Ezekiel (Book and Person). III. Judaism. B. Rabbinic Judaism', in *Encyclopedia of the Bible and Its Reception*, vol. 8: *Essenes–Fideism*, cols 595–8. Berlin: De Gruyter.

Stenzel, Meinrad. 1942. 'Der Bibelkanon des Rufin von Aquileja'. *Biblica* 23: 43–61.

Stone, Timothy J. 2013. *The Compilational History of the Megilloth: Canon, Contoured Intertextuality and Meaning in the Writings*. Tübingen: Mohr Siebeck.

Strack, H.L., and Günter Stemberger. 1996. *Introduction to the Talmud and Midrash*, 2nd edn. Minneapolis, MN: Fortress.

Stuart, Moses. 1845. *Critical History and Defence of the Old Testament Canon*. Andover, MA: Allen, Morrill and Wardell.

Stuckenbruck, Loren T. 2011. 'Apocrypha and the Septuagint: Exploring the Christian Canon', in *Die Septuaginta und das frühe Christentum*, eds Thomas Schott Caulley and Hermann Lichtenberger, pp. 177–201. Tübingen: Mohr Siebeck.

Stuckenbruck, Loren T. 2013. 'The *Book of Enoch*: Its Reception in Second Temple Jewish and in Christian Tradition'. *Early Christianity* 4: 7–40.

Stuhlhofer, Franz. 1988. *Der Gebrauch der Bibel von Jesus bis Euseb: eine statistische Untersuchung zur Kanongeschichte*. Wuppertal: R. Brockhaus.

Sundberg, Albert C. 1964. *The Old Testament of the Early Church*. Cambridge, MA: Harvard University Press.

Sundberg, Albert C. 1973. 'Canon Muratori: A Fourth-Century List'. *Harvard Theological Review* 66: 1–41.

Sundberg, Albert C. 1996. 'The Old Testament of the Early Church Revisited', in *Festschrift in Honor of Charles Speel*, eds Thomas J. Sienkewicz and James E. Betts, pp. 88–110. Monmouth, IL: Monmouth College.

Sweeney, Marvin A. 2011. 'The Problem of Ezekiel in Talmudic Literature', in *After Ezekiel: Essays on the Reception of a Difficult Prophet*, eds Andrew Mein and Paul M. Joyce, pp. 11–23. New York: T&T Clark.

Talmon, Shemaryahu and Yigael Yadin. 1999. *Masada VI: The Yigael Yadin Excavations 1963–1965*. Jerusalem: Israel Exploration Society.

Talshir, Zipora. 2001. 'Several Canon-Related Concepts Originating in Chronicles'. *Zeitschrift für die Alttestamentliche Wissenschaft* 113: 386–403.

Tanner, Norman P. 1990. *Decrees of the Ecumenical Councils*, 2 vols. Washington, D.C.: Georgetown University Press.

Taylor, Finian D. 1978. 'Augustine of Hippo's Notion and Use of the Apocrypha'. Ph.D. thesis, University of Notre Dame.

Thiele, Walter. 1987. *Vetus Latina: Die Reste der altlateinischen Bibel 11/2: Sirach (Ecclesiasticus)*. Freiburg: Herder.

Thielman, Frank. 1998. 'The Place of the Apocalypse in the Canon of St. Gregory Nazianzen'. *Tyndale Bulletin* 49.1: 155–7.

Thompson, Edward Maunde. 1912. *An Introduction to Greek and Latin Palaeography*. Oxford: Oxford University Press.

Tigchelaar, Eibert. 2003. 'Is the Liar Bar Kokhba? Considering the Date and Provenance of the Greek (Ethiopic) *Apocalypse of Peter*', in *The Apocalypse of Peter*, eds J. N. Bremmer and István Czachesz, pp. 63–77. Leuven: Peeters.

Tite, Philip L. 2012. *The Apocryphal Epistle to the Laodiceans: An Epistolary and Rhetorical Analysis*. Texts and Editions for New Testament Study 7. Leiden: Brill.

Tornau, Christian, and Paolo Cecconi. 2014. *The Shepherd of Hermas in Latin: Critical Edition of the Oldest Translation Vulgata*. Berlin: De Gruyter.

Tov, Emanuel. 2004. *Scribal Practices and Approaches Reflected in the Texts Found in the Judean Desert*. Leiden: Brill.

Tov, Emanuel. 2008. *Hebrew Bible, Greek Bible, and Qumran: Collected Essays*. Tübingen: Mohr Siebeck.

Tov, Emanuel. 2010. *Revised Lists of the Texts from the Judaean Desert*. Leiden: Brill.

Tov, Emanuel. 2012. *Textual Criticism of the Hebrew Bible*, 3rd edn. Minneapolis, MN: Fortress.

Trebolle, Julio. 2000. 'A "Canon within a Canon": Two Series of Old Testament Books Differently Transmitted, Interpreted and Authorized'. *Revue de Qumran* 19: 383–99.

Trebolle Barrera, Julio. 2002. 'Origins of a Tripartite Old Testament Canon', in *The Canon Debate*, eds Lee Martin McDonald and James A. Sanders, pp. 128–45. Peabody, MA: Hendrickson.

Tregelles, Samuel P. 1867. *Canon Muratorianus: The Earliest Catalogue of the Books of the New Testament*. Oxford: Oxford University Press.

Trobisch, David. 1989. *Die Enstehung der Paulusbriefsammlung: Studien zu den Anfängen christlicher Publizistik.* Göttingen: Vandenhoeck & Ruprecht.

Trobisch, David. 1994. *Paul's Letter Collection: Tracing the Origins.* Minneapolis, MN: Fortress.

Tuckett, Christopher. 2012. *2 Clement: Introduction, Text, and Commentary.* Oxford: Oxford University Press.

Turner, C.H. 1891. 'Appendix', in *Studia Biblica et Ecclesiastica*, vol. 3, pp. 304–25. Oxford: Oxford University Press.

Turner, C.H. 1912a. 'A Fragment of an Unknown Latin Version of the Apostolic Constitutions. (Book VIII 41–End: Lagarde 274.26–281.9.) From a MS in the Chapter Library of Verona LI foll. 139*b*–146*a*'. *Journal of Theological Studies* 13: 492–505.

Turner, C.H. 1912b. 'Introduction to the Fragment Printed Above, pp. 492–505'. *Journal of Theological Studies* 13: 505–10.

Turner, C.H. 1912c. 'Latin Lists of the Canonical Books. IV. An Early Version of the Eighty-Fifth Apostolic Canon. From MS Veron. LI foll. 155*b*, 156*a*'. *Journal of Theological Studies* 13: 511–12.

Turner, C.H. 1913. 'A Primitive Edition of the Apostolic Constitutions and Canons: An Early List of Apostles and Disciples'. *Journal of Theological Studies* 15: 53–65.

Turner, C.H. 1914. 'Notes on the *Apostolic Constitutions*. I. The Compiler an Arian'. *Journal of Theological Studies* 16: 54–61.

Turner, C.H. 1915. 'Notes on the *Apostolic Constitutions*. II. The Apostolic Canons'. *Journal of Theological Studies* 16: 523–38.

Turner, C.H. 1920. 'Notes on the *Apostolic Constitutions*. III. The Text of Cod. Vat. 1506'. *Journal of Theological Studies* 21: 160–8.

Turner, C.H. 1930. 'Notes on the *Apostolic Constitutions*. III. The Text of the Eighth Book'. *Journal of Theological Studies* 31: 128–41.

Ulrich, Eugene. 2002. 'The Notion and Definition of Canon', in *The Canon Debate*, eds Lee Martin McDonald and James A. Sanders, pp. 21–35. Peabody, MA: Hendrickson.

Ulrich, Eugene C. 2003a. 'The Non-Attestation of a Tripartite Canon in 4QMMT'. *Catholic Biblical Quarterly* 65: 202–14.

Ulrich, Eugene C. 2003b. 'Qumran and the Canon of the Old Testament', in *The Biblical Canons*, eds J.-M. Auwers and H.J. De Jonge, pp. 57–80. Leuven: Leuven University Press.

Ulrich, Eugene C. 2010. 'Methodological Reflections on Determining Scriptural Status in First Century Judaism', in *Rediscovering the Dead Sea Scrolls: An Assessment of Old and New Approaches and Methods*, ed. Maxine L. Grossman, pp. 145–61. Grand Rapids, MI: Eerdmans.

Ulrich, Eugene C. 2015. *The Dead Sea Scrolls and the Developmental Composition of the Bible.* Leiden: Brill.

Unger, Dominic J. and Irenaeus M.C. Steenberg. 2012. *St. Irenaeus of Lyons: Against the Heresies.* Ancient Christian Writers 64. New York: Newman.

Unnik, W.C. van. 1949. 'De la règle Μήτε προσθεῖναι μήτε ἀφελεῖν dans l'histoire du canon'. *Vigiliae Christianae* 3: 1–36.

Van Minnen, Peter. 2003. 'The Greek *Apocalypse of Peter*', in *The Apocalypse of Peter*, eds J.N. Bremmer and István Czachesz, pp. 15–39. Leuven: Peeters.

VanderKam, James C. 1996. '1 Enoch, Enochic Motifs, and Enoch in Early Christian Literature', in *The Jewish Apocalyptic Heritage in Early Christianity*, eds James C. VanderKam and William Adler, pp. 33–101. Minneapolis, MN: Fortress.

VanderKam, James C. 1998. 'Authoritative Literature in the Dead Sea Scrolls'. *Dead Sea Discoveries* 5: 382–402.

VanderKam, James C. 2000. *From Revelation to Canon: Studies in the Hebrew Bible and Second Temple Literature*. Leiden: Brill.

VanderKam, James C. 2010. 'Moses Trumping Moses: Making the Book of *Jubilees*', in *The Dead Sea Scrolls: Transmission of Traditions and Production of Texts*, eds Sarianna Metso, Hindy Najman, and Eileen Schuller, pp. 25–44. Leiden: Brill.

VanderKam, James C. 2012. *The Dead Sea Scrolls and the Bible*. Grand Rapids, MI: Eerdmans.

Verheyden, Joseph. 2003. 'The Canon Muratori: A Matter of Dispute', in *The Biblical Canons*, eds J.-M. Auwers and H.J. de Jonge, pp. 487–556. Leuven: Leuven University Press.

Verheyden, Joseph. 2007. 'The *Shepherd of Hermas*', in *The Writings of the Apostolic Fathers*, ed. Paul Foster, pp. 63–71. London: T&T Clark.

Verheyden, Joseph. 2013. 'The New Testament Canon', in *The New Cambridge History of the Bible*, vol. 1: *From the Beginnings to 600*, eds James Carleton Paget and Joachim Schaper, pp. 389–411. Cambridge: Cambridge University Press.

Von Lips, Hermann. 2004. *Der neutestamentliche Kanon: Seine Geschichte und Bedeutung*. Zürich: Theologischer Verlag Zürich.

Vööbus, Arthur. 1975. *The Synodicon in the West Syrian Tradition I*. Corpus Scriptorum Christianorum Orientalium 367. Louvain: Secrétariat du CorpusSCO.

Wagschal, David. 2015. *Law and Legality in the Greek East: The Byzantine Canonical Tradition, 381–883*. Oxford: Oxford University Press.

Warren, David H. 1999. 'The Greek Language of the Apocryphal Acts of the Apostles: A Study in Style', in *The Apocryphal Acts of the Apostles*, eds François Bovon, Ann Graham Brock, and Christopher R. Matthews, pp. 101–24. Cambridge, MA: Harvard University Press.

Wasserman, Tommy. 2006. *The Epistle of Jude: Its Text and Transmission*. Stockholm: Almqvist & Wiksell.

Wasserman, Tommy. 2010. 'A Comparative Textual Analysis of P^4 and $P^{64}+^{67}$'. *TC: A Journal of Biblical Textual Criticism* 15: 1–26.

Watson, Francis. 2013. *Gospel Writing: A Canonical Perspective*. Grand Rapids, MI: Eerdmans.

Watson, Francis. 2016a. *The Fourfold Gospel: A Theological Reading of the New Testament Portraits of Jesus*. Grand Rapids, MI: Baker.

Watson, Francis. 2016b. 'Towards a Redaction-Critical Reading of the Diatessaron Gospel'. *Early Christianity* 7: 95–112.

Wayment, Thomas A. 2013. *The Text of the New Testament Apocrypha (100–400 CE)*. New York: Bloomsbury.

Weber, Robert and Roger Gryson, eds. 2007. *Biblia Sacra iuxta vulgatam versionem*, 5th edn. Stuttgart: Deutsche Bibelgesellschaft.

Weeks, Stuart D., Simon Gathercole, and Loren T. Stuckenbruck. 2004. *The Book of Tobit: Texts from the Principal Ancient and Medieval Traditions, with Synopsis, Concordances, and Annotated Texts in Aramaic, Hebrew, Greek, Latin, and Syriac*. Berlin: De Gruyter.

Wermelinger, Otto. 1984. 'Le canon des Latins au temps de Jérôme et d'Augustin', in *Le Canon de l'Ancien Testament: Sa formation et son histoire*, eds Jean-Daniel Kaestli and Otto Wermelinger, La Monde de la Bible 10, pp. 153–96. Geneva: Labor et Fides.

Westcott, Brooke Foss. 1889. *A General Survey of the Canon of the New Testament*, 6th edn. Cambridge: Macmillan.

Westcott, Brooke Foss. 1896. *A General Survey of the History of the Canon of the New Testament*, 7th edn. New York: Macmillan.

Williams, David S. 2015. '1 Maccabees', in *The T&T Clark Companion to the Septuagint*, ed. James K. Aitken, pp. 261–72. New York: Bloomsbury.

Williams, Megan Hale. 2006. *The Monk and the Book: Jerome and the Making of Christian Scholarship*. Chicago, IL: University of Chicago Press.

Wilson, Gerald H. 1985. *The Editing of the Hebrew Psalter*. Chico, CA: Scholars Press.

Wolfenson, L.B. 1924. 'Implications of the Place of the Book of Ruth in Editions, Manuscripts, and Canon of the Old Testament'. *Hebrew Union College Annual* 1: 151–78.

Wooden, R. Glenn. 2015. '2 Esdras', in *The T&T Clark Companion to the Septuagint*, ed. James K. Aitken, pp. 195–202. New York: Bloomsbury.

Wordsworth, John. 1901. *The Ministry of Grace: Studies in Early Church History with Reference to Present Problems*. London: Longmans, Green, and Co.

Wright, Benjamin G. 2000. 'Ben Sira, Book of', in *Encyclopedia of the Dead Sea Scrolls*, vol. 1, eds Lawrence H. Schiffman and James C. VanderKam, pp. 91–3. Oxford: Oxford University Press.

Wright, W. 1870 1871 1872. *Catalogue of Syriac Manuscripts in the British Museum Acquired since the Year 1838*. London: Gilbert and Rivington.

Wyrick, Jed. 2004. *The Ascension of Authorship: Attribution and Canon Formation in Jewish, Hellenistic, and Christian Traditions*. Cambridge, MA: Harvard University Press.

Yardeni, Ada. 2002. *The Book of Hebrew Script: History, Palaeography, Script Styles, Calligraphy and Design*. New Castle, DE: Oak Knoll.

Young, Frances M. with Andrew Teal. 2010. *From Nicaea to Chalcedon: A Guide to the Literature and Its Background*, 2nd edn. Grand Rapids, MI: Baker.

Zahn, Molly M. 2011. *Rethinking Rewritten Scripture: Composition and Exegesis in the 4Q Reworked Pentateuch Manuscripts*. Leiden: Brill.

Zahn, Theodor. 1888–1892. *Geschichte des neutestamentlichen Kanons*, 2 vols. Erlangen: A. Dichert.

Zahn, Theodor. 1900. 'Das Neue Testament Theodors von Mopsuestia und der ursprüngliche Kanon der Syrer'. *Neue kirchliche Zeitschrift* 11: 788–806.

Zevit, Ziony. 1998. 'The Second–Third Century Canonization of the Hebrew Bible and Its Influence on Christian Canonization', in *Canonization and Decanonization*, eds Arie van der Kooij and Karel van der Toorn, pp. 133–60. Leiden: Brill.

Ziegler, Joseph, ed. 1980. *Sapientia Iesu Filii Sirach*. Septuaginta Vetus Testamentum Graecum, vol. XII/2, 2nd edn. Göttingen: Vandenhoeck & Ruprecht.

Zsengellér, J. 1998. 'Canon and the Samaritans', in *Canonization and Decanonization: Papers Presented to the International Conference of the Leiden Institute for the Study of Religions (LISOR) held at Leiden 9–10 January 1997*, eds A. van der Kooij and K. van der Toorn, pp. 161–71. Leiden: Brill.

Ancient Literature Index

Gallagher and Meade, *The Biblical Canon Lists from Early Christianity: Texts and Analysis*

Modern Author Index